THIRD EDITION

PSYCHOLOGY

A Concise Introduction

THIRD EDITION

PSYCHOLOGY

A Concise Introduction

Richard A. Griggs
University of Florida

Worth Publishers

Senior Publisher: Catherine Woods
Executive Editor: Kevin Feyen
Associate Managing Editor: Tracey Kuehn
Project Editor: Leigh Renhard
Marketing Manager: Lindsay Johnson
Production Manager: Sarah Segal
Media and Supplements Editor: Peter Twickler
Art Director, Cover Designer: Babs Reingold
Interior Designers: Lissi Sigillo and Lyndall Culbertson
Chapter Opener Paintings: Nancy Olivier
Cover Painting: Ravenna Taylor
Illustration Coordinator: Bill Page
Illustrations: Matthew Holt
Photo Editor: Ted Szczepanski
Composition: MPS Limited, a Macmillan Company
Printing and Binding: Quad/Graphics Taunton

Library of Congress Cataloging-in-Publication Data Control Number: 2010931645

ISBN-13: 978-1-4292-6155-5
ISBN-10: 1-4292-6155-2

Worth Publishers
41 Madison Avenue
New York, NY 10010
www.worthpublishers.com

To Henry, my canine kindred spirit

While death ends a life, it does not end a relationship

You will remain with me forever in my heart and on my mind

About the Author

Richard A. Griggs is Professor Emeritus of Psychology at the University of Florida. After earning his Ph.D. in cognitive psychology at Indiana University, he went to the University of Florida, where he has spent his entire academic career. He has won numerous teaching awards at the University of Florida and was named APA's Society for the Teaching of Psychology Teacher of the Year for 4-year Colleges and Universities in 1994. He served on the Editorial Board of *Teaching of Psychology* for over a decade, as a *Contemporary Psychology* Consulting Editor for textbook reviews, and as an Associate Editor of *Thinking and Reasoning*. His two main research areas are human reasoning and the teaching of psychology. He has published over 100 journal articles, reviews, and book chapters, including 31 in *Teaching of Psychology*. He was also one of the originators and developers of the Society for the Teaching of Psychology's online resource, *A Compendium of Introductory Psychology Textbooks,* and the editor of Volume 3 of the Society's *Handbook for Teaching Introductory Psychology*. When he isn't busy with professional activities, he likes to relax at home with his wife Sherri, also a psychologist. His main pastimes are golf, reading, and fitness.

Brief Contents

Contents

Preface

Those of us who teach introductory psychology have the privilege and the challenge of introducing students to our discipline, which is more expansive than ever as research proliferates in many areas. This task has become increasingly problematic in recent years as the authors of introductory textbooks have struggled to keep pace, resulting in books that are more comprehensive, longer, and thus more difficult to complete in one term. The choices of which topics to assign and to what depth to cover them have become more difficult for teachers. We end up either omitting entire chapters or asking students to read chapters at a pace too hurried for optimal learning. Further, introductory textbooks have become much more expensive, leading some students to not even purchase them. As an introductory psychology teacher, I have grappled with these critical issues. *Psychology: A Concise Introduction* is the result of my own search for a textbook that includes the essential core content in psychology but is also economical in both size and cost.

Chapter Topics. To make the most informed choices of chapter topics, I consulted Benjamin Miller and Barbara Gentile's national survey of 761 introductory psychology teachers at 490 schools (Miller & Gentile, 1998). They asked teachers to rate the importance of and need for coverage of 25 different topics in their courses. Since my first chapter covers psychology as a science, I chose the highest-rated topics in Miller and Gentile's study as the subjects of the other nine chapters. To maintain the book's brevity, I paired sensation with perception and cognitive development with social development in single chapters. The topic order is the standard one—introduction/methods, neuroscience, sensation/perception, learning, memory, thinking/intelligence, developmental psychology, personality, social psychology, and abnormal psychology. Because the topics of emotion, motivation, and states of consciousness were rated just below the chosen topics, I included sections on emotion and consciousness in the neuroscience chapter and motivation in the learning chapter. My choices of chapter topics were further validated by Scott Bates's analysis of topic coverage for 107 introductory psychology course syllabi (Bates, 2004). His topic coverage findings based on syllabi analysis match my chapter topic choices almost perfectly.

Pedagogical Program. In writing *Psychology: A Concise Introduction,* I have tried to offer solid topical coverage in an engaging, conversational style. The content in each chapter has been reduced to the core content within that topic domain. Illustrations are full-color and pedagogically sound. Students will find this book easy to learn from. It incorporates both pedagogical aids and study guide exercises to structure their learning. My choice of pedagogical aids was primarily based on recent research findings about student perception of the use and importance of the many aids employed in textbooks. I included the aids that students report valuing and using in their learning. Each chapter begins with an overview in the form of a topical outline, and key terms are identified by boldface type and then defined both in the text and in a marginal glossary. Detailed summaries are provided at the end of each major chapter section. Study guide exercises begin with Concept Check questions at the end of each chapter section. These questions lead students to think more deeply about the material in that section. For example, a question may ask students to contrast concepts to understand differences between them or to demonstrate their understanding of a concept by applying it in a novel situation. At the end of each chapter there is a list of key terms and a Key Terms Exercise to test student knowledge of these terms. A multiple-choice Practice Test on the chapter's content follows the Key Terms Exercise. Answers to this test along with answers to the Key Terms Exercise and the sectional Concept Checks are provided at the end of each chapter. These exercises combined with the pedagogical aids should foster sufficient review and self-assessment, eliminating the need for and additional expense of a separate study guide.

Third Edition Changes. Reaching the goal of a textbook that could be covered in a single term at a reasonable price without sacrificing essential content was a challenge, but based on the overwhelmingly positive market response and user reviews, the publisher and I seem to have been successful. With only 10 chapters, *Psychology: A Concise Introduction* has fit nicely into introductory courses on both semester and quarter systems. The breadth of the audience for the text has also been gratifying. It has been used successfully at all types of colleges and universities, from two-year schools to research institutions. Given this success and to maintain the text's basic goal, the content was expanded and revised only where necessary. Reviewers and users that I have been in contact with almost unanimously wanted no major content changes, especially new chapters. Therefore, the 10 chapters (those topics taught most frequently by introductory teachers) remain the same, and content additions were made judiciously.

The second edition revisions were well received, so my third edition revisions are along the same lines. I only made revisions that enhanced the text's pedagogical program or visual persona, were absolutely necessary due to recent research findings, contributed toward more closure on a particular topic, or had substantial value to student readers. Thus, I have added more summary review tables (especially in the neuroscience and sensation/perception chapters), more visuals (historical photos and pedagogically valuable illustrations and cartoons), updated content where necessary (e.g., Burger's recent replication of Milgram's original disobedience findings), added content that provides better closure on a topic (e.g., coverage of "theory of mind" to the section on social development) or that has value to students in their everyday lives (e.g., Gerd Gigerenzer's work on how to interpret positive results for medical screening tests).

In this new edition, the visual pedagogical program was expanded and strengthened throughout the text. Because this program is an integral part of the learning process, I carefully examined each figure, table, illustration, photo, and cartoon to ensure that it served a clear pedagogical function, and any needing revision were redone. In addition, we added over 20 new instructive figures and tables and over 40 new illustrations, historical photos, and cartoons to further improve the pedagogical value of the visual program. The text's interior design was also revised to have a cleaner look and thus enhance its use. Because of their success in the first two editions, the specific pedagogical aids employed (those that research has found students report valuing and using in their learning) and the structure of the integrated study guide remain the same. All of the questions in the Concept Check sections, Key Terms Exercises, and multiple-choice Practice Tests were re-evaluated and revised if necessary. In addition, some new Concept Check questions were added to further enhance student learning. In sum, I think that you will find both the visual art program and integrated study guide even more pedagogically effective in this revised edition, and of critical importance, students will find this new edition even easier to learn from.

As with the first two editions, the textbook's smaller size and lower cost allow teachers the option of adding supplemental readings to customize their courses to fit their own goals and interests. To facilitate the task of finding supplemental materials, Worth offers many supplements for this purpose.

Supplements

For Instructors

Instructor's Resource Manual, Andrew N. Christopher, Albion College; Pam Marek, Kennesaw State University

Thoroughly updated from the last edition, this manual provides a variety of resources to help you plan your course and class sessions. Resources include sample course syllabi, annotated chapter outlines and lecture guides with tips on how to present the material, effective classroom activities (including both in-class activities and homework assignments) drawn from established sources as well as the authors' own experiences, and suggestions for using Worth courseware, including *PsychSim 5.0,* all of Worth's video resources for introductory psychology, and the textbook's **Book Companion Site.**

Printed *Test Bank,* Cynthia S. Koenig, St. Mary's College of Maryland; Pam Marek, Kennesaw State University; Sherri L. Jackson, Jacksonville University; and Richard A. Griggs, University of Florida

Tied to the pages of *Psychology: A Concise Introduction,* **Third Edition,** and considerably larger for the third edition, the printed *Test Bank* provides over 1,500 multiple-choice factual/definitional and conceptual questions.

Diploma Computerized Test Bank (Windows and Macintosh on one CD-ROM)

The **Diploma CD-ROM** guides you through the process of creating a test, allowing you to add an unlimited number of questions, edit questions, format a test, scramble questions, and include pictures and multimedia links. The accompanying **Gradebook** enables you to record student grades throughout your course and includes the capacity to track student records, view detailed analyses of test items, curve tests, generate reports, add weights to grades, and more. The CD-ROM provides the access point for **Diploma Online Testing** as well as Blackboard- and WebCT-formatted versions of the **Test Bank.**

For Classroom Presentation

ActivePsych **Instructor's Classroom Exercise CD-ROMs** include interactive activities designed for in-class presentation and group participation, with a robust library of new clips and animations. These activities require very little instructor preparation (just load the CD and launch the activity) and are designed to foster class discussion and critical thinking. The *ActivePsych* suite of instructor presentation CD-ROMs includes the following:

Two powerful types of classroom activities: **32 Flash-based interactive demonstrations** are designed to promote classroom discussion and critical thinking; **22 PowerPoint-based demonstrations, inventories, and surveys** are designed to assess student understanding of various psychological topics. (These demonstrations work easily with the **iClicker Classroom Response System**.)

iClicker Radio Frequency Classroom Response System iClicker is Worth's polling system, created by educators for educators. This radio frequency system is the hassle-free way to make your class time more interactive. The system allows you to pause to ask questions and instantly record responses, as well as take attendance, direct students through lectures, gauge students' understanding of the material, and much more.

PowerPoint Slide Sets

There are three PowerPoint slide sets to accompany the text. For each chapter, we offer a set that features chapter outlines, a set that includes chapter art and illustrations, and a final lecture presentation set that merges detailed chapter outlines with text illustrations and artwork from outside sources. Each set can be used directly or customized to fit your needs.

Expanded and Improved Book Companion Site
www.worthpublishers.com/griggs

The *password-protected Instructor Site* offers a full array of teaching resources, including a new suite of PowerPoint slides, electronic lecture guides, an online quiz grade book, and links to additional tools.

Enhanced Course Management Solutions (WebCT, Blackboard, Desire2Learn, Angel) allow adopters to access all of this edition's teaching and learning resources in one central location (via their course management system) through one seamless, guided experience.

Digital Media Archive, Second Edition Drawn from a variety of sources, the new edition of the **Digital Media Archive** includes more than 30 short video clips plus numerous new animations. These clips are available in MPEG format for easy import into PowerPoint presentations.

Scientific American **Frontiers Teaching Modules, Third Edition**, edited by Martin Bolt. The Third Edition offers 15 edited clips from *Scientific American* **Frontiers** segments produced between 2003 and 2005.

Worth Digital Media Archive
Available in CD-ROM and DVD formats; Faculty Guide also available
This presentation tool contains 42 digitized video clips of classic experiments and research. Footage includes animations, Albert Bandura's Bobo doll research, Harold Takooshian's bystander studies, Harry Harlow's monkey experiments, Stanley Milgram's obedience studies, and Ulric Neisser's selective attention research. The **Digital Media Archive** clips on CD-ROM are available in MPEG for optimal visual presentation with QuickTime and Windows Media Player and are compatible with Microsoft PowerPoint software.

The *Scientific American* Frontiers Video Collection, Second Edition
Available on CD-ROM and DVD formats; Faculty Guide also available
Hosted by Alan Alda, this enriched video collection from the highly praised *Scientific American* **Frontiers** series features a number of prominent psychologists, including Benjamin Beck, Renée Baillargeon, Barry Beyerstein, Paula Tallal, Michael Gazzaniga, Helen Neville, Linda Bartoshuk, Carlyle Smith, Scott Campbell, Patricia Murphy, James McGaugh, Irene Pepperberg, Steven Pinker, Karl Rosengren, Philip Zelazo, Janet Astington, Joan Peskin, Ray Hyman, Caroline Keating, Barbara Rothbaum, Hunter Hoffman, Sally Boysen, Larry Cahill, and Ron Schusterman. This collection is an excellent way to show students how psychological research is actually conducted.

For Students

PsychPortal has an interactive ebook, videos, animations, and simulations, and is an innovative learning space that combines a powerful quizzing engine with unparalleled media resources. PsychPortal conveniently offers all the functionality you need to support your online or hybrid course, yet it is flexible, customizable and simple enough to enhance your traditional course.

The Student Video Tool Kit for Introductory Psychology offers footage of classic experiments to illustrate key psychological concepts, as well as the most current and cutting-edge clips from the BBC's motion picture gallery, allowing students to witness psychological science as it comes to life. The clips are all accompanied by questions to assess students' understanding. **The Student Video Tool Kit** can be assigned for work outside the classroom and student performance can be accessed through an online grade book. It can be packaged with *Psychology: A Concise Introduction,* **Third Edition.** Adopters of *Psychology: A Concise Introduction* who choose to package **The Student Video Tool Kit** with the text will also receive **The Instructor Video Tool Kit for Introductory**

Psychology. Available on CD-ROMs or DVD, **The Instructor Video Tool Kit** contains more than 120 digitized video clips that can be easily imported into PowerPoint or other presentation resources for classroom lectures.

Book Companion Site
www.worthpublishers.com/griggs
The *Psychology: A Concise Introduction,* **Third Edition, Companion Web site** offers students a virtual study guide, 24 hours a day, seven days a week. These resources are free and do not require any special access codes or passwords. The site includes self-tests, review materials, annotated Web links, simulations, and demonstrations.

PsychSim 5.0, Thomas E. Ludwig, Hope College, CD-ROM
Developed by leading multimedia author Thomas Ludwig, *PsychSim* offers students a unique way to better understand the major concepts of general psychology. **Version 5.0** contains 42 modules that place the student in the role of experimenter (for example, conditioning a rat, probing the hypothalamus electrically, or working in a sleep lab) or as a participant (for example, responding to tests of memory and visual illusions or interpreting facial expressions) in simulated research. Other simulations provide dynamic tutorials or demonstrations of important principles and processes. Through *PsychSim,* students develop a much deeper understanding of core psychological concepts by engaging in the discipline's classic experiments. *PsychSim 5.0* is available to students on CD-ROM with an accompanying booklet. Twenty *PsychSim* modules are also available through the companion Web site.

Additional Reading for Students
All of the following can be packaged with *Psychology: A Concise Introduction,* **Third Edition,** for a nominal additional cost.

Scientific American Reader to Accompany *Psychology: A Concise Introduction*
To provide a relevant and inexpensive supplementary reader to *Psychology: A Concise Introduction* I went through the *Scientific American* database and selected 10 recent articles that best complement the 10 chapters in the text. The articles are sequenced to match the chapter topic order, and the chapter related to each article will adequately prepare the student to read the article. The *Scientific American Reader* provides another tool for enhancing lectures, encouraging discussion, and emphasizing the relevance of psychology to everyday life.

Pursuing Human Strengths: A Positive Psychology Guide, Martin Bolt, Calvin College
Martin Bolt's workbook aims to help students build up their strengths. Closely following the research, this book provides a brief overview of nine positive traits, such as hope, self-respect, commitment, and joy. It also offers self-assessment activities that help students gauge how much of the trait they have developed, and research-based suggestions for how they might work further toward fostering these traits.

Critical Thinking Companion, **Second Edition, Jane Halonen, University of West Florida; Cynthia Gray, Alverno College**
Tied to the main topics in introductory psychology, this handbook includes six categories of critical thinking exercises—pattern recognition, practical problem solving, creative problem solving, scientific problem solving, psychological reasoning, and perspective taking.

Acknowledgments

First, I would like to thank all the reviewers who gave generously of their time and expertise in working on the first three editions of *Psychology: A Concise Introduction*. I am especially thankful to my colleague **Jeff Farrar** for his very thoughtful work on Chapter 7. My gratitude extends to the following reviewers for their invaluable contributions.

Nancy Bales
Gavilan College

Kathleen Briggs
University of Minnesota

Andrew N. Christopher
Albion College

Sarah Cooper
Ohlone College

Deanna Dodson
Lebanon Valley College

Marjan Ghahramanlou
Community College of Baltimore County–Catonsville

Bill Godsil
Santa Monica College

Vernon Haynes
Youngstown State University

Jeffrey Henriques
University of Wisconsin–Madison

Brian J. Hock
Austin Peay State University

Sherri L. Jackson
Jacksonville University

Angela Kelling
Georgia Institute of Technology

Gary Klatsky
Oswego State University of New York

Eric Landrum
Boise State University

David McDonald
University of Missouri–Columbia

Gary Nallan
University of North Carolina–Asheville

John Norland
Blackhawk Technical College

Susan O'Donnell
George Fox University

Nicole Peck
Kansas State University

Mark Seely
Saint Joseph's College

Albert F. Smith
Cleveland State University

Tirza Shulman
Kansas State University

Inger Thompson
Glendale Community College

Stephen A. Truhon
Austin Peay State University

Sandra Wilcox
California State University–Dominguez Hills

Clive D. L. Wynne
University of Florida

I am also indebted to my supplements author team—**Andrew N. Christopher, Cynthia S. Koenig,** and **Pam Marek.** I truly appreciate their hard work and commitment to excellence.

At Worth Publishers, I am indebted to the many editorial and production people who worked on this revision. These people are listed on the copyright page, but special thanks go to **Tracey Kuehn** (Associate Managing Editor), **Leigh Renhard** (Project Editor), **Ted Szczepanski** (Photo Editor), and **Sarah Segal** (Production Manager) who together skillfully managed the text's production, and **Babs Reingold** (Art Director) who supervised the development of the book's beautiful cover and its art and design program. I would also like to specifically thank **Nancy Olivier** for her beautiful chapter opening art and **Ravenna Taylor** for the gorgeous cover art. In addition, I appreciate the dedication and efforts of my copy editor **Francine Almash,** my meticulous proofreader **Jean Erler,** and my indexer, **Alexandra Nickerson.** My deepest thanks go to **Kevin Feyen,** my current Editor, and **Marge Byers** and **Renee Altier,** my two previous Editors, for their insightful and invaluable guidance of this project throughout the first three editions.

Finally, my thanks extend to my wife, Sherri. Her love, encouragement, and unflagging support kept me going through all three editions of this text.

THIRD EDITION

PSYCHOLOGY

A Concise Introduction

1 The Science of Psychology

What do you think psychologists do? If you are like most people, when you think of a psychologist, you think of a therapist counseling people who have problems. If I asked you to name a psychologist, you would probably name Sigmund Freud. However, Freud and psychologists who work as therapists are not the focus of this book. They will be discussed, but they are only a part of psychology's story. Psychology is a science, not just a mental health profession. The subjects of this scientific study are you, me, all humans. Some psychologists may use other animals in their research, but their main goal is usually still to understand humans. **Psychology** is the science of behavior and mental processes. Psychologists attempt to understand all aspects of both our observable behavior, such as speech and physical movement, and internal mental processes, such as remembering and thinking, which cannot be directly observed. Psychologists may be found in any number of roles, including teaching, research-ing, consulting, and yes, counseling troubled people. This book, however, will focus on the research done by psychological scientists, the process by which they've accomplished that research, and what we've learned from their work.

psychology The science of behavior and mental processes.

Psychological researchers study everything about us from how our brain works and how we see and hear to how we reason and make decisions. The American Psychological Association lists 54 different divisions of psychology, and psycholo-gists specialize in studying each of these different aspects of our behavior and mental processing. To learn more about these various subfields and careers in psychology, visit www.apa.org/careers/resources/guides/careers.aspx. Although there are many diverse areas within psychology, there are only four major research perspectives for studying these topics. We will begin with a general overview of these four perspectives and then provide descriptions of the major research methods that psychologists use regardless of their perspective. Understanding these perspectives and the research methods used by psychologists will allow you to start thinking like a psychologist (like a scientist).

Note that there are other perspectives in psychology that are primarily clinical in nature (related to psychological therapy). We will discuss the psychoanalytic perspective (which emphasizes the interaction of unconscious forces and child-hood experiences in personality development) and the humanistic perspective (which emphasizes the personal growth motive) in Chapter 8, Personality Theories and Assessment.

The Four Major Research Perspectives

There are four major research perspectives—biological, cognitive, behavioral, and sociocultural. It's important to understand that these perspectives are comple-mentary. The research findings from the major perspectives fit together like the pieces of a jigsaw puzzle to give us a more complete picture. No particular perspective is better than the others, and psychologists using the various perspectives work together to provide a more complete explanation of our behav-ior and mental processing.

The best way to understand how the major research perspectives differ is to consider the major goal of psychologists—to explain human behavior and mental processes. To explain means to know the causes of our behavior and mental processes. To facilitate your understanding of these perspectives, I discuss them in two different pairs based on the type of causal factors that they emphasize—internal factors or external factors. The biological perspective and the cognitive perspective focus on causes that stem from within us (internal factors); the behavioral perspective and the sociocultural perspective focus on causes that stem from outside us (external factors). We'll also briefly consider developmental psychology, a research field that provides a nice example of how these perspectives complement one another.

Perspectives Emphasizing Internal Factors

The biological perspective and the cognitive perspective focus on internal factors. In the case of the **biological perspective,** our physiological hardware (especially the brain and nervous system) is viewed as the major determiner of behavior and mental processing. The genetic and evolutionary bases of our physiology are also important. In contrast, for the **cognitive perspective,** the major explanatory focus is on how our mental processes, such as perception, memory, and problem solving, work and impact our behavior. To contrast this perspective with the biological perspective, you can think of these mental processes as the software, or programs, of the brain (the hardware).

The biological perspective. We are biological creatures; therefore, looking for explanations in terms of our biology makes sense. Biological psychologists look for causes within our physiology, our genetics, and human evolution. They argue that our actions and thoughts are functions of our underlying biology. Let's consider an example of what most people would term a "psychological" disorder, depression. Why do we get depressed? A biological psychologist might focus on a deficiency in the activity of certain chemicals in the nervous system as a cause of this problem. Therefore, to treat depression using this perspective, the problem with the chemical deficiency would have to be rectified. How? Antidepressant drugs such as Prozac or Zoloft might be prescribed. These drugs increase the activity of the neural chemicals involved, and this increased activity might lead to changes in our mood. If all goes well, a few weeks after beginning treatment, we begin to feel better. Thus, our mood is at least partly a function of our brain chemistry. Of course, many nonbiological factors can contribute to depression, including unhealthy patterns of thinking, learned helplessness, and disturbing life circumstances. It's important to remember that employing psychology's complementary perspectives in addressing research and clinical issues provides the most complete answer.

biological perspective A research perspective whose major explanatory focus is how the brain, nervous system, and other physiological mechanisms produce behavior and mental processes.

cognitive perspective A research perspective whose major explanatory focus is how mental processes, such as perception, memory, and problem solving, work and impact behavior.

In addition to the impact of brain chemistry, biological psychologists also study the involvement of the various parts of the brain and nervous system on our behavior and mental processes. For example, they have learned that our "eyes" are indeed in the back of our head. Biological psychologists have found that it is the back part of our brain that allows us to see the world. So, a more correct expression would be that "our eyes are in the back of our brain." The brain is not only essential for vision, but it is also the control center for almost all of our behavior and mental processing. In Chapter 2, you will learn how the brain manages this incredibly difficult task as well as about the roles of other parts of our nervous system and the many different chemicals that transmit information within it.

The cognitive perspective. Cognitive psychologists study all aspects of cognitive processing from perception to the higher-level processes, such as problem solving and reasoning. Let's try a brief exercise to gain insight into one aspect of our cognitive processing. I will name a category, and you say aloud as fast as you can the first instance of that category that comes to mind. Are you ready? The first category is FRUIT. If you are like most people, you said apple or orange. Let's try another one. The category is PIECE OF FURNITURE. Again, if you are like most people, you said chair or sofa. Why, in the case of FRUIT, don't people say pomegranate or papaya? How do we have categories of information organized so that certain examples come to mind first for most of us? In brief, cognitive research has shown that we organize categorical information around what we consider the most typical or representative examples of a category (Rosch, 1973). These examples (such as apple and orange for FRUIT) are called prototypes for the category and are retrieved first when we think of the category.

A broader cognitive processing question concerns how memory retrieval in general works. Haven't you been in the situation of not being able to retrieve information from memory that you know you have stored there? This can be especially frustrating in exam situations. Or think about the opposite—an event or person comes to mind seemingly out of the blue. Why? Even more complex questions arise when we consider how we attempt to solve problems, reason, and make decisions. For example, here's a series problem with a rather simple answer, but most people find it very difficult: What is the next character in the series OTTFFSS_? The answer is not "O." Why is this problem so difficult? The progress that cognitive psychologists have made in answering such questions about cognitive processing will be discussed in Chapter 5, on memory, and Chapter 6, on thinking and intelligence (where you can find the answer to the series problem).

Perspectives Emphasizing External Factors

Both the behavioral perspective and the sociocultural perspective focus on external factors in explaining human behavior and mental processing. The **behavioral perspective** emphasizes conditioning of our behavior by environmental events, and there is more emphasis on explaining observable

behavioral perspective A research perspective whose major explanatory focus is how external environmental events condition observable behavior.

sociocultural perspective A research perspective whose major explanatory focus is how other people and the cultural context impact behavior and mental processes.

behavior than on unobservable mental processes. The **sociocultural perspective** also emphasizes the influence of the external environment, but it more specifically focuses on the impact of other people and our culture as the major determiners of our behavior and mental processing. In addition to conditioning, the sociocultural perspective equally stresses cognitive types of learning, such as learning by observation or modeling, and thus focuses just as much on mental processing as observable behavior.

The behavioral perspective. According to the behavioral perspective, we behave as we do because of our past history of conditioning by our environment. There are two major types of conditioning, classical (or Pavlovian) and operant. You may be familiar with the most famous example of classical conditioning—Ivan Pavlov's dogs (Pavlov, 1927/1960). In his research, Pavlov sounded a tone and then put food in a dog's mouth. The pairing of these two environmental events led the dog to salivate to the tone in anticipation of the arrival of the food. The salivary response to the tone was conditioned by the sequencing of the two environmental events (the sounding of the tone and putting food in the dog's mouth). The dog learned that the sound of the tone meant food was on its way. According to behaviorists, such classical conditioning can explain how we learn fear and other emotional responses, taste aversions, and many other behaviors.

Classical conditioning is important in determining our behavior, but behaviorists believe operant conditioning is even more important. Operant conditioning involves the relationship between our behavior and its environmental consequences (whether they are reinforcing or punishing). Simply put, if we are reinforced for a behavior, its probability will increase; if we are punished, the probability will decrease. For example, if you ask your teacher a question and he praises you for asking such a good question and then answers it very carefully, you will tend to ask more questions. However, if the teacher criticizes you for asking a stupid question and doesn't even bother to answer it, you will probably not ask more questions. Environmental events (such as a teacher's response) thus control behavior through their reinforcing or punishing nature. Both types of conditioning, classical and operant, will be discussed in Chapter 4. The point to remember here is that environmental events condition our behavior and are the causes of it.

The sociocultural perspective. This perspective focuses on the impact of other people (individuals and groups) and our cultural surroundings on our behavior and mental processing. We are social animals, therefore other people are important to us and thus greatly affect what we do and how we think. None of us is immune to these social "forces." Haven't your thinking and behavior been impacted by other people, especially those close to you? Our coverage of sociocultural research will emphasize the impact of these social forces on our behavior and mental processing.

To help you understand the nature of sociocultural research, let's consider a famous set of experiments that attempted to explain the social forces operating during a tragic, real-world event—the Kitty Genovese murder in 1964 (Latané & Darley, 1970). Kitty Genovese was brutally attacked, stabbed, and murdered while trying to enter her apartment building late at night. The attack was a prolonged one in which the attacker left and came back at least three times over a half-hour period. Kitty screamed and pleaded for help, but none was forthcoming. Some people living in the building heard her screams for help, but no one helped. Someone finally called the police, but it was too late. The attacker had fled, and Kitty was dead. Exactly how many people witnessed the attack and failed to help is not clear. Initially reported as 38, more recent analysis of the available evidence indicates that the number may have been much smaller (Manning, Levine, & Collins, 2007). Regardless, no one acted until it was too late. To explain why these people didn't help, researchers manipulated the number of bystanders present in follow-up experiments. Their general finding is called the bystander effect—the probability of a victim receiving help in an emergency is higher when there is only one bystander than when there are many. In brief, other bystanders may lead us not to help. How do we apply this effect to the Kitty Genovese murder? The bystanders to the murder led each other not to help. Each felt that someone else would do something and that surely someone else had already called the police. This research, along with studies of other intriguing topics that involve social forces such as why we conform and obey even when it may lead to destructive behavior, will be detailed in Chapter 9, on social psychology.

Now you have at least a general understanding of the four major research perspectives, summarized in Table 1.1. Remember, these perspectives are complementary, and, when used together, help us to gain a more complete understanding of our behavior and mental processes. Developmental psychology (the scientific study of human development across the lifespan) is a research area that nicely illustrates the benefits of using multiple research perspectives to address experimental questions. A good example is the study of how children acquire language. Initially, behavioral learning principles of reinforcement and imitation were believed to be sufficient to account for language acquisition. Although these principles

Table 1.1	The Four Major Research Perspectives in Psychology	
Research Perspective	**Major Explanatory Focus**
Biological	How our physiology (especially the brain and nervous system) produces our behavior and mental processes and how genetics and evolution have impacted our physiology
Cognitive	How our mental processes, such as perception, memory, and problem solving, work and how they impact our behavior
Behavioral	How external environmental events condition our observable behavior
Sociocultural	How other people and the cultural context impact our behavior and mental processes

clearly do play a role (Whitehurst & Valdez-Menchaca, 1988), most developmental language researchers now recognize that biology, cognition, and the sociocultural context are also critical to language learning (Pinker, 1994; Tomasello, 2003). Studies of the brain, for example, indicate that specific brain areas are involved in language acquisition. Research has also revealed that cognitive processes are important as well. For example, as children acquire new concepts, they learn the names that go with them and thus expand their vocabulary. In addition, it has been shown that the sociocultural context of language helps children to learn about the social pragmatic functions of language. For instance, they use a variety of pragmatic cues (such as an adult's focus of attention) for word learning. Thus, by using all four research perspectives, developmental researchers have gained a much better understanding of how children acquire language. We will learn in Chapter 7 (Developmental Psychology) that our understanding of many developmental questions has been broadened by the use of multiple research perspectives.

Subsequent chapters will detail the main concepts, theories, and research findings in the major fields of psychology. As you learn about these theories and research findings, beware of the **hindsight bias (I-knew-it-all-along phenomenon)**—the tendency, after learning about an outcome, to be overconfident in one's ability to have predicted it. Research has shown that after people learn about an experimental finding, the finding seems obvious and very predictable (Slovic & Fischhoff, 1977). Almost any conceivable psychological research finding may seem like common sense after you learn about it. If you were told that research indicates that "opposites attract," you would likely nod in agreement. Isn't it obvious? Then again, if you had been told that research indicates that "birds of a feather flock together," you would probably have also agreed and thought the finding obvious. Hindsight bias works to make even a pair of opposite research conclusions both seem obvious (Teigen, 1986). Be mindful of hindsight bias as you learn about what psychologists have learned about us. It may lead you to think that this information is more obvious and easier than it actually is. You may falsely think that you already know much of the material and then not study sufficiently, leading to disappointment at exam time. The hindsight bias even works on itself. Don't you feel like you already knew about this bias? Incidentally, social psychology researchers have found that birds of a feather DO flock together and that opposites DO NOT attract (Myers, 2002).

Psychologists' conclusions are based upon scientific research and thus provide the best answers to questions about human behavior and mental processing. Whether these answers sometimes seem obvious or sometimes agree with common sense is not important. What is important is understanding how psychologists conduct this scientific research in order to get the best answers to their questions. In the next section, we discuss their research methods.

hindsight bias (I-knew-it-all-along phenomenon) The tendency, after learning about an outcome, to be overconfident in one's ability to have predicted it.

Section Summary

In this section, we learned that there are four major research perspectives in psychology. Two of them, the biological perspective and the cognitive perspective, focus on internal causes of our behavior and mental processing. The biological perspective focuses on causal explanations in terms of our physiology, especially the brain and nervous system. The cognitive perspective focuses on understanding how our mental processes work and how they impact our behavior. The biological perspective focuses on the physiological hardware, while the cognitive perspective focuses more on the mental processes or software of the brain.

The behavioral perspective and the sociocultural perspective emphasize external causes. The behavioral perspective focuses on how our observable behavior is conditioned by external environmental events. The sociocultural perspective emphasizes the impact that other people (social forces) and our culture have on our behavior and mental processing.

Psychologists use all four perspectives to get a more complete explanation of our behavior and mental processing. None of these perspectives is better than the others; they are complementary. Developmental psychology is a research field that nicely illustrates their complementary nature.

We also briefly discussed the hindsight bias, the I-knew-it-all-along phenomenon. This bias leads us to find outcomes as more obvious and predictable than they truly are. You need to beware of this bias when learning the basic research findings and theories discussed in the remainder of this text. It may lead you to think that this information is more obvious and easier than it actually is. It is important that you realize that psychologists have used scientific research methods to conduct their studies, thereby obtaining the best answers possible to their questions about human behavior and mental processing.

ConceptCheck | 1

> **Explain how the biological and cognitive research perspectives differ in their explanations of human behavior and mental processing.**

> **Explain how the behavioral and sociocultural research perspectives differ in their explanations of human behavior and mental processing.**

Research Methods Used by Psychologists

Regardless of their perspective, psychology researchers use the same research methods. These methods fall into three categories—descriptive, correlational, and experimental. The experimental method is used most often because it allows the researcher to explore cause–effect relationships. Remember, the main goal of psychology is to explain (through cause–effect relationships) human behavior and mental processes. However, sometimes researchers can't conduct experiments. For example, it is obviously unethical to set up an experiment testing the effects of passive smoking on children. Who would knowingly subject a group of children to cigarette smoke? In such situations, psychologists can learn a lot by employing the other methods—descriptive and correlational. Researchers can carefully observe and describe the health effects on one child in a family of smokers, or they can study many families in search of relationships (correlations) between parental smoking and childhood infections. These other research methods also provide data for developing hypotheses (testable predictions about cause–effect relationships) to examine in experimental research. We'll discuss the three types of methods in the following order: descriptive, correlational, and experimental.

Descriptive Methods

There are three types of **descriptive methods:** observational techniques, case studies, and survey research. The main purpose of all three methods is to provide objective and detailed descriptions of behavior and mental processes. However, these descriptive data only allow the researcher to speculate about cause–effect relationships—to develop hypotheses about causal relationships. Such hypotheses must then be tested in experiments. With this important limitation in mind, we'll consider the three descriptive methods one at a time.

Observational techniques. Observational techniques exactly reflect their name. The researcher directly observes the behavior of interest. Such observation can be done in the laboratory. For example, children's behavior can be observed using one-way mirrors in the laboratory. However, behavior in the laboratory setting may not be natural. This is why researchers often use **naturalistic observation,** a descriptive research method in which behavior is observed in its natural setting, without the researcher intervening in the behavior being observed. Researchers use naturalistic observation when they are interested in how humans or other animals behave in their natural environments. The researcher attempts to describe both objectively and thoroughly the behaviors that are present and the relationships among these behaviors. There have been many well-known observational studies of other species of animals in their natural habitats. You are probably familiar with some of them—Dian Fossey's study of mountain gorillas in Africa, on which the movie, *Gorillas in the Mist,* was based, and Jane Goodall's study of chimpanzees in Africa (Fossey, 1983; Goodall, 1986). This method is not used only for the observation of other species of animals. Observational studies of human behavior are conducted in many natural settings such as the workplace and school, and in social settings such as bars.

Observational techniques do have a major potential problem, though. The observer may influence or change the behavior of those being observed. This is why observers must remain as unobtrusive as possible, so that the results won't be contaminated by their presence. To overcome this possible shortcoming, researchers use participant observation. In **participant observation,** the observer becomes part of the group being observed. Sometimes naturalistic observation

descriptive methods Research methods whose main purpose is to provide objective and detailed descriptions of behavior and mental processes.

naturalistic observation A descriptive research method in which the behavior of interest is observed in its natural setting, and the researcher does not intervene in the behavior being observed.

participant observation A descriptive research method in which the observer becomes part of the group being observed.

studies that start out with unobtrusive observation end up as participant observation studies. For example, Dian Fossey's study of gorillas turned into participant observation when she was finally accepted as a member of the group. However, in most participant observation studies, the observer begins the study as a participant, whether in a laboratory or natural setting. You can think of this type of study as comparable to doing undercover work. A famous example of such a study involved a group of people posing as patients with symptoms of a major mental disorder to see if doctors at psychiatric hospitals could distinguish them from real patients (Rosenhan, 1973). It turned out that the doctors couldn't do so, but the patients could. Once admitted, these "pseudopatients" acted normally and asked to be released to see what would happen. Well, they weren't released right away. We will find out what happened to them in Chapter 10.

THE FAR SIDE® By GARY LARSON

"Well, well—another blonde hair. ... Conducting a little more 'research' with that Jane Goodall tramp?"

The Far Side® by Gary Larson © 1987 FarWorks, Inc. All Rights Reserved. The Far Side® and the Larson® signature are registered trademarks of FarWorks, Inc. Used with permission.

Case studies. Detailed observation is also involved in a case study. In a **case study,** the researcher studies an individual in depth over an extended period of time. In brief, the researcher attempts to learn as much as possible about the individual being studied. A life history for the individual is developed, and data for a variety of tests are collected. The most common use of case studies is in clinical settings with patients suffering specific deficits or problems. The main goal of a case study is to gather information that will help in the treatment of the patient. The results of a case study cannot be generalized to the entire population. They are specific to the individual that has been studied. However, case study data do allow researchers to develop hypotheses that can then be tested in experimental research. A famous example of such a case study is that of the late Henry Molaison, an amnesic (Scoville & Milner, 1957). He was studied by nearly

case study A descriptive research method in which the researcher studies an individual in depth over an extended period of time.

survey research A descriptive research method in which the researcher uses questionnaires and interviews to collect information about the behavior, beliefs, and attitudes of particular groups of people.

100 investigators (Corkin, 2002) and is often referred to as the most studied individual in the history of neuroscience (Squire, 2009). For confidentiality purposes while he was alive (he died in 2008 at the age of 82), only his initials, H. M., were used to identify him in the hundreds of studies that he participated in for over five decades. Thus, we will refer to him as H. M. His case will be discussed in more detail in Chapter 5 (Memory), but let's consider some of his story here to illustrate the importance of case studies in the development of hypotheses and the subsequent experimental work to test these hypotheses.

For medical reasons, H. M. had his hippocampus (a part of the brain below the cortex) and the surrounding areas surgically removed at a young age. His case study included testing his memory capabilities in depth after the operation. Except for some amnesia for a period preceding his surgery (especially events in the days immediately before the surgery), he appeared to have normal memory for information that he had learned before the operation, but he didn't seem to be able to form any new memories. For example, if he didn't know you before his operation, he would never be able to remember your name regardless of how many times you met with him. He could read a magazine over and over again without ever realizing that he had read it before. Such memory deficits led to the hypothesis that the hippocampus plays an important role in the formation of new memories; later experimental research confirmed this hypothesis (Cohen & Eichenbaum, 1993).

We will learn exactly what role the hippocampus plays in memory in Chapter 5. Remember, researchers cannot make cause–effect statements based on the findings of a case study, but they can formulate hypotheses that can be tested in experiments.

Survey research. The last descriptive method is one that you are most likely already familiar with, survey research. You have probably completed surveys either over the phone, via the mail, or in person during an interview. **Survey research** uses questionnaires and interviews to collect information about the behavior, beliefs, and attitudes of particular groups of people. It is assumed in survey research that people are willing and able to answer the survey questions accurately. However, the wording, order, and structure of the survey questions may lead the participants to give biased answers (Schwartz, 1999). For example, survey researchers need to be aware of the social desirability bias, our tendency to respond in socially approved ways that may not reflect what we actually think or do. This means that questions need to be constructed carefully to minimize such biases. Developing a well-structured, unbiased set of survey questions is a difficult, time-consuming task, but one that is essential to doing good survey research.

"Next question: I believe that life is a constant striving for balance, requiring frequent tradeoffs between morality and necessity, within a cyclic pattern of joy and sadness, forging a trail of bittersweet memories until one slips, inevitably, into the jaws of death. Agree or disagree?"

Another necessity in survey research is surveying a representative sample of the relevant **population,** the entire group of people being studied. For many reasons (such as time and money), it is impossible to survey every person in the population. This is why the researcher only surveys a **sample,** the subset of people in a population participating in a study. For these sample data to be meaningful, the sample has to be representative of the larger relevant population. If you don't have a representative sample, then generalization of the survey findings to the population is not possible.

One ill-fated survey study of women and love (Hite, 1987) tried to generalize from a nonrepresentative sample (Jackson, 2009). Shere Hite's sample was drawn mainly from women's organizations and political groups, plus some women who requested and completed a survey following the researcher's talk-show appearances. Because such a sample is not representative of American women in general, the results were not either. For example, the estimates of the numbers of women having affairs and disenchanted in their relationships with men were greatly overestimated. To obtain a representative sample, survey researchers usually use random sampling.

In **random sampling,** each individual in the population has an equal opportunity of being in the sample. To understand the "equal opportunity" part of the definition, think about selecting names from a hat, where each name has an equal opportunity for being selected. In actuality, statisticians have developed procedures for obtaining a random sample that parallel selecting names randomly from a hat. Think about how you would obtain a random sample of first-year students at your college. You couldn't just sample randomly from those first-year students in your psychology class. All first-year students wouldn't have an equal opportunity to be in your sample. You would have to get a complete list of all first-year students from the registrar and then sample randomly from it. The point to remember is that a survey study must have a representative sample in order to generalize the research findings to the population.

Correlational Studies

In a **correlational study,** two variables are measured to determine if they are related (how well either one predicts the other). A **variable** is any factor that can take on more than one value. For example, age, height, grade point average, and intelligence test scores are all variables. In conducting a correlational study, the researcher first gets a representative sample of the relevant population. Next, the researcher takes the two measurements on the sample. For example, the researcher could measure a person's height and their intelligence test score.

population The entire group of people that a researcher is studying.

sample The subset of a population that actually participates in a research study.

random sampling A sampling technique that obtains a representative sample of a population by ensuring that each individual in a population has an equal opportunity to be in the sample.

correlational study A research study in which two variables are measured to determine if they are related (how well either one predicts the other).

variable Any factor that can take on more than one value.

The correlation coefficient. To see if the variables are related, the researcher calculates a statistic called the **correlation coefficient,** a statistic that tells us the type and the strength of the relationship between two variables. Correlation coefficients range in value from –1.0 to +1.0. The sign of the coefficient, + or –, tells us the type of relationship, positive or negative. A **positive correlation** indicates a direct relationship between two variables—low scores on one variable tend to be paired with low scores on the other variable, and high scores on one variable tend to be paired with high scores on the other variable. Think about the relationship between height and weight. These two variables are positively related. Taller people tend to be heavier. SAT scores and first-year college grades are also positively correlated (Linn, 1982). Students who have higher SAT scores tend to get higher grades during their first year of college.

A **negative correlation** is an inverse relationship between two variables—low scores on one variable tend to be paired with high scores on the other variable, and high scores on one variable tend to be paired with low scores on the other variable. A good example of a negative correlation is the relationship for children between time spent watching television and grades in school—the more time spent watching television, the lower the school grades (Ridley-Johnson, Cooper, & Chance, 1983). As you know if you have ever climbed a mountain, elevation and temperature are negatively correlated—as elevation increases, temperature decreases. In summary, the sign of the coefficient tells us the type of the relationship between the two variables—positive (+) for a direct relationship or negative (–) for an inverse relationship.

The second part of the correlation coefficient is its absolute value, from 0 to 1.0. The strength of the correlation is indicated by its absolute value. Zero and absolute values near 0 indicate no relationship. As the absolute value increases to 1.0, the strength of the relationship increases. Please note that the sign of the coefficient does not tell us anything about the strength of the relationship. Coefficients do not function like numbers on the number line, where positive numbers are greater than negative numbers. With correlation coefficients, only the absolute value of the number tells us about the relationship's strength. For example, –.50 indicates a stronger relationship than +.25. As the strength of the correlation increases, researchers can predict the relationship with more accuracy. If the coefficient is + (or –) 1.0, we have perfect predictability. Virtually all correlation coefficients in psychological research have an absolute value less than 1.0. Thus, we usually do not have perfect predictability so there will be exceptions to these relationships, even the strong ones. These exceptions do not, however, invalidate the general trends indicated by the correlations. They only indicate that the relationships are not perfect. Because the correlations are not perfect, such exceptions have to exist.

correlation coefficient A statistic that tells us the type and the strength of the relationship between two variables. The sign of the coefficient (+ or –) indicates the type of correlation—positive or negative, respectively. The absolute value of the coefficient (0.0 to 1.0) represents the strength of the correlation, with 1.0 being the maximum strength.

positive correlation A direct relationship between two variables.

negative correlation An inverse relationship between two variables.

Scatterplots. A good way to understand the predictability of a coefficient is to examine a **scatterplot**—a visual depiction of correlational data. In a scatterplot, each data point represents the scores on the two variables for each partici-

> **scatterplot** A visual depiction of correlational data in which each data point represents the scores on the two variables for each participant.

pant. Several sample scatterplots are presented in Figure 1.1 (page 14). Correlational studies usually involve a large number of participants, therefore there are usually a large number of data points in a scatterplot. Because those in Figure 1.1 are just examples to illustrate how to interpret scatterplots, there are only 15 points in each one. This means there were 15 participants in each of the hypothetical correlational studies leading to these scatterplots.

The scatterplots in Figure 1.1(a) and (b) indicate perfect 1.0 correlations—(a) a perfect positive correlation and (b) a perfect negative correlation. All of the points fall on the same line in each scatterplot, which allows us to predict one variable from the other perfectly by using the equation for the line. This means that you have maximal predictability. Please note that the difference between (a) and (b) is the direction of the data points (line). If the data points show an increasing trend (go from the bottom left to the top right of the scatterplot) as in (a), it is a positive relationship. Low scores on one variable tend to be paired with low scores on the other variable, and high scores with high scores. This is a direct relationship. However, if the data points show a decreasing trend (go from the top left to the bottom right) as in (b), there is a negative relationship. Low scores tend to be paired with high scores, and high scores with low scores. This is an inverse relationship.

The scatterplot in Figure 1.1(c) indicates no relationship between the two variables. There is no direction to the data points in this scatterplot. They are scattered all over in a random fashion. This means that we have a correlation near 0 and minimal predictability. Now consider (d) and (e). First, you should realize that (d) indicates a positive correlation because of the direction of the data points from the bottom left to the top right and that (e) indicates a negative correlation because of the direction of the scatter from the top left to the bottom right. But what else does the scatter of the data points tell us? Note that the data points in (d) and (e) neither fall on the same line as in (a) and (b) nor are they scattered all about the graph with no directional component as in (c). Thus, scatterplots (d) and (e) indicate correlations with strengths somewhere between 0 and 1.0. As the amount of scatter of the data points increases, the strength of the correlation decreases. So, how strong would the correlations represented in (d) and (e) be? They would be fairly strong because there is not much scatter. Remember, as the amount of scatter increases, the strength decreases and so does predictability. When the scatter is maximal as in (c), the strength is near 0, and we have little predictability.

The third-variable problem. Strong correlations give us excellent predictability, but they do not allow us to draw cause-effect conclusions about the relationships between the variables. I cannot stress this point enough. Correlation is necessary but not sufficient for causation to exist. Remember, correlational data

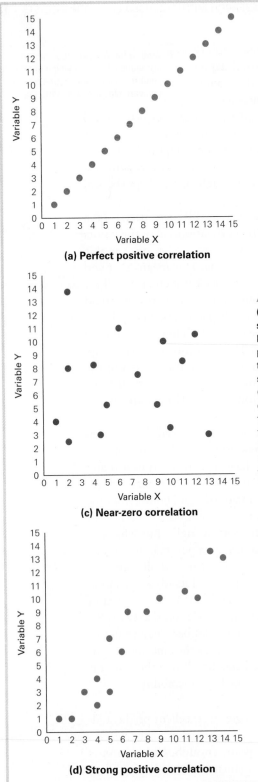

(a) Perfect positive correlation

(c) Near-zero correlation

(d) Strong positive correlation

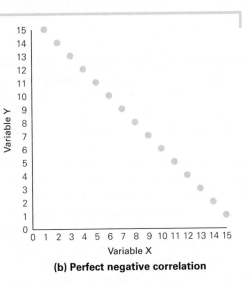

(b) Perfect negative correlation

▲ **Figure 1.1** I Some Sample Scatterplots I (a) and (b) are examples of perfect correlations because there is no scatter—all of the data points in each plot fall on the same line. The correlation in (a) is positive because the data points show an increasing trend (go from bottom left to top right) and is negative in (b) because the data points show a decreasing trend (go from top left to bottom right). (c) is an example of a near-zero correlation because the data points are scattered all over and do not show a directional trend. (d) is an example of a strong positive correlation because there is not much scatter and the data points have an increasing trend. (e) is an example of a strong negative correlation because there is not much scatter and the data points show a decreasing trend.

(e) Strong negative correlation

do not allow us to conclude anything about cause–effect relationships. Only data collected in well-controlled experiments allow us to draw such conclusions. This does not mean that two correlated variables cannot be causally related, but rather that we cannot determine this from correlational data. Maybe they are; maybe they are not. Correlational data do not allow you to decide if they are or are not. Let's see why.

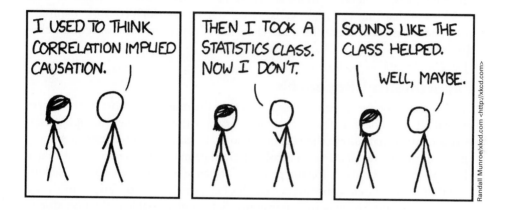

To understand this point, let's consider the negative correlation between self-esteem and depression. As self-esteem decreases, depression increases. But we cannot conclude that low self-esteem causes depression. First, it could be the reverse causal relationship. Isn't it just as likely that depression causes low self-esteem? Second, and of more consequence, isn't it possible that some third factor is responsible for the relationship between the two variables? For example, isn't it possible that some people have a biological predisposition for both low self-esteem and depression or that both self-esteem and depression are the result of a brain chemistry problem? Both self-esteem and depression could also stem from some current very stressful events. Such alternative possibilities are examples of the **third-variable problem**—another variable may be responsible for the relationship observed between two variables. In brief, such "third variables" are not controlled in a correlational study, making it impossible to determine the cause for the observed relationship.

To make sure you understand the third-variable problem, here is a very memorable example (Li, 1975, described in Stanovich, 2004). Because of overpopulation problems, a correlational study was conducted in Taiwan to identify variables that best predicted the use of contraceptive devices. Correlational data were collected on many different variables, but the researchers found that use of contraceptive devices was most strongly correlated with the number of electrical appliances in the home! Obviously having electrical appliances such as television sets, microwave ovens, and toasters around does not cause people to use birth control. What third variable might be responsible

> **third-variable problem** An explanation of a correlation between two variables in terms of another (third) variable that could possibly be responsible for the observed relationship between the two variables.

for this relationship? Think about it. A likely one is level of education. People with a higher education tend to be both better informed about birth control and to have a higher socioeconomic status. The former leads them to use contraceptive devices, and the latter allows them to buy more electrical appliances. To control for the effects of such third variables, researchers conduct an experiment in which they manipulate one variable and measure its effect upon another variable while controlling other potentially relevant variables. Researchers must control for possible third variables so that they can make cause-effect statements. Such control, manipulation, and measurement are the main elements of experimental research, which is described next.

Experimental Research

The key aspect of experimental research is that the researcher controls the experimental setting. The only factor that varies is what the researcher manipulates. It is this control that allows the researcher to make cause–effect statements about the experimental results. This control is derived primarily from two actions. First, the experimenter controls for the possible influence of third variables by making sure that they are held constant across all of the groups or conditions in the experiment. Second, the experimenter controls for any possible influences due to the individual characteristics of the participants, such as intelligence, motivation, and memory, by using **random assignment**—randomly assigning the participants to groups in an experiment in order to equalize participant characteristics across the various groups in the experiment. If the participant characteristics of the groups are on average equivalent at the beginning of the experiment, then any differences between the groups at the end of the experiment cannot be attributed to such characteristics.

Please note the differences between random assignment and random sampling. Random sampling is a technique in which a sample of participants that is representative of a population is obtained. Hence it is used not only in experiments but also in other research methods such as correlational studies and surveys. Random assignment is only used in experiments. It is a control measure in which the researcher randomly assigns the participants in the sample to the various groups or conditions in an experiment. Random sampling allows you to generalize your results to the relevant population; random assignment controls for possible influences of individual characteristics of the participants on the behavior(s) of interest in an experiment. These differences between random sampling and random assignment are summarized in Table 1.2.

random assignment A control measure in which participants are randomly assigned to groups in order to equalize participant characteristics across the various groups in an experiment.

independent variable In an experiment, the variable that is a hypothesized cause and thus is manipulated by the experimenter.

Designing an experiment. When a researcher designs an experiment, the researcher begins with a hypothesis (the prediction to be tested) about the cause-effect relationship between two variables. One of the two variables is assumed to be the cause, and the other variable is the one to be affected. The **independent variable** is the hypothesized cause, and

Table 1.2 Differences Between Random Sampling and Random Assignment	
Random Sampling	**Random Assignment**
A sampling technique in which a sample of participants that is representative of the population is obtained	A control measure in which participants in a sample are randomly assigned to the groups or conditions in an experiment
Used in experiments and some other research methods such as correlational studies and surveys	Used only in experiments
Allows researcher to generalize the findings to the relevant population	Allows researcher to control for possible influences of individual characteristics of the participants on the behavior(s) of interest

the experimenter manipulates it. The **dependent variable** is the variable that is hypothesized to be affected by the independent variable and thus is measured by the experimenter. Thus, in an **experiment** the researcher manipulates the independent variable and measures its effect on the dependent variable while controlling other potentially relevant variables. If there is a causal relationship between the independent and dependent variables, then the measurements of the dependent variable are dependent on the values of the independent variable, hence the name dependent variable. Sometimes the researcher hypothesizes more than one cause or more than one effect so he manipulates more than one independent variable or measures more than one dependent variable. To help you understand this terminology and the mechanics of an experiment, I'll describe an example.

Let's consider the simplest experiment first—only two groups. For control purposes, participants are randomly assigned to these two groups. One of the groups will be exposed to the independent variable, and the other will not. The group exposed to the independent variable is called the **experimental group,** and the group not exposed to the independent variable is called the **control group.** Let's say the experimenter's hypothesis is that aerobic exercise reduces anxiety. The independent variable that will be manipulated is aerobic exercise, and the dependent variable that will be measured is level of anxiety. The experimental group will participate in some aerobic exercise program, and the control group will not. To measure any possible effects of the aerobic exercise on anxiety, the experimenter must measure the anxiety levels of the participants in each group at the beginning of the study before the independent variable is manipulated, and then again after the manipulation. If the two groups are truly equivalent, the level of anxiety for each group at the beginning of the study should be essentially the

dependent variable In an experiment, a variable that is hypothesized to be affected by the independent variable and thus is measured by the experimenter.

experiment A research method in which the researcher manipulates one or more independent variables and measures their effect on one or more dependent variables while controlling other potentially relevant variables.

experimental group In an experiment, the group exposed to the independent variable.

control group In an experiment, the group not exposed to the independent variable.

same. If the aerobic exercise does reduce anxiety, then we should see this difference in the second measurement of anxiety at the end of the experiment.

The independent and dependent variables in an experiment must be operationally defined. An **operational definition** is a description of the operations or procedures the researcher uses to manipulate or measure a variable. In our sample experiment, the operational definition of aerobic exercise would include the type and the duration of the activity. For level of anxiety, the operational definition would describe the way the anxiety variable was measured (for example, a participant's score on a specified anxiety scale). Operational definitions not only clarify a particular experimenter's definitions of variables, but also allow other experimenters to attempt to replicate the experiment more easily.

Let's go back to our aerobic exercise experiment. We have our experimental group and our control group, but this experiment really requires a second control group. The first control group (the group not participating in the aerobic exercise program) provides a baseline level of anxiety to which the anxiety of the experimental group can then be compared. In other words, it controls for changes in the level of anxiety not due to aerobic exercise. However, we also need to control for what is called a **placebo effect**—improvement due to the expectation of improving because of receiving treatment. The placebo effect can arise not only from a conscious belief in the treatment but also from subconscious associations between recovery and the experience of being treated (Niemi, 2009). For example, stimuli that a patient links with getting better, such as a doctor's white lab coat or the smell of an examining room, may induce some improvement in the patient's condition. In addition, giving a medication a popular brand name, prescribing more frequent doses, using placebo injections rather than pills, or indicating that it is expensive can boost the effect of a placebo (Niemi, 2009; Stewart-Williams, 2004; Waber, Shiv, Carmon, & Ariely, 2008).

The reduction of anxiety in the experimental group participants in our aerobic exercise experiment may be partially or completely due to a placebo effect. This is why researchers add a control group called the placebo group to control for the possible placebo effect. A **placebo group** is a group of participants who believe they are receiving treatment, but they are not. They get a **placebo**—an inactive pill or a treatment that has no known effects. For example, the participants in a placebo group in the aerobic exercise experiment would be told that they are getting an antianxiety drug, but they would only get a placebo (in this case, a pill that has no active ingredient). The complete design for the aerobic exercise experiment including the experimental, placebo, and control groups is shown in Figure 1.2. For the experimenter to conclude that there is a placebo effect, the reduction of anxiety in the placebo group would have to be significantly greater than the reduction for the control group. For the experimenter to conclude that the reduction of anxiety in the experimental group is due to aerobic exercise and

operational definition A description of the operations or procedures that a researcher uses to manipulate or measure a variable.

placebo effect Improvement due to the expectation of improving because of receiving treatment.

placebo group A control group of participants who believe they are receiving treatment, but who are only receiving a placebo.

placebo An inactive pill or a treatment that has no known effects.

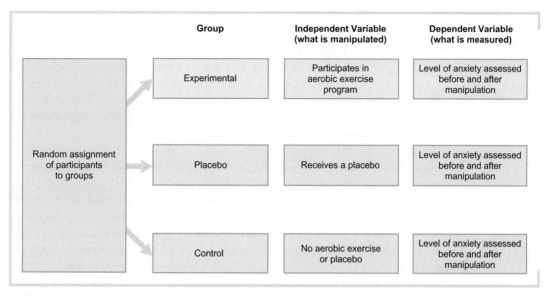

Group	Independent Variable (what is manipulated)	Dependent Variable (what is measured)
Experimental	Participates in aerobic exercise program	Level of anxiety assessed before and after manipulation
Placebo	Receives a placebo	Level of anxiety assessed before and after manipulation
Control	No aerobic exercise or placebo	Level of anxiety assessed before and after manipulation

Random assignment of participants to groups

▲ **Figure 1.2** I Design of Aerobic Exercise and Anxiety
Experiment I Participants are randomly assigned to groups in order to
equalize participant characteristics across the groups. The placebo group
controls for the placebo effect, and the control group provides a baseline
level of anxiety reduction for participants who do not participate in the aerobic exercise program or receive a placebo. The level of anxiety reduction for
each group is determined by comparing the measurements of the dependent variable (level of anxiety) before and after manipulating the independent
variable (aerobic exercise).

not a placebo effect, it would have to be significantly greater than that observed
for the placebo group.

Now you may be wondering what is meant by "significantly greater." This is
where statistical analysis enters the scene. We use what are called **inferential
statistical analyses**—statistical analyses that allow researchers to draw conclusions
about the results of their studies. Such analyses tell the researcher the probability
that the results of the study are due to random variation (chance). Obviously, the
experimenter would want this probability to be low. Remember, the experimenter's
hypothesis is that the manipulation of the independent variable (not chance) is
what causes the dependent variable to change. In statistics, a "significant" finding
is one that has a probability of .05 (1/20) or less that it is due to chance. Thus,
a significant finding is one that is probably not due to chance.

Statistical significance tells us that a result probably did not
occur by chance, but it does not insure that the finding has
practical significance or value in our everyday world. A statistically significant finding with little practical value sometimes
occurs when very large samples are used in a study. With such
samples, very small differences among groups may be significant. Belmont and Marolla's (1973) finding of a birth-order

inferential statistical analyses
Statistical analyses that allow
researchers to draw conclusions
about the results of a study by determining the probability the results are
due to random variation (chance).
The results are statistically significant if this probability is .05 or less.

double-blind procedure A control measure in an experiment in which neither the experimenters nor the participants know which participants are in the experimental and control groups.

effect for intelligence test scores is a good example of such a finding. Belmont and Marolla analyzed intelligence test data for almost 400,000 19-year-old Dutch males. There was a clear birth-order effect: First borns scored significantly higher than second borns, second borns higher than third borns, and so on. However, the score difference between these groups was very small (only a point or two) and thus not of much practical value. So remember, statistically significant findings do not always have practical significance.

The aerobic exercise experiment would also need to include another control measure, the double-blind procedure. In the **double-blind procedure,** neither the experimenters nor the participants know which participants are in the experimental and control groups. This procedure is called "double blind" because both the experimenters and participants are blind to (do not know) the participant group assignments. It is not unusual for participants to be blind to which group they have been assigned. This is especially critical for the placebo group participants. If they were told that they were getting a placebo, there would be no expectation for getting better and no placebo effect. But why should the experimenters not know the group assignments of the participants? This is to control for the effects of experimenter expectation (Rosenthal, 1966, 1994). If the experimenters knew which condition the participants were in, they might unintentionally treat them differently and thereby affect their behavior. In addition, the experimenters might interpret and record the behavior of the participants differently if they needed to make judgments about their behavior (their anxiety level in the example study). The key for the participant assignments to groups is kept by a third party and then given to the experimenters once the study has been conducted.

"It was more of a 'triple-blind' test. The patients didn't know which ones were getting the real drug, the doctors didn't know, and I'm afraid, *nobody* knew."

Now let's think about experiments that are more complex than our sample experiment with its one independent variable (aerobic exercise) and two control groups. In most experiments, the researcher examines multiple values of the independent variable. With respect to the aerobic exercise variable, the experimenter might examine the effects of different amounts or different types of aerobic exercise. Such manipulations would provide more detailed information about the effects of aerobic exercise on anxiety. An experimenter might also manipulate more than one independent variable. For example, an experimenter might manipulate diet as well as aerobic exercise. Different diets (high-protein vs. high-carbohydrate diets) might affect a person's level of anxiety in different ways. The two independent variables (diet and aerobic exercise) might also interact to determine one's level of anxiety. An experimenter could also increase the number of dependent variables. For example, both level of anxiety and level of depression could be measured in our sample experiment, even if only aerobic exercise were manipulated. If aerobic exercise reduces anxiety, then it might also reduce depression. As an experimenter increases the number of values of an independent variable, the number of independent variables, or the number of dependent variables, the possible gain in knowledge about the relationship between the variables increases. Thus, most experiments are more complex in design than our simple example with an experimental group and two control groups. In addition, many experimental studies including replications are necessary to address just one experimental question. Researchers now, however, have a statistical technique called **meta-analysis** that combines the results for a large number of studies on one experimental question into one analysis to arrive at an overall conclusion. Because a meta-analysis involves the results of numerous experimental studies, its conclusion is considered much stronger evidence than the results of an individual study in answering an experimental question.

The various research methods that have been discussed are summarized in Table 1.3. Their purposes and data-gathering procedures are described. Make sure you understand each of these research methods before going on to the next section, where we'll discuss how to understand research results. If you feel that you don't understand a particular method, go back and reread the information about it until you do.

meta-analysis A statistical technique that combines the results of a large number of studies on one experimental question into one analysis to arrive at an overall conclusion

Table 1.3	Summary of Research Methods	
Research Method	**Goal of Method**	**How Data Are Collected**
Laboratory observation	Description	Unobtrusively observe behavior in a laboratory setting
Naturalistic observation	Description	Unobtrusively observe behavior in its natural setting
Participant observation	Description	Observer becomes part of the group whose behavior is being observed
Case study	Description	Study an individual in depth over an extended period of time
Survey	Description	Representative sample of a group completes questionnaires or interviews to determine behavior, beliefs, and attitudes of the group
Correlational study	Prediction	Measure two variables to determine whether they are related
Experiment	Explanation	Manipulate one or more independent variables in a controlled setting to determine their impact on one or more measured dependent variables

Section Summary

Research methods fall into three categories—descriptive, correlational, and experimental. There are three descriptive methods—observation, case studies, and surveys. Observational studies can be conducted in the laboratory or in a natural setting (naturalistic observation). Sometimes participant observation is used. In participant observation, the observer becomes a part of the group being observed. The main goal of all observation is to obtain a detailed and accurate description of behavior. A case study is an in-depth study of one individual. Hypotheses generated from case studies in a clinical setting have often led to important experimental findings. Surveys attempt to describe the behavior, attitudes, or beliefs of particular populations (groups of people). It is essential in conducting surveys to ensure that a representative sample of the population is obtained for the study. Random sampling in which each person in the population has an equal opportunity to be in the sample is used for this purpose.

Descriptive methods only allow description, but correlational studies allow the researcher to make predictions about the relationships between variables. In a correlational study, two variables are measured and these measurements are compared to see if they are related. A statistic, the correlation coefficient, tells us both the type of the relationship (positive or negative) and the strength of the relationship. The sign of the coefficient (+ or –) tells us the type, and the absolute value of the coefficient (0 to 1.0) tells us the strength. Zero and values near zero indicate no relationship. As the absolute value approaches 1.0, the strength increases. Correlational data may also be depicted in scatterplots. A positive correlation is indicated by data points that extend from the bottom left of the plot to the top right. Scattered data points going from the top left to the bottom right indicate a negative correlation. The strength is reflected in the amount of scatter—the more the scatter, the lower the strength. A correlation of 1.0 gives us perfect predictability about the two variables involved, but it does not allow us to make cause–effect statements about the variables. This is because "third" variables may be responsible for the observed relationship.

To draw cause-effect conclusions, the researcher must conduct well-controlled experiments. In a simple experiment, the researcher manipulates the independent variable (the hypothesized cause) and measures its effect upon the dependent variable (the variable hypothesized to be affected). These variables are operationally defined so that other researchers understand exactly how they were manipulated or measured. In more complex experiments, more than one independent variable is manipulated or more than one dependent variable is measured. The experiment is conducted in a controlled environment in which possible third variables are held constant; the individual characteristics of participants are controlled through random assignment of participants to groups or conditions. Other controls used in experiments include using a control group that is not exposed to the experimental manipulation, a placebo group, which receives a placebo to control for the placebo effect, and the double-blind procedure to control for the effects of experimenter and participant expectation. The researcher uses inferential statistics to interpret the results of an experiment. These statistics determine the probability that the results are due to chance. For the results to be statistically significant, this probability has to be very low, .05 or less. Statistically significant results, however, may or may not have practical significance or value in our everyday world. Because most experimental questions lead to many studies including replications, meta-analysis, a statistical technique that combines the results of a large number of experiments on one experimental question into one analysis, can be used to arrive at an overall conclusion.

ConceptCheck | 2

> ➤ **Explain why the results of a case study cannot be generalized to a population.**
>
> ➤ **Explain the differences between random sampling and random assignment.**
>
> ➤ **Explain how the scatterplots for correlation coefficients of +.90 and −.90 would differ.**
>
> ➤ **Waldman, Nicholson, Adilov, and Williams (2008) found that autism prevalence rates among school-aged children were positively correlated with annual precipitation levels in various states. Autism rates were higher in counties with higher precipitation levels. Try to identify some possible third variables that might be responsible for this correlation.**
>
> ➤ **Explain why a double-blind procedure is necessary in an experiment in which there is a placebo group.**

How to Understand Research Results

Once we have completed an experiment, we need to understand our results and to describe them concisely so that others can understand them. To do this, we need to use statistics. There are two types of statistics—descriptive and inferential. We described inferential statistics when we discussed how to interpret the results of experimental studies. In this section, we will be discussing **descriptive statistics**—statistics used to describe the data of a research study in a concise fashion. The correlation coefficient that we discussed earlier is a descriptive statistic that allows us to describe the results of a correlational study precisely. For experimental findings, we need two types of descriptive statistics to summarize our data—measures of central tendency and measures of variability. In addition, a researcher often constructs a frequency distribution for the data. A **frequency distribution** depicts, in a table or a graph, the number of participants receiving each score for a variable. The bell curve, or normal distribution, is the most famous frequency distribution. We begin with the two types of descriptive statistics necessary to describe a data set: measures of central tendency and measures of variability.

> **descriptive statistics** Statistics that describe the results of a research study in a concise fashion.
>
> **frequency distribution** A depiction, in a table or figure, of the number of participants (frequency) receiving each score for a variable.

Descriptive Statistics

In an experiment, the data set consists of the measured scores on the dependent variable for the sample of participants. A listing of this set of scores, or any set of numbers, is referred to as a distribution of scores, or a distribution of numbers. To describe such distributions in a concise summary manner, we use two types of descriptive statistics: measures of central tendency and measures of variability.

Measures of central tendency. The measures of central tendency define a "typical" score for a distribution of scores. There are three measures of central tendency (three ways to define the "typical" score)—mean, median, and mode. The first is one that you are already familiar with—the mean or average. The **mean** is the numerical average for a distribution of scores. To compute the mean, you merely add up all of the scores and divide by the number of scores. A second measure of central tendency is the **median**—the score positioned in the middle of the distribution of scores when all of the scores are listed from the lowest to the highest. If there is an odd number of scores, the median is the middle score. If there is an even number of scores, the median is the halfway point between the two center scores. The final measure of central tendency, the **mode,** is the most frequently occurring score in a distribution of scores. Sometimes there are two or more scores that occur most frequently. In these cases, the distribution has multiple modes. Now let's consider a small set of scores to see how these measures are computed.

Let's imagine a class with five students who just took an exam. That gives us a distribution of five test scores: 70, 80, 80, 85, and 85. First, let's compute the mean or average score. The sum of all five scores is 400. Now divide 400 by 5, and you get the mean, 80. What's the median? It's the middle score when the scores are arranged in ascending order. Because there is an odd number of scores (5), it's the third score—80. If there had been an even number of scores, the median would be the halfway point between the center two scores. For example, if there had been only four scores in our sample distribution (70, 80, 85, and 85), the median would be the halfway point between 80 and 85, 82.5. Now, what's the mode or most frequently occurring score? For the distribution of five scores, there are two numbers that occur twice, so there are two modes—80 and 85. This kind of distribution is referred to as a bimodal distribution (a distribution with two modes). Remember that a distribution can have one or more than one mode.

Of the three measures of central tendency, the mean is the one that is most commonly used. This is mainly because it is used to analyze the data in many inferential statistical tests. The mean can be distorted, however, by a small set of unusually high or low scores. In this case, the median, which is not distorted by such scores, should be used. To understand how atypical scores can distort the mean, let's consider changing one score in our sample distribution of five scores. Change 70 to 20. Now, the mean is 70 (350/5). The median remains 80, however; it hasn't changed. This is because the median is only a positional score. The mean is distorted because it has to average in the value of any unusual scores.

Measures of variability. In addition to knowing the typical score for a distribution, you need to determine the variability between the scores. There are two measures of variability—the range and the standard deviation. The range is the simpler to compute. The **range** is simply the difference

▌ **mean** The numerical average of a distribution of scores.

▌ **median** The score positioned in the middle of a distribution of scores when all of the scores are arranged from lowest to highest.

▌ **mode** The most frequently occurring score in a distribution of scores.

▌ **range** The difference between the highest and lowest scores in a distribution of scores.

between the highest and lowest scores in the distribution. For our sample distribution with five scores, it would be 85 minus 70, or 15. However, like the mean, unusually high or low scores distort the range. For example, if the 70 in the distribution had been a 20, the range would change to be 85 minus 20, or 65. This would not be a good measure of the distribution's variability because four of the five scores are 80 or 85, not very different.

standard deviation The average extent that the scores vary from the mean for a distribution of scores.

The measure of variability used most often is the standard deviation. In general terms, the **standard deviation** is the average extent that the scores vary from the mean of the distribution. If the scores do not vary much from the mean, the standard deviation will be small. If they vary a lot from the mean, the standard deviation will be larger. In our example of five test scores with a mean of 80, the scores (70, 80, 80, 85, and 85) didn't vary much from this mean, therefore the standard deviation would not be very large. However, if the scores had been 20, 40, 80, 120, and 140, the mean would still be 80; but the scores vary more from the mean, therefore the standard deviation would be much larger.

The standard deviation and the various other descriptive statistics that we have discussed are summarized in Table 1.4. Review this table to make sure you understand each statistic. The standard deviation is especially relevant to the normal distribution, or bell curve. We will see in Chapter 6, on thinking and intelligence, that intelligence test scores are actually determined with respect to standard deviation units in the normal distribution. Next we will consider the normal distribution and the two types of skewed frequency distributions.

Table 1.4 Summary of Descriptive Statistics	
Descriptive Statistic	**Explanation of Statistic**
Correlation coefficient	A number between –1.0 and +1.0 whose sign indicates the type (+ = positive and – = negative) and whose absolute value (0 to 1.0) indicates the strength of the relationship between two variables
Mean	Numerical average for a distribution of scores
Median	Middle score in a distribution of scores when all scores are arranged in order from lowest to highest
Mode	Most frequently occurring score or scores in a distribution of scores
Range	Difference between highest and lowest scores in a distribution of scores
Standard deviation	Average extent to which the scores vary from the mean for a distribution of scores

Frequency Distributions

A frequency distribution organizes the data in a score distribution so that we know the frequency of each score. It tells us how often each score occurred. These frequencies can be presented in a table or visually in a figure. We'll consider visual depictions. For many human traits (such as height, weight, and intelligence), the frequency distribution takes on the shape of a bell curve. In fact, if a large number of people are measured on almost anything, the frequency distribution will visually approximate a bell-shaped curve. Statisticians call this bell-shaped frequency distribution, shown in Figure 1.3, the **normal distribution.**

Normal distributions. There are two main aspects of a normal distribution. First, the mean, the median, and the mode are all equal because the normal distribution is symmetric about its center. You do not have to worry about which measure of central tendency to use because all of them are equal. The same number of scores fall below the center point as above it. Second, the percentage of scores falling within a certain number of standard deviations of the mean is set. About 68 percent of the scores fall within 1 standard deviation of the mean; about 95 percent within 2 standard deviations of the mean; and over 99 percent within 3 standard deviations of the mean.

These percentages are what give the normal distribution its bell shape. The percentages hold regardless of the size of the standard deviation for a normal distribution. Figure 1.4 (page 27) shows two normal distributions with the same mean but different standard deviations. Both have bell shapes, but the distribution with the smaller standard deviation (A) is taller. As the size of the standard deviation increases, the bell shape becomes shorter and wider (like B).

> **normal distribution** A frequency distribution that is shaped like a bell. About 68 percent of the scores fall within 1 standard deviation of the mean, about 95 percent within 2 standard deviations of the mean, and over 99 percent within 3 standard deviations of the mean.

▲ **Figure 1.3 I The Normal Distribution I** In a normal distribution, the mean, the median, and the mode are all equal because the distribution is perfectly symmetrical about its center. In addition, about 68 percent of the scores fall within 1 standard deviation of the mean, about 95 percent within 2 standard deviations of the mean, and over 99 percent within 3 standard deviations of the mean.

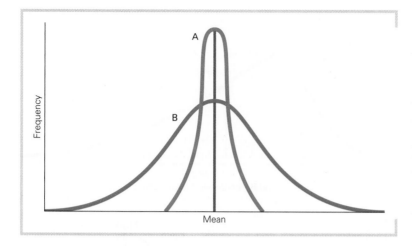

The percentages of scores and the number of standard deviations from the mean always have the same relationship in a normal distribution. This allows you to compute percentile ranks for scores. A **percentile rank** is the percentage of scores below a specific score in a distribution of scores. If you know how many standard deviation units a specific score is above or below the mean in a normal distribution, you can compute that score's percentile rank. For example, the percentile rank of a score that is 1 standard deviation above the mean is roughly 84 percent. Remember, a normal distribution is symmetric about the mean so that 50 percent of the scores are above the mean and 50 percent are below the mean. This means that the percentile rank of a score that is 1 standard deviation above the mean is greater than 50 percent (the percent below the mean) + 34 percent (the percent of scores from the mean to +1 standard deviation).

Now I'll let you try to compute a percentile rank. What is the percentile rank for a score that is 1 standard deviation below the mean? Remember that it is the percentage of the scores below that score. Look at Figure 1.3. What percentage of the scores is less than a score that is 1 standard deviation below the mean? The answer is about 16 percent. You can never have a percentile rank of 100 percent because you cannot outscore yourself, but you can have a percentile rank of 0 percent if you have the lowest score in the distribution. The scores on intelligence tests and the SAT are based on normal distributions, therefore percentile ranks can be calculated for these scores. We will return to the normal distribution when we discuss intelligence test scores in Chapter 6.

Skewed distributions. In addition to the normal distribution, two other types of frequency distributions are important. They are called skewed distributions, which are frequency distributions that are asymmetric in shape. The two major types of skewed distributions are illustrated in Figure 1.5. A **right-skewed distribution** is a frequency distribution in which there are some unusually high scores

percentile rank The percentage of scores below a specific score in a distribution of scores.

right-skewed distribution An asymmetric frequency distribution in which there are some unusually high scores that distort the mean to be greater than the median.

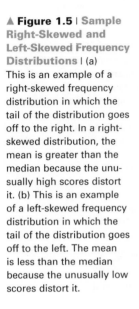

▲ **Figure 1.5** | Sample **Right-Skewed and Left-Skewed Frequency Distributions** | (a) This is an example of a right-skewed frequency distribution in which the tail of the distribution goes off to the right. In a right-skewed distribution, the mean is greater than the median because the unusually high scores distort it. (b) This is an example of a left-skewed frequency distribution in which the tail of the distribution goes off to the left. The mean is less than the median because the unusually low scores distort it.

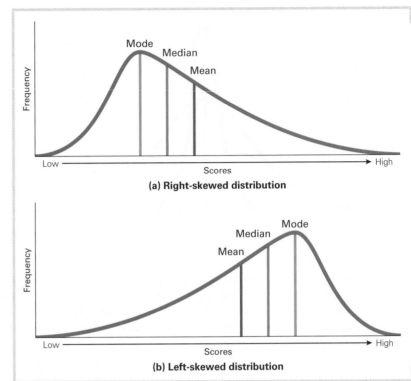

[shown in Figure 1.5(a)]. A **left-skewed distribution** is a frequency distribution in which there are some unusually low scores [shown in Figure 1.5(b)]. An easy way to remember the difference is that the tail of the right-skewed distribution goes off to the right, and the tail of the left-skewed distribution goes off to the left. A right-skewed distribution is also called a positively skewed distribution (the tail goes toward the positive end of the number line); a left-skewed distribution a negatively skewed distribution (the tail goes toward the negative end of the number line).

Now that we have defined right-skewed and left-skewed distributions, let's consider some examples of each type of distribution so that we get a better understanding of these distributions. As you read these examples, visually think about what the distributions would look like. Remember, the tail of a right-skewed distribution goes to the right (the high end of the scale), and the tail of a left-skewed distribution goes to the left (the low end of the scale). A good example of a right-skewed distribution is people's incomes. The incomes of most people tend to be on the lower end of possible incomes, but some people make a lot of money, with very high incomes increasingly rare. Another example is family size in the United States. The size of most families is 3 or 4, some are 5 or 6, and greater than 6 is increasingly rare. Age at retirement is an example of a left-skewed distribution. Most people retire in their mid to late 60s or early 70s, some

left-skewed distribution An asymmetric frequency distribution in which there are some unusually low scores that distort the mean to be less than the median.

retire in their 50s, and relatively few in their 40s or earlier. Another example would be scores on a relatively easy exam. Most students would get As or Bs (high scores), some would get Cs, a few Ds, and hardly any Fs.

Because unusually high or low scores distort a mean, such distortion occurs for the means of skewed distributions. The mean for a right-skewed distribution is distorted toward the tail created by the few high scores and therefore is greater than the median. The mean for the left-skewed distribution is distorted toward the tail created by the few low scores and therefore is less than the median. When you have a skewed distribution, you should use the median because atypical scores in the distribution do not distort the median. This means that you need to know the type of frequency distribution for the scores before deciding which measure of central tendency—mean or median—is more appropriate. Beware, sometimes the inappropriate measure of central tendency for skewed distributions (the mean) is used to mislead you (Huff, 1954). Paulos (2006) in an article subtitled, "It's mean to ignore the median" describes a good example of such misuse from the political arena in the early 2000s. Republicans touted the economy's growth since 2000 using the mean increase in family income in the United States whereas the Democrats pushed the economy's lackluster growth using the median increase in family income. If the distribution of increase in family incomes across all levels of socioeconomic status was skewed, then the median would be the appropriate statistic to use. The distribution was indeed skewed, severely left-skewed. The growth in family income not only eluded the lower and middle classes, but by and large, it passed up the upper-middle class as well. The huge increases in income went mainly to those with already huge incomes. Thus, in this case the median was the appropriate statistic to use.

Skewed distributions are also important to understand because various aspects of everyday life, such as medical trends (mortality rates for various diseases), are often skewed. Let's consider a famous example of the importance of understanding skewed distributions (Gould, 1985). Stephen Jay Gould, a noted Harvard scientist, died of cancer in 2002. However, this was 20 years after he was diagnosed with abdominal mesothelioma cancer and told that this type of cancer had "a median mortality rate of 8 months after diagnosis." Most people would think that they would only have about 8 months to live if given this median statistic. However, Gould realized that his expected chances depended upon the type of frequency distribution for the deaths from this disease. Because the statistic is reported as a median rather than a mean, the distribution is skewed. Now, if you were Gould, which type of skewed distribution would you want—right or left? Many people at first think they would want left-skewed, but you wouldn't want this distribution because everyone would be dead within less than a year. Look at its shape in Figure 1.5(b). If it is 8 months from the origin to the median, then it is less than 4 months from the median to the end of the distribution. You would want a severely right-skewed distribution with a long tail to the right, going on for years. This is what Gould found the distribution to be when he examined the medical literature on the disease. The distribution had a tail that stretched out to the right for many years beyond the median, and Gould was fortunate to be out in this long tail, living for 20 more years after getting the diagnosis. When he did die, it was from a different type of cancer (Blastland & Dilnot, 2009).

In confronting his illness, Gould was thinking like a scientist. Such thinking provided him and the many readers of his article on the subject with a better understanding of a very difficult medical situation. Thinking like a scientist allows all of us to gain a better understanding of ourselves, others, and the world we all inhabit. Such thinking, along with the accompanying research, has enabled psychological scientists to gain a much better understanding of human behavior and mental processing. We describe the basic findings of this research in the remainder of the book. You will benefit not only from learning about these findings, but also from thinking more like a scientist in your daily life.

Section Summary

To understand research findings, psychologists use statistics—a branch of mathematics that provides procedures for the description and analysis of data. In this section, we were concerned with descriptive statistics. Measures of central tendency allow a researcher to describe the "typical" score for a distribution of scores concisely. There are three such measures: mean, median, and mode. The mean is merely the arithmetical average. The median is the middle score when the distribution is arranged in ascending or descending order. The mode is the most frequently occurring score. Of these three measures, the mean is used most often. However, if unusually high or low scores in the distribution distort the mean, then the median should be used. In addition to describing the typical score, we need to determine the variability of the scores. We could use the range—the difference between the highest and lowest scores—but unusually low or high scores distort it. The measure of variability most often used is the standard deviation, the average extent that the scores vary from the mean of the distribution.

The standard deviation is especially relevant to the normal (bell-shaped) frequency distribution. Sixty-eight percent of the scores in a normal distribution fall within 1 standard deviation of the mean, 95 percent within 2 standard deviations, and over 99 percent within 3 standard deviations. These percentages hold true regardless of the value of the standard deviation. They also enable us to compute the percentile rank for a specific score in a normal distribution. The percentile rank for a score is the percentage of the scores below it in the distribution of scores. All distributions are not symmetric like the normal distribution. Two important nonsymmetric distributions are the right-skewed and left-skewed distributions. In a right-skewed distribution, there are some unusually high scores; in a left-skewed distribution, there are some unusually low scores. In both cases, the mean is distorted, therefore the median should be used.

ConceptCheck | 3

> **Explain what measures of central tendency and measures of variability tell us about a distribution of scores.**

> **Explain why the normal distribution has a bell shape.**

> **Explain the relationship between the mean and median in a right-skewed distribution and in a left-skewed distribution.**

Chapter Key Terms

You should know the definitions of the following key terms from the chapter. They are listed in the order in which they appear in the chapter. For those you do not know, return to the relevant section of the chapter to learn them. When you think that you know all of the terms, complete the matching exercise based on these key terms.

psychology

biological perspective

cognitive perspective

behavioral perspective

sociocultural perspective

hindsight bias (I-knew-it-all-along phenomenon)

descriptive methods

naturalistic observation

participant observation

case study

survey research

population

sample

random sampling

correlational study

variable

correlation coefficient

positive correlation

negative correlation

scatterplot

third-variable problem

random assignment

independent variable

dependent variable

experiment

experimental group

control group

operational definition

placebo effect

placebo group

placebo

inferential statistical analyses

double-blind procedure

meta-analysis

descriptive statistics

frequency distribution

mean

median

mode

range

standard deviation

normal distribution

percentile rank

right-skewed distribution

left-skewed distribution

Key Terms Exercise

Identify the correct term for each of the following definitions. The answers to this exercise follow the answers to the Concept Checks at the end of the chapter.

1. An explanation of a correlation between two variables in terms of another variable that could possibly be responsible for the observed relationship between the two variables.

_____

2. A control measure in an experiment in which neither the experimenters nor the participants know which participants are in the experimental and control groups.

_____

3. The score positioned in the middle of a distribution of scores when all of the scores are arranged from lowest to highest.

_____

4. An asymmetric frequency distribution in which there are some unusually high scores that distort the mean to be greater than the median.

_____

5. Improvement due to the expectation of improving because of receiving treatment.

_____

6. An inverse relationship between two variables.

_____

7. A control measure in an experiment in which participants are randomly assigned to groups in order to equalize participant characteristics across the various groups in the experiment.

_____

8. The percentage of scores below a specific score in a distribution of scores.

_____

9. A research perspective whose major explanatory focus is how the brain, nervous system, and other physiological mechanisms produce our behavior and mental processes.

_____

10. A description of the operations or procedures that a researcher uses to manipulate or measure a variable.

_____

11. The tendency, after learning about an outcome, to be overconfident in one's ability to have predicted it.

_____

12. A visual depiction of correlational data in which each data point represents the scores on the two variables for each participant.

_____

13. The entire group of people that a researcher is studying.

_____

14. The difference between the highest and lowest scores in a distribution of scores.

_____

15. Statistical analyses that allow researchers to draw conclusions about the results of a study by determining the probability the results are due to random variation (chance).

_____

Practice Test Questions

The following are practice multiple-choice test questions on some of the chapter content. The answers are given after the Key Terms Exercise answers at the end of the chapter. If you guessed on a question or incorrectly answered a question, restudy the relevant section of the chapter.

1. Which of the following major research perspectives focuses on conditioning by external environmental events as the major cause of our behavior?
   a. biological
   b. cognitive
   c. behavioral
   d. sociocultural

2. Which of the following would be the best procedure for obtaining a representative sample of the students at your school?
   a. sampling randomly among students in the student union
   b. sampling randomly among students studying in the library
   c. sampling randomly among the students who belong to Greek organizations
   d. sampling randomly from a list of all the students enrolled at your school

3. Which of the following research methods allow(s) the researcher to draw cause–effect conclusions?
   a. descriptive
   b. correlational
   c. experimental
   d. all of the above

4. Height and weight are _____ correlated; elevation and temperature are _____ correlated.
   a. positively; positively
   b. positively; negatively
   c. negatively; positively
   d. negatively; negatively

5. Which of the following correlation coefficients indicates the STRONGEST relationship?

   a. +.75

   b. −.81

   c. +1.25

   d. 0.00

6. Manipulate is to measure as _____ is to _____.

   a. positive correlation; negative correlation

   b. negative correlation; positive correlation

   c. independent variable; dependent variable

   d. dependent variable; independent variable

7. In an experiment, the _____ group participants receive an inactive treatment but are told that the treatment will help them.

   a. experimental

   b. control

   c. placebo

   d. third-variable

8. The most frequently occurring score in a distribution of scores is the _____, and the average score is the _____.

   a. mode; mean

   b. mean; mode

   c. median; mean

   d. mean; median

9. About _____ percent of the scores in a normal distribution are between −1 standard deviation and +1 standard deviation of the mean.

   a. 34   b. 68

   c. 95   d. 99

10. In a left-skewed distribution, the mean is _____ than the median; in a right-skewed distribution, the mean is _____ than the median.

    a. greater; greater

    b. greater; less

    c. less; greater

    d. less; less

11. Shere Hite's failure to use _____ resulted in misleading findings for her women and love survey study.

    a. a placebo group

    b. a double-blind procedure

    c. random assignment

    d. random sampling

12. Professor Jones noticed that the distribution of students' scores on his last biology exam had an extremely small standard deviation. This indicates that:

    a. the exam was given to a very small class of students.

    b. the exam was a poor measure of the students' knowledge.

    c. the students' scores tended to be very similar to one another.

    d. the students' mean exam score was less than the median exam score.

13. In a normal distribution, the percentile rank for a score that is 1 standard deviation below the mean is roughly _____%.

    a. 16

    b. 34

    c. 68

    d. 84

14. Dian Fossey's study of gorillas is an example of _____.

    a. naturalistic observation

    b. participant observation

    c. naturalistic observation that turned into participant observation

    d. a case study

15. Which of the following types of scatterplots depicts a weak, negative correlation?

    a. a lot of scatter with data points going from top left to bottom right

    b. very little scatter with data points going from top left to bottom right

    c. a lot of scatter with data points going from bottom left to top right

    d. very little scatter with data points going from bottom left to top right

Chapter Concept Check Answers

Concept Check I 1

- Both of these research perspectives empha-size internal causes in their explanations of human behavior and mental processing. The biological perspective emphasizes the role of our actual physiological hardware, especially the brain and nervous system, while the cognitive perspective empha-sizes the role of our mental processes, the "programs" of the brain. For example, biological explanations will involve actual parts of the brain or chemicals in the brain. Cognitive explanations, however, will involve mental processes such as percep-tion and memory without specifying the parts of the brain or chemicals involved in these processes. Thus, the biological and cognitive perspectives propose explana-tions at two different levels of internal factors, the actual physiological mecha-nisms and the mental processes resulting from these mechanisms, respectively.

- Both of these research perspectives empha-size external causes in their explanations of human behavior and mental processing. The behavioral perspective emphasizes condition-ing of our behavior by external environmen-tal events while the sociocultural perspective emphasizes the impact of other people and our culture on our behavior and mental processing. Thus, these two perspectives emphasize different types of external causes. In addition, the behavioral perspective emphasizes the conditioning of observable behavior while the sociocultural perspective focuses just as much on mental processing as observable behavior and on other types of learning in addition to conditioning.

Concept Check I 2

- The results of a case study cannot be generalized to a population because they are specific to the individual who has been studied. To generalize to a population, you need to include a representative sample of the population in the study. However, the results of a case study do allow the researcher to develop hypotheses about cause-effect relationships that can be tested in experimental research to see if they apply to the population.

- Random sampling is a method for obtaining a representative sample from a population. Random assignment is a control measure for assigning the members of a sample to groups or conditions in an experiment. Random sampling allows the researcher to generalize the results from the sample to the population; random assignment con-trols for individual characteristics across the groups in an experiment. Random assignment is used only in experiments, but random sampling is used in experi-ments and some other research methods such as correlational studies and surveys.

- There would be the same amount of scatter of the data points in each of the two scat-terplots because they are equal in strength (.90). In addition, because they are strong correlations, there would not be much scat-ter. However, the scatter of data points in the scatterplot for +.90 would go from the bottom left of the plot to the top right; the scatter for −.90 would go from the top left of the plot to the bottom right. Thus, the direction of the scatter would be different in the two scatterplots.

- Some possible third variables that could serve as environmental triggers for autism among genetically vulnerable children stem from the children being in the house more and spending less time outdoors because of the high rates of precipitation. According to the authors of the study, such variables would include increased television and video viewing, decreased vitamin D levels because of less exposure to sunlight, and increased exposure to household chemi-cals. In addition, there may be chemicals in the atmosphere that are transported to the surface by the precipitation. All of these variables could serve as third variables and possibly account for the correlation.

- The double-blind procedure is necessary in experiments with placebo groups for two reasons. First, the participants in the placebo group must think that they are receiving a treatment that will help, or a placebo effect would not be possible. Thus, they cannot be told that they received a placebo. Second, the experimenter must be blind in order to control for the effects of experimenter expectation (for example, unintentionally judging the behavior of participants in the experimental and placebo groups differently because of knowing their group assignments).

Concept Check | 3

- Measures of central tendency tell us what a "typical" score is for the distribution of scores. The three central tendency measures give us different definitions of "typical." The mean is the average score; the median is the middle score when all of the scores are ordered by value; and the mode is the most frequently occurring score. Measures of variability tell us how much the scores vary from one another, the variability between scores. The range is the difference between the highest and lowest scores, and the standard deviation is the average extent that the scores vary from the mean for the set of scores.

- It has a bell shape because the scores are distributed symmetrically about the mean with the majority of the scores (about 68 percent) close to the mean (from −1 standard deviation to +1 standard deviation). As the scores diverge from the mean, they become symmetrically less frequent, giving the distribution the shape of a bell.

- In a right-skewed distribution, the mean is greater than the median because the unusually high scores in the distribution distort it. The opposite is true for the left-skewed distribution. The mean is less than the median because the unusually low scores in the distribution distort it.

Answers to Key Terms Exercise

1. third-variable problem
2. double-blind procedure
3. median
4. right-skewed distribution
5. placebo effect
6. negative correlation
7. random assignment
8. percentile rank
9. biological perspective
10. operational definition
11. hindsight bias (I-knew-it-all-along phenomenon)
12. scatterplot
13. population
14. range
15. inferential statistical analyses

Answers to Practice Test Questions

1. c; behavioral
2. d; sampling randomly from a list of all the students enrolled at your school
3. c; experimental
4. b; positively; negatively
5. b; −.81
6. c; independent variable; dependent variable
7. c; placebo
8. a; mode; mean
9. b; 68
10. c; less; greater
11. d; random sampling
12. c; students' scores tended to be very similar to one another
13. a; 16
14. c; naturalistic observation that turned into participant observation
15. a; a lot of scatter with data points going from top left to bottom right

2 Neuroscience

Our brain controls almost everything we do. It is responsible for our perception, consciousness, memory, language, intelligence, and personality—everything that makes us human. This would seem to be a daunting job for an organ that only weighs about three pounds. The brain, however, has been estimated to consist of about 100 billion nerve cells, called neurons (Thompson, 2000). Each neuron may receive information from thousands of other neurons; therefore, the number of possible communication connections between these billions of neurons is in the trillions! This complexity may never be completely understood, but it's an intriguing puzzle—human brains trying to understand how human brains work.

"The body is made up of millions and millions of crumbs"

In this chapter on neuroscience (the scientific study of the brain and nervous system), we will first examine neurons, the building blocks of the nervous system. We will look at how neurons transmit and integrate information, and how drugs and poisons interrupt these processes (and change our behavior and mental processes). We will also consider how some diseases and disorders are related to transmission problems.

Once we understand how neurons work, we will consider the hierarchical structure of the nervous system, discussing its various subsystems—the central nervous system and the peripheral nervous system—along with the body's other major communication system, the endocrine glandular system. We will also consider emotions and the role of the autonomic nervous system, a division of the peripheral nervous system, in explaining how our emotional experiences are generated.

Next, the major parts of the brain (vast collections of neurons) and their functions will be detailed. We will focus mainly on the cerebral cortex, the seat of higher mental functioning in humans. Last, we will consider what consciousness is and what brain activity during sleep (a natural break from consciousness) tells us about the five stages of sleep and the nature of dreaming.

The Neuron

Why are psychologists interested in how neurons work? Isn't this biology and not psychology? The answer is that it's both. Humans are biological organisms. To understand our behavior and mental processes, we need to understand their biological underpinnings, starting with the cellular level, the neuron. How we feel, learn, remember, and think all stem from neuronal activity. So, how a neuron works and how neurons communicate are crucial pieces of information in solving the puzzle of human behavior and mental processing.

In explaining how a neuron works, we will talk about how neurons communicate with each other. We have a fairly good understanding of how information is transmitted, but we do not have as good an understanding of exactly how these vast communication networks of neurons oversee what we do and make us what we are. These more complex questions are the remaining key pieces of the puzzle to be solved. In this section, we will cover the part of the story that is best understood—how the building blocks of the nervous system, the neurons, work. We begin with a discussion of the neuron's structure and parts.

The Structure of a Neuron

The brain and the nervous system are composed of two types of cells—neurons and glial cells. **Neurons** are responsible for information transmission throughout the nervous system. They receive, send, and integrate information within the brain and the rest of the nervous system. **Glial cells** (or **glia,** Greek for "glue") constitute the support system for the neurons. For example, glial cells take away the waste products of neurons, keep the neurons' chemical environment stable, and insulate them, allowing neurons to do their work more efficiently. The number of neurons we have is impressive, but we have about 10 times more glial cells to support the work of billions of neurons. Thus, around 90% of the cells in the brain are glial cells. Glial cells are only about one-tenth as large as neurons, so they take about the same amount of space as neurons (Kalat, 2007).

Recent research is questioning the idea that glial cells merely provide a support system for neurons (Fields, 2004, 2009; Koop, 2009). It appears that not only do neurons and glial cells communicate but also that glial cells communicate with each other in a separate but parallel network to the neuronal network, influencing the brain's performance. Glial cells also appear to influence the formation of synapses and to aid in determining which neuronal connections get stronger or weaker over time, which is essential to learning and to storing memories. In addition, glial cells may play an important role in mental disorders such as schizophrenia and depression and in neurodegenerative diseases such as Parkinson's and Alzheimer's. Whereas neuroscientists are excited by all of these possibilities and the prospect of doing research on these cells that have been largely ignored until recently, neurons are still viewed as the most important cells for communication within the human nervous system and thus will be the focus of our discussion.

Neurons all have the same basic parts and structure, and they all operate the same way. A generic neuron with all of the important parts identified is depicted in Figure 2.1. The three main components of a neuron are the dendrites, cell body, and axon. Let's first get a general idea of the main functions of these three parts and their relationships to each other.

▨ **neurons** Cells that transmit information within the nervous system.

▨ **glial cells (glia)** Cells in the nervous system that comprise the support system for the neurons.

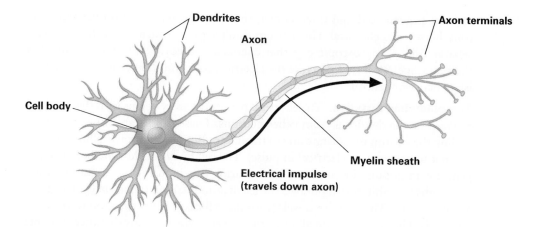

▲ **Figure 2.1** | **The Structure of a Neuron** | The three main parts of a neuron are the dendrites, cell body, and axon. The dendrites receive information from other neurons and pass it along to the cell body. The cell body decides whether the information should be passed on to other neurons. If it decides it should, then it does so by means of an electrical impulse that travels down the axon—the longer, thin fiber coming out of the cell body. The pictured neuron has a myelinated axon. Please note that there are periodic gaps where there is no myelin. The impulse jumps from one gap to the next down the axon. When the impulse reaches the axon terminals, it triggers chemical communication with other neurons.

Dendrites are the fibers that project out of the cell body like the branches of a tree. Their main function is to receive information from other neurons. The dendrites pass this information on to the **cell body,** which contains the nucleus of the cell and the other biological machinery that keeps the cell alive. The cell body also decides whether or not to pass the information from the dendrites on to other neurons. If the cell body decides to pass along the information, it does so by way of the **axon**—the long, singular fiber leaving the cell body. At its end, the axon subdivides into axon terminals, branchlike endings. The main function of the axon is to conduct information from the cell body to the axon terminals in order to trigger the transmission of information with other neurons. Axons vary greatly in length, with the longest ones going from the spinal cord to the toes. Given this general understanding of the parts of the neuron, let's look more closely at exactly how they are involved in transmitting information.

dendrites Fibers projecting out of the cell body of a neuron whose function is to receive information from other neurons.

cell body The part of the neuron that contains its nucleus and the other biological machinery to keep the cell alive and that decides whether or not to generate a neural impulse in order to pass incoming information on to other neurons.

axon The long, singular fiber projecting out of the cell body of a neuron whose function is to conduct the neural impulse from the cell body to the axon terminals triggering chemical communication with other neurons.

How Neurons Communicate

The first point to note in learning about how neurons communicate with each other (and sometimes with muscles and glands) is that the process is partly electrical and partly chemical. Within a neuron, it's electrical—an actual electrical impulse is generated and travels down the axon. Communication between neurons, however, is chemical. The neurons don't actually touch each other. They are separated by a microscopic gap that chemical molecules travel across to carry their message. We'll first describe the electrical part and then explain this "chemistry" between neurons.

The electrical impulse. The electrical part of the story begins with the messages received by the dendrites from other neurons. These inputs are either excitatory (telling the neuron to generate an electrical impulse) or inhibitory (telling the neuron not to generate an electrical impulse). The cell body decides whether or not to generate an impulse by continually calculating this input. If the excitatory input outweighs the inhibitory input by a sufficient amount, then the cell body will generate an impulse. The impulse travels from the cell body down the axon to the axon terminals. This impulse is an all-or-nothing event, which means that there is either an impulse or there is not; and if there is an impulse, it always travels down the axon at the same speed regardless of the intensity of the stimulus input. So, how are the varying intensities of stimuli (for example, a gentle pat on the cheek versus a slap) encoded? The answer is straightforward. The intensity of the stimulus determines how many neurons generate impulses and the number of impulses that are generated each second by the neurons. Stronger stimuli (a slap rather than a pat) lead to more neurons generating impulses and generating those impulses more often.

The impulses in different neurons travel down the axon at varying rates up to around 200 miles per hour (Dowling, 1998). This may seem fast, but it is much slower than the speed of electricity or computer processing. A major factor determining the impulse speed for a particular neuron is whether or not its axon is encased in a **myelin sheath**—an insulating layer of a white fatty substance. With no myelin sheath, the impulse travels slowly down the axon in a continuous fashion, like a fuse burning down on a stick of dynamite. The rate is faster in axons encased in myelin because the impulse can only be regenerated at the periodic gaps in the sheath where there is no myelin. A myelinated axon (like the one in Figure 2.1) looks like a string of sausages with gaps between the sausages. The impulse "leaps" from gap to gap instead of traveling continuously down the axon. To understand why this is faster, think about walking across a room in a heel-to-toe fashion (continuously touching the heel of your advancing foot to the toes of your lagging foot) versus taking long strides to get to the other side. Striding is clearly much faster.

Damage to this myelin sheath will result in serious problems. For example, multiple sclerosis causes deterioration of the myelin sheath that encases neuronal axons. This means that impulses can no longer leap down the axon, or eventually even travel down the axon, so information transmission is greatly slowed. People with multiple sclerosis experience incapacitating behavioral changes, such as difficulty in moving. Sadly, there is presently no cure for multiple sclerosis.

Given its white color, myelin is also responsible for the distinction between white matter and gray matter in the brain. Myelinated axons make up the "white" matter; unmyelinated cell bodies and dendrites make up the "gray" matter.

myelin sheath An insulating layer covering an axon that allows for faster neural impulses.

Why the distinction? Myelination creates a whitish appearance because of the white color of the myelin. Unmyelinated parts of a neuron appear grayish. If we were able to look at the two cerebral hemispheres of the brain, they would appear grayish because we are mainly looking at the billions of cell bodies that make up their outside layer. Hence, the expression, "Use your gray matter."

Chemical communication between neurons. What happens when the electrical impulse reaches the axon terminals? The answer is depicted in Figure 2.2.

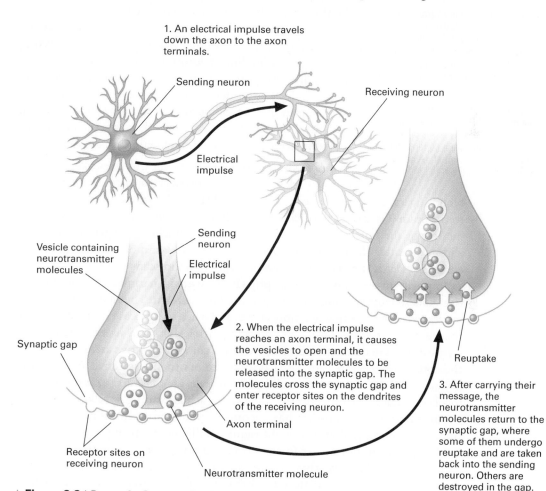

1. An electrical impulse travels down the axon to the axon terminals.

Sending neuron

Receiving neuron

Electrical impulse

Vesicle containing neurotransmitter molecules

Sending neuron

Electrical impulse

Synaptic gap

2. When the electrical impulse reaches an axon terminal, it causes the vesicles to open and the neurotransmitter molecules to be released into the synaptic gap. The molecules cross the synaptic gap and enter receptor sites on the dendrites of the receiving neuron.

Reuptake

3. After carrying their message, the neurotransmitter molecules return to the synaptic gap, where some of them undergo reuptake and are taken back into the sending neuron. Others are destroyed in the gap.

Axon terminal

Receptor sites on receiving neuron

Neurotransmitter molecule

▲ **Figure 2.2** | **Synaptic Communication Between Neurons** | Neurons communicate with each other chemically. As explained in the figure, there are three steps. (1) When the electrical impulse in a neuron reaches the axon terminals, it causes neurotransmitter molecules in the terminal vesicles to be released into the synaptic gap between neurons. (2) These molecules cross the gap and fit into receptor sites on the dendrites of other neurons, thereby carrying their messages. (3) The neurotransmitter molecules then go back into the gap, where they are either taken up by the sending neuron (reuptake) to be used again or are destroyed by enzymes.

■ **neurotransmitter** A naturally occurring chemical in the nervous system that specializes in transmitting information between neurons.

■ **synaptic gap (synapse)** The microscopic gap between neurons across which neurotransmitters travel to carry their messages to other neurons.

■ **positron emission tomography (PET) scan** A visual display of the activity levels in various areas in the brain generated by detecting the amount of positron emission created by the metabolization of radioactive glucose in each area.

■ **functional magnetic resonance imaging (fMRI)** A computerized image of the activity levels of various areas in the brain generated by detecting the amount of oxygen brought to each area.

In the axon terminals, there are tiny vesicles (sacs) containing a **neurotransmitter,** a naturally occurring chemical in our nervous system that specializes in transmitting information. When the impulse reaches the sending neuron's axon terminals, it causes the vesicles to open and the neurotransmitter molecules to come out and go into the **synaptic gap** (or **synapse**), the microscopic gap between neurons. Two thousand of these tiny synaptic gaps would fit comfortably inside the thinnest of human hairs (Lynch & Granger, 2008). The neurotransmitter molecules cross the gap and enter receptor sites on the dendrites of other neurons. This is achieved by what is termed binding—neurotransmitter molecules fit into the dendrite receptor sites on the receiving neuron like a key fits into a lock. After delivering their message, the molecules go back into the gap. Some are destroyed by enzymes in the gap, but others undergo reuptake—they are taken back into the axon terminals of the sending neuron to be used again.

Brain scans. In order to carry out this essential communication work, neurons require oxygen and other nutrients like blood sugars. This is why about 20 percent of the body's blood supply is pumped to the brain (Gazzaniga, Ivry, & Mangun, 2002), and the brain consumes about a quarter of the body's oxygen (Ackerman, 2004). Without oxygen, neurons die within minutes. Neurons doing more work require even more oxygen and nutrients. This fact is the key to how various types of brain scans work.

In **positron emission tomography (PET) scans,** a harmless dose of radioactive glucose (sugar) is introduced into the bloodstream. The radioactive glucose moves to those areas that are more active, and when the glucose is metabolized by the neurons, it emits positrons (atomic particles emitted by radioactive substances) that are detected and measured by a computer. Active areas show up on the computer-generated image as brighter colors than less active areas. In this manner, PET scans are used to tell us which areas are most active, and thus more involved, while a person performs some task, such as reading or talking.

Another type of scan that has become popular, **functional magnetic resonance imaging (fMRI),** does not require radioactivity being introduced into the bloodstream, but rather focuses on the amount of oxygen brought to the various areas. The areas that are more active are provided with more oxygen through increased blood flow to them. The fMRI detects these areas with increased bloodflow and highlights them in its computerized image of brain activity. Variations in bloodflow are depicted as variations in color in the image. Like PET scans, fMRI is used to study the functions of various brain parts and locations. Actually, fMRI is preferred over PET scans because it is noninvasive and produces a much sharper picture. Historically, we learned about brain function only by observation of brain-damaged individuals and postmortem comparisons of damaged and normal brains. Modern brain scans have allowed us to learn about structures and functions while the neurons are still healthy and active.

Neurotransmitters, Drugs, and Poisons

Fifty to 100 different chemicals in our nervous system function as neurotransmitters (Valenstein, 2005). In this section, we will look at seven of them that we know quite a bit about—acetylcholine, dopamine, serotonin, norepinephrine, GABA (gamma-aminobutyric acid), glutamate, and endorphins. We'll identify some of the behaviors and mental processes in which each of these neurotransmitters plays a major role, provide some examples of how poisons and drugs bring about their effects by impacting the synaptic communication process for particular neurotransmitters, and explain how some disorders and diseases may result from excessive activity or a deficit in activity for particular neurotransmitters. In the discussions of drugs and poisons, we will use the agonist versus antagonist distinction. An **agonist** is a drug or poison that increases the activity of one or more neurotransmitters; an **antagonist** is a drug or poison that decreases the activity of one or more neurotransmitters. We'll see that agonists and antagonists bring about their effects in many different ways.

Acetylcholine. **Acetylcholine (ACh)** is a neurotransmitter involved in learning, memory, and muscle movement. When it is located in the brain, it impacts learning and memory. Alzheimer's patients tend to have lower levels of ACh. At muscle junctures throughout our body, ACh leads to muscle contractions, allowing us to move the various parts of our body. Its role in muscle movement shows how poisons work in agonistic or antagonistic ways to impact the normal level of neurotransmitter activity. There are several poisons that paralyze us (prevent muscle movement) by preventing ACh from fulfilling its movement function. Let's look at three such poisons and see how they achieve this same effect, but in different ways.

First, consider botulinum poison (sometimes called botulin), a toxin involved in food poisoning. Botulinum poison is an antagonist that blocks the release of ACh at muscle junctures, leading to paralysis and, if not treated, death. The chest and diaphragm muscles become paralyzed, so the victim cannot breathe. An extremely mild form of this poison is what is used in the Botox treatment for facial wrinkling, where the facial muscles are temporarily paralyzed, thus smoothing them. Curare, the poison that South American Indians put on the tips of their spears and arrows, paralyzes by occupying the receptor sites for ACh, thereby preventing the ACh molecules from getting in and delivering their message. Like botulinum poison, curare is an antagonist for ACh and can kill by paralyzing critical muscles. Another poison, black widow spider venom, is an agonist for ACh, and can also lead to death by paralysis. Black widow spider venom causes the continuous release of ACh, flooding the synapse. This initial effect is agonistic, leading to uncontrollable convulsive movement due to the

agonist A drug or poison that increases the activity of one or more neurotransmitters.

antagonist A drug or poison that decreases the activity of one or more neurotransmitters.

acetylcholine (ACh) A neurotransmitter involved in learning, memory, and muscle movement.

dopamine A neurotransmitter involved in arousal and mood states, thought processes, and physical movement.

Parkinson's disease A disease in which the person has movement problems such as muscle tremors, difficulty initiating movements, and rigidity of movement. These movement problems stem from a scarcity of dopamine in the basal ganglia.

blood–brain barrier A protective mechanism by which the blood capillaries supplying the brain create a barrier that prevents dangerous substances access to the brain.

L-dopa A drug for Parkinson's disease that contains the precursors to dopamine so that once it is in the brain, it will be converted to dopamine.

heightened ACh activity, but death occurs through paralysis after the supply of ACh has been exhausted. But don't worry. There's enough poison in a black widow spider bite to kill other insects, but humans rarely die from such bites.

Dopamine. Dopamine is a neurotransmitter that impacts our arousal and mood states, thought processes, and physical movement, but in a very different way than ACh. Low levels of dopamine in the basal ganglia, brain structures that we will discuss later in the chapter, lead to **Parkinson's disease,** which causes movement problems such as muscle tremors, difficulty initiating movements, and rigidity of movement. Actor Michael J. Fox and boxer Muhammad Ali both suffer from Parkinson's disease. Physicians first attempted to treat Parkinson's disease by injecting dopamine through the bloodstream. This did not work, however, because dopamine could not get through the **blood–brain barrier**—a protective mechanism by which the blood capillaries supplying the brain create a barrier that prevents dangerous substances from accessing the brain. The downside is that some good substances, such as dopamine in the case of Parkinson's disease, also cannot gain access. However, **L-dopa,** a drug for Parkinson's disease, can pass through the blood–brain barrier. It contains the precursors to dopamine, so once in the brain L-dopa is converted to dopamine. Thus, L-dopa functions as an agonist for dopamine by increasing its production. However, L-dopa is not effective for all Parkinson's patients, and as Parkinson's disease progresses, L-dopa becomes less effective for those it does help.

There are also side effects of L-dopa that resemble some of the symptoms of schizophrenia—a psychotic disorder in which a person loses touch with reality and suffers from perceptual and cognitive processing deficits, such as hallucinations, false beliefs, and deficits in attention. This makes sense, however, because one of the main explanations for schizophrenia involves an excess of dopamine activity, and dopamine impacts our thought processes. In fact, traditional antipsychotic drugs for schizophrenia work antagonistically by globally blocking receptor sites for dopamine so that dopamine cannot enter them, thereby reducing its level of activity. Conversely, some of the side effects of these antipsychotic drugs resemble the movement symptoms of Parkinson's disease, because these powerful drugs also lessen the activity of the dopamine in the movement system involving the basal ganglia.

The effects of addictive stimulants (such as amphetamines and cocaine) illustrate dopamine's involvement in our arousal and mood states. For example, amphetamines act as agonists for dopamine activity by continually stimulating the release of dopamine from axon terminals, thereby depleting it. Similarly, cocaine creates an agonistic effect by blocking the reuptake of dopamine, which means dopamine accumulates in the synapse. Cocaine thus prolongs its effect on other neurons by forcing dopamine to deliver its message to these neurons repeatedly, thereby using it up. The downside is that these dopamine-caused "high" arousal states are temporary and are followed by "crashes" created by the shortage of dopamine that follows. The pleasurable mood effects of these addictive stimulants are thought to arise from the release of dopamine in the brain's reward centers. Other addictive drugs such as painkillers, caffeine, and nicotine also increase dopamine activity in these centers.

Serotonin and norepinephrine. In addition to dopamine, cocaine blocks the reuptake of **serotonin** and **norepinephrine**—neurotransmitters involved in levels of arousal and mood, sleep, and eating. These two neurotransmitters play a major role in mood disorders such as depression. The best known and most prescribed antidepressant drugs, such as Prozac, Paxil, and Zoloft, are **selective serotonin reuptake inhibitors (SSRIs)**—antidepressant drugs that achieve their agonistic effect by selectively blocking just the reuptake of serotonin. SSRIs only partially block reuptake (unlike cocaine) so they do not exhaust the neurotransmitter supply and there are no subsequent "crashes." Some other antidepressant drugs, such as Cymbalta, Pristiq, and Effexor, work by blocking the reuptake of both serotonin and norepinephrine. These drugs are called **selective serotonin and norepinephrine reuptake inhibitors (SSNRIs)**. SSRIs, SSNRIs, and other types of antidepressant drugs will be discussed more fully in the section on biomedical therapies in Chapter 10.

GABA and glutamate. GABA (gamma-aminobutyric acid) is the main inhibitory neurotransmitter in the nervous system. Thus, its primary role is to keep the brain from becoming too aroused. It works like the brakes on a car by preventing mental processes or behavior from going unchecked. For example, it lowers arousal and anxiety and helps regulate movement. Antianxiety drugs (tranquilizers) are agonists for GABA, increasing GABA activity and thereby lowering anxiety. Lack of GABA activity may also contribute to epilepsy, a brain disorder leading to uncontrolled movement and convulsions. Tranquilizers, such as Valium and Librium, sometimes also serve as antiepileptic treatments because they have been found to block epileptic convulsions.

Glutamate is the main excitatory neurotransmitter in the nervous system. It is involved in memory storage and pain perception. Excessive glutamate activity, however, can be dangerous, leading to the death of neurons. For example, strokes lead to overstimulation of glutamate synapses and the subsequent loss of neurons that literally excite themselves to death. Deficient glutamate activity can also cause problems. Glutamate levels that drop too low can even cause coma. Research has also found that abnormal levels of glutamate activity may play a central role in the neurochemistry of schizophrenia (Kalat, 2007). Hence, antipsychotic drugs that impact glutamate activity levels are presently undergoing clinical trials by pharmaceutical companies.

serotonin and norepinephrine
Neurotransmitters involved in levels of arousal and mood, sleep, and eating.

selective serotonin reuptake inhibitors (SSRIs) Antidepressant drugs that achieve their agonistic effect on serotonin by selectively blocking its reuptake.

selective serotonin and norepinephrine reuptake inhibitors (SSNRIs) Antidepressant drugs that achieve their agonistic effect on serotonin and norepinephrine by selectively blocking their reuptake.

GABA (gamma-aminobutyric acid) The main inhibitory neurotransmitter in the nervous system. It is involved in lowering arousal and anxiety and regulating movement.

glutamate The main excitatory neurotransmitter in the nervous system. It is involved in memory storage, pain perception, strokes, and schizophrenia.

endorphins A group of neuro-transmitters that are involved in pain relief and feelings of pleasure.

Endorphins. **Endorphins** are a group of neurotransmitters that are involved in pain relief and feelings of pleasure. They represent the nervous system's natural painkillers. When endorphins are released, we feel less pain and experience a sense of euphoria. Endorphins, therefore, help explain good feelings such as the "runner's high." Higher than normal endorphin levels have been found in runners following a marathon (Mahler, Cunningham, Skrinar, Kraemer, & Colice, 1989). Morphine and heroin are painkilling drugs that achieve their agonistic effects by binding to endorphin receptors, thereby increasing endorphin activity (Pert & Snyder, 1973). (Actually, the word "endorphin" is a contraction of the words "endogeneous," which means originating within, and "morphine.") These painkillers also trigger the brain's reward centers, causing the release of dopamine.

Endorphins may also play a role in biologically explaining placebo effects on pain. Remember, as we discussed in Chapter 1, a placebo drug is an inert substance that has no pharmacological effect. The expectation of improvement created by taking the placebo may stimulate the release of endorphins, resulting in an actual decrease in pain. Similarly, stimulation of endorphins may partially explain how acupuncture, the Chinese medical practice of inserting needles at specified sites of the body, leads to pain relief (Pert, 1999).

All of the neurotransmitters that we have discussed are summarized in Table 2.1 along with some of the behaviors and mental processes in which they play a major role.

Table 2.1	Neurotransmitters and Some of Their Functions
Neurotransmitter	**Involved in:**
Acetylcholine (Ach)	Learning, memory, muscle movement
Dopamine	Arousal and mood states, thought processes, physical movement
Serotonin and Norepinephrine	Levels of arousal and mood, sleep, eating
GABA (main inhibitory neurotransmitter)	Lowering arousal and anxiety, regulating movement
Glutamate (main excitatory neurotransmitter)	Memory storage, pain perception, strokes, schizophrenia
Endorphins	Pain relief and feelings of pleasure

Frank and Ernest

2006 Thaves/Distributed by NEA, Inc.

Section Summary

In this section, we discussed how billions of neurons, the building blocks of the nervous system, work and communicate with each other. All three parts of a neuron are involved. The dendrites receive the information from other neurons and pass it on to the cell body, which decides whether or not to pass the information on to other neurons. If the information is to be passed on, an electrical impulse is generated and travels down the axon. When this impulse reaches the axon terminals, neurotransmitter molecules are released and travel across the synaptic gap, carrying the message to other neurons, and then are destroyed or return to the sending neuron to be used again. It is this chemical communication that allows the neurons to transmit and integrate information within the nervous system, giving us our perceptions, feelings, memories, and thoughts, as well as our ability to move. Glial cells aid in this information transmission process by serving as a support system for the neurons.

Acetylcholine (ACh), dopamine, serotonin, norepinephrine, GABA, glutamate, and endorphins are seven major neurotransmitters that impact many important aspects of our behavior and mental processing. Some disorders and diseases stem from excessive activity or a deficit in activity for particular neurotransmitters. In addition, drugs and poisons achieve their effects by changing the activity level of particular neurotransmitters in either agonistic or antagonistic ways. Agonists increase the level of neurotransmitter activity; antagonists decrease it. This neuronal chemistry is the source of all of our behavior and mental processes, but we are only aware of its products (our behavior and mental processing) and not the intercellular chemistry itself. In the next section, we will consider the nervous system at a more global level by examining its major subdivisions—the central nervous system and the peripheral nervous system. We will also discuss the body's other major communication system—the endocrine glandular system.

ConceptCheck | 1

- ► Explain why you can think of a neuron as a miniature decision-making device.

- ► Explain why neural impulses are faster in neurons with myelinated axons than in those with unmyelinated axons.

- ► Explain why drugs that block the reuptake of neurotransmitters are considered agonists.

- ► Explain why treatment of Parkinson's disease with L-dopa leads to some side effects that resemble the thought disorder symptoms of schizophrenia and why the side effects of traditional antipsychotic drugs lead to side effects resembling Parkinson's disease.

The Nervous System and the Endocrine System

In this section, we will present an overview of the nervous system and the other major communication system of the body, the endocrine glandular system. We will also discuss the three types of neurons in the nervous system. An overview diagram of the major subdivisions of the nervous system is given in Figure 2.3. The two major parts are the **central nervous system (CNS),** made up of the brain and spinal cord, and the **peripheral nervous system (PNS),** the remainder of the nervous system throughout the body, linking the CNS with the body's sensory receptors, muscles, and glands. One part of the peripheral nervous system, the autonomic nervous system, plays an important role in emotional experiences. We will learn how it does so once we learn more about the general nature of the nervous system and its major divisions and the body's other major communication system, the endocrine glandular system.

central nervous system (CNS) The brain and spinal cord.

peripheral nervous system (PNS) The part of the nervous system that links the CNS with the body's sensory receptors, muscles, and glands.

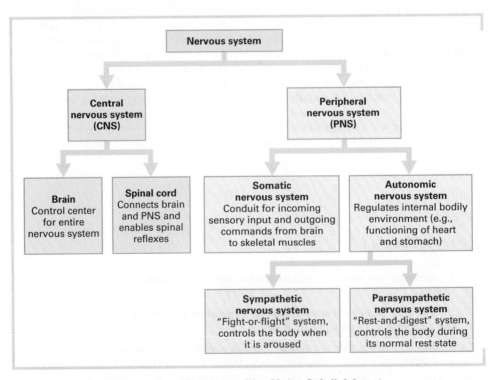

▲ **Figure 2.3** | The Nervous System and Its Major Subdivisions | The nervous system first divides into the central nervous system (the spinal cord and brain) and the peripheral nervous system (the remainder of the nervous system throughout the body). The peripheral nervous system has two parts—the somatic (or skeletal) nervous system and the autonomic nervous system. The autonomic nervous system also has two parts—the sympathetic nervous system and parasympathetic nervous system.

There are three types of neurons in the nervous system. **Interneurons,** which integrate information within the CNS by communicating with each other, are only in the CNS. Interneurons also intervene within the spinal cord between sensory and motor neurons that are only in the PNS. **Sensory neurons** carry information to the CNS from sensory receptors (such as the rods and cones in the eyes), muscles, and glands. **Motor neurons** carry movement commands from the CNS out to the rest of the body. Bundles of sensory neurons are called sensory nerves. Most enter the CNS through the spinal cord, while some (from the head) enter the brain directly through holes in the cranium (the skull around the brain). Collections of the motor neurons are called motor nerves. They exit the CNS through the spinal cord or, for the head, from the cranium. To begin to understand the role that these neurons play, we'll next discuss the CNS and the role of the spinal cord.

interneurons Neurons that integrate information within the CNS through their communication with each other and between sensory and motor neurons in the spinal cord.

sensory neurons Neurons in the PNS that carry information to the CNS from sensory receptors, muscles, and glands.

motor neurons Neurons in the PNS that carry movement commands from the CNS out to the rest of the body.

spinal cord The conduit between the brain and the PNS for incoming sensory data and outgoing movement commands to the muscles.

spinal reflex A simple automatic action of the spinal cord not requiring involvement of the brain, such as the knee-jerk reflex.

The Central Nervous System

Both parts of the CNS, the spinal cord and the brain, are totally encased in bone—the spinal cord within the spinal column and the brain within the cranium—for protective reasons. In addition, for further protection, both are surrounded by cerebrospinal fluid for cushioning. We will detail the spinal cord's role in the CNS here, and then discuss the brain in the last section of this chapter.

The **spinal cord** spans from the stem of the brain down through the neck and the center of the spinal column. The spinal cord has two main functions. First, it serves as the conduit for both incoming sensory data and outgoing movement commands to the muscles in the body. This is why a spinal cord injury, such as that suffered by actor Christopher Reeve, may result in paralysis and difficulty in breathing. Second, it provides for spinal reflexes. A **spinal reflex** is a simple automatic action not requiring involvement of the brain. A good example is the knee-jerk reflex in which a leg jerks forward when the knee is tapped. Only sensory neurons and motor neurons are involved in this reflex. The knee-jerk reflex might appear to have no use, but it is an example of a stretch reflex that is important to maintaining our posture and for lifting objects.

For most spinal reflexes, however, interneurons are also involved. Sensory neurons connect with interneurons in the spinal cord, which then connect with motor neurons. The sensory information is also sent up to the brain by way of interneurons, but the brain is usually not involved. A good example of such a spinal reflex is the withdrawal reflex. When we touch something extremely hot or painful, we jerk away. These reflexes normally occur without interference from the brain so that they can occur rapidly. The brain can stop a spinal reflex by sending commands to override the reflexive response, but for obvious reasons it usually chooses not to interfere.

The brain is the control center for the entire nervous system, but it couldn't perform this job without agents to carry out its commands and to provide information about the activities of the rest of the body and the world outside. We will next discuss the PNS, the system that provides these supportive functions for the brain.

The Peripheral Nervous System

Not only does the PNS gather information about the external environment and the body's internal environment for the brain through the sensory nerves, it also serves as the conduit for the brain's commands to the rest of the body through the motor nerves. To carry out these tasks, the PNS has two parts working in concert with each other—the somatic (or skeletal) nervous system and the autonomic nervous system.

The **somatic (skeletal) nervous system** carries sensory input from receptors to the CNS and relays commands from the CNS to the skeletal muscles to control their movement. Skeletal muscles are those that are attached to bone, such as the muscles of the arms and legs. As we have already discussed, the primary neurotransmitter for these muscles is acetylcholine. The **autonomic nervous system** regulates the functioning of our internal environment (glands and organs such as the stomach, lungs, and heart). The somatic nervous system is thought of as voluntary, but the autonomic system is usually thought of as involuntary, operating on automatic (hence the name, autonomic) to maintain our internal functioning such as heartbeat, respiration, and digestion. This is why we are generally unaware of what the autonomic nervous system is doing.

The autonomic system has two parts—the sympathetic nervous system and the parasympathetic nervous system. These two systems normally work together to maintain a steady internal state. However, the **sympathetic nervous system** is in control when we are very aroused, as in an emergency, and prepares us for defensive action. The **parasympathetic nervous system** takes over when the aroused state ends to return the body to its normal resting state. Some effects of each part of this dual autonomic system on the glands and muscles that they impact are shown in Table 2.2. In general, the sympathetic nervous system expends energy, and the parasympathetic nervous system conserves energy. The two systems are connected to essentially the same glands and organs, but generally lead to opposite effects. For example, the sympathetic leads to pupil dilation, accelerated heartbeat, and inhibited digestion; the parasympathetic leads to pupil contraction, slowed heartbeat, and stimulated digestion. Given these actions, the sympathetic nervous system is usually referred to as the "fight-or-flight" system; it prepares us for one of these two actions in times of emergency. In contrast, the parasympathetic nervous system has sometimes been called the "rest-and-digest" system (Dowling, 1998).

▌ **somatic (skeletal) nervous system** The part of the PNS that carries sensory input from receptors to the CNS and relays commands from the CNS to skeletal muscles to control their movement.

▌ **autonomic nervous system** The part of the PNS that regulates the functioning of our internal environment (glands and organs like the heart, lungs, and stomach).

▌ **sympathetic nervous system** The part of the autonomic nervous system that is in control when we are highly aroused, as in an emergency, and need to prepare for defensive action.

▌ **parasympathetic nervous system** The part of the autonomic nervous system that returns the body to its normal resting state after having been highly aroused, as in an emergency.

Table 2.2 Some Functions of the Sympathetic and Parasympathetic Nervous Systems

Sympathetic Nervous System	Parasympathetic Nervous System
Dilates pupils	Contracts pupils
Contracts blood vessels	Dilates blood vessels
Speeds heart rate	Slows heart rate
Speeds breathing	Slows breathing
Inhibits salivation	Activates salivation
Inhibits digestion	Stimulates digestion
Activates sweat glands	Inhibits sweat glands

The sympathetic and parasympathetic divisions of the autonomic nervous system work together to coordinate our internal functioning, including our heart, stomach, and glandular activity. In general, the sympathetic system arouses and expends energy while the parasympathetic system calms and conserves energy.

The Endocrine Glandular System

The **endocrine glandular system,** the body's other major communication system, is not part of the nervous system, but these two systems are connected in order to maintain normal internal functioning. The endocrine glandular system works with the autonomic nervous system in responding to stress, and it also plays an important role in such basic behaviors as sex and eating and in normal bodily functions, such as metabolism, reproduction, and growth.

The endocrine glandular system communicates through messengers in the bloodstream. Endocrine glands secrete chemical substances within the body into the bloodstream; exocrine glands (such as sweat and tear glands) secrete substances outside the body. The substances secreted by the endocrine glands are hormones. A **hormone** is a chemical messenger produced by the endocrine glands and carried by the bloodstream to target sites throughout the body. Some hormones (adrenalin and noradrenalin secreted by the adrenal glands) are chemically similar to some neurotransmitters (epinephrine and norepinephrine), but neurotransmitters are released at their targets (other neurons), while hormones have to travel through the bloodstream to reach their targets. For example, the male sex hormone, testosterone, travels from the male sex glands through the bloodstream to target sites in facial skin to stimulate hair growth.

The endocrine glandular system is controlled by its connection with a part of the brain called the hypothalamus (to be discussed in the next section). The hypothalamus controls the most influential gland in the endocrine system, the **pituitary gland,** which releases hormones essential for human growth, and also releases hormones that direct

▮ **endocrine glandular system** The body's other major communication system. Communication is achieved through hormones that are secreted by the endocrine glands and travel through the bloodstream to their target sites.

▮ **hormone** A chemical messenger that is produced by an endocrine gland and carried by the bloodstream to target tissues throughout the body.

▮ **pituitary gland** The most influential gland in the endocrine glandular system. It releases hormones for human growth and hormones that direct other endocrine glands to release their hormones.

other endocrine glands to release their hormones. For example, it is the pituitary gland that directs a male's sex glands to secrete testosterone. The pituitary gland, located near the base of the brain, thus functions like the master of the endocrine system, which is why it is sometimes referred to as the "master gland." The hypothalamus, through its control of the pituitary gland, is thus able to regulate the endocrine glandular system.

Other endocrine glands—such as the thyroid gland, the adrenal glands, the pancreas, and the sex glands—are located throughout the body. The thyroid gland, which affects our growth and maturation among other things, is located in the neck. The adrenal glands, which are involved in our metabolism and help to trigger the "fight-or-flight" response with commands from the autonomic nervous system, are situated above the kidneys. The pancreas, located between the kidneys, is involved in digestion and maintaining our blood-sugar levels. The testes (in males) and ovaries (in females) secrete sex hormones. The major endocrine glands along with their main functions are depicted in Figure 2.4.

Emotions and the Autonomic Nervous System

We all experience anger, fear, joy, love, hate, and many other emotions. Emotions play an important part in our lives, and the autonomic nervous system, especially

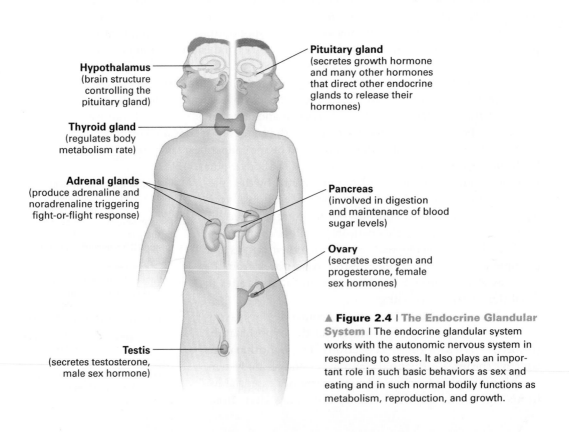

Hypothalamus
(brain structure
controlling the
pituitary gland)

Pituitary gland
(secretes growth hormone
and many other hormones
that direct other endocrine
glands to release their
hormones)

Thyroid gland
(regulates body
metabolism rate)

Adrenal glands
(produce adrenaline and
noradrenaline triggering
fight-or-flight response)

Pancreas
(involved in digestion
and maintenance of blood
sugar levels)

Ovary
(secretes estrogen and
progesterone, female
sex hormones)

Testis
(secretes testosterone,
male sex hormone)

▲ **Figure 2.4 I The Endocrine Glandular System** I The endocrine glandular system works with the autonomic nervous system in responding to stress. It also plays an important role in such basic behaviors as sex and eating and in such normal bodily functions as metabolism, reproduction, and growth.

the sympathetic division, plays an important role in how we experience and express emotions. Think about the heightened state of arousal and the bodily feelings that accompany various emotions. For example, we may feel our blood pressure rising, our heart pounding, our body trembling, or butterflies in our stomach. Such bodily arousal and feelings stem from autonomic nervous system activity, which prepares us for our emotional reactions. But exactly what is an emotion, and how do emotions arise?

The three components of emotion. Psychologists usually define an **emotion** as a complex psychological state that involves three components: (1) a physical component—a state of physiological arousal triggered by the autonomic nervous system; (2) a behavioral component—outward expression of the emotion, including facial expressions, movements, and gestures; and (3) a cognitive component—our appraisal of the situation to determine which emotion we are experiencing and how intensely we are experiencing it.

First, let's consider the physical component of emotion. In emotional situations the autonomic nervous system increases our physiological arousal. The sympathetic nervous system goes into its "fight-or-flight" mode—our heart rate and breathing increase, our blood pressure surges, we start sweating, our pupils dilate, we begin trembling, our digestion stops, and so on. This aroused state prepares us to react emotionally to the situation, whether our reaction is to run from an attacker, hug a loved one, or laugh at a roommate's joke. Different emotions seem to lead to subtly different patterns of autonomic nervous system arousal (Levenson, 1992). The language we use to describe different emotional states reflects the different patterns in arousal states for these emotions (Oatley & Duncan, 1994). For example, we say we are "hot under the collar" when angry, but that we have "cold feet" when afraid. These descriptions parallel differences in body temperature for these two basic emotions; we have a higher than normal body temperature when we are angry and a lower one when we are afraid.

The behavioral component of emotion is the product of the somatic nervous system. It provides the nonverbal, expressive behavior for the emotion—our facial expressions, such as smiles and frowns, and our body language, such as clenching our fists. Some emotion researchers have proposed a facial-feedback hypothesis, which assumes that the facial muscles send messages to the brain, allowing the brain to determine which emotion is being experienced (Izard, 1990; Soussignan, 2002). For example, when we see someone we truly care for and haven't seen for some time, we automatically start smiling; signals about this facial expression are sent to the brain to help the brain determine what emotion is being experienced. In fact, there is even evidence that watching another person's facial expressions causes a reciprocal change in our own facial muscles (Dinberg & Thunberg, 1998). If they smile, we smile. Signals are sent not only from the facial muscles but also from the entire motor nervous system to the brain, contributing to the cognitive appraisal component of the emotion.

emotion A complex psychological state that involves a state of physiological arousal, an outward behavioral expression of the emotion, and a cognitive appraisal of the situation to determine the specific emotion and its intensity.

James-Lange theory A theory of emotion proposing that an emotion is determined from a cognitive appraisal of the physiological arousal and behavioral responses which occur first.

Cannon-Bard theory A theory of emotion proposing that an emotion is determined from simultaneously occurring physiological arousal, behavioral responses, and cognitive appraisal.

Schachter-Singer two-factor theory A theory of emotion proposing that an emotion is determined by cognitive appraisal of the physiological arousal and the entire environmental situation.

The cognitive component of emotion appraises the situation to determine what emotion we are experiencing. We perceive the changes in bodily arousal and behavioral responses within the situational context, and then, using the knowledge we have stored in memory about emotions, we determine what emotion we are experiencing. For example, if your hands are sweating, you feel butterflies in your stomach, your mouth is dry, and you are about to give a speech to a large crowd, then your brain will easily deduce that you are anxious.

Next, we will consider how this cognitive component interacts with the physical and behavioral components to produce our emotional experiences as we contrast some of the major theories of emotion.

Theories of emotion. Many theories have been proposed over the last century to explain emotion. We'll consider three of them—the James-Lange theory, the Cannon-Bard theory, and the Schachter-Singer two-factor theory. To see how these theories differ, we'll contrast them with what is referred to as the "commonsense" explanation of emotion, which proposes that the subjective experience of the emotion triggers the physiological arousal and behavioral response. For example, you are out hiking and you see a bear (an emotion-provoking stimulus). The commonsense view would say that you cog-

Bettmann/Corbis

William James

The Royal Library of Denmark, Dept. of Maps, Prints and Photographs.

Carl Lange

nitively recognize a dangerous situation and react emotionally by realizing you are afraid. This emotional feeling of fear triggers the arousal of the autonomic nervous system—for example, your heart races and you start sweating—and a behavioral response—you back away slowly. (Don't run from a bear. It triggers their chase instincts.) The commonsense view proposes the following order of events—you realize you are afraid, and then the physiological arousal and behavioral response follow. Our heart races and we start sweating and back away because we are afraid.

American psychologist William James and Danish psychologist Carl Lange developed one of the earliest theories of emotion (Lange & James, 1922). They disagreed with the order of events proposed by the commonsense theory and argued that the emotional feeling does not precede, but rather follows, the physiological arousal and behavioral response. According to the **James-Lange theory,** physiological arousal and backing away are responses to the stimulus of seeing the bear. You then interpret these autonomic and behavioral responses as the emotion fear. You determine that you are afraid because you are sweating, your heart is racing, and you are backing away. The emotional feeling occurs after, and as a result of, the arousal and behavioral responses. The particular emotion experienced depends upon the specific arousal and response patterns.

Walter Cannon, the physiologist most responsible for discovering the functions of the autonomic nervous system (Kalat, 2007), had different ideas about the role of arousal in emotion. He and another physiologist, Philip Bard, developed what is called the **Cannon-Bard theory** (Bard, 1934; Cannon, 1927). This theory argues that arousal patterns for different emotions are too physiologically alike to be used to determine which emotion is being experienced. Instead, they proposed that an emotion-provoking stimulus (the bear) sends messages simultaneously to the peripheral nervous system and the brain. The autonomic nervous system produces the physiological arousal responses such as our heart racing; the motor nervous system produces the behavioral response (backing away); and the brain produces the emotional feeling (fear). These three responses occur simultaneously, but independently. So, according to the Cannon-Bard theory, the arousal and behavioral responses do not cause the emotional feeling, and the emotional feeling does not cause the responses. They all happen at the same time.

Walter Cannon

Bettmann/Corbis

Subsequent research on these two theories has not strongly supported either one but has indicated that the cognitive component may play a larger role than previously thought. These early theories did not emphasize this component. The last theory of emotion that we will discuss, Stanley Schachter and Jerome Singer's two-factor theory, illustrates the emerging importance of the cognitive component (Schachter & Singer, 1962). Schachter and Singer agreed with the James-Lange theory that arousal was a central element in our experience of emotion, but also with the Cannon-Bard theory that physiological arousal is too similar to distinguish different emotions. According to the **Schachter-Singer two-factor theory,** there are two important ingredients in determining the emotion—physiological arousal and cognitive appraisal. The physiological arousal tells us how intense the emotion is, while the cognitive appraisal of the entire situation (the arousal responses such as our heart racing, the behavioral response of backing away, and the situational aspect of being alone with the bear) allows us to identify (label) the emotion, leading to the emotional feeling (fear). In the two-factor theory, cognitive appraisal precedes the emotion. This is different from the Cannon-Bard assumption that arousal and the emotion occur simultaneously. The two-factor theory is contrasted with the three earlier theories in Figure 2.5.

Philip Bard

JHMI Medical Archive

Stanley Schachter

Columbia University Library

Schachter and Singer's experimental work to test their theory only provided partial support, but their theory has spurred much discussion and research on the role of cognitive appraisal in emotion. As mentioned earlier, the autonomic arousal patterns for some emotions are not the same, but some argue that these pattern differences may be too small to allow the differentiation of most emotions (Lang, 1994). However, these

Jerome Singer

Courtesy Daniel Singer

▲ **Figure 2.5** | Theories of Emotion | The commonsense theory argued that our feeling of fear causes our physiological arousal and behavioral responses. The James-Lange theory proposed just the opposite—our physiological arousal and behavioral responses cause us to feel afraid. According to the Cannon-Bard theory, the physiological and behavioral responses and the feeling of fear occur simultaneously. The Schachter-Singer two-factor theory asserted that cognitive appraisal of the physiological arousal and behavioral responses and the entire situation leads to the identification (labeling) of the emotion (fear), which leads to our feeling of fear.

emotions also lead to different patterns of brain activity (Damasio et al., 2000). Could these patterns be used to differentiate emotions?

To help resolve this question, Joseph LeDoux (1996, 2000) proposes that there are different brain systems for different emotions. Some emotional responses might be the product of a brain system that operates as a reflex system without cognitive appraisal. Fear is probably such an emotion. LeDoux actually has some evidence that the fear response can be generated almost instantaneously—before higher-level cognitive appraisal of the situation could occur. Such fast responding would have survival value from an evolutionary point of view by allowing us to make quick, defensive responses to threats without having to wait on slower, cognitive appraisal.

Other emotions, however, may entail using a brain system that relies on cognitive appraisal and the use of past emotional experiences in this appraisal. This system would be responsible for more complex emotions, such as love or guilt, that do not require an instant response. In sum, this theory not only accommodates much of what we know about emotion but also provides a general framework for research on the roles of various brain structures in generating our emotions. We now turn to a discussion of these brain structures and what we presently know about them and their roles not only in emotion but also in thought, language, memory, and the many other information-processing abilities we possess.

Section Summary

In this section, we dicussed the two major communication systems within the body—the nervous system, which uses neurotransmitters to communicate, and the endocrine glandular system, which uses slower-acting hormones to communicate. The nervous system is composed of two main divisions—the central nervous system (CNS), which consists of the brain and spinal cord, and the peripheral nervous system (PNS), which links the CNS with the body's sensory receptors, muscles, and glands. Sensory neurons carry information from the PNS to the CNS, and motor neurons carry movement commands from the CNS to parts of the PNS. The spinal cord not only serves as the conduit for this information but also is responsible for spinal reflexes, automatic actions not requiring involvement of the brain. Interneurons integrate all information processing within the CNS.

The PNS has two parts that work in concert with each other—the somatic nervous system carries sensory information to the CNS and relays commands from the CNS to skeletal muscles to control their movement, and the autonomic nervous system regulates our internal environment. To do this, the autonomic system has two parts working together—the sympathetic nervous system, which expends energy, and the parasympathetic nervous system, which conserves energy. The sympathetic is in control during emergencies to help us prepare for defensive action; once the emergency is over, the parasympathetic helps us return to our normal resting state.

The endocrine glandular system is not part of the nervous system, but the two systems work together to maintain normal internal functioning. The endocrine glandular system plays an important role in many basic behaviors, such as eating and sex, and normal bodily functions, such as metabolism, growth, and reproduction. The brain controls the endocrine glandular system through the hypothalamus, which controls the master gland within the system, the pituitary gland.

We also discussed how the autonomic nervous system plays a critical role in the physical component of our emotional experiences by triggering a state of physiological arousal, which prepares us for our emotional reactions. An emotion is the result of the interplay between this physical component, a behavioral component (the outward expression of the emotion), and a cognitive component (an appraisal of the entire situation to determine which emotion we are experiencing). The major explanations of emotion have varied in the proposed relationships among these three components, as well as their importance. More recent theories of emotion, such as Schachter and Singer's two-factor theory, have emphasized the importance of the cognitive appraisal component, and the idea that cognition must precede emotion. However, this is not always the case. LeDoux's proposal that different brain systems may be responsible for different emotional responses (those requiring cognitive appraisal versus those that do not) can account for both emotional reactions in which cognition precedes emotion, and those in which emotion precedes cognition.

ConceptCheck | 2

> Explain the differences between sensory neurons, motor neurons, and interneurons with respect to location and function.

> Explain why the sympathetic nervous system has been referred to as the "fight-or-flight" system and the parasympathetic nervous system as the "rest-and-digest" system.

> Explain how hormones differ from neurotransmitters.

> Explain why the pituitary gland is referred to as the "master gland."

> Explain how the James-Lange theory and the Cannon-Bard theory of emotion differ.

The Brain

The brain has evolved from the brain stem structures that link the brain to the spinal cord all the way up to the cerebral cortex. As we go up the brain stem, processing gets more complex. In fact, it is the very top, the cerebral cortex, that differentiates our brains from those of all other animals. The cerebral cortex enables such complex processes as decision making, language, and perception. Even so, all of the structures below the cerebral cortex are essential for normal behavior and mental processing. This will become clearer as we discuss each structure's role in this complex, interactive system we call the brain.

Going Up the Brain Stem

Between the spinal cord and the cortex, there are two sets of brain structures—the central core and the limbic system. The brain stem and structures near the brain stem (cerebellum, thalamus, and basal ganglia) can be thought of as the central core of the brain. Surrounding the top border of the brain stem are the limbic system structures—the hypothalamus, hippocampus, and amygdala. Our discussion will start with the central core structures going up the brain stem to the limbic system structures.

The central core. Figure 2.6 shows the central core brain structures. The brain stem spans from the spinal cord up to the thalamus. The first brain stem structure is the **medulla,** which links the spinal cord to the brain. The medulla is involved in regulating essential body functions such as heartbeat, breathing, blood pressure, digestion, and swallowing. This is why damage to the medulla can result in death. A drug overdose, which suppresses proper functioning of the medulla, can also lead to death. Just above the medulla where the brain stem bulges sits the **pons.** Along with the medulla, the pons serves as a passageway for neural

medulla A brain stem structure involved in many essential body functions, such as heartbeat, breathing, blood pressure, digestion, and swallowing.

pons A brain stem structure that serves as a bridge between the cerebellum and the rest of the brain and is involved in sleep and dreaming.

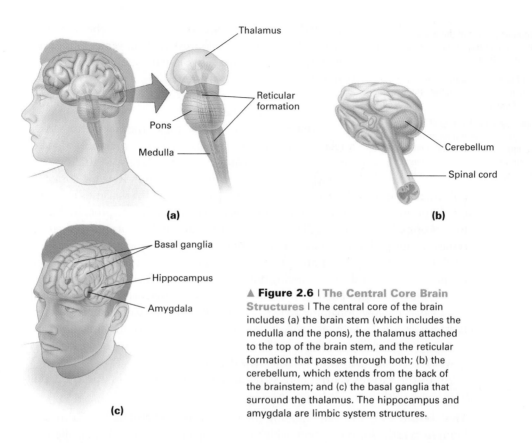

(a)

Thalamus

Reticular formation

Pons

Medulla

(b)

Cerebellum

Spinal cord

(c)

Basal ganglia

Hippocampus

Amygdala

▲ **Figure 2.6** | **The Central Core Brain Structures** | The central core of the brain includes (a) the brain stem (which includes the medulla and the pons), the thalamus attached to the top of the brain stem, and the reticular formation that passes through both; (b) the cerebellum, which extends from the back of the brainstem; and (c) the basal ganglia that surround the thalamus. The hippocampus and amygdala are limbic system structures.

signals to and from higher areas in the brain. The pons (Latin for "bridge") functions as a bridge between the cerebellum and the rest of the brain and is involved in sleep and dreaming.

The **reticular formation** is a network of neurons running up the center of the brain stem and into the thalamus that is involved in controlling our different levels of arousal and awareness. This function was demonstrated by Moruzzi and Magoun (1949) in research with cats. When they stimulated a sleeping cat's reticular formation, the cat awoke and entered a very alert state. When they severed the connections of the reticular formation with higher brain structures, however, the cat went into a coma from which it could never be awakened. The reticular formation also plays a role in attention by deciding which incoming sensory information enters our conscious awareness.

The **cerebellum** is involved in the coordination of our movements, our sense of balance, and motor learning. Cerebellum means "little brain" in Latin, and it looks like two minihemispheres attached to the rear of the brain stem. The cerebellum coordinates all of our movements, such as walking, running, and dancing. Damage to the cerebellum will lead to very unsteady, unbalanced movement.

▮ **reticular formation** A network of neurons running up the center of the brain stem that is responsible for our different levels of arousal and consciousness.

▮ **cerebellum** A part of the brain involved in the coordination of our movements, sense of balance, and motor learning.

thalamus A part of the brain that serves as a relay station for incoming sensory information.

basal ganglia A part of the brain that is involved in the initiation and execution of movements.

limbic system A group of brain structures (hypothalamus, hippocampus, and amygdala) that play an important role in our survival, memory, and emotions.

Alcohol depresses the functioning of the cerebellum, which is why it leads to the uncoordinated movements typical of someone who is drunk. This is why some of the tests for being drunk involve coordinated movement. The cerebellum is also the location of motor learning, such as how to ride a bicycle or to type.

The **thalamus,** located at the top of the brain stem, serves as a relay station for incoming sensory information. As such, it sends each type of sensory information (visual, auditory, taste, or touch) to the appropriate location in the cerebral cortex. The only type of sensory information that does not pass through the thalamus is olfactory (smell) information. Smell information goes directly from the receptors in our nose to the cortex. The **basal ganglia** are on the outer sides of the thalamus and are concerned mainly with the initiation and execution of physical movements. Like the cerebellum, the basal ganglia are affected by alcohol, and so make the movements required by tests for drunken driving difficult to execute. The basal ganglia are actually a group of various interacting brain regions. As we discussed earlier in this chapter, abnormally low dopamine activity in one region of the basal ganglia results in Parkinson's disease. Another disease that involves difficulty in controlling movements is Huntington's chorea, which stems from problems in another region of the ganglia in which there are GABA and acetylcholine deficits.

All of the various central core structures are summarized in Table 2.3 along with some of their major functions.

The limbic system. Surrounding the top border (or "limbus" in Latin) of the brain stem is the **limbic system,** which is made up of the hypothalamus, the amygdala, and the hippocampus. These limbic structures play an important role in our survival, memory, and emotions. Figure 2.7 shows the three parts of the limbic

Table 2.3 Central Core Structures and Some of Their Functions	
Central Core Structure	**Functions**
Medulla	Involved in essential body functions, such as heartbeat, breathing, blood pressure, and swallowing
Pons	Serves as bridge between cerebellum and rest of brain and involved in sleep and dreaming
Reticular Formation	Responsible for our different levels of arousal and consciousness
Cerebellum	Involved in coordination of our movements, sense of balance, and motor learning
Thalamus	Serves as relay station for incoming sensory stimuli (except for olfactory sensory information)
Basal Ganglia	Involved in initiation and execution of movements

system. The **hypothalamus** is a very tiny structure, weighing about half an ounce, which is named after its location—below the thalamus ("hypo" means "below" in Greek). The hypothalamus controls the pituitary gland (and so directs activity in the endocrine glandular system) and the autonomic nervous system to maintain the body's internal environment, such as regulating body temperature. It also plays a major role in regulating basic drives such as eating, drinking, and sex. Thus, this tiny structure plays a huge role in both our behavior and our survival.

▲ **Figure 2.7** | **The Limbic System** | Positioned around the top of the brain stem is the limbic system—the hypothalamus, hippocampus, and amygdala.

The **hippocampus** is involved in the formation of memories. Hippocampus may seem like a rather strange name, but like many parts of the brain, it was given a name that matched its visual appearance. The hippocampus looks somewhat like a seahorse, and "hippocampus" means "seahorse" in Greek. Recall the case study of H. M. that we discussed in Chapter 1. H. M. had his left and right hippocampal structures removed for medical reasons and as a result suffered severe memory deficits (Corkin, 1984). Subsequent research on H. M. and other amnesics has shown the hippocampus to be critical for the formation of certain types of new memories (Cohen & Eichenbaum, 1993), which we will discuss in Chapter 5.

The hippocampus has also been found to have the capacity to generate new neurons, a process called neurogenesis (Gage, 2003; Kempermann & Gage, 1999). The research group most responsible for demonstrating neurogenesis in humans is led by Fred Gage. Given that brain imaging techniques cannot detect neuronal growth and that ethics prohibit neurosurgery to detect such growth in humans, Gage and his colleagues developed a very clever way to demonstrate that such growth exists. BrdU is a traceable substance that has been used in cancer treatment to track how rapidly the disease is spreading. BrdU is integrated into the DNA of cells preparing to divide. Hence it becomes part of the DNA of the new cells and all future descendents of the original dividing cells. Thus, BrdU functions as a marker for new cells. Because BrdU cannot be administered to healthy people, Gage and his colleagues examined postmortem hippocampal tissue of cancer patients who had been injected with BrdU before their deaths, and new noncancerous cells with BrdU were found (Eriksson et al., 1998; van Praag, Schinder, Christie, Toni, Palmer, & Gage, 2002). Although the purposes of neurogenesis in the hippocampus of humans are not yet clear, some research suggests that it may play a key role in depression (Jacobs, van Praag, & Gage, 2000a, 2000b). We will consider this hypothesis in Chapter 10 (Abnormal Psychology).

Located just in front of the hippocampal structures are the **amygdala** left and right structures. Amygdala means

▮ **hypothalamus** A part of the brain that is involved in regulating basic drives such as eating, drinking, and sex. It also directs the endocrine glandular system through its control of the pituitary gland and the autonomic nervous system to maintain the body's internal environment.

▮ **hippocampus** A part of the brain involved in the formation of memories.

▮ **amygdala** A part of the brain that is involved in emotions by influencing aggression, anger, and fear and by providing the emotional element of our memories and the interpretation of emotional expressions in others.

Table 2.4	Limbic System Structures and Some of Their Functions
Limbic System Structure	**Functions**
Hypothalamus	Involved in regulating basic drives such as eating, drinking, and sex, directing the endocrine glandular system, and maintaining the body's internal environment
Hippocampus	Involved in the formation of memories and via neurogenesis may play a role in depression
Amygdala	Involved in emotions by influencing aggression, anger, and fear and by providing emotional element of our memories and the interpretation of emotional expressions in others

"almond" in Greek, and these structures look like almonds. The amygdala plays a major role in regulating our emotional experiences, especially fear, anger, and aggression. It is also responsible for generating quick emotional responses directly, without cortical involvement (LeDoux, 2000). The first evidence for the amygdala's role in emotional behavior was done on wild, rather violent rhesus monkeys (Klüver & Bucy, 1939). The monkeys' amygdalas were surgically removed. The surgery transformed the monkeys into calm, tame animals, clearly changing their emotional behavior. Other research has indicated that the amygdala also provides the emotional element in our memories and guides our interpretation of the emotional expressions of others (LeDoux, 1996).

All three structures in the limbic system are summarized in Table 2.4 along with some of their major functions.

Processing in the Cerebral Cortex

All of the brain structures that we have discussed so far are important to our behavior and survival. The most important brain structure, however, is the **cerebral cortex,** the control and information-processing center for the nervous system. This is where perception, language, memory, decision making, and all other higher-level cognitive processing occur. The cerebral cortex physically envelops all of the other brain structures, except for the lowest parts of the brain stem and cerebellum. It is by far the largest part of the brain, accounting for about 80 percent of its total volume (Kolb & Whishaw, 2001). The cerebral cortex consists of layers of interconnected cells that make up the "bark" or covering of the brain's two hemispheres, which are called cerebral hemispheres. The two hemispheres are separated on top by a deep gap but joined together farther down in the middle by the **corpus callosum,** a bridge of neurons that allows the two hemispheres to communicate.

cerebral cortex The layers of interconnected cells covering the brain's two hemispheres. This is the control and information-processing center for the nervous system; it is where perception, memory, language, decision making, and all other higher-level cognitive processing occur.

corpus callosum The bridge of neurons that connects the two cerebral hemispheres.

The cerebral cortex is very crumpled in appearance with all sorts of bulges and gaps. This allows more cortical surface area to fit inside our rather small skull. If we were to unfold the cerebral cortex to check the amount of surface area, we would find the area to be about the size of four sheets of notebook paper or one newspaper page. Think about this. You couldn't fit four sheets of paper into your pants pocket unless you crumpled them up. This is the same principle that applies to fitting the large surface area of the cerebral cortex into the small space within the skull. It is this large amount of surface area in the cerebral cortex that not only allows our complex cognitive processing but also differentiates our brains from those of all other animals. To see where different types of processing occur in the cerebral cortex, we need to learn the geography of the two hemispheres. This geography is rather simple in that the outer surface of each hemisphere is divided into four defined parts, called lobes, which we will discuss first.

The four lobes. Figure 2.8 shows the four lobes in the left hemisphere. They are the same in the right hemisphere and are named after the specific bone area in the skull covering each of them. Two distinctive fissures (gaps) serve as boundary markers for three of the lobes. The central fissure (also called the fissure of Rolando) runs down the center of each hemisphere, and the lateral fissure (also called the Sylvian fissure) runs back along the side of each hemisphere. The **frontal lobe** is the area in front of the central fissure and above the lateral fissure, and the **parietal lobe** is the area located behind the central fissure and above the lateral fissure. The **temporal lobe** is located beneath the lateral fissure. The remaining lobe is the **occipital lobe,** which is located in the lower back of each hemisphere. Brynie (2009) explains how to find your occipital lobes. Run your hand up the back of your neck until you come to a bump and then place your palm on the bump. Your palm is squarely

Courtesy of R. A. Poldrack, Harvard Medical School.

The cerebral cortex of the human brain is very crumpled. This allows more cortical surface area to fit inside our rather small skull. The actual surface area, if unfolded, is about the size of four sheets of notebook paper.

▌ **frontal lobe** The area in each cerebral hemisphere in front of the central fissure and above the lateral fissure. The motor cortex is in this lobe.

▌ **parietal lobe** The area in each cerebral hemisphere in back of the central fissure and above the lateral fissure. The somatosensory cortex is in this lobe.

▌ **temporal lobe** The area in each cerebral hemisphere located beneath the lateral fissure. The primary auditory cortex is in this lobe.

▌ **occipital lobe** The area located in the lower back of each cerebral hemisphere. The primary visual cortex is in this lobe.

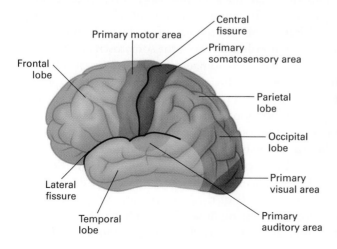

▲ **Figure 2.8 | The Four Lobes and the Sensory-Motor Processing Areas |** This figure shows the four lobes in the left hemisphere. They are exactly the same areas in the right hemisphere. The central fissure separates the frontal lobe from the parietal lobe, and the temporal lobe is located beneath the lateral fissure running along the side of the hemisphere. The occipital lobe is toward the lower back of the hemisphere. The motor cortex is the strip in the frontal lobe directly in front of the central fissure; the somatosensory cortex is the strip in the parietal lobe directly behind the central fissure. Primary auditory processing occurs in the temporal lobe, and primary visual processing in the occipital lobe.

over the occipital lobes. The frontal lobes are the largest of the lobes. Their location is easy to remember because they are in the front of the hemispheres and directly behind our forehead. Now that we know these four areas, we can see what we have learned about what type of processing occurs in each of them. We begin with the well-defined areas for producing voluntary movement of different parts of the body, such as raising a hand or making a fist, and for processing various types of sensory input, such as touch, visual, and auditory information.

The motor cortex. The **motor cortex,** the frontal lobe strip of cortex directly in front of the central fissure in each hemisphere, allows us to move different parts of our body. The two motor cortex strips are related to the body by contralateral control—each hemisphere controls the voluntary movement of the opposite side of the body. This means that the motor strip in the left hemisphere controls movement in the right side of the body, and the motor strip in the right hemisphere controls movement in the left side of the body. It is also interesting that the amount of space allocated to a specific body part in the motor cortex is not related to the actual size of the body part, but rather to the complexity and precision of movement of which that part is capable. Smaller parts that can make complex movements, such as our fingers, get a large amount of space, and larger parts, such as our torso, that cannot make complex movements do not get much space. Figure 2.9 illustrates this with what is called a homunculus ("little man" in Greek)—a body depiction with the size of each body part proportional to its amount of area in the motor cortex and not its actual size. Note that the body parts are arranged in a toe-to-head fashion spanning from the top of the motor strip to the bottom. It is as if the homunculus is hanging by its toes over the side of the hemisphere.

The somatosensory cortex. The **somatosensory cortex,** the parietal lobe strip of cortex directly behind the central fissure in each hemisphere, is where our body sensations of pressure, temperature, limb position, and pain are processed. "Somato" is Greek for body. Somatosensory, then, refers to the body senses. In addition to information about touch, the somatosensory cortex receives input about temperature and pain and information from the muscles and joints that allow us to monitor the positions of the various parts of the body. As in the motor cortex, there are contralateral relationships between the somatosensory strips and sides of the body. The somatosensory strip in the left hemisphere interprets the body sensory information for the right side of the body, and the strip in the right hemisphere interprets this information for the left side of the body. In addition, the amount of space within these strips is not allocated by the size of the body part. In the somatosensory cortex, it is allocated in accordance with the sensitivity of the body part—the more sensitive, the more space. For example, the lips and other parts of the face are more sensitive, so they have larger processing areas than body parts, such as our torso, that are not as sensitive. The homunculus for the

motor cortex The strip of cortex in each cerebral hemisphere in the frontal lobe directly in front of the central fissure, which allows us to move different parts of our body.

somatosensory cortex The strip of cortex in each cerebral hemisphere in the parietal lobe directly in back of the central fissure, which allows us to sense pressure, temperature, and pain in different parts of our body as well as the position of our body parts.

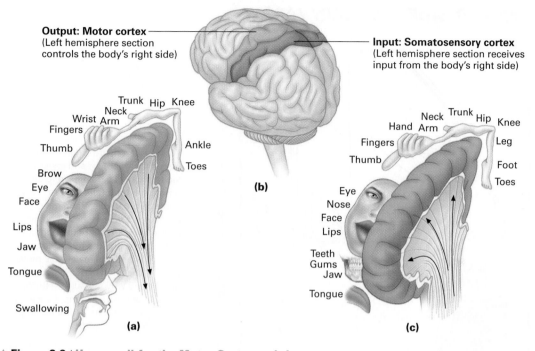

Output: Motor cortex
(Left hemisphere section
controls the body's right side)

Input: Somatosensory cortex
(Left hemisphere section receives
input from the body's right side)

(b)

(a)

(c)

▲ **Figure 2.9** I Homunculi for the Motor Cortex and the Somatosensory Cortex I These homunculi are for the left hemisphere. This means that the motor strip controls the right side of the body, and the somatosensory strip receives signals from the right side of the body. The amount of space for each body part in the motor strip is based on the complexity and precision of movement for that part, and the amount of space for each body part in the somatosensory strip is related to the part's sensitivity. For both strips, the body is arranged from foot to head starting from the top of the hemisphere. (Adapted from Penfield & Rasmussen, 1968.)

somatosensory strip is given in Figure 2.9. Like the motor strip, the body is arranged from toe to head, starting at the top of the strip.

The visual cortex and the auditory cortex. There are two other important areas for processing sensory information in Figure 2.8 (page 63) that we haven't discussed yet. These are the primary processing areas for our two major senses, seeing and hearing. The visual cortex is located in the occipital lobes at the back of the hemispheres, and the auditory cortex is in the temporal lobes. Figure 2.8 shows where they are located in the left hemisphere. They have the same locations in the right hemisphere. These processing areas for visual and auditory information are only the locations of the primary (initial) processing of visual and auditory information. These primary areas pass the results of their analyses on to areas in the other lobes to complete the brain's interpretation of the incoming visual or auditory information. These secondary cortical processing areas are part of what is termed the association cortex.

The four cerebral lobes and the type of sensory/motor processing that occurs in each lobe are summarized in Table 2.5 (page 66).

THE FAR SIDE® By GARY LARSON

"Whoa! *That* was a good one! Try it, Hobbs—just poke his brain right where my finger is."

Where is the neurosurgeon's finger? To get the right foot and lower right leg to move, it would have to be poking the top of the motor cortex in the left frontal lobe. Remember that the motor cortex in the left hemisphere controls movement of the right half of the body, and the motor cortex in the right hemisphere controls movement of the left half of the body. To understand why it would be the top of the motor cortical strip, look at the homunculus for the left motor strip in Figure 2.9 (page 65).

Table 2.5	The Four Cerebral Lobes and Type of Sensory/Motor Processing in Each Lobe
Cerebral Lobe	**Type of Sensory/Motor Processing**
Frontal	Includes motor cortex, which allows us to move the different parts of our body
Parietal	Includes somatosensory cortex where our body sensations of touch, temperature, limb position, and pain are processed
Temporal	Includes primary auditory cortex where auditory sensory information is initially processed
Occipital	Includes primary visual cortex where visual sensory information is initially processed

The association cortex. Most of the cortex (about 70 percent) is referred to as the **association cortex**—all the areas of the cerebral cortex, except those devoted to primary sensory or motor processing. This is where all the higher-level processing such as decision making, reasoning, perception, speech, and language occurs. These areas were named the association cortex because higher-level processing requires the association (integration) of various types of information. Scientists have studied the association cortex for over a century, but they are only beginning to understand the functions of some of the association areas (helped greatly by the recently developed scanning technologies, such as PET scans and fMRI).

During the nineteenth century and most of the twentieth century, scientists mainly learned about these association areas by studying the behavior of people who had suffered brain damage in accidents and strokes, or had brain surgery for medical reasons. Their behavioral and mental processing deficits were related to the particular cortical areas where damage or surgery had occurred. A railroad worker's tragic accident in 1848 gave us some hints as to what type of processing occurs in our frontal lobes (Macmillan, 2000). Phineas Gage was taking a break from tamping some blasting powder into a rock with a metal tamping iron. He was distracted and the tamping iron slipped, generating some sparks that caused the powder to explode. The explosion caused the metal tamping iron, which was 3 feet 7 inches long, 1¼ inches in diameter, and 13½ pounds in weight, to fly through his left cheek and head, exiting through his frontal lobes.

Gage survived, but his personality was greatly changed. As his doctor and friends pointed out, "Gage was no longer Gage" (Fleischman, 2002). He became very irresponsible, impulsive, and disorderly; had great difficulty making decisions and reasoning; and cursed regularly. This led neuroscientists to hypothesize that the frontal lobes played a major role in such behaviors. Subsequent collaborative evidence from similar cases and from studies using other techniques such as brain scans confirmed that this is the case (Klein & Kihlstrom, 1998). The frontal lobes play a major role in our planning, decision making, judgment, impulse control, and personality, especially its emotional aspects. Actually, the areas destroyed in Gage's frontal lobes were essentially those that were disconnected from the rest of the brain in the infamous lobotomies performed on hundreds of patients in mental hospitals in the middle part of the twentieth century. The frontal lobes may also be partially responsible for the bad

> **association cortex** All of the cerebral cortex except those areas devoted to primary sensory processing or motor processing. This is where all the higher-level cognitive processing that requires the association (integration) of information, such as perception and language, occurs.

Phineas Gage's doctor had this picture of the tamping iron and Phineas's skull taken in 1868 to document the case. Seeing the iron and the skull side by side makes it difficult to believe that Gage survived, but he did. He died 12 years later in 1860 at age 36, probably from hypothermia stemming from an epileptic seizure (Fleischman, 2002).

Courtesy, Woburn Public Library, Woburn MA/Glennon Archives

Hanna Damasio, M.D., University of Iowa and *Science*.

Using neuroimaging and the measurements of Phineas Gage's skull taken from his medical records, Damasio, Grabowski, Frank, Galaburda, and Damasio (1994) reconstructed the probable path of the tamping rod through Gage's brain.

decisions and risky behavior of teenagers because frontal lobe development is not complete until the late teens and possibly even the early 20s (Sabbagh, 2006).

What happened to Phineas Gage? While it has proved very difficult to fill in all of the details of Gage's subsequent life, Fleischman (2002) provides a general account. Following his recovery, Phineas tried to return to his job as railroad foreman, but because of the "new" Gage's vulgar, unreliable behavior, the railroad let him go. It appears that for a brief period of time he traveled around New England exhibiting himself along with the tamping iron, possibly ending up in P. T. Barnum's American Museum sideshow in New York City. After this, because he got along very well with horses, he worked for awhile in a livery stable in New Hampshire near his hometown. In 1852 he traveled, taking the tamping iron with him, to South America to care for horses and be a stagecoach driver in Chile. Because of health issues he returned in 1859 to California where his family had moved, and after recovering, he found work as a farmhand. In 1860 he began suffering epileptic seizures (likely due to slow changes in his brain tissue damaged in the railroad accident), and at that time, physicians could not control such seizures. These seizures killed him, 11½ years after the accident. The immediate cause of death was probably hypothermia (the body cannot control its internal temperature) created by the seizures. If you want to find out more about Phineas Gage, go to www.deakin.edu.au/hmnbs/psychology/gagepage, a Web site maintained by Malcolm Macmillan, the world's leading authority on Gage, or read Macmillan's book, *An odd kind of fame: Stories of Phineas Gage.*

Broca's area An area in the cerebral cortex responsible for fluent speech production. It is in the left frontal lobe of the majority of people, regardless of handedness.

Early brain researchers also analyzed the brains of deceased people, relating a person's brain analysis to their behavior while living. Using this technique, two nineteenth-century researchers, Paul Broca and Karl Wernicke, studied people with aphasias—speech and language dysfunctions—and made some major discoveries about where speech and language abilities occur in the brain. By examining the brains of deceased persons who had lost their ability to speak fluently while alive, Paul Broca, a French brain researcher, identified an area in the left frontal lobe that is named after him, **Broca's area,** which is responsible for fluent speech production (see Figure 2.10). Damage to Broca's area leads to Broca's aphasia—the inability to generate fluent speech while maintaining the ability to understand speech and read silently.

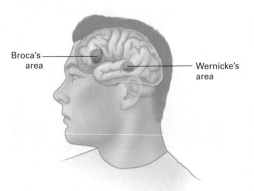

Broca's area

Wernicke's area

▲ **Figure 2.10 | Broca's Area and Wernicke's Area |** Broca's area and Wernicke's area are responsible for speech production and the comprehension of speech and text, respectively. They are located only in the left hemisphere for the majority of both left- and right-handed people.

Broca's area is only in the left hemisphere in the majority of people, both right-handed and left-handed (unlike the sensory and motor processing areas that are in each hemisphere). This means that speech production seems to be a specialization of the left hemisphere (the comparable area in the right hemisphere is usually not used for speech production). So, what is this area in the right hemisphere used for? One possible answer that has been offered is singing and music. People with Broca's area damage often retain these abilities (Besson et al., 1998). This means that singing and speaking seem to originate from different areas of the brain. What about Broca's area in deaf people who use sign language? Will damage to Broca's area impact their ability to use sign language? The answer is yes. Broca's area seems important for both the production of speech and its complement in the deaf, sign language (Corina, 1998).

> ▌ **Wernicke's area** An area in the cerebral cortex responsible for comprehension of speech and text. It is in the left temporal lobe of the majority of people, regardless of handedness.

People with damage to Broca's area do not have a problem understanding the speech of other people or reading silently, which means these skills must involve other areas. One of these areas is in the left temporal lobe and is named after its discoverer, Karl Wernicke, a German researcher. **Wernicke's area** is responsible for the comprehension of speech and reading. Figure 2.10 shows exactly where this area is located. Damage to this area leads to Wernicke's aphasia—incoherent speech and the inability to understand the speech of others and to read. Wernicke's area functions as the understanding center for incoming speech and text.

Like Broca's area, Wernicke's area is only in the left temporal lobe of the majority of people (regardless of handedness). Many people have the misconception that these speech and language centers normally reside in the hemisphere opposite to a person's handedness. This is only the case for a very small number of right-handers and some left-handers, however. Speech and language centers are located in the left hemisphere for about 95 percent of right-handers and 70 percent of left-handers (Springer & Deutsch, 1998).

Next, we will consider the question of whether there are any hemispheric specializations other than speech and language.

Specializations of the Left and Right Hemispheres

Are there any other abilities specific to only one of the two hemispheres of the brain? To try to answer this question, researchers have examined patients who have had their corpus callosum, the cortical bridge between the two hemispheres, severed as a medical treatment for severe cases of epilepsy. William Van Wagenen performed the first split-brain surgery in 1940 (Gazzaniga, 2008). Not many people have had this surgery, and because of improved medications and other modes of treatment for epilepsy, it is done even more rarely now. The rationale behind this surgery was that the epileptic seizures would be lessened in severity if they were confined to only one hemisphere. Indeed, the surgery did provide this benefit. However, it also created a group of people in which the two hemispheres of the brain could not communicate. They are usually referred to as "split-brain" people, and they make up an ideal group for studying the question of hemispheric specialization. First, we will discuss the general experimental procedure that has been used to study this question.

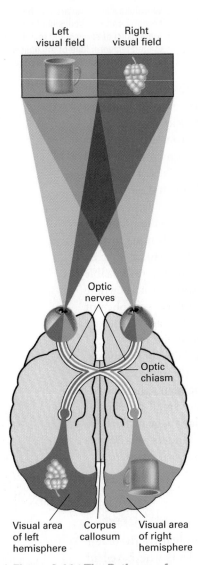

Left visual field   Right visual field

Optic nerves

Optic chiasm

Visual area of left hemisphere   Corpus callosum   Visual area of right hemisphere

▲ **Figure 2.11** I **The Pathways for Processing Information in the Left and Right Visual Fields** I The information from the left visual field goes to the right half of each eye and then to the right hemisphere. The information in the right visual field goes to the left half of each eye and then to the left hemisphere. Half of the fibers from each eye cross over at the optic chiasm to go to the opposite hemisphere—the right half in the left eye go to the right hemisphere and the left half in the right eye go to the left hemisphere.

Studying the two hemispheres. To understand the experimental procedure for studying the two hemispheres, we first need to understand how the visual fields, the eyes, and the cerebral hemispheres are related. These relationships are shown in Figure 2.11. Our field of vision has two halves—the left visual field (what is to the left of center in our field of vision) and the right visual field (what is to the right of center in our field of vision). Light waves from the left visual field go to the right half of each eye, and those from the right visual field go the left half of each eye. Each visual field is processed by half of each eye. The right half of each eye connects with the right hemisphere, and the left half of each eye with the left hemisphere. This means that the eyes and the hemispheres, with respect to processing incoming visual information, are not contralaterally related. Rather, the visual information in half of each eye goes to each hemisphere. The visual information in the right halves goes to the right hemisphere, and the visual information in the left halves goes to the left hemisphere. Thus, information in the left visual field goes only to the right hemisphere, and information in the right visual field goes only to the left hemisphere. The following diagram should help you remember this processing sequence:

| Left visual field | Right half of each eye | Right hemisphere |
| Right visual field | Left half of each eye | Left hemisphere |

This relationship between the visual fields and the hemispheres is important because it allows information that is presented briefly in one visual field to go to only one hemisphere. With split-brain people, the information cannot be transferred to the other hemisphere because the corpus callosum connecting their two hemispheres has been severed. By examining how split-brain people can identify the presented information (orally, visually, or by touch), researchers can study the hemispheric specialization question.

Recall that the speech and language centers (Broca's and Wernicke's areas) are only in the left hemisphere of the vast majority of people. This would mean that a split-brain person should only be able to identify information orally when it is presented briefly in the right visual field (it is this field that feeds information to the left hemisphere). In fact, this is what has been found with split-brain people. For example, if a picture of a spoon were flashed briefly in the left visual field, a split-brain person would not be able to say that it was a spoon. But if we blindfolded the split-brain person and asked her to identify the flashed object from a group of objects by touch with the left hand, the split-brain person can do this (Gazzaniga, 1992). Remember that the somatosensory strip in the right hemisphere is connected to the left hand. However, even after identifying the spoon as the object presented, a split-brain person would not be able to identify it orally if asked what was in her left hand. What would happen if the blindfolded split-brain person were asked to move the object from her left hand to her right hand? She would now say that she was holding a spoon. The information that it was a spoon would be gathered through touch by her right hand and sent to the somatosensory strip in her left hemisphere, allowing her to transfer this information to the speech centers in the left hemisphere.

Split-brain people are also sometimes asked to identify the presented information by pointing with the appropriate hand (left hand for right hemisphere, right hand for left hemisphere). A clever use of this methodology involves simultaneously presenting different objects to each hemisphere. For example, an orange might be shown in the right visual field so it goes to the left hemisphere, and an apple in the left visual field so it goes to the right hemisphere. If then asked to use the left hand to identify what was presented, the split-brain person would point to the apple; but if she had been asked to use the right hand, she would have pointed to the orange. In each case, the nonresponding hemisphere would be baffled by the other hemisphere's response.

What we know about the left and right hemispheres. The two most prominent researchers on split-brain questions have been Roger Sperry and Michael Gazzaniga. Sperry led most of the early split-brain research and in 1981 won the Nobel Prize in Physiology or Medicine for his discoveries concerning the functional specializations of the cerebral hemispheres. Sperry's student, Michael Gazzaniga, who conducted the first studies with human split-brain participants in the early 1960s at the California Institute of Technology under the guidance of Sperry and neurosurgeon Joseph Bogen, has continued this line of inquiry for the past five decades (Gazzaniga, 2005, 2008). Now let's see what these studies with split-brain participants have told us about hemispheric specialization.

Roger Sperry

Ron Meyer/Caltech Archives

We know that the speech and language centers are specialties of the left hemisphere. This is why the left hemisphere is sometimes referred to as the verbal hemisphere. This does not mean, however, that the right hemisphere has no verbal ability. It can't produce speech, but it can understand simple verbal material. In addition, the left hemisphere is better at mathematical skills and logic, while the right is better at spatial perception, solving spatial problems (block design), and drawing. Face recognition is also a right-hemisphere specialization.

Michael Gazzaniga

Courtesy Michael Gazzaniga

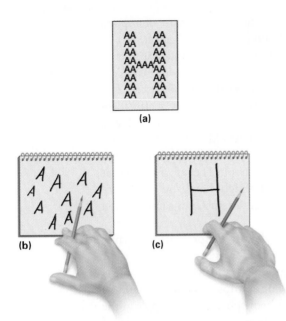

▲ Figure 2.12 | Sample hierarchical stimulus and recall results for such stimuli by brain-damaged patients | (a) The sample hierarchical stimulus is a capital **H** made up of little **A**s. (b) Patients with right hemisphere damage (dependent on the left hemisphere) could remember the details of the hierarchical stimulus (the **A**s) but not the overall pattern **(H)**. (c) Patients with left hemisphere damage (dependent upon the right hemisphere) could remember the overall pattern **(H)** but not its details (the **A**s). (Adapted from MacNeilage, Rogers, and Vallortigara, 2009.)

In general, the left hemisphere is more analytic, analyzing wholes into their elements or pieces; the right hemisphere processes information in a more holistic fashion, combining pieces into wholes. The right gets the big picture (the "forest"); the left focuses on the smaller details (the "trees"). This information-processing style difference between the two hemispheres is sometimes referred to as global versus local processing.

Support for this general processing style difference between the hemispheres has been corroborated by research with brain-damaged patients using hierarchical stimuli developed by David Navon (1977). These hierarchical stimuli consist of a large letter (the global, holistic level) that is composed of smaller versions of another letter (the local or analytic level). See the example in Figure 2.12a in which the large letter **H** is composed of smaller **A**s. Delis, Robertson, and Efron (1986) used such stimuli to study perceptual encoding in brain-damaged patients. The patients were asked to study the hierarchical stimulus and then redraw it from memory after a brief period of distraction. The patients with right hemisphere damage who were dependent on their left hemisphere often drew **A**s unsystematically scattered about the page (see Figure 2.12b). They remembered the constituent elements of the original stimulus but not the overall pattern. In contrast, the patients with left hemisphere damage who were dependent on their right hemisphere often drew a large capital **H** but with no **A**s (see Figure 2.12c). They remembered the global pattern but not the constituent elements. Thus, the right hemisphere specializes in synthesizing global, holistic patterns whereas the left hemisphere specializes in analyzing the details of a stimulus. Fink et al. (1996) have also observed this hemispheric processing style difference in PET scan data when normal participants were attending to either the global or local level of Navon hierarchical figures.

This processing difference along with all of the other specialization differences that have been observed in split-brain people have led to the expressions "left-brained" and "right-brained" to refer to people who seem to excel at the skills normally attributed to left and right hemispheres, respectively. We must remember, however, that these differences in hemispheric performance are for people whose two hemispheres can no longer communicate. When normal people are performing a task, the two hemispheres are constantly interacting and sharing information. There is no forced separation of labor as in the split-brain person. It may be the case that one hemisphere tends to play a larger role in some tasks, but both hemispheres are involved (Corballis, 2007; Hellige, 1993). This is why it is not very accurate to say someone is "left-brained" or "right-brained." It is best not to make the distinction. Nearly all of us are "whole-brained."

> **consciousness** An individual's subjective awareness of their inner thinking and feeling and their external environment.

Consciousness and the Sleeping Brain

There are many questions left for neuroscientists to answer about the brain and its many functions, but the most intriguing questions concern human consciousness— What is consciousness and what underlies it? Probably the best way to think about **consciousness** is as a person's subjective awareness of his inner thinking and feeling as well as his immediate surroundings. Thus, consciousness is both internal (one's thoughts and feelings) and external (what's going on in one's environment).

Most brain (and bodily) functioning goes on without our conscious awareness. For example, you are presently recognizing the letters and words in this paragraph, but you are not consciously aware of the actual processing required to accomplish this recognition. You are only consciously aware of the results of the recognition process (the meaningful collection of words). Even if you wanted to, you couldn't become consciously aware of this processing by the brain. Think about the billions of neurons communicating with each other within your brain and nervous system at this very moment. You cannot become aware of activity at this neuronal level of processing. Our consciousness is privy to only some of the results of this processing.

We can describe waking consciousness as our tuning in to both our internal and external worlds, but questions about exactly what underlies it (how it is generated) or why it evolved remain open for debate. Similarly, we are still pondering the question of why we experience sleep—a natural, altered state of consciousness. We do, however, have some better answers to questions about what the brain is doing during sleep. Electrical recordings of brain activity during sleep allow us to measure different stages of sleep and to tell us when we are dreaming. So first we'll examine the stages of sleep and how they are related to dreaming. Then, we will briefly discuss theories that have been proposed to explain why we sleep and why we dream.

The five stages of sleep. The various stages of sleep have been determined by monitoring the electrical activity in the brain using an electroencephalograph (EEG). Small electrodes are attached to the scalp and connected to recording equipment that produces a real-time graph of electrical activity in the cortex of the brain. In Figure 2.13 on the following page, a sample EEG for the awake, relaxed state is shown along with sample EEGs for the five stages of sleep. As we slip into sleep and pass through the first four stages, our brain waves change, in general becoming progressively slower, larger, and more irregular, especially in Stages 3 and 4. Stage 1 sleep, which lasts about 5 minutes, is followed by about 20 minutes of Stage 2 sleep, which is characterized by periodic bursts of rapid activity called sleep spindles. Some researchers believe these spindles represent the activity of a mechanism that lessens the brain's sensitivity to sensory input and thus keeps the person asleep. The fact that older people's sleep contains fewer spindles and is interrupted

▲ Figure 2.13 | Sleep Stages and the Brain Waves Associated with Each Stage | The various stages of sleep are indicated by changes in the brain waves in the EEG recordings. As you pass from awake to deep sleep (Stages 3 and 4), the brain waves get larger and slow down. After deep sleep, you ascend back through Stages 3 and 2 into REM sleep, for which the waves are more rapid and resemble those of Stage 1.

▍ REM (rapid eye movement) sleep
The stage of sleep that is characterized by rapid eye movements and brain wave patterns that resemble those for an awake state and in which most dreaming occurs. REM sleep is sometimes referred to as paradoxical sleep because the bodily muscles are immobilized but much of the brain is highly active.

by more awakenings during the night is consistent with this explanation.

Next are the two stages comprising slow-wave sleep—the brief, transitional sleep of Stage 3 and then the deep sleep of Stage 4. These two stages, especially Stage 4, are characterized by delta waves—large, slow brain waves. You are now completely asleep and this initial period of slow-wave sleep lasts for about 30 minutes. In deep sleep, the parasympathetic nervous system dominates. So, muscles relax, heart rate slows, blood pressure declines, and digestion is stimulated. Mysteriously, the brain is still monitoring environmental information, though it is outside our conscious awareness. If a sensory stimulus is important, such as a baby's cry, or very strong, such as a slamming door or a breaking glass, it will break through the perceptual barrier created by sleep and awaken us.

Near the end of your first period of deep sleep (about an hour after falling asleep), you return through Stages 3 and 2 and enter **REM (rapid eye movement) sleep,** the most fascinating stage of sleep. REM sleep is characterized by very rapid waves somewhat like those of Stage 1 sleep. However, you are still sound asleep. REM sleep is sometimes referred to as paradoxical sleep because the muscles are relaxed, but other body systems and the brain are active, following a waking pattern. Heart rate rises, breathing is more rapid, eyes move back and forth rapidly under closed eyelids, and one's genitals become aroused. The brain is also highly active; both oxygen consumption and cerebral blood flow increase. Strangely, given all of this internal activity, the muscles are relaxed, leaving the body essentially paralyzed except for occasional muscle twitching.

REM sleep indicates the beginning of dreaming; it is the stage during which most dreaming occurs. How do we know this? If people are awakened during Stages 1 through 4, they only occasionally report dreaming; but if awakened during REM sleep, people usually recall dreams that they were having. This is as true for people who say they dream as for those who say they rarely do so, which means that we all dream whether we realize it or not. This first bout of REM sleep typically lasts about 10 minutes and completes the first sleep cycle of the night. The cycle of stages, in which we move out of and back into REM sleep, repeats itself about every 90 minutes throughout the night. Deep sleep (Stages 3 and 4) gets briefer and eventually disappears, as Stage 2 and REM sleep periods get longer with each sleep cycle. Over the course of the night, you have four or five REM sleep periods, amounting to about 20 to 25 percent of your sleep time (Figure 2.14).

We spend about 2 hours a night dreaming, which works out to about 6 years of dreaming across our lifetime, given current life expectancies. We don't remember many of our dreams, though. The dreams we do remember are usually from our last phase of REM sleep, right before we wake up. Many dreams are highly emotional and unpleasant. For example, people often dream of being attacked or pursued. This may be due to the fact that the frontal lobes (responsible for rational thought) are shut down during REM

▲ **Figure 2.14 | The Pattern of Sleep-Stage Cycles During a Night's Sleep** | After passing through the first four stages of sleep, we return through Stages 3 and 2 to enter REM sleep. This completes the first sleep-stage cycle. As this cycle is repeated throughout a typical night's sleep, the deep sleep stages (3 and 4) get briefer and disappear, and the Stage 2 and REM sleep periods get longer.

sleep, but the amygdala and the hippocampus, the limbic system structures responsible for emotion and memory, are active, creating the irrational imagery and emotional experiences of our dream world. Given the strong visual nature of dreams, what are the dreams of blind people like? Research indicates that people born blind or who go blind very early in life do not have visual dreams. Their dreams are just as emotional, but involve other sensations, especially sounds.

Why do we sleep and dream? We do not know why we sleep, but we know that we need sleep. You cannot cheat sleep; it will always overcome you. Inadequate sleep has a high cost. Sleep-deprived people have impaired concentration and a general bodily feeling of weakness and discomfort, and they may even hallucinate. Sleep deprivation also suppresses your immune system, lessening your ability to fight off infection and disease. Sleep-deprived people are also more vulnerable to accidents. For example, traffic accidents increase following the shortened sleep accompanying the 1-hour time change in the spring (Coren, 1993). All of this may help explain why people who typically sleep 7 or 8 hours outlive those who are chronically sleep deprived (Dement, 1999). College students are notorious for being sleep deprived, with as many as four out of five not getting adequate sleep. Beware of sleep deprivation and its negative effects. Sleep deprivation makes it more difficult to concentrate, study, and take exams. So, creating a large sleep debt will, in simple terms, "make you stupid" (Dement, 1999, p. 231).

We clearly need sleep. How much, however, varies greatly with individuals. On the average, though, we spend about a third of our lives sleeping. Why? Three possible answers have been proposed, and the actual answer probably involves all three. First, sleep seems to serve a restorative function by allowing the brain and body time to rest and recuperate from the daily wear and tear of our existence. Sleep is necessary for optimal functioning. Second, sleep helps us process what we learn. It allows the brain the opportunity to consolidate our day's experiences into our memory banks for later retrieval and use. Indeed, there is research evidence that memory is often strengthened and enhanced following a period of sleep (Stickgold & Ellenbogen, 2009). REM sleep is especially important in relation to memory. Disruption of REM sleep (by being constantly awakened during this stage) following learning impairs our memory for this learning (DuJardin, Guerrien, & LeConte, 1990). Disruption of other sleep stages does not impair memory similarly. Third, sleep may have evolved as an adaptive process. It served a protective function for our ancestors, increasing their survival by keeping them safe from predators during the night and from the dangers of wandering around cliffs in the dark. Those who stayed in their caves and slept had a better chance of surviving and passing on their genes.

So, sleep has clear advantages. But why do we dream? One answer is the critical role of REM sleep in learning—providing the opportunity for memory consolidation of new information (Stickgold, Hobson, Fosse, & Fosse, 2001). Other answers to the question of why we dream have also been proposed. About a hundred years ago, Sigmund Freud proposed that dreams were disguised outlets for the inner conflicts of our unconscious (Freud 1900/1953a). But given its lack of scientific support, the Freudian view has been rejected by most contemporary sleep researchers. There are many contemporary theories of why we dream, but all have their critics. One explanation, however, that has received much attention is the activation-synthesis theory (Hobson, 2003; Hobson & McCarley, 1977; Hobson, Pace-Scott, & Stickgold, 2000). This physiological theory proposes that neurons in the pons fire spontaneously during REM sleep, sending random signals to various areas in the cortex and the emotional areas in the limbic system. The signals are random, but the brain tries to make sense of them and produce a meaningful interpretation. Thus, a dream is the brain's synthesis of these signals. However, because the signals evoke random memories and visual images, the brain has a difficult time weaving a coherent story, often resulting in the bizarre and confusing nature of our dreams. This relates to a major criticism of the theory: dream content is more coherent, consistent over time, and concerned with waking problems and anxieties than the activation-synthesis theory would predict (Domhoff, 2003). Criticisms aside, this theory has led to a wide body of research on the neurological stuff that dreams are made of and thus greatly increased our knowledge of the physiological basis of dreaming.

Although sleep researchers do not agree about why we dream, they do agree that REM sleep is essential. This is clearly demonstrated by the REM sleep rebound effect—a significant increase in the amount of REM sleep following deprivation of REM sleep. The fact that REM sleep and the rebound effect are observed in other mammals implies a definite biological need for this type of sleep. Exactly what that need is, however, remains an open question.

Section Summary

In this section, we discussed many of the major structures in the brain. Between the spinal cord and the cerebral hemispheres, there are two sets of brain structures—the central core and limbic system. The central core is made up of the medulla, pons, and reticular formation (parts of the brain stem) and the cerebellum, thalamus, and basal ganglia (structures near the brain stem). The medulla regulates essential body functions, such as breathing and blood pressure, and the pons serves as a bridge between the cerebellum and the rest of the brain. The reticular formation is involved in controlling different levels of arousal and awareness. The cerebellum is involved in the coordination of movement and motor learning, the thalamus serves as a relay station for incoming sensory information, and the basal ganglia are involved in the initiation and execution of physical movements. Surrounding the top of the brain, the limbic system structures (hypothalamus, hippocampus, and amygdala) play important roles in our survival, memory, and emotions.

As we move up the brain stem to the cerebral hemispheres, the functioning gets more complex. It is the top cortical layer that gives us all of our complex abilities (such as language, perception, and decision making) and makes us "human." Each cerebral hemisphere is divided into four lobes—frontal, parietal, temporal, and occipital. The motor cortex in the frontal lobes allows us to move different parts of our body. The somatosensory cortex in the parietal lobes is where our body sensations of touch, temperature, limb position, and pain are processed. Both the motor cortex and the somatosensory cortex are related to the two sides of our body in a contralateral fashion—the left hemisphere controls the movement of, and processes body sensations from, the right side of the body, and the right hemisphere does so for the left side of the body. The primary visual cortex is in the occipital lobes, and the primary auditory cortex is in the temporal lobes. The remaining area in the two hemispheres, about 70 percent of the cortex, is called the association cortex. All of the higher-level cognitive processing, including perception and decision making, occurs in the association cortex. Such processing requires the association of various types of information.

Research has shown that the frontal lobes play a major role in our planning, reasoning, impulse control, and personality—especially its emotional aspects. We have also learned that the speech and language areas are only in the left hemisphere in the majority of people, regardless of handedness. Broca's area in the left frontal lobe is responsible for speech production, and Wernicke's area in the left temporal lobe is responsible for the comprehension of speech and text. In addition, research on split-brain people (whose hemispheres cannot communicate because they have had their corpus callosum surgically severed) has shown that there are processing differences between the two hemispheres. For example, the left specializes in speech, language, mathematical skills, and logic; the right specializes in spatial perception, face recognition, and drawing. In addition, the right hemisphere specializes in processing stimuli at the holistic, global level whereas the left hemisphere analyzes stimuli into their elements or pieces. We must remember, however, that in normal people, the two hemispheres are constantly interacting. One hemisphere may play a more major role in some tasks, but both hemispheres are involved.

Neuroscientists have much more to learn not only about the brain but also about consciousness, a person's awareness of his inner thinking and feeling and his external environment. We have learned much about sleep, a natural altered state of consciousness, through the use of EEG recordings of the brain's electrical activity while sleeping. Such recordings indicate the occurrence of five different stages of sleep, with the REM (rapid eye movement) sleep stage as the one during which most dreaming occurs. We can't yet explain definitively why we sleep or why we dream, but both are clearly essential. Sleep-deprived people suffer many consequences ranging from impaired concentration to weakened immune systems. A rebound effect for REM sleep (a significant increase in REM sleep) follows REM sleep deprivation.

ConceptCheck | 3

➤ Explain where in the cerebral cortex (which hemisphere, lobe, area in the lobe, and part of that area) is active when you feel a slap on the left cheek of your face.

➤ Explain which areas in the cerebral cortex are involved and how they are involved when you shadow (repeat aloud) someone's speech.

➤ Explain what types of behavioral deficits would be observed in a person who suffered damage to her cerebellum.

➤ Explain how you could demonstrate that a split-brain person knows what was briefly flashed in his left visual field, even though he cannot say what was flashed.

➤ This 400-year-old painting, *Vertumnus*, was done by Giuseppe Arcimboldo, a sixteenth-century Italian painter who is best known for creating imaginative portraits from such objects as fruits, vegetables, flowers, books, and other objects. *Vertumnus* is a portrait of Rudolf II of Prague made from fruits, flowers, and vegetables. Let's use this portrait to test your understanding of both the processing differences between the two hemispheres and the relationship between the visual fields and the hemispheres. Suppose *Vertumnus* is flashed briefly in the left visual field of a split-brain person and he is instructed to point with the appropriate hand to what he saw given the choice of the two words "face" and "fruits." Which hand would he use and which word would he point to? Why? Now suppose the painting had been flashed briefly in his right visual field. Which hand would he use and which word would he point to? Why?

Giuseppe Arcimboldo/Wikipedia

➤ Explain why REM sleep is sometimes referred to as paradoxical sleep.

Study Guide

Chapter Key Terms

You should know the definitions of the following key terms from the chapter. They are listed in the order in which they appear in the chapter. For those you do not know, return to the relevant section of the chapter to learn them. When you think that you know all of the terms, complete the matching exercise based on these key terms.

neurons
glial cells (glia)
dendrites
cell body
axon
myelin sheath
neurotransmitter
synaptic gap (synapse)
positron emission tomography (PET) scan
functional magnetic resonance imaging (fMRI)
agonist
antagonist
acetylcholine (ACh)
dopamine
Parkinson's disease
blood–brain barrier
L-dopa
serotonin
norepinephrine
selective serotonin reuptake inhibitors (SSRIs)
selective serotonin and norepinephrine reuptake inhibitors (SSNRIs)

GABA (gamma-aminobutyric acid)
glutamate
endorphins
central nervous system (CNS)
peripheral nervous system (PNS)
interneurons
sensory neurons
motor neurons
spinal cord
spinal reflex
somatic (skeletal) nervous system
autonomic nervous system
sympathetic nervous system
parasympathetic nervous system
endocrine glandular system
hormone
pituitary gland
emotion
James-Lange theory
Cannon-Bard theory
Schachter-Singer two-factor theory

medulla
pons
reticular formation
cerebellum
thalamus
basal ganglia
limbic system
hypothalamus
hippocampus
amygdala
cerebral cortex
corpus callosum
frontal lobe
parietal lobe
temporal lobe
occipital lobe
motor cortex
somatosensory cortex
association cortex
Broca's area
Wernicke's area
consciousness
REM (rapid eye movement) sleep

Key Terms Exercise

Identify the correct key term for each of the following definitions. The answers to this exercise follow the answers to the Concept Checks at the end of the chapter.

1. A chemical messenger that is produced by an endocrine gland and carried by the bloodstream to target sites throughout the body.

   _____

2. The part of the brain involved in the coordination of our movements, sense of balance, and motor learning.

   _____

3. An insulating layer of a white fatty substance on an axon that allows for faster neural impulses.

_____

4. A visual display that shows the activity of various areas in the brain by detecting the level of positron emission arising from radioactive glucose being metabolized in each area.

_____

5. A naturally occurring chemical within the nervous system that specializes in transmitting information between neurons.

_____

6. The areas in the cerebral cortex not devoted to primary sensory processing or motor processing.

_____

7. A drug or poison that decreases the activity of one or more neurotransmitters.

_____

8. The part of the peripheral nervous system that carries sensory input from receptors to the CNS and relays commands from the CNS to skeletal muscles to control their movement.

_____

9. The bridge of neurons that connects the two cerebral hemispheres.

_____

10. The major inhibitory neurotransmitter in the nervous system.

_____

11. Cells in the nervous system that comprise the support system for the neurons.

_____

12. Drugs that achieve their agonistic effect on serotonin by selectively blocking its reuptake.

_____

13. A group of neurotransmitters that are involved in pain relief and feelings of pleasure.

_____

14. A brain stem structure involved in many essential body functions, such as heartbeat, breathing, blood pressure, digestion, and swallowing.

_____

15. The area in each cerebral hemisphere in back of the central fissure and above the lateral fissure. The somatosensory cortex is in this lobe.

_____

Practice Test Questions

The following are practice multiple-choice test questions on some of the chapter content. The answers are given after the Key Terms Exercise answers at the end of the chapter. If you guessed or incorrectly answered a question, restudy the relevant section of the chapter.

1. The main function of the _____ is to receive information from other neurons.
   a. dendrites
   b. cell body
   c. axon
   d. axon terminals

2. Which of the following is an agonist?
   a. curare
   b. GABA
   c. botulinum poison
   d. amphetamine

3. An SSRI works by blocking the reuptake of _____.
   a. dopamine
   b. serotonin
   c. norepinephrine
   d. GABA

4. Which type of neuron carries information from the CNS to the PNS?
   a. sensory neuron
   b. motor neuron

c. interneuron

d. glial

5. Which of the following is an action of the parasympathetic nervous system?

a. pupil dilation

b. stimulation of digestion

c. accelerated heartbeat

d. raised blood sugar levels

6. The actions of the pituitary gland are controlled by the _____.

a. hippocampus

b. amygdala

c. hypothalamus

d. medulla

7. The limbic system consists of the _____.

a. thalamus, hypothalamus, and amygdala

b. hypothalamus, medulla, and reticular formation

c. amygdala, hypothalamus, and hippocampus

d. basal ganglia, amygdala, and cerebellum

8. In the majority of people, Broca's area is located in the _____ hemisphere, and Wernicke's area is located in the _____ hemisphere.

a. right; right

b. right; left

c. left; right

d. left; left

9. Information in a person's left visual field goes to the _____ half of each eye and then to the _____ hemisphere.

a. left; left

b. left; right

c. right; right

d. right; left

10. Which of the following stages of sleep is referred to as paradoxical sleep?

a. Stage 2

b. Stage 3

c. Stage 4

d. REM sleep

11. The _____ theory of emotion proposes that the physiological arousal and behavioral responses and the emotional feeling all occur simultaneously but independently.

a. Schachter-Singer two-factor

b. Cannon-Bard

c. James-Lange

d. "commonsense"

12. At dinner, when John picks up his fork, his _____ nervous system controls the movement of his fingers. His _____ nervous system regulates his stomach and controls the digestion of food.

a. autonomic; autonomic

b. autonomic; somatic

c. somatic; autonomic

d. somatic; somatic

13. Damage to the right hemisphere will most likely disrupt a person's ability to _____.

a. balance a checkbook

b. recognize faces

c. do logic problems

d. give speeches

14. Botulinum poisoning (food poisoning) causes paralysis by blocking the release of ____, and curare paralyzes by occupying the receptor sites for _____.

a. acetylcholine; acetylcholine

b. acetylcholine; GABA

c. GABA; acetylcholine

d. GABA; GABA

15. The amount of space devoted to each part of the body in the motor cortex is _____.

a. proportional to the actual size of that part of the body

b. proportional to the complexity and precision of movement of which that part of the body is capable

c. the same for all body parts

d. greater for your torso than for your hands

Chapter Concept Check Answers

Concept Check | 1

- We can think of the neuron as a miniature decision-making device because the cell body of the neuron has to decide whether or not to generate an electrical impulse based on the incoming information from other neurons. If the excitatory input outweighs the inhibitory input by a sufficient amount, the cell body will decide to generate an impulse.

- Neural impulses are faster in neurons with myelinated axons than unmyelinated axons because the electrical impulse leaps from gap to gap in the myelin sheath rather than traveling continuously down the axon.

- Drugs that block the reuptake of neurotransmitters are considered agonists because they keep the neurotransmitters active in the synaptic gap (they keep carrying their messages over and over again to the receiving neuron), which increases the activity of the neurotransmitters.

- L-dopa leads to side effects that resemble the thought disorder symptoms of schizophrenia because L-dopa increases the activity of dopamine in the brain and the schizophrenic symptoms are the result of too much dopamine activity. Similarly, traditional antipsychotic drugs lead to side effects resembling Parkinson's disease symptoms because these drugs globally reduce the activity of dopamine in the brain. Thus, dopamine activity in the movement system involving the basal ganglia is reduced, leading to movement problems similar to those of Parkinson's disease.

Concept Check | 2

- With respect to location, sensory neurons and motor neurons are only in the PNS, and interneurons are only in the CNS. With respect to function, sensory neurons carry information to the CNS from the sensory receptors and internal organs, muscles, and glands of the body. Motor neurons carry movement commands from the CNS out to the rest of the body. Interneurons integrate the information within the CNS.

- The sympathetic nervous system is referred to as the "fight-or-flight" system because it prepares us for these actions in an emergency situation. The parasympathetic nervous system is referred to as the "rest-and-digest" system because its actions (the opposite of those in the sympathetic nervous system) allow us to rest and let functions such as digestion go back to normal.

- Both hormones and neurotransmitters are chemical messengers, but the hormones are much slower because they carry their message through the bloodstream to their distant targets. Neurotransmitters are released within the nervous system directly to their targets.

- The pituitary gland is referred to as the "master gland" because it releases hormones that direct the other endocrine glands to release their hormones. It functions like the master of the endocrine system.

- According to the James-Lange theory of emotion, we use the autonomic arousal and behavioral responses to determine the emotion. The emotional feeling occurs after and as a result of these responses. The specific emotion experienced depends upon the particular pattern of the arousal and behavioral responses. But, according to the Cannon-Bard theory, arousal patterns are too similar to be used to differentiate specific emotions. Cannon and Bard propose that arousal, behavioral response, and emotional feeling occur simultaneously and independently. Thus, contrary to the James-Lange theory, the arousal and behavioral responses and the emotional feeling happen at the same time.

Concept Check | 3

- To feel a slap on the left cheek of your face, the area devoted to the cheek in the lower half of the somatosensory cortical strip in the parietal lobe in the right hemisphere would be activated. Refer to Figure 2.9 to see the exact location of the cheek in the somatosensory homunculus and thus the activation. Remember that the activation would be at this location in the right hemisphere because your left cheek was slapped.

- When you shadow someone's speech, the auditory sensory input from the person's speech goes first to the primary auditory cortex in the temporal lobes, next to Wernicke's area to be understood, and then to Broca's area to produce the appropriate motor programs, which are then sent to the motor cortex, which then executes the programs to activate your speech muscles to produce the speech.

- A person who suffered damage to her cerebellum would have problems in motor coordination and balance. Her movements would be jerky and uncoordinated, and she would have great difficulty maintaining her balance.

- You would ask him to identify the object by the sense of touch with his left hand. He could identify it by matching the tactile input (the information gathered from touching the object) with his knowledge of what had been presented, both in the right hemisphere.

- If *Vertumnus* were flashed briefly in a split-brain person's left visual field, it would be processed in his right hemisphere. Hence he would use his left hand to respond because the right hemisphere's motor cortex controls that hand. Because the right hemisphere specializes in face recognition and engages in visual, holistic processing, he would point to "face" because the overall global impression of the painting is a face. However, if the painting had been flashed briefly in his right visual field, he would use his right hand because the painting would be processed in the left hemisphere, which controls that hand. Because the left hemisphere engages in analytic processing of the elements of a stimulus, the painting would be analyzed into its component elements (fruits, flowers, and vegetables) so he would point to "fruits," one of the main elements of the face. Gazzaniga has actually conducted some experimental trials using some of Archimboldo's paintings with a split-brain participant and found these predicted results.

- REM sleep is sometimes referred to as paradoxical sleep because your bodily muscles are relaxed and immobilized, but many parts of your brain are active with both oxygen consumption and cerebral blood flow increasing. The brain appears to be awake, but you are behaviorally asleep.

Answers to Key Terms Exercise

1. hormone
2. cerebellum
3. myelin sheath
4. PET scan
5. neurotransmitter
6. association cortex
7. antagonist
8. somatic (skeletal) nervous system
9. corpus callosum
10. GABA
11. glial cells (glia)
12. selective serotonin reuptake inhibitors (SSRIs)
13. endorphins
14. medulla
15. parietal lobe

Answers to Practice Test Questions

1. a; dendrites
2. d; amphetamine
3. b; serotonin
4. b; motor neuron
5. b; stimulation of digestion
6. c; hypothalamus
7. c; amygdala, hypothalamus, and hippocampus
8. d; left; left
9. c; right; right
10. d; REM sleep
11. b; Cannon-Bard
12. c; somatic; autonomic
13. b; recognize faces
14. a; acetylcholine; acetylcholine
15. b; proportional to the complexity and precision of motor movement of which that part of the body is capable

3

Sensation and Perception

magine what you would be like if you couldn't see, hear, taste, smell, or feel. You could be described as alive only in the narrowest sense of the word. You would have no perceptions, memories, thoughts, or feelings. We understand the world through our senses, our "windows" to the world. Our reality is dependent upon the two basic processes of sensation and perception. To understand this reality, we must first understand how we gather (sense) and interpret (perceive) the information that forms the foundation for our behavior and mental processing. Sensation and perception provide us with the information that allows us both to understand the world around us and to live in that world. Without them, there would be no world; there would be no "you."

▲ **Figure 3.1** | **Turning the Tables, An Example of a Misperception** | The two tabletops appear to have different dimensions and shapes. Surprisingly, however, they are identical. To convince yourself, measure one and then compare it to the other. Even knowing this, you cannot make your brain see them as identical. (From Shepard, 1990.)

Perception does not exactly replicate the world outside. Our "view" of the world is a subjective one that the brain constructs by using assumptions and principles, both built-in and developed from our past perceptual experiences. This means that sometimes our view of the world is inaccurate. Consider the tops of the two tables depicted in Figure 3.1. Do they appear to be the same shape and size? They don't appear to be identical, but they are! If we trace one of the tabletops and then place the tracing on the other one, it will fit perfectly. As pointed out by Lilienfeld, Lynn, Ruscio, and Beyerstein (2010), "Seeing is believing, but seeing isn't always believing correctly (p. 7)." We will revisit this illusion and its explanation later in the chapter; but, in general, this illusion is the result of the brain's misinterpretation of perspective information about the two tables (Shepard, 1990). The important point for us is that the brain is misperceiving reality and that even with the knowledge that these two tabletops are identical, you will not be able to suppress the misperception your brain produces. Your brain, not you, controls your perception of the world. The brain doesn't work like a photocopy machine during perception. The brain interprets during perception; our perception is its interpretation. Beauty is not in the eye of the beholder, but rather in the brain of the beholder.

To understand how sensation and perception work, we must first look at how the physical world outside and the psychological world within relate to each other. This pursuit will take us back to the experimental roots of psychology and the work of nineteenth-century German researchers in psychophysics. These researchers were not psychologists but rather physiologists and physicists. They used experimental methods to measure the relationship between the physical properties of stimuli and a person's psychological perception of those stimuli (hence the term *psychophysics*). Psychophysical researchers (psychophysicists) demonstrated that our mental activity could be measured quantitatively. Following a discussion of some of their major findings, we will take a look at how our two primary senses, vision and hearing, gather and process information from the environment, specifically focusing on how we see color and how we distinguish the pitch of a sound. Last, we will detail the general process of visual perception by examining how the brain organizes and recognizes incoming visual information, makes distance judgments to enable depth perception, and sometimes constructs misperceptions (illusions) as in Figure 3.1.

How the Physical World Relates to the Psychological World

Just as the name implies, psychophysical research focuses on the relationship between the physical world and the psychological world. Early psychophysical researchers attempted to answer basic questions concerning how we process the intensities of physical energy forms such as light waves and sound waves. We will discuss three questions that they addressed in their research—the detection question, the difference question, and the scaling question.

The detection and difference questions examine limits on our sensory processing. The detection question is concerned with the limits on our ability to detect very faint signals. How intense does a light have to be for us to see it? How intense does a sound have to be for us to hear it? Similarly, the difference question is concerned with limits on our detection abilities, but in this case with our ability to detect very small differences between stimuli. What is the smallest difference in brightness between two lights that we can see? What is the smallest difference in loudness between two sounds that we can hear? The scaling question is not concerned with sensory processing limits, but rather with how we perceive the magnitudes (intensities) of clearly detectable stimuli. What is the relationship between the actual physical intensities of stimuli and our psychological perceptions of these intensities? For example, if we double the physical intensity of a light, do we see it as twice as bright? If we double the intensity of a sound, do we hear it as twice as loud? The answer to both of these questions is, surprisingly, "no." If our perception does not reflect the actual changes in intensities, then how are the perceived changes related to the actual changes? The scaling question asks how our perceptual scaling of stimulus intensities is related to the actual physical scaling of stimulus intensities.

The Detection Question

What's the dimmest light we can see or the softest sound we can hear? To answer such questions about the limits of our detection abilities, early psychophysicists varied the amount of energy in a sensory stimulus (the intensity of a light or sound) and asked a person to answer "yes" or "no" as to whether the stimulus (the light or the sound) was detected. They attempted to measure the minimum amount of energy necessary for detection, what they called the absolute threshold. They reasoned that a person would always detect a stimulus that contained at least this threshold amount of energy. In other words, the person would say "no"

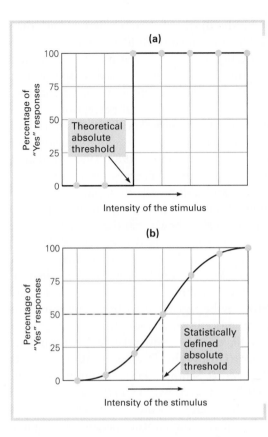

(a)

(b)

▲ **Figure 3.2** | Theoretical and Observed Absolute Thresholds | (a) This is a depiction of the result that psychophysical researchers thought they would observe in their detection studies. Theoretically, the absolute threshold is the minimum amount of physical energy in a stimulus (the minimum intensity of a stimulus) necessary to detect it. If a stimulus does not have this much energy, it should never be detected. If it has this much energy or more, it should always be detected. (b) This is a depiction of the result that psychophysical researchers actually obtained. There was no amount of physical energy in a stimulus that led to the kind of responding depicted in (a). Instead, the responding looked more like a flattened-S shape. Thus, the absolute threshold was defined statistically as the minimum amount of energy in a stimulus detected 50 percent of the time.

to all stimuli with less than this amount of energy and "yes" to all stimuli with this amount or more. Figure 3.2(a) depicts a plot of the result that psychophysical researchers thought they would observe.

Absolute threshold. The experimental results, however, did not fit this prediction. There was no abrupt transition point from responding "no" to responding "yes." Instead, the percentage of the time that a person said "yes" increased gradually as the amount of energy in the stimulus increased. This pattern of responding is depicted in Figure 3.2(b). Given this result, psychophysicists had to use a statistical definition to define the **absolute threshold,** the minimum amount of energy in a sensory stimulus detected 50 percent of the time. In other words, the absolute threshold is the amount of energy that has an equal probability of being detected or not detected. Using this definition, researchers have found that humans are pretty good detectors of weak stimuli. For example, we are able to see a candle flame on a mountain at a distance of 30 miles on a dark clear night with no other lights present and hear the tick of a watch under quiet conditions at a distance of 20 feet (Galanter, 1962).

Defining the absolute threshold in this way creates a strange definition of subliminal (*limen* means threshold in

absolute threshold The minimum amount of energy in a sensory stimulus detected 50 percent of the time.

Latin, so "subliminal" means below threshold) stimuli—stimuli detected less than 50 percent of the time. This means that subliminal stimuli are ones detected up to 49 percent of the time. Such a definition clearly does not match what people commonly take subliminal to mean: not consciously detected. Based on this everyday definition, however, some interesting questions about subliminal processing arise. Is there any empirical evidence for subliminal perception (perception without conscious awareness)? Is there any empirical evidence for subliminal persuasion (advertisers influencing consumer behavior with subliminal stimuli)? The answer to this last question is a clear "no" (Moore, 1988, 1992; Pratkanis, 1992; Pratkanis & Greenwald, 1988; Trappey, 1996). There is no need to worry that television, music, and other media are subliminally manipulating us. But what about those claims that subliminal tapes can improve your memory, help you to lose weight, and so on? Research has also shown that the tapes don't have the effects claimed (Greenwald, Spangenberg, Pratkanis, & Eskenazi, 1991).

Research in well-controlled laboratory settings (Bar & Biederman, 1998; Marcel, 1983), however, has demonstrated, with respect to subliminal perception, that sensory input can definitely be registered without our conscious awareness. Such perception is short-lived, though, and doesn't seem to have any consequential, long-term impact on our behavior (Greenwald, Draine, & Abrams, 1996; Greenwald, Klinger, & Schuh, 1995). Subliminal perception should not be confused with extrasensory perception (ESP), perception without using our known senses, such as mental telepathy (perceiving another person's thoughts). Just as there is no reliable evidence for subliminal persuasion, neither is there any such evidence for ESP (Druckman & Swets, 1988; Milton & Wiseman, 1999). After decades of research, no one has ever demonstrated a single, reproducible ESP finding. Over three decades ago, James Randi, a magician and master debunker of paranormal claims, offered $10,000 to anyone who could demonstrate ESP ability under controlled conditions. He later upped it to $1 million. He still has his money. (For more information, go to the "One Million Dollar Paranormal Challenge" icon at Randi's Web site, www.randi.org.)

signal detection theory A theory that assumes that the detection of faint sensory stimuli depends not only upon a person's physiological sensitivity to a stimulus but also upon his decision criterion for detection, which is based on nonsensory factors.

Signal detection theory. Contemporary psychophysical researchers believe that the detection of faint signals involves decision making, as well as sensory processing, so they use signal detection theory to examine a person's detection of very faint sensory stimuli (Green & Swets, 1966; Swets, 1964). According to **signal detection theory,** our ability to detect a faint sensory signal (stimulus) is a decision-making process that depends upon a person's physiological sensitivity to the signal and upon a person's decision-making criterion, which is based on non-sensory factors such as personality traits, expectations, alertness, and motivation. A person must make a decision about the sensory evidence that is available. Is there sufficient evidence to say a signal was present? This is like the decision a juror has to make in a trial. The juror has to decide, based upon the evidence presented, whether the defendant is guilty or not guilty. Based on their personalities and beliefs, jury members may use very different decision-making criteria (need varying amounts of evidence before deciding guilt). Similarly, people may have equal physiological sensitivity to sensory signals, but come to different decisions about whether they detected them or not because they use different criteria for their decisions.

The task used by signal detection researchers is different from that used to measure the absolute threshold. Instead of presenting a faint signal of varying intensity on each trial, either a signal of constant faint intensity is presented on a trial or no signal is presented, and the observer decides that a signal was presented and responds "yes" or that no signal was presented and responds "no." Thus, there are four possible events that could occur on a trial: detecting a signal when one was presented (a hit), saying a signal was presented when it was not (a false alarm), failing to detect a signal when one was presented (a miss), or correctly saying a signal was not presented when it was not (a correct rejection). Two of these events (hit and correct rejection) are correct responses by the observer, and two (false alarm and miss) are errors. All four events are depicted in Table 3.1.

Using the data for these four outcomes over a large number of trials, a signal detection theoretical analysis provides two quantitative measures, one for a person's physiological sensitivity to faint sensory signals and one for his decision criterion (how much evidence is needed for a "yes" response). The importance of the former measure is obvious, but why is the latter measure of value? Consider a sample detection task in the real world—looking at an X-ray to determine whether a faint spot indicating cancer is present or not. Remember, there are two possible errors in a detection decision—saying a signal is present when it is not (a false alarm) and saying a signal is not present when it is (a miss). The costs of either of these errors could be great. In the X-ray example, a false alarm might lead to additional (and unnecessary) clinical tests and possibly unnecessary surgery; a miss might lead to no treatment and death.

The measurement of a person's decision criterion tells us about these two error rates. For example, a person with a very lax decision criterion (a tendency to say "yes" with little evidence, a "yea" sayer) will make many false alarms but

Table 3.1	**Four Possible Outcomes in a Signal Detection Study**	
	Signal	
	Present	**Absent**
Observer's Response "Yes"	Hit	False Alarm
"No"	Miss	Correct Rejection

have few misses because he is saying "yes" most of the time. The opposite is true for a person with a very strict decision criterion (a tendency to only say "yes" when there is much evidence, a "nay" sayer). A strict criterion leads to many misses but few false alarms because the observer is saying "no" most of the time. So, depending upon the cost of each type of error, a person can change his decision criterion to lessen the cost. The bottom line is that our perception of even a faint signal is a subjective process impacted by non-sensory factors. With this understanding of limitations on our ability to detect faint sensory signals, let's see what psychophysical researchers have found out about our ability to detect very small differences between signals—the difference question.

The Difference Question

What's the smallest difference in brightness between two lights or in loudness between two sounds that we can detect? To answer such questions about how much difference there needs to be between stimuli to perceive them as different, psychophysicists vary the amount of difference in physical energy between two clearly detectable stimuli (two lights or two sounds) and ask a person to answer "yes" or "no" as to whether the stimuli (lights or sounds) are different. With this procedure, these early psychophysical researchers thought that they could measure a person's threshold for perceiving a difference in intensity between two stimuli. However, as with absolute threshold measurement, the results did not reveal a set threshold amount, so the **difference threshold** had to be defined statistically as the minimum difference between two stimuli detected 50 percent of the time. Another name for the difference threshold is the just noticeable difference, or jnd.

Weber's law. When measuring a person's difference threshold, psychophysicists presented two stimuli on each trial and varied the amount of difference between them across trials. It is important to understand how they manipulated the amount of difference across trials. To do this, they kept the intensity of one stimulus the same on every trial and changed the intensity of the other stimulus across trials. They called the stimulus whose intensity remained the same the standard stimulus, and the stimulus whose intensity changed across trials the comparison stimulus. For example, the standard stimulus for judging differences in lifted weights might be 20 pounds, and the comparison stimuli would be various weights less than or greater than 20 pounds. On one trial the comparison weight might be 19.5 pounds, 21 pounds on the next trial, and so forth.

Ernst Weber, a nineteenth-century German psychophysicist, discovered that difference thresholds and the standard stimulus intensities used to measure them have a very lawful relationship. Simply put, **Weber's law** says that for each type of sensory judgment that we can make, the measured difference threshold is a constant fraction of the standard stimulus

difference threshold The minimum difference between two sensory stimuli detected 50 percent of the time. The difference threshold is also sometimes referred to as the just noticeable difference, or jnd.

Weber's law For each type of sensory judgment that we can make, the measured difference threshold is a constant fraction of the standard stimulus value used to measure it. This constant fraction is different for each type of sensory judgment.

value used to measure it. The constant is different for each type of judgment. For example, for judging brightness of lights the constant is .08, but it is .05 for loudness of tones (Teghtsoonian, 1971). A smaller constant means that smaller differences can be detected for that type of sensory judgment. To understand Weber's law, let's consider perceiving differences in lifted weights. The constant for lifted weights is .02, or 1/50. If the standard stimulus used to determine the difference threshold were 100 pounds, the threshold would be 2 pounds. If the standard were 200 pounds, the threshold would be 4 pounds. What would the difference threshold be for a standard stimulus of 1000 pounds? It would be 20 pounds (1/50 of 1000). Researchers have found that Weber's law holds for most types of sensory judgments but not for very low-intensity or high-intensity stimuli (Gescheider, 1976).

In everyday life, Weber's law means that our ability to perceive a difference is relative to the constant background intensity. For example, in a dimly lit room, a little bit of light will be noticed; but in a brightly lit room, it will take a much greater increase in light to be noticed. In both cases, however, the proportion of the background intensity necessary to see an increase in brightness will be the same. The bottom line is that we notice proportional differences and not absolute differences. But when we perceive differences between stimuli that are well above threshold level, are the perceived differences in magnitude the same as the actual differences in the physical intensities of the stimuli? This is the scaling question.

The Scaling Question

The detection question and the difference question were concerned with thresholds and with the perception of very weak stimulus intensities or very small differences between stimulus intensities. The events occurring in normal perception are well above threshold levels; therefore, it is important to understand how we perceive the changing intensities of these everyday events that are well above our thresholds. To do so, we need to understand the scaling question—How do perceptual scales of measurement relate to physical scales of measurement? For almost all types of sensory judgment, the scales of measurement are not equivalent. They are lawfully related, however.

Stevens's power law. S. S. Stevens, a twentieth-century American researcher, conducted experiments in which he had people estimate the magnitudes of many types of sensory stimuli. Through these experiments, he discovered how the perceived magnitude of a stimulus is related to its actual physical magnitude (Stevens, 1962, 1975). By relating the perceived magnitude judgments to the actual physical intensities, Stevens found that the perceived magnitude of a stimulus (the perceived brightness of a light or loudness of a sound) is equal to its actual physical intensity raised to some constant power for each type of sensory judgment. This relationship is called **Stevens's power law.**

Stevens's power law The perceived magnitude of a stimulus is equal to its actual physical intensity raised to some constant power. The constant power is different for each type of sensory judgment.

Now let's try to figure out what this means by considering some different types of sensory judgment. First, if the constant power for a type of sensory judgment were 1, the perceived magnitude would actually equal the physical magnitude. However, this is seldom the case, though it does happen when we judge line lengths. If a line is doubled in length, we perceive its length as doubled. For almost all types of sensory judgments, however, the constant power that the physical intensity has to be raised to is either less than or greater than 1, which means that the perceived magnitude is less or greater, respectively, than the actual physical magnitude. Brightness and loudness magnitude judgments are good examples of when the perceived magnitude is less than the actual magnitude. To perceive a light as twice as bright, its actual intensity has to be increased eight- to ninefold. A good example of the perceived magnitude being greater than actual physical magnitude is the judgment of electric shock intensities. If shock intensity is doubled, we perceive the increase as much more than double, about 10 times as great.

The bottom line for almost all types of sensory judgments is that our perception of stimulus magnitude does not match the actual physical world. Our perception is a transformation that is created within us. But why would our perceptions be rescaled? One explanation involves thinking about the adaptive value of such sensory processing (Goldstein, 2007). Lessening our perception of dramatic increases in sensory intensities such as light and sound serves a protective function for our eyes and ears. Increasing the perceived intensities of dangerous stimuli like electric shock would alert us to possible dangers before they seriously affected us. Both types of rescaling would tend to pay dividends in terms of our survival; hence Stevens's power law may be partially understandable as an adaptation enhancing our survival.

Another phenomenon that helps us to understand how we process the intensity of stimuli is **sensory adaptation**—our sensitivity to unchanging and repetitious stimuli disappears over time. For example, when we first put our watch on our wrist, we are aware of it, but that sensitivity disappears quickly. Why? Our senses are set to detect changes in the environment, and therefore they adapt to continuous or repeated presentation of a stimulus with decreasing responsiveness. Like Stevens's power law, sensory adaptation makes sense from an evolutionary viewpoint. It is more important for our survival to detect environmental changes than things that don't change. Changes are more likely to signal danger. There are some limits on sensory adaptation, though. We don't adapt to extremely intense, especially painful stimuli, such as a severe toothache or incredibly loud noises. We also don't usually adapt to unchanging visual stimuli; our eyes are constantly moving so their visual images continue to change.

To help you to integrate the information in this section, the three psychophysical questions along with the answers we have described are summarized in Table 3.2. If anything in this table is not clear to you, restudy the relevant material before going on to the next section.

▌ **sensory adaptation** Our sensitivity to unchanging and repetitious stimuli disappears over time.

Table 3.2	Three Psychophysical Questions and Answers
Psychophysical Questions	**Answers**
Detection Question: What is the minimum amount of energy in a stimulus that humans can detect?	Absolute threshold: the minimum amount of energy in a stimulus that can be detected 50% of the time
	Signal detection theory: detection of faint stimuli depends not only upon physiological sensitivity to a stimulus but also upon a person's decision criterion for detection, which is based on non-sensory factors
Difference Question: What is the minimum difference in stimulus energy between two stimuli that humans can detect?	Difference threshold: the minimum difference in stimulus energy between two stimuli that can be detected 50% of the time
	Weber's law: the measured difference threshold is a constant fraction of the standard stimulus used to measure it and this constant is different for each type of sensory judgment
Scaling Question: How are human perceptual scales of measurement related to physical scales of measurement?	Stevens's power law: the perceived magnitude of a stimulus is equal to its actual physical intensity raised to some constant power for each type of sensory judgment

Section Summary

In this section, we discussed some of the basic findings from psychophysical research. We considered three psychophysical questions—the detection, difference, and scaling questions. To answer the detection question, psychophysical researchers measured the absolute threshold, the minimum stimulus intensity that can be detected 50 percent of the time. Using this definition, researchers have found humans to be pretty good detectors of faint signals. However, because they view the detection task as a decision-making process involving a response criterion, sensory researchers prefer to use signal detection theory to describe our detection abilities. Using this type of analysis, both an observer's decision criterion and her sensitivity to faint sensory stimuli can be identified. Thus, if the costs of a particular observer's errors (false alarms or misses) are high, the observer's criterion can be changed to reduce these rates. Regardless of the type of analysis, researchers have failed to find any reliable evidence for subliminal persuasion or extrasensory perception.

To answer the difference question, psychophysicists measured the difference threshold, the minimum difference in stimulus intensity between two stimuli that can be detected 50 percent of the time. It turns out that difference thresholds and the standard stimulus intensities used to measure them have a relationship called Weber's law—the measured difference threshold is a constant proportion of the standard stimulus value used in its measurement. This constant is different for each type of sensory judgment, and a smaller constant indicates that smaller differences can be detected for that type of sensory judgment.

Surprisingly, research on the scaling question has indicated that the relationship between perceived stimulus magnitudes and the actual physical magnitudes is almost always not an equivalent one. According to Stevens's power law, to equal the perceived intensity, the actual physical intensity has to be raised to some constant power, and this constant is different for each type of sensory judgment. When this constant power is 1, the perceived intensity equals the actual intensity. This, however, seldom occurs, but it is the case for line-length judgments. Almost all of the time the constant is less or greater than 1, which means that the perceived intensity is less or greater, respectively, than the actual physical intensity. Brightness and loudness are examples of perceived magnitude judgments being less than the actual physical magnitudes, and electric shock is an example of magnitude judgments being greater. One explanation of Stevens's power law involves its adaptive value with respect to our survival. Such an explanation can also account for sensory adaptation, our decreasing sensory responsiveness to constant, nonextreme stimuli.

ConceptCheck | 1

➤ Why were absolute and difference thresholds given statistical definitions?

➤ According to signal detection theory, what would happen to a person's false alarm and miss rates if the person switched from a very lax to a very strict decision criterion?

➤ What does a really large constant fraction in Weber's law tell us about our ability to judge differences?

➤ Why is it adaptive for the constant exponent in Stevens's power law to be greater than 1 for physical energies that are dangerous to us at high intensities?

How We See and How We Hear

Our two most dominant senses are vision and hearing. This section will first discuss how our eyes and ears gather and process information from the environment. Visual and auditory stimuli are physical energies in the form of waves—light waves and sound waves. We need to understand the characteristics of these waveforms to understand how visual and auditory stimuli are processed, so we need to discuss them first. A typical waveform and its primary characteristics (wavelength, frequency, and amplitude) are illustrated in Figure 3.3.

Wavelength refers to the distance in one cycle of a wave, from one crest to the next. Different wavelengths of light lead to varying perceptions of color. Humans can perceive wavelengths roughly from 400 to 700 nanometers (nm), or billionths of a meter. As the wavelengths decrease from 700 nm, the resulting hues go from red through the colors of the spectrum down to violet. One way to remember the order of these colors is by remembering the name ROY G. BIV, which stands for Red, Orange, Yellow,

wavelength The distance in one cycle of a wave, from one crest to the next.

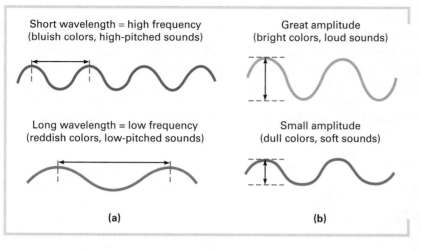

I A Typical Waveform and Its Characteristics I Wavelength is the distance of one complete cycle of the wave, from one crest to the next. A wave's frequency refers to the number of times it can cycle in 1 second—the longer the wave, the lower the frequency. The amplitude of the wave refers to the amount of energy in the wave, which is the height of the wave at its crest.

Green, Blue, Indigo, and Violet. **Amplitude** refers to the amount of energy in a wave, its intensity, which is the height of the wave at its crest. For light waves, the amplitude determines the brightness of the light. Different amplitudes lead to different levels of brightness; the greater the amplitude, the brighter the light.

For auditory stimuli, the frequency of the waveform rather than its length is used. **Frequency** refers to the number of times the waveform cycles in 1 second. Longer wavelengths have lower frequencies, and shorter wavelengths have higher frequencies. The frequency of a sound wave determines its pitch, the quality of sound that we describe as high or low. For example, female voices usually have a higher pitch than male voices. Humans can perceive sound wave frequencies from about 20 to 20,000 hertz (Hz), the number of cycles of the sound wave in one second. This unit of measurement's name, hertz, comes from a nineteenth-century German physicist named Heinrich Hertz, who studied sound. The amplitude of a sound wave corresponds to our perception of its loudness. As the amplitude of a wave increases, its perceived loudness increases.

The brain cannot process physical energies such as light waves and sound waves. There are receptor cells in our eyes and ears that specialize in **transduction**—converting physical energy into neural signals that the brain can understand. This conversion is the first step in processing incoming sensory information. Following transduction, the incoming visual and auditory signals undergo further processing on their way to the brain, and within the brain before we see and hear the brain's interpretations of these signals. Next, we will take a closer look at transduction and the initial information processing in the eyes and ears, focusing on how we see color and how we distinguish the pitches of sounds.

amplitude The amount of energy in a wave, its intensity, which is the height of the wave at its crest.

frequency The number of times a wave cycles in 1 second.

transduction The conversion of physical energy into neural signals that the brain can understand.

How the Eye Works

The light-sensitive receptor cells are located in the retina at the very back of the eye; therefore, light waves have to travel through almost the entire eye before transduction occurs. Figure 3.4 shows the path of the light and each of the parts of the eye that we will discuss. The cornea is the clear, tough covering on the front of the eye that starts bending the light waves that will eventually have to be focused on the retina. The light waves pass through the cornea and the pupil,

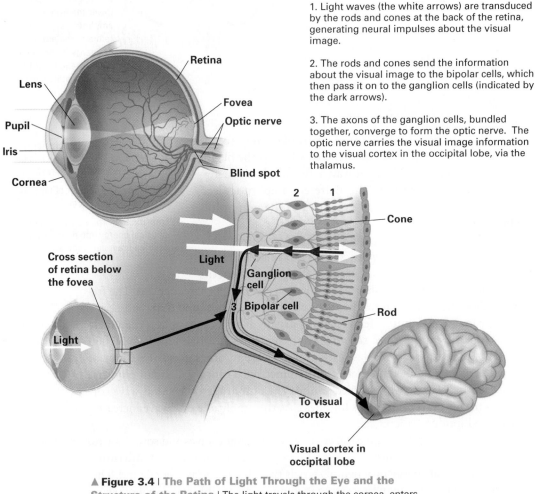

1. Light waves (the white arrows) are transduced by the rods and cones at the back of the retina, generating neural impulses about the visual image.

2. The rods and cones send the information about the visual image to the bipolar cells, which then pass it on to the ganglion cells (indicated by the dark arrows).

3. The axons of the ganglion cells, bundled together, converge to form the optic nerve. The optic nerve carries the visual image information to the visual cortex in the occipital lobe, via the thalamus.

▲ **Figure 3.4** | **The Path of Light Through the Eye and the Structure of the Retina** | The light travels through the cornea, enters through the pupil whose size is controlled by the iris, and is focused on the retina by the lens. Here, as explained in the figure, the light waves are (1) transduced into neural signals describing the visual image; and (2) these signals are sent to the bipolar cells, which forward them to the ganglion cells whose axons bundle together to form the optic nerve, which (3) carries the signals back to the occipital lobes in the brain, via the thalamus, to be interpreted.

a tiny hole through which the light waves enter the eye. The iris is a colored muscle that both gives eyes their color and controls the size of the pupil, which determines how much light enters. To lessen the amount of entering light, the iris will constrict (lessen) the size of the pupil, and to increase the amount of entering light, it will dilate (increase) the pupil's size. A completely dilated pupil lets in about 16 times as much light as one that is completely constricted (Matlin & Foley, 1997).

The light then passes through the transparent lens, which is responsible for **accommodation**—the focusing of the light waves from objects of different distances directly on the retina. This process is called accommodation because the lens changes its shape (accommodates) in order to focus objects at different distances. When looking at distant objects (at least 20 feet away), the lens is in its unaccommodated flattest state, which allows the light waves to be focused on the retina. When we look at objects that are nearer, the lens accommodates by becoming thicker in order to focus the light waves properly on the retina. Because light travels in straight lines, the retinal image will be inverted and reversed. The brain, however, rearranges this image to its correct orientation for our perception.

If the image is not properly focused on the retina because of defects in the lens or the shape of the eyeball, problems in vision arise. **Nearsightedness** occurs when the light waves from distant objects come into focus in front of the retina, which blurs the images of these objects. **Farsightedness** is created by the opposite focusing problem—light waves from nearby objects come into focus behind the retina, resulting in blurred images. So, in nearsightedness, we have difficulty viewing distant objects, but can see near objects well; in farsightedness, we have difficulty viewing near objects, but can see far objects well. Farsightedness is similar to what happens to our vision as we age; the lens loses its ability to accommodate for nearby objects. Older people find it difficult to focus on near objects, so they have to get reading glasses and hold objects at a distance to help in seeing them.

The structure of the retina. Except for the visual image being reversed and inverted, no visual processing occurs until the light waves reach the retina, which is only a mere half-millimeter thick (Brynie, 2009). As shown in Figure 3.4, the **retina,** the light-sensitive layer of the eye, is composed of three layers of cells—ganglion, bipolar, and receptor (the rods and cones). The light waves pass through the ganglion and bipolar cells before reaching the rods and cones, where visual processing begins. The light waves are absorbed by photopigments (light-sensitive chemicals) within these receptor cells, creating patterns of neural impulses that describe the visual image. This neural information is conveyed to the bipolar cells, which in turn send it along to the ganglion cells. The optic nerve, the axons of the ganglion cells bundled together, exits the eye carrying the information along the visual pathways to the brain. Where the optic nerve exits each eye, we

accommodation The focusing of light waves from objects of different distances directly on the retina.

nearsightedness A visual problem in which the light waves from distant objects come into focus in front of the retina, blurring the images of these objects.

farsightedness A visual problem in which the light waves from nearby objects come into focus behind the retina, blurring the images of these objects.

retina The light-sensitive layer of the eye that is composed of three layers of cells—ganglion, bipolar, and receptor (rods and cones).

▲ **Figure 3.5** | **Find Your Blind Spots** | To find the blind spot in your left eye, hold the book at arm's length in front of you, close your right eye and stare at the orange on the right with your left eye, and keep staring at the orange while you move the book slowly toward you. The apple should disappear when it falls on the blind spot in your left eye, somewhere between 6 to 12 inches from your eye. To find the blind spot in your right eye, this time close the left eye and stare at the apple on the left with you right eye as you move the book slowly toward you. This time the orange should disappear when it falls upon the blind spot in your right eye.

SergiyN/Fotolia.com

April D/Fotolia.com

have a blind spot—a retinal area with no receptor cells, preventing us from seeing anything there. To experience the blind spots in each of your eyes, follow the instructions in Figure 3.5. Why don't we normally notice the blind spot in each eye? The brain fills them in by using top-down processing, which we will discuss in the next section (Churchland & Ramachandran, 1996).

The optic nerve carries the visual information to the thalamus, which is responsible for directing it to the primary visual cortex in our occipital lobes to be processed. But how does the visual cortex interpret this message from the retina? David Hubel and Torsten Wiesel's innovative research in which they recorded patterns of electrical impulses in individual neurons in the visual cortex of cats provided the answer. They were awarded the Nobel Prize in Physiology or Medicine in 1981 for their discoveries concerning information processing in the visual system. The story of their collaboration along with reprints of all of their key publications can be found in Hubel and Wiesel's *Brain and visual perception: The story of a 25-year collaboration* (2004). Because this cortical processing is very involved, we'll just describe the general nature of this very counterintuitive processing.

Essentially, the brain recognizes a visual object (a process called pattern recognition) by breaking it down into its elementary features, such as angles and diagonal lines. Cortical cells called feature detectors then recognize these elementary features. Finally, the elementary features are put back together again, so that the whole object can be recognized. For example, to recognize △, it is

Ira Wyman/Sygma/Corbis

David Hubel and Torsten Wiesel

broken down into its features (possibly, /, _, and \), which are recognized and then regrouped into the proper relationship. Strange isn't it? To recognize an object, the object is broken down into its parts and then put back together again in order to identify it. Even stranger is that there are separate processing systems for form, color, distance, and motion information, which the brain somehow coordinates and unifies into our seamless perception of the world (Ratey, 2001).

rods Receptor cells in the retina that are principally responsible for dim light and achromatic vision.

cones Receptor cells in the retina that are principally responsible for bright light and color vision.

fovea A tiny pit in the center of the retina filled with cones.

Rods and cones. There are two types of visual receptor cells, rods and cones, in the retina. They are called rods and cones because of their actual physical shapes. Their functions are also very different. **Rods** are principally responsible for dim light and achromatic (colorless) vision, and **cones** for bright light and color vision. Rods outnumber cones about 20 to 1 (Kalat, 2007). There are about 120 million rods and only 6 million or so cones in each eye. Cones are more centrally located in the retina than rods. They are located in the **fovea,** a tiny pit in the center of the retina, and in the periphery of the retina on each side of the fovea. Rods are only located in the periphery, and the proportion of rods to cones increases with increasing distance from the fovea. The major differences between rods and cones are summarized in Table 3.3.

The difference in location of rods (peripheral) and cones (central) helps us to determine where we should focus an object for the best visual acuity (resolution of detail). In normal or brighter light when the cones are mainly responsible for our vision, the object should be focused on the fovea, which is packed with cones. Cones provide a clearer picture of an object. Why? Cones, especially foveal cones, tend to have more direct routes than the rods to the bipolar and ganglion cells for the retinal information that they process. For example, typically one foveal cone communicates with one bipolar cell, but several rods communicate with one bipolar cell. This means that the information that the rods send forward has been averaged across several retinal positions, leading to a less

Table 3.3 Differences Between Rods and Cones	
Rods	**Cones**
120 million in each eye	6 million in each eye
Located mainly in periphery of retina	Located mainly in fovea and central retina
Primarily responsible for dim light vision	Primarily responsible for bright light vision
Responsible for achromatic (colorless) vision	Responsible for chromatic (color) vision
Lead to low visual acuity	Lead to high visual acuity

clear picture of the retinal image. Foveal cones do not have to do such averaging; therefore, the retinal image they send forward is more detailed and clearer. The cones in the periphery just outside of the fovea do some averaging but far less than the rods.

But where should we focus an object in dim light conditions? The answer is in the periphery of the retina rather than the fovea. Why? This is where the rods are more densely located, and they are mainly responsible for our vision when not much light is available. We shouldn't look directly at the object when there isn't much light, but rather focus a little to the side of it so that it will be projected onto the periphery of the retina. The image won't be as clear as when we can use our cones, but it is the best we can do in dim light. The major role of the rods in dim light vision is also apparent in **dark adaptation,** the process by which the rods and cones through internal chemical changes become more and more sensitive to light in dim light conditions. The cones adapt quickly (in 5 to 10 minutes), but need more light to function, so they do not really help us to see in dim light. It takes longer for the rods to adapt (20 minutes or so), but they slowly help us to see in dim light. Normally, however, we have enough light for our cones to be working. That is why we see the world in vivid color. But how do the cones do this, and what else is involved in producing our perception of color? These are the questions we discuss next.

How We See Color

How we see color can be explained by combining two rather simple theories of color vision, the trichromatic theory and the opponent-process theory. We will consider each one separately and then how the two work together to explain color vision.

Trichromatic theory of color vision. Trichromatic theory, as the word trichromatic implies, proposes that there are three colors involved. **Trichromatic theory** assumes that there are three types of cones, activated best by short, medium, or long wavelengths of light, roughly corresponding to blue, green, and red. Indeed, research indicates that there are three types of cones, each containing a slightly different photopigment that is maximally sensitive to blue, green, or red wavelengths of light (Wald, 1964). The trichromatic theory assumes that all of the many colors that we can perceive are mixtures of various proportions of these three cone activities. If all three types of cones are equally active, we see white (the sum of the three wavelengths of light). Trichromatic theory played a role in the creation of the television screen, which consists of microscopic red, green, and blue dots. The colors we see on the screen are the product of how these three types of dots are activated by the television broadcast and how the light-emitting dots activate our three types of cones.

dark adaptation The process by which the rods and cones through internal chemical changes become more and more sensitive to light in dim light conditions.

trichromatic theory A theory of color vision that assumes that there are three types of cones, each only activated by wavelength ranges of light corresponding roughly to blue, green, and red. It further assumes that all of the various colors that we can see are mixtures of various levels of activation of the three types of cones. If all three are equally activated, we see white.

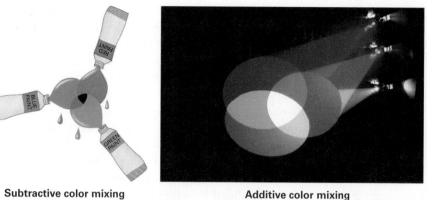

Subtractive color mixing

(a)

Additive color mixing

(b)

Fritz Goro/Time Life Pictures/Getty Images

▲ **Figure 3.6** | **Subtractive and Additive Mixtures** | (a) In a subtractive mixture, some wavelengths are absorbed (subtracted) and so do not get reflected from the mixture. For example, mixing equal amounts of red, green, and blue paints is a subtractive mixture. The intersection of all three colors appears black. (b) Mixing equal amounts of red, green, and blue wavelengths of light, however, is an additive mixture in which all the wavelengths are directly mixed together, producing different different results than mixing paints of these three colors. For example, the intersection of all three wavelengths appears white. The binary additive mixtures are also counterintuitive. For example, the additive mixture of equal proportions of red and green wavelengths of light appears yellow.

It is important to realize that the proposed mixtures of the primary colors are **additive mixtures**—different wavelengths of light are directly mixed together. In additive mixtures, all of the wavelengths of light reach the retina and are added together. The resulting colors are very different than those for **subtractive mixtures,** such as mixing paints. In subtractive mixtures, some wavelengths are absorbed (subtracted) and so do not get reflected from the mixture to the retina. For example, if we mix red, green, and blue paints together in equal amounts, the result is black (no light reflected). A mixture of equal proportions of red, green, and blue wavelengths of light, however, appears white. These subtractive and additive mixtures are shown in Figure 3.6.

There are color phenomena that trichromatic theory has difficulty explaining. We know that red-green and blue-yellow are pairs of **complementary colors,** wavelengths that when added together produce white. This means we cannot produce an additive mixture that is perceived to be reddish-green or a bluish-yellow. Trichromatic theory can't explain why such colors can't be produced if every color is an additive mixture of the three primary colors. In addition, this theory has difficulty explaining how we see complementary-color afterimages. For example, if we stare at a solid red square for a while and then look at a white sheet of paper, we will see a solid green square. Why?

> **additive mixtures** Direct mixtures of different wavelengths of light in which all of the wavelengths reach the retina and are added together.
>
> **subtractive mixtures** Mixtures of wavelengths of light in which some wavelengths are absorbed (subtracted) and so do not get reflected from the mixtures to the retina.
>
> **complementary colors** Wavelengths of light that when added together produce white.

opponent-process theory A theory of color vision which assumes that there are three opponent-process cell systems (red-green, blue-yellow, and black-white) that process color information after it has been processed by the cones. The colors in each system oppose one another in that if one color is stimulated, the other is inhibited.

Opponent-process theory of color vision. To explain such phenomena, researchers developed a second theory, the opponent-process theory (Hurvich & Jameson, 1957). The **opponent-process theory** assumes that there are three opponent-process cell systems helping us to see color and that they are located at the post-receptor level of processing (after cone processing), which would mean along the visual pathways from the bipolar cells to the brain. The systems are the pairs, red-green and blue-yellow, plus a black-white (levels-of-brightness) system. The colors within each system oppose each other—if one is stimulated, the other one is inhibited. For example, there are blue-yellow opponent-process cells stimulated by blue light and inhibited by yellow light, and others that are stimulated by yellow and inhibited by blue. Researchers have found that some ganglion cells as well as some cells in the thalamus and visual cortex respond in accordance with opponent-process theory (DeValois & DeValois, 1975; Engel, 1999; Gegenfurtner & Kiper, 2003). Thus, we know that such cell systems exist.

Opponent-process theory can easily explain why we can't see a reddish-green or a bluish-yellow. The complementary colors involved in each case cannot both be simultaneously stimulated. They cancel each other out. The theory can also explain complementary color afterimages. When you stare at one of the two colors in an opponent-process system for awhile, the part of that system responsible for processing this color gets fatigued and has to stop and recover. This is why we see the complementary color in the system when we look at a white surface—the other color is recovering and cannot oppose it. A good example is the American red, white, and blue flag. If we stare at a picture of this flag for a while and then switch our attention to a white sheet of paper, we see a complementary green, black, and yellow flag! If you stare at the green, black, and yellow flag in Figure 3.7 for about 40 seconds and then look at the white space next to it, what do you see?

▲ **Figure 3.7 | Demonstration of Complementary Afterimage |** Stare at the flag below for awhile and then look at the white space to its right. You should see the American flag.

Table 3.4	Three Theories of Color Vision
Theory	**Explanation of Color Vision**
Trichromatic theory	There are three types of cones, each only activated by wavelength ranges of light corresponding roughly to blue, green, and red; all colors are mixtures of various levels of activation of these three types of cones
Opponent-process theory	There are three opponent-process cell systems (red-green, blue-yellow, and black-white) which process color information after it has been processed by the cones; the colors in each system oppose one another (if one is stimulated, the other is inhibited)
Composite theory	Color information is processed by the cones according to trichromatic theory, but color information is processed at the post-receptor cell level according to opponent-process theory

There is research that supports both trichromatic theory and opponent-process theory, so the best explanation for how we see color involves both theories, but at different locations in the visual pathways (Boynton, 1988). Color information is processed by the cones according to trichromatic theory, but color information is processed at the post-receptor cell level (by bipolar, ganglion, thalamic, and cortical cells) according to the opponent-process theory. This simple composite theory is a good example of competing theories becoming complementary theories. All three theories of color vision are summarized in Table 3.4.

This brief discussion of how we see color shows how visual input from the environment is processed, analyzed, and reconfigured, starting with its initial processing in the retina and as it continues along the visual pathways to the brain to be interpreted. Next, we will consider how such processing of auditory information enables us to hear.

How the Ear Works

The auditory sensory system is a mechanical (vibratory) system with the receptor cells located in the inner portion of each ear. As you can see in Figure 3.8 (page 104), the ear is divided into three sections—the outer ear, middle ear, and inner ear. The parts of each section are also shown in Figure 3.8 (page 104). The pinna, the external part of the ear, collects sounds and funnels them through the auditory canal to the tympanic membrane (the eardrum), which marks the boundary between the outer ear and middle ear. The sound waves produce vibrations in the eardrum, and these vibrations create a chain reaction that moves the malleus, incus, and stapes (more commonly referred to as the hammer, anvil, and stirrup given their shapes), the three tiny bones in the middle ear (the three smallest bones in the human body). The movement of the stapes creates vibrations of the oval window, a membrane covering an opening into the inner ear.

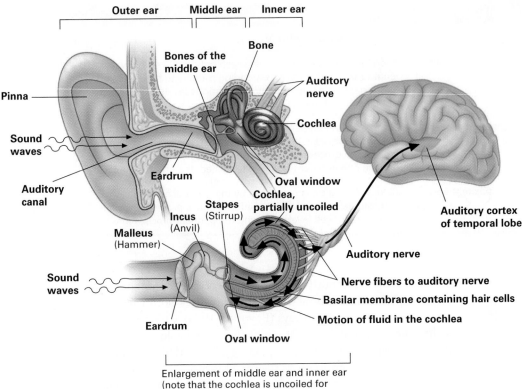

Enlargement of middle ear and inner ear
(note that the cochlea is uncoiled for
explanatory purposes, but not in reality)

▲ **Figure 3.8** | **The Path of Sound Through the Ear** | Sound is
conducted through the ear by way of air pressure changes. After entering
through the pinna, the sound waves create vibrations in the eardrum that
lead to movement of the three tiny bones in the middle ear. This movement
leads to vibration of the oval window that leads to movement of the fluid
in the inner ear, displacement along the basilar membrane, and movement
of the hair cells within the membrane. The movement of these hair cells
creates the neural signals that are taken to the primary auditory cortex in
the temporal lobes by the auditory nerve via the thalamus.

The cochlea is a snail-shaped structure in the inner ear that contains the receptor
cells for hearing. Tiny **hair cells** that line the basilar membrane (a membrane that
extends the length of the cochlea) are the receptors for hearing. There are not nearly
as many hair cells as there are rods and cones in the eyes, only about 16,000 hair cells
in each ear (Matlin & Foley, 1997). The vibrations of the oval window displace fluid
within the cochlea, which causes movement of the basilar membrane and thus movement of the hair cells in the membrane. The auditory message is coded according to
how these tiny hair cells move. This motion of the hair cells gets translated into neural impulses that get passed on to the auditory nerve cells that
carry the information to the thalamus, which directs the information to the primary auditory cortex in the temporal lobes.

▌ **hair cells** The receptor cells for
hearing. They line the basilar membrane inside the cochlea.

Hearing loss caused by damage to these hair cells or the auditory nerve fibers is called **nerve deafness.** Such damage is most often caused by continued exposure to extremely loud noises and aging. This type of deafness is much more difficult to treat than **conduction deafness,** hearing loss caused by damage to the mechanical system carrying the auditory information to the cochlea. For example, puncturing an eardrum can lead to conduction deafness. Hearing aids can often help to alleviate this type of deafness.

Now that we have a basic understanding of how the ear works and how auditory information gets coded and processed, we'll consider an important aspect of this complex coding, how we distinguish different pitches.

How We Distinguish Pitch

Remember that pitch is the quality of sound that we describe as high or low and is determined by the frequency of a sound wave. We can perceive sound wave frequencies from about 20 to 20,000 Hz. Each of the frequencies in this rather large range corresponds to a different pitch that we can perceive. The best explanation of how we perceive this range of pitches parallels the story of how we see different colors. We will find that to get the best explanation, two theories will need to be combined—place theory and frequency theory. First, we will consider each of the two theories, and then how they go together.

Place theory assumes that there is a specific place along the basilar membrane, starting from the oval window, which will respond maximally to a particular frequency. Thus, the brain will know the frequency by knowing the location of peak activity along the basilar membrane. In some ingenious experiments on the cochleas from human cadavers, Georg von Békésy discovered that each frequency generates a traveling wave that moves along the basilar membrane and peaks at a particular location (Békésy, 1960). Starting at the oval window and 20,000 Hz, the pitch goes down as the peak activity moves down the basilar membrane. These peak locations tell the brain the frequencies of the incoming auditory stimuli.

Frequency theory assumes that the frequency of the sound wave is mimicked by the firing rate of the hair cells across the entire basilar membrane. For example, if the frequency were 100 Hz, the firing rate for the membrane would be 100 impulses per second. The brain would know the frequency by the basilar membrane's firing rate in reaction to the auditory stimulus.

Now let's see why and how we put theories together to get a better explanation of pitch perception. First, research has found that specific locations along the basilar membrane correlate well with the frequencies of sound waves, except for lower pitches (< 500 Hz). For these lower pitches, the firing rate of the basilar membrane mimics the frequency. This means

nerve deafness Hearing loss created by damage to the hair cells or the auditory nerve fibers in the inner ear.

conduction deafness Hearing loss created by damage to one of the structures in the ear responsible for mechanically conducting the auditory information to the inner ear.

place theory A theory of pitch perception which assumes that there is a specific location along the basilar membrane that will maximally respond to a particular frequency, thereby indicating the pitch to the brain. As this location goes down the basilar membrane from the oval window, the pitch goes down from 20,000 Hz to 20 Hz.

frequency theory A theory of pitch perception that assumes that the frequency of the sound wave is mimicked by the firing rate of the entire basilar membrane.

Table 3.5	Theories of Pitch Perception
Theory	**Explanation of Pitch Perception**
Place theory	There is a specific location along the basilar membrane that will maximally respond to a particular frequency, thereby indicating the pitch to the brain
Frequency theory	The frequency of the sound wave is mimicked by the firing rate of the entire basilar membrane, thereby indicating the pitch to the brain
Composite theory	Lower frequencies (< 500 Hz) are processed according to frequency theory, higher frequencies (> 5,000 Hz) are processed according to place theory, and for frequencies between from 500 to 5,000 Hz, both theories are working

that place theory can explain how we hear the entire range of pitches except for low pitches, but frequency theory can explain how we hear these low pitches. Is frequency theory only able to explain how we perceive pitches below 500 Hz? No, the upper limit on firing rate is 5,000 times per second. There is a maximum firing rate for nerve cells, about 1,000 times per second. However, with the addition of the **volley principle,** in which the cells take turns firing to increase the maximum firing rate for the group of cells, frequency theory could explain our perception of frequencies up to about 5,000 Hz (Zwislocki, 1981). Because 5,000 times per second is the upper limit for the firing rate using the volley principle, frequency theory would not be able to explain how we perceive higher frequencies of 5,000 to 20,000 Hz.

volley principle Cells taking turns firing will increase the maximum firing rate for a group of cells.

Combining the two theories gives us a composite theory that fits the research findings on pitch perception. Frequency theory explains the perception of lower frequencies (< 500 Hz), and place theory explains how we perceive higher frequencies (> 5,000 Hz). This means that the brain uses the firing rate to differentiate the low frequencies and the location of maximal hair cell activity along the basilar membrane to distinguish the high frequencies. For the range of frequencies in between (roughly 500 to 5,000 Hz), both sources of information work, giving us double coverage and better pitch perception. This is fortunate because this range of frequencies contains the sounds most important to us—for example, human speech. All three theories of pitch perception are summarized in Table 3.5.

Section Summary

In this section, we discussed our two most dominant senses—vision and hearing. Stimuli for both senses occur in the form of waves, light waves and sound waves, respectively. For light waves, different wavelengths lead to the perception of different colors, and the amplitude of the wave determines the level of perceived brightness. With respect to sound waves, wave frequency determines the pitch that we perceive, and wave amplitude determines our perception of loudness. The brain cannot process such physical energy forms, hence receptor cells (rods and cones in the retina and hair cells in the basilar membrane within the cochlea) transduce (convert) the physical energy into neural signals that the brain can understand.

Light waves pass through many parts of the eye before being transduced by the rods and cones at the back of the retina. Once transduced, the neural signals are carried by the optic nerve to the thalamus, which sends them to the primary visual cortex where they are interpreted. In this interpretation process, the object is broken down into its elemental features, which are recognized by feature detectors, and then the features are combined so that the whole object can be recognized. The cones and rods divide the initial visual processing. Cones are responsible for bright light and color vision; rods are responsible for dim light and achromatic vision.

There are two competing explanations for how we see color—trichromatic theory and opponent-process theory. Trichromatic theory proposes three types of cones, each responding to ranges of wavelengths corresponding to red, green, and blue. All other colors are derived from varying proportions of these three primaries. Research indicates that we do have these three types of cones. Opponent-process theory assumes that there are three types of cell systems (red-green, blue-yellow, and black-white) at the post-receptor level that help us to see color. Being complementary pairs, the colors within each system oppose (cancel) each other. Opponent-process theory can explain complementary color phenomena that the trichromatic theory cannot. The combination of these two theories provides the best explanation of color vision. The trichromatic theory explains how the cones operate, and the opponent-process theory explains how cells in the visual pathways operate after the cones have done their initial processing.

The auditory system is a mechanical vibratory system with the hair cell receptors located within the basilar membrane in the cochlea. Incoming vibrations result in fluid displacement in the cochlea that causes movement of these hair cells. The nature of these hair cell movements creates the auditory message that gets carried by the auditory nerve, by way of the thalamus, to the primary auditory cortex for interpretation. Damage to these hair cells or the auditory nerve results in nerve deafness, which is very difficult to treat. Damage to one of the structures conducting the auditory information to the inner ear causes conduction deafness, which is easier to treat.

To explain how we perceive pitch, two theories are necessary. We can perceive a fairly large range of frequencies, 20 to 20,000 Hz. Place theory, which assumes that there are specific locations along the basilar membrane correlated with each frequency, explains how we hear high pitches (frequencies above 5,000 Hz). Frequency theory, which assumes that the firing rate of the hair cells mimics the incoming frequency information, explains how we hear low pitches (frequencies less than 500 Hz). Frequency theory (with the addition of the volley principle) and place theory both operate to give us better pitch perception for moderate pitches (frequencies from 500 to 5,000 Hz).

ConceptCheck | 2

> Explain the difference between nearsightedness and farsightedness with respect to focusing problems.

> Explain what opponent-process theory would predict that you would see if you stared for a minute at a flag with alternating yellow and white stripes and a rectangular patch of green in the center and then looked at a white sheet of paper.

> Explain why longer sound waves lead to lower frequencies and shorter ones lead to higher frequencies.

> Explain why neither the place theory nor the frequency theory by itself can explain human perception of pitch from 20 to 20,000 Hz.

How We Make Sense of What We See

So far we have learned that sensory structures such as the eyes and ears are designed to receive and begin processing various aspects of stimuli from our external environment. These structures transduce the raw data from the environment into neural impulses that the brain can understand. This initial information gathering and recoding by the sensory structures is usually referred to as **sensation,** and the resulting interpretation by the brain, **perception.** These two processes, however, are not quite as distinct as their definitions make them sound. They work together in more of an interactive way. A consideration of bottom-up and top-down processing for visual perception should help you to understand this interaction. Following this discussion, we'll consider perceptual organization and constancy, two processes essential for bringing order to incoming visual information. Last, we'll discuss distance perception, how the brain manages to give us the third dimension of depth in our perception of the world.

sensation The initial information gathering and recoding by the sensory structures.

perception The interpretation by the brain of sensory information.

Bottom-up Processing and Top-down Processing

Perception is the product of bottom-up and top-down processing. **Bottom-up processing** refers to the processing of incoming sensory input as it travels up from the sensory structures to the brain. It is called bottom-up because it is coming from the senses up to the brain. Bottom-up processing starts with the transduction of the incoming sensory signals. You can think of bottom-up processing as bringing the sensory input from the environment to the brain to be interpreted. However, the perceptual systems in the brain do not just randomly search through billions of possibilities to recognize the sensory input that is sent up. The search is greatly narrowed by **top-down processing**—the brain's use of

bottom-up processing The processing of incoming sensory information as it travels up from the sensory structures to the brain.

top-down processing The brain's use of knowledge, beliefs, and expectations to interpret sensory information.

▲ **Figure 3.9 | Perceptual Organization and Top-down Processing |** Do you see a meaningful object in this figure? There is one. It is a Dalmatian dog sniffing the ground. Can you find it? To do so, your perceptual top-down processing mechanisms will have to organize some of the features of the figure to match your knowledge of what such a dog looks like. If you are having trouble locating the Dalmatian, it is outlined for you at the end of the chapter. Once you see it, you won't have any difficulty seeing it the next time. Your top-down processing mechanisms will know how to organize the features so you perceive it.

knowledge, beliefs, and expectations to interpret the sensory information. It is referred to as top-down because it is coming from the top (the brain) back down to the sensory structures. To understand the difference between these two types of processing, think about listening to someone speak in a language that is foreign to you. You have bottom-up processing in that you hear the sounds. You cannot interpret this sensory input, however, because you do not have top-down processing (comprehension of the foreign language is not part of your knowledge base).

To further your understanding of these two types of processing, look at Figure 3.9. Do you see a meaningful pattern? If not, then your top-down processing is letting you down. There's a Dalmatian dog sniffing the ground. The dog's head is in the very center of the figure. To see it, your top-down processing has to organize various features in the figure successfully to fit your knowledge of what such a dog looks like. Once your brain does this, you won't have trouble seeing it the next time you look at this figure. You'll have the necessary top-down processing. If you are having trouble locating the Dalmatian, it is outlined for you at the end of this chapter.

The subjective nature of perception is due to this top-down processing. Our past experiences, beliefs, and expectations bias our interpretations of sensory input. Perceptual set and the use of contextual information in perception are two good examples of this biasing effect of top-down processing. **Perceptual set** occurs when we interpret an ambiguous stimulus in terms of how our past experiences have "set" us to perceive it. Our top-down processing biases our interpretation so that we're not even aware of the ambiguity. Let's consider how we perceive close plays in sporting events. Don't we usually see them in favor of "our" team? We are set by past experiences to see them in this biased way. This means that

perceptual set The interpretation of ambiguous sensory information in terms of how our past experiences have set us to perceive it.

▲ **Figure 3.10** | **A Context Effect on Perception** |
The interpretations of the ambiguous characters composing the second item in the first series and the fourth item in the second series are determined by the context created by the items on each side of them. In the first series, these items are letters so the interpretation of the ambiguous characters is a letter, B. In the second series, the items are numbers so the interpretation is a number, 13. (Adapted from Coren, Ward, & Enns, 2004, used by permission of John Wiley & Sons, Inc.)

A, B, C, D, E, F

10, 11, 12, 13, 14

past experiences guide our perception with top-down processing. In other words, we see it "our way."

Contextual effects are even stronger examples of top-down processing guiding perception. A **contextual effect** on perception occurs when we use the present context of sensory input to determine its meaning. Figure 3.10 shows a simple example of such contextual effects. Most people see the top line of characters as the alphabetic sequence A, B, C, D, E, F, and the second line as the numeric sequence 10, 11, 12, 13, 14. But if we now look at the characters creating the B and the 13, they are the same in each case. The context created by each line (alphabetic versus numeric) determined our interpretation. If surrounded by letters, the characters were interpreted as the letter B; if surrounded by numbers, the characters were interpreted as the number 13.

Context is a crucial contributor to perception. Without contextual information, the brain may not be able to decide upon an interpretation. What about the following characters: IV? They could be alphabetical (the letters I and V) or numeric (the Roman numeral for 4). Inserted into a sentence with other words, such as "Jim was in the hospital and hooked up to an IV," we would perceive them as letters. However, if they were inserted into the sentence, "Edward IV was the King of England in the fifteenth century," we would perceive their numerical meaning. The addition of contextual information provides top-down processing that allows the brain to resolve such ambiguities in normal perception.

Perceptual Organization and Perceptual Constancy

Perceptual organization and constancy are essential processes for bringing order to the incoming sensory input. Let's consider perceptual organization first. To be interpreted, the bits of incoming sensory data must be organized into meaningful wholes—shapes and forms. Some German psychologists working in the early part of the twentieth century developed many principles that explain how the brain automatically organizes visual input into meaningful holistic objects. Because the German word *gestalt* translates as "organized whole," these psychologists became known as Gestalt psychologists. To the Gestalt psychologists, these organized wholes are more than just the sum of their parts. A good example of this is stroboscopic movement, the perceptual creation of motion from a rapidly presented series of slightly

contextual effect The use of the present context of sensory information to determine its meaning.

▲ **Figure 3.11** | An Example of Figure-Ground Ambiguity | Do you see a white vase or two blue facial silhouettes looking at each other? You can see both, but only one at a time. When you switch your perception from one to the other, your brain is switching how the input is organized with respect to figure and ground. When you see a vase, the vase is the object; but when you see the two faces, the vase becomes the background.

varying images. For example, we see smooth motion when watching a movie, but in actuality there are only still picture frames being shown rapidly in succession. The motion we perceive emerges from the parts, the still frames, but is not present in them. To explain how we organize our visual input into holistic objects, Gestalt psychologists proposed many different organizational principles. We will consider two major ones—the figure-and-ground principle and the principle of closure.

Gestalt psychologists developed a basic rule for perceptual organization, the **figure-and-ground principle**—the brain organizes the sensory input into a figure or figures (the center of attention) and ground (the less distinct background). To get a better understanding of this principle, let us examine the image in Figure 3.11. This reversible figure-ground pattern was introduced by Danish Gestalt psychologist Edgar Rubin in 1915. What is the figure and what is the ground? These keep changing. We see a vase as a white object on a colored background, but then we see two silhouettes facing each other on a white background. In this case, the brain keeps switching its figure and ground organization for these sensory data. This is called a reversible pattern because the figure and ground reverse in the two possible interpretations. What is figure in one interpretation becomes the background in the other. Without any context, top-down processing cannot determine which interpretation is the correct one.

▮ **figure-and-ground principle** The Gestalt perceptual organizational principle that the brain organizes sensory information into a figure or figures (the center of attention) and ground (the less distinct background).

The ambiguous vase-silhouettes illustration helps us to understand the figure-and-ground principle, but ambiguity can also be due to the possibility of more than one object on the same background. The features of the object may allow more than one interpretation. A classic example of such an ambiguity is given in Figure 3.12 (page 112). Do you see an old woman or a young woman?

▲ **Figure 3.12 | An Example of an Organizational Perceptual Ambiguity |** Do you see the head and shoulders of an old woman or a young woman? If you're having trouble seeing the old woman, she has a large nose, which is located below and to the left of the center of the figure. The old woman's large nose is the chin and jaw of the younger woman. Now can you see both of them? Because there is no contextual information to determine a correct interpretation, your perception will keep switching from one interpretation to the other.

Wikipedia

Wikipedia

▲ **Figure 3.13 | Two More Organizational Perceptual Ambiguities |** On the left is a young/old woman ambiguity taken from a German postcard from 1888. The ambiguity on this puzzle card is like the one in Figure 3.12. Can you see both the young woman and the old woman? Their head positions are just like those in Figure 3.12. The old woman's big nose is the chin and jaw of the younger woman. On the right is a similar perceptual ambiguity but that allows the perception of both a young man and an old man. If you're having difficulty seeing both men, the old man's big nose is the chin and jaw of the younger man just like in the ambiguous women's version. The two men, however, are facing to the right and not to the left like the two women.

The young woman is looking back over her right shoulder, and the old woman's chin is down on her chest. Actually, depending upon how you organize the features, you can see both, but not simultaneously. If you are able to see both, your top-down processing will keep switching your perception because there is no contextual information to determine which interpretation is correct.

This young/old woman organizational ambiguity is often credited to British cartoonist W. E. Hill who published it in a humor magazine in 1915, but it appears that Hill adapted it from an original concept that was popular throughout the world on postcards and trading cards in the nineteenth century. The earliest known depiction of the young/old woman ambiguity is on an anonymous German postcard from 1888 shown on the left in Figure 3.13 (Weisstein, 2009). Can you perceive both the young woman and the old woman? Having identified them in Hill's illustration should have facilitated their perception on this card. As in Hill's illustration, the old woman's large nose is the chin and lower jaw of the younger woman. Botwinick (1961) created the male version of this figure (shown on the right in Figure 3.13) and entitled it "Husband and Father-in-Law" because the title of Hill's female ambiguous figure was "Wife and Mother-in-Law." If you're having trouble perceiving the two men, the older man's big nose (like the older woman's big nose) is the chin and lower jaw of the younger man; but the two men are facing in the opposite direction of the two women in Hill's illustration.

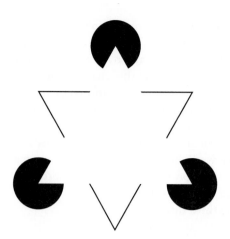

▲ **Figure 3.14** | An Example of a Subjective Contour | Does there appear to be a very bright triangle overlying three black circles and another triangle? This brighter-appearing triangle isn't really there. It is a subjective contour created by your brain in its perception of the three black circles with a chunk missing (the three Pac Man–like characters). To demonstrate that this overlying brighter triangle is truly not there, cover up everything in the display but the horizontal blank center. When you do this, you will not see any difference in level of brightness across the horizontal center of the display. If the whiter triangle were really there, you would see differences in brightness.

Another important Gestalt perceptual organizational principle is **closure,** which refers to the tendency to complete (close) incomplete figures to form meaningful objects. You've already seen some examples of closure in Figures 3.9 and 3.10. Closure was used to perceive the Dalmatian dog in Figure 3.9 (page 109) and to perceive the ambiguous characters in Figure 3.10 (page 110) as the letter B in the alphabetic context. In order to close a figure, we use top-down knowledge. Sometimes, however, the brain goes too far in using closure and creates figures where none exist. Such figures are called **subjective contours**—lines or shapes that are perceived to be present but do not really exist (Kanizsa, 1976). The white triangle that seems to be overlying three black circles and another triangle in Figure 3.14 is a subjective contour. Only three 45° angles and three black circles with a chunk missing are present. In perceiving these stimuli, the brain creates an additional object, the second triangle, by filling in the missing parts of the sides of this triangle; but this triangle doesn't really exist. The caption for Figure 3.14 explains how to demonstrate that the overlying triangle is really not there. Because 4-month-old infants also see such subjective contours (Ghim, 1990), it appears that our brains are hardwired to make sense of missing information by using top-down processing to fill in what should be there (Hood, 2009).

In addition to being able to organize and group sensory input to form meaningful objects, the brain must be able to maintain some type of constancy in its perception of the outside world, and it does. **Perceptual constancy** refers to the perceptual stability of the size, shape, brightness, and color for familiar objects seen at varying distances, different angles, and under different lighting conditions. These various types of constancy are referred to as size, shape, brightness, and color constancy, respectively. The retinal images for familiar objects change under different visual conditions such as different viewing angles or distances. For example, the size of a car doesn't shrink in our perception as it drives away. The

closure The Gestalt perceptual organizational principle that the brain completes (closes) incomplete figures to form meaningful objects.

subjective contour A line or shape that is perceived to be present but does not really exist. The brain creates it during perception.

perceptual constancy The perceptual stability of the size, shape, brightness, and color for familiar objects seen at varying distances, different angles, and under different lighting conditions.

size of its retinal image shrinks, but its size in our perception doesn't change. The brain adjusts our perceptions in accordance with what we have learned about the outside world. We know that the car's size doesn't change and realize that it is just farther away from us. Perceptual constancy must override this changing sensory input to maintain an object's normal size, shape, brightness, and color in our perception of the object. Perceptual constancy is a very adaptive aspect of visual perception. It brings order and consistency to our view of the world.

Perceptual organization and perceptual constancy are essential processes in perception. Without them, our perceptions would be meaningless fragments in a constant state of flux. Constancy and organization bring meaning and order to them. However, neither of these aspects explains another crucial part of visual perceptual processing—how we perceive the third dimension: depth.

I have no depth perception. Is there a cop standing on the corner, or do you have a tiny person in your hair?

Dan Piraro, reprinted with permission of King Features Syndicate.

Depth Perception

Depth perception involves the judgment of the distance of objects from us. The brain uses many different sources of relevant information or cues to make judgments of distance. These cues may require both eyes (binocular cues) or only one eye (monocular cues).

The major binocular cue is retinal disparity. To understand retinal disparity, first consider that our two eyes are not in the same place on our face. Each eye (retina) takes in a slightly different view of the world. The difference (disparity) between these two views of each retina provides information about the distance of an object from us. It allows the brain to triangulate the distance from us. The **retinal disparity** cue refers to the fact that as the disparity (difference) between the two retinal images increases, the distance from us decreases.

To understand this, hold up your right hand in front of you and form a fist but extend your index finger upward. If you hold it stationary and focus on it, and now close one eye, and then rapidly open it and close the other one a few times, your finger will appear to move. If you now move the finger closer to you and repeat the rapid closing and opening of the eyes one at a time, again, the finger appears to move, but now much more because the retinal views of the finger are more disparate. When right in front of your eyes, you see maximal movement because the disparity between the two retinal images is at its maximum.

There are several monocular cues, but we will discuss only a couple of them so that you have some understanding of how such cues work. **Linear perspective** refers to the fact that as parallel lines recede away from us, they appear to converge—the greater the distance, the more they converge. For example, think about looking down a set of railroad tracks or a highway.

depth perception Our ability to perceive the distance of objects from us.

retinal disparity A binocular depth cue referring to the fact that as the disparity (difference) between the two retinal images of an object increases, the distance of the object from us decreases.

linear perspective A monocular depth cue referring to the fact that as parallel lines recede away from us, they appear to converge—the greater the distance, the more they seem to converge. Sometimes referred to as perspective convergence.

The tracks and the two sides of the road appear to converge as they recede away from us. Because convergence is involved, this cue is sometimes referred to as perspective convergence. Another monocular cue that is easy to understand is **interposition**—if one object partially blocks our view of another, we perceive it as closer. Near objects partially overlap farther ones.

interposition A monocular depth cue referring to the fact that if one object partially blocks our view of another, we perceive it as closer to us.

Monocular cues, binocular cues, and various distance-judging principles the brain uses are normally valid distance indicators. However, sometimes these cues and principles lead the brain to create misperceptions. We refer to such misperceptions as illusions—misperceptions of reality. Two illusions are illustrated in Figure 3.15. The first is called the Ponzo illusion because it was first demonstrated by the Italian psychologist Mario Ponzo in 1913. The two horizontal bars are identical in size, but the top one appears larger. The other illusion is the Terror Subterra illusion (Shepard, 1990). The pursuing monster (the higher one) looks larger than the pursued monster, but the two monsters are identical in size. In addition to this size illusion, the identical faces of the two monsters are sometimes misperceived as expressing different emotions, such as rage in the pursuer and fear in the pursued monster. How are distance cues involved in these misperceptions of size in these two illusions?

(a) **(b)**

▲ **Figure 3.15** | **The Ponzo and Terror Subterra Illusions** | (a) The two red bars in the Ponzo illusion are identical in size. However, the top bar appears to be larger. (b) The two monsters in the Terror Subterra illusion are identical in size, but the pursuing monster (the top one) appears to be larger. To convince yourself that the two bars and the two monsters are identical, trace one of the bars (monsters) on a thin sheet of paper and then slide the tracing over the other bar (monster). Both illusions seem to be caused by the brain's misinterpretation of the relative distance from us of the two bars in (a) and the two monsters in (b). See the text for the complete explanation.

To see how distance cues are involved in these illusions, we must first consider how the brain relates the retinal image size of an object to the object's distance from us. As an object gets farther away from us, its size on the retina decreases. This is simple geometry, and the brain uses this geometric principle in creating our perception of the object. Now consider the situation in which two objects have equal retinal image sizes, but distance cues indicate to the brain that one of the objects is farther away. What would the brain conclude from this information? Using the principle relating retinal image size to distance, it would conclude that the object farther away must be larger. This is the only way that its retinal image size could be equal to that of the object closer to us. Thus, the brain enlarges the size of the more distant object in our perception of the objects. However, if the cues provided incorrect distance information and the objects were really equidistant from us, then we would see a misperception, an illusion. The brain incorrectly enlarged the object that it had mistakenly judged to be farther away. This is comparable to something we have experienced in working math problems: plug an incorrect value into an equation and get the problem wrong. This is essentially what the brain is doing when it uses incorrect information about distance, leading to a mistake in perception. It is important to realize that our brain's computing of the retinal image size and distance from us of objects is done at the unconscious level of processing. We are privy only at a conscious perceptual level to the product of our brain's calculations.

Now let's apply this explanation to our sample illusions. Think about the Ponzo illusion shown in Figure 3.15a (page 115). If this illusion is due to the brain's using incorrect distance information about the two horizontal lines, which cue that we described is responsible? That's right—linear perspective. The convergence of the railroad tracks normally indicates increasing distance. Given this cue information, the brain incorrectly assumes that the top bar is farther away. Because the two horizontal bars are the same size and truly equidistant from us, they are the same size on our retinas. Because their retinal images are of equal size but the brain thinks that the bars are at varying distances from us, it incorrectly distorts the top bar (the one assumed to be farther away) to be larger in our perception, or, should I say, misperception.

The Terror Subterra illusion shown in Figure 3.15b (page 115) can be explained in the same way. Monocular depth cues, mainly linear perspective, lead the brain to judge the pursuing monster to be farther away. Given that the retinal image sizes of the two monsters are equal because the two monsters are identical and equidistant from us and that the pursuing monster is incorrectly judged to be farther away, the brain enlarges the pursuing monster in our conscious perception, resulting in the illusion. As in the Ponzo illusion, the brain applies the valid principle relating retinal image size to the distance of objects from us, but uses incorrect distance information and thus creates a misperception.

The Müller-Lyer illusion depicted in Figure 3.16(a) is another example of an illusion created by the brain misapplying the geometry relating retinal image

(a)

(b)

▲ **Figure 3.16 | The Müller-Lyer Illusion |** (a) The two vertical line segments are equal in length. However, the one with the arrow feather endings on the left appears longer than the one with the arrowhead endings on the right. (b) Like the illusions in Figure 3.15, this illusion is created by the brain misapplying the geometry relating the retinal image size of objects and their distance from us. Based on its experiences with receding and projecting corners as illustrated here, our brain mistakenly thinks that the line with arrow feather endings is a receding corner and thus farther from us than the line with arrowhead endings, which our brain thinks is a projecting corner. Because the retinal images of the two lines are identical, the brain incorrectly lengthens the arrow feather line in our conscious perception.

size to distance from us (Gregory, 1968). As in the other two illusions, the brain mistakenly thinks that the line on the left with arrow feather endings is farther away than the line on the right with arrowhead endings. Why? In this case, the brain is using a relationship between distance and different types of corners that it has learned from its past perceptual experience. The line with arrow feather endings has the appearance of a corner that is receding away from us (like the corners where two walls meet in a room), while the line with arrowhead endings has the appearance of a corner that is jutting out toward us (like the corners where two sides of a building meet). These two types of corners are illustrated in Figure 3.16(b). Thus, based on its past experience with such corners, the brain believes that the line with arrow feather endings is farther away.

However, in reality, the line with the arrow feather endings is not farther away. The two vertical lines are identical in length and equidistant from us; therefore, their two retinal images are identical. Given the identical retinal images and the incorrect judgment about relative distance, the brain incorrectly enlarges the line with arrow feather endings so that we perceive it as being longer. In support of this explanation, cross-cultural researchers have found that people who live in physical environments without such distance-indicating corners are far less susceptible to seeing the illusion (Segall, Campbell, & Herskovits, 1963, 1966; Stewart, 1973).

The Turning the Tables illusion in Figure 3.1 (page 85) also arises because our brain gives us a three-dimensional interpretation of a two-dimensional drawing (Shepard, 1990). Perspective cues indicate that the long side of the table on the left goes back in depth whereas the long side of the table on the right is more nearly at right angles to our line of sight. Thus, if the table on the left goes back in depth, the brain will think that its retinal image must be foreshortened (appear shorter than it really is) because this is what happens in true three-dimensional viewing. The fact the retinal images of the two tabletops, however, are identical in length thus implies that the real length of the table on the left must be greater than the real length of the table on the right (and vice versa for the short sides of the two tables given their depth interpretations by the brain). Because these inferences about orientation, depth, and length are made automatically by the brain, we remain powerless to eliminate the illusion even though we know that the tabletops are identical. The drawing of the tables automatically triggers the brain to make a three-dimensional interpretation, and we cannot choose to see the drawing as what it is, a pattern of lines on a flat piece of paper.

The moon illusion can also be explained in a similar way (Restle, 1970). The illusion is that the moon appears to be larger on the horizon than when it is overhead at its zenith. But the moon is the same size and at the same distance from us whether it is on the horizon or overhead. This means that the moon's larger size on the horizon has to be an illusion. The objects near the horizon lead

Paul Souders/The Image Bank/Getty Images

The Moon Illusion I The moon on the horizon appears much larger than it does when it is overhead, higher up in the sky, but this is an illusion. The moon is the same size and remains the same distance from us regardless of where it is in the sky. Objects near the horizon lead the brain to think that the horizon moon is farther away than when it is overhead, so the brain mistakenly enlarges its size in our perception because the retinal images of the horizon and overhead moons are the same size.

the brain to think that the moon is farther away when it is near the horizon than when it is overhead. Because the retinal images of the moon at these two locations are the same and the brain mistakenly thinks that the horizon moon is farther away, it distorts the moon's size to appear much larger in our perception than when it is overhead. It really isn't, and it is easy to see that this is the case.

To make the moon on the horizon shrink, we can roll up a sheet of cardboard into a viewer and look at the moon through this viewer so that we only see the moon and not any of the objects on the horizon. The moon will appear to shrink dramatically in size because the brain will no longer be led astray in its judgment of distance for the horizon moon. In creating such size misperceptions, the brain is using a valid principle, but faulty information about the relative distance. The overall result (our perception) is incorrect. In summary, the distance cues and principles the brain uses to give us an accurate view of the external world work almost all of the time, but these same cues and principles sometimes cause misperceptions.

Section Summary

In this section, we looked at visual perception in more detail. Bottom-up and top-down processing are both necessary for smooth and efficient perception. While top-down processing is adaptive, as illustrated by perceptual constancy, it is also responsible for the subjective nature of perception. Perceptual bias and contextual perceptual effects are good examples of how our past experiences, beliefs, and expectations guide our interpretation of the world.

Perceptual organization and perceptual constancy are essential processes for giving order to incoming sensory input. Gestalt psychologists proposed many principles that guide the organization of sensory input into meaningful holistic objects, such as the figure-and-ground and closure principles. In addition to organizing the sensory input into meaningful objects, the brain must maintain constancy in its perception of the world. To achieve perceptual constancy, the brain uses top-down processing to change sensory input to maintain an object's normal size, shape, brightness, and color in our perception of the object.

Depth perception (the judgment of the distance of objects from us) is a crucial part of visual perception. To judge depth, the brain uses information from binocular cues, such as retinal disparity, and monocular cues, such as linear perspective and interposition. The brain's perception of object size is related to its distance from us. As an object gets farther away from us, its size on our retina decreases. However, sometimes the brain applies this geometric principle relating retinal image size to distance and creates a misperception (an illusion). The Ponzo, Terror Subterra, Müller-Lyer, Turning the Tables, and moon illusions are good examples of such misapplication. In each case, the brain incorrectly judges that the two objects involved in the illusion, which have equal retinal image sizes, are at varying distances, and so mistakenly makes the object judged to be farther away larger in our perception.

ConceptCheck | 3

> Explain why perceptual processing requires both bottom-up and top-down processing.

> Explain how the top-down processing involved in context effects on perception is similar to that involved in using the Gestalt organizational principle of closure.

> Explain why seeing one of your professors in a local grocery store makes it more difficult to recognize her.

> Explain why the brain's application of the geometric relationship between retinal image size of an object and its distance from us leads the brain to create the Ponzo, Müller-Lyer, and moon illusions.

Study Guide

Chapter Key Terms

You should know the definitions of the following key terms from the chapter. They are listed in the order in which they appear in the chapter. For those you do not know, return to the relevant section of the chapter to learn them. When you think that you know all of the terms, complete the matching exercise based on these key terms.

absolute threshold	cones	perception
signal detection theory	fovea	bottom-up processing
difference threshold	dark adaptation	top-down processing
Weber's law	trichromatic theory	perceptual set
Stevens's power law	additive mixtures	contextual effect
sensory adaptation	subtractive mixtures	figure-and-ground principle
wavelength	complementary colors	closure
amplitude	opponent-process theory	subjective contour
frequency	hair cells	perceptual constancy
transduction	nerve deafness	depth perception
accommodation	conduction deafness	retinal disparity
nearsightedness	place theory	linear perspective
farsightedness	frequency theory	interposition
retina	volley principle	
rods	sensation	

Key Terms Exercise

Identify the correct key term for each of the following definitions. The answers to this exercise follow the answers to the Concept Checks at the end of the chapter.

1. The focusing of light waves from objects of different distances directly on the retina.

2. A visual problem in which the light waves from nearby objects are focused behind the retina, blurring the images of these objects.

3. A theory of color vision which assumes that there are three types of cones, each activated only by wavelength ranges of light corresponding roughly to blue, green, and red.

4. The brain's use of knowledge, beliefs, and expectations to interpret sensory information.

5. The Gestalt perceptual organizational principle that the brain completes incomplete figures to form meaningful objects.

6. Our sensitivity to unchanging and repetitious stimuli disappears over time.

7. Hearing loss created by damage to one of the structures in the ear responsible for carrying the auditory information to the inner ear.

_____

8. The number of times a waveform cycles in 1 second.

_____

9. The perceived magnitude of a stimulus is equal to its actual physical intensity raised to a constant power, and this constant power is different for each type of sensory judgment.

_____

10. The minimum difference between two sensory stimuli detected 50 percent of the time.

_____

11. Wavelengths of light that when added together produce white.

_____

12. A theory of pitch perception which assumes that the frequency of the sound wave is mimicked by the firing rate of the entire basilar membrane.

_____

13. A line or shape that is perceived to be present but does not really exist. The brain creates it during perception.

_____

14. The perceptual stability of the size, shape, brightness, and color for familiar objects seen at varying distances, different angles, and under different lighting conditions.

_____

15. The process by which the rods and cones, through internal chemical changes, become more and more sensitive to light in dim light conditions.

_____

Practice Test Questions

The following are practice multiple-choice test questions on some of the chapter content. The answers are given after the Key Terms Exercise answers at the end of the chapter. If you guessed or incorrectly answered a question, restudy the relevant section of the chapter.

1. The amount of energy in a sensory stimulus detected 50 percent of the time is called the _____.
   a. difference threshold
   b. absolute threshold
   c. false alarm rate
   d. miss rate

2. If a person is using a very strict criterion for a signal detection task, the false alarm rate will be _____, and the miss rate will be _____.
   a. high; high
   b. high; low
   c. low; high
   d. low; low

3. According to Weber's law, if $c = 1/50$, then the difference threshold for a standard stimulus of 100 units would be _____.
   a. 1
   b. 2
   c. 5
   d. 10

4. Red wavelengths of light are _____, and violet wavelengths of light are _____.
   a. long; long
   b. long; short
   c. short; long
   d. short; short

5. The rods in the retina are responsible for _____ vision, and the cones are responsible for _____ vision.
   a. color; dim light
   b. bright light; dim light
   c. color; bright light
   d. dim light; color

6. According to the opponent-process theory of color vision, if you stared at a blue circle for a while and then looked at a white surface, you would see a circular _____ afterimage.

   a. blue
   b. green
   c. yellow
   d. black

7. Transduction of sound waves into neural impulses is performed by the_____.

   a. eardrum
   b. oval window
   c. malleus, incus, and stapes
   d. hair cells in the basilar membrane

8. The best explanation for how we perceive low pitches (< 500 Hz) is the _____ theory, and the best explanation for how we perceive high pitches ($> 5,000$ Hz) is the _____ theory.

   a. place; place
   b. place; frequency
   c. frequency; place
   d. frequency; frequency

9. Perceptual set is a good example of _____.

   a. the figure-ground principle
   b. perceptual constancy
   c. bottom-up processing
   d. top-down processing

10. Which of the following is a binocular depth cue?

    a. linear perspective
    b. interposition
    c. retinal disparity
    d. all of the above

11. What is the purpose of transduction?

    a. increasing the intensity of a stimulus so it is easier for the brain to detect
    b. translating physical energy into neural signals that the brain can understand
    c. determining whether or not a stimulus is detectable
    d. integrating visual signals with auditory signals

12. Damage to the hair cells in the cochlea causes _____ deafness, and _____ occurs when light waves from distant objects come into focus in front of the retina.

    a. nerve; nearsightedness
    b. conduction; nearsightedness
    c. nerve; farsightedness
    d. conduction; farsightedness

13. Even though the image of your dog on your retina changes as your dog runs to fetch a stick, you do not perceive your dog as getting smaller. Which process of perception explains this phenomenon?

    a. perceptual set
    b. perceptual constancy
    c. dark adaptation
    d. accommodation

14. Perceiving either a vase or two facial silhouettes looking at each other was used to illustrate the Gestalt principle of _____; perceiving two ambiguous characters numerically as 13 or alphabetically as the letter B was used to illustrate_____.

    a. closure; subjective contours
    b. figure and ground; contextual effects
    c. closure; contextual effects
    d. figure and ground; subjective contours

15. Although Henry's watchband was bothering him when he first put it on, a short while later he did not even notice he was wearing it. This illustrates _____.

    a. accommodation
    b. sensory adaptation
    c. subliminal perception
    d. perceptual constancy

Chapter Concept Check Answers

Concept Check | 1

- The two types of threshold were given statistical definitions because the experimental data did not permit an absolute definition. There was no none-to-all point of change in the results that were observed when psychophysical researchers attempted to measure the absolute and difference thresholds.

- In switching from a very lax to a very strict decision criterion, a person's false alarm rate would go down and the miss rate would go up. These changes would be due to the person's changing from saying "yes" most of the time to saying "no" most of the time.

- A really large constant fraction in Weber's law would indicate that difference judgments for that type of sensory judgment are not very good; a larger proportion of the standard stimulus is necessary for a difference to be perceived.

- It is adaptive for the exponent to be greater than 1 for dangerous physical energy forms because we would then perceive weak input of that type to be much more intense than it really is. This would possibly allow us to escape before being exposed to more intense energy of that type.

Concept Check | 2

- In nearsightedness, we have difficulty viewing distant objects because their images come into focus in front of the retina; in farsightedness, we have difficulty viewing near objects because their images come into focus behind the retina. The focusing problems could be due to defects in the lens or the shape of the eyeball.

- After staring at the flag with alternating yellow and white stripes and a block of green in the middle, the yellow, white, and green parts of the three opponent-process systems would be fatigued and thus unable to oppose the blue, black, and red parts of these systems when you stared at the white sheet of paper. Thus, instead of seeing white, you would see an afterimage of a flag with alternating blue and black stripes and a block of red in the middle. Once the opposing parts of the three systems recovered, the flag afterimage would disappear, and you would see the white surface.

- Longer wavelengths lead to lower frequencies because such wavelengths can only cycle a small number of times per second. Similarly, shorter wavelengths lead to higher frequencies because they can cycle more times per second.

- Neither theory by itself can explain how we hear the entire range of pitches, 20 to 20,000 Hz, because each theory is unable to explain pitch perception for a particular part of this range. Place theory cannot explain how we perceive low pitches (< 500 Hz) because there are no places of maximal firing along the basilar membrane for these frequencies. The firing rate of the entire membrane mimics these frequencies. Similarly, frequency theory cannot explain how we perceive high pitches, those greater than 5,000 Hz, because there is a physiological limit on the firing rate for cells. Even if the volley principle is employed, this limit is about 5,000 times per second. This means that the hair cells could not generate firing rates to match the high frequencies.

Concept Check | 3

- Perceptual processing requires both types of processing because without bottom-up processing you would have nothing to perceive and without top-down processing you would have no knowledge to use to interpret the bottom-up input.

- The similarity is that, in both cases, the brain uses top-down processing to complete the perception. In context effects, the brain uses the present context to complete the perception by determining what would be meaningful in that particular context. In closure, the brain uses the incomplete part of an object to determine what the remaining part should be in order for it to be a meaningful object.

- It is more difficult to recognize your professor because she is in a very different context. Your brain is thrown for a "perceptual loop" because she doesn't fit in this context (outside the classroom). This is why it takes your brain longer to find the relevant top-down knowledge.

- The retinal image sizes of the two objects in each case are equal because the two objects are actually equal in size and are equidistant from us. Available distance cues, however, lead the brain to believe mistakenly that one of the two objects in each case is farther away. Therefore, the brain enlarges the size of the object that it thinks is more distant because this would have to be the case in order for the geometric relationship between retinal image size and distance from us to hold. For example, in the Ponzo illusion, the linear perspective distance cue leads the brain to think that the top horizontal bar is farther away. Because the two horizontal bars have identical retinal image sizes, the brain then uses the geometric relationship and mistakenly creates an illusion by making the top bar larger in our perception.

Answers to Key Terms Exercise

1. accommodation
2. farsightedness
3. trichromatic theory
4. top-down processing
5. closure
6. sensory adaptation
7. conduction deafness
8. frequency

9. Stevens's power law
10. difference threshold
11. complementary colors
12. frequency theory
13. subjective contour
14. perceptual constancy
15. dark adaptation

Answers to Practice Test Questions

1. b; absolute threshold
2. c; low; high
3. b; 2
4. b; long; short
5. d; dim light; color
6. c; yellow
7. d; hair cells in the basilar membrane
8. c; frequency; place
9. d; top-down processing
10. c; retinal disparity
11. b; translating physical energy into neural signals that the brain can understand
12. a; nerve; nearsightedness
13. b; perceptual constancy
14. b; figure and ground; contextual effects
15. b; sensory adaptation

Now go back to Figure 3.9 on page 109, and you should easily see the dalmatian dog.

4 Learning

O ur ability to learn seems boundless. We continue to learn new things every day, and we continually use the products of our past learning. Our learning affects how we perceive, remember, think, and behave. In this chapter, we will focus on what psychologists have learned about how we learn.

In general, two types of psychologists—behavioral psychologists and cognitive psychologists—have studied learning, and they have gone about their research in very different ways. Behavioral psychologists have focused on the learning of associations through classical conditioning and operant conditioning. Classical conditioning involves learning associations between events in our environment, such as that the smell of the turkey roasting in the oven signals that a delicious meal will follow. Operant conditioning focuses on learning associations between our behavior and its environmental consequences, such as that additional studying usually leads to better grades. Cognitive psychologists studying learning are interested in the more complex type of learning involved in human memory—how we encode information into our memory system, store it over time, and later retrieve it for use. A cognitive psychologist would be interested in how you learn the information in this textbook and what type of study technique would lead to the best memory for this information.

In this chapter, we will first focus on what behavioral psychologists have discovered about learning associations through classical conditioning and operant conditioning. Then we will consider some of the biological constraints upon such learning and also begin a discussion of the cognitive approach to learning (covered in detail in the next chapter on how we remember).

Learning Through Classical Conditioning

Does the name "Pavlov" ring a bell? If you understand this really bad joke, then you are already somewhat familiar with **classical conditioning**—learning that one stimulus signals the arrival of another stimulus. A stimulus (plural: stimuli) is any sight, sound, smell, taste, or body sensation that a human or animal can perceive. You know from Chapter 1 that Pavlov's dogs salivated to the sound of a tone (the first stimulus) because they learned to expect food in their mouth (the second stimulus) after hearing the tone. This may not sound like the research of a Nobel Prize–winning scientist, but it was important work that had a great impact on our understanding of how we learn. Classical conditioning is sometimes referred to as Pavlovian conditioning because Pavlov was the first researcher to study this type of learning systematically. So, let's take a closer look at Pavlov's research to gain an understanding of classical conditioning and its importance in learning.

The Elements and Procedures of Classical Conditioning

Ivan Pavlov was a Russian physiologist who won a Nobel Prize in 1904 for his earlier work on the physiology of digestion. Pavlov studied the digestive processes of dogs. During

▌ **classical conditioning** Acquiring a new response (the conditioned response) to a previously neutral stimulus (the conditioned stimulus) that reliably signals the arrival of an unconditioned stimulus.

This is a photograph of Pavlov's experimental laboratory. Look at the dog's left cheek. Pavlov devised a surgical insert that diverted the dog's saliva to exit its cheek so it could be measured accurately.

these experiments, the dogs were strapped into harnesses and had tubes inserted in their cheeks to measure salivation, the initial step in the digestive process. Pavlov had cleverly found a way to divert the saliva so that it was excreted through the dogs' cheeks. As part of this research, the dogs were given food (meat powder) and then the amount of saliva was measured. During this research, Pavlov made an accidental discovery. He noticed that the dogs started to salivate before the meat powder was even put in their mouths. For example, the dogs salivated when they heard the footsteps of his assistants bringing the meat powder. Pavlov wanted to know why, and this became the focus of his research for the remainder of his career. So what exactly did he do?

Unconditioned stimulus (UCS) and unconditioned response (UCR). First, let's consider why the dogs salivated when the meat powder was put in their mouths. This is a reflexive response—when food is put in your mouth, you salivate. Dogs do it, I do it, you do it. This is called a **reflex**—a stimulus-response pair (food in the mouth and salivation) in which the stimulus automatically elicits the response. The reflexive stimulus (food in the mouth) that elicits the automatic response (salivation) is referred to as the **unconditioned stimulus (UCS),** and the response automatically elicited by the UCS is referred to as the **unconditioned response (UCR).** The key word is "unconditioned." This means that no learning was necessary for this stimulus (the food, in our example) to elicit the response (salivation, in our example). It's a naturally occurring reflex. Now let's examine how such reflexes are used to achieve conditioning.

Conditioned stimulus (CS) and conditioned response (CR). Pavlov began with a neutral stimulus, a stimulus that does not naturally elicit the to-be-conditioned response. Pavlov used various neutral stimuli, such as a tone generated by a tuning fork, a light, and a touch on the leg, in his conditioning research on dogs (Pavlov, 1927/1960). Before conditioning, his dogs did not automatically salivate to these stimuli. They had to learn (be conditioned) to do this. To achieve such conditioning, the neutral stimulus (for example, a tone) is presented just before the UCS (the food). What does "just before" mean? This can mean a few seconds, but the optimal time interval between the onsets of the two stimuli is usually very brief, only a half-second to 1 second (Mazur,

▌ **reflex** A stimulus-response pair in which the stimulus (the unconditioned stimulus) automatically elicits the response (the unconditioned response).

▌ **unconditioned stimulus (UCS)** The stimulus in a reflex that automatically elicits an unconditioned response.

▌ **unconditioned response (UCR)** The response in a reflex that is automatically elicited by the unconditioned stimulus.

1998). In addition, the two stimuli usually need to be paired together for several trials. Nevertheless, there are some exceptions in which classical conditioning can be obtained without a close temporal pairing of the CS and UCS and in only a small number of trials, sometimes only one. The primary exception is taste aversion, which we will discuss in the last section of this chapter when we discuss biological constraints on learning.

Once the conditioning occurs (signaled in Pavlov's research by the dog salivating to the sound of the tone before the meat powder is put into its mouth), the neutral stimulus is referred to as the **conditioned stimulus (CS).** This previously neutral stimulus (the tone) comes to elicit a new response (salivating) after repeated pairings with the unconditioned stimulus (meat powder in the dog's mouth). The learned response (salivating) to the conditioned stimulus (the tone) is called the **conditioned response (CR).** The conditioned response (salivating) is a preparatory response for the impending UCS (meat powder in the dog's mouth).

To firm up your understanding of the elements of classical conditioning, let's consider another example, conditioning of the eyeblink response, which is often used in classical conditioning research with humans. A neutral stimulus, such as a tone, is presented just before a mild puff of air to a person's eye (the UCS). Initially, an eyeblink (the UCR) occurs reflexively in response to the air puff (the UCS), but with repeated pairings of the tone followed shortly thereafter by the air puff, the previously neutral stimulus (the tone) becomes the conditioned stimulus (the CS) and now elicits a new response, an eyeblink (the CR), in advance of the air puff. In this case, the eyeblink serves as an adaptive, defensive response to the air puff.

Delayed and trace conditioning. The timing of the relationship of the CS and UCS is a critical factor in classical conditioning. The conditioned stimulus (the tone) is presented just before the UCS (the meat powder in Pavlov's experiments) because the conditioning involves learning that this stimulus is a reliable predictor for the arrival of the UCS (Rescorla, 1988). Thus, presenting the UCS before the CS (called backward conditioning) or presenting the UCS and CS at the same time (called simultaneous conditioning) typically leads to no conditioning or poor

conditioned stimulus (CS) The stimulus that comes to elicit a new response (the conditioned response) in classical conditioning.

conditioned response (CR) The response that is elicited by the conditioned stimulus in classical conditioning.

conditioning because the CS in these two cases would not be a good predictor of the UCS (Powell, Symbaluk, & MacDonald, (2002). The CS has to clearly predict the UCS by being presented first or conditioning usually will not occur. There are two ways to present the CS first: delayed and trace conditioning.

In **delayed conditioning,** the CS remains on until after the UCS is presented, so that the two stimuli occur at the same time. The tone would be turned on and not turned off until after the meat powder was placed in the dog's mouth. This procedure is called "delayed" because turning off (taking away) the CS is delayed until after the UCS starts. In **trace conditioning,** there is a period of time between turning off the CS and the onset of the UCS (called the trace interval), when neither stimulus is present. In Pavlov's case, this would mean turning the tone on and then off, waiting a brief period of time, and then putting the meat powder in the dog's mouth. For the association between stimuli to be learned, the animal or human (dog in Pavlov's case) must maintain a "memory trace" of the CS (the tone) to pair with the later-occurring UCS (the meat powder). This is why it is called trace conditioning.

Delayed conditioning is the most effective procedure for classical conditioning, but trace conditioning can be almost as effective if the trace interval between stimuli is very short (Powell, Symbaluk, & MacDonald, 2002). It also appears that for trace conditioning, processing by both the cerebellum and hippocampus is essential for successful conditioning whereas for delayed conditioning, only processing by the cerebellum is necessary (Clark & Squire, 1998). In trace conditioning, processing by the hippocampus is necessary to establish a memory trace of the CS so that it can be associated with the UCS following the trace interval (Bangasser, Waxler, Santollo, & Shors, 2006). In addition, it appears that delayed conditioning can be accomplished without conscious awareness of the temporal relationship between the CS and UCS, but trace conditioning cannot (Clark & Squire, 1998).

The entire classical conditioning process is diagrammed in Figure 4.1. Study the diagram to make sure you understand the four elements that are involved in classical conditioning—the UCS, UCR, CS (the former neutral stimulus), and CR. To ensure that you understand, next we'll consider another famous example of classical conditioning, the "Little Albert" study.

delayed conditioning A classical conditioning procedure in which the conditioned stimulus precedes the unconditioned stimulus and remains present until after the unconditioned stimulus is presented so that the two stimuli occur together.

trace conditioning A classical conditioning procedure in which the conditioned stimulus precedes the unconditioned stimulus but is removed before the unconditioned stimulus is presented so the two stimuli do not occur together.

The Little Albert study. John Broadus Watson, an American psychologist in the early part of the twentieth century, was the founder of behavioral psychology (Watson, 1913, 1919). He was very impressed with classical conditioning and its potential use to make psychology an objective science of behavior. To examine the possible role of such conditioning in human emotional responses such as fear, Watson and his research assistant, Rosalie Rayner, conducted a study

Before Conditioning

Unconditioned Stimulus (UCS)   elicits   Unconditioned Response (UCR)

Neutral Stimulus (NS)   Does not elicit to-be-conditioned response

During Conditioning Trials

Present   Neutral Stimulus (NS)   just before

Unconditioned Stimulus (UCS)   (which automatically elicits UCR)

After Conditioning

Conditioned Stimulus (CS; former NS)   elicits   Conditioned Response (CR)

▲ **Figure 4.1** I **The Elements of Classical Conditioning** I In classical conditioning, you start with a reflex—an unconditioned stimulus (UCS) that automatically elicits an unconditioned response (UCR). To condition a new response to a neutral stimulus, the neutral stimulus is presented just before the unconditioned stimulus. After several pairings, the neutral stimulus elicits a new response called the conditioned response (CR). The neutral stimulus is now referred to as the conditioned stimulus (CS).

on an infant named Albert (Watson & Rayner, 1920). When the conditioning phase of the study began, Albert was 11 months old.

Let's think about the Little Albert study in terms of the four elements of classical conditioning—UCS, UCR, CS, and CR. As a neutral stimulus, the researchers used a white laboratory rat. Albert was not afraid of the rat. In fact, when he saw the rat before the conditioning, he moved toward it and touched it. What was the reflex that Watson and Rayner used? While Albert was looking at the white rat, Watson quietly sneaked behind him with an iron bar and a hammer and clanged them together. Albert's reflexive response, the UCR, was the fear-avoidance response (crying and trying to crawl away) to this unexpected loud noise, the UCS. Watson and Rayner paired the sight of the white rat (the neutral stimulus that became the CS) with the unexpected loud noise (the UCS) several times until the sight of the white rat started eliciting the fear-avoidance response (crying and trying to crawl away from the rat). It took only seven pairings.

This study was unethical, of course. Psychologists would not be allowed to conduct such a study today. Ironically, however, at that time Watson was criticized more by animal rights activists for his research with rats than he was for the Little Albert study (Buckley, 1989). Are you wondering whatever became of Albert? Sadly, no one knows (Harris, 1979). We do know that Watson and Rayner did not decondition Little Albert's fear-avoidance response.

Archives of the History of American Psychology

Courtesy of Professor Benjamin Harris, University of Wisconsin–Parkside.

In the photograph on the left, Little Albert did not display any fear of the white rat before the classical conditioning trials but rather attempted to play with it. However, following the conditioning trials in which the sight of the white rat was paired with an unexpected loud noise, he acquired a fear response to the rat. In the second photograph, he is generalizing this conditioned fear response to a rabbit.

One of Watson's former students, Mary Cover Jones, demonstrated that such a fear *could* be deconditioned (Jones, 1924). She deconditioned a pre-existing fear of rabbits in a 3-year-old boy named Peter. In Chapter 10, we will discuss a behavioral therapy for treating fear disorders (called phobias) that is based upon Jones's work. In addition, Elsie Bregman in 1934 showed that there could be limits to conditioning such fear responses. In her study, she was unable to condition infants to fear inanimate objects such as wooden blocks and cloth curtains. These results suggest possible biological predispositions to learn certain fears more easily than others. We will return to this idea in the last section of this chapter in our discussion of biological constraints on learning.

It is important to realize that classical conditioning is not only involved in conditioning negative emotional responses such as fear, but can also be used to develop positive emotional responses to stimuli. For example, classical conditioning is used in advertising to condition positive attitudes and feelings toward products (Allen & Shimp, 1990; Grossman & Till, 1998; Olson & Fazio, 2001). Think about advertisements that pair celebrities with products. Pairing popular professional basketball players like Michael Jordan and LeBron James with Nike products in advertisements is a good example. Both of these athletes were paid millions of dollars for their Nike endorsements. Why? The advertisers attempt to use our positive feelings about these celebrities to condition positive responses to their products. The celebrity serves as the UCS, and the product as the CS. John Watson pioneered this type of advertising when he worked as a psychology consultant for the J. Walter Thompson advertising agency in New York following his dismissal from academics (Buckley, 1989). Watson was forced to leave the academic life after he had an extramarital affair with his research assistant on the Little Albert study, Rosalie Rayner.

General Learning Processes in Classical Conditioning

We have seen how classical conditioning works: A new, learned response (the CR) is elicited by the CS in preparation for the arrival of the UCS. This response learning is also referred to as **acquisition,** acquiring a new response—the CR to the CS. But what happens after acquisition? Will this new response (fear-avoidance in the Little Albert study) be generalized to other stimuli (say, white rabbits) that are similar to the CS (a white rat)? If so, can we learn to discriminate and respond this way only to specific stimuli (white rats)? Will this response (fear-avoidance) continue to occur when the CS (a white rat) is no longer paired with the UCS (the unexpected loud noise)? To answer such questions, we now turn to a discussion of the other general learning processes that follow acquisition in classical conditioning.

Extinction and spontaneous recovery. What do you think would happen to the CR if the UCS no longer followed the CS? Would the CR now be "unlearned"? Remember that in classical conditioning the CS reliably signals that the UCS is coming. If the CS no longer serves this function, then the CR is no longer necessary so it is no longer made. No preparation is needed because the UCS is no longer presented. For example, in Pavlov's work the dog would eventually stop salivating to the tone when the tone no longer signaled that the meat powder was coming. In the Little Albert study, Albert's fear of a white rat would have diminished after it no longer signaled that the loud, unexpected noise was coming. This unlearning process is called **extinction,** the diminishing of the CR when the UCS no longer follows the CS.

A visual comparison of the acquisition and extinction processes is given in Figure 4.2 (a and b, page 134). The strength of the CR increases during acquisition, but it decreases during extinction. Note, however, that during the extinction process, the CR mysteriously increases somewhat in strength following a rest interval. This is called **spontaneous recovery,** a partial recovery in strength of the CR following a break during extinction trials. As extinction continues, however, the recovery observed following the rest intervals continues to decrease until it is minimized. For example, the dog would salivate very little or not at all to the tone, and Albert would show little or no fear of the white rat. The spontaneous recovery that occurs during the extinction process indicates, as Pavlov had concluded, that the CR may not be totally lost during extinction, but only greatly weakened or inhibited. Research since Pavlov's time has demonstrated that this is indeed the case (Bouton, 1994; Rescorla, 1996).

Stimulus generalization and discrimination. In addition to acquisition, extinction, and spontaneous recovery, there are two other general learning processes involving the CR—stimulus generalization and discrimination. Let's consider generalization first. It's easy to understand. After acquisition of a CR (salivating) to a CS (a tone), we observe

acquisition (in classical conditioning) Acquiring a new response (the conditioned response) to the conditioned stimulus.

extinction (in classical conditioning) The diminishing of the conditioned response when the unconditioned stimulus no longer follows the conditioned stimulus.

spontaneous recovery (in classical conditioning) A partial recovery in strength of the conditioned response following a break during extinction training.

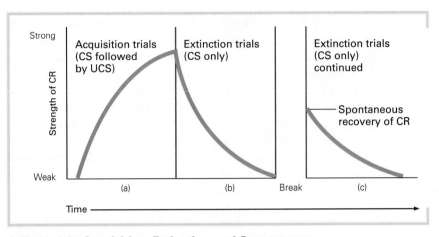

▲ **Figure 4.2** | **Acquisition, Extinction, and Spontaneous Recovery** | Panel (a) depicts the acquisition of the CR. Note that during acquisition, the UCS follows the CS on each trial. Acquisition of the CR is reflected in the increase in its strength across conditioning trials. Extinction is depicted in panel (b). On extinction trials, the UCS never follows the CS. This process is reflected in the decrease of the strength of the CR across extinction trials. Note, however, that when a break is taken during extinction training, there is a temporary partial recovery in strength of the CR following the break, depicted in panel (c). This partial recovery is called spontaneous recovery. The amount of recovery lessens as extinction training continues.

generalization. In **stimulus generalization,** stimuli similar to the CS elicit the CR. The more similar the stimulus is to the CS, the stronger the response will be. Generalization is an adaptive process. Classical conditioning would not be a very useful type of learning if it only allowed us to learn relationships between specific stimuli. If a dog bites you, isn't it more adaptive to generalize the fear-avoidance response to other dogs (especially dogs similar to the one that bit you)?

To understand generalization, let's consider Pavlov's research with dogs. Assume Pavlov classically conditioned a dog to give the salivary response to a tone with a pitch of 1000 Hz. (Remember from Chapter 3 that this represents a sound wave that cycles 1000 times per second.) To test for generalization, the CS (the 1000 Hz tone) and the other stimuli (tones with higher and lower frequencies) are presented, but the UCS (the meat powder) does not follow any of them. The strength of the CR (the amount of salivation) to each of these stimuli is measured. So what would happen if a 1025 Hz or a 975 Hz tone were presented? The dog would probably give a fairly strong salivary response to these tones because they are very similar to the original CS of 1000 Hz. But the strength of the CR (the amount of salivation) would go down as the generalization test tones get farther away from the original CS of 1000 Hz. This generalization function is illustrated in Figure 4.3. Ignore the discrimination function in the figure for now. We will discuss it shortly.

Notice how symmetric the generalization test results are around the original CS value (1000 Hz) in Figure 4.3. This is because the generalization test tones could be varied symmetrically in frequency above and below the original CS

stimulus generalization (in classical conditioning) The elicitation of the conditioned response to stimuli that are similar to the conditioned stimulus. The more similar the stimulus is to the conditioned stimulus, the stronger the response.

▲ **Figure 4.3** | **Stimulus Generalization and Discrimination** | These are idealized stimulus generalization and discrimination results following classical conditioning of the salivary response (CR) in dogs to a CS tone of 1000 Hz. The strength of the CR to generalization test stimuli (all tones except the 1000 Hz tone) decreases as the similarity of the test stimulus to the original CS decreases. These generalization responses, however, can be extinguished through discrimination training in which the UCS (food) only follows the 1000 Hz tone. The CR to each of the other tones will be extinguished except for the tones so similar to the 1000 Hz tone (975 Hz and 1025 Hz) that the dog does not perceive them as different.

tone. But think about the Little Albert study by Watson and Rayner. Their original CS was a white rat. What do you think they used to test for generalization? They used other animals—a rabbit, as we've seen, and a dog (neither was white)—but they also used some less similar inanimate objects, including a bearded Santa Claus mask, a sealskin coat, human hair, a package of white cotton, and some wooden blocks. The generalization stimuli did not vary symmetrically around the white rat, but the same pattern of generalization results were observed. As the generalization test stimuli became less similar to the CS (the white rat), the strength of the CR (the fear-avoidance response) decreased. The response to the other animals and the coat was stronger than the responses to the mask and hair. Similarly, the response to the white cotton was even less, and was nonexistent for the toy blocks.

Sometimes we overgeneralize and need to narrow our responding to a specific stimulus or smaller set of stimuli. In the case of the dog bite, we might overgeneralize and fear any dog. This wouldn't be rational, so we would need to learn to discriminate dogs that might bite us from those who would not. Such discrimination learning can be thought of as the opposite of generalization. Generalization leads to the CR being given to a broader set of stimuli; discrimination leads to the CR being given to a narrower set of stimuli. In classical conditioning, **stimulus discrimination** is the elicitation of the CR only by the CS or only by a small set of highly similar

stimulus discrimination (in classical conditioning) The elicitation of the conditioned response only by the conditioned stimulus or only by a small set of highly similar stimuli that includes the conditioned stimulus.

stimuli that includes the CS. In the dog bite example, this would be learning only to fear potentially dangerous dogs.

Discrimination training is used to teach stimulus discrimination. We will discuss the simplest case—learning to give the CR only to the original CS. This is not only the easiest type of discrimination training to understand, but it is also the procedure used to determine the sensory abilities of animals. In this type of discrimination training, the UCS follows only the original CS, the one stimulus to which you want the animal or human to respond (give the CR). None of the other stimuli used in the training are followed by the UCS. During discrimination training, you present many different stimuli numerous times, but the UCS only follows the original CS. What do you think happens? What normally happens to the CR when the UCS is removed in classical conditioning? It is extinguished. This is what discrimination training does; it diminishes the responding to the other stimuli.

Idealized results of stimulus discrimination training for a CS tone of 1000 Hz in our Pavlovian classical conditioning example are shown in Figure 4.3 (page 135). As you can see, responding is centered at 1000 Hz, as it is for the stimulus generalization results. However, unlike the generalization results, the responding following discrimination training is to a much narrower range of stimulus frequencies. The animal has learned only to salivate to the 1000 Hz tone and tones very similar to it (975 Hz and 1025 Hz). Why does the animal salivate at all to any stimulus other than the 1000 Hz tone? It wouldn't if it had perfect pitch perception and could discriminate all frequencies, but it can't. Thus, the animal salivates to this narrow range of frequencies because it has difficulty differentiating them. This is why discrimination training can be used to learn what nonverbal animals (and human infants) can discriminate. If they respond to stimuli the same way, then it is assumed that they cannot differentiate between the stimuli.

All five of the general learning processes for classical conditioning are summarized in Table 4.1. If any of these processes are not clear to you, restudy the discussions of those processes in the text and their visual depictions in Figures 4.2 (page 134) and 4.3 (page 135) to solidify your understanding. You want to ensure that you understand these learning processes for classical conditioning because they will be redefined for operant conditioning in the next section.

Table 4.1	General Learning Processes in Classical Conditioning
Learning Process	**Explanation of Process**
Acquisition	Acquiring a new response (the conditioned response) to the conditioned stimulus
Extinction	Diminishing of the conditioned response when the unconditioned stimulus no longer follows the conditioned stimulus
Spontaneous recovery	Partial recovery in strength of the conditioned response following a break during extinction training
Stimulus generalization	Elicitation of the conditioned response by stimuli that are similar to the conditioned stimulus (the more similar, the stronger the response)
Stimulus discrimination	Elicitation of the conditioned response only by the conditioned stimulus or only by a small set of highly similar stimuli that includes the conditioned stimulus

Section Summary

In this section, we discovered that one way we learn about the world is by noting associations between various stimuli in our environment. This is called classical conditioning. Classical conditioning occurs when a conditioned stimulus (CS) reliably predicts the arrival of an unconditioned stimulus (UCS), which reflexively elicits an unconditioned response (UCR). In Pavlov's research, for example, a tone (CS) predicted the arrival of meat powder (UCS) that automatically elicited a salivary response (UCR). The optimal way to pair the two stimuli together in classical conditioning is called delayed conditioning. The CS is presented shortly before the UCS, but the CS continues so that the two stimuli occur together (the tone is turned on and left on until the meat powder is put in the dog's mouth). The learning is the acquisition of a new response, the conditioned response (CR) to the CS (the dog starts salivating to the sound of the tone).

Once this new response is acquired, it will be generalized to stimuli similar to the CS (tones similar in frequency to the particular tone used as the CS in conditioning). Although this generalization of the CR is an adaptive process, we can learn to discriminate the CS (the particular tone used in conditioning) from other stimuli (tones) except those highly similar to the CS. In discrimination learning, we learn that the CS is the only stimulus that is followed by the UCS. When the UCS no longer follows a stimulus, the CR (salivation) is extinguished (no longer given). However, the CR temporarily increases in strength following breaks during the extinction process. This is known as spontaneous recovery and indicates that the CR may still be available in a weakened or inhibited form.

ConceptCheck | 1

> At about the same time that Pavlov accidentally discovered classical conditioning and began studying it, an American graduate student at the University of Pennsylvania, Edwin Twitmyer, was conducting his doctoral research (see Twitmyer, 1974). Twitmyer was examining the strength of the knee-jerk reflex and how this reflex might be affected by other physiological factors, such as clenching one's fists. During some of his trials, a bell would ring to signal to the participant to clench his fists, then a hammer would strike the participant's knee, the knee would jerk, and the amount of knee jerk would be measured. After many of these trials, Twitmyer noticed that a participant's knee might jerk before the hammer hit it. It jerked in response to the bell! Like Pavlov, he had accidentally discovered a case of classical conditioning. Identify the UCS, UCR, CS, and CR in this strange case of classical conditioning.

> Explain why Watson and Rayner's Little Albert study is an example of the delayed conditioning procedure, not the trace conditioning procedure.

> Explain why generalization and discrimination can be thought of as opposites.

> Explain which other general learning process is used in discrimination training.

Learning Through Operant Conditioning

In the last section, we described classical conditioning—learning about associations between stimuli in our environment. In this section, we will consider another important type of conditioning, **operant conditioning**—learning to associate behaviors with their consequences. Behaviors that are reinforced (lead to satisfying consequences) will be strengthened, and behaviors that are punished (lead to unsatisfying consequences) will be weakened. The behavior that is reinforced or punished is referred to as the operant response because it "operates" on the environment by bringing about certain consequences. We are constantly "operating" on our environment and learning from the consequences of our behavior. For example, in meeting someone whom you like and want to date, your behavior (what you say and how you act) will either lead to satisfying consequences (a date) or unsatisfying consequences (no date). Satisfying consequences will lead you to act that way again in the future; unsatisfying consequences will lead you to change your behavior.

▌ **operant conditioning** Learning to associate behaviors with their consequences. Behaviors that are reinforced (lead to satisfying consequences) will be strengthened, and behaviors that are punished (lead to unsatisfying consequences) will be weakened.

Research on how we learn associations between behaviors and their consequences started around the beginning of the twentieth century. American psychologist Edward Thorndike studied the ability of cats and other animals to learn to escape from puzzle boxes (Thorndike, 1898, 1911). In these puzzle boxes, there was usually only one way to get out (for example, pressing a lever would open the door). Thorndike would put a hungry animal in the box, place food outside the box (but in sight of the animal), and then record the animal's behavior. If the

Edward Thorndike used puzzle boxes like the one shown here in his classic learning studies with cats. The boxes varied in how difficult they were for the cats to escape from. The pictured box was one of the easier boxes—pulling on a looped string raised the bolt to open the door. More difficult boxes required the cat to make more than one response. The results of these puzzle box experiments led Thorndike to develop the law of effect.

animal pressed the lever, as a result of its behavior it would manage to escape the box and get the food (satisfying effects). The animal would tend to repeat such successful behaviors in the future when put back into the box. However, other behaviors (for example, pushing the door) that did not lead to escaping and getting the food would not be repeated.

Based on the results of these puzzle box experiments, Thorndike developed what he termed the **law of effect**—any behavior that results in satisfying consequences tends to be repeated, and any behavior that results in unsatisfying consequences tends not to be repeated. In the 1930s, B. F. (Burrhus Frederic) Skinner, the most influential of all behaviorists, redefined the law in more objective terms and started the scientific examination of how we learn through operant conditioning (Skinner, 1938). Let's move on to Skinner's redefinition and a description of how operant conditioning works.

Learning Through Reinforcement and Punishment

To understand how operant conditioning works, we first need to learn Skinner's redefinitions of Thorndike's subjective terms, "satisfying" and "unsatisfying" consequences. A **reinforcer** is defined as a stimulus that increases the probability of a prior response, and a **punisher** as a stimulus that decreases the probability of a prior response. Therefore, **reinforcement** is defined as the process by which the probability of a response is increased by the presentation of a reinforcer following the response, and **punishment** as the process by which the probability of a response is decreased by the presentation of a punisher following the response. "Reinforcement" and "punishment" are terms that refer to the process by which certain stimuli (consequences) change the probability of a behavior; "reinforcer" and "punisher" are terms that refer to the specific stimuli (consequences) that are used to strengthen or weaken the behavior.

Let's consider an example. If you operantly conditioned your pet dog to sit by giving her a food treat each time she sat, the food treat would be the reinforcer, and the process of increasing the dog's sitting behavior by using this reinforcer would be called reinforcement. Similarly, if you conditioned your dog to stop jumping on you by spraying her in the face with water each time she did so, the spraying would be the punisher, and the process of decreasing your dog's jumping behavior by using this punisher would be called punishment.

Just as classical conditioning is best when the CS is presented just before the UCS, immediate consequences normally produce the best operant conditioning (Gluck, Mercado, & Myers, 2008). Timing affects learning. If there is a significant delay between a behavior and its consequences, conditioning is very difficult. This is true for both reinforcing and punishing consequences. The learner tends

law of effect A principle developed by Edward Thorndike that says that any behavior that results in satisfying consequences tends to be repeated and that any behavior that results in unsatisfying consequences tends not to be repeated.

reinforcer A stimulus that increases the probability of a prior response.

punisher A stimulus that decreases the probability of a prior response.

reinforcement The process by which the probability of a response is increased by the presentation of a reinforcer.

punishment The process by which the probability of a response is decreased by the presentation of a punisher.

to associate reinforcement or punishment with recent behavior; and if there is a delay, the learner will have engaged in many other behaviors during the delay. Thus, a more recent behavior is more likely to be associated with the consequences, hindering the conditioning process. For instance, think about the examples we described of operantly conditioning your pet dog to sit or to stop jumping on you. What if you waited 5 or 10 minutes after she sat before giving her the food treat, or after she jumped on you before spraying her. Do you think your dog would learn to sit or stop jumping on you very easily? No, the reinforcer or punisher should be presented right after the dog's behavior for successful conditioning.

Normally then, immediate consequences produce the best learning. However, there are exceptions. For example, think about studying now for a psychology exam in two weeks. The consequences (your grade on the exam) do not immediately follow your present study behavior. They come two weeks later. Or think about any job that you have had. You likely didn't get paid immediately. Typically, you are paid weekly or biweekly. What is necessary to overcome the need for immediate consequences in operant conditioning is for the learner to have the cognitive capacity to link the relevant behavior to the consequences regardless of the delay interval between them. If the learner can make such causal links, then conditioning can occur over time lags between behaviors and their consequences.

Positive and negative reinforcement and punishment. Both reinforcement and punishment can be either positive or negative, creating four new terms. Let's see what is meant by each of these four new terms—positive reinforcement, negative reinforcement, positive punishment, and negative punishment. To understand these terms, we first have to understand that positive and negative do not have their normal meanings in this context. The word "positive" means that a stimulus is presented; the word "negative" means that a stimulus is removed. In both positive reinforcement and positive punishment, a stimulus is presented; in both negative reinforcement and negative punishment, a stimulus is removed. Next, we need to understand that there are two types of stimuli that could be presented or removed: appetitive and aversive stimuli. An **appetitive stimulus** is a stimulus that the animal or human finds pleasant (has an appetite for). An **aversive stimulus** is a stimulus that the animal or human finds unpleasant, the opposite of appetitive. Food, money, and good grades are examples of appetitive stimuli for most of us, and strong electric shock, bad grades, and sickness are examples of aversive stimuli for most people.

Now that we know what positive and negative mean, and the difference between appetitive and aversive stimuli, we can understand the meanings of positive and negative reinforcement and punishment. General explanations for each type of reinforcement and punishment are given in Figure 4.4. In **positive reinforcement,** an appetitive stimulus is presented, but in **positive punishment,** an aversive stimulus is presented. An

appetitive stimulus A stimulus that is pleasant.

aversive stimulus A stimulus that is unpleasant.

positive reinforcement Reinforcement in which an appetitive stimulus is presented.

positive punishment Punishment in which an aversive stimulus is presented.

	Positive	**Negative**
Reinforcement	Appetitive stimulus presented	Aversive stimulus removed
Punishment	Aversive stimulus presented	Appetitive stimulus removed

▲ **Figure 4.4** | **Positive and Negative Reinforcement and Punishment** |
"Positive" means that something is presented, and "negative" means that something is taken away. Reinforcement means that the behavior is strengthened, and punishment means that the behavior is weakened. In positive reinforcement, an appetitive stimulus is presented, and in positive punishment, an aversive stimulus is presented. In negative reinforcement, an aversive stimulus is removed, and in negative punishment, an appetitive stimulus is removed.

example of positive reinforcement would be praising a child for doing the chores. An example of positive punishment would be spanking a child for not obeying the rules.

Similarly, in negative reinforcement and negative punishment, a stimulus is taken away. In **negative reinforcement,** an aversive stimulus is removed; in **negative punishment,** an appetitive stimulus is removed. An example of negative reinforcement would be taking Advil to get rid of a headache. The removal of the headache (an aversive stimulus) leads to continued Advil-taking behavior. An example of negative punishment would be taking away a teenager's driving privileges (an appetitive stimulus) after she breaks curfew. The removal of the driving privileges (an appetitive stimulus) leads to better adherence to the curfew in the future.

In all of these examples, however, we only know if a stimulus has served as a reinforcer or a punisher and led to reinforcement or punishment if the target behavior keeps occurring (reinforcement) or stops occurring (punishment). For example, the spanking would be punishment if the disobedient behavior stopped, and the praise reinforcement if the chores continued to be done. However, if the disobedient behavior continued, the spanking would have to be considered reinforcement; and if the chores did not continue to be done, the praise would have to be considered punishment. This is an important point. What serves as reinforcement or punishment is relative to each individual, in a particular context, and at a particular point in time. While it is certainly possible to say that

negative reinforcement Reinforcement in which an aversive stimulus is removed.

negative punishment Punishment in which an appetitive stimulus is removed.

What type of operant conditioning is going on here? Be careful. Think about it from the perspectives of both the child and the parents. For the child, it's positive reinforcement. The child is crying to get something pleasant (sleeping with the parents). For the parents, it's negative reinforcement. They let the child sleep with them in order to remove something they find unpleasant, the crying.

primary reinforcer A stimulus that is innately reinforcing.

secondary reinforcer A stimulus that gains its reinforcing property through learning.

behavior modification The application of classical and operant conditioning principles to eliminate undesirable behavior and to teach more desirable behavior.

certain stimuli usually serve as reinforcers or punishers, they do not inevitably do so. Think about money. For most people, $100 would serve as a reinforcer, but it might not for Bill Gates (of Microsoft), whose net worth is in the billions. Remember, whether the behavior is strengthened or weakened is the only thing that tells you whether the consequences were reinforcing or punishing, respectively.

Primary and secondary reinforcers. Behavioral psychologists make a distinction between primary and secondary reinforcers. A **primary reinforcer** is innately reinforcing, reinforcing since birth. Food and water are good examples of primary reinforcers. Note that "innately reinforcing" does not mean "always reinforcing." For example, food would probably not serve as a reinforcer for someone who has just finished eating a five-course meal. Innately reinforcing only means that the reinforcing property of the stimulus does not have to be learned. In contrast, a **secondary reinforcer** is not innately reinforcing, but gains its reinforcing property through learning. Most reinforcers fall into this category. Examples of secondary reinforcers are money, good grades, and applause. Money would not be reinforcing to an infant, would it? Its reinforcing nature has to be learned through experience.

Behaviorists have employed secondary reinforcers in token economies in a variety of institutional settings, from schools to institutions for the mentally challenged (Allyon & Azrin, 1968). Physical objects, such as plastic or wooden tokens, are used as secondary reinforcers. Desired behaviors are reinforced with these tokens, which then can be exchanged for other reinforcers, such as treats or privileges. Thus, the tokens function like money in the institutional setting, creating a token economy. A token economy is an example of **behavior modification**—the application of conditioning principles, especially operant principles, to eliminate undesirable behavior and to teach more desirable behavior. Like token economies, other behavior modification techniques have been used successfully for many other tasks, from toilet training to teaching autistic children (Kazdin, 2001).

Reinforcement without awareness. According to behavioral psychologists, reinforcement should strengthen operant responding even when people are unaware of the contingency between their responding and the reinforcement. Evidence that this is the case comes from a clever experiment by Hefferline, Keenan, and Harford (1959). Participants were told that the purpose of the study was to examine the effects of stress on body tension and that muscular tension would be evaluated during randomly alternating periods of harsh noise and soothing music. Electrodes were attached to different areas of the participants' bodies to measure muscular tension. The duration of the harsh noise, however, was not really random. Whenever a participant contracted a very small muscle in their left thumb, the noise was terminated. This muscular response was imperceptible and could only be detected by the electrode mounted at the muscle. Thus, the participants did not even realize when they contracted this muscle.

There was a dramatic increase in the contraction of this muscle over the course of the experimental session. The participants, however, did not realize this, and none had any idea that they were actually in control of the termination of the harsh noise. This study clearly shows that operant conditioning can occur without a person's awareness. It demonstrated this using negative reinforcement (an increase in the probability of a response that leads to the removal of an aversive stimulus). The response rate of contracting the small muscle in the left thumb increased and the aversive harsh noise was removed when the response was made. Such conditioning plays a big role in the development of motor skills, such as learning to ride a bicycle or to play a musical instrument. Muscle movements below our conscious level of awareness but key to skill development are positively reinforced by our improvement on the skill.

Pessiglione et al. (2008) provide a more recent demonstration of operant conditioning without awareness for a decision-making task. In brief, participants learned to choose contextual cues predicting monetary reinforcement (winning money) relative to those predicting punishment (loss of money) without conscious perception of these cues. Thus, they learned cue-outcome associations without consciously perceiving the cues. The procedure involved visual masking, which you may not understand. When a visual stimulus is masked, it is exposed briefly (maybe 50 msec) and followed immediately by another visual stimulus that completely overrides it, thereby masking (preventing conscious perception) of the first stimulus.

In this experiment, after being exposed to a masked contextual cue (an abstract novel symbol masked by a scrambled mixture of other cues) flashed briefly on a computer screen, a participant had to decide if he wanted to take the risky response or the safe response. The participant was told that the outcome of the risky response on each trial depended upon the cue hidden in the masked image. A cue could either lead to winning £1(British currency), losing £1, or not winning or losing any money. If the participant took the safe response, it was a neutral outcome (no win or loss). Participants were also told that if they never took the risky response or always took it, their winnings would be nil and that because they could not consciously perceive the cues, they should follow their intuition in making their response decisions. All of the necessary precautions and assessments to ensure that participants did not perceive the masked cues were taken. Overall, participants won money in the task, indicating that the risky response was more frequently chosen following reinforcement predictive cues relative to punishment predictive cues.

In addition to this recent demonstration of operant conditioning without awareness, there have been several demonstrations of classical conditioning without awareness (Clark & Squire, 1998; Knight, Nguyen, & Bandetti, 2003; Morris, Öhman, & Dolan, 1998; Olsson & Phelps, 2004). Using delayed conditioning, Clark and Squire, for example, successfully conditioned the eyeblink response in both normal and amnesic participants who were not aware of the tone–air puff relationship. Participants watched a movie during the conditioning trials, and postconditioning testing indicated that they had no knowledge of the CS-UCS association.

CRAIG SWANSON © WWW.PERSPICUITY.COM

▌ **shaping** Training a human or animal to make an operant response by reinforcing successive approximations of the desired response.

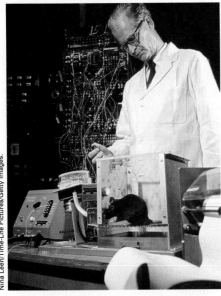

B. F. Skinner and one of his operant conditioning chambers, a "Skinner box." When the rat presses the lever, an electrical relay system is activated and reinforcement (such as a food pellet) is delivered. In addition to a lever, operant chambers may contain other response mechanisms, such as a key for a pigeon to peck.

General Learning Processes in Operant Conditioning

Now that we have a better understanding of how we learn through reinforcement and punishment, let's consider the five general learning processes in operant conditioning that we discussed in the context of classical conditioning—acquisition, extinction, spontaneous recovery, generalization, and discrimination. Because some of the examples of these processes are concerned with operant conditioning of animals, it's important to know how such animal research is conducted. It's also important to learn how to read cumulative records because they are used to measure and depict operant responding in the general learning processes.

For control purposes, behavioral psychologists conduct much of their laboratory research on nonhuman animals. In conducting their experiments with animals, operant conditioning researchers use operant chambers, which resemble large plastic boxes. These chambers are far from simple boxes, though. Each chamber has a response device (such as a lever for rats to press or a key for pigeons to peck), a variety of stimulus sources (such as lamps behind the keys to allow varying colors to be presented on them), and food dispensers. Here, "key" refers to a piece of transparent plastic behind a hole in the chamber wall. The key or other response device is connected to a switch that records each time the animal responds. Computers record the animal's behavior, control the delivery of food, and maintain other aspects of the chamber. Thus, the operant chamber is a very controlled environment for studying the impact of the animal's behavior on its environment. Operant chambers are sometimes referred to as "Skinner boxes" because B. F. Skinner originally designed this type of chamber.

What if the animal in the chamber does not make the response that the researcher wants to condition (for example, what if the pigeon doesn't peck the key)? This does happen, but behavioral researchers can easily deal with this situation. They use what they call **shaping;** they train the animal to make the response they want by reinforcing successive approximations of the desired response. For example, consider the key-peck response for a pigeon. The researcher would watch the behavior of the pigeon and would begin the shaping by reinforcing the pigeon for going in the general area of the key. This would get the pigeon near the key. The researcher would then reinforce the pigeon any time its head was in the area of the key. The pigeon would keep its head near the key and would probably occasionally touch the key. Then the researcher would reinforce the pigeon for touching the key. As you can see, by reinforcing such successive approximations of the desired behavior, the animal can be shaped to make the desired response. This training by successive approximations is just as successful with humans and is also used to shape human operant responding.

> **cumulative record** A record of the total number of operant responses over time that visually depicts the rate of responding.

> **acquisition** (in operant conditioning) The strengthening of a reinforced operant response.

> **extinction** (in operant conditioning) The diminishing of the operant response when it is no longer reinforced.

Responding in an operant conditioning experiment is depicted in a cumulative record. A **cumulative record** is a record of the total number of responses over time. As such, it provides a visual depiction of the rate of responding. Figure 4.5 shows how to read a cumulative record. The slope of the record indicates the response rate. Remember that the record visually shows how the responses cumulate over time. If the animal is making a large number of responses per unit of time (a fast response rate), the slope of the record will be steep. The cumulative total is increasing quickly. When there is no responding (the cumulative total remains the same), the record is flat (no slope). As the slope of the record increases, the response rate gets faster. Now let's see what cumulative records look like for some of the general learning processes.

Acquisition, extinction, and spontaneous recovery. The first general process, **acquisition,** refers to the strengthening of the reinforced operant response. What would this look like on the cumulative record? Figure 4.6(a, page 146) shows that the response rate increases over time. This looks very similar to the shape of the acquisition figure for classical conditioning (see Figure 4.2, page 134), but remember the cumulative record is reporting cumulative responding as a function of time, not the strength of the response. Thus, **extinction,** the diminishing of the operant response when it is no longer reinforced, will look different than it did for classical conditioning. Look at Figure 4.6(b, page 146). The decreasing slope of the record indicates that the

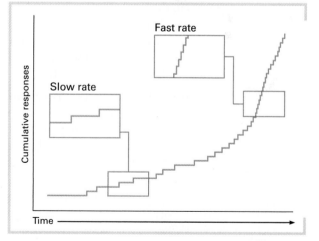

▲ **Figure 4.5 | How to Understand a Cumulative Record |** By measuring how responses cumulate over time, a cumulative record shows the rate of responding. When no responses occur, the record is flat (has no slope). As the number of responses increases per unit of time, the cumulative total rises more quickly. The response rate is reflected in the slope of the record. The faster the response rate, the steeper the slope of the record.

▲ Figure 4.6 | Cumulative Record Illustrations of Acquisition, Extinction, and Spontaneous Recovery | (a) This is an acquisition cumulative record; the responding rate increases as learning occurs so the cumulative record has a fairly steep slope reflecting this increase. (b) This is an extinction cumulative record; the responding rate has essentially fallen to zero. A flat cumulative record indicates extinction. (c) This is an example of spontaneous recovery—a burst of responding following a break in extinction training. As the extinction training continues, the record will return to flat (no responding).

response is being extinguished; there are fewer and fewer responses over time. The response rate is diminishing. When the record goes to flat, extinction has occurred. However, as in classical conditioning, there will be **spontaneous recovery,** the temporary recovery of the operant response following a break during extinction training. This would be indicated in the record by a brief period of increased responding following a break in extinction training. However, the record would go back to flat (no responding) as extinction training continued. This is shown in Figure 4.6(c).

Let's think about acquisition, extinction, and spontaneous recovery with an example that is familiar to all of us—vending machines. We learn that by putting money into a certain vending machine, we can get a candy bar. We acquire the response of inserting money into this particular machine. One day, we put in money, but no candy comes out. This is the case the next few times we visit the machine. Soon, we stop putting our money in the machine. Our responding is being extinguished. However, after a few more days (a break), we go back and try again. This is comparable to spontaneous recovery. We hope the machine has been repaired, and we'll get that candy bar. If so, our response rate will return to its previous level; if not, our response rate will continue along the extinction trail.

Discrimination and generalization. Now let's consider discrimination and generalization. To understand discrimination in operant conditioning, we need first to consider the **discriminative stimulus**—the stimulus that has to be present for the operant response to be reinforced or punished. The discriminative stimulus "sets the occasion" for the response to be reinforced or punished (rather than elicits the response as in classical conditioning). Here's an example. Imagine a rat in an experimental operant chamber. When a light goes on and the rat presses the lever, food is delivered. When the light is not on, pressing the lever does not lead to food delivery. In brief, the rat learns when pressing the lever will be reinforced with food. This is **stimulus discrimination**—learning to give the operant

spontaneous recovery (in operant conditioning) The temporary recovery of the operant response following a break during extinction training.

discriminative stimulus (in operant conditioning) The stimulus that has to be present for the operant response to be reinforced.

stimulus discrimination (in operant conditioning) Learning to give the operant response only in the presence of the discriminative stimulus.

response (pressing the lever) only in the presence of the discriminative stimulus (the light). A high response rate in the presence of the discriminative stimulus (the light) and a near-zero rate in its absence would indicate that the discrimination was learned.

Now we can consider **stimulus generalization,** giving the operant response in the presence of stimuli similar to the discriminative stimulus. Let's return to the example of the rat learning to press the lever in the presence of a light. Let's make the light a shade of green and say that the rat learned to press the lever only in the presence of that particular shade of green light. What if the light were another shade of green, or a different color like yellow?

Table 4.2	General Learning Processes in Operant Conditioning
Learning Process	**Explanation of Process**
Acquisition	Strengthening of a reinforced operant response
Extinction	Diminishing of the operant response when it is no longer reinforced
Spontaneous recovery	Temporary recovery in the operant response rate following a break during extinction training
Stimulus generalization	Giving the operant response in the presence of stimuli similar to the discriminative stimulus (the more similar, the higher the response rate)
Stimulus discrimination	Learning to give the operant response only in the presence of the discriminative stimulus

Presenting similar stimuli (different colored lights) following acquisition constitutes a test for generalization. The extent of responding to a generalization stimulus reflects the amount of generalization to that stimulus. As with classical conditioning (see Figure 4.3, page 135), there is a gradient of generalization in operant conditioning—as the generalization test stimulus becomes less similar to the discriminative stimulus,

stimulus generalization (in operant conditioning) Giving the operant response in the presence of stimuli similar to the discriminative stimulus. The more similar the stimulus is to the discriminative stimulus, the higher the operant response rate.

the response rate for the operant response goes down. A stimulus discrimination function similar to the one observed for classical conditioning would also be observed after additional discrimination training that involved teaching discrimination of the discriminative stimulus (the light) from other stimuli of the same class (lights of different colors).

All five of the general learning processes for operant conditioning are summarized in Table 4.2. If any of these processes are not clear to you, restudy the discussions of those processes in the text to solidify your understanding. Also make sure that you understand how these learning processes in operant conditioning differ from those in classical conditioning (summarized in Table 4.1, page 136).

Now that we understand the general processes involved in operant conditioning, we need to consider the question of how operant responding is maintained following acquisition. Will the responding be maintained if it is reinforced only part of the time? If so, what's the best way to do this? Such questions require an understanding of what are called reinforcement schedules.

> **continuous schedule of reinforcement** Reinforcing the desired operant response each time it is made.

> **partial schedule of reinforcement** Reinforcing the desired operant response only part of the time.

> **partial-reinforcement effect** The finding that operant responses that are reinforced on partial schedules are more resistant to extinction than those reinforced on a continuous schedule.

> **fixed-ratio schedule** A partial schedule of reinforcement in which a reinforcer is delivered each time a fixed number of responses are made. The fixed number can be any number greater than one.

> **variable-ratio schedule** A partial schedule of reinforcement in which the number of responses it takes to obtain a reinforcer varies on each trial but averages to a set number across trials.

Partial-Reinforcement Schedules in Operant Conditioning

The reinforcement of every response is called a **continuous schedule of reinforcement.** But we aren't reinforced for every response in everyday life. In real life, we experience **partial schedules of reinforcement,** in which a response is only reinforced part of the time. Partial-reinforcement schedules lead to the **partial-reinforcement effect.** Responses that are reinforced according to a partial schedule rather than a continuous schedule are more resistant to extinction. Incidentally, Skinner accidentally discovered the partial-reinforcement effect when he was short of food reinforcement for his experimental work and was forced to use partial reinforcement instead of continuous reinforcement (Skinner, 1956). To understand this effect, we first need to consider the four major aspects of partial-reinforcement schedules—ratio, interval, fixed, and variable.

Partial-reinforcement schedules can be based on either the number of responses made or on the amount of time that has elapsed. A ratio schedule is based on the number of responses made, and an interval schedule is based on the amount of time that has elapsed. In addition, the number of responses or the amount of elapsed time can be fixed or variable. In a fixed schedule, the number of responses required for a ratio schedule or the amount of time needed for an interval schedule is fixed. Similarly, for a variable schedule, the number of responses required for a ratio schedule and amount of time for an interval schedule varies on each trial. In summary, there are four types of partial schedules—fixed ratio, variable ratio, fixed interval, and variable interval. Let's look first at ratio schedules.

Ratio schedules. In a **fixed-ratio schedule,** a reinforcer is delivered after a fixed number of responses are made. The number of responses must be greater than one. (A fixed-ratio schedule that only required one response to get a reinforcer would be a continuous schedule of reinforcement). In a laboratory experiment, for example, a rat might have to press the lever 10 times (the fixed ratio) before the delivery of a reinforcer (usually food). To get another reinforcer, 10 more presses would be necessary, and so on. A good example from everyday life is piecework in a factory in which a worker has to make a certain number of items (say two wallets) before receiving any pay. The worker makes two wallets and then receives a certain amount of money. Then he or she must make two more to be paid that amount of money again. Just as the rat has to make responses (press the lever) in the operant chamber, the worker has to make responses (in this case, make actual products) to get reinforced.

In a **variable-ratio schedule,** the number of responses it takes to obtain a reinforcer varies on each trial but averages to be a certain number across trials. The human, rat, or other animal never knows exactly how many responses will be necessary to get the next reinforcer. A rat might have to press a lever 10 times to get a reinforcer, then 21 times, then 6 times, and so on. The exact number of responses necessary to get a reinforcer varies. A good example in everyday life is the way a slot machine is programmed. The person playing the slot machine knows that it will eventually pay off but does not know how many responses (insertions of money into the slot machine) are necessary to get that payoff.

Ratio schedules lead to high rates of responding because the number of responses determines reinforcement; the more they respond, the more they are reinforced. Cumulative records for the two ratio schedules are given in Figure 4.7. The slopes for the two ratio schedules are steep, which indicate a high rate of responding. Look closely after each reinforcement presentation (indicated by a tick mark), and you will see very brief pauses after reinforcement, especially for the fixed-ratio record. These pauses indicate that the animal took a short break from responding following the reinforcement. These pauses occur more often for

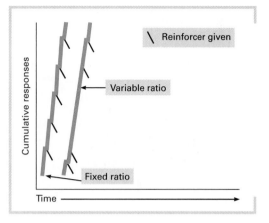

▲ **Figure 4.7** | **Cumulative Records for Fixed-Ratio and Variable-Ratio Schedules of Partial Reinforcement** | Both ratio schedules lead to high rates of responding as indicated by the steep slopes of the two cumulative records. Each tick mark indicates when a reinforcer was delivered. As you can see, the tick marks appear regularly in the record for the fixed-ratio schedule, but irregularly in the record for the variable-ratio schedule. A fixed-ratio schedule leads to short pauses after reinforcement, but these pauses don't occur as often for a variable-ratio schedule.

the fixed-ratio schedule because the number of responses that must be made to get another reinforcer is known. Thus, the animal or human can rest before starting to respond again. These pauses get longer as the fixed number of responses gets larger.

Interval schedules. Now let's consider interval schedules. Do you think the cumulative records for the two interval schedules will have steep slopes like the two ratio schedules? Will there be any flat sections in the record indicating no responding? Let's see. In a **fixed-interval schedule,** a reinforcer is delivered following the first response after a set interval of time has elapsed. Please note that the reinforcement does not automatically appear after the fixed interval of time has elapsed; the reinforcement merely becomes obtainable after the fixed interval. A response must be made in order to get the reinforcement. Let's consider an example. We could fix the time interval at 1 minute for our example of a rat pressing a lever in an operant chamber. This means that a food pellet would be delivered following the first lever press after 1 minute had elapsed. After another minute elapsed following the response and another lever press was made, another reinforcer would be delivered. This pattern would continue—1 minute elapses, a response is made, a reinforcer is given. Before predicting what the cumulative record for this type of schedule should look like, let's think about a fixed-interval schedule example with students.

In most of your classes, you are given periodic scheduled exams (for example, an exam every 4 weeks). To understand how such periodic exams represent a fixed-interval schedule,

fixed-interval schedule A partial schedule of reinforcement in which a reinforcer is delivered after the first response is given once a set interval of time has elapsed.

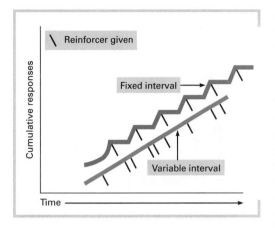

▲ **Figure 4.8** | **Cumulative Records for Fixed-Interval and Variable-Interval Schedules of Partial Reinforcement** | As in Figure 4.7 (page 149), the tick marks indicate when reinforcers were delivered for each of the two schedules. The flat sections following reinforcements for the fixed-interval schedule indicate periods when little or no responding occurred. Such pauses do not occur for a variable-interval schedule. A variable-interval schedule leads to steady responding.

think of studying as the targeted response, and an acceptable grade on the exam as the reinforcer. Think about how much you would study during each of the 4-week intervals before each test. Think about the average study behavior across students in the class for each day during that 4-week interval. There probably wouldn't be much studying during the first week or two, and the amount of study would increase dramatically (cramming) right before each exam. Think about what the cumulative record for this sort of responding would look like. There would be long periods with little responding (essentially flat sections) right after each exam, and then there would be a dramatic burst of responding (a steep slope) right before each exam. Now look at the record for the fixed-interval schedule in Figure 4.8. It looks just like this. This is also what the record would look like for a rat pressing a lever on this type of schedule for a food reinforcer.

Now imagine that you are the teacher of a class in which students had this pattern of study behavior. How could you change the students' study behavior to be more regular? The answer is to use a **variable-interval schedule** in which a reinforcer is delivered following a response after a different time interval on each trial (in our example, each exam), but the time intervals across trials average to be a set time. This would translate in our example to unscheduled surprise exams. Think about how students' study behavior would have to change to do well on the exams with this new schedule. Students would have to study more regularly because a test could be given at any time. Their studying would be steadier over each interval. They wouldn't have long periods of little or no studying. Now look at the cumulative record for the variable-interval schedule in Figure 4.8. The flat sections appearing in the fixed-interval schedule are gone. The slope of the record indicates a steady rate of responding (studying). Why? The answer is simple—the length of the interval varies across trials (between exams in the example). It might be very brief or very long. The students don't know. This is why the responding (studying) becomes steady.

The four types of partial-reinforcement schedules and their respective effects on response rate are summarized in Table 4.3. As you review the information in this table for each type of schedule, also review the cumulative record for the schedule in either Figure 4.7 (page 149) or 4.8 to see visually the impact of that type of schedule upon responding.

Let's compare the cumulative records for the four types of partial-reinforcement schedules given in Figures 4.7 (page 149) and 4.8. What conclusions can we draw? First, ratio schedules

▌ **variable-interval schedule** A partial schedule of reinforcement in which the time that must elapse on each trial before a response will lead to the delivery of a reinforcer varies from trial to trial but averages to a set time across trials.

Table 4.3	Four Partial-Reinforcement Schedules and Their Effects on Response Rate	
Schedule	**Effect on Response Rate**
Fixed-ratio (reinforcer is delivered after a fixed number of responses are made)	High rate of responding with pauses after receiving reinforcement
Variable-ratio (reinforcer is delivered after a variable number of responses are made)	High rate of responding with fewer pauses after receiving reinforcement than for a fixed-ratio schedule
Fixed-interval (reinforcer is delivered after the first response is given once a fixed interval of time has elapsed)	Little or no responding followed by a high rate of responding as the end of the interval nears
Variable-interval (reinforcer is delivered after the first response is given once a variable interval of time has elapsed)	Steady rate of responding during the interval

lead to higher rates of responding than interval schedules. Their slopes are much steeper. This is because ratio schedules depend on responding and interval schedules depend on time elapsing. Second, variable schedules lead to fewer breaks (no responding occurring) after reinforcements than fixed schedules. This is because with variable schedules it is not known how many responses will have to be made or how much time will have to elapse before the next reinforcement.

Now let's think about partial-reinforcement schedules in terms of a general learning process—extinction. Remember the partial-reinforcement effect that we described at the beginning of this section—partial schedules of reinforcement are more resistant to extinction than are continuous schedules. This means that responding will not be extinguished as quickly after using one of the partial schedules as it would be with a continuous schedule. Obviously, it is easier to extinguish the response if the reinforcement had been given continuously for every response in the past. If a response is made and doesn't get reinforced, the responder knows immediately something is wrong because they have always been reinforced after each response. With partial schedules, if a response is made and doesn't get reinforced, the responder doesn't know that anything is wrong because they have not been reinforced for every response. Thus, it will take longer before extinction occurs for the partial schedules because it will take longer to realize that something is wrong.

Do you think there are any differences in this resistance to extinction between the various partial schedules of reinforcement? Think about the fixed schedules versus the variable schedules. Wouldn't it be much more difficult to realize that something is wrong on a variable schedule? On a fixed schedule, it would be easy to notice that the reinforcement didn't appear following the fixed number of responses or fixed time interval. On a variable schedule, however, the disappearance of reinforcement would be very difficult to detect because it's not known how many responses will have to be made or how much time has to elapse. Think about the example of a variable-ratio schedule with the rat pressing a lever. Because there is no fixed number of responses that have to be made, the rat wouldn't realize that its responding was being extinguished. It could be that the number of lever presses necessary to get the next reinforcement is very large. Because of such uncertainty, the variable schedules are much more resistant to extinction than the fixed schedules.

Motivation, Behavior, and Reinforcement

We have just learned about how reinforcement works and that partial-reinforcement schedules are powerful. But what initiates our behavior and guides it toward obtaining reinforcement? The answer is **motivation,** the set of internal and external factors that energize our behavior and direct it toward goals. Its origin is the Latin word *movere,* meaning to set in motion. Motivation moves us toward reinforcement by initiating and guiding our goal-directed behavior. There are several explanations of how motivation works. We will first consider a few general theories of motivated behavior and then a distinction between two types of motivation and reinforcement, extrinsic versus intrinsic.

Theories of motivation. One explanation of motivation, **drive-reduction theory,** proposes that first, a bodily need (such as hunger) creates a state of bodily tension called a drive; then, motivated behavior (seeking food) works to reduce this drive by obtaining reinforcement (food) to eliminate this need and return the body to a balanced internal state. Drives are disruptions of this balanced bodily state. We are "pushed" into action by these unpleasant drive states. They motivate our behavior to reduce the drive. Drive-reduction theory does a good job of explaining some of our motivated behaviors, especially those concerned with biological needs, such as hunger and thirst; but it cannot explain all motivated behavior. Our behaviors are clearly motivated by factors other than drive reduction. Even eating and drinking aren't always cases of drive-reduction motivation. What if you accidentally run into someone that you really want to date and she/he asks you to lunch, but you had eaten a full lunch 15 minutes earlier? You would probably eat another lunch, wouldn't you? We eat for reasons other than hunger. Similarly, I'm sure that you often have drinks without being truly thirsty. And is it really a "thirst" for knowledge that motivates your study behavior? A complementary theory, the incentive theory of motivation, has been proposed to account for such behavior.

In contrast to being "pushed" into action by internal drive states, the **incentive theory** of motivation proposes that we are "pulled" into action by incentives, external environmental stimuli that do not involve drive reduction. The source of the motivation, according to incentive theory, is outside the person. Money is an incentive for almost all of us. Good grades and esteem are incentives that likely motivate much of your behavior to study and work hard. Incentive theory is much like

motivation The set of internal and external factors that energize our behavior and direct it toward goals.

drive-reduction theory A theory of motivation that proposes that our behavior is motivated to reduce drives (bodily tension states) created by unsatisfied bodily needs to return the body to a balanced internal state.

incentive theory A theory of motivation which proposes that our behavior is motivated by incentives, external stimuli that we have learned to associate with reinforcement.

operant conditioning. Your behavior is directed toward obtaining reinforcement.

Another explanation of motivation, **arousal theory,** extends the importance of a balanced internal environment in drive-reduction theory to include our level of physiological arousal and its regulation. According to arousal theory, our behavior is motivated to maintain an optimal level of arousal, which varies within individuals (Zuckerman, 1979). When below the optimal level, our behavior is motivated to raise our arousal to that level. We seek stimulation. We might, for example, go see an action movie. If overaroused, then our behavior is motivated to lower the arousal level. We seek relaxation, so we might take a nap or a quiet walk. So in arousal theory, motivation does not always reduce arousal as in drive-reduction theory, but rather regulates the amount of arousal (not too much, not too little).

In addition, arousal theory argues that our level of arousal affects our performance level, with a certain level being optimal. Usually referred to as the **Yerkes-Dodson law** because Robert Yerkes and James Dodson (1908) originally proposed it, this relationship between level of arousal and performance quality is rather simple. Shown in Figure 4.9, it is an inverted U-shaped relationship. Increased arousal will aid performance to a point (the optimal amount of arousal), after which further arousal impairs performance. Think about exams. You need to be aroused to do well on them; but if you are too aroused, your performance will be negatively affected.

To solidify your understanding of these three theories of motivation, they are summarized in Table 4.4.

Extrinsic motivation versus intrinsic motivation. Motivation researchers make a distinction between **extrinsic motivation,** the desire to perform behavior to obtain an external reinforcer or to avoid an

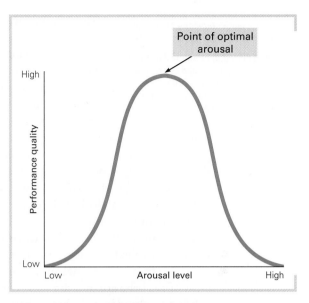

▲ **Figure 4.9** | **The Yerkes-Dodson Law** | The Yerkes-Dodson law is very straightforward. As arousal increases, the quality of performance increases—up to the point of optimal arousal. Further increases in arousal are detrimental to performance

arousal theory A theory of motivation which proposes that our behavior is motivated to maintain an optimal level of physiological arousal.

Yerkes-Dodson law A law describing the relationship between the amount of arousal and the performance quality on a task—increasing arousal up to some optimal level increases performance quality on a task, but increasing arousal past this point is detrimental to performance.

extrinsic motivation The desire to perform a behavior for external reinforcement.

Table 4.4	Theories of Motivation
Theory	**Explanation**
Drive-reduction theory	Our behavior is motivated to reduce drives (bodily tension states) created by unsatisfied bodily needs to return the body to a balanced internal state
Incentive theory	Our behavior is motivated by incentives (external stimuli that we have learned to associate with reinforcement)
Arousal theory	Our behavior is motivated to maintain an optimal level of physiological arousal

intrinsic motivation The desire to perform a behavior for its own sake.

overjustification effect A decrease in an intrinsically motivated behavior after the behavior is extrinsically reinforced and then the reinforcement discontinued.

external aversive stimulus, and **intrinsic motivation,** the desire to perform a behavior for its own sake. In cases of extrinsic motivation, reinforcement is not obtained from the behavior, but as a result of the behavior. In intrinsic motivation, the reinforcement is provided by the activity itself. Think about what you are doing right now. What is your motivation for studying this material? Like most students, you want to do well in your psychology class. You are studying for an external reinforcer (a good grade in the class), so your behavior is extrinsically motivated. If you enjoy reading about psychology and studying it for its own sake and not to earn a grade (and I hope that you do), then your studying would be intrinsically motivated. It is not an either-or situation. Both types of motivation are probably involved in your study behavior, but the contribution of each type varies greatly for each student.

The reinforcers in cases of extrinsic motivation—such as food, money, and awards—are called extrinsic reinforcers. They do not originate within the task itself, but come from an external source. In the case of intrinsic motivation, the enjoyment of the behavior and the sense of accomplishment from it are labeled intrinsic reinforcers. Paradoxically, researchers have found that extrinsic reinforcement will sometimes undermine intrinsically motivated behavior (Deci, Koestner, & Ryan, 1999; Lepper & Henderlong, 2000; Tang & Hall, 1995). This is referred to as the **overjustification effect,** a decrease in an intrinsically motivated behavior after the behavior is extrinsically reinforced and then the reinforcement is discontinued.

The overjustification effect has been demonstrated for people of all ages, but let's consider an example from a study with nursery-school children (Lepper, Greene, & Nisbett, 1973). The children liked drawing with felt-tipped pens and did so during play periods (they were intrinsically motivated to engage in such drawing). Once this was established, some of the children were given extrinsic reinforcement—"Good Player" awards—for their drawing under the guise that someone was coming to look at the children's drawings. Other children were not given this extrinsic reinforcement for drawing. A week later, when no certificates were being given for the felt-tip drawings, the children who had not been extrinsically reinforced continued to draw with the felt-tip pens, but those who had been reinforced spent much less time drawing, illustrating the overjustification effect. What leads to this effect?

Extrinsic reinforcement (the awards for the children) provides unnecessary justification for engaging in the intrinsically motivated behavior (drawing with the felt-tip pens). A person's intrinsic enjoyment of an activity provides sufficient justification for their behavior. With the addition of the extrinsic reinforcement, the person may perceive the task as overjustified and then attempt to understand their true motivation (extrinsic versus intrinsic) for engaging in the activity. It is this cognitive analysis of motivation that leads to the decrease in engaging in the activity. In this cognitive analysis, the person overemphasizes the importance of the extrinsic motivation to their behavior. For example, the person may perceive the extrinsic reinforcement as an attempt at controlling their behavior, which may lead them to stop engaging in the activity to maintain their sense of choice. A person might also think that the reinforcement makes the activity more like work (something one does for extrinsic reinforcement) than play (something one does for its own sake), lessening their enjoyment of the activity and leading them to cease engaging in it.

The overjustification effect indicates that a person's cognitive processing influences their behavior and that such processing may lessen the effectiveness of extrinsic reinforcers. Don't worry, though, about the overjustification effect influencing your study habits (assuming that you enjoy studying). Research has shown that performance-contingent extrinsic reinforcers (such as your grades, which are contingent upon your performance) are not likely to undermine studying (Eisenberger & Cameron, 1996; Tang & Hall, 1995). This means that the extrinsic reinforcement is not likely to impact intrinsic motivation if the extrinsic reinforcement is dependent upon doing something well versus just doing it.

The overjustification effect imposes a limitation on operant conditioning and its effectiveness in applied settings. It tells us that we need to be careful in our use of extrinsic motivation so that we do not undermine intrinsic motivation. It also tells us that we must consider the possible cognitive consequences of using extrinsic reinforcement. In the next section, we continue this limitation theme by first considering some biological constraints on learning and then some cognitive research that shows that reinforcement is not always necessary for learning.

Section Summary

In this section, we learned about operant conditioning, in which the rate of a particular response depends on its consequences, how it operates on the environment. Immediate consequences normally produce the best operant conditioning, but there are exceptions to this rule. If a particular response leads to reinforcement (satisfying consequences), the response rate increases; if a particular response leads to punishment (unsatisfying consequences), the rate decreases. In positive reinforcement, an appetitive (pleasant) stimulus is presented, and in negative reinforcement, an aversive (unpleasant) stimulus is removed. In positive punishment, an aversive (unpleasant) stimulus is presented; in negative punishment, an appetitive (pleasant) stimulus is removed.

In operant conditioning, cumulative records (visual depictions of the rate of responding) are used to report behavior. Reinforcement is indicated by an increased response rate on the cumulative record, and extinction (when reinforcement is no longer presented) is indicated by a diminished response rate leading to no responding (flat) on the cumulative record. As in classical conditioning, spontaneous recovery of the response (a temporary increase in response rate on the cumulative record) is observed following breaks in extinction training. Discrimination and generalization involve the discriminative stimulus, the stimulus in whose presence the response will be reinforced. Thus, discrimination involves learning when the response will be reinforced. Generalization involves responding in the presence of stimuli similar to the discriminative stimulus—the more similar the stimulus, the greater the responding.

We learned about four different schedules of partial reinforcement—fixed ratio, variable ratio, fixed interval, and variable interval. All of these partial-reinforcement schedules, especially the variable ones, lead to greater resistance to extinction than does a continuous reinforcement schedule. This is the partial-reinforcement effect. In addition, we learned that ratio schedules lead to faster rates of responding than interval schedules and that variable schedules lead to fewer pauses in responding.

We also learned about motivation, which moves us toward reinforcement by initiating and guiding our goal-directed behavior. We considered three theories of motivation. First, drive-reduction theory proposes that drives—unpleasant internal states of tension—guide our behavior toward reinforcement so that the tension is reduced. Second, incentive theory asserts that our behavior is motivated by incentives—environmental stimuli that are associated with reinforcement. Third, arousal theory emphasizes the importance of physiological arousal and its regulation to motivation. Our behavior is motivated to maintain an optimal level of arousal. In addition, our level of arousal affects how well we perform tasks and solve problems. According to the Yerkes-Dodson law, increased arousal up to some optimal amount aids performance, but additional arousal is detrimental.

We also learned about the overjustification effect, in which extrinsic (external) reinforcement sometimes undermines intrinsic motivation, the desire to perform a behavior for its own sake. In the overjustification effect, there is a substantial decrease in an intrinsically motivated behavior after this behavior is extrinsically reinforced and then the reinforcement discontinued. This effect seems to be the result of the cognitive analysis that a person conducts to determine the true motivation for their behavior. The importance of the extrinsic reinforcement is overemphasized in this cognitive analysis, leading the person to stop engaging in the behavior. Thus, the overjustification effect imposes a cognitive limitation on operant conditioning and its effectiveness.

ConceptCheck | 2

> Explain what "positive" means in positive reinforcement and positive punishment and what "negative" means in negative reinforcement and negative punishment.

> Explain why it is said that the operant response comes under the control of the discriminative stimulus.

> Explain why a cumulative record goes to flat when a response is being extinguished.

> Explain why the partial-reinforcement effect is greater for variable schedules than fixed schedules of reinforcement.

> Explain why the overjustification effect is a cognitive limitation on operant conditioning.

Biological and Cognitive Aspects of Learning

In our discussion of the classical conditioning of emotional responses, we mentioned biological predispositions to learning certain fears. Humans seem prepared to learn fears of animals or heights much easier than fears of toy blocks or curtains. Animals (snakes or spiders) are more dangerous to us than toy blocks, so such predispositions make evolutionary sense (Seligman, 1971). Are there any other predispositions that affect classical conditioning and are there any biological constraints on operant conditioning? In addition to addressing these questions about the biological aspects of learning, we will also discuss cognitive research on latent learning and learning through modeling that questions whether reinforcement is necessary for learning. Let's start with the biological research.

Biological Preparedness in Learning

Do you have any taste aversions? Have you stopped eating a certain food or drinking a certain liquid because you once got miserably sick after doing so? If you have a really strong aversion, you may feel ill even when you think about that food or drink. If the illness involved a specific food from a particular restaurant, you may have even generalized the aversion to the restaurant. Just as we are biologically prepared to learn certain fears more than others (Öhman & Mineka, 2001), we are also prepared to learn taste aversions. Our preparedness to learn to fear objects and situations dangerous to us (animals and heights) and to avoid foods and drinks that make us sick has adaptive significance. Such learning enhances our chances of survival. It makes biological sense then that we should be predisposed to such learning. To see how psychologists have studied such predispositions, let's take a closer look at some of the early research on taste aversion.

Taste aversion. John Garcia and his colleagues conducted some of the most important early research on taste aversion in the 1960s. Their research challenged the prevailing behaviorist argument that an animal's capacity for conditioning is not limited by its biology (Garcia, 2003). Garcia benefited from an accidental discovery while studying the effects of radiation on rats (Garcia, Kimeldorf, Hunt, & Davies, 1956). The rats would be moved from their home cages to experimental chambers for the radiation experiments. The radiation made the rats nauseous, and they would get very sick later back in their home cages. The rats, however, would still go back into the experimental chambers where they had been radiated, but they would no longer drink the water in these chambers. Why? The water bottles in the chambers were made of a different substance than those in the home cages—plastic versus glass. So, the water the rats drank in the experimental chambers had a different taste than that in their home cages, and the rats had quickly learned an aversion to it. They paired the different taste with their later sickness. Rats do not have the cognitive capacity to realize that they were radiated and that it was the radiation that made them sick. Note that the rats did not get sick immediately following the drinking or the radiation. The nausea came hours later. This means that learning a taste aversion is a dramatic counterexample to the rule that the UCS (sickness) in classical conditioning must immediately follow the CS (the different-tasting water) for learning to occur (Etscorn & Stephens, 1973). In fact, if the CS-UCS interval is less than a few minutes, a taste aversion will not be learned (Schafe, Sollars, &

John Garcia

Bernstein, 1995). This makes sense because spoiled or poisoned food typically does not make an animal sick until a longer time period has elapsed.

So how did Garcia and his colleagues use these taste aversion results for rats to demonstrate biological preparedness in learning? Garcia and Koelling (1966) showed that the rats would not learn such aversions for just any pairing of cue and consequences. Those that seemed to make more biological sense (different-tasting water paired with later sickness) were easily learned, but other pairings that didn't make biological sense did not even seem learnable. For example, they examined two cues that were both paired with sickness through radiation: (1) sweet-tasting water, or (2) normal-tasting water accompanied by clicking noises and flashing lights when the rats drank. The rats who drank the sweet-tasting water easily learned the aversion to the water, but the rats who drank normal-tasting water with the accompanying clicking noises and flashing lights did not. The rats just couldn't learn to pair these environmental auditory and visual cues with their later sickness; this pairing didn't make any biological sense to the rats. It's important for rats to learn to avoid food and water that will make them sick, but in a natural environment, noises and lights don't typically cause sickness for rats.

This doesn't mean that other animals might not be predisposed to learn auditory or visual aversions. For example, many birds, such as quail, seem to learn visual aversions rather easily. A clever study demonstrated this difference among animals in types of learning predispositions. In this study, both quail and rats drank dark blue, sour-tasting water prior to being made ill (Wilcoxon, Dragoin, & Kral, 1971). Later, the animals were given a choice between dark blue water that tasted normal and sour-tasting water that visually appeared normal. The birds only avoided the dark blue water, and the rats only avoided the sour-tasting water. In general, an animal is biologically predisposed to learn more easily those associations that are relevant to its environment and important to its survival (Staddon & Ettinger, 1989). Rats are scavengers, so they eat whatever is available. They encounter many novel foods, so it makes biological sense that they should be prepared to learn taste aversions easily to enhance their survival. Birds hunt by sight, so visual aversions are more relevant to their survival. There are also biological preparedness effects on operant conditioning. We'll take a look at one of the most important—instinctual drift.

Instinctual drift. Keller and Marian Breland, two of Skinner's former students, discovered an important biological preparedness effect on operant conditoning (Breland & Breland, 1961). The Brelands, who became animal trainers, employed operant conditioning to train thousands of animals to do all sorts of tricks. In doing this training, they discovered what has become known as **instinctual drift**—the tendency of an animal to drift back from a learned operant response to an object to an innate, instinctual response. For example, the Brelands used food reinforcement to train some animals to pick up oversized coins and put them in a bank. The Brelands did this with both pigs and raccoons. However, they observed that once the coins became associated with the food reinforcement, both types of animal drifted back

instinctual drift The tendency for an animal to drift back from a learned operant response to an innate, instinctual reponse to an object.

As shown in these photos, pigs are biologically predisposed to root out their food, and raccoons are biologically predisposed to wash their food. Thus, when the Brelands operantly conditioned pigs and raccoons to pick up over-sized coins and put them in a bank using food reinforcement, the animals sometimes "misbehaved" (reverted back to these instinctual responses that were part of their food gathering behaviors). The pigs pushed the coins with their snouts, and the raccoons rubbed the coins together in their forepaws. Reverting back to an innate, instinctual response from a learned operant response is called instinctual drift.

to instinctual responses that were part of their respective food-gathering behaviors. The pigs began to push the coins with their snouts, and the raccoons started to rub the coins together in their forepaws. These more natural responses interfered with the Brelands' operant training.

The important point of these findings is that biologically instinctual responses sometimes limit or hinder our ability to condition other, less natural responses. The Brelands' work demonstrates a biological preparedness effect upon operant conditioning. Biological predispositions show that animals will learn certain associations (those consistent with their natural behavior) more easily than others (those less consistent with their natural behavior). Also note that this "misbehavior" of the pigs and the raccoons (their instinctual responses) continued without reinforcement from the trainers. In fact, it prevented the animals from getting reinforcement. This aspect of the Brelands' work relates to the more general question of whether we can learn without reinforcement, which we will discuss in the next section.

Latent Learning and Observational Learning

Cognitively oriented learning researchers are interested in the mental processes involved in learning. These researchers have examined the question of whether we can learn without reinforcement in their studies of latent learning and observational learning. We'll consider some of the classic research on these two types of learning.

Latent learning. Think about studying for an exam in one of your courses. What you have learned is not openly demonstrated until you are tested on it by the exam. You learn, but you do not demonstrate the learning until reinforcement

Edward Tolman

▌ **latent learning** Learning that occurs but is not demonstrated until there is incentive to do so.

for demonstrating it (a good grade on the exam) is available. This is an example of what psychologists call **latent learning,** learning that occurs but is not demonstrated until there is incentive to do so. This is what Edward Tolman was examining in his pioneering latent-learning research with rats.

In this research, food-deprived rats had to negotiate a maze, and the number of wrong turns (errors) that a rat made was counted (Tolman & Honzik, 1930a, b, and c). In one study, there were three different groups of rats and about three weeks (one trial per day) of maze running. Food (reinforcement) was always available in the goal box at the maze's end for one group but never available for another group. For the third group, there was no food available until the 11th day. What happened? First, the number of wrong turns decreased over trials, but it decreased much more rapidly for the group who always got food reinforcement through the first 10 trials. Second, the performance for the group that only started getting food reinforcement on the 11th day improved immediately on the next day (and thereafter), equaling that of the group that had always gotten food reinforcement (see Figure 4.10). It appears that the third group of rats had been learning the maze all along, but did not demonstrate their learning until the food reinforcement was made available. The rats' learning had been latent. They had learned a cognitive map (a mental representation) of the maze, and when they needed to use it (when reinforcement became available), they did. This explanation was tested further by blocking the optimal route to the goal box to see if the rats would use their cognitive map to take the next best route. The rats did.

P. BYRNES.

"Bathroom" Sure, it's just down the hall to the left, jog right, left, another left, straight past two more lefts, then right, and it's at the end of the third corridor on your right."

Observational learning. If such cognitive maps are within the abilities of rats, then it shouldn't be surprising that much of the learning by humans doesn't involve conditioning through direct experience. **Observational learning (modeling)**—learning by observing others and imitating their behavior—plays a major role in human learning (Bandura, 1973). For example, observational learning helps us learn how to play sports, write the letters of the alphabet, and drive a car. We observe others and then do our best to imitate their behavior. We also often learn our attitudes and appropriate ways to act out our feelings by observing good and bad models. Today's sports and movie stars are powerful models for such learning.

Albert Bandura's famous experiments on learning through modeling involved a Bobo doll, a large inflated clown doll, and kindergarten-age children as participants (Bandura, 1965; Bandura, Ross, & Ross, 1961, 1963a, 1963b). In one

▌ **observational learning (modeling)** Learning by observing others and imitating their behavior.

▲ **Figure 4.10** | Latent Learning | There were three different groups of rats, and each rat received one trial per day in a maze. Latent learning is evident for the rats who did not receive reinforcement until Day 11. Once reinforcement (a food reward in the goal box at the end of the maze) was given, these rats demonstrated their prior learning of the maze on the first 11 days by immediately (on Day 12) doing as well as the rats that had been regularly reinforced. They had learned a cognitive map of the maze, and when reinforcement became available, they used it. This learning remained latent (present but not evident) until their maze-running behavior was reinforced. (From Tolman & Honzik, 1930c.)

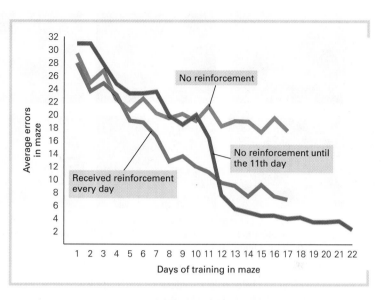

experiment, some of the children in the study were exposed to an adult who beat, kicked, and yelled at the Bobo doll. After observing this behavior, the child was taken to a room filled with many appealing toys, but the experimenter upset the child by saying that these toys were being saved for other children. The child was then taken to a room that contained a few other toys, including the Bobo doll. Can you guess what happened? The child started beating on the Bobo doll just as the adult model had done. The children even repeated the same words that they heard the model use earlier while beating the doll. Children who had not observed the abusive adult were much less likely to engage in such behavior.

But what would happen if a child were exposed to a model that acted gently toward the Bobo doll? In another experiment, Bandura had children observe either an aggressive model, a gentle model, or no model. When allowed to play in a toy room that included a Bobo doll, what happened? The children exposed to the aggressive model acted more aggressively toward the doll than the children with no model, and the children with the gentle model acted more gently toward the doll than the children with no model. In general, the children's behavior with the doll was guided by their model's behavior. But the models in these experiments were not reinforced or punished for their behavior. Would this make a difference?

Bandura examined this question in another experiment. The young children watched a film of an adult acting aggressively toward the Bobo doll, but there were three different versions of the film. In one version, the adult's behavior was reinforced; in another, the behavior was punished; and in the third, there were no consequences.

Albert Bandura

Courtesy of Albert Bandura

Courtesy of Albert Bandura, Stanford University

These photographs of the children in the Bobo doll experiments imitating the violent behavior of the adult model show the powerful influence of observational learning.

The children's interactions with the Bobo doll varied depending upon which film the child had seen. The children who had watched the adult get reinforced for aggressive behavior acted more aggressively toward the Bobo doll than those who had seen the model act with no consequences. In addition, the children who had watched the adult get punished were less likely to act aggressively toward the doll than the children who had not been exposed to any consequences for acting aggressively toward the doll. The children's behavior was affected by the consequences witnessed in the film. Then Bandura cleverly asked the children if they could imitate the behavior in the film for reinforcement (snacks). Essentially, all the children could do so. This is an important point. It means that the children all learned the behavior through observation regardless of whether the behavior was reinforced, punished, or neither.

Much of the research on observational learning since Bandura's pioneering studies has focused on the question of whether media violence leads people to behave more aggressively. There is clearly an abundance of violence on television and in other media. It has been estimated that the average child has viewed 8,000 murders and 100,000 other acts of violence on television alone by the time he finishes elementary school (Huston et al., 1992). But do we learn to be more aggressive from observing all of this violence on television and in other media? Literally hundreds of studies have addressed this question, and as you would expect, the findings are complicated. Leading scientists reviewing this literature, however, came to the following general conclusion: "Research on violent television and films, video games, and music reveals unequivocal evidence that media violence increases the likelihood of aggressive and violent behavior in both immediate and long-term contexts" (Anderson et al., 2003). Although the empirical evidence linking media violence to elevated aggression is clear-cut (Murray, 2008), media exposure is not a necessary and sufficient cause of violence—not all viewers will be led to violence (Bushman & Anderson, 2001). However, because so many people (literally millions) are exposed to media violence, the effect on society can be immense even if only a small percentage of viewers are affected. If say only 1% of viewers are affected and behave more aggressively, this means that hundreds of thousands of people would be more likely to commit aggressive acts. Media violence is clearly a societal problem that needs to be addressed.

Recent research has also found neurons that provide a neural basis for observational learning. These **mirror neurons** are neurons that fire both when performing an action and when observing another person perform that same action. When you observe someone engaging in an action, similar mirror neurons are firing in both your brain and in the other person's brain. Thus, these neurons in your brain are "mirroring" the behavior of the person you are observing. Mirror neurons were first discovered in macaque monkeys via electrode recording by Giacomo Rizzolatti and his colleagues at the University of Parma in the mid-1990s (Iacoboni, 2009), but it is not normally possible to study single neurons in humans because this would require attaching electrodes directly to the brain. Using fMRI and other scanning techniques,

THE FAR SIDE® By GARY LARSON

© 1981 FarWorks, Inc. All Rights Reserved/Dist. by Creators Syndicate

neuroscientists, however, have observed that the same cortical areas in humans are involved when performing an action and observing that action (Rizzolatti & Craighero, 2004). These brain areas are referred to as mirror neuron systems. Because both human and nonhuman primates learn much through observation and imitation, the mirror neuron systems provide a way through which observation could be translated into action (Iacoboni, 2005). In addition to providing a neural basis for observational learning, researchers speculate that mirror neuron systems may also play a major role in empathy and understanding the intentions and emotions of others (Iacoboni, 2009) and represent the basic neural mechanism from which language evolved (Rizzolatti & Arbib, 1998; Rizzolatti & Craighero, 2004). Some researchers even think that there may be a link between mirror neuron deficiency and social disorders, namely autism in which children have difficulty in social interactions (Dapretto et al., 2006).

Observational learning, like latent learning, emphasizes the role of cognitive processes in learning. Just as the rats seemed to have a cognitive map of the maze, the children seemed to have a cognitive model of the actions of the adult models and their consequences. Cognitive psychologists have

mirror neurons Neurons that fire both when performing an action and when observing another person perform that same action.

studied the development of such mental representations and their storage in memory and subsequent retrieval from memory in their attempts to understand how the human memory system works. We will take a detailed look at the human memory system in Chapter 5.

Section Summary

In this section, we learned about some of the effects of biological preparedness on learning and about latent learning and observational learning in which direct reinforcement is not necessary. Research on taste aversion indicated that rats could easily learn aversions to different-tasting water when it was paired with later sickness, but could not learn to pair auditory and visual cues with such sickness. This finding indicates that animals may be biologically predisposed to learn those associations that are important to their survival more easily than arbitrary associations. Similarly, the Brelands found in their animal training work that animals drift back to their instinctual responses from conditioned arbitrary ones, a phenomenon called instinctual drift. Findings such as these highlight the impact of biological predispositions upon learning.

Research has shown that reinforcement is not necessary for learning to occur. Tolman's research with rats running mazes showed that without reinforcement, rats could learn a cognitive map of the maze that they could then use very efficiently when reinforcement became available at the end of the maze. This was an instance of latent learning, learning that is not demonstrated until there is an incentive to do so. Albert Bandura's pioneering research on observational learning showed that much of human learning also doesn't involve direct experience. The children in his study all learned a model's behavior through observation, regardless of whether the behavior was reinforced, punished, or neither. Research in observational learning since Bandura's studies has extended his findings by linking media violence to an increased likelihood of aggression in viewers. Other recent research by neuroscientists has led to the discovery of mirror neuron systems that provide a neural basis for observational learning.

ConceptCheck | 3

> Explain why the ease of learning taste aversions is biologically adaptive for humans.

> Given Garcia and Koelling's (1966) findings (discussed in this section) for pairing the cues of sweet-tasting water and normal-tasting water accompanied by clicking noises and flashing lights when rats drank with a sickness consequence, what do you think they observed when they paired these two cues with an immediate electric shock consequence instead of the sickness consequence? Justify your answer in terms of biological preparedness in learning.

> Explain why it would be easier to operantly condition a behavior that is "natural" for an animal than one that isn't natural.

> Explain the relationship between latent learning and reinforcement.

> Explain how reinforcing and punishing models influenced observers in Bandura's research.

Study Guide

Chapter Key Terms

You should know the definitions of the following key terms from the chapter. They are listed in the order in which they appear in the chapter. For those you do not know, return to the relevant section of the chapter to learn them. When you think that you know all of the terms, complete the matching exercise based on these key terms.

classical conditioning
reflex
unconditioned stimulus (UCS)
unconditioned response (UCR)
conditioned stimulus (CS)
conditioned response (CR)
delayed conditioning
trace conditioning
acquisition (in classical conditioning)
extinction (in classical conditioning)
spontaneous recovery (in classical conditioning)
stimulus generalization (in classical conditioning)
stimulus discrimination (in classical conditioning)
operant conditioning
law of effect
reinforcer
punisher
reinforcement

punishment
appetitive stimulus
aversive stimulus
positive reinforcement
positive punishment
negative reinforcement
negative punishment
primary reinforcer
secondary reinforcer
behavior modification
shaping
cumulative record
acquisition (in operant conditioning)
extinction (in operant conditioning)
spontaneous recovery (in operant conditioning)
discriminative stimulus (in operant conditioning)
stimulus discrimination (in operant conditioning)
stimulus generalization (in

operant conditioning)
continuous schedule of reinforcement
partial schedule of reinforcement
partial-reinforcement effect
fixed-ratio schedule
variable-ratio schedule
fixed-interval schedule
variable-interval schedule
motivation
drive-reduction theory
incentive theory
arousal theory
Yerkes-Dodson law
extrinsic motivation
intrinsic motivation
overjustification effect
instinctual drift
latent learning
observational learning (modeling)
mirror neurons

Key Terms Exercise

Identify the correct term for each of the following definitions. The answers to this exercise follow the answers to the Concept Checks at the end of the chapter.

1. A classical conditioning procedure in which the conditioned stimulus precedes the unconditioned stimulus but the two stimuli do not occur together.

_____

2. A stimulus that gains its reinforcing property through learning.

_____

3. In operant conditioning, giving the operant response in the presence of stimuli similar to the discriminative stimulus.

_____

4. The stimulus that comes to elicit a new response in classical conditioning.

_____

5. The finding that operant responses reinforced on partial schedules are more resistant to extinction than those reinforced on a continuous schedule.

_____

6. A stimulus that is unpleasant.

_____

7. Training an animal or human to make an operant response by reinforcing successive approximations to the desired response.

_____

8. A partial schedule of reinforcement in which the number of responses it takes to obtain a reinforcer varies on each trial but averages to a set number across trials.

_____

9. A partial schedule of reinforcement in which the time that must elapse on each trial before a response will lead to the delivery of a reinforcer varies from trial to trial but averages to a set time across trials.

_____

10. The application of classical and operant conditioning principles to eliminate undesirable behavior and to teach more desirable behavior.

_____

11. The desire to perform a behavior for external reinforcement.

_____

12. Punishment in which an aversive stimulus is presented.

_____

13. A principle developed by Edward Thorndike that says that any behavior that results in satisfying consequences tends to be repeated and that any behavior that results in unsatisfying consequences tends not to be repeated.

_____

14. A partial recovery in strength of the conditioned response following a break during extinction training.

_____

15. The diminishing of the operant response when it is no longer reinforced.

_____

Practice Test Questions

The following are practice multiple-choice test questions on some of the chapter content. The answers are given after the Key Terms Exercise answers at the end of the chapter. If you guessed or incorrectly answered a question, restudy the relevant section of the chapter.

1. In Pavlov's classical conditioning research, a tone was used as the _____, and food inserted in the mouth served as the _____.
   a. UCS; CS
   b. CS; UCS
   c. UCR; CR
   d. CR; UCR

2. In classical conditioning, the diminishing of the CR following removal of the UCS is called _____.
   a. acquisition
   b. discrimination
   c. extinction
   d. generalization

3. In stimulus generalization in classical conditioning, the strength of the CR _____, as the similarity of the generalization stimulus to the _____ increases.
   a. increases; CS
   b. decreases; CS
   c. increases; UCS
   d. decreases; UCS

4. In reinforcement, the probability of a behavior _____; in punishment the probability of a behavior _____.
   a. increases; increases
   b. increases; decreases
   c. decreases; increases
   d. decreases; decreases

5. Negative reinforcement occurs when an _____ stimulus is _____.
   a. appetitive; presented
   b. appetitive; removed
   c. aversive; presented
   d. aversive; removed

6. Which of the following is the best example of a primary reinforcer?
   a. a cheeseburger
   b. a grade of "A" on an exam
   c. praise from your teacher
   d. winning the lottery

7. The stimulus in whose presence a response will be reinforced is called the _____ stimulus in operant conditioning.
   a. generalization
   b. discriminative
   c. acquisition
   d. extinction

8. Piecework in a factory is an example of a _____ schedule of reinforcement; a slot machine is an example of a _____ schedule of reinforcement.
   a. variable-ratio; fixed-interval
   b. fixed-interval; variable-ratio
   c. fixed-ratio; variable-ratio
   d. variable-ratio; fixed-ratio

9. The Brelands' difficulties in training animals was the result of _____.
   a. the partial reinforcement effect
   b. instinctual drift
   c. a token economy
   d. latent learning

10. Tolman's research with rats in mazes indicated the occurrence of _____.

   a. observational learning
   b. latent learning
   c. the partial-reinforcement effect
   d. instinctual drift

11. Which of the following is an example of a secondary reinforcer?
   a. money
   b. a money order
   c. a check
   d. all of the above

12. The _____ effect is a decrease in an intrinsically motivated behavior after the behavior is extrinsically reinforced and the reinforcement discontinued.
   a. overjustification
   b. partial reinforcement
   c. shaping
   d. instinctual drift

13. A steep cumulative record in operant conditioning indicates _____, and a flat cumulative record indicates _____.
   a. a slow rate of responding; no responding
   b. a slow rate of responding; a fast rate of responding
   c. a fast rate of responding; no responding
   d. a fast rate of responding; a slow rate of responding

14. The results of Bandura's "Bobo doll" studies illustrate _____, and Tolman and Honzik's studies of latent learning indicate the importance of _____ in maze learning by rats.
   a. observational learning; the overjustification effect
   b. observational learning; cognitive maps
   c. the partial reinforcement effect; the overjustification effect
   d. the partial reinforcement effect; cognitive maps

15. Continuing to take Advil because it alleviates headaches is an example of _____, and no longer parking in "No Parking"

zones because you lost money in fines for doing so is an example of _____.

a. positive punishment; positive reinforcement

b. positive reinforcement; positive punishment

c. negative punishment; negative reinforcement

d. negative reinforcement; negative punishment

Chapter Concept Check Answers

Concept Check | 1

- The UCS was the hammer striking the participant's knee, and the UCR was the participant's knee jerk in response to the hammer strike. The CS was the bell ringing, and the CR was the participant's knee jerk in response to this bell.

- The Little Albert study is an example of using the delayed classical conditioning procedure because the CS (the white rat) was presented before the UCS (the loud, unexpected noise) and remained there until the UCS was presented. If the white rat had been taken away before the unexpected loud noise, then the study would have been an example of using the trace classical conditioning procedure.

- Generalization and discrimination can be thought of as opposites because generalization is the broadening of the conditioned response to other stimuli, whereas discrimination is the narrowing of the response to only the stimulus followed by the UCS and those stimuli so similar to this stimulus that they cannot be discriminated from it.

- Extinction is used during discrimination training. The responses to all stimuli except the original CS are diminished because the UCS does not follow any of them. However, if a stimulus cannot be discriminated from the CS, the response to it is not extinguished.

Concept Check | 2

- "Positive" refers to the presentation of a stimulus. In positive reinforcement, an appetitive stimulus is presented; in positive pun-

ishment, an aversive stimulus is presented. "Negative" refers to the removal of a stimulus. In negative reinforcement, an aversive stimulus is removed; in negative punishment, an appetitive stimulus is removed.

- The operant response comes under the control of the discriminative stimulus because it is only given in the presence of the discriminative stimulus. The animal or human learns that the reinforcement is only available in the presence of the discriminative stimulus.

- A cumulative record goes flat when a response is extinguished because no more responses are made; the cumulative total of responses remains the same over time. Thus, the record is flat because this total is not increasing at all. Remember that the cumulative record can never decrease because the total number of responses can only increase.

- The partial-reinforcement effect is greater for variable schedules than fixed schedules because there is no way for the person or animal to know how many responses are necessary (on a ratio schedule) or how much time has to elapse (on an interval schedule) to obtain a reinforcer. Thus, it is very difficult to realize that reinforcement has been withdrawn and so the responding is more resistant to extinction. On fixed schedules, however, you know how many responses have to be made or how much time has to elapse because these are set numbers or amounts of time. Thus, it is easier to detect that the reinforcement has been withdrawn, so fixed schedules are less resistant to extinction.

- The overjustification effect is a cognitive limitation on operant conditioning because it is the result of a person's cognitive analysis of their true motivation (extrinsic versus intrinsic) for engaging in an activity. In this analysis, the person overemphasizes the importance of the extrinsic reinforcement. For example, the person might now view the extrinsic reinforcement as an attempt at controlling their behavior and stop the behavior to maintain their sense of choice.

Concept Check | 3

- Learning taste aversions quickly and easily is adaptive because it increases our chances of survival. If we eat or drink something that makes us terribly sick, it is adaptive to no longer ingest that food or drink because we might die. We have a greater probability of surviving if we learn such aversions easily.

- The rats easily learned (stopped drinking the water) when the normal-tasting water accompanied by clicking noises and flashing lights was paired with immediate electric shock, but they did not when the sweet-tasting water cue was paired with this consequence. In terms of biological preparedness, the former pairing makes biological sense to the rats whereas the latter pairing does not. In a natural environment, audiovisual changes typically signal possible external dangers, but sweet-tasting water typically does not. External cues (noises and flashing lights) paired with an external dangerous consequence (shock) makes more biological sense than an internal cue (taste) paired with an external consequence (shock). For learning to occur, external cues should be paired with external consequences, and internal cues with internal consequences.

- It would be easier to operantly condition a "natural" response because it would lower the probability that instinctual drift will interfere with the conditioning. Because an animal would already be making its natural response to the object, there would be no other response to drift back to. In addition, the natural response to the object would be easier to shape because it would be given sooner and more frequently than an unnatural response.

- Latent learning occurs without direct reinforcement, but such learning is not demonstrated until reinforcement is made available for the learned behavior.

- In Bandura's work, reinforcing the model increased the probability that the observed behavior would be displayed, and punishing the model decreased the probability that the observed behavior would be displayed. But Bandura demonstrated in both cases that the behavior was learned. The reinforcement or punishment only affected whether it was displayed.

Answers to Key Terms Exercise

1. trace conditioning
2. secondary reinforcer
3. stimulus generalization
4. conditioned stimulus
5. partial-reinforcement effect
6. aversive stimulus
7. shaping
8. variable-ratio schedule
9. variable-interval schedule
10. behavior modification
11. extrinsic motivation
12. positive punishment
13. law of effect
14. spontaneous recovery (in classical conditioning)
15. extinction (in operant conditioning)

Answers to Practice Test Questions

1. b; CS; UCS
2. c; extinction
3. a; increases; CS
4. b; increases; decreases
5. d; aversive; removed
6. a; a cheeseburger
7. b; discriminative
8. c; fixed ratio; variable ratio
9. b; instinctual drift
10. b; latent learning
11. d; all of the above
12. a; overjustification
13. c; a fast rate of responding; no responding
14. b; observational learning; cognitive maps
15. d; negative reinforcement; negative punishment

5

Memory

magine what life would be like without memory. Everything would be constantly new. There would be no past experiences. We would have no top-down processing. Even the present would be a state of massive confusion because we couldn't use what we know, our memory, to interpret the world. Everything would be new and unfamiliar. So, instead of being critical of memory when we forget things, we should be thankful that we have it. Our memories may fail us sometimes, but they are essential for life as we currently experience it. Without memory, we would be lost in the present.

The study of memory is not only an extension of the study of sensation and perception discussed in Chapter 3 (top-down processing using stored memories enables current perceptions, and new memories are formed from these perceptions), but it is also an extension of the discussion of the learning processes in Chapter 4 (the learning involved in human memory is more complex than the associational learning involved in conditioning). In this chapter, we will focus on the memory processes essential to learning as we normally think about it—learning from books and other media. The material in this chapter will have a practical use—by finding out how memory works, you will be able to improve yours.

To help understand how your memory works, we begin with a discussion of the most influential model of our memory system—the three-stage model. Then, the focus will turn to how we get information into our memory system—a process called encoding. In this section, we will examine ways to improve memory through better encoding. Next, we will consider encoding's companion process—retrieval, the process of getting information out of memory. In this section on retrieval, we will learn that memory is a constructive process and can be manipulated. We will also consider the question of whether information stored in memory is ever lost. Is the information truly no longer available or is it just not accessible at a particular point in time? Here we will also discuss false memories and the controversial topic of repressed memories of childhood abuse. But before considering these more complex issues in memory, let's get a basic overview of how our memory system works by considering the classic three-stage model.

Three-Stage Model of Memory

The three-stage model of our memory system has guided much of the research on memory since the late 1960s (Atkinson & Shiffrin, 1968). Diagrams depicting this memory model typically use a series of boxes to indicate the stages of information processing, and arrows connecting the boxes to show the flow of information within the system. Figure 5.1 (page 172) is an informational flow chart for the three-stage memory model. In general, information enters from the physical environment through our senses into sensory memory and flows from sensory memory to short-term memory to long-term memory and then back to short-term memory when we need to use it. In this section, we will discuss each of these three stages of information processing and how the stages interact to provide us with memory. The initial stage of processing, sensory memory, is roughly comparable

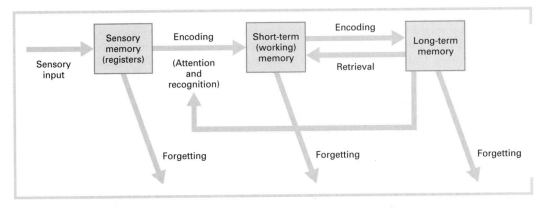

▲ **Figure 5.1** | **Three-stage model of memory** | Information from the physical environment enters the sensory registers through each of our senses (vision, hearing, taste, smell, and touch). This set of registers is referred to collectively as sensory memory. These registers are temporary storage places for sensory information until it can be attended to, recognized, and moved further along in the memory system. Sensory information that is not attended to is quickly forgotten. The information in each register that we attend to goes on to be recognized and enters the second stage of memory, short-term memory, which is comparable to our present awareness. Top-down processing (using information stored in long-term memory) guides this encoding of sensory input from sensory memory into short-term memory. If attended to and studied, information in short-term memory will be encoded into long-term memory where it is stored for later use. If not attended to, the information will be forgotten. To use the information stored in long-term memory, we bring it back into short-term memory (a process called retrieval). If we cannot retrieve such information, it is said to be forgotten. Later in the chapter we will consider explanations for such forgetting.

to what we called sensation in Chapter 3. Information in this stage is bottom-up sensory input that hasn't been recognized yet. So let's begin by discussing how memory researchers have demonstrated that a sensory-memory stage exists and how information is processed in this stage.

Sensory Memory

Sensory memory (SM) consists of a set of registers, where we temporarily store incoming sensory information from the physical environment until we can attend to it, interpret it, and move it to the next stage of memory processing (short-term memory). We have a register for each of our senses—vision, hearing, taste, smell, and touch.

The sensory information stored temporarily in these registers has not yet been recognized. Once it is recognized and we are consciously aware of it, it has moved into the next memory stage, short-term memory. Vision is our dominant sense, so we'll focus on the visual sensory register, commonly referred to as iconic memory, to help you understand how these registers work.

sensory memory (SM) The set of sensory registers, one for each of our senses, that serve as holding places for incoming sensory information until it can be attended to, interpreted, and encoded into short-term memory.

A good way to think about **iconic memory** is that it is photographic memory but for less than 1 second. An exact copy of the visual information exists in iconic memory, but only for a very brief period of time. We cannot attend to everything we see; therefore, the visual information in the register that we attend to gets recognized and goes on to short-term memory, and the unattended information in the register fades away and is quickly forgotten. We said that iconic memory lasts less than a second. This means that its duration (how long information can remain in a memory stage if not attended to) is less than a second. How do we know this? We will examine how research psychologists have answered this duration question and a similar capacity question (how much information can be held in a memory stage at one time) for each of the three memory stages. We'll start with a discussion of how the capacity and duration answers for iconic memory were found. Two different experimental procedures, one direct and one inferential, have been used. We'll consider the direct one, the temporal integration procedure, first, because it is easier to understand.

> **iconic memory** The visual sensory register that holds an exact copy of the incoming visual input but only for a brief period of time, less than 1 second.

> **temporal integration procedure** An experimental procedure in which two meaningless visual patterns that produce a meaningful pattern if integrated are presented sequentially with the time delay between their presentations varied.

The temporal integration procedure. In the **temporal integration procedure,** two random meaningless dot patterns are presented sequentially at the same visual location with a brief time delay between them. When these two meaningless patterns are integrated, a meaningful pattern is produced. So, if the meaningful pattern is seen, this means that the two patterns must have been integrated in our memory system (since the two patterns were not presented simultaneously).

To see how this works, let's consider an example. Look at the first two dot patterns (a and b) in Figure 5.2. Neither has any meaning by itself. Each is just a random dot pattern. However, if you integrate the two patterns (as shown in c), you see a meaningful pattern—the letters V O H. If the first two patterns were shown simultaneously in the same visual location on a screen so that they were integrated, you would see V O H; but if they were presented sequentially, the only way you could see the three letters is if the two meaningless dot patterns are integrated somewhere within your memory system. This is exactly what happens. The two patterns are integrated in iconic memory. However, this is only the case if the

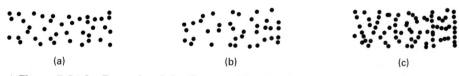

(a)   (b)   (c)

▲ **Figure 5.2 | An Example of the Temporal Integration Procedure |** In this experimental procedure, two meaningless patterns (such as a and b) are shown sequentially at the same visual location. If the time interval between the two patterns is less than a second, a meaningful pattern (in this example, the letters V O H) is seen. The meaningful pattern can only be perceived when the two other patterns are integrated, so this integration must be taking place within our memory system, in what we call the visual sensory register or iconic memory. (From Eriksen & Collins, 1967.)

Sperling's full-report procedure An experimental procedure in which, following the brief presentation of a matrix of unrelated consonants, the participant has to attempt to recall all of the letters in the matrix.

Sperling's partial-report procedure An experimental procedure in which, following the brief presentation of a matrix of unrelated consonants, the participant is given an auditory cue about which row of the matrix to recall.

interval between the two patterns is very brief, less than a second (Eriksen & Collins, 1967). Participants in these experiments do not see the meaningful pattern when the two dot patterns are separated by more than a second. The first pattern has already faded from the visual register, and the two patterns cannot be integrated in iconic memory.

This pattern of results using the temporal integration procedure is also observed for larger dot patterns (Hogben & Di Lollo, 1974). People see the meaningful integrated pattern if the interval between these larger patterns is less than a second. Hence the capacity of the visual sensory register must be fairly large or these more complex patterns couldn't be integrated in iconic memory. Thus, the capacity of iconic memory is large, but its duration is very brief, less than a second.

Sperling's full- and partial-report procedures. We find the same results when we use a very different experimental procedure devised by George Sperling (1960). On each trial in Sperling's research, participants were presented with a different matrix of unrelated consonants for 50 milliseconds, a very brief interval but long enough to process visual information. Different size matrices were used, but in our explanation we will consider 3 × 3, nine-letter matrices (as illustrated in Figure 5.3). The task was to report the letters in the matrix briefly flashed on each trial, but Sperling used two different report procedures. In **Sperling's full-report procedure,** the participant had to try to report the entire matrix of letters. Over trials, participants recalled 4.5 letters on average, usually those letters in the top row and the left section of the second row. However, participants also reported (subjectively) that they sensed the entire matrix, but that it had faded from memory by the time they reported the 4 or 5 letters. This sounds like iconic memory, doesn't it? Let's see how Sperling indirectly demonstrated through inference that the remaining unreported letters were indeed in iconic memory by using his partial-report procedure.

In **Sperling's partial-report procedure,** the participant only had to report a small part of the presented letter matrix, a row indicated by an auditory cue on each trial. A high-pitched tone indicated that the top row was to be recalled, a

▲ **Figure 5.3 I A 3 × 3 Letter Matrix Like Those Used in Sperling's Iconic Memory Research I** On each trial, a different letter matrix was shown for 50 milliseconds. In the full-report procedure, participants attempt to recall all of the letters in the matrix. In the partial-report procedure, participants get an auditory cue following the matrix that tells them which row to report—high-pitched tone, recall top row; medium-pitched tone, recall middle row; and low-pitched tone, recall bottom row. The row that is cued is varied randomly across trials, so the participant has no way of knowing which row will be cued on any particular trial. In addition, the time between the letter matrix presentation and the auditory cue is varied.

L	Z	Q
R	B	P
S	K	N

medium-pitched tone the middle row, and a low-pitched tone the bottom row. These tones were easy to discriminate, so the participant had no difficulty in determining which row was indicated for recall. The letter matrix was different on every trial; therefore, the participant could not learn the matrix. In addition, the cued row was varied randomly across trials; therefore, the participant had no way of knowing which row would be cued on any particular trial. Regardless, when the auditory cue was given immediately after the brief presentation of the letter matrix, participants recalled the indicated row 100 percent of the time. From this result, we can infer that all of the rows must have been present in iconic memory; that is, an exact copy of the letter matrix must have been in iconic memory.

Based on the experimental results for the temporal integration procedure, what do you think would happen when Sperling inserted a time delay between the letter matrix and the auditory cue? Remember, the duration of iconic memory was estimated to be less than a second. Sperling found that as this time delay increased (up to 1 second), participants' recall of the cued row worsened. This meant that the matrix was fading quickly from memory. We can conclude, then, based on two very different experimental procedures, that there is a visual sensory register and that it seems to hold an exact copy of the visual stimulus (indicating a large capacity), but only for a very brief time, less than a second (a very brief duration).

To get a feel for how iconic memory works in nonlaboratory situations, let's think about seeing a bolt of lightning. It's not really a singular, continuous bolt. It is actually three or more bolts that overlap in our iconic memory and lead to the perception of the single flash of lightning. If you turn off the lights and have a friend quickly move a flashlight in a circular motion, you see a circle of light. Why? Again, iconic memory is at work; it isn't a continuous stream of light, but that's what you see. This has larger implications. It is iconic memory that allows us to see the world as continuous and not as a series of unconnected snapshots.

All of our senses have sensory registers that have large capacities with very brief durations. For example, the auditory sensory register, called echoic memory, that processes sounds has a duration of 4–5 seconds, slightly longer than the duration of iconic memory (Darwin, Turvey, & Crowder, 1972; Glucksberg & Cowen, 1970). These sensory registers are what enable continuous perception of the physical environment. Collectively, these registers make up sensory memory, the first step of information processing in the three-stage memory model. However, when we think about memory, we aren't usually thinking about sensory memory. We're thinking about memory with a much longer duration. So let's take a look at the next major stage of processing in the memory system—short-term memory, which has a little greater duration.

Three or four bolts of lightning overlap in our iconic memory, leading to the perception of one continuous bolt.

Short-Term Memory

Short-term memory (STM) is the memory stage in which the recognized information from sensory memory enters consciousness. We rehearse the information in short-term memory so we can transfer it into more permanent storage (long-term memory) and remember it at some later time. We also bring information from long-term memory back into short-term memory to use it to facilitate rehearsal, solve problems, reason, and make decisions; thus short-term memory is thought of as working memory (Baddeley, 1992, 2001, 2003; Engle, 2002). It is the workbench of the memory system. It is where you are doing your present conscious cognitive processing. What you're thinking about right now as you read this sentence is in your short-term memory. As you work to understand and remember what you are reading, you are using your short-term working memory. The capacity of this type of memory is rather small. Humans just can't process that many pieces of information simultaneously in consciousness. In addition, the information in this stage is in a rather fragile state and will be quickly lost from memory (in less than 30 seconds) if we do not concentrate on it. This is why it is called short-term memory. Now that we have a general understanding of the nature of this stage of memory, let's see how researchers have learned about its capacity and duration.

The capacity of short-term memory. To assess the capacity of short-term memory, researchers have used the **memory span task.** In this task, the participant is presented a series of items one at a time and has to remember the items in the order that they were presented. The list items could be any of several types of stimuli such as unrelated letters or words. On each trial, the specific list items change. For example, if words are used, then it is a different list of words on each trial. What have researchers found? George Miller provided the answer in his classic 1956 paper, "The Magical Number Seven, Plus or Minus Two: Some Limits on Our Ability to Process Information." Your **memory span** is defined as the average number of items you can remember across a series of memory span trials. Humans remember 7 ± 2 (5 to 9) chunks of information on memory span tasks. To see what Miller meant by the term "chunk," let's consider the memory span task.

In the memory span task, different types of items can be used. If the items were unrelated letters, most participants would remember 5 to 9 unrelated letters. But if the items were three-letter acronyms (meaningful abbreviations like ABC or USA) or words (like dog or boy), participants would remember 5 to 9 three-letter acronyms or words (15 to 27 letters). In this latter case, participants remember more letters than in the first case, but they remember the same number of meaningful units. This is what is meant by the term "chunk." A **chunk** is a meaningful unit in memory. The capacity limit in short-term memory is in terms of

short-term memory (STM) The memory stage with a small capacity (7 ± 2 chunks) and brief duration (< 30 seconds) that we are consciously aware of and in which we do our problem solving, reasoning, and decision making.

memory span task A memory task in which the participant is given a series of items one at a time and then has to recall the items in the order in which they were presented.

memory span The average number of items an individual can remember across a series of memory span trials.

chunk A meaningful unit in a person's memory.

chunks, 7 ± 2 chunks. So if the chunks are larger for a particular type of material (words vs. letters), we remember more information but not more chunks. Experts in a particular area, such as chess masters, have larger chunks for information in their area of expertise (Chase & Simon, 1973). In the case of a chess master, for example, several chess pieces on the board form a chunk whereas for chess novices, each piece is a separate chunk.

The duration of short-term memory. Now let's consider the duration of short-term memory, less than 30 seconds. Why is the duration of short-term memory said to be less than 30 seconds if this type of memory is equivalent to our conscious workspace? If we choose to do so, we could keep information in our consciousness for as long as we want, clearly longer than 30 seconds. The duration estimate refers to how long information can stay in short-term memory if we cannot attend to it. To measure this duration, researchers developed the distractor task (Brown, 1958; Peterson & Peterson, 1959). In the **distractor task,** a small amount of information (three unrelated consonants such as CWZ) is presented, the participant is immediately distracted from concentrating on the information for a brief interval of time, and then the information must be recalled. How is the participant distracted? A number is immediately presented, and the participant has to count rapidly aloud backward by 3s (or by some other interval). Counting backward rapidly occupies the short-term work space and prevents the participant from attending to the three letters. The experimenter varies the length of the distraction period. When the distraction period is over, the participant must try to recall the letters. What happens? Some typical data are presented in Figure 5.4.

As you can see in Figure 5.4, the estimated duration for information in short-term memory is rather brief, less than 30 seconds. To relate this to everyday life, think about looking up a new phone number. You find the number in the phone book. It goes into your iconic memory, and you attend to it and recognize it. It enters your conscious short-term memory. You start to concentrate on it so you can dial the number. Now what would happen to that number if you heard someone screaming outside and you ran to see what had happened? Chances are that you would forget the phone number (just like participants forget the three consonants in studies using the distractor task), and then have to look it up again.

> **distractor task** A memory task in which a small amount of information is briefly presented and then the participant is distracted from rehearsing the information for a variable period of time, after which the participant has to recall the information.

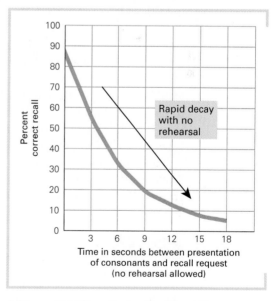

▲ **Figure 5.4 | Results for the Short-Term Memory Distractor Task |** This figure shows how forgetting in short-term memory occurs over time. As the length of the distractor interval increases, forgetting increases very rapidly. In less than 30 seconds, recall is essentially zero. (From Peterson & Peterson, 1959.)

maintenance rehearsal A type of rehearsal in short-term memory in which the information is repeated over and over again in order to maintain it.

long-term memory (LTM) The memory stage in which information is stored for a long period of time (perhaps permanently) and whose capacity is essentially unlimited.

Information in short-term memory is in a temporary storage state, and we need to concentrate on it to prevent it from being lost. Usually we use maintenance rehearsal to accomplish this. **Maintenance rehearsal** is repeating the information in short-term memory over and over again in order to maintain it. For example, in the case of the phone number, we rehearse it over and over again to ourselves until we dial it.

Maintaining information in short-term memory is usually not our goal, certainly not when we are trying to learn. Our goal is to put that information into long-term storage so that we can retrieve and use it in the future. In the last two major sections of this chapter, we will look at the process of encoding information from short-term memory into long-term memory and of retrieving that information from long-term memory at some later time. But first we need to get an overview of long-term memory, the last memory stage in the three-stage model.

Long-Term Memory

When we use the word "memory," we normally mean what psychologists call long-term memory. **Long-term memory (LTM)** allows storage of information for a long period of time (perhaps permanently), and its capacity is essentially unlimited. Remember the trillions of possible synaptic connections in the brain that we discussed in Chapter 2? They represent the capacity of long-term memory. The brain's memory storage capacity has been estimated to be around 2.5 petabytes (a million gigabytes), which would be enough to hold three million hours of television shows if your brain worked like a video recorder (Reber, 2010). You would have to leave the television running continuously for more than 300 years to use up all that storage. We will consider the duration or permanence of information in long-term memory in more detail later in this chapter when we consider theories of forgetting.

The durations and capacities for all three stages of memory are summarized in Table 5.1. Review these so that you have a better understanding of how these three stages differ. Next, let's consider different types of long-term memories.

Table 5.1	Durations and Capacities of the Three Memory Stages	
Memory Stage	**Duration**	**Capacity**
Sensory Memory	<1 sec for iconic memory; 4–5 seconds for echoic memory	Large
Short-Term Memory	Up to 30 secs without rehearsal	7 ± 2 chunks
Long-Term Memory	A long time (perhaps permanently)	Essentially unlimited

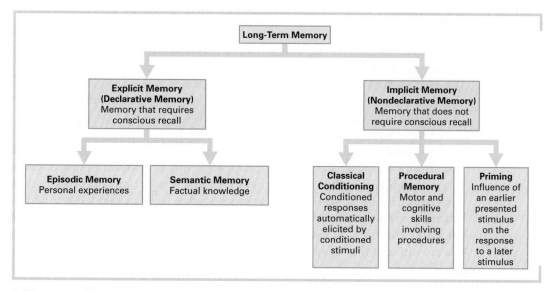

▲ **Figure 5.5** I Types of Long-Term Memory

Types of long-term memories. Memory researchers make many distinctions between various types of long-term memories (Squire, 2004). The first distinction is between memories that we have to recall consciously and make declarative statements about and those that don't require conscious recall or declarative statements (see Figure 5.5). What if someone asked you, "Who was the first president of the United States?" You would retrieve the answer from your long-term memory and consciously declare, "George Washington." This is an example of what is called **explicit (declarative) memory**—long-term memory for factual knowledge and personal experiences. Explicit memory requires a conscious explicit effort to remember. A further distinction is made in explicit memory between **semantic memory,** memory for factual knowledge, and **episodic memory,** memory of personal life experiences (Tulving, 1972). Remembering that George Washington was the first president of the United States (semantic memory) is very different than remembering your first kiss (episodic memory).

Explicit memory is contrasted with **implicit (nondeclarative) memory.** Implicit memory is long-term memory that influences our behavior, but does not require conscious awareness or declarative statements. Implicit memory happens automatically, without deliberate conscious effort. For example, you remember how to drive a car and you do so without consciously recalling and describing what you are doing as you drive. Some implicit memories (like driving a car, typing, or hitting a tennis ball) are referred to as

▪ **explicit (declarative) memory** Long-term memory for factual knowledge and personal experiences. This type of memory requires a conscious effort to remember and entails making declarations about the information remembered.

▪ **semantic memory** Explicit memory for factual knowledge.

▪ **episodic memory** Explicit memory for personal experiences.

▪ **implicit (nondeclarative) memory** Long-term memory for procedural tasks, classical conditioning, and primary effects. This type of memory does not require conscious awareness or the need to make declarations about the information remembered.

procedural memories because they have a physical procedural aspect (the execution of an ordered set of movements) to them. In contrast with declarative explicit memories, procedural implicit memories are like knowing "how" versus knowing "what." Not all implicit memories, however, are procedural memories (see Figure 5.5). We learned about another type of implicit memory, classical conditioning, in Chapter 4. Classically conditioned responses elicited automatically by conditioned stimuli are also implicit memories.

Another type of nonprocedural implicit memory is priming. In **priming,** an earlier stimulus influences the response to a later stimulus. Priming is classed as implicit memory because it occurs independent of a person's conscious memory for the priming stimulus. There are several experimental priming procedures, but let's consider one called repetition priming so that you can gain a better understanding of how priming works. In repetition priming, a person first studies a list of words and then at some later time is asked to complete a list of word fragments with the first word that comes to mind for each fragment. For example, the fragment *s _ c _ _ _* might be presented. The likelihood that the person answers *s o c i a l* (the primed word because the word *social* was on the earlier word list) is much higher than for unprimed words, such as *s o c c e r* or *s o c k e t*, that fit the fragment but were not on the list. Such priming occurs even when people had not recognized the list word on an earlier recognition test (Tulving, Schacter, & Stark, 1982). Thus, priming occurs when explicit memory for the word does not, which means that priming is an involuntary, nonconscious implicit process. Graf, Squire, and Mandler (1984) provided further evidence that priming is an implicit, nonconscious type of memory. They found that amnesics who had no explicit memory for new information could perform as well as normal adults on a repetition priming word fragment task even though the amnesics had no conscious memory of having seen the words before.

Next we'll see how other memory research with amnesics has allowed us to further differentiate explicit and implicit memory and even discover what parts of the brain seem to be involved in each type of memory.

Amnesia, the loss of long-term memories. There is some evidence from the studies of **amnesics,** people with severe memory deficits following brain surgery or injury, that explicit and implicit memories are processed in different parts of the brain. We will focus our discussion of amnesics on the most studied amnesic in psychological research, H. M., whom we discussed briefly in Chapter 1. When H. M. was 7 years old, he was hit by a bicyclist and suffered a brain injury that later led to severe epileptic seizures in his teens (Hilts, 1995). In 1953 at the age of 27, H. M. had his hippocampus and surrounding temporal lobe areas removed with the hope of reducing his epileptic seizures. The seizures were reduced, but the operation drastically affected his long-term memory. Before the operation, he had normal short-term memory and long-term memory. After the operation, he had normal short-term memory,

▓ **procedural memory** Implicit memory for cognitive and motor tasks that have a physical procedural aspect to them.

▓ **priming** The implicit influence of an earlier presented stimulus on the response to a later stimulus. This influence is independent of conscious memory for the earlier stimulus.

▓ **amnesic** A person with severe memory deficits following brain surgery or injury.

above-average intelligence, and no perceptual or language deficits, but he didn't seem able to store any new information in long-term memory (Scoville & Milner, 1957). For example, H. M. could read the same magazine over and over again and think it was a new magazine each time. If he did not know someone before his operation and that person introduced herself to him and then left the room for a few minutes, he would not know the person when she returned. Even Brenda Milner and Suzanne Corkin, the two neuroscientists who studied H. M. for decades, had to introduce themselves anew each time they met with him.

H. M. suffered from **anterograde amnesia**—the inability to form new explicit long-term memories following surgery or trauma to the brain. Anterograde amnesia is contrasted with **retrograde amnesia**—the disruption of memory for the past, especially episodic information for events before, especially just before, brain surgery or trauma. Such amnesia is typical in cases of brain concussions. H. M. suffered some retrograde amnesia, especially for the several days preceding the surgery, but this was mild compared to his severe, pervasive anterograde amnesia.

The late Henry Gustav Molaison, better known as H. M. in the hundreds of studies in which he participated.

Remember, as we just learned, amnesics have shown implicit repetition priming effects. So what about H. M.? Although he didn't form any new explicit long-term memories (but see O'Kane, Kensinger, & Corkin, 2004), did he too form new implicit memories? The answer is a resounding yes (Corkin, 2002). Let's briefly consider some of the experiments demonstrating this. H. M. demonstrated implicit procedural memory on a mirror-tracing task. In this task, you have to trace a pattern that can be seen only in its mirror image, which also shows your tracing hand moving in the direction opposite to its actual movement. This is a difficult motor task, but there is a practice effect in that the number of errors decreases across practice sessions. H. M.'s performance on this task showed a normal practice effect even when months elapsed between the sessions (Gabrieli, Corkin, Mickel, & Growdon, 1993). However, he did not remember ever having done this task and had to have the instructions repeated each session. Corkin (1968) also found that H. M. improved with practice on another manual skill learning task, one in which he had to keep a stylus on a small dot that was spinning around on a turntable. H. M. got better at this task with practice, but he had no conscious memory of his earlier experiences that led to his improved performance.

H. M. also demonstrated implicit repetition priming effects on a word fragment completion task without conscious awareness of the earlier presented priming words (Corkin, 2002) and implicit memory for a classically conditioned

▌ **anterograde amnesia** The inability to form new explicit long-term memories for events following surgery or trauma to the brain. Explicit memories formed before the surgery or trauma are left intact

▌ **retrograde amnesia** The disruption of memory for the past, especially episodic information for events before, especially just before, surgery or trauma to the brain.

The Mirror-Drawing Task The task is to trace the outline of a star (or some other shape) with a metal stylus when the star and your hand can be seen only in the mirror. Thus, the tracing movements have to be made in the direction opposite from the way in which they appear in the mirror. When the stylus moves off of the star outline (each red section in the illustrated tracing), it makes electrical contact with the underlying aluminum plate and a tracing error is recorded. There is nonconducting tape on the star outline so as long as the stylus stays on the outline, no electrical contact is made. Just like we would, H. M. improved from session to session (the number of errors he made decreased) as he gained more experience in this task. However, unlike us, he could not remember ever having performed the task before and had to have the task explained to him each session. As explained in the text, this means that he formed new implicit procedural memories for how to do the task, but he did not form new explicit episodic memories of having performed the task.

eyeblink response (Woodruff-Pak, 1993). In the latter case, after he was classically conditioned to give an eyeblink response to a tone, he could not consciously remember the conditioning episodes; however, he stored an implicit memory of the conditioned association between the tone and eyeblink. Thus, he blinked when he was exposed to the tone but had no idea why he did so. LeDoux (1996) tells the story of a similar finding with a female amnesic with memory deficits like those of H. M. She was unable to recognize her doctor (Edouard Claparède) so each day Dr. Claparède shook her hand and introduced himself. One day, however, the doctor concealed a tack in his hand so that when shaking hands, the tack pricked her. The next time the doctor tried to introduce himself and shake hands, she refused to do so but didn't know why. She had been conditioned without any explicit awareness of it.

How is it possible that H. M. and amnesics like him can form new implicit but not explicit memories? Research indicates that other parts of the brain, such as the cerebellum and cortex, and not the hippocampus are important for implicit memory formation and storage (Green & Woodruff-Pak, 2000; Krupa, Thompson, & Thompson, 1993; Squire, 2004). Implicit memory formation is functional in these amnesics because the cerebellum and the other parts of the brain necessary for such memories are intact, but explicit memory formation isn't because the hippocampus has been removed. This explanation is also one of those proposed for **infantile/child amnesia,** our inability as adults to remember events that occurred in our lives before about 3 years of age. According to this explanation, we cannot remember our

▌ **infantile/child amnesia** Our inability as adults to remember events that occurred in our lives before about 3 years of age.

experiences during this period because the hippocampus, which is crucial to the formation of episodic explicit long-term memories, is not yet fully developed. It is also important to realize that although the hippocampus is critical to the formation of such memories, it is not the final repository for these memories. As explicit memories age, the hippocampus's participation wanes (Smith & Squire, 2009). These memories are distributed throughout many areas in the cortex, but how this happens and how these memories are represented remain questions to be answered (Miller, 2005).

free recall task A memory task in which a list of items is presented one at a time and then the participant is free to recall them in any order.

primacy effect The superior recall of the early portion of a list relative to the middle of the list in a one-trial free recall task.

recency effect The superior recall of the latter portion of a list relative to the middle of the list in a one-trial free recall task.

Evidence for short-term versus long-term memory distinction. The memory findings for amnesics like H. M. also indicate that short-term memory and long-term memory are different stages of memory. H. M.'s short-term memory did not suffer any substantial deficits after the operation. For example, his memory span is within the normal range. He can repeat a telephone number with no difficulty. Researchers examining the free recall task have found additional evidence that long-term memory and short-term memory are different stages. In the **free recall task,** participants are given a list of words one at a time and then asked to recall them in any order they wish. Kirkpatrick (1894) introduced the free recall task, noting that some word positions are recalled much better than others. If recall performance for the words is plotted in terms of the order the words were presented (their position in the list—first, second, . . . , last), the figure has a very distinctive shape (Figure 5.6). The ends of the list are recalled much more often than the middle of the list. The superior recall of the early portion of the list is called the **primacy effect.** The superior recall of the latter portion of the list is called the **recency effect.**

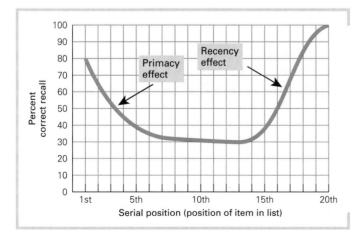

▲ **Figure 5.6 | Serial Position Effects for the Free Recall Task |** The superior recall of the first few items presented relative to those in the middle of the list is called the primacy effect. This effect is due to the fact that the primary items in the list are studied more and so have a higher probability of being in long-term memory for later recall. The recency effect refers to the superior recall of the last few items presented versus those in the middle of the list. This effect is due to the easy immediate recall of the items presently in short-term memory (those recently presented).

How do the primacy effect and recency effect relate to the distinction between short-term and long-term memory? The recency effect is caused by recall from short-term memory. Items at the end of the list, the most recent items, have a high probability of still being in short-term memory, so they can be recalled immediately and very well. The primacy effect, however, is the result of superior recall from long-term memory of the first few words in the list versus those in the middle (Rundus & Atkinson, 1970). Let's think about the task. The words are presented one at a time. The first word comes into your empty short-term memory to be rehearsed. It gets 100 percent of your attention. Then the second word appears and is rehearsed with the first word (each gets 50 percent of your attention). This goes on until short-term memory capacity is reached and each new word causes a word already in short-term memory to be bumped out. This results in the first few items on the list being rehearsed more than the later words in the middle and thus having a higher probability of being stored in long-term memory and recalled better. The items in the middle of the list come into a filled short-term memory, get little rehearsal, and thus have a low probability of being stored in long-term memory and recalled later. This is similar to what sometimes happens to students on exams. They study one topic more than another, and this translates to better test performance on the more-studied topic.

How do we know that this is so? Researchers have demonstrated that the primacy effect and the recency effect can be manipulated independently, indicating that different memory stages are involved. For example, if recall is delayed by having the participants count rapidly backward by 3s for 30 seconds, the recency effect is eliminated, but the primacy effect remains (Glanzer & Cunitz, 1966). Thus, the distractor period only disturbed recall from short-term memory. Similarly, we can eliminate the primacy effect but still observe a recency effect if we force participants to rehearse each of the list items equally by having them only rehearse each word aloud after it is presented. With equal rehearsal, the primary and middle items are recalled equally well so there is no primacy effect; and because amount of rehearsal is not critical to recall from short-term memory, a recency effect (although smaller) remains. In addition, recent fMRI neuroimaging data indicate that both short-term memory and long-term memory are involved in these serial position effects (Talmi, Grady, Goshen-Gottstein, & Moscovitch, 2005). Recognition of early items in the word list uniquely activated brain areas traditionally associated with long-term memory, but none of these areas were activated for retrieval of late items in the list.

We learned that more rehearsal leads to better long-term memory, but is better memory just a matter of more rehearsal (more study)? This question is addressed in the next section where we discuss moving information from short-term to long-term memory (what you try to do when you study). You will learn that the type of rehearsal (study method) you use is important. Thus, the information in the next section can help you to develop better study strategies and better memory.

Section Summary

In this section, we discussed the three-stage model that describes the processing of information entering from the physical environment through our senses into our memory system. In general, sensory information enters the sensory registers that comprise the first stage of processing—sensory memory. These temporary storage registers have large capacities and hold essentially exact copies of the information until we can attend to it and process it further. The duration of these registers is very brief, however. In the case of the visual sensory register, the duration is less than a second. We can only attend to part of the information in each register to process it farther into the memory system. The rest of the information fades quickly from the register and is forgotten.

The information that we attend to gets recognized and moves into our short-term memory, the second stage in the three-stage memory model. Short-term memory is like our conscious workspace. It has a small capacity (7 ± 2 chunks of information) and a brief duration (less than 30 seconds). Short-term memory is sometimes referred to as working memory because it is here that we do the work necessary to encode new information into long-term memory and to accomplish all of our other conscious activities, such as problem solving and decision making.

The third stage of processing, long-term memory, is what we normally mean when we use the word "memory." It is our long-term (perhaps permanent) repository for information. In addition, the capacity of long-term memory is essentially limitless. There are different types of long-term memories. The major distinction is between explicit memories (ones that require conscious recall and declaration) and implicit memories (those that do not require conscious recall and declaration). There are two types of explicit memories—semantic memories (our factual knowledge base) and episodic memories (our personal life experiences). There are three types of implicit memories—procedural memories that involve some type of physical or cognitive procedure, classical conditioning memories, and memories leading to priming effects.

Research findings with amnesics who have suffered hippocampal damage indicate that the hippocampus is important for explicit memory formation but not implicit memory formation. These findings also support the distinctiveness of short-term and long-term memories because these amnesics have relatively normal short-term memory. Further evidence for these two stages is provided by the primacy effect and the recency effect for free recall. The independent manipulation of these effects indicates that they are the products of recall from different memory stages.

ConceptCheck | 1

▶ Explain why you can think of the information in sensory memory as bottom-up input and the information in long-term memory as top-down input.

▶ Explain why the very brief duration of iconic memory is necessary for normal visual perception.

▶ Explain what is meant by the term "chunk" with respect to the capacity of short-term memory, 7 ± 2 chunks.

▶ Explain how the studies of H. M. indicate that he cannot form any new explicit long-term memories, but can form new implicit long-term memories.

Encoding Information into Memory

There are three essential processes in our memory system—encoding, storage, and retrieval. **Encoding** is the process of transferring information from one memory stage to the next (sensory into short-term memory and from short-term into long-term memory). **Storage** refers to the process of maintaining information in a particular stage. Storage is temporary except for long-term memory. **Retrieval** is the process of bringing information stored in long-term memory to the conscious level in short-term memory. Let's go back to the flow chart of the three-stage model of memory in Figure 5.1 (page 172). Encoding and retrieval determine the flow of information within the three-stage system. Information is first encoded from sensory memory to short-term memory where it can be stored temporarily. Information is then encoded from short-term to long-term memory where it is stored more permanently, but can be retrieved and brought back into short-term memory when we need to use it.

In this section, we will cover encoding and its role in moving information from short-term into long-term memory. Our focus will be on the best ways to achieve this transfer. We begin with a consideration of general encoding strategies.

How We Encode Information

The first distinction to consider is automatic versus effortful processing. **Automatic processing** is processing that occurs subconsciously and does not require attention. In contrast, **effortful processing** is processing that occurs consciously and requires attention. For a particular type of processing to become automatic, much practice is needed. A good example is reading. At first, learning to read is very effortful, but after years of practice it becomes easier and more automatic. Wouldn't it be nice if encoding to learn (studying) were an automatic process? It is unlikely that studying can become as automatic as reading, but we can get better at it by using better encoding strategies and practicing these strategies. In this section, we'll discuss some better ways to encode. If you practice them, your encoding (and your memory) will improve.

Levels-of-processing theory. Remember that encoding is the process of transferring information from one memory stage into another. Here we are interested in encoding from short-term to long-term memory. Encoding information into long-term memory is related to retrieving information from long-term memory. Some types of encoding lead to better retrieval. The **levels-of-processing theory** describes what types of encoding lead to better retrieval (Craik & Lockhart, 1972). This theory assumes that incoming information can be processed at different levels, from the simplistic physical level to the semantic level, and that semantic processing,

encoding The process of moving information from one memory stage to the next (from sensory memory into short-term memory or from short-term memory to long-term memory).

storage The process of maintaining information in a memory stage.

retrieval The process of bringing information stored in long-term memory into short-term memory.

automatic processing Memory processing that occurs subconsciously and does not require attention.

effortful processing Memory processing that occurs consciously and requires attention.

levels-of-processing theory A theory of information processing in memory that assumes that semantic processing, especially elaborative semantic processing, leads to better long-term memory.

especially elaborative semantic processing, leads to better memory. According to this theory, there are three general levels of processing—physical, acoustic, and semantic. To understand the differences among these three levels, consider processing the word "brain." We can process it as a string of lowercase letters. This would be the physical level. Next we could process "brain" by how it sounds, the acoustic level, which is a little deeper than the physical level. Third, we can process what "brain" means and then elaborate upon that meaning by relating it to what we know about parts of the brain and brain chemistry.

Let's consider an experiment to see how these three levels may lead to different levels of memory performance. Researchers presented participants with a long list of words one at a time, but manipulated the level of processing of the words by manipulating the task to be performed on each word (Craik & Tulving, 1975; Experiment 2). For each word, one of three types of questions had to be answered. One type of question required processing the word at a physical level (for example, "Is this word in capital letters?"). A second type of question required acoustic processing (for example, "Does the word rhyme with bear?"). The third type of question required semantic processing (for example, "Will the word fit in the sentence, The man placed the ____ on the table?"). Participants did not know that they would be tested for their memory of the words. They only thought that they had to answer a question about each word. However, the experimenter later surprised the participants with a memory test for the words. Levels-of-processing theory predicts that memory for the words that had to be processed semantically should be best, those processed acoustically next best, and those only processed physically worst. This is exactly what was found (see Figure 5.7). Long-term recognition memory was the best for the words encoded semantically, next best for those encoded acoustically, and worst for those only encoded physically.

Elaborative rehearsal. Maintenance rehearsal, the repetitive cycling of information in short-term memory, was discussed earlier in the chapter. This type of rehearsal serves to maintain information in short-term memory. Levels-of-processing theory, however, views this type of rehearsal as shallow, acoustic rehearsal. It is not very effective in producing good long-term memory for information. Semantic processing is much better. Once at the semantic level of processing, though, we should engage in **elaborative rehearsal**—rehearsing by relating the new material to information already in long-term memory. The memory organization created by the integration of the new information

▪ **elaborative rehearsal** A type of rehearsal in short-term memory in which incoming information is related to information from long-term memory to encode it into long-term memory.

▲ **Figure 5.7 | Differences in Recognition Memory for Words Processed at Different Levels |** Participants were presented a long list of words one at a time and had to answer a question about each word as it was presented. The nature of the questions led to different levels of processing—physical (how it was printed), acoustic (how it sounded), or semantic (what it meant). The level of processing dramatically affected the participants' later ability to recognize the word as one that had been on this list. (Adapted from Craik & Tulving, 1975; Experiment 2.)

with existing information leads to more successful retrieval of the information than shallower processing. This organization provides more retrieval cues (links with other information in long-term memory) for the new information, thereby facilitating its retrieval. For example, to elaborately encode the concept of elaborative rehearsal, you could relate it to other concepts that you learned recently by thinking about such things as how elaborative rehearsal is different from maintenance rehearsal, how it relates to levels-of-processing theory, and how it is an example of effortful processing. Such elaboration enables much better long-term memory.

In elaborative rehearsal, you should try to relate the new information to information you know well. Because you know yourself so well, you should elaborate by tying the new information to yourself. To learn new concepts, you should personalize them by thinking of examples of these concepts in your own experiences. It is easier to remember information that you have related to yourself. This is called the **self-reference effect,** and it is a well-established research finding (Symons & Johnson, 1997). For example, researchers have found that people can remember more words from a list if they related the words to themselves (Rogers, Kuiper, & Kirker, 1977). Participants were asked whether list words such as "generous" applied to them. Later recall of such words was very good, even better than for words processed at the semantic level (as in the Craik and Tulving study). Think about how this might work. What if the word were "honest"? You would start thinking about incidents in your life in which you were honest and in which you were not. The word would then be linked to all of these incidents, facilitating its later recall. So when you are studying a new concept, try to find examples of it in your own life. For some concepts this is easy to do; for others it isn't. However, it's worth the effort because such connections will help you to remember the concept through the self-reference effect.

Environmental effects on encoding. The fact that elaborative rehearsal improves memory stems from a larger principle—the encoding specificity principle (Tulving, 1983). In simple terms, the **encoding specificity principle** proposes that the cues present during encoding serve as the best cues for retrieval. This is why the various concepts and examples that you relate to a new concept during elaborative rehearsal help you remember the concept. They were present during encoding so they serve as good retrieval cues. Such cues are internal environmental cues; they refer to internal cognitive processing, what you were thinking about during rehearsal. Encoding specificity also applies to the external environmental cues present during encoding. Many research studies have shown that long-term memory is better when the physical study and test environments are as similar as possible. For example, in one rather dramatic demonstration of this, participants learned and were tested either underwater or on land (Godden & Baddeley, 1975). The two groups that had the same study-test environments (both were underwater or on land) remembered significantly better

▓ **self-reference effect** The superior long-term memory for information related to oneself at time of encoding into long-term memory.

▓ **encoding specificity principle** The principle that the environmental cues (both internal and external) present at the time information is encoded into long-term memory serve as the best retrieval cues for the information.

than the two groups that had their study-test environments reversed. However, you need not rush to classrooms to study. Classroom environmental effects on college exam performance are not very strong (Saufley, Otaka, & Bavaresco, 1985). Why? External environmental effects on learning diminish when the learning has taken place in several environments (Smith, Glenberg, & Bjork, 1978). In the case of exams, students have learned the relevant information in a variety of environments ranging from the classroom to nonclassroom environments, such as the library and dormitory rooms, thereby overriding the classroom environmental effect.

We have limited our discussion so far to a rather narrow definition of internal environment—a person's mental activities at the time of encoding. Broader internal environmental factors, such as a person's physiological state or mood, also impact encoding and retrieval. These effects lead to a phenomenon known as **state-dependent memory,** memory that depends upon the relationship of one's physiological state at time of encoding and retrieval. The best memory occurs when people are in the same state at retrieval as they were at encoding, and memory is hindered by state differences. For example, people under the influence of alcohol at time of encoding would recall best if under the influence at the time of retrieval. Please note, however, that memory under the influence of alcohol, regardless of the state at the time of retrieval, is very poor. It is best to encode and retrieve in a nonalcoholic state.

There are similar effects on memory that depend on the relationship between a person's emotional states, such as being happy or sad, at time of encoding and retrieval. Because one's mood is involved, these effects are referred to as **mood-dependent memory,** the retrieval of a particular memory is better when a person's mood at retrieval is the same as it was during encoding. Like state-dependency effects, mood-dependency effects furnish support for the encoding specificity principle—context is important for successful memory retrieval. There is also a related phenomenon called the **mood-congruence effect**—the tendency to recall memories that are congruent with a person's current mood. A particular mood cues memories that are consistent with that mood (Eich, 1995). We tend to remember more positive events when we are feeling good and more negative events when we are feeling down. These events have been associated with the accompanying emotions. Thus, the emotions serve as retrieval cues for the events. This congruency effect may hinder recovery in depressed people because they will tend to remember negative events and not positive ones. In

> **state-dependent memory** Long-term memory retrieval is best when a person's physiological state at the time of encoding and retrieval of the information is the same.

> **mood-dependent memory** Long-term memory retrieval is best when a person's mood state at the time of encoding and retrieval of the information is the same.

> **mood-congruence effect** Tendency to retrieve experiences and information that are congruent with a person's current mood.

Callahan

Callahan. Courtesy of Levin Represents.

"I wonder if you'd mind giving me directions. I've never been sober in this part of town before."

■ **mnemonic** A memory aid.

■ **method of loci** A mnemonic in which sequential pieces of information to be remembered are encoded by associating them with sequential locations in a very familiar room or place and then the pieces of information are retrieved by mentally going around the room (place) and retrieving the piece at each location.

fact, this is the case. Depressed patients report more memories related to illness, injury, and death than nondepressed people (Schacter, 2000). Think positively, and the mood-congruency effect will help maintain that positive attitude.

In summary, elaborative rehearsal is the most effective strategy for encoding. Research has found that actors use elaborative rehearsal including encoding specificity, mood-congruency effects, and the self-reference effect to learn their lines (Noice & Noice, 1997). They do not use shallow processing and just memorize their lines. (Neither should students try this in their courses!) Elaborative rehearsal is the key to more effective learning. It is important to practice this type of rehearsal. You should integrate information that you are trying to learn with as much other information in your knowledge base as you can, especially relating it to yourself. You will get better at this elaboration strategy as you practice it, and learning will become easier.

How to Improve Encoding

In this section, we will discuss a few more specific ways to improve memory. We'll start with some techniques to improve memory for lists and more organized sets of concepts. These techniques use a **mnemonic,** a memory aid. Mnemonics are useful for remembering lists of items, especially ordered lists, speeches, and long passages of text. We'll start with a mnemonic that was used by ancient Greek orators to remember speeches.

The Greek orators used a mnemonic called the **method of loci** (Yates, 1966). "Loci" is the plural of "locus," which means place or location. In the method of loci, the sequential pieces of information to be remembered are first associated with sequential locations in a very familiar room or place. Then, when retrieving the information, one would merely mentally go around the room (or place) and retrieve the item stored at each sequential location. The Greek orators would mentally store the major points of a speech at sequential locations in the room where they were speaking. Then, during the speech an orator would go from location to location within the room to retrieve the key points of his speech. If you were trying to remember an ordered list of items for an exam, you could pair the items systematically with locations within the classroom and then during the exam mentally go from location to location within the classroom to retrieve them. The method of loci is a type of elaborative rehearsal using mental imagery. You elaborate upon items that you want to remember by visually associating them with a series of locations that you already know well or that will be available at the time of recall.

© 1994 by Sidney Harris.

"You simply associate each number with a word, such as 'table' and 3,476,029."

All mnemonics work by using some type of elaboration. In another mnemonic, the **peg-word system,** you visually associate the items in a list with a jingle that you first memorize. The jingle is "One is a bun, two is a shoe, three is a tree, four is a door, five is a hive, six is sticks, seven is heaven, eight is a gate, nine is swine, and ten is a hen." You then associate each successive item in the list with the object for each successive number. For example, the first item on the list would be associated visually in a mental image with bun. If the word to be remembered were "dog", then you might construct an image of a big bun with a dog in it. Then, as you go through the peg words, you retrieve the associated image, so you can retrieve the list.

One might think that these mnemonic techniques require much more effort than just memorizing the information that we want to remember. But researchers have found that people using mnemonics demonstrate much better memory than those who have just attempted to memorize a list. Why? As we discussed earlier, elaborative rehearsal is better for encoding into long-term memory. Interestingly, one mnemonic that involves little elaboration has not been found to be more effective—the first-letter technique (Gruneberg & Herrmann, 1997). In the first-letter technique, you compose a word, acronym, or sentence from the first letters of the words you want to remember. The mnemonic that we suggested in Chapter 3 to use to remember the colors of the spectrum (the name ROY G. BIV—**R**ed, **O**range, **Y**ellow, **G**reen, **B**lue, **I**ndigo, **V**iolet) is an example of this technique. This mnemonic helps, but it is not as effective as the other, more elaborative mnemonics, especially for more complex information.

So what else—in addition to elaborative rehearsal and the use of mnemonics—improves encoding? There are two concepts that will help: (1) distribute study over time and do not just cram, and (2) practice makes perfect. The superior memory for spaced study versus cramming is called the **spacing (distributed study) effect.** Your memory will improve if you distribute your studying for an exam over the entire preparation interval and not just the few days before the exam (Payne & Wenger, 1996). In fact, for best results, distribute study and cram.The more you study, the more you learn. Overlearning, continuing to study material past the point of initial learning, improves memory. Remember what we said about practice and automatic processing. Continued practice will make retrieval more automatic. Such practice may not make you "perfect," but you'll definitely do better.

peg-word system A mnemonic in which the items in a list to be remembered are associated with the sequential items in a memorized jingle and then the list is retrieved by going through the jingle and retrieving the associated items.

spacing (distributed study) effect Superior long-term memory for spaced study versus massed study (cramming).

Section Summary

In this section, we discussed the most effective encoding strategy, elaborative rehearsal, which is relating new information to well-known information in long-term memory. Elaboration is most effective when we relate the new information to ourselves, the self-reference effect. Elaborative rehearsal leads to better memory because we create good retrieval cues when we integrate the new information with older, well-known information. This relates to the encoding specificity principle, which states that the best retrieval cues are those present during encoding. We learned that state-dependent memory, mood-dependent memory, and mood-congruent memory are special cases of this principle. In these cases, the physiological state and the emotional mood provide strong retrieval cues.

We also discussed how mnemonic devices, memory aid techniques, are especially effective for remembering ordered information in a list, speech, or text. The method of loci, which originated in ancient Greece, and the peg-word system are both very effective because of their use of elaboration and visual imagery. In addition, to improve memory we should engage in spaced study—distributing our elaborative study over time rather than cramming. Overlearning is also beneficial.

ConceptCheck | 2

> Explain why elaborative encoding is more effective than just memorizing.

> Explain how state-dependent memory and mood-dependent memory stem from the encoding specificity principle.

> Explain what the method-of-loci mnemonic and the peg-word system mnemonic have in common.

Retrieving Information from Memory

In the last section, we focused on how to encode information into long-term memory. In this section, we will examine how we retrieve encoded information. First, we will consider the various ways that retrieval is measured. This will be followed by a discussion of forgetting, the failure to retrieve. Here we will discuss the major theories of why our memories fail us. Then, we will examine the reconstructive nature of the retrieval process by considering the role of schemas, source misattribution, and the misinformation effect. Finally, we will discuss the problem of "false" memories.

How to Measure Retrieval

The three main methods for measuring our ability to retrieve information from long-term memory are recall, recognition, and relearning. **Recall** is a measure of retrieval that requires the reproduction of the information with essentially no retrieval cues. Common recall measures would be short-answer and essay test questions. **Recognition** is a measure of retrieval that only requires the identification of the information in the presence of retrieval cues. In a recognition test you do not have to reproduce the information, you only have to identify it. Multiple-choice and matching test questions are examples of recognition test questions. Usually such questions are easier because retrieval cues (the answers themselves) are present to help you remember the information. The third method, **relearning,** is sometimes called the savings method because it is a measure of the amount of time

recall A measure of long-term memory retrieval that requires the reproduction of the information with essentially no retrieval cues.

recognition A measure of long-term memory retrieval that only requires the identification of the information in the presence of retrieval cues.

relearning The savings method of measuring long-term memory retrieval in which the measure is the amount of time saved when learning information for the second time.

saved when learning information for the second time. The most relevant example of relearning for students is studying for a comprehensive final examination in a course. You must relearn the material. It will take you less time to relearn it, but how much less depends upon how well you learned it the first time.

Hermann Ebbinghaus conducted the first experimental studies on human memory over a hundred years ago in Germany using the relearning method (Ebbinghaus, 1885/1964). His stimulus materials were lists of nonsense syllables, groupings of three letters (consonant-vowel-consonant such as BAV) that are not words or acronyms. He used meaningless nonsense syllables because he wanted to study pure memory for the list items. His familiarity with and knowledge of words and acronyms would have affected his ability to learn and remember the lists. His

Hermann Ebbinghaus

experimental procedure was very straightforward. He would study a list of nonsense syllables until he could correctly recite the complete list without any hesitations. He then put the list aside and waited some period of time (from 20 minutes up to 31 days) and then relearned the list to the same criterion (one complete recitation without any hesitations).

To get a measure of relearning, Ebbinghaus computed what he called a savings score—the reduction in the number of trials it took him to reach criterion. For example, if it took him 10 trials to learn a list initially and only 5 to relearn it, he saved 50 percent (5 vs. 10 trials). He used many different lists of nonsense syllables and many different retention intervals (the different amounts of time between initial learning and relearning). The results were like those shown in Figure 5.8 (page 194). The forgetting curve in this figure shows that the greatest amount of forgetting occurs rather quickly and then tapers off. In Ebbinghaus's case, after about 2 days, little more forgetting occurred. This type of forgetting curve for long-term memory has been obtained over and over again in memory research (Bahrick, 1984). What causes this forgetting? Let's consider some possible explanations.

Why We Forget

There is no question that we forget. Our memories clearly fail us. This is especially problematic for exams. Haven't we all taken an exam and forgotten some information and then retrieved it after the exam was over? To understand forgetting, we must confront two questions. First, why do we forget? Second, do we really ever truly forget or do we just fail to retrieve information at a particular point in time? To answer these questions, we'll take a look at four theories of forgetting—encoding failure theory, storage decay theory, interference theory, and cue-dependent theory.

Encoding failure theory states that sometimes forgetting is not really forgetting but rather encoding failure (sometimes called pseudoforgetting). The information in question never entered long-term memory. We can't forget information

encoding failure theory A theory of forgetting that proposes that forgetting is due to the failure to encode the information into long-term memory.

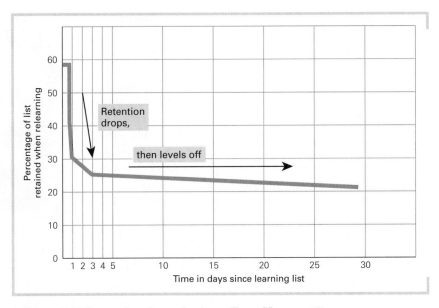

▲ **Figure 5.8** I **Forgetting Curve for Long-Term Memory** I The course of long-term forgetting usually takes on the shape of this figure—a rapid steep decrease that then levels off. In Ebbinghaus's memory research with nonsense syllables, the amount of time he saved relearning the material decreased dramatically for the first 2 days following initial learning and then leveled off after that. (Adapted from Ebbinghaus, 1885/1964.)

that never entered long-term memory (that we never encoded into long-term memory). This would be like trying to locate a particular book in a library when the library never purchased it. For a good example of encoding failure, take the common penny. How well do you remember its features? Take a few minutes and try to draw the front and back of a penny. If you're like the participants in Nickerson and Adams's (1979) study, you'll find this difficult to do. There are eight critical features on a penny, and Nickerson and Adams found the median number recalled and located correctly to be just three. As a second exercise, consider Figure 5.9. Which one of these pennies is the real penny? Nickerson and Adams found that most Americans do not know. Why? They probably never encoded the details of the penny, so just as they cannot draw a penny correctly, they cannot pick out the real one from fake ones. If we do not encode information into long-term memory, we obviously will not be able to remember it.

The other three theories of forgetting deal with information that was encoded into long-term memory, but that we cannot retrieve. The storage decay theory suggests that forgetting occurs because of a problem in the storage of the information. The **storage decay theory** assumes that the biological representation of the memory gradually decays

storage decay theory A theory of forgetting that proposes that forgetting is due to the decay of the biological representation of the information and that periodic usage of the information will help to maintain it in storage.

▲ **Figure 5.9 | An Example of Encoding Failure** | Can you identify the real penny? Most Americans cannot. Why? The answer is likely encoding failure. Most of us are not that interested in coins and have never bothered to encode the exact features of a penny into long-term memory, so we have difficulty in choosing the real penny. This may be referred to as forgetting, but it is more appropriately called encoding failure. You can't really forget something that you did not put into long-term memory. The first penny (a) is the real penny. (From Nickerson & Adams, 1979.)

over time and that periodic usage of the information will help to maintain it in storage. This latter assumption reflects the "use it or lose it" principle. This theory proposes that we forget because the information is no longer available in long-term memory. We forget because we cannot possibly remember it. The memory trace has decayed away. This would be like trying to get a particular book from a library, but finding that its pages had rotted away.

The other two theories of forgetting propose that there are retrieval problems and not a problem with storage. Both assume that the forgotten information is still available in long-term memory, but cannot be retrieved. Each of the theories proposes a different reason for why the information cannot be retrieved. **Interference theory** proposes that other information interferes and makes the forgotten information inaccessible. In our library book example, this would be comparable to boxes of books blocking access to the location where the book is located. This theory proposes two types of such interference: (1) **proactive interference**—the disruptive effect of prior learning on the retrieval of new information, and (2) **retroactive interference**—the disruptive effect of new learning on the retrieval of old information. Let's consider a couple of examples. Think about changing phone numbers after having a particular number for many years. When asked for your phone number, remembering the old one interferes with retrieving the new one. This would be proactive interference. The disruptive effect is from prior learning (your old phone number). For an example of retroactive interference, think about being at a party with many people you do not know. You meet someone that you want to talk to later, but

interference theory A theory of forgetting that proposes that forgetting is due to other information in memory interfering and thereby making the to-be-remembered information inaccessible.

proactive interference The disruptive effect of prior learning on the retrieval of new information.

retroactive interference The disruptive effect of new learning on the retrieval of old information.

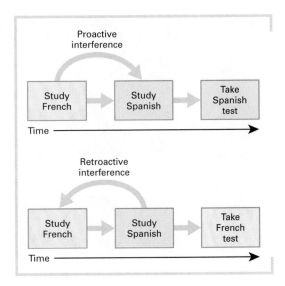

▲ **Figure 5.10** I **Proactive and Retroactive Interference** I In the proactive interference example, prior learning (French) disrupts memory for newly learned information (Spanish). In the retroactive interference example, new learning (Spanish) disrupts memory for information learned earlier (French).

after meeting her, you are introduced to several other people. Now you cannot remember her name. The names of the people that you met after her are interfering with your retrieval of her name. This is retroactive interference because it is a case of the disruptive effect of new learning on the retrieval of old information. An additional example of each type of interference is given in Figure 5.10.

Cue-dependent theory also assumes that forgetting stems from not gaining access to the desired information (Tulving, 1974). According to cue-dependent theory, we forget because the cues necessary for retrieval are not available. The information is available, but we cannot access it because we cannot find it. The cues we need to locate it are not available. This is like trying to find a particular book in a library without its call number and a map of the library stacks. We wouldn't have the cues necessary to locate it, so we would likely not be able to do so. Successful retrieval is dependent upon the availability of the retrieval cues.

So there are many reasons why we forget. The four major theories are summarized in Table 5.2, but how can you apply this knowledge to enhance your learning? First, sometimes we forget because we do not encode the information into long-term memory. You should be especially wary of this reason when you are preparing for your class exams. You need to study thoroughly to avoid encoding failure on exams. Second, we may forget if information that is encoded and stored in long-term memory isn't periodically recalled and refreshed. The information can fade away over time. Think about what you have learned in the various courses that you have taken so far in college. After a course is over, you may sometimes feel like you retained little of that information for very long. If you want to retain more of it for a longer period of time, you need to regularly recall and use it. Third, the information that we are trying to retrieve may still

cue-dependent theory A theory of forgetting that proposes that forgetting is due to the unavailability of the retrieval cues necessary to locate the information in long-term memory.

Table 5.2	Four Theories of Forgetting
Theory	**Explanation of Forgetting**
Encoding Failure Theory	Forgetting is due to the failure to encode the information into long-term memory
Storage Decay Theory	Forgetting is due to the decay of the biological representation of the information in long-term memory
Interference Theory	Forgetting is due to the interference of other information in long-term memory, making the forgotten information inaccessible
Cue-dependent Theory	Forgetting is due to the unavailability of the retrieval cues necessary to locate the information in long-term memory

be there, but we forget because other information may interfere with our retrieval of it or we may not have the necessary retrieval cues available to find it. Elaboration during encoding and overlearning will help to reduce these retrieval problems.

The next section concerns the information that we do retrieve. Is it accurate or is it distorted? The answer is that it is often distorted. How does this occur? It occurs because retrieval is reconstructive and not exact. Let's take at look at the retrieval process to see how its reconstructive nature may distort our memories.

The Reconstructive Nature of Retrieval

The act of remembering is an act of reconstruction. Memory does not work like a tape recorder or a video recorder. Retrieval is not like playback. Our memories are far from exact replicas of past events. If you read a newspaper this morning, do you remember the stories that you read in the paper word for word? We usually encode the gist or main theme of the story along with some of the story's highlights. Then, when we retrieve the information from our memory, we reconstruct a memory of the story using the theme and the highlights.

Our retrieval reconstruction is guided by what are called **schemas**—frameworks for our knowledge about people, objects, events, and actions. These schemas allow us to organize our world. For example, what happens when you enter a dentist's office or what happens when you go to a restaurant to eat? You have schemas in your memory for these events. The schemas tell us what normally happens. For example, consider the schema for eating out in a restaurant (Schank & Abelson, 1977). First, a host or hostess seats you and gives you a menu. Then the waitperson gets your drink order, brings your drinks, and then takes your meal order. Your food arrives, you eat it, the waitperson brings the bill. You pay it, leave a tip, and go. These schemas allow us to encode and retrieve information about the world in a more organized, efficient manner.

schemas Frameworks for our knowledge about people, objects, events, and actions that allow us to organize and interpret information about our world.

The first experimental work on schemas and their effects on memory was conducted by Sir Frederick Bartlett in the first half of the twentieth century (Bartlett, 1932). Bartlett had his participants study some stories that were rather unusual. He then tested their memory for these stories at varying time intervals. When the participants recalled the stories, they made them more consistent with their own schemas about the world. For example, one story did not say anyone was wounded in the battle described, but participants recalled that many men were wounded, fitting their schemas for battles. Unusual details were normalized. For example, participants recalled incorrectly that the men in another story were fishing rather than hunting seals. In addition, the stories were greatly shortened in length when recalled. Strangely, the participants did not even realize that they were changing many of the details of the stories. In fact, the parts that they changed were those that they were most confident about remembering.

Bartlett's participants had reconstructed the stories using their schemas and did not even realize it. The main point to remember is that they distorted the stories in line with their schemas. Why? Schemas allow us to encode and retrieve information more efficiently. It would be impossible to encode and retrieve the exact details of every event in our lives. That's why we need organizing schemas to guide us in this task, even though they do not provide an exact copy of what happened. This seems a small cost given the benefits provided by organizing memory in terms of schemas.

Memory can be further distorted in reconstruction by source misattribution and the misinformation effect. **Source misattribution** occurs when we do not remember the true source of a memory and attribute the memory to the wrong source. Maybe you dream something and then later misremember that it actually happened. You misattribute the source to actual occurrence rather than occurrence in a dream. Source information for memories is not very good. You need to beware of this when writing papers. You may unintentionally use another person's ideas and think they are yours. You have forgotten their source. Even if source misattribution is unintentional, it is still plagiarism.

A famous case of source misattribution involved noted developmental psychologist Jean Piaget (Loftus & Ketcham, 1991). For much of his life, Piaget believed that when he was a child, his nursemaid had thwarted an attempt to kidnap him. He remembered the attempt, even remembered the details of the event. When the nursemaid finally admitted to making up the story, Piaget couldn't believe it. He had reconstructed the event from the many times the nursemaid recounted the incident and misattributed the source to actual occurrence. This is like thinking that something we dreamed really occurred. The source of the memory is misattributed.

Source misattribution results in what is called a **false memory,** an inaccurate memory that feels as real as an accurate memory. False memories can also be the result of the misinformation effect. The **misinformation effect** occurs when a memory is distorted by subsequent exposure to misleading information. Elizabeth Loftus and her colleagues have

source misattribution Attributing a memory to the wrong source, resulting in a false memory.

false memory An inaccurate memory that feels as real as an accurate memory.

misinformation effect The distortion of a memory by exposure to misleading information.

provided many demonstrations of the misinformation effect. These studies usually involve witnessing an event and then being tested for memory of the event but being given misleading information at the time of the test. Let's consider an example.

Loftus and John Palmer (1974) showed participants a film of a traffic accident and then later tested their memory for the accident. The test included misleading information for some of the participants. For example, some participants were asked, "How fast were the cars going when they smashed into each other?" and others were asked, "How fast were the cars going when they hit each other?" Participants who were asked the question with the word "smashed" estimated the speed to be much higher than those who were asked the question with the word "hit." In addition, when brought back a week later, those participants who had been questioned with the word "smashed" more often thought that they had seen broken glass in the accident when in fact there was none. The key theme of this line of research is that our memories for events are distorted by exposure to misinformation. The resulting false memories seem like real memories.

SPECIAL GUEST

BRUNDAGE MORNALD, OF BATTLE CREEK, MONTANA

UNDER HYPNOSIS, MR. MORNALD RECOVERED LONG-BURIED MEMORIES OF A PERFECTLY NORMAL, HAPPY CHILDHOOD.

Lee Lorenz/The New Yorker Collection/www.cartoonbank.com

False memories have important implications for use of eyewitness testimony in criminal cases and for the controversy over memories of childhood sexual abuse that have supposedly been repressed but then are "recovered" in adulthood. The Loftus and Palmer research example shows us that eyewitness testimony is subject to error and manipulation by misleading information. Between 1989 and 2007, for example, 201 prisoners in the United States were freed because of DNA evidence; and 77% of these prisoners had been mistakenly identified by eyewitnesses (Hallinan, 2009). Many of these overturned cases rested on the testimony of two or more mistaken eyewitnesses. Eyewitnesses not only often misidentify innocent people as criminals but they also often do so with the utmost confidence, and jurors tend to heavily weigh an eyewitness's confidence when judging their believability.

Clearly, certain types of interrogation, including the way questions are worded, could lead to false memories. With respect to the repressed memory controversy, many memory researchers are skeptical and think that these "recovered" memories may describe events that never occurred (like the kidnapping attempt on Piaget as a child). Instead, they may be false memories that have been constructed and may even have been inadvertently implanted by therapists during treatment sessions. In fact, researchers have demonstrated that

Dr. Elizabeth Loftus has conducted research on eyewitness testimony and the inaccuracies in memory retrieval for over 30 years. Given her expertise in this area, she has testified as an expert witness in over 200 court cases, including many high-profile cases such as the trial of serial killer Ted Bundy (Neimark, 1996).

such implanting is possible (Loftus, Coan, & Pickrell, 1996; Loftus & Ketchum, 1994). We must remember, however, that demonstrating the possibility of an event does not demonstrate that it actually happened. So, are all memories of childhood sexual abuse false? Absolutely not. Sexual abuse of all kinds is unfortunately all too real. The important point for us is that the research on false memory has provided empirical evidence to support an alternative explanation to the claims for recovered memories, and will help to sort out the true cases from the false.

Section Summary

In this section, we considered the three ways to measure retrieval—recall, recognition, and relearning. In recall, the information has to be reproduced, but in recognition it only has to be identified. In relearning, the time one saves in relearning information is the measure of memory. For all three retrieval measures, forgetting from long-term memory levels off after a rapid initial burst of forgetting.

There are four major theories that address the question of why we forget. Encoding failure theory assumes that the information is never encoded into long-term memory, so it is not there to be retrieved. The storage decay theory assumes that the information is encoded but that it decays during storage so that it is no longer available to be retrieved. The other two theories assume that the information is still available in long-term memory, but cannot be accessed. Interference theory assumes that the retrieval failure is due to other information blocking our retrieval. This interfering information could be older information interfering with the retrieval of new information (proactive interference) or new information interfering with the retrieval of older information (retroactive interference). The other theory, cue-dependent theory, assumes that the cues necessary to retrieve the information are not available, meaning that the information cannot be located in long-term memory.

Memory is a reconstructive process guided by our schemas—organized frameworks of our knowledge about the world. The use of schemas along with source misattribution problems and the misinformation effect can lead to false memories, inaccurate memories that feel as real as accurate memories. Such false memories create questions about the accuracy of eyewitness testimony and the validity of supposed repressed memories of childhood abuse.

ConceptCheck | 3

> Explain the difference between recall and recognition as methods to measure retrieval.

> Explain how the four major theories of forgetting differ with respect to the availability versus accessibility of the forgotten information.

> Explain how schemas help to create false memories.

> Explain how source misattribution and the misinformation effect lead to false memories.

Study Guide

Chapter Key Terms

You should know the definitions of the following key terms from the chapter. They are listed in the order in which they appear in the chapter. For those you do not know, return to the relevant section of the chapter to learn them. When you think that you know all of the terms, complete the matching exercise based on these key terms.

sensory memory (SM)
iconic memory
temporal integration procedure
Sperling's full-report procedure
Sperling's partial-report procedure
short-term memory (STM)
memory span task
memory span
chunk
distractor task
maintenance rehearsal
long-term memory (LTM)
explicit (declarative) memory
semantic memory
episodic memory
implicit (nondeclarative) memory
procedural memory

priming
amnesic
anterograde amnesia
retrograde amnesia
infantile/child amnesia
free recall task
primacy effect
recency effect
encoding
storage
retrieval
automatic processing
effortful processing
levels-of-processing theory
elaborative rehearsal
self-reference effect
encoding specificity principle
state-dependent memory
mood-dependent memory
mood-congruence effect

mnemonic
method of loci
peg-word system
spacing (distributed study) effect
recall
recognition
relearning
encoding failure theory
storage decay theory
interference theory
proactive interference
retroactive interference
cue-dependent theory
schemas
source misattribution
false memory
misinformation effect

Key Terms Exercise

Identify the correct key term for each of the following definitions. The answers to this exercise follow the answers to the Concept Checks at the end of the chapter.

1. The principle that states that the cues (both internal and external) present at the time information is encoded into long-term memory serve as the best retrieval cues for the information.

_____

2. A measure of long-term memory retrieval that requires the reproduction of the information with essentially no retrieval cues.

_____

3. The disruptive effect of new learning on the retrieval of old information.

_____

4. The visual sensory register that holds an exact copy of the incoming visual input

but only for a very brief period of time—less than a second.

_____

5. A meaningful unit in memory.

_____

6. Long-term memory for factual knowledge and personal experiences that requires a conscious effort to remember and that entails making declarations about the information remembered.

_____

7. The inability to form new explicit long-term memories for events following surgery or trauma to the brain.

_____

8. A type of rehearsal in short-term memory in which incoming information is related to information from long-term memory to encode it into long-term memory.

_____

9. Superior long-term memory for spaced study versus massed study (cramming).

_____

10. Frameworks of knowledge about people, objects, events, and actions that allow us to organize and interpret information about our world.

_____

11. Explicit memory for personal experiences.

_____

12. A theory of forgetting that proposes that forgetting is due to the unavailability of the retrieval cues necessary to locate the information in long-term memory.

_____

13. An experimental procedure in which, following the brief presentation of a matrix of unrelated consonants, the participant

is given an auditory cue about which row of the matrix to recall.

_____

14. Our inability as adults to remember events that occurred in our lives before about 3 years of age.

_____

15. A memory task in which the participant is given a series of items one at a time and then has to recall the items in the order in which they were presented.

_____

Practice Test Questions

The following are practice multiple-choice test questions on some of the chapter content. The answers are given after the Key Terms Exercise answers at the end of the chapter. If you guessed or incorrectly answered a question, restudy the relevant section of the chapter.

1. Which of the following types of memory holds sensory input until we can attend to and recognize it?
   a. short-term memory
   b. sensory memory
   c. semantic memory
   d. episodic memory

2. Our short-term memory capacity is _____ ± 2 chunks.
   a. 3
   b. 5
   c. 7
   d. 9

3. Which of the following types of memory has the shortest duration?
   a. sensory memory
   b. short-term memory
   c. semantic memory
   d. episodic memory

4. Procedural memories are _____ memories and thus are probably processed in the _____.

a. explicit; hippocampus

b. explicit; cerebellum

c. implicit; hippocampus

d. implicit; cerebellum

5. Which of the following leads to the best long-term memory?

a. maintenance rehearsal

b. elaborative rehearsal

c. physical processing

d. acoustic processing

6. The primacy and recency effects in free recall demonstrate that we have the greatest difficulty recalling the words _____ of a list.

a. at the beginning

b. at the end

c. in the middle

d. at the beginning and end

7. Which of the following is not a mnemonic aid?

a. method of loci

b. peg-word system

c. temporal integration procedure

d. first-letter technique

8. An essay test measures _____, and a multiple-choice test measures _____.

a. recall; recall

b. recall; recognition

c. recognition; recall

d. recognition; recognition

9. Which of the following theories of forgetting argues that the forgotten information was in long-term memory but is no longer available?

a. encoding failure theory

b. storage decay theory

c. interference theory

d. cue-dependent theory

10. Piaget's false memory of a kidnapping attempt when he was a child was the result of _____.

a. infantile amnesia

b. source misattribution

c. encoding failure

d. storage decay

11. After learning the phone number for Five Star Pizza, Bob cannot remember the phone number he learned last week for the Donut Connection. After living in Los Angeles for three years, Jim is unable to remember his way around his hometown in which he had lived the previous 10 years prior to moving to Los Angeles. Bob is experiencing the effects of _____ interference, and Jim is experiencing the effects of _____ interference.

a. proactive; proactive

b. proactive; retroactive

c. retroactive; proactive

d. retroactive; retroactive

12. Per levels-of-processing theory, which of the following questions about the word "depressed" would best prepare you to correctly remember tomorrow that you had seen the word in this practice test question today?

a. How well does the word describe you?

b. Does the word consist of 10 letters?

c. Is the word typed in capital letters?

d. Does the word rhyme with obsessed?

13. The forgetting curve for long-term memory in Ebbinghaus's relearning studies with nonsense syllables indicates that _____.

a. the greatest amount of forgetting occurs rather quickly and then it levels off

b. little forgetting occurs very quickly and the greatest amount occurs later after a lengthy period of memory storage

c. forgetting occurs at a uniform rate after learning

d. little forgetting ever occurs

14. In the Loftus and Palmer experiment, participants were shown a film of a traffic accident and then later tested for their memory of it. The finding that memory differed based upon the specific words used in the test questions illustrated _____.

a. state-dependent memory

b. source misattribution

c. the self-reference effect

d. the misinformation effect

15. The results for the experiment in which word lists were studied either on land or underwater and then recalled either on land or underwater provide evidence for ____.

a. source misattribution

b. encoding specificity

c. proactive interference

d. retroactive interference

Chapter Concept Check Answers

Concept Check | 1

- As pointed out in Chapter 3, bottom-up processing is the processing of incoming sensory information from the physical environment. This is what occupies sensory memory so it is bottom-up input. Also, as pointed out in Chapter 3, top-down processing uses the information in our long-term knowledge base to interpret the bottom-up input. Thus, long-term memory can be thought of as providing top-down input because it is the repository of our knowledge base and past experiences.

- The duration of iconic memory must be very brief because if it were not, our visual sensory register would get overloaded quickly, leading to successive visual images overlapping in the register. Thus, we wouldn't perceive the world normally because it would be a constant mix of conflicting overlapping images.

- A "chunk" is a meaningful unit in our memory; for example, a single letter, an acronym, and a word each comprise one chunk. We have a memory span of 7 ± 2 unrelated letters, acronyms, or words.

- H. M. demonstrated a practice effect on the mirror-drawing task and the manual skill learning task in which he had to keep a stylus on a small dot that was spinning around on a turnable, but he did not consciously remember ever having done either task.

This shows that he formed new implicit long-term memories for how to do these tasks because his performance on the tasks improved as he gained experience on them but that he did not form new explicit long-term memories for actually having done the tasks because he could not remember ever doing these tasks. H. M. also demonstrated repetition priming effects on a word fragment completion task without conscious awareness of the earlier presented priming words. Thus, he demonstrated implicit long-term memory for the words on the word fragment completion task but he had no explicit long-term memory for having seen them before. In another study, he was classically conditioned to give an eyeblink response to a tone. After the conditioning, whenever he was exposed to the tone, he gave the eyeblink response; but he did not consciously remember ever having been conditioned. This finding shows that he formed new implicit long-term memories of the association between the tone and eyeblink but did not form any new explicit long-term memories for the conditioning episodes.

Concept Check | 2

- Elaborative encoding is more effective than memorizing because the process of elaboration ties the new information to older, well-known information. This older information provides many good retrieval cues for the new information. Thus, elaborative encoding provides both more retrieval cues and better ones than memorizing.

- State-dependent memory and mood-dependent memory are both instances of the encoding specificity principle operating because in each case, maximal similarity in study-test physiological states or moods leads to the best long-term memory.

- Both mnemonics relate the new information to a well-known sequence. In each mnemonic you step through the sequence and retrieve the list item tied to that step. In the case of the method of loci, sequential locations within a well-known room or place are used whereas in the peg-word system, the steps are part of a well-learned jingle (one is a bun, two is a shoe, . . .). Thus, both mnemonics use elaborative rehearsal.

Concept Check I 3

- In recall, the information has to be reproduced. In recognition, the information only has to be identified.

- Encoding failure theory and storage decay theory assume the forgotten information is not available in long-term memory. Both the interference and cue-dependent theories of forgetting assume it is still available but not accessible.

- Schemas help to create false memories because in using them, we tend to replace the actual details of what happened with what typically happens in the event that the schema depicts. As Bartlett found in his schema research, this is especially true for unusual details. This means that schemas tend to normalize our memories and lead us to remember what usually happens and not exactly what did happen.

- Source misattribution leads to false memories because we don't really know the source of a memory. The event may never have occurred, but we think that it did because we misattributed the source of the memory. The misinformation effect leads to false memories through the effect of misleading information being given at the time of retrieval. We incorporate this misleading information for an event into our memory and thus create a false memory for it.

Answers to Key Terms Exercise

1. encoding specificity principle
2. recall
3. retroactive interference
4. iconic memory
5. chunk
6. explicit memory
7. anterograde amnesia
8. elaborative rehearsal
9. spacing (distributed study) effect
10. schemas
11. episodic memory
12. cue-dependent theory
13. Sperling's partial-report procedure
14. infantile/child amnesia
15. memory span task

Answers to Practice Test Questions

1. b; sensory memory
2. c; 7
3. a; sensory memory
4. d; implicit; cerebellum
5. b; elaborative rehearsal
6. c; in the middle
7. c; temporal integration procedure
8. b; recall; recognition
9. b; storage decay theory
10. b; source misattribution
11. d; retroactive; retroactive
12. a; How well does the word describe you?
13. a; the greatest amount of forgetting occurs rather quickly and then it levels off
14. d; the misinformation effect
15. b; encoding specificity

6

Thinking and Intelligence

I n this chapter, we will consider how we use the information in our memories to think. **Thinking** is the processing of information to solve problems and make judgments and decisions. Because these processes are important aspects of intelligent thinking, we will also consider intelligence testing and some of the controversies surrounding the concept of intelligence. We will start our discussion with the most basic, higher-level cognitive process—problem solving. You will be asked to solve several problems. You will learn more from these exercises if you try to solve each problem before reading about its solution.

Problem Solving

A problem is a situation in which there is a goal, but it is not clear how to reach the goal. There are well-defined and ill-defined problems (Gilhooly, 1996). A **well-defined problem** is a problem with clear specifications of the start state (where you are), goal state (where you want to be), and the processes for reaching the goal state (how to get there). An **ill-defined problem** is a problem lacking clear specification of the start state, goal state, or the processes for reaching the goal state. Board games such as Monopoly and Scrabble represent well-defined problems. Their start states and goal states, along with the processes of moving from one to the other (the rules of the game), are all clearly specified. Getting your roommate to help clean the apartment would be an ill-defined problem. The start state and goal state are fairly well-defined, but the processes for moving between them are not. Most problems we confront are ill-defined, and to solve them we need to define the missing parts. We'll see that blocks to solving problems may arise in this definition process.

Before learning about some of these obstacles to problem solving, I would like you to attempt to solve the following problems. You may recognize one of the series problems from Chapter 1. Don't worry if you find these problems difficult; most people do. I will explain why.

thinking The processing of information to solve problems and make judgments and decisions.

well-defined problem A problem with clear specifications of the start state, goal state, and the processes for reaching the goal state.

ill-defined problem A problem lacking clear specification of either the start state, goal state, or the processes for reaching the goal state.

> (a) **Instructions: For each of these two series problems, your goal is to predict the next alphabetic character in each of the series. The answer to the first series is not "O."**
>
> OTTFFSS?
> EOEREXN?

(b) Instructions: Connect the nine circles using four straight lines without lifting your pen or pencil from the paper or retracing any of your lines. You should attempt this problem on a separate sheet of paper so that you can keep a record of your attempts. Once you have a four-straight-line solution, the next goal is to connect the nine circles with three straight lines using the same constraints as in the four-straight-line version.

Blocks to Problem Solving

Problem solving can be divided into two general steps: (1) interpreting the problem and (2) trying to solve the problem. For many problems, the path to a solution is blocked in the first step by incorrectly interpreting the problem. This is like answering a test question too quickly, only to find out later that you misinterpreted the question. If you are working with such a misinterpretation, you will probably fail to solve the problem. The two nine-circle problems are good examples of problems that often lead to misinterpretations. Let's see how.

fixation The inability to create a new interpretation of a problem.

Interpreting the problem. Look at your failed attempts at solving the nine-circle problem involving four straight lines. Did you try to keep your lines within the mental square created by the circles? Most people do, and you cannot solve the problem this way (Wickelgren, 1974). Not only do most people create this misinterpretation, but they also continue to use it even though they make no progress toward solving the problem. This inability to "think outside the box" and create a new interpretation of a problem is called **fixation.** Reread the instructions. You were not required to keep your lines within this mental square. Any or all of the four lines can extend outside this space. The lines only have to be straight and connect all nine circles. Knowing this, try again to solve the problem. Draw a straight line that goes

"Thinking outside of the box is difficult for some people. Keep trying."

down through the first column of circles and continues on outside of the mental square. When you bring your next line back up, also continue it outside of the mental square. This should start you on your way to a solution, though it may still be elusive (Weisberg & Alba, 1981).

What about the second nine-circle problem—connecting all nine circles with three straight lines? If you didn't solve it, think about the assumptions that you made when you interpreted the problem. This problem is even more difficult, because you may have made two mistakes in your interpretation and fixated on them, making the problem impossible to solve. First, as in the four-straight-line problem, you might have assumed that you needed to keep your lines within the mental square created by the circles. Second, you might have assumed that the lines need to go through the centers of the circles. Neither assumption is valid. Now try to solve this problem knowing that both of these assumptions are misinterpretations. Try drawing three straight lines that do not go through the centers of the circles and that travel outside the mental square. It might help to imagine using a very long ruler to draw your lines. If you're still stumped on either one of these problems, look at the sample solutions at the end of the chapter.

Another obstacle to problem solving is **functional fixedness**—the inability to see that an object can have a function other than its typical one. This type of fixation also occurs during the problem definition stage. Functional fixedness limits our ability to solve problems that require using an object in a novel way (Duncker, 1945). This often happens to us in our everyday life. Maybe we need a screwdriver, but one isn't available. We have other things such as coins that could function as a screwdriver, but we may not think about using them in this novel way. Or, what if you just did some grocery shopping, and as you are about to walk out it starts raining hard. You have no umbrella. How can you avoid getting soaked? You bought some large trash bags, but you may not think about using one as a raincoat to protect you from the rain. To combat functional fixedness, we should systematically think about the possible, novel uses of all the various objects in the problem environment. This is bound to increase our ability to solve the continual problems that come up in our daily lives.

Solving the problem. Problem misinterpretation and functional fixedness are good examples of the negative impact that our past experiences can have on our ability to solve current problems. Our past experience with problem solving can also lead to a phenomenon known as **mental set**—the tendency to use previously successful solution strategies without considering others that are more appropriate for the current problem. Mental set is especially common for strategies that have been used recently. Consider the two letter-series problems on page 207. If you had difficulty solving them, mental set may be what

▇ **functional fixedness** The inability to see that an object can have a function other than its typical one in solving a problem.

▇ **mental set** Tendency to use previously successful problem-solving strategies without considering others that are more appropriate for the current problem.

insight A new way to interpret a problem that immediately yields the solution.

hindered you (Griggs, 2003). You probably attempted to solve these two problems with strategies that you have used successfully in the past with series problems. You may have viewed the letters in the series as single entities and looked for relationships between them. This strategy does not include viewing each of the letters as part of some larger entity. You cannot solve the series unless you do so. For the first series problem, you should think of the letters as the first letters in the words of a well-known ordering. It's as easy as 1-2-3.

The solution: These are the first letters in the sequence of number words—**O**ne, **T**wo, **T**hree, **F**our, **F**ive, **S**ix, **S**even—so the answer is E for **E**ight. This should help you to solve the second series problem, but don't fall prey to mental set and try to find another well-known ordering in which these are the first letters of the words in the sequence. You need to look for another solution strategy. Because of mental set, you probably don't see the strategy, but it's directly related to the solution to the first series. The letters in the second series are the last letters in the number words—on**E**, tw**O**, thre**E**, up to seve**N**. The answer is T for eigh**T**. What's the lesson to be learned? Don't cling to solution strategies that have worked in the past, but which are not presently working. Try new approaches.

Sometimes when searching for new approaches to a problem, we may experience what has been called **insight**—a new way to interpret a problem that immediately gives the solution. This rapid understanding is the key to the solution. Insight is sometimes referred to as an "Aha!" or "Eureka!" experience. Try the following problem from Knoblich and Oellinger (2006). You may experience insight in solving it. The solution is given at the end of the chapter.

Instructions: The equation shown is not correct. To create a correct equation, you can move only one matchstick (but not remove it). Only Roman numerals and the three operators, +, −, and = are allowed.

There are many potential blocks to problem solving, and it takes a very conscious effort to overcome them. Ask yourself questions such as the following: Is my interpretation of the problem unnecessarily constraining? Can I use any of the objects in the problem in novel ways to solve the problem? Do I need a new type of solution strategy? If we do not make this effort, we are engaged in what is called mindless behavior—rigid, habitual behavior in which we fail to attend carefully to the details of the present situation (Langer, 1989, 1997). To be good problem solvers, we need to be open to new interpretations of problems and to new ways to use objects to solve problems. We will also need to develop a broader, more effective set of solution strategies, which is our next topic.

Solution Strategies

Just as problem solving can be divided into two steps, solution strategies can be divided into two types—algorithms and heuristics. An **algorithm** is a step-by-step procedure that guarantees a correct answer to a problem. For example, when we solve a math problem with long division, we are using an algorithm. If we execute the steps correctly, we will get the correct answer. For many problems, however, we may not know the algorithm or an algorithm for the problem may not exist. To solve the problem in such cases, we have to use a **heuristic,** a solution strategy that seems reasonable given our past experiences with solving problems, especially similar problems. Think of a heuristic as an educated guess.

algorithm A step-by-step problem-solving procedure that guarantees a correct answer to a problem.

heuristic A problem-solving strategy that seems reasonable given one's past experience with solving problems, especially similar problems, but does not guarantee a correct answer to a problem.

Sometimes you may even know the algorithm for a problem, but you don't use it because its execution would be too time-consuming. Instead you may try some heuristics, and they might pay off with a quicker answer, or they may lead to no answer or an incorrect one. This is the crucial difference between an algorithm and a heuristic. An algorithm guarantees a correct answer (if it's the correct algorithm for the problem and you execute it correctly), but a heuristic makes no guarantees. Let's consider some problems (anagram word puzzles) for which you likely know the algorithm, but because it would usually be too difficult to execute, you use heuristics instead. In an anagram puzzle, the letters of a word are presented in a scrambled order, and the problem is to rearrange them to determine the word. Now, what's the algorithm for such puzzles? Generate each possible sequence of the letters and check to see if each sequence is a word. This sounds simple, but it isn't. For example, there are over 5,000 possible sequences of the letters for a seven-letter anagram! So unless there are only a few letters in the anagram, we use heuristics based upon our knowledge of the English language. For example, we know that the letter U usually follows the letter Q and that certain letters such as B and C don't follow one another in words. We attempt to create words with the letters following such principles. To understand this strategy, let's work a couple of anagram puzzles. As you try to solve them, think about the strategy you are using.

Instructions: Rearrange the letters in each anagram puzzle to form a meaningful word in the English language.

1. L O S O G C Y H Y P   2. T E R A L B A Y

The first puzzle is rather easy. The answer is especially relevant to this text. It's PSYCHOLOGY. Your use of heuristics was probably successful and led to a quick answer. The second puzzle is more difficult. Your use of heuristics may have failed and didn't yield a solution. Even so, you probably didn't switch to using the algorithm. You probably kept trying to find a solution by using heuristics. As you can see, heuristics might pay off with quick answers, but they may lead to no answer as in the second anagram puzzle. Now think about the algorithmic strategy. There are over 40,000 sequences for the eight letters in the second anagram puzzle; therefore, generating each of them to check if it's a word would take far more time and effort than we are willing to spend. However, if you did so, you would find that the answer is BETRAYAL.

Now let's consider three particular heuristics that are used fairly often in problem solving—the anchoring and adjustment, working backward, and means-end analysis heuristics. We'll start with the anchoring and adjustment heuristic.

The anchoring and adjustment heuristic. To help you to understand this heuristic, let's try an estimation problem taken from Plous (1993). The task involved in this problem would be impossible to execute. It is only a hypothetical problem that examines how we make estimates.

> **Estimate how thick a sheet of paper that is 0.1 millimeter thick would be if it were folded in on itself 100 times.**

Most people estimate the thickness to be only a few yards or so, which is not even close to the correct answer: 0.1 millimeter $\times$ 2^{100}, which equals 800 trillion times the distance between the earth and the sun (Plous, 1993)! Why do we underestimate this thickness by so much? We are most likely using the **anchoring and adjustment heuristic** in which an initial estimate is used as an anchor and then this anchor is adjusted up or down. The difficulty in using the anchoring and adjustment heuristic is that we tend to attach too much importance to the starting anchor amount and do not adjust it sufficiently (Tversky & Kahneman, 1974). The folding problem is a good illustration of this bias. If you double the thickness of the sheet of paper a few times, you still have a rather small thickness. Using this small thickness as an anchor for making your estimate, you do not adjust the estimate sufficiently and usually guess only a few yards. In this case, the anchoring and adjustment heuristic leads us to ignore the fact that the powers of 2 grow exponentially as we double them and become very large very quickly.

anchoring and adjustment heuristic A heuristic for estimation problems in which one uses his or her initial estimate as an anchor estimate and then adjusts the anchor up or down (often insufficiently).

This estimation problem was only a hypothetical exercise, but it shows how we fail to adjust the anchor enough when using the anchoring and adjustment heuristic. Anchoring is a very robust psychological phenomenon and has been shown to influence judgments in a variety of domains such as making judgments in personal injury cases (Chapman & Bornstein, 1996), negotiating (Ritov, 1996), and playing the stock market (Paulos, 2003). In the real world, anchoring may have costs attached to it. A good example that you may have experienced is the inclusion of minimum payment information on credit card statements. These minimum payment amounts can act as psychological anchors (Stewart, 2009; Thaler & Sunstein, 2008). In a hypothetical bill-paying experiment manipulating the inclusion of minimum payment information, Stewart (2009) found that the inclusion of this information led to significant reductions in partial payment amounts, which in the real world would lead to increased interest charges. We should also beware of using this heuristic when meeting people. Our first impression of a person is similar to forming an anchor. We must be sure to process subsequent information about the person carefully and adjust our impression (anchor) sufficiently. Remember, the anchoring and adjustment heuristic leads us to fail to adjust the anchor enough. So do not become too attached to an anchor when making judgments and decisions.

Working backward. Working backward is a heuristic that you may have learned to use in your math classes. The **working backward heuristic** is attempting to solve a problem by working from the goal state backward to the start state (Wickelgren, 1974). In math problems, this translates to working backward from the answer to the given information in the problem. To see how this heuristic would work, consider the following problem (Sternberg & Davidson, 1982):

> **Water lilies growing in a pond double in area every 24 hours. On the first day of spring, only one lily pad is on the surface of the pond. Sixty days later, the pond is entirely covered. On what day is the pond half covered?**

Did you solve it? It is impossible to solve this problem working in a forward direction. However, if you work backward by starting with the fact that the pond is entirely covered on the sixtieth day, you can solve it rather easily. Just ask yourself how much of the pond would be covered on the fifty-ninth day if the pond were entirely covered on the sixtieth day. The answer is half. The working backward heuristic is ideal for problems that have many possible paths from the start state, but only one path (or a few) going backward from the goal state.

Means-end analysis. A good heuristic for working forward on a problem is means-ends analysis. In **means–end analysis,** the problem is broken down into subgoals and we work toward decreasing the distance to the goal state by achieving these subgoals. Consider the following Tower of Hanoi problem. It is a well-defined problem. The start state,

working backward heuristic A problem-solving heuristic in which one attempts to solve a problem by working from the goal state back to the start state.

means–end analysis heuristic A problem-solving heuristic in which the distance to the goal state is decreased systematically by breaking the problem down into subgoals and achieving these subgoals.

the goal state, and the rules for moving from the start state to the goal state are all clearly specified.

> **Instructions: The problem is to create the same configuration of disks on Peg C as is on Peg A in the starting state. Rules, however, govern your moves. You can only move one disk at a time, and you cannot place a larger disk on top of a smaller disk. Try to solve this problem efficiently by minimizing the number of moves that have to be made. The most efficient solution involves seven moves.**

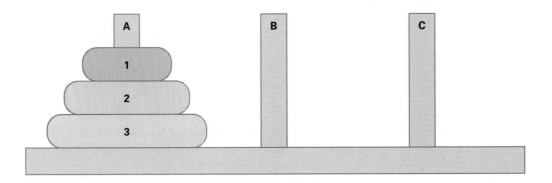

Let's try to use means-end analysis to solve the problem. What would be the first subgoal? You have to get Disk 3 on Peg C. You cannot, however, achieve this immediately so you have to set up another subgoal. What is it? You have to get Disk 1 on top of Disk 2 on Peg B. You cannot achieve this immediately either so what is the next subgoal? Yes, you have to get Disk 2 on Peg B. To achieve this you need to get Disk 1 off Disk 2 and not on Peg B. How do you achieve this subgoal? By now you should have the idea. Go ahead and finish solving the problem. It takes a minimum of seven moves. (The list of moves is given at the end of this chapter.)

The specific solution steps to a Tower of Hanoi problem with a certain number of disks can be varied by manipulating the start and goal states (which peg the disks are on and which peg they need to be moved to, respectively). Such changes allow researchers to see if problem performance is enhanced with practice on various versions of the problem. As you would expect, they found that people do get more efficient in solving these problems with practice. Interestingly though, this practice effect is also shown by anterograde amnesics, such as H. M. (who was described in Chapter 5). They too can learn to solve the Tower of Hanoi problem more efficiently with practice, but they have no recollection each time of ever having seen the problem before (Squire & Cohen, 1984). Why? As we learned in Chapter 5, these amnesics form implicit procedural memories from practice in solving a problem because their cerebellum is intact, but no explicit episodic memories of working on the problem are formed because the hippocampus is critical for forming such memories and these amnesics have had their hippocampus removed.

Given the solution to the 3-disk Tower of Hanoi problem described above, let's consider a 64-disk Tower of Hanoi problem. Everything is the same except the number of disks—64 instead of 3. What is your estimate of the minimum number of moves necessary to solve the 64-disk version? Don't read further until you derive an estimate. If you used the anchoring and adjustment heuristic to derive an estimate, you probably greatly underestimated the answer. You probably derived a rather small anchor based on the 3-disk version that required only seven moves and then failed to adjust it upward sufficiently. The minimum number of moves for the Tower of Hanoi problems is $2^n - 1$, where n is the number of disks (Raphael, 1976). Thus, for 3 disks, it is 7, $2^3 - 1$. Now do you see the problem with your estimate? The answer for 64 disks is $2^{64} - 1$, or trillions of moves! Did the anchoring and adjustment heuristic lead you astray again?

The events in our everyday lives are not as well-defined as the allowable moves in a Tower of Hanoi problem. They are uncertain. They have varying probabilities of occurring. We have to learn how to think in a probabilistic world. Such thinking involves estimating event probabilities (uncertainties). The heuristics we have discussed so far are not usable for this type of judgment. The heuristics that we do use to make these probability judgments and, more generally, how we think under uncertainty are the main topics of the next section.

Section Summary

In this section, we discussed how problems are either well-defined or ill-defined. Well-defined problems provide clear definitions of the start and goal states, and the processes for reaching the goal state from the start state. Ill-defined problems do not. Everyday problems tend to be ill-defined; therefore, interpreting the problem is necessary. Such interpretation may block problem solving. Blocks can be caused by problem misinterpretation, functional fixedness, or mental set. These blocks are all examples of the negative impact of our past experience on problem solving. We must make a mindful effort to overcome these blocks or our problem solving will suffer.

When attempting to solve a problem, we use either an algorithm that guarantees us a correct answer or heuristics that may lead to a quick solution or possibly to no solution. We prefer to use heuristics because they are less time-consuming. In addition, we may not know the appropriate algorithm for a problem or one may not even exist. Sometimes heuristics can lead to errors. A good example is the anchoring and adjustment heuristic for making estimates. The error in this case stems from our failure to adjust our initial anchor sufficiently.

The working backward heuristic is especially useful for problems that have many paths going forward from the start state but only one (or a few) going backward from the goal state. Means-ends analysis is a useful heuristic for almost any type of problem. In this heuristic, you move forward by achieving subgoals that continue to reduce the distance between the start state and goal state.

Concept**Check** | 1

> ➤ Explain how functional fixedness and mental set are examples of the negative impact of past experience.

> ➤ Explain why we tend to use heuristics and not algorithms even though algorithms guarantee correct solutions.

> ➤ Explain how the anchoring and adjustment heuristic may lead you to make a serious error in estimation.

Thinking Under Uncertainty

We live in an uncertain world; everything that happens has a probability. For example, there is a probability for whether it will rain today and another probability for whether you will get an "A" in this class. The probability of an event is the likelihood that it will happen. Probabilities range from 0 (never happens) to 1 (always happens), but they are usually uncertain, somewhere between 0 and 1. An event with a probability of 0.5 is maximally uncertain because it is equally likely to occur and not to occur. Because we live in an uncertain world, we have to learn to estimate the probabilities (uncertainties) of various events. But how do we do this? Let's try to estimate some probabilities.

Consider this: Does the letter *r* occur more often as the first letter or third letter in English words? To answer this question, you need to make a judgment about the probability of one event (*r* occurring as the first letter) in relation to the probability of a second event (*r* occurring as the third letter). Think about how you would estimate these probabilities. One way to proceed would be to compare the ease of thinking of words beginning with *r* versus having *r* in the third position. Isn't it easier to think of words beginning with *r*? Does this mean that such words occur more often and that this event is more probable? If you think so, you are using a heuristic (words that are more available in our memory are more probable) to answer the probability question. When we discuss the main heuristics that humans use to judge probabilities, we'll return to this problem and see if this heuristic led us to the correct answer.

In addition to judging the uncertainty of events in our environment, we attempt to reduce our uncertainty about the world by trying to find out how various events are related to each other. For example, is the amount of arthritis pain related to the weather? To answer such questions, we develop and test hypotheses about how the events in our world are related. Such hypothesis testing allows us to learn about the world. Many of our beliefs are the conclusions that we have arrived at from testing such hypotheses. However, we usually don't test our hypotheses in well-controlled formal experiments the way that psychologists do. Instead we conduct subjective, informal tests of our hypotheses. Obviously, such a nonscientific approach may be biased and result in incorrect conclusions and erroneous beliefs. A good example is belief in the paranormal. If you are like most college students, you probably believe in at least one paranormal phenomenon, such as mental telepathy, clairvoyance, or psychokinesis (Messer & Griggs, 1989). But, as you learned in Chapter 3, there is not one replicable scientific finding for any of these phenomena. We'll discuss how such erroneous beliefs might arise from our subjective hypothesis testing method.

We also often engage in hypothesis testing in various medical situations. One very common instance is testing the hypothesis that we have a specific disease given a positive result on a medical screening test for the disease. This actually amounts to trying to compute a conditional probability, which for most people (doctors and patients) is not that easy. Research that we will discuss shows that both doctors and patients tend to greatly overestimate such probabilities. To help you more accurately assess your chances of having the disease in this situation, we'll teach you a relatively simple way to compute such probabilities. But first let's see how we judge probabilities in general and how these judgments might be biased.

Judging Probability

Cognitive psychologists Amos Tversky and Daniel Kahneman identified two heuristics that we often use to make judgments about probabilities—the representativeness heuristic and the availability heuristic (Tversky & Kahneman, 1974). It is important to point out that these two heuristics usually lead to reasonably good judgments, but

Amos Tversky   Daniel Kahneman

Courtesy of Greymayer Award, University of Louisville and the Tversky family

Courtesy of Greymayer Award, University of Louisville and Daniel Kahneman

Daniel Kahneman was awarded the Nobel Prize in Economic Sciences in 2002 for the groundbreaking research on heuristics that we partially describe here. His collaborator Amos Tversky would surely have shared the Nobel Prize with him, but he died in 1996, and Nobel committees are prohibited from awarding prizes posthumously. As we will learn, Kahneman and Tversky's research demonstrated that people often make decisions using heuristics rather than complete rational analysis. Kahneman's prize was in Economic Sciences because this research had important applications to economic theory and because there is no Nobel Prize awarded in Psychological Sciences. Incidentally, Kahneman was the first person with a doctorate from a psychology department to win a Nobel Prize. Other Nobel Prize winners that we have mentioned (Roger Sperry, David Hubel, and Torsten Wiesel) all received their degrees in other disciplines such as zoology and medicine. Herbert Simon, another cognitive psychologist, who won the Nobel Prize in Economic Sciences in 1978 received his degree in Political Science.

they sometimes lead to errors. Why? The major reason is that a heuristic can lead us to ignore information that is extremely relevant to the particular probability judgment. To understand, let's consider the following problem (Tversky & Kahneman, 1983).

> **You will read a brief description of Linda, and then you will be asked to make a judgment about her. Here's the description:**
>
> **Linda is 31 years old, single, outspoken, and very bright. She majored in philosophy. As a student, she was deeply concerned with issues of discrimination and social justice, and also participated in antinuclear demonstrations.**
>
> **Which of the following alternatives is more likely?**
>
> **Linda is a bank teller.**
>
> **Linda is a bank teller and active in the feminist movement.**

The representativeness heuristic. To decide which alternative is more probable, most people would use what is called the **representativeness heuristic**—a rule of thumb for judging the probability of membership in a category by how well an object resembles (is representative of) that category. Simply put, the rule is: the more representative, the more probable. Using this heuristic, most people judge that the second alternative (Linda is a bank teller and active in the feminist movement) is more likely than the first alternative. Why? Linda resembles someone active in the feminist movement more than she resembles a bank teller. However, it is impossible for the second alternative to be more likely than the first. Actually the description of Linda is totally irrelevant to the probability judgment!

▮ **representativeness heuristic** A heuristic for judging the probability of membership in a category by how well an object resembles (is representative of) that category (the more representative, the more probable).

Let's look at the set diagram in Figure 6.1. This diagram illustrates what is known as the conjunction rule for two different uncertain events (in this case, being a bank teller and being active in the feminist movement). The conjunction

▲ **Figure 6.1** | **The Overlapping Set Diagram for the Linda Problem** | The overlap (the green area) of the two sets (all bank tellers and all people active in the feminist movement) indicates the probability of being both a bank teller and active in the feminist movement. Because this area is a subset (part) of each of the two sets, its probability has to be less than that for either of the two sets. This is the conjunction rule.

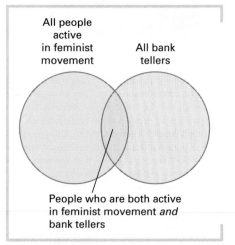

All people active in feminist movement

All bank tellers

People who are both active in feminist movement *and* bank tellers rule is that the likelihood of the overlap of two uncertain events (the green section of the diagram) cannot be greater than the likelihood of either of the two events because the overlap is only part of each event. This means that all of the tellers who are active in the feminist movement make up only part of the set of all bank tellers. Because the set of bank tellers is larger and includes those tellers who are active in the feminist movement, it is more likely that someone is a bank teller than someone is a bank teller and active in the feminist movement. Judging that it is more likely that Linda is a bank teller and active in the feminist movement illustrates the **conjunction fallacy**—incorrectly judging the overlap of two uncertain events to be more likely than either of the two events. By using the representativeness heuristic, we overlook a very simple principle of probability, the conjunction rule. This illustrates the shortcoming of using such heuristics—overlooking essential information for making the probability judgment.

Using the representativeness heuristic also leads to the **gambler's fallacy**—the erroneous belief that a chance process is self-correcting in that an event that has not occurred for a while is more likely to occur. Suppose a person has flipped eight heads in a row and we want to bet $100 on the next coin toss, heads or tails. Some people will want to bet on tails because they think it more likely, but in actuality the two events are still equally likely. One of the most famous examples of the gambler's fallacy occurred in a Monte Carlo casino in 1913 when a roulette wheel landed on black 26 times in a row (Lehrer, 2009). During that run, most people bet against black since they felt that red must be "due." They assumed that the roulette wheel would somehow correct the imbalance and cause the wheel to land on red. The casino ended up making millions of francs. "The wheel has no mind, no soul, no sense of fairness...Yet, we often treat it otherwise" (Vyse, 1997, p. 98).

Why do people commit the gambler's fallacy? Again, they are using the representativeness heuristic (Tversky & Kahneman, 1971). People believe that short sequences (the series of eight coin tosses or the 26 spins of the roulette wheel) should reflect the long-run probabilities. Simply put, people believe random sequences, whether short or long, should look random. This is not the case. Probability and the law of averages only hold in the long run, not the short run. In addition, the long run is indeed very long—infinity. The representativeness heuristic leads us to forget this.

Why are we so prone to using the representativeness heuristic and making judgments based only on categorical resemblance? The answer is tied to the fact that the mind categorizes information automatically. Categorization is just another name for pattern recognition, an automatic process that we discussed in Chapter 3. The brain constantly recognizes (puts into categories) the objects, events, and people in our world. Categorization is one of the brain's basic operational principles, so it shouldn't be surprising that we may judge categorical probabilities in the same way that we recognize patterns. This is how the brain normally operates. In addition to probability judgments, the

conjunction fallacy Incorrectly judging the overlap of two uncertain events to be more probable than either of the two events.

gambler's fallacy Incorrectly believing that a chance process is self-correcting in that an event that has not occurred for a while is more likely to occur.

representativeness heuristic can lead us astray in judging the people we meet because our first impression is often based on categorical resemblance. We tend to categorize the person based on the little information we get when we meet him or her. Remember that this initial judgment is only an anchor, and we need to process subsequent information carefully in order to avoid misjudgment of the person.

The availability heuristic. Let's go back to the judgment that you made earlier. Does the letter *r* appear more often as the first letter or third letter in English words? Actually, the letter *r* appears twice as often as the third letter in words than as the first letter. However, if you used the availability heuristic that was described, you would judge the reverse to be the case (that *r* occurs more often as the first letter). The **availability heuristic** is the rule of thumb that the more available an event is in our memory, the more probable it is (Tversky & Kahneman, 1973). We can think of more words beginning with the letter *r* than with *r* in the third position because we organize words in our memories by how they begin. This does not mean that they are more frequent, but only that it is easier to think of them. They are easier to generate from memory. The opposite is the case—words with *r* in the third position are more frequent. This is actually true for seven letters: *k, l, n, r, v, x,* and *z* (Tversky & Kahneman, 1973).

Remember that a heuristic does not guarantee a correct answer. The availability heuristic may often lead to a correct answer; but as in the letter *r* problem, events are sometimes more easily available in our memories for reasons other than how often they actually occur. An event may be prominent in our memories because it recently happened or because it is particularly striking or vivid. In such cases, the availability heuristic will lead to an error in judgment. Think about judging the risk of various causes of death. Some causes of death (airplane crashes, fires, and shark attacks) are highly publicized and thus more available in our memories, especially if they have occurred recently. Using the availability heuristic, we judge them to be more likely than lesser publicized, less dramatic causes of death such as diabetes and emphysema, which are actually more likely but not very available in our memories (Lichtenstein, Slovic, Fischhoff, Layman, & Combs, 1978). In fact, the probability of dying from falling airplane parts is 30 times greater than that of being killed by a shark (Plous, 1993). The lesson to be learned here is that greater availability in memory does not always equal greater probability.

Availability in memory also plays a key role in what is termed a dread risk. A dread risk is a low-probability, high-damage event in which many people are killed at one point in time. Not only is there direct damage in the event, but there is secondary, indirect damage mediated through how we psychologically react to the event. A good example is our reaction to the September 11, 2001, terrorist attacks (Gigerenzer, 2004, 2006). Fearing dying in a terrorist airplane crash because the September 11 events were so prominent in our memories, we reduced our air travel and increased our automobile travel, leading to a significantly greater number of fatal traffic accidents than

availability heuristic A heuristic for judging the probability of an event by how available examples of the event are in memory (the more available, the more probable).

Because airplane crashes are so visually dramatic and highly publicized by the media, they tend to be very available in our memories. This availability leads us to greatly overestimate our likelihood of dying in a plane crash.

usual. It is estimated that about 1,600 more people needlessly died in these traffic accidents (Gigerenzer, 2006). These lives could have been saved had we not reacted to the dread risk as we did. We just do not seem to realize that it is far safer to fly than to drive. National Safety Council data reveal that you are 37 times more likely to die in a vehicle accident than on a commercial flight (Myers, 2001).

Clearly there are shortcomings with the heuristics that we use to judge probabilities (uncertainties). Although these heuristics usually serve us well, beware of their shortcomings. Make sure you have not overlooked relevant probability information when using the representativeness heuristic, and try to think beyond prominence in memory when using the availability heuristic. Are there also shortcomings with the way we try to reduce our uncertainty and learn about the world through hypothesis testing? We now turn to this question.

Hypothesis Testing

In Chapter 1, we discussed the experimental research method that psychologists use to test their hypotheses about human behavior and mental processing. Like psychologists, we too have beliefs about the relationships between the variables in our environment (hypotheses), and we too collect data to test these beliefs. However, we don't use the experimental method discussed in Chapter 1. So what do we do? How do people test their hypotheses and thus reduce their uncertainty about the world? British researcher Peter Wason devised two problems to examine this question—the 2-4-6 task and the four-card selection task.

Confirmation bias. In the 2-4-6 task, you are presented the number sequence "2-4-6" and asked to name the rule that the experimenter used to generate that sequence (Wason, 1960). Before presenting your hypothesized rule (your answer), you are allowed to generate as many sequences of three numbers as you want and get feedback on whether each conforms to the experimenter's rule. When you think that you know the rule, you tell the experimenter. Before we describe how people perform on this task, think about how you would proceed. What would be your first hypothesis for the rule and what sequences of three numbers would you generate to test your hypothesized rule?

Most of the participants do not name the correct rule. They devise a hypothesis (e.g., "numbers increasing by 2") and proceed to test the hypothesis by generating series that conform to it (e.g., 8-10-12). In other words, they test their hypotheses by trying to confirm them. Did you do this? People do not test their hypotheses by trying to disconfirm them (e.g., generating the sequence 10-11-12 for the hypothesis "numbers increasing by 2"). The tendency to seek evidence that confirms one's beliefs is called **confirmation bias.** This bias is pervasive in our everyday hypothesis testing, so it is not surprising that it occurs on the 2-4-6 task. The 2-4-6 task serves to highlight the inadequacy of the confirmation bias as a way to test a hypothesis. To truly test a hypothesis, we must try to disconfirm it. We should attempt to disconfirm each hypothesis that we generate. The experimenter's rule for the 2-4-6 task was a very simple, general rule, so most sequences that people generated conformed to it. What was it? The rule was simply any three increasing numbers; how far apart the numbers were did not matter.

Now let's look at the four-card selection task (Wason, 1966, 1968). Try the problem before reading further.

The four cards below have information on both sides. On one side of a card is a letter, and on the other side is a number.

Consider this rule: If a card has a vowel on one side, then it has an even number on the other side.

Select the card or cards that you definitely must turn over to determine whether the rule is true or false for these four cards.

Well, if you're like most people, you haven't answered correctly. The correct response rate for this problem is usually less than 10 percent (Griggs & Cox, 1982). The most frequent error is to select the cards showing A and 4. The card showing A is part of the correct solution, but the card showing 4 is not. You should select the cards showing A and 7. Why? First, you should decide what type of card would falsify the rule. The rule states that if a card has a vowel on one side, it has to have an even number on the other side. Therefore, a card with a vowel on one side and an odd number on the other side would falsify the rule. Now do

confirmation bias The tendency to seek evidence that confirms one's beliefs.

you see why the answer is A and 7? An odd number on the other side of the A card would falsify the rule, and so would a vowel on the other side of the 7 card. No matter what is on the other side of the K and 4 cards, the rule is true.

So why do people select the cards showing A and 4? As in the 2-4-6 task, people focus on confirmation and select cards to verify the rule (show that it is true). They choose the cards showing A and 4 because they incorrectly think that the rule must hold in both directions (it doesn't) and they must verify that it does so. They choose the card showing a vowel (A) to verify that it has an even number on the other side and the card showing an even number (4) to verify that it has a vowel on the other side. Instead of deducing what will falsify (disconfirm) the rule, people merely try to confirm it (confirmation bias).

Research on the 2-4-6 task and the four-card selection task show that people try to confirm hypotheses. Confirmation bias, however, is not limited to the 2-4-6 and four-card selection tasks, but extends to many aspects of our daily lives such as jury decisions, physicians' diagnoses, and the justification of governmental policies (Nickerson, 1998). In addition, it leads to other cognitive difficulties. For example, confirmation bias may lead us to perceive illusory correlations between events in our environment (Chapman, 1967; Chapman & Chapman, 1967). An **illusory correlation** is the erroneous belief that two variables are statistically related when they actually are not. If we believe a relationship exists between two things, then we will tend to notice and remember instances that confirm this relationship. Let's consider an example.

Many people erroneously believe that a relationship exists between weather changes and arthritis. Why? They focus on instances when the weather changes and their arthritic pain increases. To determine if this relationship actually exists, we need to consider the frequency of all four possible events, the two that confirm the hypothesis and the two that disconfirm it. In our example, the two confirming instances would be (1) when the weather changes and arthritic pain changes, and (2) when the weather does not change and arthritic pain does not change. The two disconfirming instances are (1) when the weather changes but arthritic pain does not, and (2) when the weather does not change but arthritic pain changes. When the frequencies of all four events are considered, it turns out that there isn't a relationship between these two variables. The confirming events are not more frequent than the disconfirming events (Redelmeier & Tversky, 1996).

Confirmation bias is likely responsible for many of our erroneous beliefs. Science provides better answers than informal, biased hypothesis testing. When our beliefs are contradicted by science, as in the case of belief in paranormal events, we should think about our hypothesis testing procedure versus that of the scientist. We may have only gathered evidence to support our belief. We have to be willing to accept that our beliefs may be wrong. This is not easy for us to do. We suffer from **belief perseverance**—the tendency to cling to our beliefs in the face of contradictory evidence (Anderson, Lepper,

illusory correlation The erroneous belief that two variables are statistically related when they actually are not.

belief perseverance The tendency to cling to one's beliefs in the face of contradictory evidence.

▌ **person-who reasoning** Questioning a well-established research finding because one knows a person who violates the finding.

& Ross, 1980). Our beliefs constitute a large part of our identity; therefore, admitting that we are wrong is very difficult.

Such denial is illustrated by **person-who reasoning**—questioning a well-established finding because we know a person who violates the finding (Nisbett & Ross, 1980; Stanovich, 2004). A good example is questioning the validity of the finding that smoking leads to health problems because we know someone who has smoked most of his or her life and has no health problems. Such reasoning also likely indicates a failure to understand that these research findings are probabilities. Such research findings are not certain; they do not hold in absolutely every case. Exceptions to these sorts of research findings are to be expected. Person-who reasoning is not valid, and we shouldn't engage in it.

Testing medical hypotheses. As we pointed out, confirmation bias seems to impact physicians' testing of hypotheses during the diagnostic process (Nickerson, 1998). Physicians (and patients) also seem to have difficulty in interpreting positive test results for medical screening tests, such as for various types of cancer and HIV/AIDS (Gigerenzer, 2002). They often overestimate the probability that a patient has a disease based on a positive test result. When considering what a positive result for a screening test means, you are testing the hypothesis that a patient actually has the disease being screened for by determining the probability that the patient has the disease given a positive test result. Because you will be considering the results of medical screening tests throughout your lifetime and will inevitably get some positive results, you should understand how to compute this conditional probability in order to know your chances of actually having the disease. Because this computation is not a very intuitive process, I will show you a straightforward way to do it so that you can make more informed medical decisions.

Much of the research on how successful doctors and patients are at correctly interpreting a positive result for a medical screening test and how they can improve their performance has been conducted by Gerd Gigerenzer and his colleagues (Gigerenzer, 2002; Gigerenzer & Edwards, 2003; Gigerenzer, Gaissmaier, Kurz-Milne, Schwartz, & Woloshin, 2007). Both doctors and patients have been found to overestimate these conditional probabilities. An older study by Eddy (1982) with 100 American doctors as the participants illustrates this overestimation finding; but before considering it, some explanation is necessary. In medicine, probabilities are often expressed in percentages rather than as numbers between 0 and 1.0. Three terms relevant to screening tests, the base rate for a disease and the sensitivity and false positive rates for the test, also need to be explained. The base rate (prevalence) of a disease is simply the probability with which it occurs in the population. The sensitivity rate for a screening test is the

Oliver Hartung /The New York Times/Redux

Gerd Gigerenzer

probability that a patient tests positive if she has the disease, and the false positive rate is the probability that a patient tests positive if she does not have the disease. Now consider Eddy's problem. You should try to estimate the probability asked for in the problem before reading on.

> **Estimate the probability that a woman has breast cancer given a positive mammogram result and a base rate for this type of cancer of 1%, a sensitivity rate for the test of 80%, and a false positive rate for the test of 9.6%.**

What was your estimate? If you acted like the doctors, you overestimated the probability. Almost all of the doctors estimated this probability to be around 75%. The correct answer, however, is much less, only around 8%. Hoffrage and Gigerenzer (1998) replicated Eddy's finding with even more shocking results. Physicians' estimates ranged from 1% to 90%, with a 90% chance of breast cancer being the most frequent estimate. Given the doctors' overestimation errors, think of how many women who tested positive in this case would have been unnecessarily alarmed had this been real life and not an experiment. Think about the possible consequences, which are far from trivial—emotional distress, further testing, biopsy, more expense, and maybe even unnecessary surgery. To correctly compute the conditional probability that someone has the disease *given* a positive test result, Gigerenzer recommends that you convert all of the percentages (probabilities) into natural frequencies, simple counts of events. According to Gigerenzer, natural frequencies represent the way humans encoded information before probabilities were invented and are easier for our brains to understand. In brief, they make more sense to us. To convert to natural frequencies, we begin by supposing there is a sample of women who have had the screening test. It's best to suppose a large, even number such as 1,000 because such numbers allow an easier conversion to natural frequencies. Assuming a sample of 1,000 women, we can then proceed to convert Eddy's percentages into natural frequencies and compute the conditional probability.

> **Given a base rate of 1%, we would expect 10 (1% of 1,000) women to have breast cancer.**
>
> **Of these 10, we expect 8 (80% of 10) to test positive because the test has a sensitivity rate of 80%. The results for these 8 women are called true positives because these women have breast cancer and their test results were positive. The test results for the other 2 women are called false negatives because these women have breast cancer but their test results were negative.**
>
> **Among the 990 (1,000 – 10) women without breast cancer, 95 (9.6% of 990) will test positive given the 9.6% false positive rate. The results for these 95 women are called false positives because these women do not have cancer but their test results were positive. The results for the remaining 895 women are called true negatives because these women do not have cancer and their test results were negative.**

> **Thus, 103 (8 + 95) women in the sample of 1,000 will test positive, but only 8 are true positives. Thus, the conditional probability that a woman testing positive actually has cancer is the percentage of positive test results that are true positives, 8/103 = .077 (7.7%).**

Hoffrage and Gigerenzer (1995) found that once they presented the numbers as natural frequencies to doctors, the majority suddenly understood the problem. Do you? If not, the solution steps are visually illustrated in the natural frequency tree diagram in Figure 6.2. Read through the steps in the tree diagram and then read through them again in the text. After doing this, you should better understand how to do such calculations.

It should be clear to you now that a positive result for a medical screening test does not necessarily mean that you have the disease. You might or you might not. It is natural to assume the worst when faced with a positive test result, but it may be more probable that you do not have the disease. There is uncertainty, and the hypothesis that you have the disease must be tested by computing the conditional probability that you do given the positive test result. You now know how to do this by representing the base, sensitivity, and false positive rates as natural frequencies and using these frequencies to compute the probability. Combine a low incidence rate (for example, 1 or 2%) with just a modest false positive rate (for

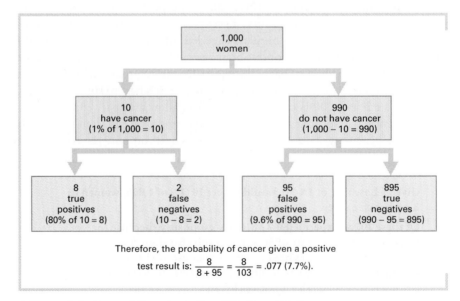

Therefore, the probability of cancer given a positive test result is: $\dfrac{8}{8+95} = \dfrac{8}{103} = .077$ (7.7%).

▲ **Figure 6.2** I **Natural Frequency Tree Diagram for Cancer Problem in Eddy (1982)** I This tree diagram visually illustrates the solution steps necessary to solve Eddy's (1982) cancer problem by converting all of the relevant probability information to natural frequencies as suggested by Gigerenzer (2002). Remember, the probability that a person has a disease given a positive screening test result for that disease is the percentage of positive test results that are true positives. (Source: Gerd Gigerenzer, Director of Max Planck Institute for Human Development, Berlin) example, 10%) for a screening test, and there will be many false positives (Mlodinow, 2008). A good example is mammography with young women. In this case, a positive mammogram is actually more likely *not* to indicate cancer. For more detailed coverage of interpreting screening test results and understanding other medical statistics, see Gigerenzer (2002) and Woloshin, Schwartz, and Welch (2008).

Section Summary

In this section, we learned that when we make probability judgments, we often use the representativeness and availability heuristics. When using the representativeness heuristic, we judge the likelihood of category membership by how well an object resembles a category (the more representative, the more probable). This heuristic can lead us to ignore extremely relevant probability information such as the conjunction rule. The availability heuristic leads us to judge the likelihood of an event by its availability in memory (the more available, the more probable). We may make errors with the availability heuristic because events may be highly prominent in our memories because of their recent occurrence or because they are particularly vivid and not because they occur more often.

We also considered that when we test hypotheses about our beliefs, we tend to suffer from confirmation bias (the tendency to seek evidence that confirms our beliefs). This bias may lead us to have erroneous beliefs based on illusory correlations, believing two variables are related when they actually are not. To prevent this, we should attempt to disconfirm our hypotheses and beliefs rather than confirm them. Even in the face of contradictory evidence, we tend to persevere in our beliefs and ignore the evidence, or we engage in denial through invalid person-who statistical reasoning (thinking that a well-established finding should not be accepted because there are some exceptions to it). Lastly we discussed medical hypothesis testing, specifically how to compute the conditional probability that a person actually has a disease that is being screened for given a positive test result. Research indicates that both doctors and patients tend to overestimate such probabilities. The conversion of the relevant probability information, however, to natural frequencies greatly facilitates the computation of these conditional probabilities.

Concept**Check** | 2

> Explain how using the representativeness heuristic can lead to the conjunction fallacy.

> Explain how using the availability heuristic can lead to the misjudgment of the probabilities of various causes of death.

> Explain how confirmation bias can lead to the perception of an illusory correlation.

> Given a base rate of 2% for a disease and a false positive rate of 10% and a sensitivity rate of 90% for the screening test for the disease, use natural frequencies to compute the conditional probability that a person actually has the disease given a positive test result.

Intelligent Thinking

The types of thinking that we have discussed so far—problem solving, judgment, and hypothesis testing—are important aspects of intelligent thinking, or what we call intelligence. We have a pretty good idea of what intelligence is, and we can recognize examples of intelligent thinking. However, finding a definition of intelligence that most psychologists can agree upon is not that easy. The definition of intelligence is controversial, and intelligence tests and their use are even more controversial. Their fairness and usefulness are constantly questioned. In this section, we will examine two of the major questions concerning intelligence and intelligence tests. First, is intelligence one general ability or is it a set of specific mental abilities? Second, is intelligence due to genetics or experience? To put these two discussions into proper perspective, we will first consider the historical development of intelligence tests and then the characteristics of a good intelligence test.

Intelligence Tests

The first attempts to develop intelligence tests took place in late nineteenth-century England and in early twentieth-century France. From the start, intelligence testing was enmeshed in the nature-versus-nurture controversy—is intelligence innate (set by genetics) or is it nurtured by one's environmental experiences? You will see that the major intelligence theorists tended to favor one side or the other. As each theorist's work is described, his bias will be pointed out.

The history of intelligence tests. In late nineteenth-century England, Sir Francis Galton was trying to develop an intelligence test for the purpose of eugenics, selective reproduction to enhance the capacities of the human race (Fancher, 1985). Galton clearly fell on the nature side of the nature–nurture debate. He believed in the genetic determination of intelligence and thought he could measure intelligence by measuring various aspects of the human brain and nervous system. Galton assumed that more intelligent people would have more acute senses, greater strength, and faster reactions to stimuli, so he devised a series of tests measuring these physical traits and tested thousands of people. As you might guess, Galton's tests were not good predictors of intelligent thinking.

Probably more significant to intelligence testing was Galton's invention of the basic mathematics behind correlational statistics (what he termed "co-relations") that are used for numerous aspects of testing from assessing genetic contributions to a test's validity (Gardner, Kornhaber, & Wake, 1996). Before Galton, correlational statistics did not exist. Actually, his disciple, Karl Pearson, formalized Galton's ideas to allow computation of the correlation coefficient (Fancher, 1985), which we discussed in Chapter 1.

In France at the beginning of the twentieth century, Alfred Binet and his assistant Theophile Simon were working on the problem of academic retardation. France had recently introduced mass public education, and

Bettman/Corbis

Sir Francis Galton

the French government asked Binet to develop a test to diagnose children whose intellectual development was subnormal and who would not be able to keep up with their peers in school. This test, published in 1905, was the first accepted test of intelligence (Fancher, 1985). The test calculated a child's performance as an intellectual level, or mental age, that then could be used in diagnosing academic retardation. Mental age is the age typically associated with a child's level of test performance. If a child's mental age were less than his or her chronological (actual) age, the child would need remedial work. The fact that Binet developed what he termed "mental orthopedics"—remedial work for children classified as subnormal—clearly illustrates his bent toward the nurture side of the nature–nurture debate.

Alfred Binet

The next major figure in intelligence test development, Lewis Terman, had Galton's nature bias, but he used Binet and Simon's test. Working at Stanford University, Terman revised the intelligence test for use with American schoolchildren. This revision, first published in 1916, became known as the Stanford-Binet (Terman, 1916). To report Stanford-Binet scores, Terman used the classic intelligence quotient formula suggested by William Stern, a German psychologist (Stern, 1914). The **intelligence quotient (IQ)** formula was the following: IQ = (mental age/chronological age) × 100. Multiplying by 100 centered the scale at 100. When a child's mental age (as assessed by the test) was greater than the child's chronological age (actual age), the child's IQ was greater than 100; when chronological age was greater than mental age, the child's IQ was less than 100. The IQ formula, however, is no longer used to compute a person's intelligence test score on the Stanford-Binet. How intelligence test scores are computed is explained in our discussion of the next major figure of intelligence testing, David Wechsler.

> ▐ **intelligence quotient (IQ)** (mental age/chronological age) × 100.

David Wechsler was working as Chief Psychologist at Bellevue Hospital in New York City in the 1930s and was in charge of testing thousands of adult patients from very diverse backgrounds (Fancher, 1985). Like Binet, Wechsler thought that intelligence was nurtured by one's environment. Given that most of his patients were undereducated, he wanted to get a much broader assessment of their abilities. The Stanford-Binet wasn't well-suited for his purposes, because it only provided a single measure of abilities related to academic performance (IQ) and wasn't primarily designed to assess adult intelligence. The IQ formula was especially not relevant for adults because at some point the mental age levels off but chronological age keeps increasing. A person's IQ would automatically go down with age regardless of one's mental abilities.

Given all of these problems, Wechsler developed his own test, the Wechsler

Lewis Terman

David Wechsler

Bellevue Scale, in 1939 (Gardner, Kornhaber, & Wake, 1996). This test became known as the Wechsler Adult Intelligence Scale (WAIS) in 1955 and is appropriate for ages 16 and older. Wechsler also developed the Wechsler Intelligence Scale for Children (WISC) in 1949 for children aged 6 to 16. Both tests (the WAIS and WISC) provide finer analyses of a person's abilities by providing test scores for a battery of not only verbal tests (such as vocabulary and word reasoning) but also performance (nonverbal) tests (such as block design, matrix reasoning, and visual puzzles). An item similar to those on the WAIS nonverbal Visual Puzzles subtest and one similar to those on the WISC nonverbal Matrix Reasoning subtest are given in Figure 6.3a and 6.3b, respectively. The WAIS and WISC are now in their fourth editions, and the Stanford-Binet is in its fifth. Like Wechsler's tests, the latest edition of the Stanford-Binet provides a broader assessment of intelligence, including nonverbal subtests.

▲ **Figure 6.3** I **Sample Performance (Nonverbal) Test Items** I (a) This is a nonverbal test item similar to those on the WAIS Visual Puzzles subtest. (b) This is a nonverbal test item similar to those on the WISC Matrix Reasoning subtest. (Source: www.pearsonassessments.com)

Deviation IQ scores. Wechsler also devised a better way to report intelligence test scores, deviation IQ scores. Like IQs, deviation IQs involve standardization. **Standardization** is the process that allows test scores to be interpreted by providing test norms. To standardize a test, the test must be given to a representative sample of the relevant population. The scores of this sample then serve as the test norms for interpretation. For example, Terman standardized the original Stanford-Binet on American children of various ages. Any child's raw test score could be compared to the standardization norms to calculate the child's mental age and IQ. Because of the problems in the IQ formula for adults, however, Wechsler decided to use his standardization data differently. He collected standardization data for various adult age groups. The data for each age group form a normal distribution (see Figure 6.4).

To calculate a person's deviation IQ, Wechsler compared the person's raw test score to the standardization normal distribution of raw scores for that person's age group. He calculated how far the raw score was from the mean raw score in terms of standard deviation units from the mean. To make the deviation scores resemble IQ formula scores, he set the mean to 100 and the standard deviation to 15. He then defined a person's **deviation IQ score** as 100 plus or minus (15 × the number of standard deviation units a person's raw test score is from the mean for the relevant age group norms). For example, if a person's raw test score fell 1 standard deviation above the mean for his or her age group, he or she would have a deviation IQ score of 100 plus (15 × 1), or 115. The deviation IQ scale for the WAIS is illustrated in Figure 6.4. The same scale is used for the WISC but with

▌ **standardization** The process that allows test scores to be interpreted by providing test norms.

▌ **deviation IQ score** 100 plus or minus (15 × the number of standard deviations the person is from the raw score mean for their standardization group).

▲ **Figure 6.4 | Deviation IQ Scores on the WAIS |** Deviation IQ scores for the WAIS are indicated for the mean, and 1 to 3 standard deviations above or below the mean. To make deviation IQ scores resemble IQ scores, the mean was set at 100 points and the standard deviation at 15 points.

standardization data for various child age groups; a similar deviation IQ scale with the standard deviation set at 16 is used for scoring the Stanford-Binet intelligence test.

Reliability and validity. In addition to being standardized, a good test must also be reliable and valid. **Reliability** is the extent to which the scores for a test are consistent. This may be assessed in various ways. In the test–retest method, the test is given twice to the same sample, and the correlation coefficient for the two sets of scores is computed. If the test is reliable, this coefficient should be strongly positive. Remember from Chapter 1 that a strong correlation coefficient approaches 1.0, hence acceptable reliability coefficients should be around .90 or higher. The reliability coefficients for the major intelligence tests, the WAIS, WISC, and Stanford-Binet, are at this level (Kaufman, 2000).

If multiple forms of the test are available, then alternate-form reliability can be assessed. Alternate-form reliability is determined by giving different forms of the test to the same sample at different times and computing the correlation coefficient for performance on the two forms. A third type of reliability assessment involves consistency within the test. If the test is internally consistent, then performance on the two halves of the test (odd versus even items) should be strongly positively correlated. This type of reliability is called split-half reliability because performance on half of the test items (the odd-numbered items) is compared to performance on the other half (the even-numbered items).

In addition to reliability, a test should have validity. **Validity** is the extent to which a test measures what it is supposed to measure or predicts what it is supposed to predict. The former type of validity is called content validity, and the latter, predictive validity. Content validity means that the test covers the content that it is supposed to cover. Experts decide this. All course exams should have content validity (be on the content that was assigned). Predictive validity means that the test predicts behavior that is related to what is being measured by the test; for example, an intelligence test should predict how well a child does in school. Children and teenagers higher in intelligence should do better on average than children and teenagers lower in intelligence, and this is the case for the intelligence tests that we have discussed. These tests all have good predictive validity. It is important to note that if a test is valid, then it will also be reliable. However, the reverse is not true. A test may be reliable, but not valid. A good example is measuring the circumference of the head as an indicator of intelligence. This number would be consistent across two measurements and therefore reliable, but it does not predict intelligent behavior (does not have predictive validity).

Intelligence test scores are among the most valid predictors of academic performance and job performance across just about every major occupation studied (Neisser et al., 1996; Sackett, Schmitt, Ellingson, & Kabin, 2001; Schmidt & Hunter, 1998). Not only do intelligence tests have good predictive validity, but they also are *not* biased against women or minorities. As Lilienfeld, Lynn, Ruscio, and Beyerstein (2010)

▌ **reliability** The extent to which the scores for a test are consistent.

▌ **validity** The extent to which a test measures what it is supposed to measure or predicts what it is supposed to predict.

point out, the belief that these tests are biased in this way is a widespread myth and that the research on this belief indicates that intelligence tests and other standardized abilities tests, such as the SAT, are not biased against women or minorities. A task force of the American Psychological Association (Neisser et al., 1996) and two National Academy of Science panels (Hartigan & Wigdor, 1989; Wigdor & Garner, 1982) reached this same conclusion. In sum, the question of intelligence test bias has been settled about as conclusively as any scientific controversy can be (Gottfredson, 1997, 2009; Sackett, Bornerman, & Connelly, 2008).

Psychologists agree on what an intelligence test should predict, but they do not agree on how intelligence should be defined. Is intelligence one general ability or many specific abilities? Does intelligence involve more than just mental abilities? Are there multiple types of intelligence? Different psychologists answer these questions in different ways based on their definitions of intelligence. The other major controversy concerning intelligence is the nature–nurture debate on the basis of intelligence. Galton's work marked the beginning of this debate, and the debate is still with us today, over a century later. It is to these two controversies that we now turn.

Controversies About Intelligence

The argument over whether intelligence is a single general ability or a collection of specific abilities has been around for over a hundred years. Many theorists have argued that intelligence comprises multiple abilities, but the exact number of abilities or types of intelligence proposed has varied from 2 to over 100. In our discussion, we'll consider a few of the more prominent theories, first considering those that propose that intelligence is one or more mental abilities and then theories that define intelligence more broadly, including more than just mental abilities as assessed by intelligence tests.

Theories of intelligence. Mental ability theories of intelligence began with Charles Spearman (1927), who argued that intelligence test performance is a function of two types of factors: (1) a g factor (general intelligence), and (2) some s factors (specific intellectual abilities such as reasoning). Spearman thought that the g factor was more important because it was relevant across the various mental abilities that make up an intelligence test, and that the s factors were more pertinent to specific subtests of an intelligence test. Spearman's theory was based on his observation that people who did well on one subtest usually did well on most of the subtests, and people who did poorly usually did so on most of the subtests. Individuals did not do equally well on all of the various subtests, however, indicating the secondary effects of the s factors or specific abilities on the various subtests. Contemporary research has shown the g factor to be a good predictor of performance both in school and at work (Gottfredson, 2000a, 2000b).

In contrast, one of Spearman's contemporaries, L. L. Thurstone, argued that specific mental abilities (like Spearman's s factors) were more important (Thurstone, 1938). Based on his research, he argued that there were seven primary

factor analysis A statistical technique that identifies clusters of test items that measure the same ability (factor).

mental abilities—verbal comprehension, number facility, spatial relations, perceptual speed, word fluency, associative memory, and reasoning. Thurstone identified these primary abilities by using **factor analysis,** a statistical technique that identifies clusters of test items that measure the same ability (factor). Spearman also used factor analysis, so why the difference in theories? Basically, they emphasized different aspects of the analysis. Thurstone emphasized the specific factor clusters whereas Spearman emphasized the correlations across the various clusters.

Later, Raymond Cattell (a student of Spearman) and John Horn proposed a slightly different type of mental ability theory that has mainly influenced researchers in aging (Cattell, 1987; Horn & Cattell, 1966, 1967). They propose that the *g* factor should be viewed as two types of intelligence: (1) fluid intelligence and (2) crystallized intelligence. Fluid intelligence refers to abilities independent of acquired knowledge, such as abstract reasoning, logical problem solving, and the speed of information processing. Crystallized intelligence refers to accumulated knowledge and verbal and numerical skills. This theory has interested researchers in aging because crystallized intelligence increases with experience and formal education and grows as we age; fluid intelligence is not influenced by these factors and actually declines with age. We will return to this theory in Chapter 7 when we consider how intelligence changes across the life span.

All of the theories we have discussed so far focus on definitions of intelligence as mental abilities assessed by standard intelligence tests such as the Stanford-Binet and WAIS. Three major contemporary theories by Howard Gardner (1983, 1993, 1999), Robert Sternberg (1985, 1988, 1999), and Keith Stanovich (2009a, b) extend this definition to include other types of ability. We'll consider Gardner's first. According to Gardner's theory of multiple intelligences, there are eight independent intelligences—linguistic, logical-mathematical, spatial, musical, bodily-kinesthetic, intrapersonal, interpersonal, and naturalistic. Brief descriptions of each of these intelligences are given in Table 6.1.

Table 6.1	Brief Descriptions of Gardner's Eight Intelligences
Linguistic	Language ability as in reading, writing, and speaking
Logical-mathematical	Mathematical problem solving and scientific analysis
Spatial	Reasoning about visual spatial relationships
Musical	Musical skills such as the ability to compose and understand music
Bodily-kinesthetic	Skill in body movement and handling objects
Intrapersonal	Understanding oneself
Interpersonal	Understanding other people
Naturalist	Ability to discern patterns in nature

The linguistic and logical-mathematical intelligences seem to fit with other definitions of intelligence in terms of mental abilities, but the other six are controversial; many psychologists see these as talents or skills and not really types of intelligence. In addition, many of these intelligences are difficult to quantify (such as intrapersonal intelligence) and present measurement problems.

According to Sternberg's triarchic theory of intelligence, there are three types of intelligence—analytical, practical, and creative. Analytical intelligence is essentially what is measured by standard intelligence tests, the skills necessary for good academic performance. However, the other two types of intelligence are not really measured by standard intelligence tests. Practical intelligence could be equated with good common sense or "street smarts." Creative intelligence is concerned with the ability to solve novel problems and deal with unusual situations. Sternberg's intelligences are all types of mental ability, but the inclusion of practical and creative intelligences broadens our conception of intelligence by including mental abilities that seem to have more applicability in the nonacademic world.

Cognitive researcher Keith Stanovich (2009a, b) argues that intelligence is a meaningful, useful construct and, unlike Gardner and Sternberg, is not interested in expanding the definition of intelligence. Rather he argues that intelligence is only one component of good thinking and thus by itself is not sufficient to explain such thinking. The other critical component is our ability to think and act rationally, which is not assessed by standard intelligence tests. Further, these two components are independent so you can be intelligent and not act rationally and vice-versa. This is why smart people sometimes do foolish things. Stanovich coined the term "dysrationalia" to describe this failure to think and behave rationally despite having adequate intelligence.

One cause of dysrationalia is that we tend to be cognitive misers, taking the easy way out to avoid thinking too much. This is the reason we have developed a whole set of heuristics and biases (many such as anchoring, representativeness, and confirmation bias were discussed earlier in this chapter) to limit the amount of thinking that we need to engage in. As we have learned, these short-cut strategies provide rough and ready answers that are right sometimes but often wrong. Another source of dysrationalia is what Stanovich calls the mindware gap which occurs when we haven't learned the appropriate mindware (specific knowledge, such as an understanding of probability, and cognitive rules and strategies, such as scientific thinking, that are necessary to think rationally). According to Stanovich, many intelligent people never acquire the appropriate mindware. Finally, given such causes, Stanovich thinks that rational thinking and behavior can be taught and that it ought to be taught at every stage of the educational system.

The six theories of intelligence that we have discussed are briefly summarized in Table 6.2 (page 236). Next we will consider the controversial nature–nurture debate on the basis of intelligence.

Table 6.2	Theories of Intelligence
Theorist	**Theory Summary**
Spearman	Intelligence is mainly a function of a general intelligence (*g*) factor
Thurstone	Intelligence is a function of seven primary mental abilities—verbal comprehension, number facility, spatial relations, perceptual speed, word fluency, associative memory, and reasoning
Cattell and Horn	There are two types of intelligence—crystallized intelligence, which refers to accumulated knowledge and verbal and numerical skills, and fluid intelligence, which refers to abilities independent of acquired knowledge, such as abstract reasoning, logical problem solving, and speed of information processing
Gardner	Intelligence is defined as eight independent intelligences—linguistic, logical-mathematical, spatial, musical, bodily-kinesthetic, intrapersonal, interpersonal, and naturalist
Sternberg	Intelligence is defined as three types of abilities—analytical, creative, and practical
Stanovich	Intelligence is not sufficient for good thinking; rationality, which is independent of intelligence, is also necessary

Nature versus nurture. Not only can't psychologists agree upon the definition of intelligence, they also argue about its origins—the nature-versus-nurture debate that we discussed earlier. This debate was popularized by Galton, a strong proponent of the nature side of the argument, over a century ago. Most contemporary psychologists, however, believe that both heredity (nature) and environmental experiences (nurture) are important. The disagreement now is over the relative contribution of each part (nature and nurture) to intelligence. We'll take a brief look at how some psychologists have tried to settle this disagreement.

First, we'll consider the results of genetic similarity studies. Genetic similarity between people varies from 100 percent similarity between identical twins to 50 percent between fraternal twins and between siblings (brothers and sisters) to 0 percent between two unrelated people. If intelligence were due to heredity, the average correlations between intelligence scores should decrease as genetic similarity decreases. Researchers have found this to be the case (Bouchard & McGue, 1981). The average correlation coefficient drops from +.86 for identical twins to essentially 0 for unrelated people. The data, however, also show effects of environment. For example, if identical twins are raised apart (adopted into different families), the average correlation between their intelligence test scores drops to +.72, indicating the importance of sharing similar environments.

Let's consider two more of these findings to see how the effects of both heredity and environment are indicated. The average correlation between fraternal twins raised together (+.60) is less than that for identical twins reared apart

(+.72), indicating the influence of heredity; but the average correlation is greater than that for ordinary siblings reared together (+.47), indicating environmental influences. Remember that the amount of genetic similarity for fraternal twins and ordinary siblings is the same, 50 percent. This means that the greater correlation for fraternal twins (+.60 versus +.47) must be due to environmental factors. The fraternal twins are the same age; hence their environmental experiences are more similar than those for ordinary siblings of different ages. As these two findings indicate, heredity and environment work together to influence intelligence test scores.

Researchers have also looked at adopted children and the correlations between their scores with both their adoptive and biological parents. The modest correlation between the intelligence test scores of adopted children with their adoptive parents disappears as the children age (McGue, Bouchard, Iacono, & Lykken, 1993). The reverse is true, however, for the correlation between the scores for adopted children and their biological parents. It increases (Plomin, DeFries, McClearn, & Rutter, 1997). This stronger relationship between a person's intelligence and that of his or her biological parents means that nature plays a larger role in determining a person's intelligence than environmental experiences.

The results of genetic similarity studies of intelligence can also be used to estimate its **heritability,** an index of the degree that variation of a trait within a given population is due to heredity. These estimates vary, usually in the range from around 50 percent up to 70 percent (Bouchard, Lykken, McGue, Segal, & Tellegen, 1990). Thus, for a given population, 50 percent to 70 percent of the variation in their intelligence test scores is estimated to be due to heredity. However, because heritability is not 100 percent, this means that heredity and environment work together to determine intelligence (though heredity may make a larger contribution). Given this fact, recent research focuses on how heredity and environment interact to determine a person's intelligence score. The assumption is that heredity determines a **reaction range,** genetically determined limits for an individual's intelligence. Heredity places upper and lower limits on a person's intelligence, but the quality of the person's environment determines where the individual falls within this range. The principle is simple—the higher the environmental quality, the higher the person's intelligence within the reaction range.

Two points about heritability should be made clear. First, it is a group statistic and is not relevant to individual cases. For example, if the heritability estimate for intelligence for a population were 50 percent, this does not mean that 50 percent of the intelligence of an individual in the group is determined by genetics and the other 50 percent by environmental experiences. It only means that 50 percent of the variation in intelligence among people in the population is due to genetics and 50 percent of the variation is due to environmental experiences. Second, it is important to understand that heritability has nothing to do with the differences that have been observed between populations, such as the difference in scores for Asian schoolchildren

heritability An index of the degree that variation of a trait within a given population is due to heredity.

reaction range The genetically determined limits for an individual's intelligence.

versus American schoolchildren. Heritability only applies to the variation within a given population or group, not to variation between groups. Observed group differences must be analyzed individually and in a different way.

Let's examine the gap between Asian and American schoolchildren to see one way such analyses are done (Stevenson, Chen, & Lee, 1993; Stevenson & Stigler, 1992). In this case, researchers examined the group difference for children of different ages and concluded that the gap is likely due to the priority placed on education in Asian countries. Why? There doesn't seem to be a gap before the children enter school. The gap begins and increases as the children proceed through school. The Asian cultures place higher value on education, and so the children spend more time and work harder, achieving more in school and higher test scores. There seem to be clear environmental factors operating to explain this particular group difference.

As if there are not enough unanswered questions and debates about intelligence, a recent curious finding has led to yet another. It is called the "Flynn effect" because intelligence researcher James Flynn popularized it. The "Flynn effect" label was coined by Herrnstein and Murray in their book *The Bell Curve* (1994). Actually Flynn (2007) says that if he had thought to name it, he would have called it the "Tuddenham effect" because Tuddenham (1948) was the first to present convincing evidence of the effect using the intelligence test scores of U.S. soldiers in World Wars I and II. The **Flynn effect** refers to the fact that in the United States and other Western industrialized nations, average intelligence scores have improved steadily over the past century (Flynn, 1987, 1999). For example, the average score in 1918 would be equivalent to a score of 76 when compared to recent standardization norms. This translates to a gain of about three points per decade. Proposed explanations involve many environmental factors ranging from better nutrition to more education, but the explanation still remains a source of debate (Neisser, 1998).

▦ **Flynn effect** The finding that the average intelligence test score in the United States and other industrialized nations has improved steadily over the last century.

Joining this debate, Flynn has recently proposed that the effect is not due to people getting smarter overall but rather to the fact that they are getting smarter at skills that have become more important in our society over the past century, especially abstract, scientific thinking (Flynn, 2007). Our society has changed from agriculture-based to industry-based to information-based. Thus, the need to develop abstract, scientific thinking has grown as the nature of our society has changed. Flynn's hypothesis is supported by the finding that large intelligence increases have not been observed for all types of cognitive functioning. For example, the largest intelligence gains have come on intelligence subtests that involve abstract, scientific thinking, and the gains on subtests that are related to traditional

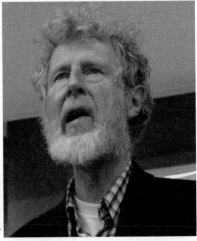

Bryce Edwards/Flickr

James Flynn

academic subjects, such as vocabulary, general knowledge, and arithmetic, have been very small. Flynn's explanation will likely not be the final word on the Flynn effect, but it seems to make enough progress in that direction that this effect is not quite the mystery that it used to be. Recent data, however, which indicate that the Flynn effect may have already ended in some industrialized nations (for example, Denmark and Norway) but is still alive in the United States (Kaufman, 2009), should maintain interest in this effect.

Section Summary

In this section, we discussed how the first attempts at developing a valid intelligence test began with Galton in late nineteenth-century England and with Binet and Simon in early twentieth-century France. Galton failed, but Binet and Simon, hired by the French government to develop a test to find children who would have difficulty in school, succeeded in 1905. Lewis Terman, working at Stanford University, revised the Binet-Simon test to use with American schoolchildren in 1916, and this test became known as the Stanford-Binet. Results for the Stanford-Binet were reported in terms of Stern's IQ formula, IQ = (mental age/chronological age) × 100. Subsequently, David Wechsler developed both the WAIS for adults and the WISC for children. Unlike the Stanford-Binet, these tests included both verbal and nonverbal subtests. In addition, Wechsler used deviation IQ scores instead of IQs to report performance on his tests. Deviation IQ scores are based on how many standard deviations a person's raw test score is above or below the raw score mean for his or her age group norms. Wechsler set the mean to 100 and the standard deviation to 15 to create deviation IQ scores that resemble IQ formula scores.

We also learned that these intelligence tests have both reliability (consistency in measurement) and predictive validity (predicting what we suppose they should predict) and are among the the most valid predictors of both academic performance and job performance. In addition, research has not supported the claim that they are biased toward women or minorities.

We also considered some of the major theories of intelligence. Most of these theories define intelligence in terms of mental abilities, but differ with respect to how many abilities are proposed. Using the results of factor analysis, Spearman thought that a general intelligence factor (the g factor) was most important, but other theorists, like Thurstone, emphasized multiple, more specific abilities in their definitions. Two recent theories have attempted to broaden the conception of intelligence and another points to the limitations of intelligence as a sufficient explanation of good thinking. Howard Gardner has proposed a theory of eight independent types of intelligence, but critics view some of these as talents or skills and not really types of intelligence. Robert Sternberg has also attempted to broaden the conception of intelligence in his triarchic theory of intelligence, which includes analytical, creative, and practical intelligences, with the latter two having more applicability in the nonacademic world. Keith Stanovich does not want to expand the definition of intelligence but rather argues that rationality in addition to intelligence is necessary for good thinking.

Last, we considered the origins of intelligence. We found that genetic similarity studies indicate that both nature (heredity) and nurture (environmental experiences) are important in determining one's intelligence. However, both heritability estimates and the results of adoption studies indicate that nature likely plays a larger role than nurture in determining intelligence. The concept of reaction range attempts to explain how heredity and environmental experiences work together to determine an individual's intelligence—heredity places limits on intellectual development, but the quality of the person's environment determines where the person's intelligence level falls within these limits. Finally, we discussed the Flynn effect—the finding that intelligence, at least as assessed by intelligence tests, has dramatically increased in the United States and other Western industrialized nations over the past century. Flynn's recent proposal that the effect is not due to people getting smarter overall but rather to the fact that they are getting smarter at skills that have become more important in our society over the past century, especially abstract, scientific thinking, has greatly reduced the mystery of this effect. Recent data also indicate that the effect may have already ended in some industrialized nations.

ConceptCheck | 3

➤ Explain why standardization of a test is necessary.

➤ Explain what a deviation IQ score is and how it differs from an IQ score.

➤ Explain how the results of studies examining the impact of genetic similarity on intelligence support both nature and nurture explanations.

➤ Explain how the more contemporary theories of intelligence proposed by Gardner, Sternberg, and Stanovich differ from the more traditional theories of intelligence (e.g., those proposed by Spearman and Thurstone).

Study Guide

Chapter Key Terms

You should know the definitions of the following key terms from the chapter. They are listed in the order in which they appear in the chapter. For those you do not know, return to the relevant section of the chapter to learn them. When you think that you know all of the terms, complete the matching exercise based on these key terms.

thinking
well-defined problem
ill-defined problem
fixation
functional fixedness
mental set
insight
algorithm
heuristic
anchoring and adjustment heuristic

working backward heuristic
means–end analysis heuristic
representativeness heuristic
conjunction fallacy
gambler's fallacy
availability heuristic
confirmation bias
illusory correlation
belief perseverance
person-who reasoning

intelligence quotient (IQ)
standardization
deviation IQ score
reliability
validity
factor analysis
heritability
reaction range
Flynn effect

Key Terms Exercise

Identify the correct term for each of the following definitions. The answers to this exercise follow the answers to the Concept Checks at the end of the chapter.

1. Incorrectly judging the overlap of two uncertain events to be more probable than either of the two events.

2. The extent to which a test measures what it is supposed to measure or predicts what it is supposed to predict.

3. A new way to interpret a problem that immediately yields the solution.

4. Questioning a well-established research finding because you know a person who violates the finding.

5. The genetically determined limits for an individual's intelligence.

6. A problem-solving heuristic in which the distance to the goal state is decreased systematically by breaking the problem down into subgoals and achieving these subgoals.

7. The tendency to use previously successful problem-solving strategies without considering others that are more appropriate for the current problem.

8. An index of the degree that variation of a trait within a given population is due to heredity.

9. The process that allows test scores to be interpreted by providing test norms.

10. Incorrectly believing that a chance process is self-correcting in that an event that has not occurred for a while is more likely to occur.

   _____

11. A problem lacking clear specification of either the start state, goal state, or the processes for reaching the goal state.

   _____

12. A heuristic for estimation problems in which one uses his or her initial estimate as an anchor estimate and then adjusts the anchor up or down (often insufficiently).

   _____

13. A problem-solving heuristic in which one attempts to solve a problem by working from the goal state back to the start state.

   _____

14. The tendency to cling to one's beliefs in the face of contradictory evidence.

   _____

15. A statistical technique that identifies clusters of test items that measure the same ability (factor).

   _____

Practice Test Questions

The following are practice multiple-choice test questions on some of the chapter content. The answers are given after the Key Terms Exercise answers at the end of the chapter. If you guessed or incorrectly answered a question, restudy the relevant section of the chapter.

1. The tendency to think of only the most typical uses of objects in a problem setting is called _____.
   a. fixation
   b. mental set
   c. functional fixedness
   d. confirmation bias

2. If you compute the area of a room by using the formula length × width = area, you are using a(n)/the _____.
   a. algorithm
   b. heuristic
   c. conjunction rule
   d. anchoring and adjustment heuristic

3. The representativeness heuristic leads us to _____.
   a. judge the probability of an event in terms of its prominence in memory
   b. judge the probability of category membership by resemblance to the category
   c. seek only evidence that confirms our beliefs
   d. maintain our beliefs even though we have been given evidence that contradicts them

4. Overestimating the probability of dying in an airplane crash is likely the result of using the _____.
   a. representativeness heuristic
   b. availability heuristic
   c. anchoring heuristic
   d. conjunction rule

5. In the 2-4-6 problem, participants demonstrate _____ in testing their hypotheses.
   a. mental set
   b. confirmation bias
   c. person-who reasoning
   d. belief perseverance

6. Mistakenly believing that two events are related is called _____.
   a. functional fixedness
   b. illusory correlation
   c. the Flynn effect
   d. the conjunction fallacy

7. Which of the following statements about test reliability and validity is false?
   a. A test can be reliable and valid.
   b. A test can be reliable but not valid.
   c. A test can be valid but not reliable.
   d. A test can be neither reliable nor valid.

8. The intelligence test scores for _____ are most strongly correlated.
   a. identical twins reared apart
   b. fraternal twins reared together
   c. siblings reared together
   d. unrelated people reared apart

9. Which of the following intelligence theorists emphasized the *g* factor?

 a. Sternberg

 b. Gardner

 c. Spearman

 d. Thurstone

10. The Flynn effect refers to the observation that average intelligence test scores in the United States and other Western industrialized nations have _____ over the past century.

 a. increased

 b. decreased

 c. stayed the same

 d. first increased but then decreased

11. Which of the following intelligence theorists proposed three types of intelligence—analytical, practical, and creative?

 a. Sternberg

 b. Gardner

 c. Thurstone

 d. Spearman

12. The folding problem in which you were asked to estimate the thickness of a 0.1 millimeter sheet of paper folded in on itself 100 times illustrates how the _____ can lead to dramatic underestimates of the correct answer to an estimation problem.

 a. representativeness heuristic

 b. availability heuristic

 c. anchoring and adjustment heuristic

 d. conjunction rule

13. A person who questions the validity of the research findings that indicate smoking leads to health problems because he knows someone who has smoked most of their life and has no health problems is using _____.

 a. the representativeness heuristic

 b. the availability heuristic

 c. person-who reasoning

 d. inferential-statistical reasoning

14. A heritability estimate of 100% for intelligence in a given population means that the variation in intelligence for this population is determined _____.

 a. solely by genetics

 b. solely by environmental experiences

 c. 50% by genetics and 50% by environmental experiences

 d. 75% by genetics and 25% by environmental experiences

15. In the Linda problem, if you judge that it is more likely that Linda is a bank teller and active in the feminist movement than that Linda is a bank teller, you are likely using the _____ heuristic and committing the _____ fallacy.

 a. availability; gambling

 b. availability; conjunction

 c. representativeness; gambling

 d. representativeness; conjunction

Chapter Concept Check Answers

Concept Check | 1

- In functional fixedness, we fixate on the normal function of an object given our past experiences with that object. Our past experience with the object may block us from seeing how to use it in a novel way. Similarly, mental set leads us to approach a problem in the same way we have approached similar problems in the past, especially the recent past. We tend to block developing a new approach because our mental set keeps us locked into the old approach based on our past experiences.

- We use heuristics rather than algorithms because algorithms tend to be time-consuming and more difficult to use. Solving anagram puzzles is a good example of a case where we know the algorithm but we do not use it unless there are only a few letters because it is too time-consuming and difficult to use.

- The anchoring and adjustment heuristic leads to a serious error in estimation when we fail to adjust our initial anchor sufficiently either up or down in magnitude. The paper-folding problem is a good example of such a failure.

Concept Check | 2

- The representativeness heuristic can lead to the conjunction fallacy by causing us to ignore the conjunction rule when making a probability judgment involving the conjunction of two uncertain events. Use of the heuristic for the Linda problem illustrates how this occurs. We focus on how much Linda resembles a feminist and ignore the conjunction rule that says that the probability that Linda is a bank teller has to be more probable than the conjunction of bank teller and active in the feminist movement.

- The availability heuristic can lead us to overestimate the risk of causes of death that are highly publicized (such as airplane crashes, fires, and shark attacks) and underestimate those that are less publicized and not as dramatic (such as diabetes and emphysema). Because the highly publicized causes are more available in our memories, we misjudge them to be more probable than the less publicized causes.

- Confirmation bias can lead to the perception of an illusory correlation by leading us to confirm our belief about the correlation by focusing only on events that confirm the belief and not on those that disconfirm the belief. To test to see if a relationship exists, we must consider the probabilities of both types of events.

- Assume that 1,000 people are screened for the disease. Given a base rate of 2% for the disease, only 20 (2% of 1,000) would actually have the disease. This means that 980 people (1,000 − 20) would not have the disease. Given a test sensitivity rate of 90%, 18 of the 20 (90% of 20) people who have the disease would test positive. Given a false positive rate of 10%, 98 (10% of 980) people who do not have the disease would test positive. Thus, there would be 116 positives (18 true positives and 98 false positives). Hence the conditional probability that someone testing positive actually has the disease is 18/116, which is .155 (15.5%).

Concept Check | 3

- Standardization of a test is necessary for the interpretation of test performance. In the standardization process, a representative sample of the relevant population takes the test and their scores are used as the norms for the test. Test takers' scores are compared to those of the standardization group in order to determine an index of performance. For example, on intelligence tests a person's performance is compared to the scores for a representative sample of the person's age group.

- A deviation IQ score is based on the standardization normal distribution of scores for each age group for an intelligence test. First, a person's raw score is determined in terms of standard deviation units above or below the mean for the person's age group. Then the person's score in terms of standard deviation units is converted to a score that resembles an IQ score. For example, on the WAIS the mean (or 0 point) is set equal to 100 and the standard deviation to 15. Thus, a person who scores 1 standard deviation above the mean in comparison to his age group norms receives a score of 100 + 15, or 115. IQ scores were based on the following formula, IQ = (mental age/chronological age) × 100. A deviation IQ tells us how well a person did relative to the standardization data for the person's age group. An IQ told us how well a child did relative to the child's own actual age.

- The results of genetic similarity studies support the nature (heredity) explanation of intelligence because as genetic similarity decreases, the average correlation between intelligence test scores also decreases. The average correlation is strongest for identical twins (about .90). However, these results also indicate that environment (nurture) plays a role. For example, the average correlation for intelligence test scores for identical twins decreases when the twins are adopted and raised apart in different environments. The twins are 100 percent genetically similar in both cases; therefore, environmental factors must be responsible for the difference in average correlations.

- The theories proposed by Gardner and Sternberg are different from the traditional theories of intelligence that we discussed in that both theorists broaden the definition of intelligence by proposing types of intelligence that are not measured by standard intelligence tests like the WAIS and Stanford-Binet. In Gardner's case, six of his proposed eight intelligences fall into this category. In Sternberg's case, two of his three proposed types of intelligence do so. However, all three of Sternberg's intelligences are types of mental ability, but this is not true for Gardner's proposed intelligences. With respect to Stanovich's theory, he doesn't want to expand the definition of intelligence like Gardner and Sternberg do, but rather argues that intelligence is only one component of good thinking. The other critical component is our ability to think and act rationally, which is not assessed by standard intelligence tests.

Answers to Key Terms Exercise

1. conjunction fallacy
2. validity
3. insight
4. person-who reasoning
5. reaction range
6. means–end analysis heuristic
7. mental set
8. heritability
9. standardization
10. gambler's fallacy
11. ill-defined problem
12. anchoring and adjustment heuristic
13. working backward heuristic
14. belief perseverance
15. factor analysis

Answers to Practice Test Questions

1. c; functional fixedness
2. a; algorithm
3. b; judge the probability of category membership by resemblance to the category
4. b; availability heuristic
5. b; confirmation bias
6. b; illusory correlation
7. c; A test can be valid but not reliable.
8. a; identical twins reared apart
9. c; Spearman
10. a; increased
11. a; Sternberg
12. c; anchoring and adjustment heuristic
13. c; person-who reasoning
14. a; solely by genetics
15. d; representativeness; conjunction

Answers to Problems

Solutions to nine-circle problems, p. 208

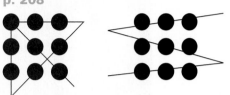

The sample four-straight-line solution is not unique. You may draw your first line from any of the other corner circles and continue from there to achieve a similar solution. The sample three-straight-line solution is taken from Adams (1986).

Solution to insight problem, p. 210

As Knoblich and Oellinger (2006) explain, most people try to create a correct equation by moving a matchstick that changes the numbers because we are taught in school that solving math problems is all about manipulating quantities. This knowledge, however, blinds us to the needed insight. To experience insight on this problem, you need to change your perspective about where the solution might lie—realize that you can also change operators. The solution lies in moving one matchstick to change the operators as shown at the bottom of this page.

Most efficient solution to Tower of Hanoi problem, p. 214

Move 1: Move Disk 1 to Peg C
Move 2: Move Disk 2 to Peg B
Move 3: Move Disk 1 to Peg B
Move 4: Move Disk 3 to Peg C
Move 5: Move Disk 1 to Peg A
Move 6: Move Disk 2 to Peg C
Move 7: Move Disk 1 to Peg C

7

Developmental Psychology

So far we have discussed perception, learning, memory, thinking, and intelligence, but we have not considered how these processes develop over the life span. This is what developmental psychologists study—how and why we change as we grow older. They examine our behavior and mental processing from conception until death. **Developmental psychology** is the scientific study of biological, cognitive, social, and personality development throughout the life span. This chapter will focus on three major types of development—biological, cognitive, and social (the next chapter will deal with personality).

■ **developmental psychology** The scientific study of biological, cognitive, social, and personality development across the life span.

Historically, a major issue for all types of development has been the nature-versus-nurture question (which we also confronted in our discussion of intelligence). As with intelligence, most psychologists now believe that nature and nurture interact to influence our development. Lingering controversial questions include exactly how nature and nurture interact and which is more important to the various aspects of our development (Harris, 1998). We will return to the nature–nurture issue at different points in the chapter.

Developmental psychologists usually divide the life span into several stages beginning with the prenatal stage and ending with late adulthood. Table 7.1 (page 248) provides a commonly used set of stages, each of which is characterized by different biological, cognitive, and social changes. Most of the major theories in developmental psychology that we will discuss are stage theories. Stage theories organize developmental change by providing the approximate age ranges at which we can expect certain types of behavior and cognitive functioning. Keep in mind, however, that the age at which individuals enter and leave stages can vary, that stage transition is probably more gradual than abrupt, and that stage definitions may vary across cultures.

This chapter is divided into discussions of different types of development, but it is important to remember that the various types of development occur simultaneously and so have an impact on each other. We begin with a discussion of the first two stages of the life span—prenatal development and infancy—to learn how development begins and progresses very early in our lives. Here we will be mainly concerned with physical development, specifically sensory and motor development. Next we will focus on our cognitive development from birth through adulthood by discussing early language development, Jean Piaget's influential stage theory of cognitive development, Lev Vygotsky's sociocultural approach to such development, and the question of whether intelligence declines across the life span.

In the last section of this chapter, we will consider social development. We will begin with a discussion of Lawrence Kohlberg's influential theory of the development of moral reasoning, then examine early social development with a discussion of the research on attachment formation, parenting styles, and theory of mind development, and conclude with a description of Erik Erikson's stage theory of social-personality development across the life span. This chapter will give you a better idea about where you are in your development, how you got there, and where you can expect to go.

Table 7.1	Dividing the Life Span into Developmental Stages
Stage	**Approximate Age Range**
Prenatal	Conception to birth
Infancy	Birth to 2 years
Childhood	2 to 12 years
Adolescence	12 to 18 years
Young adulthood	18 to 40 years
Middle adulthood	40 to 65 years
Late adulthood	65 years and over

Prenatal Development and Infancy

What happens in the prenatal environment? What sensory abilities do we have at birth? Is our brain fully developed at birth? These are the kinds of questions that we will address in this section. We know, for instance, that the brain is not fully developed at birth. Remember, we learned in the chapter on memory that we do not have any explicit memories about this period of our life because the hippocampus isn't fully developed until later. Thus, this next section should interest all of us, because we have no memory of our own life in the prenatal stage and infancy. Let's get started with the beginning of all development—the union of sperm and egg.

Prenatal Development

Human conception begins when a sperm (male reproductive cell) penetrates the membrane of an ovum or egg (female reproductive cell). Each of these reproductive cells contains genetic instructions. When the two combine, a complete set of genetic instructions is formed, half from the father and half from the mother. The fertilized egg that is formed from the union of the sperm and egg cells is called a **zygote.** All other cells in the human body develop from this single cell, and each duplicate cell carries a copy of the genetic instructions of the original zygote. The zygote develops into a growing cluster as the cells duplicate.

The **gene** is the basic unit of genetic instruction. Genes are short segments of **chromosomes,** molecules of DNA (deoxyribonucleic acid) that hold the genetic instructions for every cell in our body. Except for reproductive cells (sperm and eggs), every cell of a normal human has 23 pairs

zygote The fertilized egg that is formed from the union of the sperm and egg cells in human reproduction.

gene The basic unit of genetic instruction.

chromosomes Molecules of DNA that hold the genetic instructions for every cell in the body.

of chromosomes, one of each pair coming from the mother and one from the father. Reproductive cells receive only one member of each pair, giving them only 23 chromosomes. This means that when a sperm combines with an ovum, the zygote will have the complete 46. It is the 23rd pair of chromosomes that determines a person's sex. In a female, there are two X-shaped chromosomes (XX); in a male, there is one X-shaped chromosome and one smaller Y-shaped chromosome (XY). It is the Y chromosome that leads to the development of a male; hence the sex of the zygote is determined by which sperm, X or Y, fertilizes the ovum.

■ **identical (monozygotic) twins** Twins that originate from the same zygote.

■ **fraternal (dizygotic) twins** Twins that originate from the fertilization of two eggs at approximately the same time (two zygotes).

■ **teratogens** Environmental agents such as drugs and viruses, diseases, and physical conditions that impair prenatal development and lead to birth defects and sometimes death.

In some cases, the growing cluster of duplicated cells breaks apart early in development resulting in two clusters with identical genes. These clusters become **identical (monozygotic) twins.** They are identical because they originate from the same zygote. **Fraternal (dizygotic) twins** originate from the fertilization of two eggs at approximately the same time. Thus, fraternal twins are nonidentical and could be of different sexes and just as different as any two children with the same parents. You may be wondering why two children with the same parents can be very different in appearance. The answer is the same reason that children with different parents vary greatly in appearance—chance determines which one of the 23 pairs of chromosomes goes to a reproductive cell. This means that there are 2^{23} (8 million or so) chromosome possibilities for each reproductive cell in each parent. In addition, when the two reproductive cells unite to form the zygote, they interact to further increase the uniqueness of the zygote. This is why children from the same family can look so different.

Prenatal development (conception until birth) is divided into three stages—the germinal stage, the embryonic stage, and the fetal stage. The germinal stage begins with the formation of the zygote and ends after about 2 weeks, when the outer portion of the zygote's developing cluster of cells has attached itself to the uterine wall. This implantation leads to the formation of the placenta and umbilical cord, which allow oxygen and nutrients from the mother to enter and wastes to exit. The inner portion of the zygote becomes the developing organism, the embryo. During the embryonic stage (from 2 weeks to about 2 months), the major structures and organs of the body begin to develop, and the embryo starts to resemble a human being. During the fetal stage (from about 2 months following conception to birth), the developing organism is called a fetus, and through very rapid growth, the body structures and organs complete their growth.

Both genetic and environmental factors impact prenatal development. The nature-nurture issue is relevant, even in prenatal development. This development is mainly a function of the zygote's genetic code (nature), but it is also affected by the mother's environment (nurture). **Teratogens** are environmental agents (such as drugs or viruses), diseases (such as German measles), and physical conditions (such as malnutrition) that impair prenatal development and lead to birth defects or even death. Expectant mothers who drink alcohol, smoke, or take drugs put their developing

fetal alcohol syndrome (FAS) A syndrome affecting infants whose mothers consumed large amounts of alcohol during pregnancy, resulting in a range of severe effects including mental retardation and facial abnormalities.

sucking reflex An innate human reflex that leads infants to suck anything that touches their lips.

rooting reflex An innate human reflex that leads infants to turn their mouth toward anything that touches their cheeks and search for something to suck on.

fetuses at great risk. **Fetal alcohol syndrome (FAS)** occurs when mothers consume alcohol during pregnancy, resulting in a range of severe effects including mental retardation and facial abnormalities in the child. As alcohol consumption increases, the risk of FAS increases. However, there is no known safe limit of alcohol consumption, so the best strategy is to avoid alcohol and other teratogens entirely during pregnancy. The effects of teratogens also vary depending on when during pregnancy the fetus is exposed. Early in pregnancy a teratogen may affect the formation of the eyes, whereas later it may be the brain that is affected. There are other maternal factors that affect prenatal development. Age is one such factor. The probability of health risks to the fetus increases for mothers who are too young, 15 or younger, or too old, over 35 (Andersen, Wohlfahrt, Christens, Olsen, & Melbe, 2000; Phipps, Blume, & DeMonner, 2002).

Other risks to newborns include prematurity and low birth weight. Those that are born prematurely, before the 37th week, have a number of problems, which increase with the degree of prematurity. Major health problems of premature infants include immaturity of the lungs and the digestive and immune systems. Premature infants also have low birth weight, although some full-term infants can as well. Low birth weight increases the chances of neurological handicaps and death (Holsti, Grunau, & Whitfield, 2002). Many of the teratogens discussed above increase the likelihood of prematurity, although in about 50% of the cases there are no identifiable causes. So remember, a healthy woman providing a healthy prenatal environment enhances the probability of a healthy child.

How We Develop During Infancy

Motor development and sensory-perceptual development are the two major areas of development during infancy. We will start with an overview of our abilities at birth. Then we will discuss how these processes develop during infancy.

© Laura Dwight/Photo Edit

Motor development. The newborn comes equipped with several motor reflexes, which are unlearned responses. Some of these reflexes, such as the breathing reflex that provides us with oxygen, have obvious survival value and are permanent, but others aren't as necessary and disappear within the first year of life. Two examples of reflexes that disappear are the Babinski reflex, in which infants fan their toes upward when their feet are touched, and the grasping reflex, in which infants grasp any object that touches their palms. Two other motor reflexes, the sucking reflex and the rooting reflex, are concerned with getting nourishment and so are obviously related to survival. The **sucking reflex** leads infants to suck anything that touches their lips, and the **rooting reflex** leads infants to turn their mouths toward anything that touches their cheeks and search for something to suck on.

In this first year or so of life, infants learn to sit, stand, and walk. This is an orderly sequence; each new motor behavior builds upon previous ones. Infants learn to prop up and support their body, then to sit without support, then to crawl, then to stand while holding onto an object, then to stand without support, and finally to walk without support at somewhere around 12 months of age. It was once thought that motor development was primarily a maturational process that unfolded according to a genetic program. However, as with most achievements the process is more complex. Learning how to walk, for instance, involves the interaction of multiple factors such as increases in strength, body proportions, and balance (Thelen, 1995). During this first year, infants are also developing their perceptual abilities and learning to coordinate their body movements with perceptual input. In fact, infants learning how to move around by themselves leads to changes in depth perception (our ability to perceive the distance of objects from us). Infants who have experienced crawling develop a fear of heights and falling, whereas infants of the same age but who are not yet crawling do not show this fear (Campos, Anderson, Barbu-Roth, Hubbard, Hertenstein, & Witherington, 2000).

> **habituation** A decrease in the physiological responding to a stimulus once it becomes familiar.

Sensory-perceptual development.

Psychologists have developed a number of interesting experimental techniques to study sensory-perceptual abilities in nonverbal infants. The preferential-looking technique, a procedure used to study vision, is surprisingly simple (Fantz, 1961, 1963). Two visual stimuli are displayed side by side, and the researcher records how long the infants look at each stimulus. If the infants look at one side longer, it is inferred that they can tell the difference between the two stimuli and have a preference. Another technique involves **habituation,** a decrease in the physiological responding to a stimulus once it becomes familiar. Infants will look at a novel, unfamiliar stimulus, but this interest habituates and the infants look less and less. They get bored with it. If infants look longer at a new stimulus than an old one, then it is inferred that they must be able to perceive the difference between the two stimuli. Researchers use measures

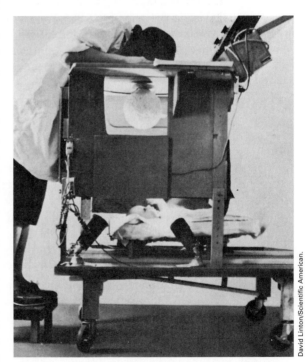

David Linton/Scientific American.

This classic experimental apparatus, called the "Fantz box," was designed by Robert Fantz about a half-century ago to study infant vision. Different stimuli were typically displayed on two side-by-side screens in the box. The researcher looked at the infant's eyes through the peephole in the top of the box and recorded the amount of time that the infant looked at each of the stimuli. The "Fantz box" has been replaced with more technologically advanced equipment providing more precise measurement, but studies using the "Fantz box" started the modern era of infant research.

other than viewing time. For example, infants intensify their sucking of a pacifier in their mouth when confronted with a novel, unfamiliar stimulus. When they habituate to the stimulus, the sucking returns to normal. Similarly, a developmental researcher may use changes in biological mechanisms, such as heart rate, to indicate infants' perceptual behavior.

Through these ingenious techniques we have learned that our five senses are functional at birth (though not fully developed). Vision, our dominant sense, is the least developed at birth. Newborns cannot see very clearly. Their visual acuity (resolution of visual detail) is estimated to be about 20/400 to 20/800 (Kellman & Banks, 1998). This means that the visual detail that a person with normal 20/20 vision can see at 400 to 800 feet is what the infant sees at 20 feet. Acuity develops rather quickly and reaches 20/20 within the first year of life. Color vision develops even sooner, by 2 to 3 months, when it becomes comparable to that of adults (Kellman & Arterberry, 1998). We also know that infants have a visual preference for faces, especially their mother's face, and other complex stimuli (Field, Cohen, Garcia, & Greenberg, 1984; Valenza, Simion, Assia, & Umilta, 1996). Infants' preference for such visual complexity may be due to the fact that such stimulation is necessary for proper development of the visual pathways and cortex during infancy (Greenough, Black, & Wallace, 1987).

Hearing in the newborn is more fully developed than vision. In fact, newborns can distinguish their mother's voice from those of others (DeCasper & Fifer, 1980). Research indicates this ability and several auditory preferences develop in the womb before birth (Dirix, Nijhuis, Jongsma, & Hornstra, 2009). Let's briefly consider one of the most famous studies indicating the effects of prenatal learning on auditory preferences after birth (DeCasper & Spence, 1986). During the last 16 weeks of pregnancy, mothers read Dr. Seuss's *The Cat in the Hat* aloud twice a day. Following birth, the researchers had the babies suck on an artificial nipple that, depending upon the infant's sucking pattern, would activate a tape of their mother reading the Dr. Seuss story or another story that the mother had never read aloud. Most of the infants sucked to hear *The Cat in the Hat*. The infants preferred the familiar story that their mothers had read to them while they were still in the womb. Infants also prefer the sound of the human voice and speech sounds versus other types of sounds. By about 6 months, an infant's hearing is comparable to that of an adult.

One of the most remarkable hearing abilities that infants possess involves speech perception. **Phonemes** are the smallest distinctive speech sounds in a language. They allow us to distinguish between different words in a language. For example, the difference between the words *pat* and *bat* is the difference in the *pa* and *ba* phonemes. In order to learn a language, infants must be able to detect these subtle differences between phonemes, and they are able to do so soon after birth. Different languages do not use all the same phonemes, and adults who are not native speakers of a particular language have difficulty detecting the speech sounds of that language. Japanese adults, for example, have trouble with the English *r* and

---

phonemes The smallest distinctive speech sounds in a language.

l sounds. Infants, in contrast, can detect all phonemes whether or not they have been exposed to them. By 12 months of age, however, they no longer can easily detect speech sounds not in their native language (Kuhl, 2004). Interestingly though, a brief amount of exposure given through live social interaction is sufficient to maintain the ability to detect nonnative phonemes (Kuhl, Tsao, & Liu, 2003). It seems as though infants come into the world prepared to learn whatever language they happen to find themselves exposed to and experience fine-tunes this ability.

The senses of smell, taste, and touch are also fairly well developed at birth. For example, infants can differentiate the smell of their mother from the smells of other people. Researchers discovered this by placing a nursing pad worn by the mother on one side of an infant and a pad worn by another woman on the other side, then measured how long the baby was turned toward each side. The infants spent more time turned toward their mother's pad (MacFarlane, 1975).

Some recent studies have indicated that infants' understanding of the physical world and their cognitive abilities may be much better than was previously thought. Researchers have demonstrated that very young infants may have an innate conceptual understanding of object movement—for instance, that objects cannot simply go through solid surfaces (Baillargeon, 1993, 2002). Other researchers have suggested that infants can perform simple mathematical operations such as addition and subtraction (Wynn, 1992). Needless to say, such claims are not without controversy—trying to understand the mind of a nonverbal infant is not an easy task (see Cohen & Marks, 2002).

Development of an infant's cognitive and perceptual abilities depends upon brain development. The brain contains about 100 billion neurons at birth, but the infant's brain is rather immature, and connections between neurons (neural networks) need to be formed. During the first few months of life, there is a large growth spurt for these connections between neurons, especially those in the cortex that control perception and cognition. Thousands of new connections are established for these neurons. The connections between the retina and the brain are a good example. Without visual experiences, these visual pathways do not develop, and vision will be permanently lost (Kalat, 2007). This is why a baby born with cataracts that prevent vision needs to have them removed as early as possible, so that normal vision will develop. During infancy, the networks of neurons that are used become stronger and those that are not used disappear (Thompson, 2000).

Section Summary

Our prenatal development starts with conception, the fertilization of an egg by a sperm to form a zygote, and proceeds through the germinal stage (first 2 weeks), the embryonic stage (2 weeks to 2 months), and the fetal stage (2 months to birth). Prenatal development is guided by the zygote's genetic code (nature), but teratogens (environmental agents such as drugs or viruses, diseases, and malnutrition) can impact the prenatal environment (nurture) and result in birth defects and even death. Other factors that affect prenatal development include fetal alcohol syndrome and the age of the mother. Prematurity and low birth weight are also risks to newborns. The newborn comes equipped with several motor reflexes, some critical for survival, such as the rooting and sucking reflexes that lead to nourishment, and some not so critical, such as the grasping reflex, which disappear within the first year of life. Within this first year, the infant learns to sit, stand, and walk in a very orderly sequence; each new motor behavior builds upon previous ones. They also learn to coordinate their body movements with perceptual input.

Although not fully developed, our five senses are functional at birth, with vision being the least developed. To study early sensory-perceptual capabilities in the nonverbal infant, researchers developed special techniques that allow them to determine what an infant can discriminate. Such research has shown, for example, that infants have the remarkable ability to discriminate phonemes, the smallest distinctive speech units in a language. Sensory-perceptual development depends upon brain development in the form of a large growth spurt of neural networks, such as between the retina and the brain. If these visual pathways do not develop in infancy, vision would be permanently lost. The neural networks that are used grow stronger, and those that are not used are eliminated.

ConceptCheck | 1

> Explain how the effects of teratogens are due to nurture and not nature.
> Explain how habituation is used to study infant sensory-perceptual skills.

How We Think Throughout Our Lives

In this section, we will examine how our cognitive abilities, such as thinking and language, develop. Because we are verbal animals and our language ability differentiates us from all other animals, we will look first at how this ability begins its development, which will lead us back to the nature–nurture issue. Next we will outline one of the most important theoretical contributions to psychology, Swiss psychologist Jean Piaget's theory of cognitive development. According to Piaget, starting at birth all of us go through the same four stages of cognitive development, each of which is qualitatively different. Next we will discuss Russian psychologist Lev Vygotsky's sociocultural approach to cognitive development. Vygotsky's approach has recently become very popular because it emphasizes the importance of social and cultural contexts in development. Last, we consider the question of whether intelligence declines throughout the adult portion of the life span.

How We Learn Language

Our ability to use language makes us unique. No other animal seems to be able to acquire and develop language ability as humans do. Although speechless at birth, our capacity for language begins to develop soon after. Children in different cultures learn to speak very different languages, but they all seem to go through the same sequence of stages. We will describe these stages of language acquisition and then consider the nature–nurture issue in explaining how language acquisition occurs.

Let's begin with the newborn infant and see how language develops. Infants are speechless, but one way they communicate is through crying. Infants cry differently, for example, to indicate hunger and pain. Crying, movement, and facial expressions allow infants to communicate fairly well. Infants also prefer **baby talk (motherese),** the different format of speech that adults use when talking with babies that involves the use of shorter sentences with a higher, more melodious pitch than normal speech. By 2 months or so, infants are making more meaningful noises such as cooing (repeating vowel sounds such as "oo" and "ah") and laughing. Infants use cooing as their response in vocal interactions with their parents.

At about 6 or 7 months, **babbling,** the rhythmic repetition of various syllables, including both consonants and vowels, begins. The syllables that are babbled are not limited to the sounds that the infant hears or those from their parents' language. However, this early babbling begins to include more and more sounds from the infant's native language over the next 6 months. The infant can now also understand some words such as "mommy" and "daddy." For example, the question "Where is mommy?" will lead the infant to look at her mother.

At about 1 year of age, infants begin to speak a few words. Their first words usually refer to their caregivers and objects in their daily environment. Sometimes, infants use a **holophrase,** a word that expresses a complete idea. A good example is children going to the door and saying "bye-bye." Vocabulary grows slowly until about 18 months, and then there is a vocabulary spurt, maybe of 100 words or more per month. This is also the period during which overextension and underextension occur. **Overextension** is the application of a newly learned word to objects that are not included in the meaning of the word. **Underextension** is the failure to apply the new word more generally to objects that are included within the meaning of the new word. A couple of examples will make these concepts clearer. A good example of overextension is children's tendency to call any male "dada," overextending the word and deflating the father's ego. Underextension frequently occurs when children do not extend the categories of "dog" and "cat" to dogs and cats beyond the family's pet dog or cat. The word is applied too narrowly. As vocabulary expands, the incidences of overextension and underextension decrease. This expansion of vocabulary reflects the influence of cognitive development since as children acquire new concepts, they learn the names that go with them.

One of the challenges children face in acquiring a vocabulary is determining the meaning of words since the context in which children hear language is often ambiguous. For

▌ **baby talk (motherese)** The different format of speech that adults use when talking with babies that involves the use of shorter sentences with a higher, more melodious pitch.

▌ **babbling** The rhythmic repetition of various syllables including both consonants and vowels.

▌ **holophrase** A word used by an infant to express a complete idea.

▌ **overextension** The application of a newly learned word to objects that are not included in the meaning of the word.

▌ **underextension** The failure to apply a new word more generally to objects that are included within the meaning of the word.

instance, if a mother points out a bird flying overhead and exclaims "look at the bird," the child has to consider many possibilities as the potential meaning of the word *bird*. For example, *bird* could refer to any object above them or any object in the sky. Research has shown, however, that children use many different types of cues to identify the speaker's intended meaning of *bird*. Some researchers have argued that children are particularly good at using social cues, such as the speaker's eye gaze, pointing, and emotional reactions to determine what the adult means when using a novel word (Baldwin & Moses, 2001; Brooks & Meltzoff, 2008; Golinkoff & Hirsh-Pasek, 2006). For instance, Tomasello, Strosberg, and Akhtar (1996) showed that children could use a speaker's emotional reaction to determine which novel object a speaker is labeling. In their task, an experimenter told 18-month-old infants that she was going to find a "toma" (a novel object). She then picked up a novel object but then rejected it and acted disappointed. She then picked up a second novel object and acted excited. She didn't name either of the two objects. The child was then shown both novel objects and asked to give the experimenter the "toma." If the child was able to use the emotional reaction of the experimenter to determine which object was the toma, she should select the object that the experimenter was excited about; and most 18-month-old children were able to do so even though it was not the first object seen.

The next step in language development is the combining of words into sentences. This begins during the vocabulary spurt between 18 and 24 months. Children engage in what is called **telegraphic speech,** using two-word sentences with mainly nouns and verbs. It is called telegraphic speech because the speech is like that in a telegram, concise and direct. Some examples are "Dada gone" and "Throw ball." These two-word statements begin to be expanded, and between the ages of 2 and 5 years, children acquire the grammar of their native language. Children learn these rules implicitly and in a very predictable order across all cultures. How they do so returns us to the nature–nurture issue.

Children acquire language early and easily, without direct instruction, and this acquisition process seems to be the same across cultures that have very different languages. This is why there is much support for the argument that language development is a genetically programmed ability (Chomsky, 1965; Pinker, 1994). Children, however, cannot develop normal speech without exposure to human speech, and it is clear that caregivers can facilitate and enhance language development, indicating that experience definitely plays a role in language acquisition. As is usually the case with the nature–nurture issue, there is some evidence for both sides; nature and nurture provide interactive influences (Elman, Bates, Johnson, Karmiloff-Smith, Paisi, & Plunkett, 1996).

One of the best illustrations of children's special skill in learning a language is the existence of a critical period for acquiring it. A critical period is a time period when learning certain skills is most easily accomplished and is thought to reflect the influence of biology (brain maturation) on development. If children do not acquire a language by a certain age, usually thought to be around the time of

▮ **telegraphic speech** Using two-word sentences with mainly nouns and verbs.

puberty or perhaps earlier, then they will not learn it as well as younger children. For example, children who are isolated from human contact prior to puberty have difficulty learning a language, even after years of later exposure. The best known example is a girl known as "Genie" (Fromkin, Krasjen, Curtiss, Rigler, & Rigler, 1974). Genie was kept tied to a potty chair for most of the first 13 years of her life. During this time, Genie heard very little language and had minimal social interactions. After she was rescued, both researchers and therapists worked hard to rehabilitate her. Although she did make some linguistic progress and was able to learn several hundred words, her grammatical development never reached typical developmental levels even after several years of trying. A similar critical period exists for children acquiring American Sign Language (ASL). Most deaf children of hearing parents are not as adept at ASL as deaf children of deaf parents because they are typically taught ASL later since their parents are not signers themselves (Newport, 1991; Senghas & Coppola, 2001). A critical period also exists for second language learning. As you may know from your own struggles to learn a second language, children have a much easier time than adults (Birdsong & Molis, 2001; Johnson & Newport, 1989).

Language development occurs during the first few years of life when the brain and cognitive abilities, such as thinking and reasoning, are also developing. When children start talking, it is easy to start thinking of them as miniature adults, but this would be a big mistake. Their cognitive abilities are not at all like those of an adult. To see how these cognitive abilities develop, we'll consider Piaget's stage theory of cognitive development, which tells us how a speechless newborn develops into a cognitively complex adult.

Piaget's Theory of Cognitive Development

Jean Piaget was a twentieth-century Swiss psychologist whose research on children's thinking led to a landmark theory of cognitive development. He was named one of the twentieth century's 20 most influential thinkers by *Time* magazine in 1999. Piaget started his career in France working with Theophile Simon (of Binet-Simon intelligence scale fame) standardizing intelligence tests (Hunt, 1993). However, he soon returned to Switzerland and began his research on how children think. Piaget did not conduct formal experiments. In his loosely structured interviews he instead posed problems for children to solve (he used his own three children in his early research), observed their actions carefully, and questioned them about their solutions. He was particularly interested in children's errors, which he thought provided insight into the child's thinking, especially into how it differed from adult thinking. He found that children of roughly the same age often gave the same wrong answers. From such data, he developed a theory of cognitive development that revolutionized our understanding of children's thinking and its development (Piaget, 1926/1929, 1936/1952, 1983).

Piaget's cognitive theory incorporated two of his interests, biology and philosophy. He assumed that cognitive development stems from a child's adaptation

Bill Anderson/Photo Researchers

Jean Piaget interacting with a child attempting to solve a problem in one of Piaget's loosely structured studies.

to the environment, and that children attempt to promote their survival by trying to learn about their environment. This means that a child is an active seeker of knowledge and gains an understanding of the world by operating on it. The child organizes this knowledge into what Piaget called **schemes** (now called schemas), which are frameworks for our knowledge about people, objects, events, and actions. Remember, we discussed these in Chapter 5. Schemas are the basic units of our knowledge that allow us to organize and interpret information about our world. In our long-term memories, we have schemas for concepts (such as books or dogs), events (such as going to a restaurant or to the dentist's office), and actions (such as riding a bicycle).

According to Piaget, cognitive adaptation involves two processes, assimilation and accommodation, both of which impact the development of schemas and thus learning. **Assimilation** is the interpretation of new experiences in terms of our existing schemas; **accommodation** is the modification of current schemas to allow for new experiences. Our earlier example of overextension—when infants call all men "dada"—would represent a child's attempt to assimilate. Children learn, however, that they need to accommodate and change their schemas. A child has only one father, but there are many men in the world. It is through accommodation that the number and complexity of a child's schemas increase and learning occurs. In accommodation, either new schemas are created for information that doesn't fit into one's present schemas or existing schemas are modified to include the new information (such as for father and men).

Piaget also proposed that major changes in children's thinking occur in stages. Each stage permits only certain kinds of thinking and involves qualitatively different cognitive functioning. Piaget further assumed that all children go through the same stages in the same order. He proposed four stages, outlined in Table 7.2. As you learn about each stage, realize that you will be changing your own schemas to accommodate all this new information about Piaget's theory. Then, after you have finished reading about the stages, look back at Table 7.2. You should easily be able to assimilate the stage descriptions into your modified schemas for Piaget's theory.

The sensorimotor stage. In the **sensorimotor stage,** from birth to about age 2, infants learn about the world through their sensory and motor interactions with it.

▌ **schemes** Piaget's term for what are now called schemas—frameworks for our knowledge about people, objects, events, and actions that allow us to organize and interpret information about our world.

▌ **assimilation** Piaget's term for the interpretation of new experiences in terms of present schemas.

▌ **accommodation** Piaget's term for the modification of present schemas to fit with new experiences.

▌ **sensorimotor stage** The first stage in Piaget's theory of cognitive development, from birth to about age 2, during which infants learn about the world through their sensory and motor interactions with it and develop object permanence.

Table 7.2 Piaget's Stages of Cognitive Development	
Stage (age range)	**Stage Description**
Sensorimotor (birth to 2 years)	Children use senses and motor abilities to learn about the world and develop object permanence.
Preoperational (2 to 6 years)	Children use symbolic thinking to understand the world but remain egocentric and lack the mental operations that allow logical thinking.
Concrete operational (6 to 12 years)	Children gain cognitive operations for logical thinking about concrete events, understand conservation, and perform mathematical operations, but they cannot reason abstractly.
Formal operational (12 years through adulthood)	Further development of cognitive operations enables adolescents to engage in abstract thinking and hypothetical-deductive reasoning.

Beginning with the simple reflexes that we discussed earlier, infants come to know the world by looking, listening, sucking, grasping, and manipulating. Infants less than 8 to 12 months old lack **object permanence,** the knowledge that an object exists independent of perceptual contact with it. For example, young infants do not understand that a toy continues to exist even if they can no longer see it. Object permanence develops over the first two years of life. Very young infants will not search for a toy that vanishes; but at about 4 to 8 months, they will sometimes search for it, especially if it is only partially hidden. At 8 to 12 months, they will search for toys even if they are completely hidden, indicating that they realize that the toy still exists even if they cannot see it. Children continue to develop their understanding of object permanence and have a fairly complete understanding by 2 years of age. Similarly, symbolic representation of objects and events starts to develop during the latter part of the sensorimotor stage. Infants begin to use words as symbols to represent known objects at around 18 months. By 18 to 24 months, infants use telegraphic speech, which represents continuing development of symbolic representation.

The preoperational stage. In the **preoperational stage,** from age 2 to age 6, children's thinking becomes more symbolic and language-based, but remains egocentric and lacks the mental operations that allow logical thinking. Preoperational children can pretend, imagine, and engage in make-believe play. They have the ability to use one thing to represent another. Preoperational children might pretend that a broom is a horse to ride, or that their finger is a toothbrush. They no longer need to be interacting with an object to think about it. For example, they now can point to a picture of a dog and say "doggie" or crawl around and pretend to be a dog by barking like a dog. Word learning also continues at a rapid pace, and children have learned thousands of

object permanence The knowledge that an object exists independent of perceptual contact with it.

preoperational stage The second stage in Piaget's theory of cognitive development, from age 2 to 6, during which the child's thinking becomes more symbolic and language-based, but remains egocentric and lacks the mental operations that allow logical thinking.

THE FAMILY CIRCUS   By Bil Keane

"Look what I can do, Grandma!"

The child in this cartoon is demonstrating egocentric behavior so he would be in Piaget's preoperational stage of cognitive development. Given his egocentrism, he thinks that everybody sees what he sees regardless of where they're at.

▌ **egocentrism** The inability to distinguish one's own perceptions, thoughts, and feelings from those of others.

▌ **conservation** The knowledge that the quantitative properties of objects (such as mass and number) remain the same despite changes in appearance.

DENNIS THE MENACE

"Cut it up into a LOT of slices, Mom. I'm really hungry!"

words by the end of the preoperational stage. Children also learn to produce narratives, descriptions of past events that have the structure of a story. However, preoperational children's thinking still has major limitations. Let's first consider what it means that their thinking is egocentric.

Egocentrism is the inability to distinguish one's own perceptions, thoughts, and feelings from those of others. This means that a preoperational child cannot perceive the world from another person's perspective. For example, preoperational children don't realize what they are doing when they block the view of the television. They assume that another's view is the same as their view. Egocentric behavior does not stem from selfishness or a lack of consideration. Preoperational children just have not developed the cognitive ability to see another person's view. It is important for parents to realize this cognitive limitation in their preoperational children. If not, they may misinterpret their children's behavior in a negative way, leading to unjust punishment of the child.

Next, to understand what Piaget meant by the lack of mental operations that allow a child to think logically, let's consider conservation. Some grasp of conservation marks the end of the preoperational stage and the beginning of the concrete operational stage. **Conservation** is the knowledge that the quantitative properties of an object (such as mass and number) remain the same despite changes in appearance. Simply put, the quantitative properties of an object do not change with a change in appearance. There are many Piagetian conservation tests, but a well-known one is the liquid/beakers problem (see Figure 7.1). In this test, the child is first shown two identical short fat beakers with equal amounts of liquid in each. With the child watching, the liquid in one of the beakers is poured into a taller, thinner beaker. Then the child is asked if the two beakers have the same amount of liquid or if one has more liquid than the other. If the child understands conservation, then he can explain why the two differently shaped beakers have an equal amount of liquid in them. No liquid was taken away or added. However, a preoperational child will say that the two beakers have different amounts and most often that the taller, thinner beaker has more liquid. Like egocentric thinking, the failure to understand conservation illustrates one of Piaget's main points—a child is not like a miniature adult with less information. A child's

Tests of Various Types of Conservation

Type of Conservation	Initial Presentation	Transformation	Question	Preoperational Child's Answer
Continuous Quantity	Two identical beakers with equal amounts of liquid.	Pour one beaker into a taller, narrower beaker.	Which beaker contains more liquid?	The taller one.
Number	Two identical rows of checkers.	Increase the space between the checkers in one row.	Which row has more checkers?	The longer one.
Mass	Two equivalent lumps of clay.	Squeeze one lump into a long, thin shape.	Which shape has more clay?	The long one.
Length	Two sticks of identical length.	Move one stick.	Which stick is longer?	The one that is farther to the right.

▲ **Figure 7.1** | **Tests of Conservation** | These are examples of tests for conservation of continuous quantity, number, mass, and length. The typical preoperational child's responses are given in the last column.

reversibility The knowledge that reversing a transformation brings about the conditions that existed before the transformation.

centration The tendency to focus on only one aspect of a problem at a time.

concrete operational stage The third stage in Piaget's theory of cognitive development, from age 6 to 12, during which children gain a fuller understanding of conservation and other mental operations that allow them to think logically, but only about concrete events.

way of thinking is very different and how it is different depends upon the child's stage of cognitive development.

A major reason why a preoperational child does not understand conservation is that the child lacks an understanding of **reversibility**—the knowledge that reversing a transformation brings about the conditions that existed before the transformation. As adults, you and I realize that you could easily pour the liquid in the taller beaker back into the shorter beaker to return to the starting state. A preoperational child does not understand this reversibility operation. A preoperational child's thinking also reflects **centration**—the tendency to focus on only one aspect of a problem at a time. In the liquid/beakers problem, for example, the child may only focus on the heights of the beakers and conclude that one has more because it is taller. Obviously, both the height and width of the beakers need to be considered in order to make a correct judgment. Other Piagetian conservation tests in addition to the liquid/beakers problem are illustrated in Figure 7.1 (page 261). Find a preoperational child around 3 to 4 years of age and try these tests. The child's responses will not only amaze you but will also give you a much better understanding of the cognitive limitations of the preoperational stage of development.

The concrete operational and formal operational stages. During the **concrete operational stage,** from about age 6 to 12, children gain a fuller understanding of conservation and other mental operations that allow them to think logically, but only about concrete events. Different forms of conservation are developed at different times. For example, conservation of continuous quantity, number, and mass are acquired rather early, but conservation of length is more difficult and is acquired later in the concrete operational stage (Vasta, Miller, & Ellis, 2004). In addition to conservation operations, concrete operational children develop other mental operations that allow them to reason logically, such as transitivity (if A > B, and B > C, then A > C) and seriation (the ability to order stimuli along a quantitative dimension, such as a set of pencils by their length).

However, all of these operations are limited to reasoning logically about concrete events. For example, transitivity is limited to having the actual objects present, such as three sticks of different lengths. Children wouldn't be able to solve the transitivity problem without the sticks physically present. Similarly, concrete objects (such as beakers of liquid) would need to be present to solve the conservation of continuous quantity problem. This means that the reasoning of concrete operational children is tied to immediate reality (what is in front of them and tangible) and not with the hypothetical world of possibility. They cannot deal with what-if and if-then problems and abstract thinking. They also do not engage in systematic deduction to solve a problem, but rather use a haphazard trial-and-error strategy.

In the **formal operational stage,** starting at age 12 or so, children gain the capacity for such hypothetical-deductive thought. According to Piaget, this capacity allows adolescents to engage not only in hypothetical thought but also in systematic deduction and tests of hypotheses, what could easily be referred to as scientific thinking. To understand the difference in thinking between concrete and formal operational children, Piaget used several scientific thinking tasks (Inhelder & Piaget, 1958).

> **formal operational stage** The last stage in Piaget's theory of cognitive development, starting at age 12 or so, during which a child gains the capacity for hypothetical-deductive thought.

In one of these tasks, children or adolescents are shown several flasks of what appear to be the same clear liquid and are told that one combination of two of these liquids would produce a blue liquid. The task is to determine the combination that would produce the blue liquid. The concrete operational children just start mixing different clear liquids together haphazardly. The formal operational children, however, proceed very differently. They develop a systematic plan for deducing what the correct combination must be by determining all of the possible combinations (hypotheses for the correct combination) and then systematically evaluating each one. To accomplish this plan, they systematically mix the liquid in one beaker with each of the other liquids. If none of these combinations produced the blue liquid, they deduce that the liquid in that beaker is not relevant to the sought-after combination and then proceed to test each of the other clear liquids in the same manner until they find the correct combination.

Formal operational adolescents can also evaluate the logic of verbal statements without referring to concrete situations; the concrete operational child can only do so with concrete evidence. For example, in one formal operational study, the experimenter asked whether a statement about some colored poker chips was true, false, or uncertain (Osherson & Markman, 1975). When the experimenter hid a chip in his hand and asked about the statement, "Either the chip is red or it is not red," the formal operational children realized that the statement was true regardless of the color of the hidden chip, but the concrete operational children were uncertain of the statement's truth status. The formal operational children understood the disjunctive logic of the statement, and the concrete operational children did not. Concrete operational children also have difficulty with propositional logic that contradicts reality (Moshman & Franks, 1986). For example, concrete operational children would judge the following reasoning to be faulty, "If cats are bigger than horses and horses are bigger than mice, then cats are bigger than mice," because the first relationship does not hold in real life. Concrete operational children are tied to the realistic truth of the content (what is) in their logical reasoning, but formal operational children are not.

Evaluation of Piaget's theory. Recent research has shown that cognitive development seems to proceed in the general sequence of stages that Piaget proposed (Lourenco & Machado, 1996). This means that Piaget's theory seems to have captured the general nature of cognitive development accurately. However, there are many issues with the specifics of Piaget's stage theory. For example, recent research has demonstrated that rudiments of many of Piaget's key concepts (such as object permanence) may begin to appear at earlier ages than Piaget proposed. Infants and young children may be more cognitively competent than Piaget theorized. Piaget's tests for the understanding of concepts may have been too complex and thus missed partial knowledge of the concept. For example, Piaget's test for object permanence required infants to reach for a hidden object. A complete understanding required the infants to search for the object after several invisible (hidden) movements. Later research that involved tracking infants' eye movements has found that infants (as young as 3 months) continue to stare at the place where the object disappeared from sight, indicating some degree of object permanence (Baillargeon, 1987).

More recent research on the formal operational stage also makes it clear that not all people reach this stage of thinking, especially in cultures that do not emphasize such thinking, and that those that do reach the stage may not always use such thinking (Dasen, 1994; McKinnon & Renner, 1971). For example, people in non-Western cultures do not usually do well on the specific scientific reasoning tasks used by Piaget, but they do very well and demonstrate formal operational thought on comparable tasks involving content that they are familiar with and that is significant within their culture (Vasta, Miller, & Ellis, 2004). Even Piaget, late in his life, realized that there were limitations on achieving formal operations (Piaget, 1972).

Other cognitive developmental researchers question whether Piaget's characterization of distinct stages of development is correct. In particular, the **information-processing approach to cognitive development** questions the existence of stages and argues that development is continuous and not comprised of distinct stages. So how do information-processing developmental psychologists explain the growth in children's cognitive abilities? They attribute this growth to developmental changes in children's information-processing abilities—how they take in, store, and use information. The information-processing approach uses a computer metaphor to describe children's thinking. Just as a computer's ability to solve problems is affected by memory and requires specific processing steps, children's problem-solving ability involves similar information processing. Information-processing researchers study factors that affect such processing. For example, developmental improvements in speed of processing (Kail, 1991), storage capacity (Pascual-Leone, 1989), and knowledge base (Schneider, 1993) have all been found to influence improvements in children's memory and thinking. As children grow older, they become increasingly more adept at information processing.

We should mention two other major criticisms of Piaget's stage theory. One is that Piaget did not consider the impact of culture and social environment on cognitive development sufficiently (Miller, 2011; Segall, Dasen, Berry, & Poortinga, 1990). The second is that Piaget's stage theory of cognitive development ends with the adolescent and the development of formal operations. Although Piaget did not address these issues, other developmental psychologists have done so. We will discuss the first issue in the next section when we examine the work of Russian

information-processing approach to cognitive development An approach to studying cognitive development that assumes cognitive development is continuous and improves as children become more adept at processing information (taking in, storing, and using information) psychologist Lev Vygotsky, whose theory did emphasize the sociocultural aspects of cognitive development. The second issue will be addressed in the section after that when we examine the question of what happens to intelligence from adolescence to old age. Does it decline as we age, especially in late adulthood? This discussion will allow us to examine two major research methods used by developmental psychologists, cross-sectional studies and longitudinal studies.

Vygotsky's Sociocultural Approach to Development

Lev Vygotsky was a Russian developmental psychologist who was a contemporary of Piaget. Both were born in 1896, but Vygotsky died of tuberculosis at a very young age, 37, and did not have the opportunity to finish developing his theory. As with Piaget's work, there was little interest in the Western world in Vygotsky's work until the 1960s. Vygotsky's approach has become especially popular recently, however, because of its sociocultural emphasis on development.

Lev Vygotsky

Vygotsky (1930, 1933, 1935/1978, 1934/1986) stressed that cognitive abilities develop through interactions with others and represent the shared knowledge of one's culture. The social aspects of Vygotsky's approach are straightforward. We are social animals, so much of our learning occurs within social interactions. In brief, we learn from other people—our parents, siblings, friends, teachers, and others. Vygotsky proposed that the culture impacts both the content and the processes of the child's cognitive development because a child's cognitive development occurs within this cultural context. Now that we have a general idea of Vygotsky's theory, let's take a look at two of his major theoretical concepts—the zone of proximal development and scaffolding.

In Vygotsky's theory, the **zone of proximal development** is the difference between what a child can actually do and what the child could do with the help of others. In Vygotsky's terms, this is the difference between the levels of actual development and potential development. It means that there are thinking skills that the child can display with the help of others but cannot perform independently. It also leads to a style of teaching called **scaffolding.** In scaffolding, the teacher adjusts the level of help in relation to the child's level of performance, while directing the child's learning progress toward the upper level of the child's zone of proximal development. The teacher gauges the amount of assistance necessary based on the learner's needs. The learning is structured in steps so that the child learns to achieve each step independently, but is guided and supported by the teacher throughout the learning process.

To illustrate these two concepts and Vygotsky's theory, let's consider the example of a child trying to solve a jigsaw puzzle (Berger, 2006). A child may appear not to be able to solve the puzzle. However, Vygotsky would say that this

zone of proximal development According to Vygotsky, the difference between what a child can actually do and what the child could do with the help of others.

scaffolding According to Vygotsky, a style of teaching in which the teacher adjusts the level of help in relation to the child's level of performance while orienting the child's learning toward the upper level of his or her zone of proximal development.

particular problem-solving task could be within the child's zone of proximal development but that she could not achieve it on her own. She needs a teacher to scaffold the task for her. How might this scaffolding proceed? The teacher would break the task down into manageable units; for example, the teacher might ask the child just to look for pieces for a particular section of the puzzle with specific suggestions about the size, shape, and colors of the relevant pieces. If this doesn't work, the teacher might actually place a few pieces in their proper places or move a few relevant pieces to their correct orientations, so their relevance is more obvious to the child. Throughout this scaffolding process, the teacher must be totally supportive of the child's progress and sensitive to how much help the child needs to progress toward solving the puzzle and how best to direct her to succeed in the next step of the solution process. After solving the puzzle, the teacher might have the child do it again, but this time with less guidance. Soon the child will be able to complete the puzzle independently. The teacher builds a scaffold to enable the child's learning. Once the learning is achieved, the scaffold is no longer necessary.

As recommended with Piaget's tests for the various types of conservation, find a young child and try to teach her how to solve a jigsaw puzzle using Vygotsky's scaffolding method. It will not only give you a better understanding of this approach but will also lead you to understand the social aspects of learning that Vygotsky stressed in his theory.

How Intelligence Changes in Adulthood

Piaget's description of intellectual development stops in adolescence with the onset of formal operations (hypothetical thought and systematic deduction), but it is important to examine what happens to intelligence across the various stages of adulthood from youth to old age. Do our cognitive abilities severely decrease across adulthood, especially in old age? The attempt to answer this question illustrates the differences between two major research methods in developmental psychology, cross-sectional studies versus longitudinal studies. In a **cross-sectional study,** people of different ages are studied and compared with one another at a single point in time. In a **longitudinal study,** the same people are studied over a long period of time. This involves collecting data periodically on the same people as they age. Longitudinal studies assess changes in people over time, whereas cross-sectional studies assess differences among age groups at a particular point in time. We will examine the use of both of these developmental research methods to answer the question about intelligence across the life span, learning the advantages and disadvantages of each.

cross-sectional study A study in which the performances of groups of participants of different ages are compared to one another.

longitudinal study A study in which performance of the same group of participants is examined at different ages.

The cross-sectional method. The early studies on this question about intelligence across the life span used the cross-sectional method. These studies used representative samples of people of various ages and consistently found that intelligence declined with age. Later studies, however, used the longitudinal method. When the same people were retested over a period of years, researchers found that intelligence did not decline with age, but remained rather stable and possibly increased until very late in life when it showed a decline. Now think about why there were two different answers to the intelligence question. First, consider the nature of a cross-sectional study and the possible problems with this method. A cross-sectional study compares people not only of different ages but also of different generations. This difference in generations can lead to what are called **cohort effects**—people of a given age (cohorts) are affected by factors unique to their generation, leading to differences in performance among generations. For example, there were significant differences in education and educational opportunities for the various generations across the twentieth century. Earlier generations generally received less education, which could certainly account for the intellectual decline observed in the cross-sectional studies. So, why would a researcher use the cross-sectional method, given such possible cohort effects? The cross-sectional method is far less time-consuming and less expensive than the longitudinal method. In addition, there is no need for continual retesting, as there is in longitudinal research.

> ▮ **cohort effects** People of a given age (cohorts) are affected by factors unique to their generation, leading to differences in performance between generations.

The longitudinal method. Now consider the longitudinal research method. Although there is no possibility of cohort effects when using the longitudinal method, it is time-consuming and expensive, and repeated testing has to be conducted. In addition, another problem arises. Participants may discontinue their participation, move far away, or die. This means that the sample changes across time, which could have an impact on the research findings if those who disappear from the sample are unlike those who stay in some relevant characteristic. How might a changing sample have led to the finding that intelligence remained fairly stable? Here's one explanation—those who survived to be tested at the older ages may have been the most intelligent and healthiest participants whose intelligence would be the most likely not to decline. This would also mean that the participants whose intelligence was likely to decline may have no longer been in the study. Given the shortcomings of both methods (see Table 7.3 on the following page), it has proven rather difficult to get a clear answer to this question of intelligence across the life span.

The type of intelligence that is being tested is also important and further complicates the search for an answer. Remember from the last chapter, in our discussion of types of intelligence, that we differentiated fluid intelligence and crystallized intelligence. Crystallized intelligence refers to accumulated knowledge, verbal skills, and numerical skills that increase with age; fluid intelligence involves abilities, such as abstract thinking and logical problem solving, that decrease with age (Horn, 1982). This difference may help to explain why scientists make their major contributions early, but historians and philosophers make theirs later in their careers.

The Seattle Longitudinal Study is a major attempt to answer the question of whether or not intelligence declines with age (Schaie, 1994, 1995). It is a large-scale longitudinal study of various intellectual abilities (such as inductive reasoning,

Table 7.3	Advantages and Disadvantages for Cross-sectional and Longitudinal Research Methods			
Research Method	**Description**	**Advantages**	**Disadvantages**	
Cross-sectional study	People of different ages are studied at a single time	Not very time-consuming or expensive	No need for continued retesting	
			Possible confounding due to cohort effects (differences in performance between age groups caused by generational differences)	
Longitudinal study	Same people are studied repeatedly over a long period of time	No possibility of cohort effects	Very time-consuming and expensive	
			Repeated testing has to be conducted	
			Possible confounding due to changes in sample over time	

word fluency, and perceptual speed) across the entire span of adulthood. It started in 1956 with more than 5,000 participants being tested every 7 years through 1998. The study is actually a combination of the longitudinal and cross-sectional methods, since groups of new participants were added periodically. This allowed the researchers to examine the possible shortcomings of both methods.

In general, the researchers found that most intellectual abilities decline somewhat by age 60, but the decline is not great until a person reaches age 80 or more (except for abilities largely dependent upon speed of processing, which clearly declines as we age). There are large individual differences, however. Those who suffer the least decline seem to be those who have stayed healthy, are in the higher socioeconomic categories, and are still involved in intellectually stimulating environments. In brief, it seems that if we work to stay healthy and cognitively stimulated, we won't suffer major deficits in our cognitive abilities until rather late in adulthood.

Section Summary

We are speechless at birth, but our capacity for language develops soon thereafter. Children of different cultures learn different languages, but they seem to go through the same sequence of stages for language acquisition. At about 12 months, infants begin to speak a few words, and then to use holophrases, words that express complete ideas. Their vocabulary grows slowly. Overextension and underextension of a word's meaning occur. A vocabulary spurt starts at about 18 months, and children engage in telegraphic speech, using two-word sentences of mainly nouns and verbs. These brief statements start to expand and between the ages of 2 to 5 years, children acquire the grammar of their native language. Children acquire language early and easily, without direct instruction, and this process seems universal. There is much support for the argument that language development is a genetically programmed ability. It is also clear that certain environmental experiences (exposure to human speech) are necessary, and that caregivers can facilitate and enhance language development.

It appears that children's thinking in general goes through a universal sequence of development. Jean Piaget's theory proposed distinct stages of cognitive development and emphasizes that the child is trying to adapt to his environment and is an active seeker of knowledge. This knowledge about the world is organized into schemas, and these schemas are developed through the processes of assimilation and accommodation.

During the sensorimotor stage (from birth to 2 years), infants learn and know about their world only through their sensory and motor interactions with it, but during this stage, object permanence develops along with language and the symbolic representation of objects and events. In the preoperational stage (from 2 to 6 years), the child's thought becomes more symbolic and language-based but remains egocentric and lacks the mental operations that allow logical thinking. For example, the child lacks the reversibility operation and so does not understand conservation. In the concrete operational stage (from about 6 to 12 years), the child gains a fuller understanding of conservation and other mental operations that allow logical thinking, but only about concrete events. In the last stage, the formal operational stage (from age 12 through adulthood), the individual gains the capacity for hypothetical and deductive thought.

Recent research indicates that many of Piaget's key concepts (such as object permanence) may begin to appear at earlier ages than Piaget proposed, but that cognitive development seems to proceed in the general sequence that he proposed. It is clear, however, that not everyone reaches formal operational thinking, especially in cultures that do not emphasize such thinking, and that those who do may not always use such thinking. In addition, the information-processing approach to cognitive development questions the existence of stages and argues that cognitive development is continuous and not comprised of stages. The information-processing approach argues that cognitive development stems from improvements in children's information-processing abilities—how they take in, store, and use information.

Piaget was not concerned with the sociocultural aspects of cognitive development, but Russian psychologist Lev Vygotsky was. Vygotsky proposed that cognitive abilities develop through interaction with others and represent shared knowledge of one's culture. According to Vygotsky, a child's zone of proximal development is the difference between what a child can actually do and what the child could do with the help of others. This is why Vygotsky recommended a style of teaching called scaffolding. The teacher structures the child's learning in steps so that the child learns each step independently, but is guided and supported by the teacher toward the upper level of the child's zone of proximal development.

Piaget and Vygotsky didn't really examine what happens to cognitive abilities across the life span, but other developmental researchers have. They have used the cross-sectional (studying people of different ages at a single time) and longitudinal (studying the same people repeatedly over a long period of time) methods, as well as the combination of the two, to do so. In general, developmental researchers have found that the ability to perform tasks that involve crystallized intelligence tends to increase with age, but that the ability to perform tasks that involve fluid intelligence shows a pattern of decline with age. Cognitive abilities that do not involve speed of processing, however, do not show dramatic decline until the age of 80 and beyond; but there are large individual differences. Those people who have stayed healthy, are in the higher socioeconomic levels, and are still involved in intellectually stimulating environments tend to see the smallest declines in intelligence as they age.

ConceptCheck | 2

▶ Explain how overextension and underextension in language development relate to Piaget's concepts of assimilation and accommodation in schema development.

▶ Explain why a child who thought that a pizza cut into eight slices was more than the same pizza cut into six slices would be in the preoperational stage of cognitive development.

▶ Explain how Vygotsky's zone of proximal development and scaffolding are related to learning and teaching.

▶ Explain the difference between the cross-sectional and longitudinal research methods.

Moral Development and Social Development

We develop cognitively and socially simultaneously, so these two types of development are difficult to separate. As Vygotsky stressed, cognitive development is best understood in its social context. In this section, we will discuss moral and social development, but we need to remember that it occurs simultaneously with cognitive development and is affected by it. Moral reasoning that involves both social and cognitive elements is a good illustration of this interactive development. For example, until a child moves away from egocentric thinking, it would be difficult for her to consider different perspectives when reasoning about the morality of a particular action. We begin our discussion of social development with a description of the major theory of moral development, Kohlberg's stage theory of moral reasoning. Then, we examine early social development with a discussion of attachment formation and parenting styles followed by a discussion of one of the most important social developments in early childhood, theory of mind. We conclude with a description of Erik Erikson's stage theory of social-personality development across the life span, from birth through late adulthood.

Kohlberg's Theory of Moral Reasoning

The most influential theory of moral reasoning is Lawrence Kohlberg's stage theory (Kohlberg, 1976, 1984). Building on an earlier theory of moral reasoning proposed by Piaget (1932), Kohlberg began the development of his theory by following in Piaget's footsteps, using stories that involved moral dilemmas to assess a child's or an adult's level of moral reasoning. To familiarize you with these moral dilemmas, consider Kohlberg's best-known story—a dilemma involving Heinz, whose wife was dying

Lawrence Kohlberg

of cancer. In brief, there was only one cure for this cancer. A local druggist had developed the cure, but he was selling it for much more than it cost to make and than Heinz could pay. Heinz tried to borrow the money to buy it, but could only get about half of what the drug cost. He asked the druggist to sell it to him cheaper or to let him pay the rest later, but the druggist refused. Out of desperation, Heinz broke into the druggist's store and stole the drug for his wife. Given this story, the person is asked if Heinz should have stolen the drug and why or why not.

Using the responses to and explanations of this and other moral dilemmas, Kohlberg found three levels of moral reasoning—preconventional, conventional, and postconventional. These levels are outlined in Table 7.4. Each level has two stages. At the **preconventional level of moral reasoning,** the emphasis is on avoiding punishment and looking out for your own welfare and needs. Moral reasoning is self-oriented. At the **conventional level,** moral reasoning is based on social rules and laws. Social approval and being a dutiful citizen are important. At the highest level, the **postconventional level,** moral reasoning is based on self-chosen universal ethical principles, with human rights taking precedence over laws, and on the avoidance of self-condemnation for violating such principles.

It is important to point out that in determining a person's level, it did not matter to Kohlberg whether the person answered yes or no to the dilemma. For

preconventional level of moral reasoning The first level of reasoning in Kohlberg's theory of moral development in which moral reasoning is based on avoiding punishment and looking out for your own welfare and needs.

conventional level of moral reasoning The second level of reasoning in Kohlberg's theory of moral development in which moral reasoning is based on social rules and laws.

postconventional level of moral reasoning The last level of reasoning in Kohlberg's theory of moral development in which moral reasoning is based on self-chosen universal ethical principles (with human rights taking precedence over laws) and the avoidance of self-condemnation for violating such principles.

Table 7.4	Kohlberg's Stage Theory of Moral Reasoning	
Level I Preconventional Morality		
Stage 1	Punishment orientation	Compliance with rules to avoid punishment
Stage 2	Reward orientation	Compliance with rules to obtain rewards and satisfy own needs
Level II Conventional Morality		
Stage 3	Good-girl/good-boy orientation	Engages in behavior to get approval of others
Stage 4	Law and order orientation	Behavior is guided by duty to uphold laws and rules for their own sake
Level III Postconventional Morality		
Stage 5	Social contract orientation	Obeys rules because they are necessary for social order but understands rules are relative
Stage 6	Universal ethical principles orientation	Concerned about self-condemnation for violating universal ethical principles based on human rights

example, in the Heinz dilemma, it did not matter whether the person said he should steal the drug or that he should not do so. The reasoning provided in the person's explanation is what mattered. Kohlberg provided examples of such explanations for each level of reasoning. To understand how Kohlberg used these responses to the moral dilemmas, let's consider sample Stage 4 rationales for stealing the drug and for not stealing the drug. The pro-stealing explanation would emphasize that it is Heinz's duty to protect his wife's life, given the vow he took in marriage. But it's wrong to steal, so Heinz would have to take the drug with the idea of paying the druggist for it and accepting the penalty for breaking the law. The anti-stealing rationale would emphasize that you have to follow the rules regardless of how you feel and regardless of the special circumstances. Even if his wife is dying, it is still Heinz's duty as a citizen to follow the law. If everyone started breaking laws, there would be no civilization. As you can see, both explanations emphasize the law-and-order orientation of this stage—if you break the law, you must pay the penalty.

Kohlberg proposed that we all start at the preconventional level as children and as we develop, especially cognitively, we move up the ladder of moral reasoning. The sequence is unvarying, but, as with Piaget's formal operational stage, we all may not make it up to the last stage. That the sequence does not vary and that a person's level of moral reasoning is age-related (and so related to cognitive development) has been supported by research.

Research also indicates that most people in many different cultures reach the conventional level by adulthood, but attainment of the postconventional level is not so clear (Snarey, 1985). There are other problems. First, it is important to realize that Kohlberg was studying moral reasoning and not moral behavior. As we will see in Chapter 9, on social psychology, thought and action are not always consistent. Ethical talk may not equate to ethical behavior. Second, some researchers have criticized Kohlberg's theory for not adequately representing the morality of women. They argue that feminine moral reasoning is more concerned with a morality of care that focuses on interpersonal relationships and the needs of others than a morality of justice, as in Kohlberg's theory. Similarly, critics have questioned the theory's universality by arguing that the higher stages are biased toward Western values. In summary, Kohlberg's theory has both support and criticism, but more importantly, it has stimulated research that continues to develop our understanding of moral development.

Attachment and Parenting Styles

As we have said before, humans are social creatures. Infants' first social relationship—between them and their primary caregivers—is important and has been carefully studied by developmental psychologists (Bowlby, 1969). This lifelong emotional bond that exists between the infants and their mothers or other caregivers is formed during the first 6 months of life and is called **attachment.** Traditionally, the primary caregiver has been the infant's

attachment The lifelong emotional bond between infants and their mothers or other caregivers, formed during the first 6 months of life.

mother, but times have changed and today the primary caregiver could be the mother, father, grandparent, nanny, or day care provider. Because attachment is related to children's later development, it is also important to examine whether children who are put in day care at a young age are at a disadvantage in comparison to those who remain at home. Following a discussion of some of the early research on attachment, we will address this question. First, we consider the question of why the attachment forms. Is it because the caregiver provides food and the attachment forms as a consequence of reinforcement?

Harry Harlow

Attachment and Harlow's monkeys. Harry Harlow used newborn monkeys in his attachment research to address this question (Harlow, 1959; Harlow & Harlow, 1962; Harlow & Zimmerman, 1959). These attachment studies were a consequence of an accidental discovery during his learning research using the infant monkeys. The infant monkeys often caught diseases from their mothers, so Harlow had separated the infant monkeys from their mothers. He gave cheesecloth blankets to the isolated infant monkeys. The infant monkeys became strongly attached to these blankets and were greatly disturbed if their "security" blankets were taken away.

After this observation, Harlow began to separate the infant monkeys from their mothers at birth and put them in cages containing two inanimate surrogate (substitute) mothers—one made of wire and one made of terry cloth. Figure 7.2 shows examples of these surrogate mothers and the motherless monkeys. Half of the monkeys received their nourishment from a milk dispenser in the wire mother and half from a dispenser in the terry cloth mother. However, all of the monkeys preferred the cloth monkey regardless of which monkey provided their nourishment. The monkeys being fed by the wire mother would only go to the wire mother to eat and then return to the cloth mother. As shown in Figure 7.2, if possible the infant monkeys would often cling to the cloth monkey while feeding from the wire

▲ **Figure 7.2** | **Harlow's Motherless Monkeys and Surrogate Mothers** | In Harry Harlow's research on the role of feeding in the attachment process, he found that contact comfort, rather than feeding, was the most important factor in the infant monkey's attachment. The infant monkeys spent most of their time on the terry cloth surrogate mother regardless of whether she provided their nourishment or not. The infant monkey would often even cling to the cloth monkey while feeding from the wire mother.

Mary Ainsworth

mother. In brief, the infant monkeys would spend most of each day on the cloth mother. The monkeys clearly had become attached to the cloth mother. Harlow concluded that "contact comfort" (bodily contact and comfort), not reinforcement from nourishment, was the crucial element for attachment formation.

In addition, the infant monkeys would cower in fear when confronted with a strange situation (an unfamiliar room with various toys) without the surrogate mother. When the surrogate mother was brought into the strange situation, the infant monkeys would initially cling to the terry cloth mother to reduce their fear, but then begin to explore the new environment and eventually play with the toys. Harlow concluded that the presence of the surrogate mother made the monkeys feel secure and therefore sufficiently confident to explore the strange situation. This situation is very similar to the strange situation procedure developed by Mary Ainsworth to study the attachment relationship in human infants (Ainsworth, 1979; Ainsworth, Blehar, Waters, & Wall, 1978). In this procedure, an infant's behavior is observed in an unfamiliar room with toys, while the infant's mother and a stranger (an unfamiliar woman) move in and out of the room in a structured series of situations. The key observations focus on the infant's reaction to the mother's leaving and returning, both when the stranger is present and absent, and on the child exploring the situation (the room and the toys in it).

secure attachment The type of attachment indicated by the infant exploring freely in the presence of the mother in the Ainsworth strange situation procedure, displaying distress when the mother leaves, and responding enthusiastically when she returns.

insecure-avoidant attachment The type of attachment indicated by the infant exploring with little interest in the mother in the Ainsworth strange situation procedure, showing only minimal distress when the mother leaves, and avoiding her when she returns.

insecure-ambivalent attachment The type of attachment indicated by the infant not exploring but seeking closeness to the mother in the Ainsworth strange situation procedure and showing high levels of distress when the mother leaves and ambivalent behavior when she returns by alternately clinging to and pushing away from her.

insecure-disorganized (disoriented) attachment The type of attachment indicated by the infant's confusion when the mother leaves and returns in the Ainsworth strange situation procedure. The infant acts disoriented, seems overwhelmed by the situation, and does not demonstrate a consistent way of coping with it.

Types of attachment. Ainsworth and her colleagues found three types of attachment relationships—secure, insecure-avoidant, and insecure-ambivalent. **Secure attachment** is indicated by the infant exploring the situation freely in the presence of the mother, but displaying distress when the mother leaves, and responding enthusiastically when the mother returns. **Insecure-avoidant attachment** is indicated by exploration but minimal interest in the mother, the infant showing little distress when the mother leaves, and avoiding her when she returns. **Insecure-ambivalent attachment** is indicated by the infant seeking closeness to the mother and not exploring the situation, high levels of distress when the mother leaves, and ambivalent behavior when she returns by alternately clinging to and pushing away from her. About two-thirds of the infants studied are found to have a secure attachment, and the other third insecure attachments. Cross-cultural research indicates that these proportions may vary across different cultures, but the majority of infants worldwide seem to form secure attachments. Later researchers have added a fourth type of insecure attachment, **insecure-disorganized (disoriented) attachment,** which is indicated

(a)

(b)

Ainsworth's Strange Situation Procedure. In part (a) of this example of the strange situation procedure, the child, Brian, explores and plays in the unfamiliar room when his mother is present. In (b), he cries and is distressed when his mother leaves the room. In (c), he is easily comforted in his mother's arms when she returns. Brian's behavior demonstrates a secure attachment with his mother.

(c)

by the infant's confusion when the mother leaves and when she returns. The infant acts disoriented, seems overwhelmed by the situation, and does not demonstrate a consistent way of coping with it (Main & Solomon, 1990).

Before putting the infants in the strange situation series, researchers observed the infant-mother relationship at home during the first 6 months of an infant's life. From such observations, they found that the sensitivity of the mother is the major determinant of the quality of the attachment relationship. A mother who is sensitive and responsive to an infant's needs is more likely to develop a secure attachment with the infant. Although the mother's caregiver style is primary, does the infant also contribute to the attachment formation? The answer is yes. Each of us is born with a **temperament,** a set of innate tendencies or dispositions that leads us to behave in certain ways. Our temperament is fundamental to our personality development and also how we interact with others (our social development). The temperaments of infants vary greatly. Some infants are more responsive, more active, and happier than others. How an infant's temperament matches the child-rearing expectations and personality of his caregiver is important in forming the attachment relationship. A good match or fit between the two enhances the probability of a secure attachment.

The type of attachment that is formed is important to later development. Secure attachments in infancy have been

temperament The set of innate tendencies or dispositions that lead a person to behave in certain ways.

▦ **authoritarian parenting** A style of parenting in which the parents are demanding, expect unquestioned obedience, are not responsive to their children's desires, and communicate poorly with their children.

▦ **authoritative parenting** A style of parenting in which the parents are demanding, but set rational limits for their children and communicate well with their children.

▦ **permissive parenting** A style of parenting in which the parents make few demands and are overly responsive to their children's desires, letting their children do pretty much as they please.

▦ **uninvolved parenting** A style of parenting in which the parents minimize both the time they spend with their children and their emotional involvement with them and provide for their children's basic needs, but little else.

linked to higher levels of cognitive functioning and social competence in childhood (Jacobsen & Hoffman, 1997; Schneider, Atkinson, & Tardif, 2001). This doesn't mean, however, that the type of attachment cannot change or that an insecure attachment cannot be overcome by later experiences. As family circumstances change, interactions change and so may the type of attachment. For example, divorce might put a child into day care, or remarriage might bring another caring adult into the family. This brings us to a very important question in our present-day society of working mothers and single parents: Is day care detrimental to the formation of secure attachments, and therefore to cognitive and social development? The general answer is no. Children in day care seem to be generally as well off as those who are raised at home (Erel, Oberman, & Yirmiya, 2000; NICHD Early Child Care Research Network, 1997, 2001). However, the effects of day care for a particular child are moderated by many variables, such as the age of the child when starting day care, the number of hours of day care per week, and the quality of the day care.

Courtesy of Diana Baumrind

Diana Baumrind

Parenting styles. Attachment formation in infants is important in shaping later development. But how do parenting styles impact development in children and adolescents? Diana Baumrind (1971, 1991) has identified four styles of parenting—authoritarian, authoritative, permissive, and uninvolved (Baumrind, 1971, 1991). **Authoritarian parents** are demanding, expect unquestioned obedience, are not responsive to their children's desires, and communicate poorly with their children. **Authoritative parents** are demanding but set rational limits for their children and communicate well with their children. **Permissive parents** make few demands and are overly responsive to their children's desires, letting their children do pretty much as they please. **Uninvolved parents** minimize both the time they spend with the children and their emotional involvement with them. They provide for their children's basic needs but little else. These parenting styles have been related to differences in cognitive and social development. Authoritative parenting seems to have the most positive effect on a child's development (Baumrind, 1996). The children of authoritative parents are not only the most independent, happy, and self-reliant, but also the most academically successful. These relationships between parenting style and child development were primarily established on white, middle-class families. Recent studies of more diverse populations and cultures suggest that these effects may vary across different ethnic and cultural groups. For instance, an authoritarian parenting style is associated with more positive outcomes for African-American girls and children of Chinese parents. The existence of these cultural differences illustrates that development is not only impacted by the immediate family but the broader cultural context in which the child lives (Bronfenbrenner, 1993).

So far we have discussed social development for the infant and child in terms of attachment and parenting styles, but such development involves others, such as friends and teachers. Friends become increasingly important and assume different functions as children age (Furman & Bierman, 1984; Simpkins, Parke, Flyr, & Wild, 2006). Early friendships are primarily due to children having similar play interests or living close together. As adolescence approaches, however, friendships begin to serve more important emotional needs, and friends provide emotional support for one another. Despite the increasing importance of friends, adolescents still value their relationships with their parents and try to uphold parental standards on major issues such as careers and education. In addition to friends, children are also part of a larger social peer network in which the social status of members varies (Asher, 1983; Jiang & Cillessen, 2005). Popular children tend to be liked by most other children and have good social skills. Children who are rejected by their peers, however, lack these social skills and often tend to be either aggressive or withdrawn. Rejected children are at increased risk for both emotional and social difficulties (Buhs & Ladd, 2001).

Theory of Mind

One of the most important social developments that occurs in early childhood is in the area of social cognition—the development of a **theory of mind.** Theory of mind refers to the understanding of the mental and emotional states of both ourselves and others. In order to have a theory of mind, children must realize that other people do not necessarily think the same thoughts, have the same beliefs, or feel the same emotions that they themselves do. Whenever we interact with others, we interpret and explain their behavior in terms of their beliefs, desires, and emotions. If a friend is angry, we might explain it by attributing it to his or her belief that we did something to upset them. It is difficult to imagine what social relationships would be like if we were unable to infer the mental and emotional states of others.

While there are many aspects of theory of mind development that begin in infancy and early childhood, one critical theory of mind accomplishment is the understanding of false beliefs (recognizing that others can have beliefs about the world that are wrong) that typically develops between 4 and 5 years of age. To test for this understanding, researchers use false-belief problems in which another person believes something to be true that the child knows is false. The question is whether the child thinks that the other person will act in accord with his false belief or with the child's correct understanding of the situation. These problems thus reveal whether the child has the understanding that different people can have different beliefs about the same situation. For example, in an unexpected location task designed to assess false belief understanding, a child sees a ball being hidden in a box by Big Bird and then Big Bird leaves the room to play outside. Next, the child observes

theory of mind The understanding of the mental and emotional states of both ourselves and others.

DENNIS THE MENACE

Dennis The Menace © 1990 Hank Ketcham Enterprises. King Features Syndicate

" I KNOW WHAT I THINK , BUT WHAT'S IMPORTANT
IS WHAT MY MOM THINKS I THINK ! "

Cookie Monster move the ball to a toy chest. The child is then asked where Big Bird will think the ball is when he comes back in from playing. A 5–year-old can accurately predict that Big Bird will think it is in the original box even though the child knows it is in the toy chest. That is, the child understands that different people can have different beliefs about the same situation. A 3-year old child typically does not understand this and would incorrectly predict Big Bird would think it is in the toy chest because younger children believe that everyone thinks like they do. Such findings are extremely robust and have been observed with different problems and in different cultures (Wellman, Cross, & Watson, 2001).

The early emergence of theory of mind understanding has led some researchers to suggest that there is a biological basis for this knowledge (Baron-Cohen, 2000). The developmental disorder of autism, in which children are primarily characterized by difficulty in social interactions, supports this biological view of theory of mind (Frith, 2003). What might be the biological basis for theory of mind development? We have already learned about one possibility. Remember, in Chapter 4 we learned that mirror neuron systems may provide the neural basis for imitation learning and play a role in empathy and the understanding of the intentions and emotions of others. Thus, early mirror neuron system deficits might cascade into developmental impairments in imitation learning and subsequently in theory of mind development, leading to autism (Iacoboni & Dapretto, 2006; Williams, Whiten, Suddendorf, & Perrett, 2001). For example, Dapretto et al. (2006) had high-functioning children with autism and normal control children undergo fMRI while imitating emotional expressions. For the autistic children, they found little activity in brain regions associated with mirror neurons. For the normal children, however, these regions were active, suggesting that a dysfunctional mirror-neuron system may underlie the social deficits observed in autism. We must remember, however, that this is presently just a hypothesis and that much more extensive research must be conducted before any firm conclusions can be made. We have primarily focused on social development during childhood and adolescence but social development continues throughout our lives. This is why we now turn to Erik Erikson's stage theory of how we develop throughout our life, from birth to old age.

Erikson's Psychosocial Stage Theory of Development

Erik Erikson's psychosocial stage theory covers the whole life span. Like Vygotsky, Erikson emphasized the impact of society and culture upon development, but Erikson's theory is different because it considered both personality development and social development. We discuss it here rather than in the next chapter, with the other personality theories, because it is a developmental theory. In fact, Erikson's inclusion of the three stages of adulthood in his theory has played a major role in the increased amount of research on all parts of the life span—not just on childhood and adolescence. However, Erikson's theory has been criticized because of the lack of solid experimental data to support it. Erikson used only observational data, which is a criticism that can be leveled against most personality theories.

Erik Erikson

Erikson divided the life span into eight stages of development, summarized in Table 7.5 on the following page (Erikson, 1950, 1963, 1968, 1980). The first five stages cover infancy, childhood, and adolescence, where Freud's theory of personality development (discussed in the next chapter) and Piaget's theory of cognitive development end. Erikson's last three stages go beyond Freud and Piaget and deal with the three stages of adulthood (young, middle, and late).

Erikson viewed our social-personality development as the product of our social interactions and the choices we make in life. At each stage, there is a major psychosocial issue or crisis that has to be resolved. Think of each stage as a "fork in the road" choice whose resolution greatly impacts our development. Each stage is named after the two sides of the issue relevant in that stage. For example, the first stage is trust versus mistrust. In this stage, infants in the first year of life are wrestling with the issue of whether they can trust or not trust others to take care of them. The resolution of each stage can end up on either side of the issue. The infant can leave the first stage either generally trusting or generally mistrusting the world. When an issue is successfully resolved, the person increases in social competence. Erikson felt that the resolution of each stage greatly impacted our personal development. Table 7.5 includes the possible resolutions for each stage.

Erikson's best-known concept, identity crisis, is part of his fifth stage. The main task of this stage is the development of a sense of identity—to figure out who we are, what we value, and where we are headed in life. As adolescents, we are confused about our identity. The distress created by the confusion is what Erikson meant by identity crisis. For most adolescents, however, it's more of a search or exploration than a crisis. Teenagers experiment with different identities in the search to find their own. If you are a traditional-age college student, you may have

Table 7.5 Erikson's Psychosocial Stages	
Stage (age range)	**Stage Description**
Trust vs. mistrust (birth to 1 year)	Infants learn that they can or cannot trust others to take care of their basic needs.
Autonomy vs. shame and doubt (1 to 2 years)	Children learn to be self-sufficient in many activities such as toilet training, walking, and exploring. If restrained too much they learn to doubt their abilities and feel shame.
Initiative vs. guilt (3 to 5 years)	Children learn to assume more responsibility by taking initiative but will feel guilty if they overstep limits set by parents.
Industry vs. inferiority (5 years to puberty)	Children learn to be competent by mastering new intellectual, social, and physical skills or feel inferior if they fail to develop these skills.
Identity vs. role confusion (adolescence)	Adolescents develop a sense of identity by experimenting with different roles. No role experimentation may result in role confusion.
Intimacy vs. isolation (young adulthood)	Young adults form intimate relationships with others or become isolated because of a failure to do so.
Generativity vs. stagnation (middle adulthood)	Middle-aged adults feel they are helping the next generation through their work and child rearing, or they stagnate because they feel that they are not helping.
Integrity vs. despair (late adulthood)	Older adults assess their lives and develop a sense of integrity if they find their lives have been meaningful, and a sense of despair if their lives do not seem meaningful.

just experienced or are still experiencing this search. Attending college and searching for a major and a career path may delay the resolution of this stage. Finding our true selves is clearly not easy. We usually explore many alternative identities before finding one that is satisfactory.

This identity stage is critical to becoming a productive adult, but development doesn't end with its resolution. Probably the greatest impact of Erikson's theory is that it expanded the study of developmental psychology past adolescence into the stages of adulthood (young, middle, and late). In young adulthood (from the end of adolescence to the beginning of middle age), a person establishes independence from her parents and begins to function as a mature, productive adult. Having established her own identity, a person is ready to establish a shared identity with another person, leading to an intimate relationship. This sequence in Erikson's theory (intimacy issues following identity issues) turns out to be most applicable to men and career-oriented women (Dyk & Adams, 1990). Many women may solve these issues in reverse order or simultaneously. For example, a woman may marry and have children and then confront the identity issues when the children become adults.

The crisis in middle adulthood (from about age 40 to 60 years) is concerned with generativity versus stagnation. "Generativity" is being concerned with the next generation and producing something of lasting value to society. Generative activity comes in many forms. In addition to making lasting contributions to society, which most of us will not do, generative activity includes rearing children, engaging in meaningful work, mentoring younger workers, and contributing to civic organizations. In Erikson's final stage in late adulthood, we conduct reviews of our lives, looking back at our lives to assess how well we have lived them. If we are satisfied with our life, we gain a sense of integrity and the ability to face death. If not, we despair and look back at our life with a sense of sadness and regret and we fear death.

Section Summary

The most influential theory of moral development is Kohlberg's stage theory of moral reasoning. Using moral dilemmas, Kohlberg proposed three levels of reasoning—preconventional, conventional, and postconventional. The first level is self-oriented, and the emphasis is on avoiding punishment and looking out for one's own needs. At the conventional level, reasoning is guided by social approval and being a dutiful citizen. At the highest postconventional level, morality is based on universal ethical principles and the realization that society's laws are only a social contract, which can be broken if they violate these more global principles. Research indicates that proceeding through the stages is related to age and cognitive development, but that most people do not reach the postconventional stage of reasoning. The theory is criticized for being based on moral reasoning and not moral behavior (since these may be very different); for being biased against women, who may focus more on a morality of care than a morality of justice; and for being biased toward Western moral values.

Social development begins with attachment, the strong emotional bond formed between an infant and his mother or primary caregiver. Harry Harlow's studies with infant monkeys and surrogate mothers found that contact comfort, and not reinforcement from nourishment, is the crucial element in attachment formation. Using the Ainsworth strange situation procedure, researchers have identified four types of attachment—secure, insecure-avoidant, insecure-ambivalent, and insecure-disorganized. The sensitivity of the caregiver to the infant and how well an infant's temperament matches the child-rearing expectations and personality of the caregiver are important to attachment formation. The majority of infants worldwide form secure attachments, and this type of attachment has been linked to higher levels of social competence and cognitive functioning in childhood. With respect to parenting styles, authoritative parenting—in which the parents are demanding but rational in setting limits for their children and communicate well with their children—seems to have the most positive effect on social and cognitive development. Recent research, however, indicates that parenting style effects may vary across ethnic and cultural groups. Friends are also important to social development, especially during adolescence when friendships serve important emotional needs.

One of the most important social developments that occurs in early childhood is the development of a theory of mind, the understanding of the mental and emotional states of both ourselves and others. One critical accomplishment in theory of mind development is the understanding of false beliefs around 4 to 5 years of age. To test for this understanding, researchers use false-belief problems in which another person believes something to be true that the child knows is false. If the child has the understanding of false beliefs, he will predict that the other person will act in accord with his false belief and not the child's correct understanding of the situation. Children without an understanding of false beliefs would make just the opposite prediction. The early emergence of theory of mind development has led some researchers to suggest that there is a biological basis for it. Mirror neuron systems are a possibility for this basis because they seem to provide the neural basis for imitation learning and play a role in empathy and the understanding of the intentions and emotions of others. Thus, early mirror neuron system deficits might lead to developmental impairments in imitation learning and subsequently theory of mind development, leading to social disorders such as autism.

With respect to social development across the life span, Erik Erikson developed an eight-stage theory of social and personality development. In each stage, there is a major psychosocial issue with two sides that has to be resolved. If the stage is resolved successfully, the person leaves the stage on the positive side of the stage issue. For example, the infant in the first year of life is dealing with the issue of trust versus mistrust. If resolved successfully, the infant will leave this stage trusting the world. Erikson stressed the fifth stage, in which a sense of identity must be developed during adolescence. This is the stage during which the identity crisis occurs. Erikson's theory is unusual in that it includes the three stages of adulthood. This inclusion played a major role in leading developmental psychologists to expand their focus to development across the entire life span.

ConceptCheck | 3

> Explain how Kohlberg would classify the following response explaining why Heinz should not steal the drug. "You shouldn't steal the drug because you'll be caught and sent to jail if you do. If you do get away with it, your conscience would bother you thinking how the police would catch up with you any minute."

> Explain why an infant's temperament is important to the process of attachment formation.

> Explain the differences between authoritarian and authoritative parenting styles.

> In the false belief problem described in the text involving Big Bird and Cookie Monster, how will a child who does not have an understanding of false beliefs answer and why will he answer in this way? How will he answer if he has an understanding of false beliefs and why will he answer in this way?

> Explain what Erikson meant by psychosocial issue or crisis.

Study Guide

Chapter Key Terms

You should know the definitions of the following key terms from the chapter. They are listed in the order in which they appear in the chapter. For those you do not know, return to the relevant section of the chapter to learn them. When you think that you know all of the terms, complete the matching exercise based on these key terms.

developmental psychology

zygote

gene

chromosomes

identical (monozygotic) twins

fraternal (dizygotic) twins

teratogens

fetal alcohol syndrome (FAS)

sucking reflex

rooting reflex

habituation

phonemes

baby talk (motherese)

babbling

holophrase

overextension

underextension

telegraphic speech

schemes

assimilation

accommodation

sensorimotor stage

object permanence

preoperational stage

egocentrism

conservation

reversibility

centration

concrete operational stage

formal operational stage

information-processing approach to cognitive development

zone of proximal development

scaffolding

cross-sectional study

longitudinal study

cohort effects

preconventional level of moral reasoning

conventional level of moral reasoning

postconventional level of moral reasoning

attachment

secure attachment

insecure-avoidant attachment

insecure-ambivalent attachment

insecure-disorganized (disoriented) attachment

temperament

authoritarian parenting

authoritative parenting

permissive parenting

uninvolved parenting

theory of mind

Key Terms Exercise

Identify the correct term for each of the following definitions. The answers to this exercise follow the answers to the Concept Checks at the end of the chapter.

1. The knowledge that an object exists independent of perceptual contact with it.

   _____

2. An innate human reflex that leads infants to turn their mouth toward anything that touches their cheeks and search for something to suck on.

   _____

3. The fertilized egg that is formed from the union of the sperm and egg cells in human reproduction.

   _____

4. Piaget's term for the modification of present schemas to fit with new experiences.

   _____

5. A style of parenting in which the parents are demanding, but set rational limits for their children and communicate well with their children.

_____

6. The type of attachment indicated by the infant exploring freely in the presence of the mother in the Ainsworth strange situation procedure, but displaying distress when the mother leaves, and responding enthusiastically when she returns.

_____

7. The different format of speech that adults use when talking with babies that involves the use of shorter sentences with a higher, more melodious pitch.

_____

8. Agents such as drugs, viruses, diseases, and physical conditions that impair prenatal development and lead to birth defects and sometimes death.

_____

9. A study in which the performance of the same group of participants is examined at different ages.

_____

10. According to Vygotsky, the difference between what a child can actually do and what the child could do with the help of others.

_____

11. The smallest distinctive speech sounds in a language.

_____

12. Using two-word sentences with mainly nouns and verbs.

_____

13. The knowledge that the quantitative properties of objects (such as mass

and number) remain the same despite changes in appearance.

_____

14. A style of teaching in which the teacher adjusts the level of help in relation to the child's level of performance while orienting the child toward the upper level of his or her zone of proximal development.

_____

15. The set of innate tendencies or dispositions that lead a person to behave in certain ways.

_____

Practice Test Questions

The following are practice multiple-choice test questions on some of the chapter content. The answers are given after the Key Terms Exercise answers at the end of the chapter. If you guessed or incorrectly answered a question, restudy the relevant section of the chapter.

1. In human conception, another name for the fertilized egg is _____.
   a. gene
   b. zygote
   c. chromosome
   d. teratogen

2. At about 6 or 7 months of age, an infant starts rhythmically repeating various syllables. This is called_____.
   a. baby talk
   b. holophrase
   c. telegraphic speech
   d. babbling

3. According to Piaget's theory of cognitive development, children are in the _____ stage if they have symbolic ability but lack conservation.
   a. sensorimotor
   b. preoperational
   c. concrete operational
   d. formal operational

4. According to Piaget, _____ is the interpretation of new experiences in terms of present schemas, and _____ is the modification of present schemas to fit with new experiences.
   a. assimilation; accommodation
   b. accommodation; assimilation
   c. reversibility; centration
   d. centration; reversibility

5. Vygotsky's term for the difference between what a child can actually do and what the child can do with the help of others is _____.
   a. zone of proximal development
   b. erogeneous zone
   c. scaffolding
   d. cohort effect

6. In a _____ study, people of different ages are studied at one point in time and compared to one another.
   a. cross-sectional
   b. longitudinal
   c. habituation
   d. scaffolding

7. According to Kohlberg, a person who complies with rules and laws to avoid punishment is in the _____ level of moral development.
   a. preconventional
   b. conventional
   c. postconventional
   d. authoritarian

8. According to Ainsworth, a child who shows little distress when the mother leaves in the strange situation procedure and neglects her when she returns has developed a(n) attachment.
   a. secure
   b. insecure-disorganized
   c. insecure-ambivalent
   d. insecure-avoidant

9. Which of the following parenting styles is most positively related to academic success, happiness, independence, and self-confidence?
   a. authoritative
   b. authoritarian
   c. permissive
   d. indifferent

10. According to Erikson's psychosocial theory, _____ is the issue that a person faces during adolescence.
    a. initiative versus guilt
    b. industry versus inferiority
    c. identity versus role confusion
    d. intimacy versus isolation

11. During the _____ stage of prenatal development (the final stage starting about 2 months after conception), the body structures and organs complete their growth.
    a. embryonic
    b. fetal
    c. germinal
    d. zygote

12. A decrease in the physiological responding to a stimulus once it becomes familiar is called _____.
    a. assimilation
    b. centration
    c. habituation
    d. conservation

13. Johnny, who is only 4 years of age, stands in front of you blocking your view of the television screen, and he does not realize that he is doing so. He thinks that his view is the same as yours. Johnny is displaying _____ and is in Piaget's _____ stage of cognitive development.
    a. egocentrism; concrete
    b. egocentrism; preoperational
    c. centration; concrete
    d. centration; preoperational

14. Michelle, who is 18 months old, has a pet dog named Sam. After she learns the name of her dog, she calls all of the dogs

she sees Sam. Michelle is demonstrating _____.

a. babbling

b. holophrase

c. underextension

d. overextension

15. Studies of intelligence in adulthood reveal that fluid intelligence abilities _____ with age, and crystallized intelligence abilities _____ with age.

a. increase; increase

b. increase; decrease

c. decrease; increase

d. decrease; decrease

Chapter Concept Check Answers

Concept Check | 1

- Teratogens are agents such as drugs, viruses, and diseases and conditions such as malnutrition that impair prenatal development and lead to birth defects or even death. Thus, they are not due to heredity (nature). They are prenatal environmental factors and therefore their effects are due to nurture.

- Habituation, a decrease in physiological responding to a stimulus once it becomes familiar, is used to determine what stimuli an infant can perceptually discriminate. The inference is that if an infant looks longer at a new stimulus than an old one, then the infant must be able to perceive the difference. In addition to looking, researchers use other measures such as changes in the rates of sucking on a pacifier and the infant's heart rate.

Concept Check | 2

- Overextension and underextension in language development involve using a word too broadly or too narrowly, respectively. Through experience we learn to extend a word's meaning correctly. Overextension can be viewed as overassimilation—incorrectly attempting to assimilate the new object into the existing schema for the word when accommodation is necessary. Underextension can be viewed as under-assimilation—failing to assimilate the new object into the existing schema for the word. In overextension, the child assimilates when he needs to accommodate, and in underextension, the child does not assimilate when he needs to assimilate.

- A child who thought that a pizza cut into eight slices was more than the same pizza cut into six slices would be in the preoperational stage because she is not demonstrating knowledge of conservation. She is centering her attention on the number of slices and not the size of the slices.

- Together these two concepts, zone of proximal development and scaffolding, comprise a teaching method. First, the zone of proximal development (the difference between what a child can actually do and what the child could do with help) is determined. Then scaffolding (adjusting the level of help in relation to the child's level of performance) is used to structure and guide the learning to the upper level of the child's zone of proximal development.

- In a cross-sectional study, groups of participants of different ages are studied at one point in time. In a longitudinal study, one group of participants is studied at many different points in time as the group ages. The cross-sectional method is less time-consuming and expensive but subject to cohort effects created by factors unique to each generation in the study. Because the same participants are tested at different ages, the longitudinal method is not subject to such effects; but due to participant attrition, sample-group changes over time may impact the results.

Concept Check | 3

- The response indicates that Heinz should not steal the drug because he would be caught and sent to jail—punished. Even if he weren't caught, his conscience would punish him. Thus, Kohlberg would classify this explanation for not stealing the drug as reflective of Stage 1 (punishment orientation) in which people comply with rules in order to avoid punishment.

- An infant's temperament is the set of innate dispositions that lead him to behave in a certain way. It determines the infant's responsiveness in interactions with care-givers, how happy he is, how much he cries, and so on. The temperaments of infants vary greatly. Those that fit the child-rearing expectations and personality of the caregivers likely facilitate attach-ment formation. Difficult infants probably do not.

- Authoritarian parents are demanding and expect unquestioned obedience, are not responsive to their children's desires, and do not communicate well with their children. Authoritative parents, however, are demanding but reasonably so. Rather than demanding blind obedience, they explain the reasoning behind rules. Unlike authoritarian parents, they are both responsive to and communicate well with their children.

- A child without understanding of false beliefs would predict that Big Bird will look for the ball in the toy chest where Cookie Monster has rehidden it because the child does not understand that others can have beliefs that disagree with his. If the child has an understanding of false beliefs, he would predict that Big Bird will look in the box where he had earlier put the ball because he realizes that others can have beliefs that disagree with his.

- Erikson thought that at each stage there is a major psychosocial issue or crisis (e.g., identity versus role confusion) that has to be resolved and whose resolution greatly impacts one's development. For each crisis, there is a positive adaptive resolution and a negative maladaptive resolution. When an issue is positively resolved, social compe-tence increases and one is more adequately prepared for the next issue.

Answers to Key Terms Exercise

1. object permanence
2. rooting reflex
3. zygote
4. accommodation
5. authoritative parenting
6. secure attachment
7. baby talk (motherese)
8. teratogens
9. longitudinal study
10. zone of proximal development
11. phonemes
12. telegraphic speech
13. conservation
14. scaffolding
15. temperament

Answers to Practice Test Questions

1. b; zygote
2. d; babbling
3. b; preoperational
4. a; assimilation; accommodation
5. a; zone of proximal development
6. a; cross-sectional
7. a; preconventional
8. d; insecure-avoidant
9. a; authoritative
10. c; identity versus role confusion
11. b; fetal
12. c; habituation
13. b; egocentrism; preoperational
14. d; overextension
15. c; decrease; increase

8

Personality Theories and Assessment

As with intelligence, psychologists cannot agree upon a definition of personality, a word that we all use and whose meaning we think we know. In its everyday usage, personality is an individual's characteristic ways of acting and thinking. If I asked you to describe the personality of your best friend or your mother, you probably would respond with a set of adjectives that capture the defining characteristics (prominent qualities) of that person's behavior, such as caring, independent, and honest. You would also probably assume that these behavioral characteristics originate from within the person, that they are internally based. For our purposes, this is a satisfactory definition of **personality**—a person's internally based characteristic ways of acting and thinking.

▌ **personality** A person's internally based characteristic ways of acting and thinking.

Psychologists call such internally based characteristics "personality traits." Each trait corresponds to a continuum on which one end is the behavioral extreme for that characteristic and the other end is its opposite. For example, the extremes for caring would be "very caring" and "very uncaring." These trait dimensions are the building blocks of personality. Individuals' personalities correspond to their patterns of traits, leading to personality differences between people. But what causes these differences? What makes us the way that we are?

Throughout history, all sorts of theories of personality differences have been proposed. For example, the ancient Greeks thought that one's mental health (personality) was a function of the balance of four humors, or bodily fluids—black bile, yellow bile, blood, and phlegm. According to Franz Gall's phrenology theory in the early nineteenth century, personality was determined by the contours and bumps of a person's head. In the twentieth century, William Sheldon's theory proposed that personality is tied to one's body type. None of these theories, however, proved very satisfactory.

Today, there are many theoretical approaches to the study of personality, but we will limit our discussion to the four major types of theories—psychoanalytic, humanistic, social-cognitive, and trait. These theories vary greatly in how they explain personality differences and in what aspects of personality they emphasize and study. Psychoanalytic theories emphasize the interaction of unconscious forces and childhood experiences in determining personality development. Humanistic theories emphasize the personal growth motive. Social-cognitive theories emphasize the importance of thought processes and interactions with others. Trait theories emphasize the role of basic personality dimensions. Because our descriptions of these theories will focus on

Bettman/Corbis

In the early nineteenth century, Franz Gall developed the phrenology theory of personality which assumed that a person's personality, could be determined by measuring the bumps on his skull. Areas that he believed were associated with particular personality traits are indicated in this phrenology chart. Although, as we learned in Chapter 2, Gall's idea that brain functions, such as language, tend to be localized is true, the size of the bumps on a person's head, however, has nothing to do with their personality.

what each one emphasizes, there will not be as much continuity as you might like across these discussions. Unfortunately, this is unavoidable given the diverse nature of these approaches.

Three of these four theoretical approaches also focus on problems in personality development; they have thus led to the development of therapies (based on the theories) to treat such problems. The prime example is psychoanalysis, developed by Freud; the humanistic approach and the social-cognitive approach have also led to well-known styles of therapy. We will discuss all of these therapies in Chapter 10, on abnormal psychology.

The trait approach is not a therapeutic approach; it is more of a descriptive approach to personality. Its primary aim is to identify the set of traits—behavioral dimensions—necessary to describe human personality. Instead of leading to styles of therapy, trait theories often lead to personality tests designed to measure their theorized dimensions of personality. This is why the trait approach is paired with personality assessment in the final section of this chapter. We will treat the other three theoretical approaches in the order that they appeared historically—psychoanalytic followed by humanistic and social-cognitive. The humanistic approach and the social-cognitive approach were both reactions to the earlier psychoanalytic and behavioral approaches; therefore, we have paired them together in the second section. We begin with Freud's psychoanalytic theory of personality, which influenced not only psychological theorizing about personality but also twentieth-century culture.

The Psychoanalytic Approach to Personality

Freud developed his landmark psychoanalytic theory of personality starting in the late nineteenth century and continuing until his death in 1939. His first solo authored book, *The Interpretation of Dreams,* came out in 1900 and was followed by more than 20 other volumes. Freud's psychoanalytic theory has been so influential that many of its important concepts—id, ego, defense mechanisms, Oedipus conflict, Freudian slip, and so on—have become part of our culture. Freud's theory is usually referred to as classical psychoanalytic theory. This distinguishes it from both other psychoanalytic theories developed by Freud's disciples and from contemporary psychodynamic theories (personality theories with a psychoanalytic base). The theories of Freud's disciples are usually called neo-Freudian theories ("neo" is Greek for new). The neo-Freudian theories shared many assumptions with classical Freudian theory, but differed in one or more important ways. The modern-day psychodynamic theories have veered even further away from Freud's original work. They still emphasize the importance of childhood experiences, unconscious thought processes, and addressing inner conflicts, but they don't use much of Freud's terminology nor do they focus on sex as the origin of personality. In this chapter, we will first discuss Freud's classical psychoanalytic theory and then describe some prominent neo-Freudian theories of personality.

Freudian Classical Psychoanalytic Theory of Personality

Freud received a medical degree from the University of Vienna and established a practice as a clinical neurologist treating patients with emotional disorders. Through his work with these patients, Freud became convinced that sex was a primary cause of emotional problems (Freud, 1905/1953b). Sex, including infantile sexuality, became a critical component of his personality theory (Freud 1900/1953a, 1901/1960, 1916 & 1917/1963, 1933/1964). To help you understand Freud's theory, we will consider its three main elements: (1) different levels of awareness, with an emphasis on the role of the unconscious; (2) the dynamic inter-play between the three parts of the personality—id, ego, and superego; and (3) the psychosexual stage theory of personality development.

Sigmund Freud

Freud's three levels of awareness. According to Freud, the mind has three levels of awareness—the conscious, the preconscious, and the unconscious. This three-part division of awareness is Freud's famous iceberg model of the mind (Figure 8.1). The iceberg's visible tip above the surface is the **conscious mind,** what you are presently

> **conscious mind** Freud's term for what you are presently aware of.

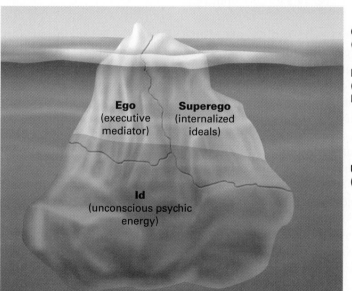

Conscious mind
(present awareness)

Preconscious mind
(outside awareness
but accessible)

Unconscious mind
(not accessible)

▲ **Figure 8.1 I Freud's Iceberg Model of the Mind I** In the iceberg model of the mind, the small part above water is our conscious mind; the part just below the surface is the preconscious; and the major portion, hidden below water, is the unconscious. A person has access only to the conscious and preconscious levels of awareness. The conscious is what the person is presently thinking about, and the preconscious is information that the person could bring into conscious awareness.

preconscious mind Freud's term for what is stored in your memory that you are not presently aware of but can access.

unconscious mind Freud's term for the part of our mind that we cannot become aware of.

id The part of the personality that a person is born with, where the biological instinctual drives reside, and that is located totally in the unconscious mind.

pleasure principle The principle of seeking immediate gratification for instinctual drives without concern for the consequences.

aware of. In memory terms, this is your short-term memory. It is what you are thinking about right now. The part of the iceberg just beneath the surface is the **preconscious mind,** what is stored in your memory that you are not presently aware of but can gain access to. In memory terms, this is your long-term memory. For example, you are not presently thinking about your birthday, but if I asked you what your birthday was, you could bring that information from the preconscious to the conscious level of awareness.

It is the third level of awareness, the unconscious, that Freud emphasized in his personality theory. In Freud's iceberg model, the large base of the iceberg that is hidden deep beneath the surface is the **unconscious mind,** the part of our mind that we cannot freely access. Freud believed this area contains the primary motivations for all of our actions and feelings, including our biological instinctual drives (such as for food and sex) and our repressed unacceptable thoughts, memories, and feelings, especially unresolved conflicts from our early childhood experiences. To better understand the role of these motivations, we need to become familiar with Freud's theory of the personality structure and his psychosexual stage theory of personality development.

Freud's three-part personality structure. Freud divided the personality structure into three parts—id, ego, and superego. These are mental processes or systems and not actual physical structures. Freud believed that personality is the product of the dynamic interaction of these three systems. The **id** is the original personality, the only part present at birth and the part out of which the other two parts of our personality emerge. As you can see in Figure 8.1 (page 291), the id resides entirely in the unconscious part of the mind. The id includes biological instinctual drives, the primitive parts of personality located in the unconscious. Freud grouped these instinctual drives into life instincts (survival, reproduction, and pleasure drives such as for food, water, and sex) and death instincts (destructive and aggressive drives that are detrimental to survival). Freud downplayed the death instincts in his theory and emphasized the life instincts, especially sex. The id contains psychic energy, which attempts to satisfy these instinctual drives according to the **pleasure principle**—immediate gratification for these drives without concern for the consequences. Thus, the id is like a spoiled child, totally self-centered and focused on satisfying these drives. For example, if you're hungry, the id, using the pleasure principle, would lead you to take any food that is available without concern for whom it belongs to.

Obviously the id cannot operate totally unchecked. We cannot go around taking anything we want to satisfy the id's drives. Our behavior is constrained by social norms and laws. We have to buy food from markets, stores, and restaurants. Our personality develops as we find ways to meet our needs within these social constraints. The second part of the personality structure, the **ego,** starts developing during the first year or so of life to find realistic outlets for the id's needs. Because the ego emerges out of the id, it derives its psychic energy from the id. The ego has the task of protecting the personality while ensuring that the id's drives are satisfied.

The ego, then, is the pragmatic part of the personality; it weighs the risks of an action before acting. The ego uses the **reality principle**—finding gratification for instinctual drives within the constraints of reality (the norms and laws of society). In order to do this, the ego spans all three levels of awareness (see Figure 8.1 on page 291). Because of its ties to the id, part of the ego must be located in the unconscious; and because of its ties to reality (the external world), part of it must be in the conscious and preconscious. The ego uses memory and conscious thought processes, such as reasoning, to carry out its job.

The ego functions as the manager or executive of the personality. It must mediate not only between the instinctual drives of the id and reality but also between these drives and the third part of the personality structure, the **superego,** which represents the conscience and idealized standards of behavior in a particular culture. The superego develops during childhood and, like the ego, develops from id energy and spans all levels of awareness. It tells the ego how one ought to act. Thus, the superego might be said to act in accordance with a morality principle. For example, if the id hunger drive demanded satisfaction and the ego had found a way to steal some food without being caught, the superego would threaten to overwhelm the individual with guilt and shame for such an act. Inevitably, the demands of the superego and the id will come into conflict, and the ego will have to resolve this turmoil within the constraints of reality. This is not an easy task.

Here is why the ego's job is so difficult. Imagine that your parents are making conflicting demands on you. For example, when you were deciding which college to attend, let's say your father wanted you to attend a state university and your mother wanted you to attend her private college alma mater. Imagine also that your boyfriend or girlfriend is adding a third level of conflicting demands (wanting to go to school together at the local community college). You want to satisfy all three, but because the demands are conflicting, it is not possible. You get anxious because there is no good resolution to the conflict. This is what often happens to the ego in its role as mediator between its three masters (id, superego, and reality). To prevent being overcome with anxiety, the ego uses what Freud called **defense mechanisms,** processes that distort reality and protect us from anxiety (Freud, 1936). The ego has many different defense mechanisms available for such self-deception, including repression, denial, displacement, and rationalization. Table 8.1 (page 294) provides descriptions and examples of several defense mechanisms.

Freud thought of repression as the primary defense mechanism. If we are unaware of unacceptable feelings, memories, and thoughts (they have been put in

ego The part of the personality that starts developing in the first year or so of life to find realistic outlets for the id's instinctual drives.

reality principle The principle of finding gratification for instinctual drives within the constraints of reality (norms of society).

superego The part of the personality that represents one's conscience and idealized standards of behavior.

defense mechanism A process used by the ego to distort reality and protect a person from anxiety.

Table 8.1	Some of Freud's Defense Mechanisms	
Defense Mechanism	**Description**	**Example**
Repression	Unknowingly placing an unpleasant memory or thought in the unconscious	Not remembering a traumatic incident in which you witnessed a crime
Regression	Reverting back to immature behavior from an earlier stage of development	Throwing temper tantrums as an adult when you don't get your way
Denial	Refusing to acknowledge anxiety-provoking realities	Refusing to accept evidence that your spouse is having an affair
Displacement	Redirecting unacceptable feelings from the original source to a safer, substitute target	Taking your anger toward your boss out on your spouse or children by yelling at them and not your boss
Sublimation	Replacing socially unacceptable impulses with socially acceptable behavior	Channeling aggressive drives into playing football or inappropriate sexual desires into art
Reaction formation	Acting in exactly the opposite way to one's unacceptable impulses	Being overprotective of and lavishing attention on an unwanted child
Projection	Attributing one's own unacceptable feelings and thoughts to others and not yourself	Accusing your boyfriend of cheating on you because you have felt like cheating on him
Rationalization	Creating false excuses for one's unacceptable feelings, thoughts, or behavior	Justifying cheating on an exam by saying that everyone else cheats

our unconscious), then we cannot be anxious about them. But it is important to remember that Freud proposed that repression occurs automatically—without conscious awareness. Once repressed, we have no conscious memory that the thought, event, or impulse ever existed. Freud believed that defense mechanisms help us to deal with anxiety. We now know, however, that we may become dependent upon defense mechanisms and not face reality. They may prevent us from facing our problems and dealing with them. The best defense mechanism may be using no defense mechanisms. Facing up to problems may allow us to see that reality is not as bad as we thought, and that consciously working to change reality is more beneficial than distorting it.

Freud believed that unhealthy personalities develop not only when we become too dependent upon defense mechanisms, but also when the id or superego is unusually strong or the ego unusually weak. In such cases, the ego cannot control the other two processes. For example, a person with a weak ego would not be able to hold the id drives in check, possibly leading to a self-centered personality. Or, a person with an overly strong superego would be too concerned with morality, possibly leading to a guilt-ridden personality. A healthy personality is one in which none of the three personality systems (id, ego, and superego) is dominating, allowing the three systems to interact in a relatively harmonious way.

In addition to imbalances between the three personality parts, Freud stressed the importance of our early childhood experiences in determining our adult personality traits. In fact, he thought that our experiences during the first six years or so of life were critical in the development of our adult personality. To understand exactly how Freud proposed that early childhood experiences impact personality, we now turn to a consideration of his psychosexual stage theory.

"Look, call it denial if you like, but I think what goes on in my personal life is none of my own damn business."

Freud's psychosexual stage theory. Freud did not spend much time observing children to help him develop his psychosexual stage theory of personality development. Freud's psychosexual stage theory was developed chiefly from his own childhood memories and from his years of interactions with his patients and their case studies, which included their childhood memories.

Two key concepts in his psychosexual theory are erogenous zone and fixation. An **erogenous zone** is the area of the body where the id's pleasure-seeking psychic energy is focused during a particular stage of psychosexual development. The erogenous zone feels good when stimulated in various ways. Thus, the erogenous zones are the body areas where instinctual satisfaction can be obtained. Each of Freud's psychosexual stages is named after the erogenous zone involved, and a change in erogenous zones designates the beginning of a new stage. For example, the first stage is called the oral stage, and the erogenous zone is the mouth area, so pleasure is derived from oral activities such as sucking. Freud proposed five stages—oral, anal, phallic, latency, and genital. They are outlined in Table 8.2 (page 296) with the erogenous zone for each stage indicated.

Freud's concept of fixation is important in understanding how he believed our childhood experiences impact our adult personality. A **fixation** occurs when a portion of the id's pleasure-seeking energy remains in a stage because of excessive or insufficient gratification of our instinctual needs during that stage of development. A person who is overindulged will want to stay and not move on, while a person who is frustrated has difficulty moving on because his needs are not met. The stronger the fixation, the more of the id's pleasure-seeking energy remains in that stage. Such fixations continue throughout the person's life and impact his behavior and personality traits. For example, a person who is fixated in the oral stage because of excessive gratification may become overly concerned with oral activities such as smoking, eating, and drinking. Because his oral needs have been overindulged, such a person may continue to depend upon others to meet his needs and thus have a dependent personality. Such a person is also likely to be gullible

erogenous zone The area of the body where the id's pleasure-seeking energies are focused during a particular stage of psychosexual development.

fixation Some of the id's pleasure-seeking energies remaining in a psychosexual stage due to excessive or insufficient gratification of instinctual needs.

■ **oral stage of psychosexual development** The first stage in Freud's theory (from birth to 18 months), in which the erogenous zones are the mouth, lips, and tongue, and the child derives pleasure from oral activities such as sucking, biting, and chewing.

■ **anal stage of psychosexual development** The second stage in Freud's theory (from 18 months to 3 years), in which the erogenous zone is the anus, and the child derives pleasure from stimulation of the anal region through having and withholding bowel movements.

or willing to "swallow" anything. We will consider some other examples of fixation as we describe the five stages.

In the **oral stage** (from birth to 18 months), the erogenous zones are the mouth, lips, and tongue, and the child derives pleasure from oral activities such as sucking, biting, and chewing. As already pointed out, a fixation would lead to having a preoccupation with oral behaviors, such as smoking, gum chewing, overeating, or even talking too much. Freud himself had such a preoccupation with smoking. He smoked 20 or so cigars a day and had numerous operations for cancer in his mouth, which eventually led to his death (Larsen & Buss, 2000). Many other personality characteristics can also stem from oral fixations. For example, a fixation created by too little gratification might lead to an excessively mistrustful person. The deprived infant has presumably learned that the world cannot be trusted to provide for basic needs.

In the **anal stage** (from about 18 months to 3 years), the erogenous zone is the anus, and the child derives pleasure from stimulation of the anal region through having and withholding bowel movements. Toilet training and the issue of control are major concerns in this stage. Parents try to get the child to have self-control during toilet training. Freud believed that fixations during this stage depend upon how toilet training is approached by the parents. Such fixations can lead to two famous adult personalities, anal retentive and anal expulsive. Both are reactions to harsh toilet training in which the parents admonish and punish the child for failures. If the child reacts to this harsh toilet training by trying to get even with the parents and withholding bowel movements, an anal-retentive personality with the traits of orderliness, neatness, stinginess, and obstinacy develops. The anal-expulsive personality develops when children rebel against harsh training and have bowel movements whenever and wherever they please. Such people tend to be sloppy, disorderly, and possibly even destructive and cruel.

Table 8.2	**Freud's Psychosexual Stages of Personality Development**	
Stage (age range)	**Erogenous Zone**	**Activity Focus**
Oral (birth to 1½ years)	Mouth, lips, and tongue	Sucking, biting, and chewing
Anal (1½ to 3 years)	Anus	Bowel retention and elimination
Phallic (3 to 6 years)	Genitals	Genital stimulation, attraction to opposite-sex parent and later identifying with same-sex parent to learn gender role and sense of morality
Latency (6 years to puberty)	No erogenous zone	Cognitive and social development
Genital (puberty through adulthood)	Genitals	Development of sexual relationships, moving toward intimate adult relationships

In the **phallic stage** (from age 3 to 6 years), the erogenous zone is located at the genitals, and the child derives pleasure from genital stimulation. According to Freud, there is much psychological conflict in this stage, including the Oedipus conflict for boys. In the **Oedipus conflict,** the little boy becomes sexually attracted to his mother and fears the father (his rival) will find out and castrate him. This parallels the Greek tragedy *Oedipus Rex,* in which Oedipus unknowingly kills his father, marries his mother, and then realizes what he's done and gouges his eyes out as punishment. Freud was much less confident about the existence of a comparable Electra conflict for girls, in which a girl is supposedly attracted to her father due to penis envy.

"During the next stage of my development, Dad, I'll be drawing closer to my mother—I'll get back to you in my teens."

Freud believed that children, especially boys, resolve conflicts in this stage by repressing their desire for the opposite-sex parent and identifying with the same-sex parent. It is in this process of **identification** that Freud believed children adopt the characteristics of the same-sex parent and learn their gender roles. For example, a little boy would adopt the behaviors and attitudes of his father. According to Freud, unsuccessful resolution of this conflict would result in a child having a conflicted gender role, sexual relationship problems with the opposite sex, and possibly a homosexual orientation. It is also during this identification process that the superego develops, as a child learns his sense of morality by adopting the attitudes and values of his parents.

Freud didn't think that the final two stages of his psychosexual theory were as important for personality development. He assumed that how a child progresses through the first three stages pretty much determined the child's adult personality. In the **latency stage** (from about age 6 to puberty), there is no erogenous zone, sexual drives become less active, and the focus is on cognitive and social development. A child of this age is most interested in school, sports, hobbies, and in developing friendships with other children of the same sex. In the **genital stage** (from puberty through adulthood), the erogenous zone is at the genitals again, and Freud believed a person develops sexual relationships in a move toward intimate adult relationships.

phallic stage of psychosexual development The third stage in Freud's theory (from 3 to 6 years), in which the erogenous zone is located at the genitals, and the child derives pleasure from genital stimulation.

Oedipus conflict A phallic stage conflict for a boy in which the boy becomes sexually attracted to his mother and fears his father will find out and castrate him.

identification The process by which children adopt the characteristics of the same-sex parent and learn their gender role and sense of morality.

latency stage of psychosexual development The fourth stage in Freud's theory (from 6 to puberty) in which there is no erogenous zone, sexual feelings are repressed, and the focus is on cognitive and social development.

genital stage of psychosexual development The fifth stage in Freud's theory (from puberty through adulthood) in which the erogenous zone is at the genitals and the child develops sexual relationships, moving toward intimate adult relationships.

Evaluation of Freud's psychoanalytic theory of personality. Freud's ideas were controversial when he first proposed them and have remained controversial over the past century. Let's consider some of the criticisms of his major concepts. First, consider Freud's "unconscious" level of awareness. Because this concept is not accessible to anyone, it is impossible to examine scientifically and thus cannot be experimentally tested. We can't observe and study a factor that we are not aware of. This criticism does not deny that unconscious processing greatly impacts thinking and behavior. It does. Think back to Chapter 3, on the human senses and perception, and to Chapter 5, on memory. Our conscious level of awareness of these important processes is like Freud's "tip of the iceberg." We have learned, however, that this iceberg is not a storehouse of instinctual drives, conflicts, and repressed memories and desires as Freud proposed. It is the location of all of our cognitive processes and the knowledge base they use—the center of our information processing. Freud was correct in pointing to unconscious processing as crucial, but he was incorrect about its role and the nature of its importance.

Freud was also correct in pointing to the importance of early childhood experience, but he was again incorrect about the nature of its importance. There is little evidence that psychosexual stages impact development, but there is evidence that many of the concepts we discussed in the last chapter, such as the connection between the type of attachment an infant forms and parenting style, are important. What about Freud's main defense mechanism, repression? Contemporary memory researchers think that it seldom, if ever, occurs (Holmes, 1990; Loftus & Ketcham, 1994; McNally, 2003). Remember the discussion of so-called recovered memories in Chapter 5, on memory? We understand today how Freud's questioning during therapy may have created such "repressed" memories in his patients. Do the other defense mechanisms fare any better? There is evidence that we do use certain defense mechanisms to ward off anxiety, though we do not necessarily do so unconsciously.

We must remember that Freud started developing his theory over 100 years ago. Our world and the state of psychological research knowledge were very different then. So, it is not surprising that Freud's theory doesn't stand up very well today. What is surprising is that he could develop a theory from such a scant database that has had such great impact on our thinking and culture. In 1999 he was on the cover of a special issue of *Time* magazine commemorating the 100 greatest thinkers and scientists of the twentieth century. We can only speculate on what his theory would be like if he had started in 1990 rather than 1890.

Neo-Freudian Theories of Personality

Even Freud's own circle of psychoanalysts disagreed with him on some aspects of his theory. These disagreements led them to develop psychoanalytic theories that accepted most of Freud's basic ideas, but differed from Freud in one or more important ways. They became known as neo-Freudian psychoanalytic theorists. In addition to Erik Erikson, whose psychosocial stage theory of development was described in the last chapter, the major neo-Freudian theorists were Carl Jung, Alfred Adler, and Karen Horney (pronounced HORN-eye). In general, these three neo-Freudian theorists, like Erikson, thought that Freud placed too much importance on psychosexual development and sexual drives and not enough emphasis on social and cultural influences on the development of personality. We discuss Jung first because, other than Freud, he is the best-known psychoanalytic theorist.

Jung's collective unconscious. Carl Jung extended Freud's notion of the unconscious to include not only the personal unconscious—each individual's instinctual drives and repressed memories and conflicts—but also the collective unconscious, the accumulated universal experiences of humankind. Each of us inherits this same cumulative storehouse of all human experience that is manifested in archetypes—symbolic images of all of the important themes in the history of humankind (such as God, the mother, and the hero). The archetypes in the collective unconscious are why myths and legends in very diverse cultures tend to have common themes. In addition to these shared universal archetypes, each of us inherits more specific ones that guide our individual personality development. Jung's theoretical concepts are rather mystical and not really scientific. His interest in the mystical side of life greatly influenced his theory, and his concepts, such as the collective unconscious and archetypes, are beyond empirical verification. These symbolic, mystical aspects of Jung's theory may be why it has been more popular in the fields of religion, anthropology, and literature than in psychology.

Carl Jung

Personality psychologists, however, have pursued some other aspects of Jung's theory. Most prominently, Jung proposed two main personality attitudes—extraversion and introversion. People's attitudes focus them toward the external, objective world (extraversion) or toward the inner, subjective world (introversion). Along with these two general outlooks, Jung proposed four functions (or cognitive styles)—sensing and intuiting for gathering information and thinking and feeling for evaluating information. Across individuals, the development of these four functions varies, with one of them being dominant. These two attitudes and four functions lead to eight possible personality types. These eight types were the basis for a personality test, the Myers-Briggs Type Indicator, developed in the 1920s by Katherine Briggs and her daughter, Isabel Myers. This test has been the primary tool for research on Jung's personality types, and it is still in use today (Myers & McCaulley, 1985). In addition, Jung's two personality attitudes, extraversion and introversion, play a central role in contemporary trait theories of personality, which we will discuss in the last section of this chapter.

Adler's striving for superiority. Another neo-Freudian theorist, Alfred Adler, disagreed with Freud's assumption that the main motivation in personality development is the satisfaction of sexual urges. Adler thought that the main motivation was what he termed "striving for superiority," the need to overcome the sense of inferiority that we feel as infants, given our totally helpless and dependent state. Adler believed that these feelings of inferiority

Alfred Adler

serve as our basic motivation. They lead us to grow and strive toward success. A healthy person learns to cope with these feelings, becomes competent, and develops a sense of self-esteem. Parental love and support help a child overcome her initial feelings of inferiority. Adler used the phrase "inferiority complex" to describe the strong feelings felt by those who never overcome the initial feeling of inferiority. People with an inferiority complex often have unloving, neglectful, or indifferent parents. The complex leads to feelings of worthlessness and a mistrust of others. Adler also defined what he termed a "superiority complex," an exaggerated opinion of one's abilities. This leads to a self-centered, vain person.

The Bettmann Archive/Corbis

Karen Horney

Horney and the need for security. Like Adler, Karen Horney focused on our early social experiences with our parents, not on instinctual biological drives. Unlike Adler, Horney's focus was on dealing with our need for security rather than a sense of inferiority. Remember the importance of a secure attachment for infants that we discussed in the last chapter, on human development? According to Horney's theory, a child's caregivers must provide a sense of security for a healthy personality to develop. Children whose parents do not lead them to feel secure would suffer from what Horney called "basic anxiety," a feeling of helplessness and insecurity in a hostile world. This basic anxiety about personal relationships may lead to neurotic behavior and a disordered personality (Horney, 1937). Horney differentiated three neurotic personality patterns—moving toward people (a compliant, submissive person), moving against people (an aggressive, domineering person), and moving away from people (a detached, aloof person). This focus of Horney and other neo-Freudian theorists on the importance of interpersonal relationships, both in childhood and in adulthood, continues in contemporary psychodynamic theory (Westen, 1998).

Section Summary

In the late-nineteenth and early-twentieth centuries, Freud developed his psychoanalytic theory of personality. He divided the mind into three levels of awareness—conscious, preconscious, and unconscious—with the unconscious (the part that we cannot become aware of) being the most important in his theory. It is the unconscious that contains life and death instinctual drives, the primary motivators for all of our actions and feelings. In addition, there are three parts of the personality structure—the id (which contains the instinctual drives and is located totally in the unconscious), the ego (the manager of the personality), and the superego (our conscience and sense of morality). The ego and the superego span all three levels of awareness. The ego attempts to find gratification for the id's instinctual drives within the constraints of the superego and reality (societal laws and norms). When the ego cannot achieve this difficult task, we become anxious. To combat such anxiety, Freud suggested that we use defense mechanisms, which protect us from anxiety by distorting reality. The primary defense mechanism is repression, unknowingly placing an unpleasant memory or thought in the unconscious, where it cannot bother us.

Freud also emphasized the importance of early childhood experience in his theory. He proposed that how successfully a child progresses through the early psychosexual stages greatly impacts his personality development. Freud proposed five psychosexual stages, with the first three being most important to our personality development. The stages—in order, with the erogenous zone (pleasure center) indicated for that stage—are oral (mouth), anal (anus), phallic (genitals), latency (no erogenous zone), and genital (genitals). A fixation, which occurs when some of the id's pleasure-seeking energies remain in a stage because of excessive or insufficient gratification, influences a person's behavior and personality for the rest of his life. For example, a person with an oral fixation will seek physical pleasure from oral activities and may be overly dependent and gullible. The important Oedipus conflict for boys (and Electra conflict for girls) in which the child is attracted to the opposite-sex parent occurs in the phallic stage of development from about age 3 to 6. Resolution of this conflict leads the child to identify with the same-sex parent and learn his or her proper gender role and sense of morality.

Neo-Freudian theorists were psychoanalytic theorists who agreed with much of Freud's theory but disagreed with some of Freud's key assumptions, which led them to develop their own versions of psychoanalytic theory. For example, Carl Jung theorized that, in addition to the personal unconscious, we have a collective unconscious that contains the accumulated experiences of humankind. Alfred Adler proposed that the main motivation was not sexual, but rather a striving for superiority in which we must overcome the sense of inferiority that we feel as infants. Failure to do so leads to an inferiority complex. Karen Horney focused her attention on our need for security as infants, rather than our sense of inferiority. She argued that if our caregivers do not help us to gain a feeling of security, we suffer from a sense of basic anxiety, which leads to various types of personality problems.

ConceptCheck | 1

> Explain, according to Freudian theory, why the ego has such a difficult job.

> Explain the difference between Freud's two defense mechanisms—reaction formation and projection.

> Explain how fixations in psychosexual development affect adult behavior and personality.

The Humanistic Approach and the Social-Cognitive Approach to Personality

Humanistic theories of personality developed during the 1960s as part of the general humanistic movement in psychology. The humanistic movement was in response to the deterministic psychoanalytic and strict behavioral psychological approaches that dominated psychology and the study of personality at that time.

As we just discussed, the classical psychoanalytic approach assumes that personality is a product of how the id's unconscious instinctual drives find satisfaction, especially during the first three psychosexual stages. The strict behavioral approach assumes that our personality and behavior are merely products of our environment, as a result of classical and operant conditioning (discussed in Chapter 4). Our personality is determined by our behavior and is conditioned by environmental events. According to both approaches, we are not in charge of our behavior and personality development. According to the psychoanalytic approach, our unconscious instinctual drives are the major motivators of our behavior and personality development. According to the behavioral approach, the environment motivates and controls our actions. In contrast, the humanistic approach emphasizes conscious free will in one's actions, the uniqueness of the individual person, and personal growth. Unlike the psychoanalytic approach's focus on our personality problems, the humanistic approach centers on the positive motivations for our actions and development, especially personal growth. To familiarize you with this approach, we will describe the theories of the two major humanistic proponents, Abraham Maslow and Carl Rogers.

At about the same time as the humanists, social-cognitive theorists rebelled against the narrowness of the strict behavioral approach to the development of personality. The behavioral approach limited itself to the factors of classical and operant conditioning for learning behaviors (personality). Social-cognitive theorists agreed that conditioning was important, but that the situation was more complex than that. Remember, Albert Bandura's work on social (observational) learning in Chapter 4 demonstrated our ability to learn from observing others without direct reinforcement, which meant that social and cognitive factors were involved in learning. The social-cognitive approach includes social and cognitive factors along with conditioning to explain personality development. Thus, the strict behavioral approach to personality is subsumed under the more extensive social-cognitive approach. Because of this, the social-cognitive approach is sometimes referred to as the social-learning approach and the cognitive-behavioral approach. We refer to it as the social-cognitive approach to note its emphasis on these two types of factors in personality development. We will describe some of the theoretical concepts of two important social-cognitive theorists, Albert Bandura and Julian Rotter, to illustrate why they think social and cognitive factors are important in personality development.

The Humanistic Approach to Personality

Abraham Maslow is considered the father of the humanistic movement. He studied the lives of very healthy and creative people to develop his theory of personality. His main theoretical emphases were psychological health and reaching one's full potential. In describing how one goes about reaching one's full potential, Maslow proposed a hierarchy of needs that motivate our behavior in this quest. Because of the motivating role of these various types of needs, Maslow's personality theory is also considered a theory of motivation.

Maslow's hierarchy of needs. An overview of Maslow's motivational hierarchy of needs, which is often depicted as a pyramid-like structure, is given in Figure 8.2. The **hierarchy of needs** is an arrangement of the innate needs that motivate behavior, from the strongest needs at the bottom of the pyramid to the weakest needs at the top of the pyramid (Maslow, 1968, 1970). From bottom to top, the needs are physiological, safety, belonging and love, esteem, and self-actualization. For obvious practical reasons, motivation proceeds from the bottom of the hierarchy to the top; lower needs are more urgent and have to be satisfied before higher needs can even be considered. On average, people seem to work their way up the hierarchy, but they also work on several levels simultaneously. The level at which the person is investing most of his effort is the one most important to a person at a particular point in time.

Abraham Maslow

Ted Polumbaum/ Time Pix/ Getty Images

As you move up in the hierarchy, the needs become more human and less basic. The most basic needs are physiological needs (such as for food and water); therefore, they form the base of the pyramid structure. At the next level, the needs to feel safe, secure, and out of danger are also relevant to our survival, but not quite as basic as physiological needs. At the next level in the hierarchy, however, needs begin to have social aspects. Love and belongingness needs (needs for affection, acceptance, family relationships, and companionship) are met through interactions with other people. Self-esteem needs at the next level in the hierarchy are concerned with achievement, mastery, and gaining appreciation from others for our achievements, as well as developing a positive self-image.

hierarchy of needs The motivational component in Maslow's theory of personality in which our innate needs that motivate our behavior are hierarchically arranged in a pyramid shape. From bottom to top, the needs are physiological, safety, belonging and love, esteem, and self-actualization.

Self-actualization need
Need to live up to one's
fullest unique potential

Esteem needs
Need for self-esteem,
achievement,
competence, and independence

Belongingness and love needs
Need to love and be loved, to
belong and be accepted

Safety needs
Need to feel safe, secure, and stable

Physiological needs
Need to satisfy hunger and thirst

▲ **Figure 8.2** | **Maslow's Hierarchy of Needs** | Needs are organized hierarchically into levels, with more pressing basic needs at the bottom of the pyramid. The level at which a person is investing most of his effort is the most important one at that particular point in time.

■ **self-actualization** The fullest realization of a person's potential.

These first four levels of needs are more deficiency-based needs, stemming from deprivation, while self-actualization at the top of the hierarchy is a growth-based need. **Self-actualization** is the fullest realization of a person's potential, becoming all that one can be. According to Maslow, the characteristics of self-actualized people include accepting themselves, others, and the natural world for what they are; having a need for privacy and only a few very close, emotional relationships; and being autonomous and independent, unquestionably democratic, and very creative. In addition, self-actualized people have what Maslow termed "peak experiences"—experiences of deep insight in which you experience whatever you are doing as fully as possible. In peak experiences, you are deeply immersed in what you are doing and feel a sense of awe and wonder. Peak experiences might, for example, arise from great music or art, or from intense feelings of love.

Maslow based his description of self-actualization on his study of about 50 people who he deemed "self-actualized." Some, such as Albert Einstein and Eleanor Roosevelt, were living so he studied them through interviews and personality tests, but others, such as Thomas Jefferson and Abraham Lincoln, were not so he used biographies and historical records to study them. Maslow was rather vague about how he conducted these "studies," however. This is why Maslow's theory has been criticized for being based on nonempirical, vague studies of a small number of people that he subjectively selected as self-actualized (Smith, 1978). His theory may have been biased toward his own idea of a healthy, self-actualized person. Regardless of these criticisms, his theory popularized the humanistic movement and led many psychologists to focus on human potential and the positive side of humankind. Carl Rogers, the other major proponent of the humanistic approach, also focused on self-actualization. Unlike Maslow, however, Rogers based his theory upon his clinical work.

Rogers's self theory. Freud's psychoanalytic theory of personality led to psychoanalysis, a type of psychotherapy used to help those suffering personality problems. Carl Rogers's self theory of personality led to another influential style of psychotherapy, client-centered (or person-centered) therapy (Rogers, 1951, 1961), which we will discuss in Chapter 10, on abnormal psychology. It is interesting to note that Rogers was a clinician in an academic setting during most of the time he was developing his theory (Schultz, 2001). His clients were not like those of psychotherapists in the private sector; he mainly dealt with young, bright people with adjustment problems. Keep this in mind as we consider his theory, since his clinical experiences likely guided its development.

Like Maslow, Rogers emphasized self-actualization, the development of one's fullest potential. He believed that this was the fundamental drive for humans. Sometimes we have difficulty in this actualization process, though, and this is the source of personality problems. How does this happen? Like Freud, Rogers believed that early experience was important, but for very different reasons. He thought that we have a strong need for positive regard—to be

Carl Rogers

accepted by and have the affection of others, especially the significant others in our life. Our parents (or caregivers) set up **conditions of worth,** the behaviors and attitudes for which they will give us positive regard. Infants and children develop their self-concept in relation to these conditions of worth in order to be liked and accepted by others and feel a sense of self-worth.

Meeting the conditions of worth continues throughout our lives. We want to be regarded positively by others so we meet their conditions. There's the problem, though. In meeting these conditions of worth, we may develop a self-concept of what others think we should be. The problem is that this self-concept might not be the same as our true, ideal self, and thus would deter self-actualization. This conflict is created by conditional positive regard, so Rogers developed the concept of **unconditional positive regard**—acceptance and approval without conditions. In addition to giving us unconditional positive regard (liking us no matter what we are like), it is important that others be empathetic (able to truly understand our feelings) and genuine with respect to their own feelings if we are to self-actualize. As we will find in Chapter 10, these characteristics are critical elements in Rogers's client-centered therapy. Rogers's self-theory is summarized in Figure 8.3.

Rogers's theory's, like Freud's theory, is based on clinical experience and is important mainly because of its application

"Just remember, son, it doesn't matter whether you win or lose—unless you want Daddy's love."

▮ **conditions of worth** The behaviors and attitudes for which other people, starting with our parents, will give us positive regard.

▮ **unconditional positive regard** Unconditional acceptance and approval of a person by others.

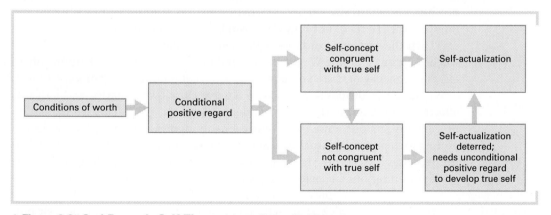

▲ **Figure 8.3** | **Carl Rogers's Self Theory** | According to Carl Rogers, the development of your self-concept is impacted by the conditions of worth set up by those people who are important to you. Their conditional positive regard may lead you to develop a self-concept that is congruent with your true self, thereby allowing you to self-actualize; or it may lead to a conflict between your developed self-concept and your true self. If there is a conflict, then you will need unconditional positive regard in order to develop your true self and self-actualize.

to therapy. Neither theory is research based. The social-cognitive approach, which we will discuss next, is research based, however. It combines elements of three of the major research perspectives—the cognitive, behavioral, and sociocultural approaches. The social-cognitive approach stresses that personality development involves learning that occurs in a social context and is mediated by cognitive processes. Let's see how.

The Social-Cognitive Approach to Personality

Social-cognitive theorists agree with behaviorists that learning through environmental conditioning contributes to personality development. However, they think that social learning (modeling) and cognitive processes, such as perception and thinking, are also involved and are actually more important to the development of our personality. To understand how modeling and cognitive processes are involved, we'll first consider the work of Albert Bandura, one of the main proponents of the social-cognitive approach.

Bandura's self-system. Bandura proposes that the behaviors that define one's personality are a product of a person's self-system (Bandura, 1973, 1986). This **self-system** is the set of cognitive processes by which a person observes, evaluates, and regulates her behavior. Social learning illustrates how this system works. Children observe the various behaviors of the models in their social environment, especially those of their parents. Given this observational learning, children may then choose, at some later time, to imitate these behaviors, especially if they were reinforced earlier. If these behaviors continue to be reinforced, children may then incorporate them into their personality. This means that there is self-direction (the child consciously chooses which behaviors to imitate). The child's behavior is not just automatically elicited by environmental stimuli. People observe and interpret the effects of not only their own behavior, but also the behavior of others. Then they act in accordance with their assessment of whether the behavior will be reinforced or not. We do not respond mechanically to the environment; we choose our behaviors based on our expectations of reinforcement or punishment.

Bandura also proposes that people observe their own behavior and judge its effectiveness relative to their own standards (Bandura, 1997). This self-evaluation process impacts our sense of **self-efficacy**—a judgment of one's effectiveness in dealing with particular situations. Success increases our sense of self-efficacy; failure decreases it. According to Bandura, our sense of self-efficacy plays a major role in determining our behavior. People generally low in self-efficacy tend to be depressed and anxious and feel helpless. People generally high in self-efficacy are confident and positive in their outlook and have little self doubt. They also have greater persistence in working to attain goals and usually achieve greater success than those with low self-efficacy. Self-efficacy parallels the story of the little engine that could. To do something, you have to think you can do it.

self-system The set of cognitive processes by which a person observes, evaluates, and regulates her behavior.

self-efficacy A judgment of one's effectiveness in dealing with particular situations.

Rotter's locus of control. Bandura's self-efficacy concept is similar to locus of control, a concept proposed by another social-cognitive theorist, Julian Rotter. According to Rotter, locus of control refers to a person's perception of the extent to which he controls what happens to him (Rotter, 1966, 1990). "Locus" means place. There are two major places that control can reside—outside you or within you. **External locus of control** refers to the perception that chance or external forces beyond your personal control determine your fate. **Internal locus of control** refers to the perception that you control your own fate. How is locus of control different from self-efficacy? People with an internal locus of control perceive their success as dependent upon their own actions, but they may or may not feel that they have the competence (efficacy) to bring about successful outcomes in various situations. For example, students may think that their own study preparation determines their exam performance, but they may not think that they have satisfactory study skills to produce good exam performance. For those with external locus of control, the self-efficacy concept isn't as relevant because such people believe that the outcomes of their actions are not affected by their actions.

Why is Rotter's locus of control concept important? Research has shown that people with an internal locus of control are psychologically and physically better off. They are more successful in school, healthier, and better able to cope with the stresses of life (Lachman & Weaver, 1998). In addition, an external locus of control may contribute to **learned helplessness,** a sense of hopelessness in which individuals think that they are unable to prevent unpleasant events (Seligman, 1975). But how does this happen? What goes on in the minds of those who become helpless? To understand, we first need to consider self-perception and the attribution process.

Self-perception. Given the impact of self-efficacy and locus of control, positive self-perception is important to healthy behavior. Our behavior, however, does not always lead to good outcomes. How then do we deal with poor outcomes and maintain positive self-perception? To understand how we do so, we need to understand **attribution,** the process by which we explain our own behavior and that of others. There are two types of attributions, internal and external. An internal attribution means that the outcome is attributed to the person. An external attribution means that the outcome is attributed to factors outside the person. Let's consider an example. You fail a psychology exam. Why? An internal attribution gives you the blame. For example, you might say, "I just didn't study enough." An external attribution would place the blame elsewhere. For example, you might say, "I knew the material, but that exam was unfair." In this case, you tend to make an external attribution. Why?

We place the blame elsewhere in order to protect our self-esteem. This attribution bias is called the **self-serving bias,** the tendency to make attributions so that one can perceive oneself favorably. If the outcome of our behavior is positive,

external locus of control The perception that chance or external forces beyond your personal control determine your fate.

internal locus of control The perception that you control your own fate.

learned helplessness A sense of hopelessness in which a person thinks that he is unable to prevent aversive events.

attribution The process by which we explain our own behavior and that of others.

self-serving bias The tendency to make attributions so that one can perceive oneself favorably.

we take credit for it (make an internal attribution). However, if the outcome is negative, we place the blame elsewhere (make an external attribution). The research evidence indicating that we use the self-serving bias is overwhelming (Myers, 2002). Think about it. Don't most of us think that we are above average in intelligence, attractiveness, and other positive characteristics? But most people can't be above average, can they? These self-enhancing perceptions created by the self-serving bias serve to maintain our self-esteem. This bias is adaptive because it protects us from falling prey to learned helplessness and depression. When negative events happen, we don't blame ourselves. Instead, we make external attributions and place the blame elsewhere.

So what type of explanatory style might lead us toward learned helplessness and depression? A pessimistic explanatory style is one answer (Peterson, Maier, & Seligman, 1993). First, the attributions of people using a pessimistic explanatory style tend to show a pattern that is the opposite of those generated by self-serving bias. Negative outcomes are given internal explanations ("I don't have any ability"), and positive outcomes external explanations ("I just got lucky"). There is more to it, however. Pessimistic explanations also tend to be stable (the person thinks that the outcome causes are permanent) and global (the causes affect most situations). Think about a person using a pessimistic explanatory style when experiencing a series of negative events. Not only would such people blame themselves (internal), but they would also think that such negative events would continue (stable) and impact most aspects of their lives (global). Such thinking could easily lead to the perception of an external locus of control and learned helplessness followed by depression. Indeed, research has found that such an explanatory style puts a person at risk for depression (Peterson & Seligman, 1984).

Section Summary

The humanistic approach to the study of personality developed as part of the humanistic movement in the 1960s in response to the rather deterministic psychoanalytic and behavioral approaches that dominated psychology at that time. In contrast to these two approaches, the humanistic theorists emphasized conscious free will in one's development and the importance of self-actualization, the fullest realization of our potential, as a major motivator of our behavior. Based on his studies of very healthy and creative people, humanistic theorist Abraham Maslow developed a hierarchy of needs that motivate our behavior and development. From bottom to top, the needs are physiological, safety, belonging and love, esteem, and self-actualization. Motivation proceeds from the bottom of the hierarchy to the top because a person cannot work toward self-actualization until the lower-level needs are met. Carl Rogers, the other major humanistic theorist, also focused on self-actualization as a major human motivation. According to Rogers, for a person to be self-actualized, the people in that person's life must set up conditions of worth that lead the person's developed self-concept to match her true self or they must give unconditional positive regard—acceptance and approval without conditions—which will allow the person to develop into her true self.

The social-cognitive approach to personality arose out of disenchantment with the rather narrow strict behavioral approach. Social-cognitive theorists agree that learning through conditioning is important, but that social learning (modeling) and cognitive processes are more important to the development of personality. For example, Albert Bandura proposed a self-system, a set of cognitive processes by which a person observes, evaluates, and regulates her behavior. Our sense of self-efficacy (our evaluation of our effectiveness in particular situations) is a key element in Bandura's theory for maintaining a healthy personality.

Julian Rotter's locus of control concept also demonstrates the importance of cognitive processing to psychological health. An external locus of control is the perception that chance or external forces beyond our personal control determine our fate. An internal locus of control is the perception that we control our own fate. People with an internal locus of control do better in school, are healthier, and are better able to cope with the stresses of life. To maintain positive self-evaluation, we also use self-serving bias in our explanations of our behavior. If the outcome of our behavior is positive, we take credit for it; if it is not, we do not. This bias is adaptive and protects us from depression. A pessimistic explanatory style—in which we take the blame for negative outcomes and not positive ones, and see these outcomes as both stable and global—is maladaptive and will likely lead to feelings of learned helplessness and depression.

ConceptCheck | 2

➤ **Explain which needs, according to Maslow, must be satisfied before a person can worry about self-actualization.**

➤ **Explain why, according to Rogers's self-concept theory, unconditional positive regard is important.**

➤ **Explain how the social-cognitive concepts of self-efficacy and locus of control are similar.**

Trait Theories of Personality and Personality Assessment

As we pointed out at the beginning of this chapter, personality **traits** are internally based, relatively stable characteristics that define an individual's personality. Traits are continuous dimensions, and people vary from each other along the dimensions for each of the various traits that make up personality. But what are the specific traits that make up human personality? Think about all of the adjectives that can describe a person. There are thousands, but this doesn't mean that thousands of traits are necessary to describe human personality. Trait theories attempt to discover exactly how many traits are necessary. You will be surprised to find out that the major trait theories propose that this number is rather small. How are such numbers derived?

Trait theorists use factor analysis (and other statistical techniques) to tell them how many basic personality factors

traits The relatively stable internally based characteristics that describe a person.

(or traits) are needed to describe human personality, as well as what these factors are. Remember, factor analysis is the statistical tool from Chapter 6 that we used to discuss the question of whether intelligence was one ability or many. Factor analysis identifies clusters of test items (in this case, on a personality test) that measure the same factor (trait). Allport and Odbert (1936) did the initial analyses, starting with 18,000 words that could be used to describe humans. Their analyses left them with around 200 clusters. Later trait researchers have reduced this number considerably; the consensus number of necessary traits is only five.

In this section, we'll consider two major trait theories that were developed using factor analysis, Hans Eysenck's three-factor theory and the Five Factor Model of personality. We'll also discuss personality assessment because personality tests are often developed to assess a theorist's proposed basic traits. The major uses for personality tests, however, are to diagnose personality problems, to aid in counseling, and to aid in making personnel decisions; therefore, we'll focus our discussion on the two main types of personality tests used, personality inventories and projective tests.

Trait Theories of Personality

According to trait theorists, basic traits are the building blocks of personality. Each trait is a dimension, a continuum ranging from one extreme of the dimension to the other. A person can fall at either extreme or anywhere in between on the continuum. An individual's personality stems from the amount of each trait that he has. This is analogous to the trichromatic theory of color vision that we discussed in Chapter 3. Remember that according to the trichromatic theory, all of the thousands of different colors that we can perceive stem from different proportions of the three primaries (red, green, and blue). In trait theories, all personalities stem from different proportions of the basic traits.

The number and kind of personality traits. Different theorists have come up with different answers to the question of how many basic personality traits there are and even what they are. For example, using factor analysis, early trait researcher Raymond B. Cattell found that 16 traits were necessary (Cattell, 1950, 1965). More recently, Hans Eysenck, also using factor analysis, has argued for only three trait dimensions (Eysenck, 1982; Eysenck & Eysenck, 1985). There are two major reasons for the different numbers—the level of abstraction and the type of data. First, the number of traits depends upon the level of abstraction in the factor analysis. For example, if you factored Cattell's 16 traits further, you would probably get something closer to Eysenck's three higher-order factors (Digman, 1990). This means that Eysenck's theory is at a more general and inclusive level of abstraction than Cattell's theory. More important, the number of traits depends upon which databases and what types of data different theorists use in their factor analysis. Different data could, of course, lead to different traits, as well as a different number of traits. Surprisingly, many contemporary trait researchers have reached something of a consensus about the number and the nature of the basic personality traits. These traits (or dimensions) are called the "Big Five." First, we'll discuss Eysenck's three-factor theory because he (unlike most trait theorists) proposes actual causal explanations for his traits, and then we'll discuss the Five Factor Model of personality.

Eysenck's three-factor theory. Hans Eysenck's three trait dimensions are extraversion–introversion, neuroticism–emotional stability, and psychoticism–impulse control. These are continuous dimensions, with extraversion, neuroticism, and psychoticism, respectively, at the high ends. Eysenck argues that these three traits are determined by heredity and proposes a biological basis for each one of them (Eysenck, 1990, 1997). Extraversion and introversion have their normal meanings, indicating differences in sociability. Extraverts are gregarious, outgoing people with lots of friends; introverts are those who are quiet, are more introspective, and tend to avoid social interaction. The biological basis for the extraversion–introversion trait is level of cortical arousal (neuronal activity). According to Eysenck, an introvert has a higher normal level of arousal in the brain than an extravert. The brains of introverts are more active. This means that an extravert has to seek out external stimulation in order to raise the level of arousal in the brain to a more optimal level.

People who are high on the neuroticism–emotional stability dimension tend to be overly anxious, emotionally unstable, and easily upset; people who are low tend to be calm and emotionally stable. Eysenck proposes differences in the sympathetic nervous system as the basis for this trait. People high on the neuroticism trait have more reactive sympathetic nervous systems. The psychoticism–impulse control trait dimension is concerned with aggressiveness, impulsiveness, empathy (seeing situations from other people's perspectives), and antisocial behavior. Eysenck assumes that a high level of testosterone and a low level of MAO, a neurotransmitter inhibitor, lead to behavior that is aggressive, impulsive, antisocial, and lacking in empathy.

Eysenck's very specific biological assumptions make his theory rather easy to test experimentally. This means that it has generated much research, and the findings have been somewhat supportive. However, most research seems to indicate that five factors, rather than three, are necessary (Funder, 2001; Goldberg, 1990; John, 1990; McCrae & Costa, 2003; Wiggins, 1996). Two of Eysenck's factors (extraversion–introversion and neuroticism–emotional stability) are among the five, and the third factor, psychoticism–impulse control, seems to be a combination of the remaining three factors. Let's see what the other three factors are.

The Five Factor Model of personality. The Five Factor Model of personality was formulated by Robert McCrae and Paul Costa (McCrae & Costa, 1999). The descriptions of the high and low ends of the five trait factors (called the Big Five) given in Table 8.3 (page 312) will give you a general understanding of the five proposed dimensions. To remember the five factors, try forming acronyms using their first letters. Order is not important. You could use OCEAN (Openness, Conscientiousness, Extraversion, Agreeableness, and Neuroticism) or CANOE (Conscientiousness, Agreeableness, Neuroticism, Openness, and Extraversion).

Table 8.3	The Big Five Personality Trait Dimensions
Dimension	**Description of High and Low Ends of Dimension**
Openness	High: independent, imaginative, broad interests, receptive to new ideas Low: conforming, practical, narrow interests, closed to new ideas
Conscientiousness	High: well-organized, dependable, careful, disciplined Low: disorganized, undependable, careless, impulsive
Extraversion	High: sociable, talkative, friendly, adventurous Low: reclusive, quiet, aloof, cautious
Agreeableness	High: sympathetic, polite, good-natured, soft-hearted Low: tough-minded, rude, irritable, ruthless
Neuroticism	High: emotional, insecure, nervous, self-pitying Low: calm, secure, relaxed, self-satisfied

(Similarly, you might use PEN to remember Eysenck's three traits, Psychoticism, Extraversion, and Neuroticism.)

Recent research indicates that these five factors are universal. They have been observed across gender, and in many diverse languages (such as English, Korean, and Turkish) and cultures (including American, Hispanic, European, African, and Asian cultures), and not just in Western industrialized societies (McCrae & Costa, 1997, 2001; Schmidt, Allik, McCrae, & Benet–Martinez, 2007). In addition, research has found that the five factors have about a 50% heritability rate across several cultures (Jang, Livesley, & Vernon, 1996; Loehlin, 1992; Loehlin, McCrae, Costa, & John, 1998), indicating a strong genetic basis. The Big Five factors also seem consistent from about age 30 to late adulthood (Costa & McCrae, 1988). Given the importance of the Big Five factors, Robert McCrae and Paul Costa have developed personality inventory assessment instruments, the NEO-PI-R, the NEO-PI-3, and the NEO-FFI, which provide personality profiles of these five factors (Costa & McCrae, 1985, 1992, 2008; McCrae, Costa, & Martin, 2005). To understand what a personality inventory test is like and how it differs from the better-known projective personality tests, we will consider personality assessment next.

Before going on to read about personality assessment, review Table 8.4, which summarizes all of the theoretical approaches to personality that we have discussed. Make sure that you know and understand the theorists and their key concepts.

Personality Assessment

Personality tests are a major tool in personality trait research, but the main uses of personality tests are to aid in diagnosing people with problems, in counseling, and in making personnel decisions. There are many types of personality tests, but we will focus on two, personality inventories and projective tests. Most of the other types of personality tests have more limited use. For example, Carl Rogers and humanistic

Table 8.4	Major Personality Theoretical Approaches	
Theoretical Approach	**Theorist**	**Key Concepts**
Psychoanalytic	Sigmund Freud	Id, ego, superego Conscious, preconscious, unconscious Pleasure principle, reality principle Defense mechanisms Psychosexual stages—oral, anal, phallic, latency, genital Erogenous zone, fixation
	Carl Jung	Collective unconscious, archetypes
	Alfred Adler	Striving for superiority, inferiority complex
	Karen Horney	Need for security, basic anxiety
Humanistic	Abraham Maslow	Hierarchy of needs, self-actualization
	Carl Rogers	Conditions of worth, unconditional positive regard, self-actualization
Social-cognitive	Albert Bandura	Self-system, self-efficacy
	Julian Rotter	Locus of control
Trait	Hans Eysenck	Three factors: Extraversion–Introversion Neuroticism–Emotional Stability Psychoticism–Impulse Control
	Robert McCrae and Paul Costa	Five Factor Model: Openness Conscientiousness Extraversion Agreeableness Neuroticism

psychologists have developed questionnaires that only address the self-concept, and Julian Rotter has developed a test that specifically assesses locus of control.

Personality inventories. A **personality inventory** is designed to measure multiple traits or, in some cases, disorders. It is a series of questions or statements for which the test taker must indicate whether they apply to him or not. The typical response format is True–False or Yes–No. Often a third response category of Can't Say or Uncertain is included. The assumption is that the person both can and will provide an accurate self-report. These tests include items dealing with specific behaviors, attitudes, interests, and values. We will discuss the MMPI, the Minnesota Multiphasic Personality Inventory (Hathaway & McKinley, 1943), revised to become the MMPI-2 in 1989 (Butcher, Dahlstrom, Graham, Tellegen, & Kaemmer, 1989). It is the most used personality test in the world (Weiner & Greene, 2008), and it has been translated into more than 100 languages.

The MMPI-2 uses a True–False–Cannot Say format with 567 simple statements (such as "I like to cook") and takes about 60 to 90 minutes to complete. Most of the statements

personality inventory An objective personality test that uses a series of questions or statements for which the test taker must indicate whether they apply to her or not.

are from the original MMPI. Some were reworded to update the item content and to eliminate sexist language, and most of the questions pertaining to religion and sexual practices were eliminated (Ben-Porath & Butcher, 1989). The MMPI was developed to be a measure of abnormal personality, with 10 clinical scales such as depression and schizophrenia. Many of the test statements have obvious connections to disorders, such as "I believe I am being plotted against," but many are just simple ordinary statements, such as "I am neither gaining or losing weight."

The MMPI test statements were chosen in the same way that Binet and Simon chose test items for their first valid test of intelligence (discussed in Chapter 6). Binet and Simon developed a large pool of possible test items and then chose only those items that differentiated fast and slow learners. Similarly, a large pool of possible test items (simple statements of all types) was developed and then only those items that were answered differently (by a representative sample of people suffering from a specific disorder versus a group of normal people) were chosen for the test. It didn't matter what each group responded and what the content of the statement happened to be; what mattered was that the two groups generally responded to the item in opposite ways. Thus, the test developers were only concerned with whether, and not why, the items were answered differently by the groups. This test construction method allowed the test developers to choose items that clearly identified the response patterns of people with 10 different disorders (such as depression and schizophrenia).

The MMPI and MMPI-2 are scored by a computer, which then generates a profile of the test taker on 10 clinical (disorder) scales. There are also test statements that comprise the basis for three validity scales, which attempt to detect test takers who are trying to cover up problems and fake profiles or who were careless in their responding. For example, there is a lie detection scale that assesses the extent to which the test taker is lying to create a particular test profile. The lie scale is based on responses to a set of test items such as "I get angry sometimes," to which most people would respond "True." The profile for a person consistently answering "False" to these questions would be invalidated.

Personality inventories like the MMPI are objective tests and are objectively scored by a computer. The computer converts the test taker's responses into a personality profile for the trait or disorder dimensions that the test is measuring. This is why the MMPI has been so popular in clinical settings for making diagnoses of personality problems. Its test construction method leads to good predictive validity for its clinical scales and its objective scoring procedure leads to reliability in interpretation. Projective personality tests, which we will discuss next, do not have good validity or reliability, but are widely used.

projective test A personality test that uses a series of ambiguous stimuli to which the test taker must respond about her perceptions of the stimuli.

Projective tests. The chances are that when personality tests are mentioned, you think of the Rorschach Inkblots Test, a projective personality test. In contrast with personality inventories, a **projective test** is a series of ambiguous stimuli, such as inkblots, to which the test taker must respond about his perceptions of the stimuli. An objective response format is not used. Test takers are asked to describe the stimulus or tell a story about it. We will discuss the two most used projective tests, the Rorschach Inkblots and the Thematic Apperception Test (TAT).

Projective tests aren't administered, scored, or interpreted in the same way as the MMPI, MMPI-2, and other objective personality inventories. They are not as objective, especially with respect to interpretation.

The most popular and widely used projective test is the Rorschach Inkblots Test (often referred to as The Rorschach), which Swiss psychiatrist Hermann Rorschach developed in 1921. There are only 10 symmetric inkblots used in the test, five in black ink on a white background and five in black and red ink on a white background. The test taker is asked what he sees in each inkblot, though the inkblots are ambiguous and have no inherent meaning. The examiner then goes through the cards and asks the test taker to clarify his responses by identifying the various parts of the inkblot that led to the response.

The assumption is that the test taker's responses are projections of his personal conflicts and personality dynamics. This means that the test taker's responses have to be interpreted, which makes the test scoring subjective and creates great variability among test scorers. In fact, one could view the test scorer's interpretations as projections themselves. The Rorschach Inkblots Test is widely used (Watkins, Campbell, Nieberding, & Hallmark, 1995), but it has yet to be demonstrated that this test is either reliable or valid (Dawes, 1994; Lilienfeld, Wood, & Garb, 2000), leading some researchers to call for a moratorium on its use (Garb, 1999).

A Simulation of a Rorschach Inkblot

Now let's consider another popular projective test, the Thematic Apperception Test (TAT), developed by Henry Murray and his colleagues in the 1930s (Morgan & Murray, 1935). The TAT consists of 31 cards (the original version had only 20), 30 with black and white pictures of ambiguous settings and one blank card (the ultimate in ambiguity). Only 10 or so of the 31 cards are used in an individual testing session. The test taker is told that this is a storytelling test and that for each picture he has to make up a story. He is to tell what has happened before, what is happening now, what

A TAT Card

the people are feeling and thinking, and how things will turn out. In scoring these responses, the scorer looks for recurring themes in the feelings, relationships, and motives of the characters in the created stories. Like the Rorschach Inkblots Test, however, it has yet to be demonstrated that the TAT scoring (interpretation) is either reliable or valid (Lilienfeld, Wood, & Garb, 2000). You are probably wondering why these two projective tests are so popular if neither has demonstrated reliability or validity. Therapists who use them believe that such tests allow them to explore aspects of the test taker's personality that the reliable and valid objective personality tests do not. These therapists tend to be psychoanalysts who believe projections are meaningful; therefore, the tests' subjective nature is not problematic for them.

Section Summary

The trait approach to personality attempts to identify the basic traits (dimensions) we need to describe human personality. These traits are the building blocks of personality. Given the basic traits, each person's personality can be viewed as her unique combination of values on these basic personality dimensions. Using factor analysis and other statistical techniques, trait theorists have proposed theories with varying numbers of basic dimensions. For example, Hans Eysenck has proposed three dimensions—psychoticism, extraversion, and neuroticism. Recent trait research indicates that five factors (the "Big Five"—openness, conscientiousness, extraversion, agreeableness, and neuroticism) are necessary. These five factors seem to be stable throughout adulthood and universal across gender and many diverse languages and cultures.

To assess personality, psychologists make use of two types of tests—personality inventories and projective tests. A personality inventory is a set of questions or statements for which the test taker must indicate whether they apply to her or not. Such objective tests usually employ a True–False–Cannot Say format. The most used personality inventory is the MMPI/MMPI-2. These tests have predictive validity for diagnosing personality problems on 10 clinical scales since the items on these tests were chosen because they differentiated normal people from people diagnosed with the 10 disorders. Projective tests are more subjective tests in which the test taker must respond about her perceptions of a series of ambiguous stimuli. The assumption is that the test taker's responses are projections of her personal conflicts and personality dynamics. Though widely used, projective tests, such as the Rorschach Inkblots Test and the TAT, have yet to be shown to be reliable or valid.

ConceptCheck | 3

▶ Explain why factor analysis can lead to different numbers of basic personality dimensions.

▶ Explain how the test construction method used to develop the MMPI ensures predictive validity for the test.

Chapter Key Terms

You should know the definitions of the following key terms from the chapter. They are listed in the order in which they appear in the chapter. For those you do not know, return to the relevant section of the chapter to learn them. When you think that you know all of the terms, complete the matching exercise based on these key terms.

personality
conscious mind
preconscious mind
unconscious mind
id
pleasure principle
ego
reality principle
superego
defense mechanism
erogenous zone
fixation

oral stage of
   psychosexual development
anal stage of
   psychosexual development
phallic stage of psychosexual
   development
Oedipus conflict
identification
latency stage of psychosexual
   development
genital stage of psychosexual
   development
hierarchy of needs

self-actualization
conditions of worth
unconditional positive regard
self-system
self-efficacy
external locus of control
internal locus of control
learned helplessness
attribution
self-serving bias
traits
personality inventory
projective test

Key Terms Exercise

Identify the correct term for each of the following definitions. The answers to this exercise follow the answers to the Concept Checks at the end of the chapter.

1. A process used by the ego to distort reality and protect a person from anxiety.

   _____

2. Unconditional acceptance and approval of a person by others.

   _____

3. A judgment of one's effectiveness in dealing with particular situations.

   _____

4. The third psychosexual stage in Freud's theory (from 3 to 6 years) in which the

erogenous zone is located at the genitals, and the child derives pleasure from genital stimulation.

   _____

5. The principle of finding gratification for instinctual drives within the constraints of reality (norms of society).

   _____

6. The part of the personality that a person is born with and that contains the biological instinctual drives and is located in the unconscious mind.

   _____

7. The process by which children adopt the characteristics of the same-sex parent and learn their gender role and sense of morality.

   _____

8. The tendency to make attributions so that one can perceive oneself favorably.

_____

9. A personality test that uses a series of ambiguous stimuli to which the test takers must respond about their perceptions of the stimuli.

_____

10. The perception that chance or external forces beyond your personal control determine your fate.

_____

11. Freud's term for the area of the body where the id's pleasure-seeking energies are focused during a particular stage of psychosexual development.

_____

12. The behaviors and attitudes for which other people, starting with our parents, will give us positive regard.

_____

13. Freud's term for what is stored in your memory that you are not presently aware of but can access.

_____

14. The process by which we explain our own behavior and that of others.

_____

15. Freud's term for the part of the personality that represents one's conscience and idealized standards of behavior.

_____

Practice Test Questions

The following are practice multiple-choice test questions on some of the chapter content. The answers are given after the Key Terms Exercise answers at the end of the chapter. If you guessed or incorrectly answered a question, restudy the relevant section of the chapter.

1. According to Freud, the _____, the executive of the personality, is located _____.
   a. ego; entirely in the unconscious
   b. ego; in all three levels of awareness
   c. superego; entirely in the unconscious
   d. superego; in all three levels of awareness

2. A woman has unacceptable feelings of hatred toward her mother, but lavishes attention and love on her. Freud would say that this is an example of _____.
   a. projection
   b. reaction formation
   c. displacement
   d. sublimation

3. Which of the following neo-Freudian theorists proposed "striving for superiority" as the primary motivation for personality development?
   a. Carl Jung
   b. Karen Horney
   c. Alfred Adler
   d. Erik Erikson

4. In Maslow's hierarchy of needs, _____ needs are at the bottom of the hierarchy, and _____ needs are at the top.
   a. physiological; self-actualization
   b. self-actualization; physiological
   c. safety; belonging and love
   d. belonging and love; safety

5. In Rogers's self theory, which of the following contributes greatly to one's self-actualization?
   a. conditional positive regard
   b. unconditional positive regard
   c. an internal locus of control
   d. an external locus of control

6. "Self-efficacy" is the answer to which of the following questions?
   a. What is the fullest realization of a person's potential?
   b. What is a sense of one's effectiveness in dealing with a particular situation?

c. What is the perception that you control your own fate?

d. What is the tendency to make attributions so that one can view one's self favorably?

7. After losing a tennis match, which of the following comments is a person most likely to make if self-serving bias is operating?

   a. "I should have practiced more."

   b. "I made too many unforced errors."

   c. "My opponent had the advantage of playing on his home court."

   d. "My mental concentration was lacking."

8. Which of the following theoretical approaches uses factor analysis to determine the number of factors necessary to describe human personality?

   a. the psychoanalytic approach

   b. the trait approach

   c. the humanistic approach

   d. the social-cognitive approach

9. Which one of Eysenck's three personality factors is not one of the "Big Five" factors?

   a. openness

   b. neuroticism

   c. psychoticism

   d. agreeableness

10. Which of the following personality tests uses True–False items and generates a profile of the test taker on 10 clinical scales?

    a. MMPI-2

    b. Rorschach Inkblots Test

    c. TAT

    d. all of the above

11. According to social-cognitive personality theorists, which of the following is least likely to lead to depression?

    a. low sense of self-esteem

    b. self-serving bias

    c. external locus of control

    d. learned helplessness

12. Which of the following trait dimensions is one of the "Big Five" personality dimensional labels?

    a. Aggressiveness

    b. Effectiveness

    c. Cheerfulness

    d. Openness

13. Inferiority complex is to basic anxiety as _____ is to _____.

    a. Adler; Horney

    b. Horney; Adler

    c. Jung; Horney

    d. Horney; Jung

14. Imagine a patient who was just diagnosed with a serious illness. According to Julian Rotter, if the patient has a strong internal locus of control, what is the patient's most likely response to the situation?

    a. "Whatever happens, it is in God's hands."

    b. "I'll just do what the doctor says and trust his judgment."

    c. "Whether I make it or not is just a matter of luck."

    d. "I want to learn about this illness and work to fight it."

15. Glenn's room looks like a tornado hit it. He is incredibly messy. His car is filled with old pizza boxes, last month's newspapers, and dirty laundry. According to Freud, Glenn is most likely fixated at the _____ stage.

    a. phallic

    b. oral

    c. anal

    d. genital

Chapter Concept Check Answers
Concept Check I 1

- According to Freud, the ego is the executive of the personality in that it must find acceptable ways within reality (society's norms) and the constraints of the superego to satisfy the instinctual drives of the id.

Finding such ways is not easy, and the ego may not be able to do its job.

- In reaction formation, the ego transforms the unacceptable impulses and behavior into their opposites; in projection they are projected onto other people. For example, consider thoughts of homosexuality in a man. In reaction formation, the man would become just the opposite in his behavior, romantically overly interested in the opposite sex. However, in projection, the homosexual feelings would be projected onto other men. He would see homosexual tendencies in other men and think they were gay, but he would not think this about himself.

- According to Freud, as a child progresses through the first three psychosexual stages (oral, anal, and phallic), he may become fixated in a stage when there is an unresolved conflict in that stage. If fixated, part of the id's pleasure-seeking energy remains at that erogenous zone and continues throughout a person's life. Thus, it will show up in the child's adult personality. For example, anal fixations will lead to the anal retentive and expulsive personality types.

Concept Check | 2

- In Maslow's hierarchy of needs, physiological, safety, belonging and love, and esteem needs have to be satisfied before the highest level need for self-actualization can be met.

- Positive regard for a person should be unconditional so that the person is free to develop her true self and thus work toward self-actualization. If our positive regard for a person is conditionalized (we set up conditions of worth for that person), then the person develops a self-concept of what others think she should be. This self may be very different from the person's true self and thus prevent self-actualization.

- Both self-efficacy and locus of control are cognitive judgments about our effectiveness in dealing with the situations that occur in our lives. Whereas self-efficacy is a person's judgment of his effectiveness in dealing with particular situations, locus of control is a more global judgment of how much a person controls what happens to him. Both a low general sense of self-efficacy and an external locus of control (i.e., the perception that forces beyond one's control determine one's fate) often lead to depression.

Concept Check | 3

- There are two major reasons that factor analysis can lead to different numbers of basic personality dimensions. The first concerns the level of abstraction at which a theorist uses the analysis. Some theorists have used a level of analysis in which some of the dimensions are still correlated (Cattell); others (Eysenck) have used higher-order factors that are not correlated. Thus, theorists may use different levels of inclusiveness, with those using more global levels leading to fewer factors. Second, and independent of level of abstraction, is what data are being analyzed. Different theorists have examined different databases. Obviously, varying input will lead to varying results even with the same type of analysis.

- The test construction method used to develop the MMPI involves only choosing test items that clearly differentiate the responding of two distinct groups. In the case of the MMPI, test items were chosen that were responded to differently by representative samples of people with 1 of 10 different disorders versus normal people. Thus, predictive validity is ensured because only test items that definitely differentiate test takers according to the purpose of the test are chosen. In the case of the MMPI, this means that various clinical personality problems, such as depression or schizophrenia, can be detected by comparing a test taker's response pattern to those of the disordered groups.

Answers to Key Terms Exercise

1. defense mechanism
2. unconditional positive regard
3. self-efficacy
4. phallic stage of psychosexual development

5. reality principle

6. id

7. identification

8. self-serving bias

9. projective test

10. external locus of control

11. erogenous zone

12. conditions of worth

13. preconscious

14. attribution

15. superego

Answers to Practice Test Questions

1. b; ego; in all three levels of awareness

2. b; reaction formation

3. c; Alfred Adler

4. a; physiological; self-actualization

5. b; unconditional positive regard

6. b; What is a sense of one's effectiveness in dealing with a particular situation?

7. c; "My opponent had the advantage of playing on his home court."

8. b; the trait approach

9. c; psychoticism

10. a; MMPI-2

11. b; self-serving bias

12. d; Openness

13. a; Adler; Horney

14. d; "I want to learn about this illness and work to fight it."

15. c; anal

9

Social Psychology

H umans are social animals. We affect each other's thoughts and actions, and how we do so is the topic of this chapter. This research area is called **social psychology**—the scientific study of how we influence one another's behavior and thinking. To understand what is meant by such social influence, we'll consider two real-world incidents in which social forces influenced behavior, and then, later in the chapter, we'll return to each incident to see how social psychologists explain them.

■ **social psychology** The scientific study of how we influence one another's behavior and thinking.

The first incident is the brutal murder of Kitty Genovese in New York City in 1964 (briefly discussed in Chapter 1). Kitty Genovese was returning home from work late one night, when she was attacked in front of her apartment building. The attack was a prolonged one over a half-hour period in which the attacker left and came back more than once. Kitty screamed for help and struggled with the knife-wielding attacker, but no help was forthcoming. Some apartment residents saw the attack and others heard her screams and pleas for help. Exactly how many residents witnessed the attack is not clear. Initially reported as 38 in *The New York Times* report, more recent analysis of the available archival evidence indicates that the number was somewhat less (Manning, Levine, & Collins, 2007). The struggle between Kitty and her attacker continued for 35 minutes before he finally fatally stabbed her. Her cries for help went unanswered. Someone finally called the police after the attacker had left, but it was too late. What social forces kept these people from acting sooner, so that Kitty Genovese's life might have been spared? Media accounts blamed apathy in the big city (Rosenthal, 1964). Social psychological researchers, however, provide a very different explanation. We will describe this explanation in the section on social influence when we discuss bystander intervention.

The second incident occurred in 1978, when over 900 people who were members of Reverend Jim Jones's Peoples Temple religious cult in Jonestown, Guyana (South America), committed mass suicide by drinking cyanide-laced Kool-Aid (though some sources say it was Flavor-Aid, a drink mix similar to Kool-Aid). These were Americans who had moved with Jones from San Francisco to Jonestown in 1977. Jonestown parents not only drank the poisoned Kool-Aid, but they also gave it to their infant children to drink. Strangely, the mass suicide occurred in a fairly orderly fashion as one person after another drank the poison. Hundreds of people went into convulsions and died within minutes. What social forces made so few of these people willing to disobey Reverend Jones's command for this unified act of mass suicide? We will return to this question in the social influence section when we discuss obedience.

The New York Times Photo Archives/Redux

Kitty Genovese

What if you had been one of those people who witnessed Kitty Genovese's murder? Would you have intervened or called the police? If you are like most people, you probably think that you would have done so. However, none of the witnesses to the attack did so until it was too late. Similarly, most people would probably say that they would not have drunk the poison at Jonestown. However, the vast majority did so. Why is there this discrepancy between what we say we would do and what we actually do? Social psychologists would say that when we just think about what our behavior would be in such a situation, we are not subject to the social forces that are operating in the actual situation. If you're in the situation, however, social forces are operating and may guide your behavior in a different way. In summary, situational social forces greatly influence our behavior and thinking. Keep this in mind as we discuss various types of social influence and social thinking.

How Others Influence Our Behavior

Social influence research examines how other people and the social forces they create influence an individual's behavior. There are many types of social influence, including conformity, compliance, obedience, and group influences. In this section, we will discuss all of these types of social influence. We start with conformity.

Why We Conform

Conformity is usually defined as a change in behavior, belief, or both to conform to a group norm as a result of real or imagined group pressure. The word "conformity" has a negative connotation. We don't like to be thought of as conformists. However, conformity research indicates that humans have a strong tendency to conform. To understand the two major types of social influence leading to conformity (informational social influence and normative social influence), we'll consider two classic studies on conformity: Muzafer Sherif's study using the autokinetic effect and Solomon Asch's study using a line-length judgment task.

The Sherif study and informational social influence. In Sherif's study, the participants thought that they were part of a visual perception experiment (Sherif, 1937). Participants in completely dark rooms were exposed to a stationary point of light and asked to estimate the distance the light moved. Thanks to an illusion called the autokinetic effect, a stationary point of light appears to move in a dark room because there is no frame of reference and our eyes spontaneously move. How far and in what direction the light appears to move varies widely among different people. During the first session in Sherif's study, each participant was alone in the dark room when making his judgments. Then, during the next three sessions, he was in the room with two other participants and could hear the others' estimates of the illusory light movement. What happened?

The average of the individual estimates varied greatly during the first session. Over the next three group sessions, however, the individual estimates converged on a common group norm. See Figure 9.1. All of the participants in the group ended up making the same estimates. What do you think would happen if you brought the participants back a year later and had them make estimates again while alone? Would their estimates regress back to their earlier individual estimates or stay

conformity A change in behavior, belief, or both to conform to a group norm as a result of real or imagined group pressure.

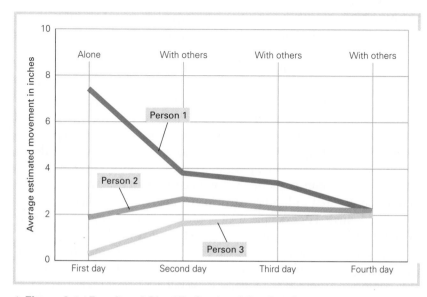

▲ **Figure 9.1** | Results of Sherif's Study of Conformity | When the three participants in Sherif's study were alone in the laboratory room on the first day, their estimates of the apparent movement of the stationary point of light varied greatly. However, once they were all together in the laboratory room from the second through the fourth day and could hear each other, their estimates converged. By the fourth day, they were all making the same judgments. (Adapted from Sherif & Sherif, 1969, p. 209.)

at the group norm? Surprisingly, they stay at the group norm (Rohrer, Baron, Hoffman, & Wander, 1954).

To understand why conformity was observed in Sherif's study, we need to consider **informational social influence.** This effect stems from our desire to be right in situations in which the correct action or judgment is not obvious and we need information. In Sherif's study, participants needed information because of the illusory nature of the judgment; thus their conformity was due to informational social influence. When a task is ambiguous or difficult and we want to be correct, we look to others for information. But what about conformity when information about the correct way to proceed is not needed? To understand this type of conformity, we need to consider Asch's study on line-length judgment and normative social influence.

The Asch study and normative social influence. Student participants in Asch's study made line-length judgments similar to the one in Figure 9.2 on page 326 (Asch, 1955). These line-length judgments are easy. If participants are alone when making these judgments, they don't make mistakes.

▌ **informational social influence**
Influence stemming from the need for information in situations in which the correct action or judgment is uncertain.

Solomon Asch

▲ **Figure 9.2** | **An Example of Asch's Line-Length Judgment Task** | The task is to judge which one of the comparison lines (1, 2, or 3) is the same length as the standard line on the left.

But in Asch's study, they were not alone. There were others in the room who were Asch's student confederates but who were playing the role of participants. Across various conditions in the study, the number of confederate participants varied from 1 to 15. On each trial, judgments were made orally, and Asch structured the situation so that confederate participants responded before the actual participant. Seating was arranged so that the actual participant was the next to last to respond. The confederate participants purposely made judgmental errors on certain trials. Asch wondered what the actual participant would do when confronted with other participants unanimously voicing an obviously incorrect judgment. For example, if all of the other participants said that "1" was the answer to the sample judgment in Figure 9.2, what would you say?

Surprisingly, a large number of the actual participants conformed to the obviously incorrect judgments offered by the confederates. About 75 percent of the participants conformed some of the time, and overall, participants conformed 37 percent of the time. Asch's results have been replicated many times and in many different countries (Bond & Smith, 1996). The correct answers are clear in the Asch judgment task, and there are no obvious reasons to conform. The students in the experimental room didn't know each other, and they were all of the same status. The judgment task was incredibly easy. Why, then, was conformity observed?

The reason for the conformity in Asch's study is **normative social influence,** an effect stemming from our desire to gain the approval and to avoid the disapproval of others. We change our behavior to meet the expectations of others and to get the acceptance of others. This is going along with the crowd. Let's think about how we could change Asch's experiment so that conformity stemmed more from informational social influence than from normative social influence. What

▌ **normative social influence** Influence stemming from our desire to gain the approval and to avoid the disapproval of others.

William Vandivert/Scientific American

Asch's Conformity Study This is a photograph taken from one of Asch's conformity experiments. The student in the middle (#6) is the actual participant. The other participants are confederates of the experimenter. As you can see, the actual participant is perplexed by the obviously incorrect responses of the confederate participants on this trial.

if the line-length judgments were all extremely difficult, and the correct answers were not clear? In this case then, the conformity would probably be even higher due to informational social influence.

Situational factors that impact conformity. Asch and other conformity researchers have found many situational factors that affect whether we conform. Let's consider three. (1) Unanimity of the group is important. It's difficult to be a minority of one, but not two. For example, Asch found that the amount of conformity drops considerably if just one of the confederate participants gives an answer—right or wrong—that differs from the rest of the group. (2) The mode of responding (voting aloud versus secret ballot) is also important. In Asch's study, if the actual participant did not have to respond aloud after hearing the group's responses, but rather could write her response, the amount of conformity dropped dramatically. So, in the various groups to which you belong, be sure to use secret ballots when voting on issues if you want the true opinions of your group members. (3) Finally, more conformity is observed from a person who is of lesser status than the other group members or is attracted to the group and wants to be a part of it. These situational factors are especially effective in driving conformity when there is a probationary period for attaining group membership.

Why We Comply

Conformity is a form of social influence in which people change their behavior or attitudes in order to adhere to a group norm. **Compliance** is acting in accordance to a direct request from another person or group. Think about how often others— your parents, roommates, friends, salespeople, and so on—make requests of you. Social psychologists have identified many different techniques that help others to achieve compliance with such requests. Salespeople, fundraisers, politicians, and anyone else who wants to get people to say "yes" use these compliance techniques. After reading this section you should be much more aware of how other people— especially salespeople—attempt to get you to comply with their requests. Of course, you'll also be better equipped to get other people to comply with your requests. As we discuss these compliance techniques, note how each one involves two requests, and how it is the second request with which the person wants compliance. We'll start our discussion with a compliance technique that you have probably encountered—the foot-in-the-door technique.

The foot-in-the-door technique. In the **foot-in-the-door technique,** compliance to a large request is gained by preceding it with a very small request. The tendency is for people who have complied with the small request to comply with the next, larger request. The principle is simply to start small and build. One classic experimental demonstration of this technique involved a large, ugly sign about driving carefully (Freedman & Fraser, 1966). People were asked directly if this ugly sign could be put in their front yards, and the vast majority of them refused. However, the

> **compliance** Acting in accordance with a direct request from another person or group.

> **foot-in-the-door technique** Compliance to a large request is gained by preceding it with a very small request.

majority of the people who had complied with a much smaller request 2 weeks earlier (for example, to sign a safe-driving petition) agreed to have the sign put in their yard. The smaller request had served as the "foot in the door." Then, when these people were approached later about the bigger request (the large, ugly sign), most of them complied with the request to put the sign in their yard.

In another study, people who were first asked to wear a pin publicizing a cancer fundraising drive were far more likely to donate to the cancer charity when asked later than were people who were asked only to contribute to the charity (Pliner, Hart, Kohl, & Saari, 1974). Why does the foot-in-the-door technique work? Its success seems to be partially due to our behavior (complying with the initial request) affecting our attitudes to be more positive about helping and to view ourselves as generally charitable people. In addition, once we have made a commitment (such as signing a safe-driving petition), we feel pressure to remain consistent (putting up the large ugly sign) with this earlier commitment.

This technique was used by the Communist Chinese during the Korean War on prisoners of war to help brainwash them about Communism (Ornstein, 1991). Many prisoners returning after the war had praise for the Chinese Communists. This attitude had been cultivated by having the prisoners first do small things like writing out some questions and then the pro-Communist answers, which they might just copy from a notebook, and maybe later writing essays in the guise of students summarizing the Communist position on various issues such as poverty. Just as the participants' attitudes changed in the Freedman and Fraser study and they later agreed to put the big, ugly sign in their yard, the POWs became more sympathetic to the Communist cause. The foot-in-the-door technique is a very powerful technique. Watch out for compliance requests of increasing size. Say no before it is too late to do so.

The door-in-the-face technique. The door-in-the-face technique is the opposite of the foot-in-the-door technique (Cialdini, Vincent, Lewis, Catalan, Wheeler, & Danby, 1975). In the **door-in-the-face technique,** compliance is gained by starting with a large, unreasonable request that is turned down and following it with a more reasonable, smaller request. The person who is asked to comply appears to be slamming the door in the face of the person making the large request. It is the smaller request, however, that the person making the two requests wants all along. For example, imagine that one of your friends asked you to watch his pet for a month while he is out of town. You refuse. Then your friend asks for what he really wanted, which was for you to watch the pet over the following weekend. You agree. What has happened? You've succumbed to the door-in-the-face technique.

The success of the door-in-the-face technique is probably due to our tendency toward reciprocity, making mutual concessions. The person making the requests appears to have made a concession by moving to the much smaller request, so shouldn't we reciprocate and comply with this smaller request? Fear that others won't view us as fair, helpful, and concerned for others likely also plays a role in this compliance technique's success. The door-in-the-face

door-in-the-face technique
Compliance is gained by starting with a large, unreasonable request that is turned down and following it with a more reasonable, smaller request.

technique seems to have even been involved in G. Gordon Liddy getting the Watergate burglary approved by the Committee to Reelect the President, CREEP (Cialdini, 1993). The committee approved Liddy's plan with a bare bones $250,000 budget after they had disapproved plans with $1 million and $500,000 proposed budgets. The only committee person who opposed acceptance had not been present for the previous two more costly proposal meetings. Thus, he was able to see the irrationality of the plan and was not subject to the door-in-the-face reciprocity influence felt by other committee members.

The low-ball technique. Consider the following scenario (Cialdini, 1993). You go to buy a new car. The salesperson gives you a great price, much better than you ever imagined. You go into the salesperson's office and start filling out the sales forms and arranging for financing. The salesperson then says that before completing the forms, she forgot that she has to get approval from her sales manager. She leaves for a few minutes and returns looking rather glum. She says regretfully that the sales manager said that he couldn't give you that great price you thought you had. The sales price has to be a higher one. What do most people do in this situation? You probably are thinking that you wouldn't buy the car. However, research on this compliance tactic, called the low-ball technique, indicates that it does work (Cialdini, Cacioppo, Bassett, & Miller, 1978).

In the **low-ball technique,** compliance to a costly request is achieved by first getting compliance to an attractive, less costly request and then reneging on it. This is similar to the foot-in-the-door technique in that a second larger request is the one desired. In the low-ball technique, however, the first request is one that is very attractive to you. You are not making a concession (as in the foot-in-the-door technique), but rather getting a good deal. However, the "good" part of the deal is then taken away. Why does the low-ball technique work? The answer is that many of us feel obligated to go through with the deal after we have agreed to the earlier deal (request) even if the deal has changed for the worse. This is similar to the pressure to remain consistent in our commitment that helps drive the foot-in-the-door technique. So remember, if somebody tries to use the low-ball technique on you, walk away. You are not obligated to comply with the new request.

■ **low-ball technique** Compliance to a costly request is gained by first getting compliance to an attractive, less costly request but then reneging on it.

that's-not-all technique Compliance to a planned second request with additional benefits is gained by presenting this request before a response can be made to a first request.

The that's-not-all technique. There's another compliance technique, which is often used in television infomercials. Just after the price for the product is given and before you can decide yes or no about it, the announcer says, "But wait, that's not all, there's more," and the price is lowered or more merchandise is included to sweeten the deal, or both. Sometimes an initial price is not even given. Rather, the announcer says something like, "How much would you pay for this incredible product?" and then goes on to sweeten the deal before you can answer. As in the low-ball technique, the final offer is the one that was planned from the start. However, you are more likely to comply and take the deal after all of the build up than if this "better" deal were offered directly (Burger, 1986). This technique is called the **that's-not-all technique**—to gain compliance, a planned second request with additional benefits is made before a response to a first request can be made. Like the door-in-the-face technique, salespeople also use this technique. For example, before you can answer yes or no to a price offered by a car salesperson, he throws in some "bonus options" for the car. As in the door-in-the-face technique, reciprocity is at work here. The seller has made a concession (the bonus options), so shouldn't you reciprocate by taking the offer, complying? We often do.

In summary, each of these compliance techniques involves two requests (see Table 9.1). In the foot-in-the-door technique, a small request is followed by a larger request. In the door-in-the-face technique, a large request is followed by a smaller request. In the low-ball technique, an attractive first request is taken back and followed by a less-attractive request. In the that's-not-all technique, a more attractive request is made before a response can be given to an initial request. In all cases, the person making the requests is attempting to manipulate you with the first request. It is the second request for which compliance is desired. The foot-in-the-door and low-ball techniques both lead to commitment to the first request with the hope that the person will feel pressure to remain true to his initial commitment and accede to the second request. The other two techniques involve reciprocity. Once the other person has made a concession (accepted our refusal in the door-in-the-face technique) or done us a favor (an even better deal in the that's-not-all technique), we think we should reciprocate and accede to the second request.

Table 9.1 Four Compliance Techniques			
Technique	**1st Request**	**2nd Request**	**Major Reason for Compliance**
Foot-in-the-door	Small	Larger	Consistency
Door-in-the-face	Large	Smaller	Reciprocity
Low-ball	Attractive	Less attractive	Consistency
That's-not-all	Attractive	More attractive	Reciprocity

Why We Obey

Compliance is agreeing to a request from a person. **Obedience** is following the commands of a person in authority. Obedience is sometimes constructive and beneficial to us. It would be difficult for a society to exist, for instance, without obedience to its laws. Young children need to obey their caretakers for their own well-being. Obedience can also be destructive, though. There are many real-world examples of its destructive nature. Consider Nazi Germany, in which millions of innocent people were murdered, or the My Lai massacre in Vietnam, in which American soldiers killed hundreds of innocent children, women, and old people. In the My Lai massacre, the soldiers were ordered to shoot the innocent villagers, and they did. The phrase, "I was only following orders" usually surfaces in such cases. When confronted with these atrocities, we wonder what type of person could do such horrible things. Often, however, it's the situational social forces, and not the person, that should bear more of the responsibility for the actions. Just as we have learned that situational factors lead us to conform and comply, we will find that such social forces can lead us to commit such acts of destructive obedience.

> ▮ **obedience** Following the commands of a person in authority.

Milgram's basic experimental paradigm. The experiments that point to social forces as causes of destructive obedience—probably the most famous and controversial ones in psychology—are Stanley Milgram's obedience studies done at Yale University in the early 1960s (Milgram, 1963, 1965, 1974). We will describe Milgram's experimental paradigm and findings in more detail than usual. It is also worth noting that Milgram was one of Asch's graduate students and actually got the initial idea for his obedience studies from conducting some of Asch's conformity studies (Blass, 2004). What exactly did Milgram do?

First, let's consider Milgram's basic experimental procedure from the perspective of a participant in this study. Imagine that you have volunteered to be in an experiment on learning and memory. You show up at the assigned time and place, where you encounter two men, the experimenter and another participant, a middle-age man. The experimenter explains that the study is examining the effects of punishment by electric shock on learning, specifically learning a list of word pairs (for example, blue—box). When tested, the learner would have to indicate for each of the first words in the word pairs, which of four words had originally been paired with it. He would press one of four switches, which would light up one of the four answer boxes located on top of the shock generator. The experimenter further explains that one participant will be the teacher and the other the learner. You draw slips for the two roles, and the other participant draws "learner," making you the teacher. You accompany the learner to an adjoining room where he is strapped into a chair with one arm hooked up to the shock generator in the other room. The shock levels in the experiment will range from 15 volts to 450 volts. The experimenter explains that high levels of shock need to be used in order for the study to be a valid test of its effectiveness as punishment. The experimenter gives you a sample shock of 45 volts so that you have some idea of the intensity of the various shock levels.

Courtesy of CUNY Graduate School and University Center

Stanley Milgram

You return to the other room with the experimenter and sit down at the shock generator, which has a switch for each level of shock, starting at 15 volts and going up to 450 volts in 15-volt increments. There are also some labels below the switches—"Slight Shock," "Very Strong Shock," "Danger: Severe Shock," and, under the last two switches, "XXX" in red. The experimenter reminds you that when the learner makes a mistake on the word pair task, you are to administer the shock by pushing the appropriate switch. You are to start with 15 volts and increase the shock level by 15 volts for each wrong answer.

The experiment begins, and the learner makes errors. Nothing else happens except for a few "Ugh!"s until at 120 volts the learner cries out that the shocks really hurt. As the shock level increases, you continue hearing him cry out, and his screams escalate with the increasing voltage (see Table 9.2). At higher levels, he protests and says that he no longer wants to participate and that he isn't going to respond anymore. After 330 volts, he doesn't respond. You turn to the experimenter to see what to do. The experimenter says to treat a nonresponse as a wrong answer and to continue with the experiment. The learner never responds again.

Table 9.2	Examples of the Learner's Protests in Milgram's Obedience Experiments with Escalated Vocal Protests
120 volts	Ugh! Hey, *this* really hurts.
150 volts	Ugh!!! Experimenter! That's all. Get me out of here. I told you I had heart trouble. My heart's starting to bother me now. Get me out of here, please. My heart's starting to bother me. I refuse to go on. Let me out.
210 volts	Ugh!! Experimenter! Get me out of here. I've had enough. I won't be in the experiment any more.
270 volts	(*Agonized scream.*) Let me out of here. Let me out of here. Let me out of here. Let me out. Do you hear? Let me out of here.
300 volts	(*Agonized scream.*) I absolutely refuse to answer any more. Get me out of here. You can't hold me here. Get me out. Get me out of here.
315 volts	(*Intensely agonized scream.*) I told you I refuse to answer. I'm no longer part of this experiment.
330 volts	(*Intense and prolonged agonized scream.*) Let me out of here. Let me out of here. My heart's bothering me. Let me out, I tell you. (*Hysterically*) Let me out of here. Let me out of here. You have no right to hold me here. Let me out! Let me out! Let me out! Let me out of here! Let me out! Let me out!

For the complete schedule of protests, see Milgram (1974), pp. 56–57.

These photos from Milgram's
obedience studies show the
shock generator that the
teacher used and the learner
being strapped into a chair
and fitted with electrodes.

This is basically the situation that Milgram's participants confronted. What would you do? If you are like most people, you say you would stop at a rather low level of shock. Before this experiment was conducted, Milgram asked various types of people (college students, nonstudent adults, and psychiatrists) what they thought they and other people would do. Inevitably, the response was that they would stop at a fairly low level of shock, less than 150 volts, that others would also do so, and that virtually no one would go to the end of the shock generator. The psychiatrists said that maybe one person in a thousand would go to the end of the shock generator.

Milgram's initial obedience finding. As you have probably already guessed, Milgram didn't find what these people predicted. For the conditions just described (learner in another room, escalated moaning and screaming, and nonresponding at higher levels of shock), almost two out of every three participants (62.5 percent) continued to obey the experimenter and administered the maximum possible shock (450 volts). This is even worse than it appears, as the learner had mentioned a slight heart condition before the experiment began and mentioned it again during his protests (see Table 9.2). Milgram replicated this finding with new participants and observed the same result—65 percent obeyed and administered the maximum shock. He also observed a 65 percent maximal obedience rate in another experiment when the learner made no vocal protests but rather just pounded the laboratory wall in protest at 300 volts and stopped pounding and responding after 315 volts. Even more frightening is Milgram's finding in a pilot study that without any auditory input (no vocal protests or pounding the wall), virtually every participant continued to obey the experimenter and administer the maximum possible shock!

It is important to realize that the learner (a confederate of the experimenter) was never really shocked. The teacher only thought he was administering the shocks. The true participants, who always drew the role of teacher, were carefully debriefed after the experiment was over and told that they did not really shock the other person. Critics of Milgram's study argue that Milgram inflicted irreparable harm on them (Baumrind, 1964). Participants were put into an emotional situation in which many of them appeared to be on the point of nervous collapse (many bit their lips, dug their fingernails into their own flesh, laughed hysterically, and pushed their fists into their foreheads). Participants also learned something disturbing about themselves—that they would follow the commands of an authority figure to harm another human being. Subsequent interviews of participants by psychiatrists, however, indicated that none of the participants had been seriously harmed by the experience (Milgram, 1964).

This difference between what we say we will do and what we actually do illustrates the power of situational social forces on our behavior. When we are not in the situation, we may say that we would act one way; however, when in the situation, we may act in the opposite way. Why does the situation have such a strong impact on our behavior? What situational factors are important? These are the questions that Milgram tried to answer in his 20 or so experiments with over 1,000 participants using variants of the procedure that I described.

Do you realize how Milgram used the foot-in-the-door technique in achieving obedience (Gilbert, 1981)? He had the participant start by administering very small shocks (beginning at 15 volts) and increased the level slowly (in 15-volt increments). The learner didn't protest these mild, early shocks. The teacher had already obeyed several times by the time the learner started his protests (at 120 volts), and by the time the shock level was high, the teacher had obeyed numerous times. Milgram's results might have been very different if he would have had participants start at a high level of shock or if the learner had protested the first few small shocks. It is also important to realize that if at any time the teacher asked the experimenter about stopping, the experimenter would respond with a series of four standardized prompts such as "Please go on" or "The experiment requires that you continue." If the teacher refused to go on, the experimenter would stop the experiment; therefore, the participants were not coerced or forced to obey.

In addition, the participants in Milgram's experiments were not college students. He conducted the study at Yale University in New Haven, Connecticut, and used volunteer participants from the New Haven community. They were paid $4, plus bus fare. The experimenter and the confederate participants were always men. In the experiments that I described and in all of his other experiments except one, Milgram used male participants from age 20 to age 50. In that one experiment, female participants served as teachers with male learners, and the maximal obedience rate was the same as with male teachers, 65 percent. This finding of no gender differences in obedience has been replicated by other researchers (Blass, 1999). Milgram's basic obedience finding has also been replicated in many different countries, including Jordan, Spain, Italy, and Austria (Blass, 1999). This means that Milgram's basic obedience-to-authority finding is definitely reliable. With this in mind, let's see what some of the situational factors are that are critical to obtaining such obedience.

Situational factors that impact obedience. Let's label the Milgram experiment that I first described as the baseline condition (the teacher and learner are in separate rooms but the teacher can hear the learner's escalated screams and protests and his refusal to continue at higher voltage levels, and the learner does not respond after 330 volts). One important factor is the physical presence of the experimenter (the person with authority). Milgram found that if the experimenter left the laboratory and gave his commands over the telephone, maximum obedience (administering the highest possible shock) dropped to 20.5 percent. The closeness of the teacher and the learner is also important (as the auditory input indicates). Remember, virtually every participant administered the maximum shock when the learner did not vocally protest or pound the wall, but only about two of every three participants did so when the teacher could hear the learner's protests or pounding. In another experiment, Milgram made the teacher and learner even closer by having them both in the same room instead of different rooms, and maximum obedience dropped to 40 percent. It dropped even further, to 30 percent, when the teacher had to administer the shock directly by forcing the learner's hand onto a shock plate. This means that obedience decreases as the teacher and learner are physically closer to each other. Oddly, though, the maximum obedience rate doesn't drop to 0 percent even when they touch; it is still 30 percent.

Some thought that the location of the experiments, at prestigious Yale University, contributed to the high maximum obedience rate. To check this hypothesis, Milgram ran the same baseline condition in a rundown office building in nearby Bridgeport, Connecticut, completely dissociated from Yale. What do you think happened? The maximum obedience rate went down, but it didn't go down much. Milgram found a maximum obedience rate of 47.5 percent. The prestige and authority of the university setting did contribute to the obedience rate, but not nearly as much as the presence of the experimenter or the closeness of the

The teacher is administering the shock to the learner by directly forcing the learner's arm on the shock plate. Even in this situation, maximal obedience was still 30 percent.

teacher and the learner. The presence of two confederate disobedient teachers dropped the obedience rate to 10 percent. To get the maximum obedience to 0 percent, Milgram set up a situation with two experimenters who at some point during the experiment disagreed. One said to stop the experiment, while the other said to continue. In this case, when one of the people in authority said to stop, all of the teachers stopped.

What about getting the maximum obedience rate to increase from that observed in the baseline condition? Milgram tried to do that by taking the direct responsibility for shocking away from the learner. Instead, the teacher only pushed the switch on the shock generator to indicate to another teacher (another confederate) in the room with the learner how much shock to administer. With this direct responsibility for shocking the learner lifted off of their shoulders, almost all of the participants (92.5 percent) obeyed the experimenter and administered the maximum shock level. This finding and all of the others that we have discussed are summarized in Table 9.3, so that you can compare them. For more detail on the experiments that were described, see Milgram (1974).

Table 9.3 Results for Some of Milgram's Experimental Conditions	
Experimental Conditions	**Percent of Maximum Obedience Observed**
Teacher and learner in different rooms, no auditory input (Pilot Study)	100
Teacher does not have direct responsibility for administering shock	92.5
Teacher and learner in different rooms and learner pounds wall at 300 volts and stops pounding and responding after 315 volts	65
Baseline condition—teacher and learner in different rooms, escalated vocal protests, and nonresponding after 330 volts	62.5; 65 in replication
Baseline condition but female participants	65
In rundown office building in Bridgeport, Connecticut	47.5
Teacher and learner in same room	40
Teacher and learner in same room and teacher has to force learner's hand onto shock plate	30
Experimenter not present	20.5
Two models of disobedience	10
Two experimenters who disagree	0

Do you think that Milgram's findings could be replicated today? Aren't people today more aware of the dangers of blindly following authority than they were in the early 1960s? If so, wouldn't they disobey more often than Milgram's participants? To test this question, Burger (2009) conducted a replication of Milgram's baseline condition. His participants were men and women who responded to newspaper advertisements and flyers distributed locally. Their ages ranged from 20 to 81 years, with a mean age of 42.9 years. Some procedural changes were necessary to obtain permission to run the study, which otherwise would not have met the current American Psychological Association guidelines for ethical treatment of human subjects. The main procedural change of interest to us was that once participants pressed the 150 volt switch and started to read the next test item, the experiment was stopped. This point was chosen because in Milgram's study, once participants went past 150 volts, the vast majority continued to obey up to the highest shock level (Burger, 2009). In a meta-analysis of data from eight of Milgram's obedience experiments, Packer (2008) also found that the 150-volt point was the critical juncture for disobedience (the voltage level at which participants were most likely to disobey the experimenter). Thus, in Burger's study, it is a reasonable assumption that the percentage of participants that go past 150 volts is a good estimate of the percentage that would go to the end of the shock generator. Of course, the experimenter also ended the experiment when a participant refused to continue after hearing all of the experimenter's prods. What do you think Burger found for male participants? What about female participants? 66.7 percent of the men continued after 150 volts, and 72.7 percent of the women did so. Although these percentages have to be adjusted down slightly because not every participant in Milgram's study who went past 150 volts maximally obeyed, these results are very close to Milgram's finding of 65% obedience for both men and women in the baseline condition. Burger's findings indicate that the average American reacted in this laboratory obedience situation today much like they did almost 50 years ago.

One criticism of Milgram's experiments was that participants were in an experiment in which they had agreed to participate and were paid for their participation. Some thought that participants may have felt an obligation to obey the experimenter and continue in the experiment because of this agreement. However, the very different levels of obedience that were observed when various situational factors were manipulated shows that these situational factors were more important in obtaining the obedience than a feeling of experimental obligation. In addition, Milgram's results have also been replicated without paying people for their participation. Let's see how this was done.

The "Astroten" study. The fascinating aspect of the "Astroten" study is that the participants did not even know they were in the study! The results, then, could hardly be due to a feeling of experimental obligation. The participants in this study were nurses on duty alone in a hospital ward (Hofling, Brotzman, Dalrymple, Graves, & Pierce, 1966). Each nurse received a call from a person using the name of a staff doctor not personally known by the nurse. The doctor ordered the nurse to give a dose exceeding the maximum daily dosage of an unauthorized medication ("Astroten") to an actual patient in the ward. This order violated many hospital rules—medication orders need to be given in person and not over the phone, it was a clear overdose, and the medication was not even authorized. Twenty-two nurses, in different hospitals and at different times, were confronted with such an order. What do you think they did? Remember that this is not an experiment. These are real nurses who are on duty in hospitals doing their jobs.

Twenty-one of the twenty-two nurses did not question the order and went to give the medication, though they were intercepted before getting to the patient. Now what do you think that the researchers found when they asked other nurses and nursing students what they would do in such a situation? Of course, they said the opposite of what the other nurses actually did. Nearly all of them (31 out of 33) said that they would have refused to give the medication, once again demonstrating the power of situational forces on obedience.

The Jonestown massacre. Given all of this research pointing to our tendency to obey people in authority, even if it is destructive, the Jonestown mass suicide orchestrated by the very charismatic Reverend Jim Jones should not be that surprising. People are willing to obey an authority, especially one with whom they are very familiar and view as their leader. Using various compliance techniques, Jones developed unquestioned faith as the cult leader and discouraged individualism. For example, using the foot-in-the-door technique he slowly increased the financial support required of Peoples Temple members until they had turned over essentially everything they had (Levine, 2003). He even used the door-in-the-face and foot-in-the-door techniques to recruit members (Ornstein, 1991). He had his recruiters ask people walking by to help the poor. When they refused, the recruiters then asked them just to donate 5 minutes of their time to

The Jonestown Massacre
These are the dead bodies of some of the over 900 members of Reverend Jim Jones's religious cult in Jonestown, Guyana, who committed mass suicide by drinking cyanide-laced Kool-Aid.

AP Photo

put letters in envelopes (door-in-the-face). Once they agreed to this small task, they were then given information about future, related charitable work. Having committed to the small task, they then returned later as a function of the consistency aspect of the foot-in-the-door technique. As they contributed more and more of their time, they became more involved in the Peoples Temple and were then easily persuaded to join.

There is one situational factor leading to the Jonestown tragedy that is not so obvious, though—the importance of Jones moving his almost 1,000 followers from San Francisco to the rain forests of Guyana, an alien environment in the jungle of an unfamiliar country (Cialdini, 1993). In such an uncertain environment, the followers would look to the actions of others (informational social influence) to guide their own actions. The Jonestown followers looked to the settlement leaders and other followers, which then helped Jones to manage such a large group of followers. With this in mind, think about the day of the commanded suicide. Why was the mass suicide so orderly and why did the people seem so willing to commit suicide? The most fanatical followers stepped forward immediately and drank the poison. People looked to others to define the correct response, which meant that they followed the lead of those who quickly and willingly drank the poison. In other words, drinking the poison seemed to be the correct thing to do. This situation reflects a "herd mentality," getting some members going in the right direction so that others will follow like cattle being led to the slaughterhouse.

How Groups Influence Us

Usually when we think of groups we think of formalized groups such as committees, sororities and fraternities, classes, or trial juries. Social psychologists, however, have studied the influences of all sorts of groups from less formal ones, such as an audience at some event, to these more formal ones. Our discussion of the influences of such groups begins with one of the earliest ones that was studied, social facilitation.

Social facilitation. How would your behavior be affected by the presence of other people, such as an audience? Do you think the audience would help or hinder? One of the earliest findings for such situations was social facilitation, improvement in performance in the presence of others. This social facilitative effect is limited, however, to familiar tasks for which the person's response is automatic (such as doing simple arithmetic problems). When people are faced with difficult unfamiliar tasks that they have not mastered (such as solving a complex maze), performance is hindered by the presence of others. Why? One explanation proposes that the presence of others increases a person's drive and arousal, and research studies have found that under increased arousal, people tend to give whatever response is dominant (most likely) in that situation (Bond & Titus, 1983; Zajonc, 1965). This means that when the task is very familiar or simple, the dominant response tends to be the correct one; thus performance improves. When

social facilitation Facilitation of a dominant response on a task due to social arousal, leading to improvement on simple or well-learned tasks and worse performance on complex or unlearned tasks when other people are present.

social loafing The tendency to exert less effort when working in a group toward a common goal than when individually working toward the goal.

diffusion of responsibility The lessening of individual responsibility for a task when responsibility for the task is spread across the members of a group.

the task is unfamiliar or complex, however, the dominant response is likely not the correct one; thus performance is hindered. This means that people who are very skilled at what they do will usually do better in front of an audience than by themselves, and those who are novices will tend to do worse. This is why it is more accurate to define **social facilitation** as facilitation of the dominant response on a task due to social arousal, leading to improvement on simple or well-learned tasks and worse performance on complex or unlearned tasks when other people are present.

Social loafing and the diffusion of responsibility. Social facilitation occurs for people on tasks for which they can be evaluated individually. Social loafing occurs when people are pooling their efforts to achieve a common goal (Karau & Williams, 1993). **Social loafing** is the tendency for people to exert less effort when working toward a common goal in a group than when individually accountable. Social loafing is doing as little as you can get away with. Think about the various group projects that you have participated in both in school and outside of school. Didn't some members contribute very little to the group effort? Why? A major reason is the **diffusion of responsibility**—the responsibility for the task is diffused across all members of the group; therefore, individual accountability is lessened.

Behavior often changes when individual responsibility is lifted. Remember that in Milgram's study the maximum obedience rate increased to almost 100 percent when the direct responsibility for administering the shock was lifted from the teacher's shoulders. This diffusion of responsibility can also explain why social loafing tends to increase as the size of the group increases (Latané, Williams, & Harkins, 1979). The larger the group, the less likely it is that a social loafer will be detected and the more the responsibility for the task gets diffused. Think about students working together on a group project for a shared grade. Social loafing would be greater when the group size is seven or eight than when it is only two or three. However, for group tasks in which individual contributions are identifiable and evaluated, social loafing decreases (Williams, Harkins, & Latané, 1981; Harkins, & Jackson, 1985). Thus, in a group project for a shared grade, social loafing would decrease if each group member is assigned and responsible for a specific part of the project.

The bystander effect and the Kitty Genovese case. Now let's think about the Kitty Genovese case described at the beginning of this chapter. Many people saw or heard the prolonged fatal attack. No one intervened until it was too late. Why? Was it big-city apathy, as proposed by many media people? Experiments by John Darley, Bibb Latané, and other social psychologists indicate that it wasn't apathy, but rather that the diffusion of responsibility, as in social loafing, played a major role in this failure to help (Latané & Darley, 1970; Latané & Nida, 1981).

Conducting experiments in which people were faced with emergency situations, Darley and Latané found what they termed the **bystander effect**—the probability of an individual helping in an emergency is greater when there is only one bystander than when there are many bystanders.

> **bystander effect** The probability of a person's helping in an emergency is greater when there are no other bystanders than when there are other bystanders.

To understand this effect, Darley and Latané developed a model of the intervention process in emergencies. According to this model, for a person to intervene in an emergency, he must make not just one, but a series of decisions, and only one set of choices will lead him to take action. In addition, these decisions are typically made under conditions of stress, urgency, and threat of possible harm. The decisions to be made are 1) noticing the relevant event or not, 2) defining the event as an emergency or not, 3) feeling personal responsibility for helping or not, and 4) deciding how to help (direct or indirect intervention). If the event is not noticed or not defined as an emergency or if the bystander does not take responsibility for helping, he will not intervene. Darley and Latané's research (e.g., Latané & Darley, 1968, and Latané & Rodin, 1969) demonstrated that the presence of other bystanders negatively impacted all of these decisions, leading to the bystander effect.

Let's take a closer look at one of these experiments (Darley & Latané, 1968) to help you better understand the bystander effect. Imagine that you are asked to participate in a study examining the adjustments you've experienced in attending college. You show up for the experiment, are led to a booth, and told that you are going to participate in a round-robin discussion of adjustment problems over the laboratory intercom. You put on earphones so that you can hear the other participants, but you cannot see them. The experimenter explains that this is to guarantee each student's anonymity. The experimenter tells you that when a light in the booth goes on, it is your turn to talk. She also says that she wants the discussion not to be inhibited by her presence, so she is not going to listen to the discussion. The study begins. The first student talks about how anxious he has been since coming to college and that sometimes the anxiety is so overwhelming he has epileptic seizures. Another student talks about the difficulty she's had in deciding on a major and how she misses her boyfriend who stayed at home to go to college. It's your turn, and you talk about your adjustment problems. The discussion then returns to the first student and as he is talking, he seems to be getting very anxious. Suddenly, he starts having a seizure and cries out for help. What would you do?

Like most people, you would likely say that you would go to help him. However, this is not what was found. Whether a participant went for help depended upon how many other students the participant thought were available to help the student having the seizure (the bystander effect). Darley and Latané manipulated this number, so there were zero, one, or four others. In actuality, there were no other students present; the dialogue was all tape-recorded. There was only one participant. The percentage of participants who attempted to help before the victim's cries for help ended decreased dramatically as the presumed number of bystanders increased, from 85 percent when alone to only 31 percent when four

▌**deindividuation** The loss of self-awareness and self-restraint in a group situation that fosters arousal and anonymity.

other bystanders who could help were assumed to be present. The probability of helping decreased as the responsibility for helping was diffused across more participants. Those participants who did not go for help were not apathetic, however. They were very upset and seemed to be in a state of conflict, even though they did not leave the booth to help. They appeared to want to help, but the situational forces (the presumed presence of other bystanders and the resulting diffusion of responsibility) led them not to do so. The bystander effect has been replicated many times for many different types of emergencies. Latané and Nida (1981) analyzed almost 50 bystander intervention studies with thousands of participants and found that bystanders were more likely to help when alone than with others about 90% of the time.

Now let's apply the bystander effect to the Kitty Genovese case. The responsibility for helping was diffused across all of the witnesses to the attack. They likely assumed that someone else probably called the police, so they didn't need to do so. A situational factor, the presence of many bystanders, resulted in no one intervening until it was too late. Based on the results of the bystander intervention studies, Kitty Genovese might have received help and possibly lived if there had been only one bystander to her attack. With the total responsibility on the one bystander's shoulders, intervention would have been far more likely.

Deindividuation. Diffusion of responsibility also seems to play a role in **deindividuation,** the loss of self-awareness and self-restraint in a group situation that fosters arousal and anonymity. The responsibility for the group's actions is defused across all the members of the group. Deindividuation can be thought of as

Deindividuation and the Ku Klux Klan
The uniform of Ku Klux Klan members, especially the hood, fosters deindividuation, the loss of self-awareness and self-restraint in a group situation that fosters arousal and anonymity. Deindividuation increases the likelihood that members will forget their moral values and act without thinking.

AP Photo/Pat Sullivan

combining the increased arousal in social facilitation with the diminished sense of responsibility in social loafing. Deindividuated people feel less restrained, and therefore may forget their moral values and act spontaneously without thinking. The result can be damaging, as seen in mob violence, riots, and vandalism. In one experiment on deindividuation, simply wearing Ku Klux Klan–type white hoods and coats led college women to deliver twice as much shock to helpless victims than did similar women not wearing Klan clothing who were identifiable by name tags (Zimbardo, 1970). Once people lose their sense of individual responsibility, feel anonymous, and are aroused, they are capable of terrible things.

> ▍ **group polarization** The strengthening of a group's prevailing opinion about a topic following group discussion about the topic.
>
> ▍ **groupthink** A mode of group thinking that impairs decision making because the desire for group harmony overrides a realistic appraisal of the possible decision alternatives.

Group polarization and groupthink. Two other group influences, group polarization and groupthink, apply to more structured, task-oriented group situations (such as committees and panels). **Group polarization** is the strengthening of a group's prevailing opinion about a topic following group discussion of the topic. The group members already share the same opinion on an issue, and when they discuss it among themselves, this opinion is further strengthened as members gain additional information from other members in support of the opinion. This means that the initially held view becomes even more polarized following group discussion.

In addition to this informational influence of the group discussion, there is a type of normative influence. Because we want others to like us, we may express stronger views on a topic after learning that other group members share our opinion. Both informational and normative influences lead members to stronger, more extreme opinions. A real-life example is the accentuation phenomenon in college students—initial differences in college students become more accentuated over time (Myers, 2002). For example, students who do not belong to fraternities and sororities tend to be more liberal politically, and this difference grows during college at least partially because group members reinforce and polarize each other's views. Group polarization for some groups may lead to destructive behavior, encouraging group members to go further out on the limb through mutual reinforcement. For example, group polarization within community gangs tends to increase the rate of their criminal behavior. Within terrorist organizations, group polarization leads to more extreme acts of violence. Alternatively, association with a quiet, nonviolent group, such as a quilter's guild, strengthens a person's tendency toward quieter, more peaceful behavior. In summary, group polarization may exaggerate prevailing attitudes among group members, leading to more extreme behavior.

Groupthink is a mode of group thinking that impairs decision making; the desire for group harmony overrides a realistic appraisal of the possible decisions. The primary concern is to maintain group consensus. Pressure is put on group members to go along with the group's view and external information that disagrees with the group's view is suppressed, which leads to the illusion of unanimity. Groupthink also leads to an illusion of infallibility—the belief that the group cannot make mistakes.

"All those in favor say 'Aye.'"
"Aye."   "Aye."   "Aye."
"Aye."   "Aye."

Given such illusory thinking, it is not surprising that groupthink often leads to very bad decisions and poor solutions to problems (Janis, 1972, 1983). The failure to anticipate Pearl Harbor, the disastrous Bay of Pigs invasion of Cuba, and the space shuttle *Challenger* disaster are a few examples of real-world bad decisions that have been linked to groupthink. In the case of the *Challenger* disaster, for example, the engineers who made the shuttle's rocket boosters opposed the launch because of dangers posed by the cold temperatures to the seals between the rocket segments (Esser & Lindoerfer, 1989). However, the engineers were unsuccessful in arguing their case with the group of NASA officials, who were suffering from an illusion of infallibility. To maintain an illusion of unanimity, these officials didn't bother to make the top NASA executive who made the final launch decision aware of the engineers' concerns. The result was tragedy.

Sadly, the NASA groupthink mentality reared its head again with the space shuttle *Columbia* disaster. It appears that NASA management again ignored safety warnings from engineers about probable technical problems. The *Columbia* accident investigation board strongly recommended that NASA change its "culture of invincibility." To prevent groupthink from impacting your group decisions, make your group aware of groupthink and its dangers, and then take explicit steps to ensure that minority opinions, critiques of proposed group actions, and alternative courses of action are openly presented and fairly evaluated.

The Challenger Explosion
Groupthink has been linked to the Challenger disaster. NASA officials, who were suffering from an illusion of infallibility, ignored the warnings of engineers who opposed the launch because of dangers posed by the cold temperatures to the seals between the rocket segments.

Section Summary

In this section, we discussed many types of social influence, how people and the social forces they create influence a person's thinking and behavior. Conformity—a change in behavior, belief, or both to conform to a group norm as a result of real or imagined group pressure—is usually due to either normative social influence or informational social influence. Normative social influence leads people to conform to gain the approval and avoid the disapproval of others. Informational social influence leads people to conform to gain information from others in an uncertain situation. Several situational factors impact the amount of conformity that is observed. For example, a nonconsensus among group members reduces the amount of conformity, and responding aloud versus anonymously increases conformity.

In conformity, people change their behavior or attitudes to adhere to a group norm, but in compliance, people act in accordance with a direct request from another person or group. We discussed four techniques used to obtain compliance. Each technique involves two requests, and it is always the second request for which compliance is desired. In the foot-in-the-door technique, a small request is followed by the desired larger request. In the door-in-the-face technique, a large first request is followed by the desired second smaller request. In the low-ball technique, the attractive first request is followed by the desired and less attractive second request. In the that's-not-all technique, a desired and more attractive second request is made before a response can be made to an initial request. The foot-in-the-door and low-ball techniques work mainly because the person has committed to the first request and complies with the second to remain consistent. The door-in-the-face and that's-not-all techniques work mainly because of reciprocity. Because the other person has made a concession on the first request, we comply with the second to reciprocate.

Obedience, following the commands of a person in authority, was the subject of Stanley Milgram's controversial experimental studies done at Yale University in the early 1960s. The studies are controversial because they demonstrate our tendency toward destructive obedience, bringing harm to others through our obedient behavior. Milgram identified numerous situational factors that determine the amount of obedience observed. For example, a very high rate of obedience is observed when the direct responsibility for one's acts is removed. Less obedience is observed when we view models of disobedience, or when another authority commands us not to obey. The "Astroten" study with nurses found a high rate of obedience in a real-world situation, indicating that it was not just a feeling of experimental obligation that led to Milgram's results. The varying amounts of obedience in relation to varying situational factors in his experiments also argue against a feeling of experimental obligation leading to Milgram findings. In addition, Milgram's baseline obedience finding has recently been replicated, demonstrating that people today react in the laboratory obedience situation like Milgram's participants did almost 50 years ago.

Even the mere presence of other people can influence our behavior. This is demonstrated in social facilitation, an improvement in simple or well-learned tasks but worse performance on complex or unlearned tasks when other people are observing us. Some group influences occur when the responsibility for a task is diffused across all members of the group. For example, social loafing is the tendency for people to exert less effort when working in a group toward a common goal than when individually accountable. Social loafing increases as the size of the group increases and decreases when each group member feels more responsible for his contribution to the group effort. Diffusion of responsibility also contributes to the bystander effect, the greater probability of an individual helping in an emergency when there is only one bystander versus when there are many bystanders. Diffusion of responsibility also contributes to deindividuation, the loss of self-awareness and self-restraint in a group situation that promotes arousal and anonymity. The results of deindividuation can be tragic, such as mob violence and rioting.

Two other group influences, group polarization and groupthink, apply to more structured, task-oriented situations, and refer to effects on the group's decision making. Group polarization is the strengthening of a group's prevailing opinion following group discussion of the topic. Like-minded group members reinforce their shared beliefs, which leads to more extreme attitudes and behavior among group members. Groupthink is a mode of group thinking that impairs decision making. It stems from the group's illusion of infallibility and its desire for group harmony, which override a realistic appraisal of decision alternatives, often leading to bad decisions.

ConceptCheck | 1

➤ Explain the difference between normative social influence and informational social influence.

➤ Explain how both the door-in-the-face technique and the that's-not-all technique involve reciprocity.

➤ Milgram found that 0 percent of the participants continued in the experiment when one of two experimenters said to stop. Based on this finding, predict what he found when he had two experimenters disagree, but the one who said to stop was substituting for a participant and serving as the learner. Explain the rationale for your prediction.

➤ According to the bystander effect, explain why you would be more likely to be helped if your car broke down on a little-traveled country road than on an interstate highway.

How We Think About Our Own and Others' Behavior

Social thinking is concerned with how we view our own attitudes and behavior and those of others. We will discuss two of the major areas of research on social thinking—attributions and attitudes. First, we will examine **attribution,** the process (briefly discussed in Chapter 8) by which we explain our own behavior and the behavior of others. In other words, what do we perceive to be the causes of our behavior and that of others? Is the behavior due to internal causes (the person) or external causes (the situation)? Remember, we show a self-serving bias when it comes to explaining our own behavior. In this section, we will revisit this bias and

▌ **attribution** The process by which we explain our own behavior and that of others.

examine two other biases in the attribution process (the fundamental attribution error and the actor-observer bias). The second major topic to be discussed is the relationship between our attitudes and our behavior. For example, do our attitudes drive our behavior, does our behavior determine our attitudes, or is it some of both? We will also consider the impact of role-playing on our attitudes and behavior.

How We Make Attributions

Imagine it's the first cold day in the fall, and you're standing in a long line for coffee at the student union coffee shop. All of a sudden, a person at the head of the line drops her cup of coffee. You turn to your friend and say "What a klutz!" inferring that this behavior is characteristic of that person. You are making an internal (dispositional) attribution, attributing the cause of dropping the cup of coffee to the person. But what if it had been you who had dropped the cup of coffee? Chances are you would have said something like, "Boy was that cup hot!" inferring that dropping the cup wasn't your fault, making an external (situational) attribution. We have different biases in the attributions we make for behavior we observe versus our own behavior. Let's look first at being an observer.

Attributions for the behavior of others. As an observer, we tend to commit the fundamental attribution error (Ross, 1977). The **fundamental attribution error** is the tendency as an observer to overestimate internal dispositional influences and underestimate external situational influences on others' behavior. Simply put, observers are biased in that they tend to attribute others' behavior to them and not the situation they are in. In the coffee example, we tend to make an internal attribution (the person is a klutz) and ignore possible external situational factors, such as the cup being really hot or slippery. The fundamental attribution error tends to show up even in experiments in which the participants are told that people are only faking a particular type of behavior. For example, in one experiment participants were told that a person was only pretending to be friendly or to be unfriendly (Napolitan & Goethals, 1979). Even with this knowledge, participants still inferred that the people were actually like the way they acted, either friendly or unfriendly.

Think about the participants in Milgram's obedience experiments. On first learning of their destructive obedient behavior, didn't you think the teachers were horrible human beings? How could they treat fellow humans in that way? Or consider the teachers themselves in these experiments. When the learners kept making mistakes, the teachers may have thought the learners were incredibly stupid and so deserved the shocks. Rape victims are sometimes blamed for provoking the rapes, and the homeless are often blamed for their poverty-stricken state. Placing such blame on victims involves the **just-world hypothesis,** the

fundamental attribution error The tendency as an observer to overestimate dispositional influences and underestimate situational influences on others' behavior.

just-world hypothesis The assumption that the world is just and that people get what they deserve.

assumption that the world is just and that people get what they deserve (Lerner, 1980). Beware of just-world reasoning. It is not valid, but is often used to justify cruelty to others.

The fundamental attribution error impacts our impressions of other people. There are two related concepts that you should also be aware of when forming impressions of others—the primacy effect and the self-fulfilling prophecy. In the **primacy effect,** early information is weighted more heavily than later information in forming an impression of another person. Beware of this effect when meeting someone new. Develop your impression slowly and carefully by gathering more information across time and from many different situations. Also be careful about the initial impressions that you make on people. Given the power of the primacy effect, your later behavior may not be able to change their initial impression of you. Try to be your true self when you first meet someone so that the primacy effect will be more accurate.

In the **self-fulfilling prophecy,** our expectations of a person elicit behavior from that person that confirms our expectations. In other words, our behavior encourages the person to act in accordance with our expectations (Jones, 1977; Rosenthal & Jacobson, 1968). For example, if you think someone is uncooperative, you may act hostile and not be very cooperative in your interactions with that person. Given your hostile behavior, the person responds by being uncooperative, confirming your expectations. The person may not really be uncooperative, however, and may only act this way in response to your behavior. However, your expectations will have been confirmed, and you will think that the person is uncooperative. Self-fulfilling prophecy is related to our tendency toward confirmation bias in hypothesis testing (see Chapter 6). Rather than acting in a manner that confirms your expectations, act in the opposite way (in the example, instead of being uncooperative, be cooperative) and see what happens. You may be surprised.

Attributions for our own behavior. Now let's consider our own behavior and making attributions. Our attribution process is biased in a different way when we are actors and not observers. Think about the example where you dropped the cup of coffee (you were the actor). You don't make a dispositional attribution ("I'm clumsy."). You make a situational attribution ("The cup was slippery."). As actors we tend to have what's called the **actor-observer bias,** the tendency to attribute our own behavior to situational influences, but to attribute the behavior of others to dispositional influences. Why this difference in attributional bias? As observers, our attention is focused on the person, so we see him as the cause of the action. As actors, our attention is focused on the situation, so we see the situation as the cause of the action. We are more aware of situational factors as actors than as observers. This

primacy effect Information gathered early is weighted more heavily than information gathered later in forming an impression of another person.

self-fulfilling prophecy Our behavior leads a person to act in accordance with our expectations for that person.

actor-observer bias The tendency to overestimate situational influences on our own behavior, but to overestimate dispositional influences on the behavior of others.

explanation is supported by the fact that we are less susceptible to the bias toward dispositional attributions with our friends and relatives, people whom we know well.

We described another attribution bias in the last chapter, the **self-serving bias**—the tendency to make attributions so that one can perceive oneself favorably. As actors, we tend to overestimate dispositional influences when the outcome of our behavior is positive and to overestimate situational influences when the outcome of our behavior is negative. In the last chapter, we were discussing this bias's role as a defense mechanism against depression. In this chapter, self-serving bias qualifies the actor-observer bias; it defines the type of attribution we make as actors based on the nature of the outcome of our actions. Think about our reaction to a test grade. If we did well, we think that we studied hard and knew the material, both dispositional factors. If we don't do very well, then we may blame the test and the teacher ("What a tricky exam." or "That test was not a good indicator of what I know."). We take credit for our successes but not our failures. Teachers also have this bias. For example, if the class does poorly on a test, the teacher thinks that the test she made up was just fine, but that the students weren't motivated or didn't study. It is important to realize that the self-serving bias and the other attribution biases do not speak to the correctness of the attributions we make, but only to the types of attributions we tend to make. This means that our attributions will sometimes be correct and sometimes incorrect.

The self-serving bias also leads us to see ourselves as "above average" when we compare ourselves to others on positive dimensions, such as intelligence and attractiveness. This tendency is exemplified in Garrison Keillor's fictional Lake Wobegon community, where, "All the women are strong, all the men are good-looking, and all the children are above average." We tend to rate ourselves unreasonably high on dimensions that we value (Mezulis, Abramson, Hyde, & Hankin, 2004). Think about it. If you were asked to compare yourself to other people on intelligence, what would you say? If you respond like most people, you would say "above average." However, most people cannot be "above average." Many of us have to be average or below average. Intelligence, like most human traits, is normally distributed with half of us below average and half of us above average.

The self-serving bias also influences our estimates of the extent to which other people think and act as we do. This leads to two effects—the false consensus effect and the false uniqueness effect (Myers, 2002). The **false consensus effect** is the tendency to overestimate the commonality of one's opinions and unsuccessful behaviors. Let's consider two examples. If you like classical music, you tend to overestimate the number of people who also like classical music, or if you fail all of your midterm exams, you tend to overestimate the number of students who also failed all of their midterms. You tend to think that your opinion and your negative behavior are the consensus opinion and behavior.

self-serving bias The tendency to make attributions so that one can perceive oneself favorably.

false consensus effect The tendency to overestimate the commonality of one's opinions and unsuccessful behaviors.

Table 9.4	Attributional Biases
Bias	**Description**
Fundamental attribution error	The tendency to overestimate dispositional influences and to underestimate situational influences on others' behavior
Actor-observer bias	The tendency to overestimate situational influences on our own behavior but to overestimate dispositional influences on others' behavior (Note: This bias is qualified by self-serving bias when explaining our own behavior.)
Self-serving bias	The tendency to make attributions so that one can perceive oneself favorably; we tend to overestimate dispositional influences on our behavior when the outcome is positive and to overestimate situational influences when the outcome is negative

false uniqueness effect The tendency to underestimate the commonality of one's abilities and successful behaviors.

attitudes Evaluative reactions (positive or negative) toward objects, events, and other people.

The **false uniqueness effect** is the tendency to underestimate the commonality of one's abilities and successful behaviors. For example, if you are a good pool player, you tend to think that few other people are. Or, if you just aced your psychology exam, you think few students did so. You think your abilities and successful behaviors are unique. The false consensus effect and the false uniqueness effect relate to the self-protective function of the self-serving bias. We want to protect and enhance our view of ourselves, our self-esteem.

All three major attributional biases (the fundamental attribution error, the actor-observer bias, and the self-serving bias) are summarized in Table 9.4.

How Our Behavior Affects Our Attitudes

In this section, we are going to consider our attitudes. In simple terms, **attitudes** are evaluative reactions (positive or negative) toward things, events, and other people. Our attitudes are our beliefs and opinions. What do you think of the Republican political party, abortion, Barack Obama, Twitter, or rap music? Have you changed any of your attitudes during your life, especially since you have been in college? Most of us do. Our attitudes often determine our behavior, but this is not always the case.

When our behavior contradicts our attitudes. Our attitudes tend to guide our behavior when the attitudes are ones that we feel strongly about, when we are consciously aware of our attitudes, and when outside influences on our behavior are not strong. For example, you may think that studying is the top priority for a student. If you do, you will likely get your studying done before engaging in other activities. However, if there is a lot of pressure from your roommates and friends to stop studying and go out, you may abandon studying for partying. But what happens when our attitudes don't guide our behavior and there isn't a lot of outside influence on our behavior? To help you understand the answer to this question, we'll consider a classic study (Festinger & Carlsmith, 1959).

Imagine that you are a participant in an experiment. You show up at the laboratory at the assigned time and the experiment turns out to be incredibly boring. For an hour, you perform various boring tasks, such as turning pegs on a pegboard over and over again or organizing spools in a box, dumping them out, and then organizing them again. When the hour is over, the experimenter explains to you that the experiment is concerned with the effects of a person's expectations on their task performance and that you were in the control group. The experimenter is upset because his student assistant hasn't shown up. She was supposed to pose as a student who has just participated in the experiment and tell the next participant who is waiting outside that this experiment was really enjoyable. The experimenter asks if you can help him out by doing this, and for doing so, he can pay you. His budget is small, though, so he can only pay you $1. Regardless, you agree to help him out and go outside and tell the waiting participant (who is really a confederate of the experimenter and not a true participant) how enjoyable and interesting the experiment was.

Before you leave, another person who is studying students' reactions to experiments asks you to complete a questionnaire about how much you enjoyed the earlier experimental tasks. How would you rate these earlier incredibly boring tasks? You are probably thinking that you would rate them as very boring, because they were. However, this isn't what researchers observed. Participants' behavior (rating the tasks) did not follow their attitude (the tasks were boring). Participants who were paid only $1 for helping out the experimenter (by lying about the nature of the experimental tasks to the next supposed participant) rated the tasks as fairly enjoyable. We need to compare this finding with the results for another group of participants who received $20 for lying about the experiment. Their behavior did follow their attitude about the tasks. They rated the tasks as boring. This is what researchers also found for another group of participants who were never asked to help out the experimenter and lie. They also rated the tasks as boring. So why did the participants who lied for $1 not rate the tasks as boring?

Before answering this question, let's consider another part of this experiment. After rating the task, participants met again with the experimenter to be debriefed, and were told the true nature of the study. Following the debriefing, the experimenter asks you to give back the money he paid you. What would you do if you were in the $20 group? You are probably saying, "No way," but remember the studies on obedience and the high rates of obedience that were observed. What actually happened? Just like all of the participants agreed to lie (whether for $1 or $20), all of the participants gave back the money, showing once again our tendency to be obedient and comply with requests of those in

cognitive dissonance theory
A theory developed by Leon Festinger that assumes people have a tendency to change their attitudes to reduce the cognitive discomfort created by inconsistencies between their attitudes and their behavior.

authority. Now let's think about why the $1 group rated the tasks differently than the $20 group.

Festinger's cognitive dissonance theory. Their behavior can be explained by Leon Festinger's **cognitive dissonance theory,** which proposes that people change their attitudes to reduce the cognitive discomfort created by inconsistencies between their attitudes and their behavior (Festinger, 1957). Let's consider a real-life example before applying this theory to the participants who were paid $1 for lying. Think about people who smoke. Most smokers have the attitude (believe) that smoking is dangerous to their health, but they continue to smoke. Cognitive dissonance theory says that smokers feel cognitive discomfort because of the inconsistency between their attitude about smoking (dangerous to their health) and their behavior (continuing to smoke). To reduce this cognitive disharmony, either the attitude or the behavior has to change. According to the cognitive dissonance theory, many smokers change their attitude so that it is no longer inconsistent with their behavior. For example, a smoker may now believe that the medical evidence isn't really conclusive. The change in the attitude eliminates the inconsistency and the dissonance it created. So now let's apply cognitive dissonance theory to the participants in the boring task study who lied for $1. Why did they rate the task as enjoyable? Their attitude was that the tasks were incredibly boring, but this was inconsistent with their behavior, lying about the tasks for only $1. This inconsistency would cause them to have cognitive dissonance. To reduce this dissonance, the participants changed their attitude to be that the tasks were fairly enjoyable. Now the inconsistency and resulting dissonance are gone.

A key aspect of cognitive dissonance theory is that we don't suffer dissonance if we have sufficient justification for our behavior (the participants who were paid $20 in the study) or our behavior is coerced. Also, cognitive dissonance sometimes changes the strength of an attitude so that it is consistent with past behavior. Think about important decisions that you have made in the past, for example, which college to attend. Cognitive dissonance theory says that once you make such a tough decision, you will strengthen your commitment to that choice in order to reduce cognitive dissonance. Indeed, the attractiveness of the alternate choices fades with the dissonance (you don't understand why you ever were attracted to the other schools) as you find confirming evidence of the correctness of your choice (you like your classes and teachers) and ignore evidence to the contrary (such as your school not being as highly rated as the other schools). Carol Tavris and Elliot Aronson (2007) provide numerous real-world examples of this cognitive dissonance–driven justification of our decisions, beliefs, and actions in their illuminating book, *Mistakes were made (but not by me)*. Recent research by Egan, Santos, and Bloom (2007) indicates that such decision rationalization even appears in children and nonhuman primates (Egan, Santos, & Bloom, 2007).

AP Photo/New School for Social Research

Leon Festinger

Bem's self-perception theory. There have been hundreds of studies on cognitive dissonance, but there is an alternative theoretical explanation for the results of some of these studies—Daryl Bem's **self-perception theory,** which proposes that when we are unsure of our attitudes we infer them by examining our behavior and the context in which it occurs

> **self-perception theory** A theory developed by Daryl Bem that assumes that when we are unsure of our attitudes, we infer them by examining our behavior and the context in which it occurs.

(Bem, 1972). According to Bem, we are not trying to reduce cognitive dissonance, but are merely engaged in the normal attribution process that we discussed earlier in this chapter. We are making self-attributions. Self-perception theory would say that the participants who lied for $1 in the boring tasks experiment were unsure of their attitudes toward the tasks. They would examine their behavior (lying for $1) and infer that the tasks must have been fairly enjoyable and interesting or else they would not have said that they were for only $1. Those paid $20 for lying would not be unsure about their attitude toward the boring tasks because they were paid so much to lie about them. According to self-perception theory, people don't change their attitude because of their behavior but rather use their behavior to infer their attitude. People are motivated to explain their behavior, not to reduce dissonance. According to self-perception theory, there is no dissonance to be reduced.

So which theory is better? Neither is really a better theory than the other. Both theories have merit and both seem to operate—but in different situations. This is similar to our earlier discussion of color vision theories, the trichromatic-color theory and the opponent-process theory in Chapter 3. Remember that trichromatic-color theory operates at the receptor cell level and opponent-process theory at the post-receptor cell level in the visual pathways. Cognitive dissonance theory seems to be the best explanation for behavior that contradicts well-defined attitudes. Such behavior creates mental discomfort, and we change our attitudes to reduce it. Self-perception theory explains situations in which our attitudes are not well-defined; we infer our attitudes from our behavior. As with the color vision theories, both cognitive dissonance theory and self-perception theory operate, but at different times.

The impact of role-playing. Now let's consider one final factor that impacts the complex relationship between our attitudes and our behavior—role-playing. We all have various social roles that we play—student, teacher, friend, son or daughter, parent, employee, and so on. Each role is defined by a socially expected pattern of behavior, and these definitions have an impact on both our behavior and our attitudes. The Stanford prison study conducted in the early 1970s at Stanford University by Philip Zimbardo was a dramatic example of this power of roles (Zimbardo, 2007). Zimbardo recruited male college students to participate in the study and renovated the basement in the Stanford psychology building to be a mock prison. He chose the most emotionally stable volunteers for the study and then randomly assigned them to the roles of prisoner and guard. The guards were given uniforms and billy clubs and instructed to enforce the rules of the mock prison. The prisoners were locked in cells and had to wear humiliating clothing (smocks with no undergarments). Such clothing was used in an attempt to simulate the emasculating feeling of being a prisoner. How did the roles of prisoner and prison guard impact the attitudes and behavior of the participants?

The participants began to take their respective roles too seriously, and after only one day of role-playing, the guards started treating the prisoners cruelly. Some of the prisoners rebelled, and others began to break down. What was only supposed to be role-playing became reality. The guards' treatment of the prisoners became both harsh and degrading. For example, some prisoners were made to clean out toilets with their bare hands. The prisoners began to hate the guards, and some of them were on the verge of emotional collapse. The situation worsened to such a degree that Zimbardo had to stop the study after 6 days. The participating college students had truly "become" guards and prisoners, and this role transformation dominated their attitudes and behavior. It is important to remember that the participants were normal male college students. This is what makes the results of this mock prison study so frightening, that these normal young men were so vulnerable to the power of the situational roles.

The Stanford prison study was conducted over 30 years ago, but new interest in this study was generated by the recent prisoner abuse at Abu Ghraib, the U.S. military prison in Iraq. Like Zimbardo's college-student guards, the American soldiers serving as prison guards engaged in dehumanizing and sadistic acts toward the prisoners. Zimbardo actually served as an expert witness in the trial of one of these soldiers and argued that situational pressures led the soldiers to commit their abusive acts. His argument, however, failed, and the soldier is now serving a sentence in a military prison. In his book, *The Lucifer Effect* (2007), Zimbardo

Philip G. Zimbardo, Inc.

A Guard Harassing a Prisoner in the Stanford Prison Study

A Guard Mistreating a Prisoner at Abu Ghraib Prison in Iraq

details the Stanford prison study, applies the findings to the behavior of the Abu Ghraib guards and some other recent incidents, and describes a 10-step program to build up our resilience to combat pressures that lead us to act abusively toward others. The Web site www.prisonexp.org also provides detailed coverage of the Stanford prison study and links to other recent writings by Zimbardo on the Abu Ghraib prison abuses.

Given the power of roles on behavior, think about how each of the various roles we play each day impacts our own attitudes and behavior. Consider the situational roles involved when you are trying to explain your own or another's behavior. They are powerful influences. As social psychologist David Myers has observed, "we are likely not only to think ourselves into a way of acting but also to act ourselves into a way of thinking" (Myers, 2002, p. 136).

Section Summary

In this section, we considered social thinking by examining how we make attributions, explanations for our own behavior and the behavior of others, and the relationship between our attitudes and our behavior. Attribution is a biased process. As observers, we commit the fundamental attribution error, tending to overestimate dispositional influences and underestimate situational influences upon others' behavior. This error seems to stem from our attention being focused on the person, so we see her as the cause of the action. When we view our own behavior, however, we fall prey to the actor-observer bias, the tendency to attribute our own behavior to situational influences, and not dispositional influences, as we do when we observe the behavior of others. The actor-observer bias stems from focusing our attention, as actors, on the situation and not on ourselves.

The actor-observer bias, however, is qualified by the self-serving bias, the tendency to make attributions so that we can perceive ourselves favorably and protect our self-esteem. As actors, we tend to overestimate dispositional influences when the outcome of our behavior is positive and to overestimate situational influences when the outcome is negative. Self-serving bias also leads us to rate ourselves as "above average" in comparison to others on positive dimensions, such as intelligence and attractiveness. It also leads to two other effects—the false consensus effect (overestimating the commonality of one's attitudes and unsuccessful behaviors) and the false uniqueness effect (underestimating the commonality of one's abilities and successful behaviors).

Attitudes are our evaluative reactions (positive or negative) toward objects, events, and other people. They are most likely to guide our behavior when we feel strongly about them, are consciously aware of them, and when outside influences on our behavior are minimized. Sometimes, however, our behavior contradicts our attitudes, and this situation often leads to attitudinal change. A major explanation for such attitudinal change is cognitive dissonance theory—we change our attitude to reduce the cognitive dissonance created by the inconsistency between the attitude and the behavior. Such change doesn't occur if we have sufficient justification for our behavior, however. A competing theory, self-perception theory, argues that dissonance is not involved. Self-perception theory proposes that we are just unsure about our attitude, so we infer it from our behavior. We are merely making self-attributions. Both theories seem to operate but in different situations. For well-defined attitudes, cognitive dissonance theory seems to be the better explanation; for weakly defined attitudes, self-perception theory is the better explanation. Both our attitudes and our behavior also seem to be greatly affected by the roles we play. These roles are defined, and these definitions greatly influence our actions and our attitudes. The results of Zimbardo's Stanford prison study dramatically illustrated this impact that roles have on us.

Concept**Check** | 2

➤ Explain how the actor-observer bias qualifies the fundamental attribution error and how self-serving bias qualifies the actor-observer bias.

➤ Explain the difference between the false consensus effect and the false uniqueness effect.

➤ Explain when cognitive dissonance theory is a better explanation of the relationship between our behavior and our attitudes and when self-perception theory is a better explanation of this relationship.

Study Guide

Chapter Key Terms

You should know the definitions of the following key terms from the chapter. They are listed in the order in which they appear in the chapter. For those you do not know, return to the relevant section of the chapter to learn them. When you think that you know all of the terms, complete the matching exercise based on these key terms.

social psychology	social facilitation	primacy effect
conformity	social loafing	self-fulfilling prophecy
informational social influence	diffusion of responsibility	actor-observer bias
normative social influence	bystander effect	self-serving bias
compliance	deindividuation	false consensus effect
foot-in-the-door technique	group polarization	false uniqueness effect
door-in-the-face technique	groupthink	attitudes
low-ball technique	attribution	cognitive dissonance theory
that's-not-all technique	fundamental attribution error	self-perception theory
obedience	just-world hypothesis	

Key Terms Exercise

Identify the correct term for each of the following definitions. The answers to this exercise follow the answers to the Concept Checks at the end of the chapter.

1. Compliance to a large request is gained by preceding it with a very small request.

   _____

2. Influence stemming from the need for information in situations in which the correct action or judgment is uncertain.

   _____

3. The tendency to underestimate the commonality of one's abilities and successful behaviors.

   _____

4. A mode of group thinking that impairs decision making because the desire for group harmony overrides a realistic appraisal of the possible decision alternatives.

   _____

5. The loss of self-awareness and self-restraint in a group situation that fosters arousal and anonymity.

   _____

6. The tendency to exert less effort when working in a group toward a goal than when individually working toward a goal.

   _____

7. Following the commands of a person in authority.

   _____

8. The probability of a person helping in an emergency is greater when there are no other bystanders than when there are other bystanders.

   _____

9. The tendency as an observer to overestimate internal dispositional influences and underestimate situational influences upon others' behavior.

   _____

10. A theory developed by Festinger that assumes people have a tendency to change their attitudes to reduce the cognitive discomfort created by inconsistencies between their attitudes and their behavior.

   _____

11. The assumption that the world is just and that people get what they deserve.

   _____

12. In impression formation, information gathered early is weighted more heavily than information gathered later in forming an impression of another person.

   _____

13. Compliance to a costly request is gained by first getting compliance to an attractive, less costly request but then reneging on it.

   _____

14. The lessening of individual responsibility for a task when responsibility for the task is spread across the members of a group.

   _____

15. A change in behavior, belief, or both to conform to a group norm as a result of real or imagined pressure.

   _____

Practice Test Questions

The following are practice multiple-choice test questions on some of the chapter content. The answers are given after the Key Terms Exercise answers at the end of the chapter. If you guessed or incorrectly answered a question, restudy the relevant section of the chapter.

1. The conformity demonstrated in Sherif's study using the autokinetic effect stems from _____ social influence, and the conformity demonstrated in Asch's study of line-length judgment stems from _____ social influence.

   a. normative; normative
   b. normative; informational
   c. informational; normative
   d. informational; informational

2. Which of the following factors increases conformity?
   a. group is not unanimous
   b. responding secretly
   c. correct action is not clear
   d. being of higher status than other group members

3. Which of the following compliance techniques involves gaining compliance to a much larger request by preceding it with a much smaller request?
   a. that's-not-all technique
   b. door-in-the-face technique
   c. low-ball technique
   d. foot-in-the-door technique

4. Which of the following situational factors in Milgram's shock experiments led to the highest maximum obedience rate?
   a. experiment conducted in a rundown office building
   b. two co-teachers disobey experimenter
   c. experimenter not present
   d. teacher has to force learner's hand onto shock plate

5. _____ is the strengthening of a group's prevailing opinion on a topic following group discussion of the topic.
   a. Deinviduation
   b. Group polarization
   c. Groupthink
   d. Social facilitation

6. Facilitation of a dominant response on a task due to social arousal is called _____.
   a. deindividuation
   b. social facilitation
   c. social loafing
   d. the bystander effect

7. When committing the fundamental attribution error, we tend to _____ the

influence of dispositional factors and
_____ the influence of situational factors.

a. overestimate; overestimate

b. overestimate; underestimate

c. underestimate; overestimate

d. underestimate; underestimate

8. With the self-serving bias, we tend to
make _____ attributions for our failures
and _____ attributions for our successes.

a. dispositional; dispositional

b. dispositional; situational

c. situational; dispositional

d. situational; situational

9. Bill likes country music and therefore
he thinks that most people like country
music. Bill's behavior is an example of
the _____.

a. fundamental attribution error

b. actor-observer bias

c. false consensus effect

d. false uniqueness effect

10. Two groups of children are told to not
play with a very attractive toy in a play-
room. One group was threatened very
severely, while the other group was only
threatened mildly. Neither group played
with the toy. According to cognitive dissonance theory, which group(s) should
later still rate the toy as very attractive?

a. severe threat group

b. mild threat group

c. neither group

d. both groups

11. Which two compliance techniques
involve the rule of reciprocity?

a. foot-in-the-door and door-in-the-face

b. low-ball and that's-not-all

c. foot-in-the-door and low-ball

d. door-in-the-face and that's-not-all

12. Conformity is higher for a person when
the group _____ the person's responses
and when the person is of _____ status
than the other group members.

a. hears; lesser

b. does not hear; lesser

c. hears; higher

d. does not hear; higher

13. The bystander effect refers to the finding
that an observer of an emergency is less
likely to help if the _____.

a. emergency takes place in a big city

b. emergency is being observed by other
people

c. observer has just endured a frustrating
experience

d. observer has been exposed to many
similar emergencies in the past

14. Which of the following comments is most
likely to be made by the leader of a group
characterized by groupthink?

a. "We have been united on matters in
the past and I hope that will continue."

b. "We will need some outside experts to
critique our decisions."

c. "It's important for each of us individually to think critically about this issue."

d. "We should probably divide into
subgroups and arrive at independent
decisions."

15. When our expectations of a person elicit
behavior from that person that confirms
our expectations, this is a case of _____.

a. self-serving bias

b. actor-observer bias

c. deindividuation

d. self-fulfilling prophecy

Chapter Concept Check Answers

Concept Check I 1

- The main difference between normative
social influence and informational social
influence concerns the need for information. When normative social influence is
operating, information is not necessary for
the judgment task (for example, the line-
length judgment task in Asch's study). The
correct answer or action is clear. People
are conforming to gain the approval
of others in the group and avoid their

disapproval. When informational social influence is operating, however, people conform because they need information as to what the correct answer or action is. Conformity in this case is due to the need for information, which we use to guide our behavior.

- In the door-in-the-face technique, the other person accepts your refusal to the first request so you reciprocate by agreeing to her second smaller request, the one she wanted you to comply with. In the that's-not-all technique, you think that the other person has done you a favor by giving you an even better deal with the second request, so you reciprocate and do her a favor and agree to the second request.

- If you predicted that the result was the same (0 percent maximum obedience), you are wrong. The result was the same as in Milgram's baseline condition, 65 percent maximum obedience. An explanation involves how we view persons of authority who lose their authority (being demoted). In a sense, by agreeing to serve as the learner, the experimenter gave up his authority, and the teachers no longer viewed him as an authority figure. He had been demoted.

- According to the bystander effect, you would be more likely to receive help on the little-traveled country road because any passing bystander would feel the responsibility for helping you. She would realize that there was no one else available to help you, so she would do so. On a busy interstate highway, however, the responsibility for stopping to help is diffused across hundreds of people passing by, each thinking that someone else would help you.

Concept Check | 2

- The actor-observer bias qualifies the fundamental attribution error because it says that the type of attribution we tend to make depends upon whether we are actors making attributions about our own behavior or observers making attributions about others' behavior. The actor-observer bias leads us as actors to make situational attributions; the fundamental attribution error leads us, as observers, to make dispositional attributions. The actor-observer bias is qualified, however, by the self-serving bias, which says that the type of attribution we make for our own actions depends upon whether the outcome is positive or negative. If positive, we tend to make dispositional attributions; if negative, we tend to make situational attributions.

- The false consensus effect pertains to situations in which we tend to overestimate the commonality of our opinions and unsuccessful behaviors. The false uniqueness effect pertains to situations in which we tend to underestimate the commonality of our abilities and successful behaviors. According to these effects, we think others share our opinions and unsuccessful behaviors, but do not share our abilities and successful behaviors. These effects both stem from the self-serving bias, which helps to protect our self-esteem.

- Cognitive dissonance theory seems to be the better explanation for situations in which our attitudes are well-defined. With the well-defined attitudes, our contradictory behavior creates dissonance; therefore, we tend to change our attitude to make it fit with our behavior. Self-perception theory seems to be the better explanation for situations in which our attitudes are weakly defined. We make self-attributions using our behavior to infer our attitudes.

Answers to Key Terms Exercise
1. foot-in-the-door technique
2. informational social influence
3. false uniqueness effect
4. groupthink
5. deindividuation
6. social loafing
7. obedience
8. bystander effect
9. fundamental attribution error
10. cognitive dissonance theory
11. just-world hypothesis

12. primacy effect
13. low-ball technique
14. diffusion of responsibility
15. conformity

Answers to Practice Test Questions

1. c; informational; normative
2. c; correct action is not clear
3. d; foot-in-the-door technique
4. a; experiment conducted in a rundown office building
5. b; Group polarization

6. b; social facilitation
7. b; overestimate; underestimate
8. c; situational; dispositional
9. c; false consensus effect
10. a; severe threat group
11. d; door-in-the-face and that's-not-all
12. a; hears; lesser
13. b; emergency is being observed by other people
14. a; "We have been united on matters in the past and I hope that will continue."
15. d; self-fulfilling prophecy

10

Abnormal Psychology

T
he scientific study of mental disorders and their treatment is called **abnormal psychology.** In this chapter, we
will detail some of the major types of disorders and
then describe the various types of therapy available to treat
them. We will also consider the important question of whether these therapies are
truly effective in treating disorders. First, however, we need to consider the diagnosis and classification processes so that you understand how disordered behavior and thinking are identified.

The Diagnosis and Classification of Mental Disorders

When psychologists say that the behavior and thinking of someone with a disorder are "abnormal," what do they mean? How do psychologists decide when
someone's behavior or thinking has crossed over the line from normal to abnormal? Psychologists use four key criteria. It is important to realize that if a person's
behavior or thinking meets one or more of these criteria, this does not necessarily
mean that the person is suffering from a disorder. This will become clear as we
discuss each of the criteria, which can be posed as questions.

First, is the behavior or thinking atypical (statistically infrequent)? Of course,
not all statistically infrequent behavior or thinking is abnormal. Consider skydiv-
ing. That's an atypical behavior in our society, but it does not mean that a person
who skydives has a disorder. Having hallucinations, however, is an atypical behavior that likely does reflect a disorder.

Second, is the behavior or thinking maladaptive? Maladaptive behavior or
thinking prevents the person from successfully functioning and adapting to life's
demands. Thus, a disordered person is not able to function in daily life. For
example, being afraid to leave one's home is atypical and maladaptive behavior
that would interfere with daily functioning.

Third, is the person or are others distressed by the behavior or thinking?
Perhaps a young man is attempting, but failing, to make a living doing odd street
stunts. His behavior is atypical and maladaptive (he will soon be penniless), but if
he is not disturbed and if his stunts are not disturbing others, then he is not
considered disordered.

Fourth, is the behavior or thinking rational? For example, a fear of birds
might be so strong that even thinking about them causes great anxiety. The
person may realize that this atypical, maladaptive, disturbing fear is not rational
but still be unable to suppress the anxiety and would therefore be considered
disordered.

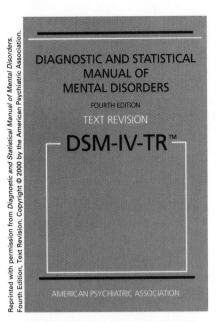

The DSM-IV-TR (published in 2000) is the latest version of the Diagnostic and Statistical Manual of Mental Disorders (DSM), the most widely used diagnostic system for mental disorders. The DSM remains a work in progress with the DSM-V scheduled for publication in 2013.

The Diagnostic and Statistical Manual

These criteria help to determine whether a person's behavior and thinking may be "abnormal," but how do we know exactly what disorder the person has? The **Diagnostic and Statistical Manual of Mental Disorders—Fourth Edition (DSM-IV),** published in 1994 by the American Psychiatric Association, is the most widely used diagnostic system for mental disorders. It bases the classification of a disorder upon behavioral and psychological symptoms and defines the diagnostic guidelines for each disorder. In 2000, there was a text revision to the DSM-IV to include some new information and eliminate some outdated language (American Psychiatric Association, 2000). This revision is usually referred to as DSM-IV-TR, but because there was little change in content, we will just refer to this fourth edition as DSM-IV. The DSM continues to be a work in progress. There is a substantial revision currently being developed, and it will be published as DSM-V in 2013.

The DSM first appeared in 1952, was only 86 pages long, and described about 60 disorders whereas the DSM-IV is over 900 pages and describes over 300 disorders (Cordón, 2005). Why has the number of disorders in the DSM increased? The major reason is that over the last half-century, we have learned a lot about various disorders and how to differentiate them; therefore, we can identify more disorders. Because of this knowledge, a major strength of the DSM-IV is that clinicians using it can make more reliable classifications than those using earlier editions, which means that clinicians agree more on a particular diagnosis for a particular patient (Nathan & Lagenbucher, 1999; Widiger, 2005). The DSM-IV also serves an important practical purpose—health insurance companies require a DSM-IV classification before paying for therapy.

The DSM-IV provides specific diagnostic criteria for each disorder. Some disorders share certain symptoms; the DSM-IV clusters these disorders into major categories. For example, several disorders that share anxiety as a symptom, such as phobic and obsessive-compulsive disorders, are categorized together as anxiety disorders. We will consider some disorders from two of the most prevalent major categories, anxiety disorders and mood disorders, and the most serious major category, schizophrenic disorders. The DSM-IV refers to the disorders in these categories as clinical disorders, what are normally called psychological or mental disorders.

The DSM-IV requires a second classification decision as to whether or not the person has a **personality disorder,** a disorder characterized by inflexible, long-standing personality

▨ **Diagnostic and Statistical Manual of Mental Disorders—Fourth Edition (DSM-IV)** The current version of the American Psychiatric Association's diagnostic and classification guidelines for mental disorders.

▨ **personality disorder** A disorder characterized by inflexible, long-standing personality traits that lead to behavior that impairs social functioning and deviates from cultural norms.

traits that lead to behavior that impairs social functioning and deviates from cultural norms. There are 10 personality disorders divided into three groups based on their symptoms (American Psychiatric Association, 2000). One group involves highly anxious or fearful behavior patterns, such as the avoidant personality, who is so overwhelmed by feelings of inadequacy and rejection that social situations are avoided. A second group involves eccentric or odd behavior patterns, such as the schizoid personality, who totally avoids social relationships and contact. The last group involves excessively dramatic, emotional, or erratic behavior patterns, such as the antisocial personality, who shows total disregard for the rights of others and the moral rules of the culture. A person with antisocial personality disorder used to be referred to as a psychopath or sociopath.

Personality disorders usually begin in childhood or adolescence and persist in a stable form throughout adulthood. They are fairly resistant to treatment and change. They need to be diagnosed, however, because they give the clinician a more complete understanding of the patient's behavior and may complicate the treatment of the patient's clinical disorder.

The Perceptual Bias of Labeling

The downside to classifying a mental disorder, regardless of the system used, is that labels are attached to people, and this biases our perception of these people in terms of the labels. Our perception is no longer objective. Think about the words that are commonly used to describe people with mental disorders—for example, "crazy," "lunatic," "deranged," "insane," or "mad." These words have strong negative connotations. Similarly, diagnostic disorder labels tend to lead to negative perceptions and interpretations of a person's behavior in terms of the label. The label guides our perception.

There is a famous study that we briefly mentioned in Chapter 1 that demonstrates the perceptual biasing effect of labeling (Rosenhan, 1973). Different researchers went to several different hospitals and faked a major symptom of schizophrenic disorders, auditory hallucinations (hearing voices). The voice in these cases was saying the words "empty," "hollow," and "thud." Other than this symptom, the researchers acted normal and only lied about their true identities. First, they wanted to see whether they would be admitted given this singular symptom. Second, they wanted to see what would happen after they were admitted if they acted normal and said that they no longer heard the voices and that they were feeling normal again. Here's what happened. In brief, the fake patients were admitted with a diagnosis of schizophrenia and their subsequent normal behavior was misinterpreted in terms of this diagnosis. For example, one person's excessive note taking was interpreted as a function of his illness when, in fact, he was just trying to take notes to document the study. Ironically, the true patients realized that the fake patients were not true patients, but the staff, guided by the diagnostic labels, did not. Even when the fake patients were released (which took a while), they carried the label "schizophrenia in remission."

Such perceptual biasing is further complicated by the misrepresentation of disordered people on television and in other media. They are often depicted as violent and dangerous to others when the vast majority of people with disorders are not a threat to anyone except maybe themselves (Applebaum, 2004; Lilienfeld, Lynn, Ruscio, & Beyerstein, 2010; Teplin, 1985). Most people with mental disorders are experiencing a troubled period in their lives and are finding it a difficult adjustment. Remember to distinguish between the person and the label. We need labels in order to know how to treat people with problems and to conduct research on these problems, but there is much more to a person than a label.

Now that we have a general understanding of the diagnostic classification system and its weaknesses, we will consider some of the major clinical disorders (labels).

Section Summary

In this section, we discussed how mental disorders are diagnosed and classified. The most widely used diagnostic system is the Diagnostic and Statistical Manual of Mental Disorders—Fourth Edition (DSM-IV). The DSM-IV bases classification upon behavioral and psychological symptoms and provides diagnostic guidelines for more than 300 disorders. A major strength of the DSM-IV is that it is more reliable than previous editions. Because some disorders share certain symptoms, the DSM-IV clusters the disorders into major categories, such as anxiety disorders. In addition to requiring an evaluation of a person's condition with respect to these clinical disorders, the DSM-IV requires a separate personality disorder diagnosis. The DSM is a work in progress, and the newest version, the DSM-V, will be available in 2013.

The downside to disorder classification is that labels are attached to people, thereby biasing our perception of these people in terms of their labels. Such perceptual biasing is further complicated by the misrepresentation of people with disorders by the media as violent and dangerous when most are not a threat to anyone except possibly themselves. Although labeling does lead to such perceptual bias, we need to use labels to know how to treat people with disorders and to conduct research on disorders.

ConceptCheck | 1

> Explain what the DSM-IV is.

> Explain the negative effect of attaching labels to disorders and why we need labels even though we know they have such effects.

Three Major Categories of Mental Disorders

As you read this section, beware of the "medical school syndrome"—the tendency to think that you have a disorder (or disease) when you read about its symptoms. Symptoms are behaviors or mental processes that indicate the presence of a disorder. The symptoms of many disorders often involve behavior and thinking that

Table 10.1	Three Major Categories of Clinical Disorders and Some Specific Disorders Within Each Category
Major Category	**Specific Disorders Within Category**
Anxiety disorders	Specific phobia, social phobia, agoraphobia, panic disorder with and without agoraphobia, generalized anxiety disorder, obsessive-compulsive disorder
Mood disorders	Major depressive disorder, bipolar disorder
Schizophrenic disorders	Schizophrenia (paranoid, disorganized, catatonic, undifferentiated, and residual subtypes)

we all experience, which may lead us to think we have the disorders. To prevent such misdiagnoses, remember the criteria that we discussed for distinguishing abnormal behavior and thinking. For example, we all get anxious or depressed (symptoms of several different disorders) at different times in our lives for understandable reasons, such as an upcoming presentation or a death in the family. These feelings of anxiety and depression only become symptoms of a disorder when they prevent us from functioning normally. We are suffering from a disorder only if our reactions to life's challenges become atypical, maladaptive, disturbing to ourselves or others, and irrational.

What causes such abnormal behavior and thinking? Most causal explanations for mental disorders are tied to the four major research approaches—biological, behavioral, cognitive, and sociocultural. None of these approaches has proven consistently better at explaining all of the various disorders, though particular approaches are sometimes better for specific disorders. Even in these cases, however, it appears best to formulate an explanation in terms of more than one kind of cause. This is usually referred to as the **biopsychosocial approach**—explaining abnormality as the result of the interaction among biological, psychological (behavioral and cognitive), and sociocultural factors. As we consider various disorders, I will provide some examples of this type of explanation. Table 10.1 outlines the three major categories of disorders, along with the specific clinical disorders within each category, that we will consider.

Anxiety Disorders

We all have experienced anxiety. Don't you get anxious at exam times, especially at final exam time? Most students do. How do you feel when you are about to give an oral presentation? Anxiety usually presents itself again. These are normal reactions, not signs of a disorder. In anxiety disorders, anxiety often occurs inexplicably and is so intense that it prevents the person from functioning normally in daily life. **Anxiety disorders** are disorders in which excessive anxiety leads to personal

biopsychosocial approach Explaining abnormality as the result of the interaction among biological, psychological (behavioral and cognitive), and sociocultural factors.

anxiety disorders Disorders in which excessive anxiety leads to personal distress and atypical, maladaptive, and irrational behavior.

specific phobia An anxiety disorder indicated by a marked and persistent fear of specific objects or situations that is excessive and unreasonable.

distress and atypical, maladaptive, and irrational behavior. We'll discuss several different anxiety disorders—specific phobias, social phobia, agoraphobia, panic disorder, generalized anxiety disorder, and obsessive-compulsive disorder.

Specific phobia. According to the DSM-IV, a **specific phobia** is indicated by a marked and persistent fear of specific objects or situations (such as snakes or heights) that is excessive and unreasonable. A selection of specific phobias are given in Table 10.2. The person realizes that the fear is excessive and unreasonable but cannot control it. Both the avoidance of the object or situation and the anxious anticipation of encountering the object or situation interfere with the person's normal life. This is important. Many of us have fears of such things as heights, snakes, and spiders, but we do not have a disorder. The anxiety and fear are not to the degree that they interfere with normal functioning and lead us to behave in maladaptive and irrational ways.

To emphasize this difference, consider this brief description of a case of a woman with a specific phobia of birds. She became housebound because of her fear of encountering a bird. Any noises that she heard within the house she thought were birds that had somehow gotten in. Even without encountering an

Table 10.2	A Selection of Specific Phobias
Phobia	**Specific Fear**
Acrophobia	Fear of heights
Aerophobia	Fear of flying
Agyrophobia	Fear of crossing streets
Arachnophobia	Fear of spiders
Claustrophobia	Fear of closed spaces
Cynophobia	Fear of dogs
Gamophobia	Fear of marriage
Gephyrophobia	Fear of crossing bridges
Hydrophobia	Fear of water
Ophidiophobia	Fear of snakes
Ornithophobia	Fear of birds
Pyrophobia	Fear of fire
Thanatophobia	Fear of death
Xenophobia	Fear of strangers
Zoophobia	Fear of animals

actual bird, the dreaded anticipation of doing so completely controlled her behavior. When she did leave her house, she would carefully back out of her driveway so that she did not hit a bird; she feared that the birds would retaliate if she did. She realized that such cognitive activity was beyond the capabilities of birds, but she could not control her fear. Her behavior and thinking were clearly abnormal.

What causes a specific phobia? One biopsychosocial answer involves both behavioral and biological factors. We learn phobias through classical conditioning and are biologically predisposed to learn some fears more easily than others. We are conditioned to fear a specific object or situation. Remember Watson and Rayner's study described in Chapter 4 in which they classically conditioned Little Albert to fear white rats? Behavioral

"Stephen's fear of heights is particularly bad today."

Naf/Cartoonstock.com

psychologists believe that the fears in specific phobias are learned the same way, but through stressful experiences in the real world, especially during early childhood. For example, a fear of birds might be due to the stressful experience of seeing Alfred Hitchcock's movie *The Birds* (in which birds savagely attack humans) at a young age. You should also remember from Chapter 4 that biological preparedness constrains learning. Certain associations (such as taste and sickness) are easy to learn, while others (such as taste and electric shock) are very difficult. This biological preparedness shows up with specific phobias in that fears that seem to have more evolutionary survival value (such as heights or animals) are more frequent than ones that do not (McNally, 1987). It is also more difficult to extinguish fears that have more evolutionary survival value (Davey, 1995).

Social phobia and agoraphobia. Most phobias are classified as specific phobias, but the DSM-IV describes two broader types of phobias, social phobia and agoraphobia.

© 2004 by Sidney Harris

social phobia An anxiety disorder indicated by a marked and persistent fear of one or more social performance situations in which there is exposure to unfamiliar people or scrutiny by others.

agoraphobia An anxiety disorder indicated by a marked and persistent fear of being in places or situations from which escape may be difficult or embarrassing.

panic disorder An anxiety disorder in which a person experiences recurrent panic attacks.

Social phobia is a marked and persistent fear of one or more social performance situations in which there is exposure to unfamiliar people or scrutiny by others. Again this is more than normal anxiety before giving a talk. The fear is excessive, unreasonable, and interferes with the person's normal functioning. For example, the person may fear eating in public and will have great difficulty managing lunch at work; she will reject all lunch and dinner invitations, greatly limiting her social opportunities. The fear may be specific to one particular social situation (such as eating in public) or more general (such as functioning inadequately with respect to all behavior in front of others), leading to the avoidance of most social situations. Social phobia is different from **agoraphobia,** the fear of being in places or situations from which escape may be difficult or embarrassing. The name of this disorder literally means fear of the marketplace; in Greek, "agora" means marketplace, and "phobia" means fear. In addition to the marketplace, situations commonly feared in agoraphobia include being in a crowd, standing in a line, and traveling in a crowded bus or train or in a car in heavy traffic. To avoid these situations, people with agoraphobia usually won't leave the security of their home.

Panic disorder. Agoraphobia usually occurs with panic disorder. **Panic disorder** is a condition in which a person experiences recurrent panic attacks—sudden onsets of intense fear. A panic attack includes symptoms such as trembling, sweating, heart palpitations, chest pain, shortness of breath, and feelings of choking and dizziness. The person is overrun with anxiety and fear. Some panic attacks occur when a person is faced with some dreaded situation (such as giving a speech), but others occur without any apparent reason. According to the DSM-IV, panic disorder can occur with or without agoraphobia. One explanation of panic disorder with agoraphobia is the fear-of-fear hypothesis: Agoraphobia is the result of the fear of having a panic attack in a public place. According to this hypothesis, agoraphobia is a case of classical conditioning in which the fear-and-avoidance response is a conditioned response to the initial panic attack.

The Scream, Munch, Edvard (1863–1944) © ARS, NY.

The Scream by Edvard Munch. This painting is typically interpreted as illustrating the intense terror in a panic attack. According to Comer (2010), the painting stems from an actual incident in Munch's life. Munch and two friends were walking on a bridge at sunset when Munch actually experienced the enormous anxiety that he brought to life in the painting.

Generalized anxiety disorder. Panic attacks occur suddenly in panic disorder. In generalized anxiety disorder, the anxiety is chronic and lasts for months. **Generalized anxiety disorder** is a disorder in which the person has excessive, global anxiety and worries that he cannot control, for a period of at least 6 months. The person just cannot stop worrying, and the anxiety is general—it is not tied to specific objects or situations as it is in a phobic disorder. About 5 percent of us will develop a generalized anxiety disorder in our lifetimes (American Psychiatric Association, 2000). Recent biological research has indicated that generalized anxiety disorder may be related to a biochemical dysfunction in the brain, that involves GABA, a neurotransmitter that we discussed in Chapter 2. Remember, GABA is the major inhibitory neurotransmitter, which means that it causes neurons to stop generating impulses. In anxiety and fear situations, more and more neurons get excited. After a while, this state of excitability in a normal person triggers the release of GABA to reduce the level of neuronal firing back to normal, which reduces the feelings of anxiety (Comer, 2010). A person with generalized anxiety disorder may have problems activating GABA, and therefore the feelings of anxiety are not reduced.

Obsessive-compulsive disorder. In **obsessive-compulsive disorder,** a person experiences recurrent obsessions or compulsions that are recognized by the person as excessive or unreasonable, but consume considerable time and cause significant distress and disruption in the person's daily life. Some people with obsessive-compulsive disorder experience only obsessions or only compulsions, but most suffer both. An **obsession** is a persistent intrusive thought, idea, impulse, or image that causes anxiety. A **compulsion** is a repetitive and rigid behavior that a person feels compelled to perform in order to reduce anxiety. The most common obsessions are concerned with contamination through germs, dirt, or other toxic substances, and the fear that something terrible, such as death or illness, is going to occur; the most frequent compulsions are excessive hand washing, bathing, and grooming (Rapoport, 1989). The lifetime prevalence rate for obsessive-compulsive disorder is only 1 to 2% (American Psychiatric Association, 2000).

It is important to realize that many people experience minor obsessions (a pervasive worry about upcoming exams) or compulsions (arranging their desks in a certain way), but they do not have this disorder. People with obsessive-compulsive disorder cannot function in their daily lives because their obsessions and compulsions consume most of the day and prevent a normal life. Normal people might go back to check to make sure that the stove was turned off once

generalized anxiety disorder An anxiety disorder in which a person has excessive, global anxiety that he or she cannot control for a period of at least 6 months.

obsessive-compulsive disorder An anxiety disorder in which the person experiences recurrent obsessions or compulsions that are perceived by the person as excessive or unreasonable, but cause significant distress and disruption in the person's daily life.

obsession A persistent intrusive thought, idea, impulse, or image that causes anxiety.

compulsion A repetitive and rigid behavior that a person feels compelled to perform in order to reduce anxiety.

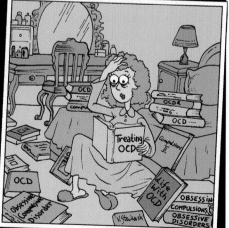

Snapshots at jasonlove.com

© Jason Love

(or even twice), but a person with an obsessive-compulsive disorder might check 50 times and in a very ritualistic manner. This is a checking compulsion—the person checks the same thing over and over again, usually a set number of times and in a particular manner. Similarly, people who suffer from a cleaning compulsion feel compelled to keep cleaning themselves. Such people might spend their day washing their hands, taking showers, and engaging in other cleaning activities. Compulsions are usually tied to obsessions. For example, the cleaning compulsion is usually tied to a contamination obsession in which people are overly concerned with avoiding contamination. To reduce the anxiety stemming from the fear of contamination, they feel compelled to keep cleaning themselves.

It is not known for sure what causes obsessive-compulsive disorder, but recent research suggests that a neurotransmitter imbalance involving serotonin may be involved. Antidepressant drugs (SSRIs) that increase serotonin activity help many patients with obsessive-compulsive disorder (Rapoport, 1991). Serotonin activity has also been linked to two parts of the brain that may be related to the disorder, the orbital region of the frontal cortex (the cortical area just above the eyes) and the caudate nucleus (an area in the basal ganglia). PET scans of these two areas indicate activity significantly greater than normal in people with obsessive-compulsive disorder (Comer, 2010). These two areas are part of a brain circuit that is involved in filtering out irrelevant information and disengaging attention, which are certainly central aspects of obsessive-compulsive disorder (Seligman, Walker, & Rosenhan, 2001). One explanation may be that serotonin works to stabilize activity in these areas. One truly bizarre case of obsessive-compulsive disorder highlights the importance of the frontal lobe region. A man with obsessive-compulsive disorder became severely depressed and attempted suicide. He shot himself in the head, but fortunately survived and was cured of his disorder. The bullet had removed some of his orbital frontal cortex and his disorder with it.

Mood Disorders

Mood disorders involve dramatic changes in a person's emotional mood that are excessive and unwarranted. Most commonly, depression is involved, but some mood disorders also involve the other extreme of mood, becoming manic. All of us have been depressed at various points in our lives and extremely happy at other times, but it is important to realize the difference between normal mood changes and abnormal ones. Let's consider depression first.

Major depressive disorder. When people say that they are depressed, they usually are referring to their feelings of sadness and downward mood following a stressful life event (such as a death in the family, the breakup of a relationship, or the loss of a job). Such mood changes are understandable and over time usually right themselves. A major depressive disorder, however, is debilitating, has an impact on every part of a person's life, and usually doesn't right itself. To be classified as having a **major depressive**

mood disorders Disorders that involve dramatic changes in a person's emotional mood that are excessive and unwarranted.

major depressive disorder A mood disorder in which the person has experienced one or more major depressive episodes.

disorder, a person must have experienced one or more major depressive episodes. A **major depressive episode** is characterized by symptoms such as feelings of intense hopelessness, low self-esteem and worthlessness, extreme fatigue, dramatic changes in eating and sleeping behavior, inability to concentrate, and greatly diminished interest in family, friends, and activities for a period of 2 weeks or more. Such people are not just down in the dumps, but rather are in a snowballing downward spiral that lasts for weeks. They lose interest in everything, even their life. Suicide is strongly related to depression and can occur at any point during or after a major depressive episode. Any comments about suicide made by people suffering a major depression should be taken seriously.

> **major depressive episode** An episode characterized by symptoms such as feelings of intense hopelessness, low self-esteem and worthlessness, extreme fatigue, dramatic changes in eating and sleeping behavior, inability to concentrate, and greatly diminished interest in family, friends, and activities for a period of 2 weeks or more.

Because it occurs so often, depression has been called the "common cold of disorders." Women suffer from major depressive disorders about twice as often as men. For women, as many as 25 percent may suffer a major depression at some time in their lives, compared with about 12 percent of men (Kessler et al., 2003). This gender difference seems to be true worldwide (Weissman et al., 1996). Recent research suggests that this gender difference for depression may be due to biological differences (Westly, 2010). The sex hormones estrogen and testosterone have different effects on the neurotransmitters involved in mood (serotonin, norepinephrine, and dopamine), leading to a difference in both emotional reaction and symptomology in women and men. The primary emotional symptom for women is sadness; but for men, it is anger often paired with irritability. Thus, female depression will be seen as depression, but male depression may be mistakenly seen as some other emotional problem, such as general frustration, and not the serious disorder that it is. This difference along with the fact that women are more likely than men to seek help almost certainly contributes to the gender difference in the clinical prevalence rates for depression.

There is also a recent argument that the high prevalence rate for depression is spurious in that it is due to overdiagnosis caused by insufficient diagnostic criteria (Horowitz & Wakefield, 2007). True mental disorders are usually rare, with very low prevalence rates, but depression has a very high prevalence rate. According to Andrews and Thomson (2009, 2010), the fact that depression has such a high prevalence rate poses an evolutionary paradox because the pressures of evolution should have led our brains to resist such a high rate of malfunction. Andrews and Thomson propose that much of what is diagnosed as depression should not be thought of as a true mental disorder (a brain malfunction) but rather as an evolutionary mental adaptation (stress response mechanism) that focuses the mind to better solve the complex life problems that brought about the troubled state. This is an intriguing hypothesis with implications not only for the diagnostic criteria for this disorder but also for the therapeutic approaches to treat it.

Traditional explanations of major depressive disorder propose both biological and psychological factors as causes. A leading biological explanation involves neurotransmitter imbalances, primarily inadequate serotonin and norepinephrine activity. Antidepressant drugs (to be discussed later in the

■ **manic episode** An episode characterized by abnormally elevated mood in which the person experiences symptoms such as inflated self-esteem with grandiose delusions, a decreased need for sleep, constant talking, distractibility, restlessness, and poor judgment for a period of at least a week.

chapter) are the most common treatment for such imbalances. There is also evidence of a genetic predisposition for this disorder. The likelihood of one identical twin getting a disorder given that the other identical twin has the disorder is the concordance rate for identical twins for the disorder. For major depressive disorder, the concordance rate for identical twins is about 50 percent (Tsuang & Faraone, 1990), much higher than the concordance rate for fraternal twins and the base rate of occurrence in the general population.

If the disorder were totally genetic in origin, however, this rate would be 100 percent. Because it isn't, nongenetic factors are also involved as causes in major depressive disorder. Cognitive factors have been found to be important. The person's perceptual and cognitive processes are assumed to be faulty, causing the depression. We discussed an example of such faulty cognitive processing in Chapter 8. Remember the pessimistic explanatory style in which a person explains negative events in terms of internal (her own fault), stable (here to stay), and global (applies to all aspects of her life) causes. Such a style, paired with a series of negative events in a person's life, will lead to learned helplessness and depression. Thus, the cause of the person's depression is her own thinking, in this case how she makes attributions. Cognitive therapies, which we will discuss later in this chapter, attempt to replace such maladaptive thinking with more adaptive thinking that will not lead to depression. These therapies have been shown to be just as effective as drug therapy in treating depression (DeRubeis et al., 2005).

Bipolar disorder. Sometimes major depressive disorder is referred to as a unipolar disorder to contrast it with bipolar disorder, another mood disorder in which the person's mood takes dramatic mood swings between depression and mania. Such disorders used to be called "manic-depressive" disorders. Experiencing a mania is not just having an "up" day. A **manic episode** is a period of at least a week of abnormally elevated mood in which the person experiences such symptoms as inflated self-esteem with grandiose delusions, a decreased need for sleep, constant talking, distractibility, restlessness, and poor judgment. The person's behavior becomes maladaptive and interferes with daily functioning.

Consider the following behavior of a person experiencing a manic episode. A postal worker stayed up all night and then went off normally to work in the morning. He returned later that morning, however, having quit his job, withdrawn all of the family savings and spent it on fish and aquariums. He told his wife that, the night before,

"Now that I've swung back to depression, I'm truly sorry for what I did when I was manic."

he had discovered a way to keep fish alive forever. He then ran off to canvass the neighborhood for possible sales. This person showed poor judgment and a decreased need for sleep, and his behavior disrupted his normal functioning (he quit his job). In the beginning, milder stages of a manic episode, some people become not only more energetic but also more creative until the episode accelerates and their behavior deteriorates.

There is no diagnosis for mania alone. It is part of a **bipolar disorder** in which recurrent cycles of depressive and manic episodes occur. A bipolar disorder is an emotional roller coaster, with the person's mood swinging from manic highs to depressive lows. There are two types of bipolar disorder. In Bipolar I disorder, the person has both major manic and depressive episodes. In Bipolar II disorder, the person has full-blown depressive episodes, but the manic episodes are milder. Bipolar I disorder is more common than Bipolar II disorder, but both disorders are rare and only affect about 1 percent of the population (Kessler et al., 1994; American Psychiatric Association, 2000).

Because the concordance rate for identical twins for bipolar disorder is so strong, 70 percent (Tsuang & Faraone, 1990), biological causal explanations are the most common. In fact, researchers are presently working on identifying the specific genes that make a person vulnerable to bipolar disorder. As with major depressive disorder, the biological predisposition shows up as neurotransmitter imbalances. In this case, the imbalances swing between inadequate activity (depression) and too much activity (mania). The most common treatment is drug therapy, and the specific drugs used will be discussed later in the chapter.

Schizophrenic Disorders

Schizophrenia is the most serious disorder that we will discuss. It is the disorder that people are usually thinking of when they use words such as "insane" and "deranged." More people are institutionalized with schizophrenia than with any other disorder, and schizophrenia is much more difficult to treat successfully than other disorders. Thankfully, only about 1 percent of the population suffer from this disorder (Gottesman, 1991). The onset of schizophrenia is usually in late adolescence or early adulthood. Men and women are equally likely to develop schizophrenia, but it tends to strike men earlier and more severely (American Psychiatric Association, 2000). Schizophrenia is more common in the lower socioeconomic classes than in the higher ones, and also for those who are single, separated, or divorced (Comer, 2010).

Schizophrenia is referred to as a **psychotic disorder** because it is characterized by a loss of contact with reality. The word "schizophrenia" is Greek in origin and literally means "split mind." This is not a bad description; in a person with schizophrenia, mental functions become split from each other and the person becomes detached from reality. The person has trouble distinguishing reality from his own

bipolar disorder A mood disorder in which recurrent cycles of depressive and manic episodes occur.

psychotic disorder A disorder characterized by a loss of contact with reality.

distorted view of the world. This splitting of mental functions, however, has led to the confusion of schizophrenia with "split personality" or multiple personality disorder (now called dissociative identity disorder in the DSM-IV), but these are very different disorders. In schizophrenia, the split is between the mental functions and their contact with reality; in multiple-personality disorder, one's personality is split into two or more distinct personalities.

The symptoms of schizophrenia. The symptoms of schizophrenia vary, but clinicians usually divide these symptoms into three categories—positive, negative, and disorganized. This use of the terms "positive" and "negative" is consistent with their use in Chapter 4, on learning. Positive means that something has been added, and negative means that something has been removed.

Positive symptoms are the more active symptoms that reflect an excess or distortion of normal thinking or behavior, including **hallucinations** (false sensory perceptions) and **delusions** (false beliefs). Hallucinations are usually auditory, hearing voices that aren't really there. Remember, the fake patients in Rosenhan's study said that they heard voices and were admitted and diagnosed as having a schizophrenic disorder. Delusions fall into several categories, such as delusions of persecution (for example, believing that one is the victim of conspiracies) or delusions of grandeur (for example, believing that one is a person of great importance, such as Jesus Christ or Napoleon). Hallucinations and delusions are referred to as positive symptoms because they refer to things that have been added. Negative symptoms refer to things that have been removed. These are deficits or losses in emotion, speech, energy level, social activity, and even basic drives such as hunger and thirst. For example, many people with schizophrenia suffer the flat affect in which there is a marked lack of emotional expressiveness. Their faces show no expression, and they speak in a monotone. Similarly, there may be a serious reduction in their quantity and quality of speech. People suffering from schizophrenia may also lose their energy and become extremely apathetic—not able to start a task, much less finish one.

Disorganized symptoms include nonsensical speech and behavior and inappropriate emotion. Disorganized speech sounds like a "word salad," with unconnected words incoherently spoken together and a shifting from one topic to another without any apparent connections. One thought does not follow the other. Those who show inappropriate emotion may smile when given terrible news. Their emotional reactions seem unsuited to the situation.

Behavior may also be catatonic—physical actions that do not appear to be goal-directed, such as assuming and maintaining postures and remaining motionless for a long period of time. Catatonic behavior takes extreme forms ranging from immobility to hyperactivity (such as rocking constantly).

According to the DSM-IV, **schizophrenia** is the presence, most of the time during at least a 1-month period, of at least two of the following symptoms—hallucinations,

▌ **hallucination** A false sensory perception.

▌ **delusion** A false belief.

▌ **schizophrenia** A psychotic disorder in which at least two of the following symptoms are present most of the time during a 1-month period—hallucinations, delusions, disorganized speech, disorganized or catatonic behavior, or negative symptoms such as loss of emotion.

Table 10.3	Five Subtypes of Schizophrenic Disorder
Subtype	**Symptoms**
Disorganized	Disorganized speech, disorganized behavior, or inappropriate emotion
Catatonic	Extreme movement symptoms ranging from excessive motor activity to posturing (immobility for long periods of time)
Paranoid	Organized cognition and emotion, but with hallucinations and delusions that are usually concerned with persecution
Undifferentiated	Mixed-bag category—symptoms fit the criteria of more than one of the above three types or none of them
Residual	There has been a past schizophrenic episode, but presently only some negative symptoms and no positive symptoms (hallucinations and delusions)

delusions, disorganized speech, disorganized or catatonic behavior, or any negative symptom (such as loss of emotion). Based on these symptoms, the DSM-IV distinguishes between five subtypes of schizophrenia (summarized in Table 10.3).

In addition to these five subtypes, clinicians have used the way the symptoms develop to make other distinctions. One distinction between chronic and acute schizophrenia deals with how quickly the symptoms developed. In chronic schizophrenia, there is a long period of development over years and the decline in the person's behavior and thinking occurs gradually. In acute schizophrenia, there is a sudden onset of symptoms that usually can be attributed to a crisis in the person's life, and the person functioned normally before the crisis with no clinical signs of the disorder. Acute schizophrenia is more of a reactive disorder, and recovery is much more likely.

Another distinction is between Type I and II schizophrenia (Crow, 1985). Type I is characterized by positive symptoms, and Type II by negative symptoms. Type I is similar to acute schizophrenia: The person has usually functioned relatively normally before the disorder strikes and there is a higher likelihood of recovery. People with Type I schizophrenia respond better to drug therapy than do those with Type II. This difference may be because the positive symptoms of Type I result from neurotransmitter imbalances, which are affected by drugs, whereas the more permanent brain abnormalities that produce the negative symptoms of Type II are not as affected by drugs.

The causes of schizophrenia. Schizophrenia probably has many different causes, and we do not have a very good understanding of any of them. Hypothesized causes inevitably involve a genetic or biological predisposition factor. There definitely appears to be a genetic predisposition to some schizophrenia; it seems to run in families, with the concordance rate for identical twins similar to that for a major depression, about 50 percent (DeLisi, 1997; Gottesman, 1991). This is significantly greater than the 17 percent concordance rate for fraternal twins. No particular genes have yet been identified, but it is possible that different genes might be involved in the different types of schizophrenia.

The concordance rate for identical twins could also be partially due to prenatal factors (Brown, 2006). One hypothesis involves prenatal viral infections. Research has found that people are at increased risk for schizophrenia if there was a flu epidemic during the middle of their fetal development (Takei, Van Os, & Murray, 1995; Wright, Takei, Rifkin, & Murray, 1995). There is even a birth month effect for schizophrenia. People born in the winter/spring months (January to April) following the fall/winter flu season are more likely to develop schizophrenia because it is more likely that they were exposed to a flu virus during fetal development (Torrey, Miller, Rawlings, & Yolken, 1997). According to the viral hypothesis, the invading virus impairs fetal brain development, making people more susceptible to developing schizophrenia later in life. The viral hypothesis is further supported by the finding that the 50 percent concordance rate in identical twins is the result of a 60 percent chance for identical twins that share the same placenta (about two-thirds of identical twins), but only a 10 percent chance for identical twins with separate placentas (Davis & Phelps, 1995). It is certainly more likely that a viral infection would affect both twins in the same placenta rather than twins in separate placentas.

Given the genetic/biological predispositions, what might be the organic problem that the person is predisposed to develop? There are two good answers—neurotransmitter imbalances and brain abnormalities. People with schizophrenia have elevated levels of dopamine activity in certain areas in the brain (Davis, Kahn, Ko, & Davidson, 1991). Autopsy and brain scan research indicates that the brains of people with schizophrenia have an excess of dopamine receptors. In addition, drugs that decrease dopamine activity reduce schizophrenic symptoms, and drugs that increase dopamine activity seem to heighten the symptoms of people with schizophrenia and produce schizophrenic symptoms in people who do not have schizophrenia. Such findings led to the development of antipsychotic drugs that are dopamine antagonists (reduce the level of dopamine activity) and help control the symptoms in many people with schizophrenia. These drugs, their side effects, and more recently developed antipsychotic drugs will be discussed in more detail when we consider biomedical therapies.

Various brain abnormalities have been found in people with schizophrenia, especially those suffering from Type II and chronic schizophrenia (Buchanan & Carpenter, 1997). For example, brain scans of those with schizophrenia often indicate shrunken cerebral tissue and enlarged fluid-filled areas. In addition, some brain areas (the thalamus) seem to be smaller than normal and the frontal lobes less active. Such brain abnormalities could be due to gene defects or prenatal factors. Birth complications (postnatal factors), such as oxygen deprivation, may also play a role in the development of these brain abnormalities (Cannon, 1997; Wright, Takei, Rifkin, & Murray, 1995).

Even given all of this biological evidence, biopsychosocial explanations are necessary to explain all of the evidence accumulated about schizophrenia. For example, if the disorder were completely genetic in origin, then the concordance rate would be 100 percent for identical twins, and it's only about 50 percent. A popular biopsychosocial explanation is the **vulnerability–stress model**—genetic, prenatal, and postnatal biological factors render a person vulnerable to schizophrenia, but environmental stress determines whether it develops or not (Gottesman, 1991). According to the vulnerability-stress model, we vary in our vulnerability to schizophrenia. A person's level of vulnerability interacts with the stressful social-cognitive events in his life to determine the likelihood of schizophrenia. Remember that schizophrenia typically strikes in late adolescence/early adulthood, periods of unusually high stress levels. There is also some evidence that dysfunctional family environments may be a contributing stress factor (Fowles, 1992).

In summary, there has been much research on the causes of schizophrenia, but we still do not have many clear answers. The only certainty is that schizophrenia is a disabling disorder with many causes. Explanations inevitably involve a biological component, making drug therapy the predominant treatment for schizophrenia. Regardless, given the person's loss of contact with reality, psychotherapies are usually difficult, if not impossible, to institute. In the next section, we will consider various types of drug therapy, along with other types of biological therapy, and the major types of psychotherapy.

> **vulnerability–stress model** A biopsychosocial explanation of schizophrenia which proposes that genetic, prenatal, and postnatal biological factors render a person vulnerable to schizophrenia, but environmental stress determines whether it develops or not.

Section Summary

In this section, we discussed three major categories of mental disorders—anxiety disorders, mood disorders, and schizophrenic disorders. Anxiety disorders are disorders in which excessive anxiety leads to personal distress and atypical, maladaptive, and irrational behavior. For each of the anxiety disorders, anxiety is involved in a different way. For example, in a specific phobic disorder, there is a marked and persistent fear of specific objects or situations that is excessive and unreasonable. There are two broader types of phobias, however—social phobia and agoraphobia. Social phobia involves a fear of social performance situations in which there is exposure to unfamiliar people or scrutiny by others. Agoraphobia is the fear of being in places or situations from which escape may be difficult or embarrassing. Agoraphobia often occurs with panic disorder, recurrent panic attacks in which the person is overwhelmed by anxiety and fear. Panic disorder can occur with or without agoraphobia.

Panic attacks occur suddenly in panic disorder, but the anxiety is chronic and global in generalized anxiety disorder. In obsessive-compulsive disorder, the person experiences recurrent obsessions (persistent thoughts that cause anxiety) and compulsions (repetitive and rigid behaviors that have to be performed to alleviate anxiety). It is not known what causes obsessive-compulsive disorder, but recent research indicates a biochemical lack of serotonin activity in two parts of the brain. SSRI antidepressants that increase serotonin activity have had some success in treating obsessive-compulsive symptoms.

Mood disorders involve dramatic changes in a person's emotional mood that are excessive and unwarranted. The most common is major depressive disorder, which is twice as frequent in women as in men. Sometimes this disorder is referred to as unipolar depression to contrast it with bipolar disorder, in which the person has recurrent cycles of depressive and manic (elevated mood) episodes. The concordance rate (the likelihood that one identical twin will get the disorder if the other twin has it) is substantial for both disorders, about 50 percent for depression and 70 percent for bipolar disorder. Neurotransmitter imbalances seem to be involved in both disorders, and cognitive factors in major depressive disorder.

Schizophrenia is the most serious disorder that we discussed. It is a psychotic disorder, which means that the person loses contact with reality. Clinicians divide schizophrenic symptoms into three categories—positive, negative, and disorganized. Based on these various types of symptoms, clinicians have identified five subtypes of schizophrenia—disorganized, catatonic, paranoid, undifferentiated, and residual. Schizophrenia seems to have many possible causes. Biological abnormalities in people with schizophrenia range from elevated dopamine activity levels to shrunken cerebral tissue, and there is also evidence that prenatal viral infections and birth complications may be involved. A popular biopsychosocial explanation of schizophrenia is the vulnerability–stress model, which proposes that genetic, prenatal, and postnatal biological factors render a person vulnerable to schizophrenia, but environmental stress determines whether it develops or not.

ConceptCheck | 2

➤ **Explain what is meant by the biopsychosocial approach and then describe a biopsychosocial explanation for specific phobic disorders.**

➤ **Explain how the two anxiety disorders, specific phobia and generalized anxiety disorder, are different.**

➤ **Explain how the concordance rates for identical twins for a major depressive disorder and for schizophrenia indicate that more than biological causes are responsible for these disorders.**

➤ **Explain the difference between schizophrenia and "split personality."**

The Treatment of Mental Disorders

Before discussing treatment for disorders (types of therapy), we need to describe the various types of mental health professionals who treat disorders. Table 10.4 lists most of the major types of mental health professionals, along with the type of credential and the typical kinds of problems they treat. States have licensing requirements for these various mental health professionals, but they do not regulate the use of labels such as "counselor." This is why you should verify that any therapist that you are considering for therapy is licensed. There is also one major difference between psychiatrists and the other health professionals. Psychiatrists are medical doctors. This means that psychiatrists can write prescriptions for medical treatment of patients. This is especially important because drug therapy is a major type of treatment for many disorders.

There are two major types of therapy, biomedical and psychological. **Biomedical therapy** involves the use of biological interventions, such as drugs, to treat disorders. **Psychotherapy** involves the use of psychological interventions to treat disorders. Psychotherapy is what we normally think of as therapy. There is a dialogue and interaction between the person and the therapist. They talk to each other. This is why psychotherapies are sometimes referred to as "talk therapies." The nature of the "talk" varies with the approach of the therapist. The behavioral, cognitive, psychoanalytic, and

biomedical therapy The use of biological interventions, such as drugs, to treat mental disorders.

psychotherapy The use of psychological interventions to treat mental disorders.

Table 10.4	Different Types of Mental Health Professionals
Type	**Credential and Job Description**
Clinical psychologist	Doctoral degree in clinical psychology; provides therapy for people with mental disorders
Counseling psychologist	Doctoral degree in psychological or educational counseling; counsels people with milder problems such as academic, job, and relationship problems
Psychiatrist	Medical degree with residency in mental health; provides therapy for people with mental disorders and is the only type of therapist who can prescribe drugs or other biomedical treatment
Psychoanalyst	Any of the above types of credential, but with training in psychoanalysis from a psychoanalytic institute; provides psychoanalytic therapy for psychological disorders
Clinical social worker	Master's or doctoral degree in social work with specialized training in counseling; provides help with social problems, such as family problems

humanistic approaches all lead to different styles of psychotherapy. In biomedical therapy, however, a drug or some other type of biological intervention is used to treat disorders. The interaction is biological, not interpersonal. As with psychotherapies, there are different types of biomedical therapy—drug therapy, electroconvulsive therapy, and psychosurgery. We will first consider these biomedical therapies and then the major types of psychotherapy.

Biomedical Therapies

Biomedical therapies for disorders have a long history, reaching back hundreds of years. Looking back, these earlier treatments may seem inhumane and cruel, but remember that we are assessing these treatments given our current state of medical and psychological knowledge, which is far superior to that available when such treatments were used. Let's consider a couple of examples.

Possibly the earliest biological treatment was trephining, which was done in the Middle Ages. In this primitive treatment, a trephine (stone tool) was used to cut away a section of the person's skull, supposedly to let evil spirits exit the body,

John W. Verano

The Granger Collection

Primitive biological therapy. The two holes in this ancient skull illustrate trephining—cutting away sections of a person's skull to let evil spirits exit the body, thus freeing the person from a disorder.

The tranquilizing chair. This treatment device was designed by Benjamin Rush, the "father of American psychiatry," in the early 1800s. Supposedly the restriction of the patient's activity and stimulation would have a calming effect by restricting the blood flow to the patient's brain. Although it seems barbaric today, it was intended as a humane alternative to the straight jacket at that time. In actuality, it did no harm nor good.

thus freeing the person from the disorder. A treatment device from the early 1800s was called the "tranquilizing chair." This device was designed by Benjamin Rush, the "father of American psychiatry," who actually instituted many humane reforms in the treatment of mental patients (Gamwell & Tomes, 1995). The treatment called for patients to be strapped into a tranquilizing chair, with the head enclosed inside a box, for long periods of time. The restriction of activity and stimulation was supposed to have a calming effect by restricting the flow of blood to the patient's brain. Such "therapies" seem absurd to us today, as does the fact that well into the nineteenth century, many mental patients were still being kept in chains in asylums, untreated. The history of therapy is a rather sad one.

Even the more contemporary biomedical treatments exist in an atmosphere of controversy. Most people have strong, negative feelings about shock therapy, and the most frequently used biomedical treatment, drug therapy, is shrouded in conflict (Valenstein, 1988). Why? Biomedical treatments are very different from undergoing psychotherapy. Direct biological interventions have a more powerful downside, because they involve possibly serious medical side effects. For example, high levels of some drugs in the blood are toxic and may even be fatal. Careful monitoring is essential. As we discuss the major types of biomedical treatments, we will include discussion of some of these potential problems. We start with drug therapy.

Drug therapy. The major medications used in drug therapy are lithium, antidepressant drugs, antianxiety drugs, and antipsychotic drugs. **Lithium** is not a drug, but rather a naturally occurring metallic element (a mineral salt) that is used to treat bipolar disorder. Lithium was actually sold as a substitute for table salt in the 1940s, but was taken off the market when reports of its toxicity and possible role in some deaths began to circulate (Valenstein, 1988). The discovery of lithium's effectiveness in combating bipolar disorder was accidental (Comer, 2010). Around 1950, John Cade, an Australian psychiatrist, injected guinea pigs with uric acid, which he thought was the cause of manic behavior, and mixed lithium with it so that the acid was more easily liquefied. Instead of becoming manic, the guinea pigs became lethargic. Later tests in humans showed that lithium stabilized the mood of patients with bipolar disorder. It is not understood exactly how lithium works (Lambert & Kinsley, 2005; Paulus, 2007), but within a rather short period of time, 1 to 2 weeks, it stabilizes mood in the majority of patients. Lithium levels in the blood must be monitored carefully, however, because of possible toxic effects—nausea, seizures, and even death (Montcrief, 1997). Because of these possibly toxic side effects, anticonvulsants (drugs used to control epileptic seizures) are now sometimes prescribed instead for people with bipolar disorder. Anticonvulsants seem to reduce bipolar disorder symptoms but have less dangerous potential side effects.

Antidepressant drugs are drugs used to treat depressive disorders. There are many different types. The first antidepressants developed were monoamine oxidase (MAO)

lithium A naturally occurring element (a mineral salt) that is used to treat bipolar disorder.

antidepressant drugs Drugs used to treat depressive disorders.

inhibitors and tricyclics (this name refers to the three-ring molecular structure of these drugs). MAO inhibitors increase the availability of the neurotransmitters norepinephrine and serotonin, which affect our mood, by preventing their breakdown (Julien, 2008). Tricyclics make the neurotransmitters norepinephrine, serotonin, and dopamine (also related to our mood) more available by blocking their reuptake during synaptic gap activity (Julien, 2008). Like lithium, the effects of both types of antidepressants were discovered accidentally when they were being tested for their impact on other problems (Comer, 2010). An MAO inhibitor was being tested as a possible treatment for tuberculosis when it was found to make the patients happier. In the case of tricyclics, their impact on depression was discovered when they were being tested as possible drugs for schizophrenia.

Research indicates that MAO inhibitors are fairly successful in combating depressive symptoms, but they are not used very often because of a potentially very dangerous side effect. Their interaction with several different foods and drinks may result in fatally high blood pressure. Tricyclics are prescribed more often than MAO inhibitors, because they are not subject to this potentially dangerous interaction. The most prescribed antidepressants by far, however, are the more recently developed selective serotonin reuptake inhibitors (SSRIs). Remember from Chapter 2 that their name describes how they achieve their effect—they selectively block the reuptake of serotonin in the synaptic gap, keeping the serotonin active and increasing its availability. The well-known antidepressant drugs Prozac, Zoloft, and Paxil are all SSRIs. The success rate of SSRIs in treatment is about the same as tricyclics, but they are prescribed more often because of milder side effects. Millions of prescriptions have been written for SSRIs, resulting in billions of dollars of sales. Prescriptions for the more recently developed selective serotonin and norepinephrine reuptake inhibitors (SSNRIs), such as Cymbalta and Effexor, that we also discussed in Chapter 2 are also on the increase. None of these various types of antidepressants, however, have immediate effects. It usually takes 3 to 6 weeks to see improvement.

There is a controversy about the effectiveness of antidepressant drugs. Some current research indicates that much of their effectiveness can be accounted for by placebo effects—improvements due to the expectation of getting better (Kirsch, 2010). Remember from Chapter 1 that a placebo is an inert substance or treatment that is given to patients who believe that it is a real treatment for their problem. An especially intriguing finding is that placebos that lead to actual physical side effects also lead to larger placebo effects. These placebo effects have sometimes

"Of course your daddy loves you. He's on Prozac—he loves everybody."

been found to be comparable to the improvement effects of antidepressant drugs (Fisher & Greenberg, 1997). Some researchers believe that this means much, if not most, of the effect found with antidepressant drugs may be due to placebo effects.

How can we make sense of these placebo effects? One possibility involves neurogenesis, which we discussed in Chapter 2. Remember, neurogenesis, the growth of new neurons, has been observed in the hippocampus in the adult brain (Jacobs, van Praag, & Gage, 2000a, 2000b). The **neurogenesis theory of depression** assumes that neurogenesis in the hippocampus stops during depression, and when neurogenesis resumes, the depression lifts (Jacobs, 2004). The question, then, is how do we get neurogenesis to resume? There are many possibilities. Research has shown that SSRIs lead to increased neurogenesis in other animals. Rats given Prozac make more neurons than rats not given Prozac. This too seems to be the case for humans taking antidepressants (Boldrini et al., 2009). The time frame for neurogenesis also fits the time frame for SSRIs to have an impact on mood. It takes 3 to 6 weeks for new cells to mature, the same time it typically takes SSRIs to improve the mood of a patient. This means that, in the case of the SSRIs, the increased serotonin activity may be responsible for getting neurogenesis going again and lifting mood.

Remember, however, what we said about disorders being biopsychosocial phenomena. It is certainly plausible that psychological factors could also have an impact on neurogenesis. Positive thinking, in the form of a strong placebo effect, might also get neurogenesis going again. A similar claim could be made for the effectiveness of cognitive psychotherapies in which therapists turn the patient's negative thinking into more positive thinking. The neurogenesis theory is only in its formative stage, but it does provide a coherent explanation of the many diverse improvement effects due to drugs, placebos, and psychotherapies.

Antianxiety drugs are drugs that treat anxiety problems and disorders. The best known antianxiety drugs, such as Valium and Xanax, are in a class of drugs called benzodiazepines. Benzodiazepines reduce anxiety by increasing the activity of the major inhibitory neurotransmitter GABA (Julien, 2008). When GABA's activity is increased, it reduces anxiety by slowing down and inhibiting neural activity, getting it back to normal levels. Unfortunately, recent evidence has shown that benzodiazepines have potentially dangerous side effects, such as physical dependence or fatal interactions with alcohol; but other types of nonbenzodiazepine antianxiety drugs have been developed with milder side effects. In addition, some antidepressant drugs, especially the SSRIs, have been very successful in treating anxiety disorders.

Antipsychotic drugs are drugs that reduce psychotic symptoms. The first antipsychotic drugs appeared in the 1950s and, as we discussed in Chapter 2, worked antagonistically by globally blocking receptor sites for dopamine,

neurogenesis theory of depression An explanation of depression that proposes that neurogenesis, the growth of new neurons, in the hippocampus stops during depression, and when it resumes, the depression lifts.

antianxiety drugs Drugs used to treat anxiety problems and disorders.

antipsychotic drugs Drugs used to treat psychotic disorders.

tardive dyskinesia A side effect of long-term use of traditional antipsychotic drugs causing the person to have uncontrollable facial tics, grimaces, and other involuntary movements of the lips, jaw, and tongue.

electroconvulsive therapy (ECT) A biomedical treatment for severe depression that involves electrically inducing a brief brain seizure.

thereby reducing its activity. These drugs greatly reduced the positive symptoms of schizophrenia but had little impact on the negative symptoms. Antipsychotic drugs revolutionized the treatment of schizophrenia and greatly reduced the number of people with schizophrenia in mental institutions. These early drugs, along with those developed through the 1980s, are referred to as "traditional" antipsychotic drugs to distinguish them from the more recently developed "new generation" antipsychotic drugs.

The traditional drugs (for example, Thorazine and Stelazine) produce side effects in motor movement that are similar to the movement problems of Parkinson's disease. In addition, there is a long-term-use side effect of traditional antipsychotic drugs called **tardive dyskinesia** in which the patient has uncontrollable facial tics, grimaces, and other involuntary movements of the lips, jaw, and tongue. The new generation antipsychotic drugs (for example, Clozaril and Risperdal) are more selective about where in the brain they reduce dopamine activity; therefore, they do not produce the severe movement side effects such as tardive dyskinesia. They also have the advantage of helping some patients' negative schizophrenic symptoms. This may be due to the fact that these drugs also decrease the level of serotonin activity. Regrettably, the new generation antipsychotic drugs have other potentially dangerous side effects and have to be monitored very carefully (Folsom, Fleisher, & Depp, 2006). Such monitoring is expensive; therefore, traditional drugs are often prescribed instead.

Recently a different type of new generation antipsychotic drug, trade name Abilify, has become available. Because of its neurochemical actions, Abilify is often referred to as a "third generation" antipsychotic drug (Julien, 2008). It achieves its effects by stabilizing the levels of both dopamine and serotonin activity in certain areas of the brain. It blocks receptor sites for these two neurotransmitters when their activity levels are too high and stimulates these receptor sites when their activity levels are too low. Thus, it works in both antagonistic and agonistic ways, depending upon what type of effect is needed. This is why it is also sometimes called a "dopamine-serotonin system stabilizer." It is too soon to make firm conclusions about Abilify, but clinical research thus far indicates that it is as effective as other new generation antipsychotic drugs and may have less severe side effects (DeLeon, Patel, & Crismon, 2004; Rivas-Vasquez, 2003). Given its neurochemical properties, Abilify is also used in the treatment of bipolar disorder.

Electroconvulsive therapy. Another type of biomedical therapy is **electroconvulsive therapy (ECT),** a last-resort treatment for the most severe cases of depression. ECT involves electrically inducing a brief brain seizure and is informally referred to as "shock therapy." ECT was introduced in 1938 as a possible treatment for schizophrenia, but it was later discovered to be effective only for depression. Electrodes are placed on one or both sides of the head, and a very brief

Electroconvulsive therapy. The patient is given an anesthetic so that she is not conscious during the procedure, as well as muscle relaxants to minimize the convulsions.

Will McIntyre/Photo Researchers

electrical shock is administered, causing a brain seizure that makes the patient convulse for a few minutes. Patients are given anesthetics so that they are not conscious during the procedure, as well as muscle relaxants to minimize the convulsions.

About 80 percent of depressed patients improve with ECT (Glass, 2001), and they show improvement somewhat more rapidly with the use of ECT than with antidepressant drugs (Seligman, 1994). This more rapid effect makes ECT a valuable treatment for suicidal, severely depressed patients, especially those who have not responded to any other type of treatment. Strangely, after more than 50 years we still do not know how ECT works in treating depression. One explanation is that, like antidepressant drugs, the electric shock increases the activity of serotonin and norepinephrine, which improves mood. ECT's effects also fit the speculative neurogenesis theory of depression. Like SSRIs, electroconvulsive shock increases neurogenesis in rats (Scott, Wojtowicz, & Burnham, 2000). This means that ECT may have an impact on neurogenesis and may do so a little more quickly than antidepressant drugs. Current research seems to indicate that ECT does not lead to any type of detectable brain damage or long-term cognitive impairment, but there is a memory-loss side effect for events just prior to and following the therapy (Calev, Guardino, Squires, Zervas, & Fink, 1995). Regardless of its clear success in treating severe depression, perhaps saving thousands of lives, ECT remains a controversial therapeutic technique because of its perceived barbaric nature. Interestingly, patients who have undergone ECT do not see it in such a negative light, and the vast majority report that they would undergo it again if their depression recurred (Goodman, Krahn, Smith, Rummans, & Pileggi, 1999; Pettinati, Tamburello, Ruetsch, & Kaplan, 1994). Much of the general public's sordid misconception of ECT likely stems from its inaccurate coverage in the entertainment media (Lilienfeld, Lynn, Ruscio, & Beyerstein, 2010).

Because of the general public's negative image of ECT, alternative neurostimulation therapies for the severely depressed are being developed. One promising

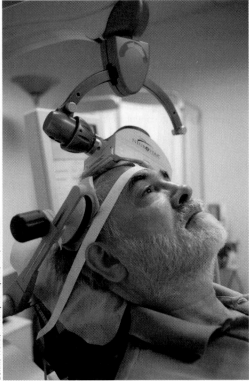

Bonnie Weller/Philadelphia Inquirer/MCT/Newscom

This man is undergoing transcranial magnetic stimulation therapy for depression. The electromagnetic coil above his left frontal lobe is transmitting magnetic pulses to stimulate neuronal activity in that area of his brain.

▓ **transcranial magnetic stimulation (TMS)** A neurostimulation therapy in which the left frontal lobe is stimulated with magnetic pulses via an electromagnetic coil placed on the patient's scalp. It is only cleared for use in cases of severe depression for which traditional treatment has not helped.

▓ **psychosurgery** A biomedical treatment in which specific areas of the brain are destroyed.

▓ **lobotomy** A type of psychosurgery in which the neuronal connections of the frontal lobes to lower brain areas are severed.

alternative is **transcranial magnetic stimulation (TMS).** In contrast with ECT, which transmits electrical impulses, TMS stimulates the brain with magnetic pulses via an electromagnetic coil placed on the patient's scalp above the left frontal lobe. This area is stimulated because brain scans of depressed patients show that it is relatively inactive. Typically a patient receives five treatments a week for 4 to 6 weeks. Unlike ECT, the patient is awake during TMS, and TMS does not produce any memory loss or other major side effects. Like ECT, it is not exactly clear how TMS works to alleviate depression, but it seems to do so by energizing neuronal activity in depressed patients' relatively inactive left frontal lobe. Although some research has shown that it may be as effective as ECT in treating severely depressed patients for whom more traditional treatments have not helped (Grunhaus, Schreiber, Dolberg, Polak, & Dannon, 2003) and the FDA has recently approved its use for this purpose, more research on this relatively new therapy and its effects is clearly needed.

Psychosurgery. An even more controversial biomedical therapy is **psychosurgery,** the destruction of specific areas in the brain. The most famous type of psychosurgery is the **lobotomy,** in which the neuronal connections of the frontal lobes to lower areas in the brain are severed. Egas Moniz, a Portuguese neurosurgeon who coined the term "psychosurgery," pioneered work on lobotomies for the treatment of schizophrenia (Valenstein, 1986). In fact, he won a Nobel prize for his work in 1949. No good scientific rationale for why lobotomies should work, or scientific evidence that they did work, was ever put forth, however. Regardless, led by Dr. Walter Freeman, thousands of lobotomies were done in the United States in the 1940s and 1950s. In 1945, Freeman developed the transorbital lobotomy technique, gaining access to the frontal lobes through the eye socket behind the eyeball with an ice-pick–like instrument, and then swinging the instrument from side to side, cutting the fiber connections to the lower brain (Valenstein, 1986). Freeman didn't even do the lobotomies in hospital operating

A transorbital lobotomy. Neurosurgeon Walter Freeman is performing a transorbital lobotomy in 1949. He is entering the patient's brain through his eye socket. Once he gains access to the brain, he will rotate the ice-pick-like instrument from side to side in order to destroy the targeted brain tissue.

Bettmann Archives

rooms. He would travel directly to the mental institutions with his bag and do several in one day. The van that Freeman traveled around in was called the "lobotomobile" (Koop, 2009). Because it renders the patient unconscious, ECT was used as the anesthetic. The arrival of antipsychotic drugs in the 1950s thankfully replaced the lobotomy as the main treatment for schizophrenia. Unfortunately, these primitive procedures had already left thousands of victims in a zombielike, deteriorated state.

Psychosurgery is still around, but it is done very infrequently and is very different from the earlier primitive lobotomies (Vertosick, 1997). For example, cingulotomies, in which dime-sized holes are surgically lesioned (burnt) in specific areas of the frontal lobes (the cingulate gyrus), are sometimes performed on patients who are severely depressed or have obsessive-compulsive disorder and who have not responded to other types of treatment. The cingulate gyrus is part of the pathway between the frontal lobes and the limbic system structures that govern emotional reactions. These new procedures bear no resemblance to the earlier lobotomies. They are done in operating rooms, using magnetic resonance imaging to guide the surgery and computer-guided electrodes with minute precision to perform the surgery. Psychosurgery is done very infrequently today because it involves irreversible brain injury. These procedures are used only in cases of serious disorders when all other treatments have failed, and only with the patient's permission.

Psychotherapies

In Chapter 8 I briefly mentioned one type of psychotherapy, psychoanalysis, developed by Sigmund Freud in the early 1900s. When thinking about psychoanalysis, we usually think of a patient lying on a couch with the therapist sitting behind the patient and taking notes about the patient's dreams and free associations. This is actually a fairly accurate description of classical psychoanalysis, but most types of psychotherapy are nothing like this. We'll discuss psychoanalysis first and then the other three major types of psychotherapy—humanistic, behavioral, and cognitive. Sometimes these four types of psychotherapy are divided according to their emphasis on insight or action. Psychoanalysis and humanistic therapies are usually referred to as insight therapies—they stress the person achieving insight into (conscious awareness and understanding of) the causes of his behavior and thinking. In contrast, behavioral and cognitive therapies are usually referred to as action therapies—they stress the actions of the person in changing his behavior or ways of thinking.

Psychoanalysis. **Psychoanalysis** is a style of psychotherapy originally developed by Sigmund Freud in which the therapist helps the person gain insight into the unconscious sources of his or her problems. Classical psychoanalysis, as developed by Freud, is very expensive and time consuming. A patient usually needs multiple sessions each week for a year or two to get to the source of her problems. Remember from Chapter 8 that Freud proposed that problems arise from repressed memories, fixations, and unresolved conflicts, mainly from early childhood. Such problems are repressed in the unconscious but continue to influence the person's behavior and thinking. The task for the psychoanalyst is to discover these underlying unconscious problems and then help the patient to gain insight into them. The difficulty with this is that the patient herself is not even privy to these unconscious problems. This means that the therapist has to identify conscious reflections of the underlying problems and interpret them. The major task of the psychoanalyst then is to interpret many sources of input—including free associations, resistances, dreams, and transferences—in order to find the unconscious roots of the person's problem.

Free association is a technique in which the patient spontaneously describes, without editing, all thoughts, feelings, or images that come to mind. For psychoanalysts, free association is like a verbal projective test. Psychoanalysts assume that free association does not just produce random thoughts but will provide clues to the unconscious conflicts leading to the patient's problems. This is especially true for resistances during free association. A **resistance** is a patient's unwillingness to discuss particular topics. For example, a patient might be free associating and say the word "mother." A resistance to this topic (his mother) would be indicated by the patient abruptly halting the association process and falling silent. The patient might also miss a therapy appointment to avoid talking about a particular topic (such as his mother) or change the subject to avoid discussion of the topic. The psychoanalyst must detect these resistances and interpret them.

The psychoanalyst also interprets the patient's dreams, which may provide clues to the underlying problem.

▌ **psychoanalysis** A style of psychotherapy originally developed by Sigmund Freud in which the therapist helps the person gain insight into the unconscious sources of his or her problems.

▌ **free association** A person spontaneously describes, without editing, all thoughts, feelings, or images that come to mind.

▌ **resistance** A person's unwillingness to discuss a particular topic during therapy.

According to Freud, psychological defenses are lowered during sleep; therefore, the unconscious conflicts are revealed symbolically in one's dreams. This means that dreams have two levels of meaning—the **manifest content,** the literal surface meaning of a dream, and the **latent content,** the underlying true meaning of a dream. It is the latent content that is important. For example, a king and queen in a dream could really represent the person's parents, or having a tooth extracted could represent castration. Another tool available to the therapist is the process of **transference,** which occurs when the patient acts toward the therapist as she did or does toward important figures in her life, such as her parents. For example, if the patient hated her father when she was a child, she might transfer this hate relationship to the therapist. In this way transference is a reenactment of earlier or current conflicts with important figures in the patient's life. The patient's conflicted feelings toward these important figures are transferred to the therapist, and the therapist must detect and interpret these transferences.

Psychoanalysis requires a lot of time because the therapist has to use these various indirect clues to build an interpretation of the patient's problem. It's similar to a detective trying to solve a case without any solid clues, such as the weapon, fingerprints, or DNA evidence. There's only vague circumstantial evidence. Using this evidence, the therapist builds an interpretation that helps the patient to gain insight into the problem. Contemporary psychoanalytic therapy, usually referred to as psychodynamic therapy, tends to be shorter, usually only lasting a few months. The therapist takes a more direct and interactive role in the therapy sessions, and there is much more emphasis on the present than the past. Regardless, both types of psychoanalysis are controversial. Critics question the validity of psychoanalysis's main constructs—unconscious conflicts and their impact on behavior and thinking.

Client-centered therapy. The most influential humanistic therapy is Carl Rogers's client-centered therapy, which is sometimes called person-centered therapy (Raskin & Rogers, 1995; Rogers, 1951). **Client-centered therapy** is a style of psychotherapy in which the therapist uses unconditional positive regard, genuineness, and empathy to help the person to gain insight into his true self-concept. Rogers and other humanists preferred to use the words "client" or "person" rather than "patient"; they thought that "patient" implied sickness, while "client" and "person" emphasized the importance of the clients' subjective views of themselves. Remember from Chapter 8 that Rogers assumed that conditions of worth set up by other people in the client's life have led the troubled person to develop a distorted self-concept, and that a person's perception of his self is critical to personality development and self-actualization (the fullest realization of one's potential). The therapeutic goal of client-centered therapy

manifest content Freud's term for the literal surface meaning of a dream.

latent content Freud's term for the underlying true meaning of a dream.

transference A person undergoing therapy acts toward the therapist as he or she did or does toward important figures in his or her life, such as his or her parents.

client-centered therapy A style of psychotherapy developed by Carl Rogers in which the therapist uses unconditional positive regard, genuineness, and empathy to help the person to gain insight into his or her true self-concept.

is to get the person on the road to self-actualization. To achieve this goal, the therapist is nondirective; she doesn't attempt to steer the dialogue in a certain direction. Instead, the client decides the direction of each session. The therapist's main task is to create the conditions that allow the client to gain insight into his true feelings and self-concept.

These conditions are exactly the same as those for healthy personality growth that were discussed in Chapter 8. The therapist should be accepting, genuine, and empathic. The therapist establishes an environment of acceptance by giving the client unconditional positive regard (accepting the client without any conditions upon his behavior). The therapist demonstrates genuineness by honestly sharing her own thoughts and feelings with the client. To achieve empathic understanding of the client's feelings, the therapist uses active listening to gain a sense of the client's feelings, and then uses mirroring to echo these feelings back to the client, so that the client can then get a clearer image of his true feelings. It is this realization of his true feelings that allows the client to get back on the road to personal growth and self-actualization. By creating a supportive environment, this style of therapy is very successful with people who are not suffering from a clinical disorder but who are motivated toward greater personal awareness and growth.

Behavioral therapy. **Behavioral therapy** is a style of psychotherapy in which the therapist uses the principles of classical and operant conditioning to change the person's behavior from maladaptive to adaptive. The assumption is that the behavioral symptoms (such as the irrational behavior of the woman with the specific phobia of birds) are the problem. Maladaptive behaviors have been learned, so they have to be unlearned and more adaptive behaviors learned instead. Behavior therapies are based on either classical or operant conditioning. We'll first describe an example of one based on classical conditioning.

Remember the Little Albert classical conditioning study by Watson and Rayner that we mentioned earlier in this chapter when we were discussing phobic disorders. As we pointed out in Chapter 4, Albert's fear of white rats was never deconditioned, but one of Watson's former students, Mary Cover Jones, later showed that such a fear could be unlearned and replaced with a more adaptive relaxation response (Jones, 1924). Jones eliminated the fear of rabbits in a 3-year-old boy named Peter by gradually introducing a rabbit while Peter was eating. Peter's pleasure response while eating was incompatible with a fear response. Over time, Peter learned to be relaxed in the presence of a rabbit. Some consider this to be the first case of behavioral therapy. Jones's work led to the development of a set of classical conditioning therapies called counterconditioning techniques. In **counterconditioning,** a maladaptive response is replaced by an

▌ **behavioral therapy** A style of psychotherapy in which the therapist uses the principles of classical and operant conditioning to change the person's behavior from maladaptive to adaptive.

▌ **counterconditioning** A type of behavioral therapy in which a maladaptive response is replaced by an incompatible adaptive response.

incompatible adaptive response. Counterconditioning therapies, such as systematic desensitization, virtual reality therapy, and flooding, have been especially successful in the treatment of anxiety disorders. These three counterconditioning therapies are referred to as exposure therapies because the patient is exposed at some point to the source of his anxiety.

Using Jones's idea that fear and relaxation are incompatible responses, Joseph Wolpe developed a behavioral therapy called systematic desensitization that is very effective in treating phobias (Wolpe, 1958). **Systematic desensitization** is a counterconditioning procedure in which a fear response to an object or situation is replaced with a relaxation response in a series of progressively increasing fear-arousing steps. The patient first develops a hierarchy of situations that evoke a fear response, from those that evoke slight fear on up to those that evoke tremendous fear. For example, a person who had a specific phobia of spiders might find that planning a picnic evoked slight fear because of the possibility that a spider might be encountered on the picnic. Seeing a picture of a spider would evoke more fear, seeing a spider on a wall 20 feet away even more. Having actual spiders crawl on her would be near the top of the hierarchy. These are just a few situations that span a possible hierarchy. Hierarchies have far more steps over which the fear increases gradually.

Joseph Wolpe

Temple University Libraries, Urban Archives, Philadelphia PA

Once the hierarchy is set, the patient is then taught how to use various techniques to relax. Once this relaxation training is over, the therapy begins. The patient starts working through the hierarchy and attempts to relax at each step. First the patient relaxes in imagined situations in the hierarchy and later in the actual situations. With both imagined and actual situations, the anxiety level of the situation is increased slowly. At some of the latter stages in the hierarchy, a model of the same sex and roughly same age may be brought in to demonstrate the behavior before the patient attempts it. For example, the model will touch the picture of a bird in a book before the patient is asked to do so. In brief, systematic desensitization teaches the patient to confront increasingly fearful situations with the relaxation response.

Virtual reality therapy is similar to systematic desensitization, but the patient is exposed to computer simulations of his fears in a progressively anxiety-provoking manner. Wearing a motion-sensitive display helmet that projects a three-dimensional virtual world, the patient experiences seemingly real computer-generated images rather than imagined and actual situations as in systematic desensitization. When the patient achieves relaxation, the simulated scene becomes more fearful until the patient can relax in the simulated presence of the feared object or

▌ **systematic desensitization** A counterconditioning exposure therapy in which a fear response to an object or situation is replaced with a relaxation response in a series of progressively increasing fear-arousing steps.

▌ **virtual reality therapy** A counterconditioning exposure therapy in which the patient is exposed in graduated steps to computer simulations of a feared object or situation.

■ **flooding** A counterconditioning exposure therapy in which the patient is immediately exposed to a feared object or situation.

■ **cognitive therapy** A style of psychotherapy in which the therapist attempts to change the person's thinking from maladaptive to adaptive.

■ **rational-emotive therapy** A type of cognitive therapy developed by Albert Ellis in which the therapist directly confronts and challenges the person's unrealistic thoughts and beliefs to show that they are irrational.

situation. Virtual reality therapy has been used successfully to treat specific phobias, social phobias, and some other anxiety disorders (Krijn, Emmelkamp, Olafsson, & Biemond, 2004).

Another counterconditioning exposure therapy, flooding, does not involve such gradual confrontation. In **flooding,** the patient is immediately exposed to the feared object or situation. For example, in the case of the spider phobia, the person would immediately have to confront live spiders. Flooding is often used instead of systematic desensitization when the fear is so strong that the person is unable to make much progress in systematic desensitization.

Behavioral therapies using operant conditioning principles reinforce desired behaviors and extinguish undesired behaviors. A good example is the token economy that we discussed in Chapter 4. A token economy is an environment in which desired behaviors are reinforced with tokens (secondary reinforcers such as gold stars or stickers) that can be exchanged for rewards such as candy and television privileges. This technique is often used with groups of institutionalized people, such as those in mental health facilities. As such, it has been fairly successful in managing autistic, retarded, and some schizophrenic institutionalized populations. For example, if making one's bed is the desired behavior, it will be reinforced with tokens that can be exchanged for treats or privileges. A token economy is more of a way to manage the daily behavior of such people than a way to cure them, but we must remember that a behavioral therapist thinks that the maladaptive behavior is the problem.

Cognitive therapy. Behavioral therapies work to change the person's behavior; cognitive therapies work on the person's thinking. **Cognitive therapy** is a style of psychotherapy in which the therapist changes the person's thinking from maladaptive to adaptive. The assumption is that the person's thought processes and beliefs are maladaptive and need to change. The cognitive therapist identifies the irrational thoughts and unrealistic beliefs that need to change and then helps the person to execute that change. Two prominent cognitive therapies are Albert Ellis's rational-emotive therapy (Ellis, 1962, 1993, 1995) and Aaron Beck's cognitive therapy (Beck, 1976; Beck & Beck, 1995).

In Ellis's **rational-emotive therapy,** the therapist directly confronts and challenges the patient's unrealistic thoughts and beliefs to show that they are irrational. These irrational, unrealistic beliefs usually involve words such as "must," "always," and "every." Let's consider a simple example. A person

Courtesy of Albert Ellis

Albert Ellis

might have the unrealistic belief that he must be perfect in everything he does. This is an unrealistic belief. He is doomed to failure, because no one can be perfect at everything they do. Instead of realizing that his belief is irrational, he will blame himself for the failure and become depressed. A rational-emotive therapist will show him the irrationality of his thinking and lead him to change his thinking to be more realistic. This is achieved by Ellis's ABC model. A refers to the Activating event (failure to be perfect at everything); B is the person's Belief about the event ("It's my fault; I'm a failure"); and C is the resulting emotional Consequence (depression). According to Ellis, A does not cause C; B causes C. Through rational-emotive therapy, the person comes to realize that he controls the emotional consequences because he controls the interpretation of the event.

Rational-emotive therapists are usually very direct and confrontational in getting their clients to see the errors of their thinking. Ellis has said that he does not think that a warm relationship between therapist and client is essential to effective therapy. Aaron Beck's form of cognitive therapy has the same therapeutic goal as Ellis's rational-emotive therapy, but the therapeutic style is not as confrontational. A therapist using **Beck's cognitive therapy** works to develop a warm relationship with the person and has a person carefully consider the objective evidence for his beliefs in order to see the errors in his thinking. For example, to help a student who is depressed because he thinks he has blown his chances to get into medical school by not having a perfect grade point average, the therapist would have the student examine the statistics on how few students actually graduate with a perfect average and the grade point averages of students actually accepted to medical school. The therapist is like a good teacher, helping the person to discover the problems with his thinking. Regardless of the style differences, both types of cognitive therapy have been especially effective at treating major depressive disorders.

Aaron T. Beck

Courtesy of Aaron T. Beck, University of Pennsylvania Medical Center

Is psychotherapy effective? Now that you understand the four major approaches to psychotherapy, let's consider this question: Is psychotherapy effective? To assess the effectiveness of psychotherapy we must consider spontaneous remission. **Spontaneous remission** is getting better with the passage of time without receiving any therapy. This means that the effect of psychotherapy must be statistically significantly greater than that due to spontaneous remission. To answer this question, researchers have used meta-analysis, a statistical technique discussed in Chapter 1 in which the results from many separate experimental studies on the same question are combined into one analysis to determine whether there is an overall effect. The results of a meta-analysis that included the results of

▌ **Beck's cognitive therapy** A type of cognitive therapy developed by Aaron Beck in which the therapist works to develop a warm relationship with the person and has the person carefully consider the evidence for his or her beliefs in order to see the errors in his or her thinking.

▌ **spontaneous remission** Getting better with the passage of time without receiving any therapy.

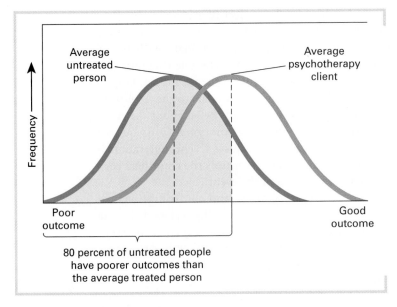

▲ Figure 10.1 |
Psychotherapy Versus No Treatment | These two normal distributions summarize the data of a meta-analysis of 475 studies on the effectiveness of psychotherapy. They show that psychotherapy is effective—the average psychotherapy client was better off than 80 percent of the people not receiving therapy. (Adapted from Smith, Glass, & Miller, 1980.)

475 studies involving many different types of psychotherapy and thousands of participants revealed that psychotherapy is effective (Figure 10.1). The average psychotherapy client is better off than about 80 percent of people not receiving any therapy (Smith, Glass, & Miller, 1980). A more recent meta-analysis of psychotherapy effectiveness studies also confirms that psychotherapy helps (Shadish, Matt, Navarro, & Phillips, 2000).

No one particular type of psychotherapy, however, is superior to all of the others. Some types of psychotherapy seem to be more effective in treating particular disorders, though. For example, behavioral therapies have been very successful in treating phobias and other anxiety disorders. Also, cognitive therapies tend to be very effective in treating depression. None of the psychotherapies, however, are very successful in treating schizophrenia.

INSIDE WOODY ALLEN

Section Summary

There are two major categories of therapy, biomedical and psychological. Biomedical therapy involves the use of biological interventions, such as drugs, to treat disorders. Psychotherapy involves the use of psychological interventions to treat disorders. Psychotherapy is what we normally think of as therapy. In psychotherapy, there is an interaction between the person and the therapist. In biomedical therapy, the interaction is biological. There are three major types of biomedical therapy—drug therapy, shock therapy, and psychosurgery. There are four major types of psychotherapy—psychoanalytic, humanistic, behavioral, and cognitive.

The major medications are lithium, antidepressant drugs, antianxiety drugs, and antipsychotic drugs. Lithium, a naturally occurring mineral salt, is the main treatment for bipolar disorder. There are four types of antidepressants—MAO inhibitors, tricyclics, SSRIs, and SSNRIs. SSRIs, which work by selectively blocking the reuptake of serotonin, are prescribed most often. Antianxiety drugs are in a class of drugs called benzodiazepines; they reduce anxiety by stimulating GABA activity that inhibits the anxiety.

There are two types of antipsychotic drugs—traditional (those developed from the 1950s through the 1980s) and new generation (developed since the 1990s). The traditional antipsychotic drugs block receptor sites for dopamine, which globally lowers dopamine activity. Because of this, these traditional drugs produce side effects in motor movement that are similar to the movement problems of Parkinson's disease. In addition, there is a long-term-use side effect of traditional antipsychotic drugs, tardive dyskinesia, in which the person has uncontrollable facial movements. The new generation drugs do not have these side effects, but they do have to be monitored very carefully because of other dangerous side effects. Such monitoring is expensive; therefore, traditional antipsychotic drugs are often prescribed instead.

Electroconvulsive therapy (ECT) that involves electrically inducing a brief brain seizure is used almost exclusively to treat severe depression. We do not know how or why this therapy works, but it is a valuable treatment for severely depressed people who have not responded to other types of treatment because it leads to somewhat faster improvement than antidepressant drugs. Given its nature, however, ECT remains shrouded in controversy. An alternative neurostimulation therapy for the severely depressed, transcranial magnetic stimulation (TMS), is not as controversial as ECT and does not produce any major side effects, but more research on its effectiveness is needed.

Even more controversial is psychosurgery, in which specific areas in the brain are actually destroyed. The most famous type of psychosurgery is the lobotomy, in which the neuronal connections of the frontal lobes to lower areas in the brain are severed. No good evidence for why such operations should work or that they did was ever put forth. The arrival of antipsychotic drugs in the 1950s replaced the lobotomy as the main treatment for schizophrenia. Psychosurgery is still around, but it is very different from what it once was and is used very infrequently, only when all other treatments have failed.

Psychotherapies can be categorized into two types—insight or action. Psychoanalytic and humanistic therapies are insight therapies; they stress the person achieving insight into the causes of her behavior and thinking. Behavioral and cognitive therapies are action therapies; they stress the actions of the person in changing her behavior and ways of thinking. The main goal of psychoanalysis, as developed by Freud, is for the therapist to uncover the unconscious sources of the person's problems by interpreting the person's free associations, dreams, resistances, and transferences. The therapist then helps the person to gain insight into the unconscious sources of her problem with this interpretation. Such classical psychoanalysis takes a long time; therefore, contemporary psychoanalytic therapists take a more direct and interactive role, emphasizing the present more than the past in order to shorten the period of therapy.

The most influential humanistic therapy is Rogers's client-centered therapy in which the therapist uses unconditional positive regard, genuineness, and empathy to help the person to gain insight into her true self-concept and get on the path to self-actualization. The therapy is client-centered, and the client decides the direction of each session. The therapist's main task is to create the conditions that allow the client to discover her true feelings and self-concept.

In behavioral therapies, the therapist uses the principles of classical and operant conditioning to change the person's behavior from maladaptive to adaptive. The assumption is that the behavioral symptoms are the problem. These behaviors were learned; therefore, they need to be unlearned and more adaptive behaviors learned. Counterconditioning exposure therapies, such as systematic desensitization, virtual reality therapy, and flooding, have been especially effective in treating anxiety disorders such as phobias. Instead of changing the person's behavior, the cognitive therapist attempts to change the person's thinking from maladaptive to adaptive. Two major kinds of cognitive therapy are Ellis's rational-emotive therapy and Beck's cognitive therapy. Both have the same therapeutic goal—changing the person's thinking to be more rational—but the therapeutic styles are very different. Rational-emotive therapy is far more confrontational and direct in its approach. Regardless, both have been very successful in treating major depressive disorders.

Using meta-analysis, a statistical technique that pools the results from many separate experimental studies on the same question into one analysis to determine whether there is an overall effect, researchers have concluded that psychotherapy is more effective than no therapy. There is no one particular type of psychotherapy that is best for all disorders, however. Rather, some types of psychotherapy seem more effective in treating particular disorders. For example, behavioral therapies tend to be effective in treating anxiety disorders, and cognitive therapies more effective in treating depression.

Concept**Check** | 3

> **Explain the difference between biomedical therapy and psychotherapy.**

> **Explain how the neurogenesis theory of depression could be considered a biopsychosocial explanation.**

> **Explain why the psychoanalyst can be thought of as a detective.**

> **Explain the difference between behavioral therapy and cognitive therapy.**

> **Explain why a control for spontaneous remission must be included in any assessment of the effectiveness of psychotherapy.**

Study Guide

Chapter Key Terms

You should know the definitions of the following key terms from the chapter. They are listed in the order in which they appear in the chapter. For those you do not know, return to the relevant section of the chapter to learn them. When you think that you know all of the terms, complete the matching exercise based on these key terms.

abnormal psychology

Diagnostic and Statistical Manual of Mental Disorders—Fourth Edition (DSM-IV)

personality disorder

biopsychosocial approach

anxiety disorders

specific phobia

social phobia

agoraphobia

panic disorder

generalized anxiety disorder

obsessive-compulsive disorder

obsession

compulsion

mood disorders

major depressive disorder

major depressive episode

manic episode

bipolar disorder

psychotic disorder

hallucination

delusion

schizophrenia

vulnerability–stress model

biomedical therapy

psychotherapy

lithium

antidepressant drugs

neurogenesis theory of depression

antianxiety drugs

antipsychotic drugs

tardive dyskinesia

electroconvulsive therapy (ECT)

transcranial magnetic therapy (TMS)

psychosurgery

lobotomy

psychoanalysis

free association

resistance

manifest content

latent content

transference

client-centered therapy

behavioral therapy

counterconditioning

systematic desensitization

virtual reality therapy

flooding

cognitive therapy

rational-emotive therapy

Beck's cognitive therapy

spontaneous remission

Key Terms Exercise

Identify the correct term for each of the following definitions. The answers to this exercise follow the answers to the Concept Checks at the end of the chapter.

1. A repetitive and rigid behavior that a person feels compelled to perform in order to reduce anxiety.

_____

2. An anxiety disorder indicated by a marked and persistent fear of being in places or situations from which escape might be difficult or embarrassing.

_____

3. An explanation of schizophrenia that proposes that genetic, prenatal, and postnatal biological factors render a person vulnerable to schizophrenia, but environmental stress determines whether it develops or not.

_____

4. A style of psychotherapy developed by Carl Rogers in which the therapist uses unconditional positive regard,

genuineness, and empathy to help the person to gain insight into his true self-concept.

5. A counterconditioning exposure therapy in which a fear response to an object or situation is replaced with a relaxation response in a series of progressively increasing fear-arousing steps.

6. Getting better with the passage of time without receiving any therapy.

7. A type of cognitive therapy developed by Albert Ellis in which the therapist directly confronts and challenges the person's unrealistic thoughts and beliefs to show that they are irrational.

8. A disorder characterized by inflexible, long-standing personality traits that lead to behavior that impairs social functioning and deviates from cultural norms.

9. A false sensory perception.

10. A mood disorder in which recurrent cycles of depressive and manic episodes occur.

11. The current version of the American Psychiatric Association's diagnostic and classification guidelines for mental disorders.

12. Explaining abnormality as the result of the interaction among biological, psychological (behavioral and cognitive), and social or cultural factors.

13. An explanation of depression that proposes that the growth of new neurons in the hippocampus stops during depression, and when it resumes, the depression lifts.

14. A person undergoing therapy acts toward the therapist as he or she did or does toward important figures in his or her life, such as parents.

15. A side effect of long-term use of traditional antipsychotic drugs causing the person to have uncontrollable facial tics, grimaces, and other involuntary movements of the lips, jaw, and tongue.

Practice Test Questions

The following are practice multiple-choice test questions on some of the chapter content. The answers are given after the answers to the Key Terms Exercise at the end of the chapter. If you guessed or incorrectly answered a question, restudy the relevant section of the chapter.

1. Which of the following is a personality disorder?
   a. schizophrenia
   b. antisocial personality
   c. bipolar disorder
   d. generalized anxiety disorder

2. _____ is the fear of being in places or situations from which escape may be difficult or embarrassing.
   a. A specific phobia
   b. Agoraphobia
   c. Social phobia
   d. Panic disorder

3. Which of the following disorders has the highest concordance rate for identical twins?
   a. bipolar disorder
   b. schizophrenia
   c. major depressive disorder
   d. The concordance rates for all of the above are the same.

4. Which of the following disorders is a (are) psychotic disorder(s)?
   a. obsessive-compulsive disorder
   b. major depressive disorder
   c. schizophrenia
   d. all of the above

5. A false sensory perception is a(n) _____, and a false belief is a(n) _____.
   a. obsession; compulsion
   b. compulsion; obsession
   c. hallucination; delusion
   d. delusion; hallucination

6. Which of the following is (are) most often used to treat bipolar disorder?
   a. SSRIs
   b. lithium
   c. new generation antipsychotic drugs
   d. MAO inhibitors

7. Tardive dyskinesia is a side effect of long-term use of _____.
   a. SSRIs
   b. traditional antipsychotic drugs
   c. lithium
   d. tricyclics

8. A _____ therapist interprets resistances and transferences to discover a person's underlying problems.
   a. psychoanalytic
   b. client-centered
   c. behavioral
   d. cognitive

9. Maladaptive behavior is to maladaptive thinking as _____ is to _____.
   a. psychoanalysis; client-centered therapy
   b. client-centered therapy; psychoanalysis
   c. behavioral therapy; cognitive therapy
   d. cognitive therapy; behavioral therapy

10. Which of the following psychotherapies is most effective in treating phobic disorders?
    a. psychoanalysis
    b. cognitive therapy

    c. behavioral therapy
    d. client-centered therapy

11. _____ is a disorder in which the person has excessive global anxiety and worry that they cannot control for a period of at least 6 months.
    a. Agoraphobia
    b. Social phobia
    c. Generalized anxiety disorder
    d. Panic disorder

12. Which of the following is a part of rational-emotive therapy?
    a. ABC model
    b. token economy
    c. free association
    d. flooding

13. Unconditional positive regard and empathy are to resistance and transference as _____ is to _____.
    a. rational-emotive therapy; Beck's cognitive therapy
    b. Beck's cognitive therapy; rational-emotive therapy
    c. psychoanalysis; client-centered therapy
    d. client-centered therapy; psychoanalysis

14. Which of the following is the best example of a biopsychosocial explanation of a mental disorder?
    a. the ABC model
    b. the vulnerability–stress model
    c. counterconditioning
    d. meta-analysis

15. Agoraphobia usually occurs in combination with _____.
    a. bipolar disorder
    b. panic disorder
    c. obsessive-compulsive disorder
    d. major depressive disorder

Chapter Concept Check Answers

Concept Check | 1

- The DSM-IV is the Diagnostic and Statistical Manual of Mental Disorders—Fourth Edition, published by the American

Psychiatric Association. It is the most widely used diagnostic system for classifying mental disorders. Basing its classification upon behavioral and psychological symptoms, it provides reliable diagnostic guidelines for over 300 disorders, grouped into major categories that share particular symptoms.

- Labels attached to people bias our perception of these people in terms of their labels. Labels for mental disorders are especially problematic because they tend to lead to negative perceptions and interpretations of a person's behavior in terms of the label. In brief, labels guide our perception. Therefore, it is important to realize that there is much more to a person than a label. However, we need labels in order to know how to treat people with disorders and to conduct research on these disorders. This is why labels are necessary.

Concept Check | 2

- A biopsychosocial explanation of a disorder entails explaining the problem as the result of the interaction of biological, psychological (behavioral and cognitive), and sociocultural factors. A good example is the explanation of specific phobia disorders in terms of a behavioral factor (classical conditioning) along with a biological predisposition to learn certain fears more easily. Thus, a psychological factor is involved in the learning of the fear but a biological factor determines which fears are easier to learn. Another good example is the vulnerability–stress explanation of schizophrenia in which one's level of vulnerability to schizophrenia is determined by biological factors, but how much stress one experiences and how one copes psychologically with the stress determines whether or not one suffers from the disorder.

- The anxiety and fear in the specific phobia disorder are exactly as the label indicates. They are specific to a certain class of objects or situations. However, the anxiety and fear in generalized anxiety disorder are not specific, but rather global. The person has excessive anxiety and worries most of the time, and the anxiety is not tied to anything in particular.

- The concordance rates for identical twins for major depressive disorder and schizophrenia are only about 1 in 2 (50 percent). If only biological genetic factors were responsible for these disorders, these concordance rates would be 100 percent. Thus, psychological and sociocultural factors must play a role in causing these disorders.

- Schizophrenia is a psychotic disorder. This means the person loses contact with reality. Thus, the split is between the person's mental functions (perception, beliefs, and speech) and reality. In "split personality," which used to be called multiple-personality disorder and is now called dissociative identity disorder in DSM-IV, one's personality is split into two or more distinct personalities.

Concept Check | 3

- In biomedical therapy, there is a direct biological intervention, via drugs or ECT, that has an impact on the biochemistry of the nervous system, or psychosurgery, in which part of the brain is actually destroyed. There is no direct impact on the client's biology in psychotherapy. Psychological interventions (talk therapies) are used to treat disorders. However, successful psychotherapy may indirectly lead to biological changes in the client's neurochemistry through more positive thinking.

- The neurogenesis theory of depression can be considered a biopsychosocial explanation because both biological and psychological factors can have an impact on the neurogenesis process that is assumed to eliminate the depression. Antidepressant drugs with their antagonistic effects on serotonin and norepinephrine are good examples of possible biological factors, and the positive thinking produced by cognitive psychotherapy is a good example of a psychological factor.

- A psychoanalyst can be thought of as a detective because she has to interpret many clues to the client's problem.

Discovering the client's problem is like solving the case. The sources of the psychoanalyst's clues are free association data, resistances, dream analysis, and transferences. The therapist uses these clues to interpret the person's problem (solve the case) and then uses this interpretation to help the person gain insight into the source of his problem.

- Both of these types of psychotherapies are very direct in their approach. However, behavioral therapies assume that the client's behavior is maladaptive and needs to be replaced with more adaptive behavior. Cognitive therapies instead hold that the client's thinking is maladaptive and needs to be replaced with more adaptive thinking. In brief, the behavioral therapist works to change the client's behavior, and the cognitive therapist works to change the client's thinking.

- Spontaneous remission is getting better with the passage of time without receiving any therapy. Thus, if it were not considered when the effectiveness of psychotherapy is being evaluated, the researcher might incorrectly assume that the improvement was due to the psychotherapy and not spontaneous remission. This is why the improvement in wellness for the psychotherapy group must be significantly (statistically) greater than the improvement for the spontaneous remission control group. If it is, then the psychotherapy has produced improvement that cannot be due to just spontaneous remission.

Answers to Key Terms Exercise

1. compulsion
2. agoraphobia
3. vulnerability–stress model
4. client-centered therapy
5. systematic desensitization
6. spontaneous remission
7. rational-emotive therapy
8. personality disorder
9. hallucination
10. bipolar disorder
11. Diagnostic and Statistical Manual of Mental Disorders—Fourth Edition (DSM-IV)
12. biopsychosocial approach
13. neurogenesis theory of depression
14. transference
15. tardive dyskinesia

Answers to Practice Test Questions

1. b; antisocial personality
2. b; Agoraphobia
3. a; bipolar disorder
4. c; schizophrenia
5. c; hallucination; delusion
6. b; lithium
7. b; traditional antipsychotic drugs
8. a; psychoanalytic
9. c; behavioral therapy; cognitive therapy
10. c; behavioral therapy
11. c; Generalized anxiety disorder
12. a; ABC model
13. d; client-centered therapy; psychoanalysis
14. b; the vulnerability–stress model
15. b; panic disorder

Glossary

abnormal psychology The scientific study of mental disorders and their treatment.

absolute threshold The minimum amount of energy in a sensory stimulus detected 50 percent of the time.

accommodation (1) In vision, the focusing of light waves from objects of different distances directly on the retina. (2) In Piagetian theory, Piaget's term for the modification of present schemas to fit with new experiences.

acetylcholine (ACh) A neurotransmitter involved in learning, memory, and muscle movement.

acquisition (in classical conditioning) Acquiring a new response (the conditioned response) to the conditioned stimulus.

acquisition (in operant conditioning) The strengthening of a reinforced operant response.

actor–observer bias The tendency to overestimate situational influences on our own behavior, but to overestimate dispositional influences on the behavior of others.

additive mixtures Direct mixtures of different wavelengths of light in which all of the wavelengths reach the retina and are added together.

agonist A drug or poison that increases the activity of one or more neurotransmitters.

agoraphobia An anxiety disorder indicated by a marked and persistent fear of being in places or situations from which escape may be difficult or embarrassing.

algorithm A step-by-step problem-solving procedure that guarantees a correct answer to a problem.

amnesic A person with severe memory deficits following brain surgery or injury.

amplitude The amount of energy in a wave, its intensity, which is the height of the wave at its crest.

amygdala A part of the brain that is involved in emotions by influencing aggression, anger, and

fear and by providing the emotional element of our memories and the interpretation of emotional expressions in others.

anal stage of psychosexual development The second stage in Freud's theory (from 18 months to 3 years), in which the erogenous zone is the anus, and the child derives pleasure from stimulation of the anal region through having and withholding bowel movements.

anchoring and adjustment heuristic A heuristic for estimation problems in which one uses his or her initial estimate as an anchor estimate and then adjusts the anchor up or down (often insufficiently).

antagonist A drug or poison that decreases the activity of one or more neurotransmitters.

anterograde amnesia The inability to form new explicit long-term memories for events following surgery or trauma to the brain. Explicit memories formed before the surgery or trauma are left intact.

antianxiety drugs Drugs used to treat anxiety problems and disorders.

antidepressant drugs Drugs used to treat depressive disorders.

antipsychotic drugs Drugs used to treat psychotic disorders.

anxiety disorders Disorders in which excessive anxiety leads to personal distress and atypical, maladaptive, and irrational behavior.

appetitive stimulus A stimulus that is pleasant.

arousal theory A theory of motivation that proposes that our behavior is motivated to maintain an optimal level of physiological arousal.

assimilation Piaget's term for the interpretation of new experiences in terms of present schemas.

association cortex All of the cerebral cortex except those areas devoted to primary sensory processing or motor processing. This is where all the higher-level cognitive processing that requires the association (integration) of information, such as perception and language, occurs.

attachment The lifelong emotional bond between infants and their mothers or other caregivers, formed during the first 6 months of life.

attitudes Evaluative reactions (positive or negative) toward objects, events, and other people.

attribution The process by which we explain our own behavior and that of others.

authoritarian parenting A style of parenting in which the parents are demanding, expect unquestioned obedience, are not responsive to their children's desires, and communicate poorly with their children.

authoritative parenting A style of parenting in which the parents are demanding, but set rational limits for their children and communicate well with their children.

automatic processing Memory processing that occurs subconsciously and does not require attention.

autonomic nervous system The part of the PNS that regulates the functioning of our internal environment (glands and organs like the heart, lungs, and stomach).

availability heuristic A heuristic for judging the probability of an event by how available examples of the event are in memory (the more available, the more probable).

aversive stimulus A stimulus that is unpleasant.

axon The long, singular fiber projecting out of the cell body of a neuron whose function is to conduct the neural impulse from the cell body to the axon terminals triggering chemical communication with other neurons.

babbling The rhythmic repetition of various syllables including both consonants and vowels.

baby talk (motherese) The different format of speech that adults use when talking with babies that involves the use of shorter sentences with a higher, more melodious pitch.

basal ganglia A part of the brain that is involved in the initiation and execution of movements.

Beck's cognitive therapy A type of cognitive therapy developed by Aaron Beck in which the therapist works to develop a warm relationship with the person and has a person carefully consider the evidence for his or her beliefs in order to see the errors in his or her thinking.

behavior modification The application of classical and operant conditioning principles to eliminate undesirable behavior and to teach more desirable behavior.

behavioral perspective A research perspective whose major explanatory focus is how external environmental events condition observable behavior.

behavioral therapy A style of psychotherapy in which the therapist uses the principles of classical and operant conditioning to change the person's behavior from maladaptive to adaptive.

belief perseverance The tendency to cling to one's beliefs in the face of contradictory evidence.

biological perspective A research perspective whose major explanatory focus is how the brain, nervous system, and other physiological mechanisms produce behavior and mental processes.

biomedical therapy The use of biological interventions, such as drugs, to treat mental disorders.

biopsychosocial approach Explaining abnormality as the result of the interaction among biological, psychological (behavioral and cognitive), and sociocultural factors.

bipolar disorder A mood disorder in which recurrent cycles of depressive and manic episodes occur.

blood–brain barrier A protective mechanism by which the blood capillaries supplying the brain create a barrier that prevents dangerous substances access to the brain.

bottom-up processing The processing of incoming sensory information as it travels up from the sensory structures to the brain.

Broca's area An area in the cerebral cortex responsible for fluent speech production. It is in the left frontal lobe of the majority of people, regardless of handedness.

bystander effect The probability of a person helping in an emergency is greater when there are no other bystanders than when there are other bystanders.

Cannon-Bard theory A theory of emotion proposing that an emotion is determined from simultaneously occurring physiological arousal, behavioral responses, and cognitive appraisal.

case study A descriptive research method in which the researcher studies an individual in depth over an extended period of time.

cell body The part of the neuron that contains its nucleus and the other biological machinery to keep the cell alive and that decides whether or not to generate a neural impulse in order to pass incoming information on to other neurons.

central nervous system (CNS) The brain and spinal cord.

centration The tendency to focus on only one aspect of a problem at a time.

cerebellum A part of the brain involved in the coordination of our movements, sense of balance, and motor learning.

cerebral cortex The layers of interconnected cells covering the brain's two hemispheres. This is the control and information-processing center for the nervous system and where perception, memory, language, decision making, and all other higher-level cognitive processing occur.

chromosomes Molecules of DNA that hold the genetic instructions for every cell in the body.

chunk A meaningful unit in a person's memory.

classical conditioning Acquiring a new response (the conditioned response) to a previously neutral stimulus (the conditioned stimulus) that reliably signals the arrival of an unconditioned stimulus.

client-centered therapy A style of psychotherapy developed by Carl Rogers in which the therapist uses unconditional positive regard, genuineness, and empathy to help the person to gain insight into his or her true self-concept.

closure The Gestalt perceptual organizational principle that the brain completes (closes) incomplete figures to form meaningful objects.

cognitive dissonance theory A theory developed by Leon Festinger that assumes people have a tendency to change their attitudes to reduce the cognitive discomfort created by inconsistencies between their attitudes and their behavior.

cognitive perspective A research perspective whose major explanatory focus is how our mental processes, such as perception, memory, and problem solving, work and impact behavior.

cognitive therapy A style of psychotherapy in which the therapist attempts to change the person's thinking from maladaptive to adaptive.

cohort effects People of a given age (cohorts) are affected by factors unique to their generation, leading to differences in performance between generations.

complementary colors Wavelengths of light that when added together produce white.

compliance Acting in accordance with a direct request from another person or group.

compulsion A repetitive and rigid behavior that a person feels compelled to perform in order to reduce anxiety.

concrete operational stage The third stage in Piaget's theory of cognitive development, from age 6 to 12, during which children gain a fuller understanding of conservation and other mental operations that allow them to think logically, but only about concrete events.

conditioned response (CR) The response that is elicited by the conditioned stimulus in classical conditioning.

conditioned stimulus (CS) The stimulus that comes to elicit a new response (the conditioned response) in classical conditioning.

conditions of worth The behaviors and attitudes for which other people, starting with our parents, will give us positive regard.

conduction deafness Hearing loss created by damage to one of the structures in the ear responsible for mechanically conducting the auditory information to the inner ear.

cones Receptor cells in the retina that are principally responsible for bright light and color vision.

confirmation bias The tendency to seek evidence that confirms one's beliefs.

conformity A change in behavior, belief, or both to conform to a group norm as a result of real or imagined group pressure.

conjunction fallacy Incorrectly judging the overlap of two uncertain events to be more probable than either of the two events.

conscious mind Freud's term for what you are presently aware of.

consciousness An individual's subjective awareness of his or her inner thinking and feeling and his or her external environment.

conservation The knowledge that the quantitative properties of objects (such as mass and number) remain the same despite changes in appearance.

contextual effect The use of the present context of sensory information to determine its meaning.

continuous schedule of reinforcement In operant conditioning, reinforcing the desired operant response each time it is made.

control group In an experiment, the group not exposed to the independent variable.

conventional level of moral reasoning The second level of reasoning in Kohlberg's theory of moral development in which moral reasoning is based on social rules and laws.

corpus callosum The bridge of neurons that connects the two cerebral hemispheres.

correlation coefficient A statistic that tells us the type and the strength of the relationship between two variables. The sign of the coefficient (+ or –) indicates the type of correlation—positive or negative, respectively. The absolute value of the coefficient (0.0 to 1.0) represents the strength of the correlation, with 1.0 being the maximum strength.

correlational study A research study in which two variables are measured to determine if they are related (how well either one predicts the other).

counterconditioning A type of behavioral therapy in which a maladaptive response is replaced by an incompatible adaptive response.

cross-sectional study A study in which the performances of groups of participants of different ages are compared to one another.

cue-dependent theory A theory of forgetting that proposes that forgetting is due to the unavailability of the retrieval cues necessary to locate the information in long-term memory.

cumulative record A record of the total number of operant responses over time that visually depicts the rate of responding.

dark adaptation The process by which the rods and cones through internal chemical changes become more and more sensitive to light in dim light conditions.

defense mechanism A process used by the ego to distort reality and protect a person from anxiety.

deindividuation The loss of self-awareness and self-restraint in a group situation that fosters arousal and anonymity.

delayed conditioning A classical conditioning procedure in which the conditioned stimulus precedes the unconditioned stimulus and remains present until after the unconditioned stimulus is presented so that the two stimuli occur together.

delusion A false belief.

dendrites Fibers projecting out of the cell body of a neuron whose function is to receive information from other neurons.

dependent variable In an experiment, a variable that is hypothesized to be affected by the independent variable and thus is measured by the experimenter.

depth perception Our ability to perceive the distance of objects from us.

descriptive methods Research methods whose main purpose is to provide objective and detailed descriptions of behavior and mental processes.

descriptive statistics Statistics that describe the results of a research study in a concise fashion.

developmental psychology The scientific study of biological, cognitive, social, and personality development across the life span.

deviation IQ score 100 plus or minus (15 × the number of standard deviations the person is from the raw score mean for their standardization group).

Diagnostic and Statistical Manual of Mental Disorders—Fourth Edition (**DSM-IV**) The current version of the American Psychiatric Association's diagnostic and classification guidelines for mental disorders.

difference threshold The minimum difference between two sensory stimuli detected 50 percent of the time. The difference threshold is also sometimes referred to as the just noticeable difference, or jnd.

diffusion of responsibility The lessening of individual responsibility for a task when responsibility for the task is spread across the members of a group.

discriminative stimulus In operant conditioning, the stimulus that has to be present for the operant response to be reinforced.

distractor task A memory task in which a small amount of information is briefly presented and then the participant is distracted from rehearsing the information for a variable period of time, after which the participant has to recall the information.

door-in-the-face technique Compliance is gained by starting with a large, unreasonable request that is turned down and following it with a more reasonable, smaller request.

dopamine A neurotransmitter involved in arousal and mood states, thought processes, and physical movement.

double-blind procedure A control measure in an experiment in which neither the experimenters nor the participants know which participants are in the experimental and control groups.

drive-reduction theory A theory of motivation that proposes that our behavior is motivated to reduce drives (bodily tension states) created by unsatisfied bodily needs in order to return the body to a balanced internal state.

effortful processing Memory processing that occurs consciously and requires attention.

ego The part of the personality that starts developing in the first year or so of life to find realistic outlets for the id's instinctual drives.

egocentrism The inability to distinguish one's own perceptions, thoughts, and feelings from those of others.

elaborative rehearsal A type of rehearsal in short-term memory in which incoming information is related to information from long-term memory to encode it into long-term memory.

electroconvulsive therapy (ECT) A biomedical treatment for severe depression that involves electrically inducing a brief brain seizure.

emotion A complex psychological state that involves a state of physiological arousal, an outward behavioral expression of the emotion, and a cognitive appraisal of the situation to determine the specific emotion and its intensity.

encoding The process of moving information from one memory stage to the next (from sensory memory into short-term memory or from short-term memory to long-term memory).

encoding failure theory A theory of forgetting that proposes that forgetting is due to the failure to encode the information into long-term memory.

encoding specificity principle The principle that the environmental cues (both internal and external) present at the time information is encoded into long-term memory serve as the best retrieval cues for the information.

endocrine glandular system The body's other major communication system. Communication is achieved through hormones that are secreted by the endocrine glands and travel through the bloodstream to their target sites.

endorphins A group of neurotransmitters that are involved in pain perception and relief.

episodic memory Explicit memory for personal experiences.

erogenous zone The area of the body where the id's pleasure-seeking energies are focused during a particular stage of psychosexual development.

experiment A research method in which the researcher manipulates one or more independent variables and measures their effect on one or more dependent variables while controlling other potentially relevant variables.

experimental group In an experiment, the group exposed to the independent variable.

explicit (declarative) memory Long-term memory for factual knowledge and personal experiences. This type of memory requires a conscious effort to remember and entails making declarations about the information remembered.

external locus of control The perception that chance or external forces beyond your personal control determine your fate.

extinction (in classical conditioning) The diminishing of the conditioned response when the unconditioned stimulus no longer follows the conditioned stimulus.

extinction (in operant conditioning) The diminishing of the operant response when it is no longer reinforced.

extrinsic motivation The desire to perform a behavior for external reinforcement.

factor analysis A statistical technique that identifies clusters of test items that measure the same ability (factor).

false consensus effect The tendency to overestimate the commonality of one's opinions and unsuccessful behaviors.

false memory An inaccurate memory that feels as real as an accurate memory.

false uniqueness effect The tendency to underestimate the commonality of one's abilities and successful behaviors.

farsightedness A visual problem in which the light waves from nearby objects are focused behind the retina, blurring the images of these objects.

fetal alcohol syndrome (FAS) A syndrome affecting infants whose mothers consumed large amounts of alcohol during pregnancy, resulting in a range of severe effects including mental retardation and facial abnormalities.

figure-and-ground principle The Gestalt perceptual organizational principle that the brain organizes sensory information into a figure or figures (the center of attention) and ground (the less distinct background).

fixation (1) In problem solving, the inability to create a new interpretation of a problem. (2) In Freudian theory, some of the id's pleasure-seeking energies remaining in a psychosexual stage due to excessive gratification or frustration of instinctual needs.

fixed-interval schedule A partial schedule of reinforcement in which a reinforcer is delivered after the first response is given once a set interval of time has elapsed.

fixed-ratio schedule A partial schedule of reinforcement in which a reinforcer is delivered each time a fixed number of responses are made. The fixed number can be any number greater than one.

flooding A counterconditioning exposure therapy in which the patient is immediately exposed to a feared object or situation.

Flynn effect The finding that the average intelligence test score in the United States and other industrialized nations has improved steadily over the last century.

foot-in-the-door technique Compliance to a large request is gained by preceding it with a very small request.

formal operational stage The last stage in Piaget's theory of cognitive development, starting at age 12 or so, during which a child gains the capacity for hypothetical-deductive thought.

fovea A tiny pit in the center of the retina filled with cones.

fraternal (dizygotic) twins Twins that originate from the fertilization of two eggs at approximately the same time (two zygotes).

free association A person spontaneously describes, without editing, all thoughts, feelings, or images that come to mind.

free recall task A memory task in which a list of items is presented one at a time and then the participant is free to recall them in any order.

frequency The number of times a wave cycles in 1 second.

frequency distribution A depiction, in a table or figure, of the number of participants (frequency) receiving each score for a variable.

frequency theory A theory of pitch perception that assumes that the frequency of the sound wave is mimicked by the firing rate of the entire basilar membrane.

frontal lobe The area in each cerebral hemisphere in front of the central fissure and above the lateral fissure. The motor cortex is in this lobe.

functional fixedness The inability to see that an object can have a function other than its typical one in solving a problem.

functional magnetic resonance imaging (fMRI) A computerized image of the activity levels of various areas in the brain generated by detecting the amount of oxygen brought to each area.

fundamental attribution error The tendency as an observer to overestimate dispositional influences and underestimate situational influences on others' behavior.

GABA (gamma-aminobutyric acid) The main inhibitory neurotransmitter in the nervous system. It is involved in lowering arousal and anxiety and regulating movement.

gambler's fallacy Incorrectly believing that a chance process is self-correcting in that an event that has not occurred for a while is more likely to occur.

gene The basic unit of genetic instruction.

generalized anxiety disorder An anxiety disorder in which a person has excessive, global anxiety that he or she cannot control for a period of at least 6 months.

genital stage of psychosexual development The fifth stage in Freud's theory (from puberty through adulthood) in which the erogenous zone is at the genitals and the child develops sexual relationships moving toward intimate adult relationships.

glial cells (glia) Cells in the nervous system that comprise the support system for the neurons.

glutamate The main excitatory neurotransmitter in the nervous system. It is involved in memory storage, pain perception, strokes, and schizophrenia.

group polarization The strengthening of a group's prevailing opinion about a topic following group discussion about the topic.

groupthink A mode of group thinking that impairs decision making because the desire for group harmony overrides a realistic appraisal of the possible decision alternatives.

habituation A decrease in the physiological responding to a stimulus once it becomes familiar.

hair cells The receptor cells for hearing. They line the basilar membrane inside the cochlea.

hallucination A false sensory perception.

heritability An index of the degree that variation of a trait within a given population is due to heredity.

heuristic A problem-solving strategy that seems reasonable given past experience with solving problems, especially similar problems, but does not guarantee a correct answer to a problem.

hierarchy of needs The motivational component in Maslow's theory of personality in which our innate needs that motivate our behavior are hierarchically arranged in a pyramid shape. From bottom to top, the needs are physiological, safety, belonging and love, esteem, and self-actualization.

hindsight bias (I-knew-it-all-along phenomenon) The tendency, after learning about an outcome, to be overconfident in one's ability to have predicted it.

hippocampus A part of the brain involved in the formation of memories.

holophrase A word used by an infant to express a complete idea.

hormone A chemical messenger that is produced by an endocrine gland and carried by the bloodstream to target tissues throughout the body.

hypothalamus A part of the brain that is involved in regulating basic drives such as eating, drinking, and sex. It also directs the endocrine glandular system through its control of the pituitary gland and the autonomic nervous system to maintain the body's internal environment.

iconic memory The visual sensory register that holds an exact copy of the incoming visual input but only for a brief period of time, less than 1 second.

id The part of the personality that a person is born with, where the biological instinctual drives reside, and that is located totally in the unconscious mind.

identical (monozygotic) twins Twins that originate from the same zygote.

identification The process by which children adopt the characteristics of the same-sex parent and learn their gender role and sense of morality.

ill-defined problem A problem lacking clear specification of either the start state, goal state, or the processes for reaching the goal state.

illusory correlation The erroneous belief that two variables are statistically related when they actually are not.

implicit (nondeclarative) memory Long-term memory for procedural tasks, classical conditioning, and priming effects. This type of memory does not require conscious awareness or the need to make declarations about the information remembered.

incentive theory A theory of motivation that proposes that our behavior is motivated by incentives, external stimuli that we have learned to associate with reinforcement.

independent variable In an experiment, the variable that is a hypothesized cause and thus is manipulated by the experimenter.

infantile/child amnesia Our inability as adults to remember events that occurred in our lives before about 3 years of age.

inferential statistical analyses Statistical analyses that allow researchers to draw conclusions about the results of a study by determining the probability that the results are due to random variation (chance). The results are statistically significant if this probability is .05 or less.

informational social influence Influence stemming from the need for information in situations in which the correct action or judgment is uncertain.

information-processing approach to cognitive development An approach to studying cognitive development that assumes cognitive development is continuous and improves as children become more adept at processing information (taking in, storing, and using information).

insecure-ambivalent attachment The type of attachment indicated by the infant not exploring but seeking closeness to the mother in the Ainsworth strange situation and showing high levels of distress when the mother leaves and ambivalent behavior when she returns by alternately clinging to and pushing away from her.

insecure-avoidant attachment The type of attachment indicated by the infant exploring with little interest in the mother in the Ainsworth strange situation procedure, showing only minimal distress when the mother leaves, and avoiding her when she returns.

insecure-disorganized (disoriented) attachment The type of attachment indicated by the infant's confusion when the mother leaves and returns in the Ainsworth strange situation procedure. The infant acts disoriented, seems overwhelmed by the situation, and does not demonstrate a consistent way of coping with it.

insight A new way to interpret a problem that immediately yields the solution.

instinctual drift The tendency for an animal to drift back from a learned operant response to an innate, instinctual response to an object.

intelligence quotient (IQ) (mental age/chronological age) $\times$ 100.

interference theory A theory of forgetting that proposes that forgetting is due to other information in memory interfering and thereby making the to-be-remembered information inaccessible.

internal locus of control The perception that you control your own fate.

interneurons Neurons that integrate information within the CNS through their communication with each other and between sensory and motor neurons in the spinal cord.

interposition A monocular depth cue referring to the fact that if one object partially blocks our view of another, we perceive it as closer to us.

intrinsic motivation The desire to perform a behavior for its own sake.

James-Lange theory A theory of emotion proposing that an emotion is determined from a cognitive appraisal of the physiological arousal and behavioral responses that occur first.

just-world hypothesis The assumption that the world is just and that people get what they deserve.

latency stage of psychosexual development The fourth stage in Freud's theory (from 6 to puberty) in which there is no erogenous zone, sexual feelings are repressed, and the focus is on cognitive and social development.

latent content Freud's term for the underlying true meaning of a dream.

latent learning Learning that occurs but is not demonstrated until there is incentive to do so.

law of effect A principle developed by Edward Thorndike that says that any behavior that results in satisfying consequences tends to be repeated and that any behavior that results in unsatisfying consequences tends not to be repeated.

L-dopa A drug for Parkinson's disease that contains the precursors to dopamine so that once it is in the brain, it will be converted to dopamine.

learned helplessness A sense of hopelessness in which a person thinks that he or she is unable to prevent aversive events.

left-skewed distribution An asymmetric frequency distribution in which there are some unusually low scores that distort the mean to be less than the median.

levels-of-processing theory A theory of information processing in memory that assumes that semantic processing, especially elaborative semantic processing, leads to better long-term memory.

limbic system A group of brain structures (hypothalamus, hippocampus, and amygdala) that play an important role in our survival, memory, and emotions.

linear perspective A monocular depth cue referring to the fact that as parallel lines recede away from us, they appear to converge—the greater the distance, the more they seem to converge. Sometimes referred to as perspective convergence.

lithium A naturally occurring element (a mineral salt) that is used to treat bipolar disorder.

lobotomy A type of psychosurgery in which the neuronal connections of the frontal lobes to lower brain areas are severed.

longitudinal study A study in which performance of the same group of participants is examined at different ages.

long-term memory (LTM) The memory stage in which information is stored for a long period of time (perhaps permanently) and whose capacity is essentially unlimited.

low-ball technique Compliance to a costly request is gained by first getting compliance to an attractive, less costly request but then reneging on it.

maintenance rehearsal A type of rehearsal in short-term memory in which the information is repeated over and over again in order to maintain it.

major depressive disorder A mood disorder in which the person has experienced one or more major depressive episodes.

major depressive episode An episode characterized by symptoms such as feelings of intense hopelessness, low self-esteem, and worthlessness, extreme fatigue, dramatic changes in eating and sleeping behavior, inability to concentrate, and greatly diminished interest in family, friends, and activities, for a period of 2 weeks or more.

manic episode An episode characterized by abnormally elevated mood in which the person experiences symptoms such as inflated self-esteem with grandiose delusions, a decreased need for sleep, constant talking, distractibility, restlessness, and poor judgment for a period of at least a week.

manifest content Freud's term for the literal surface meaning of a dream.

mean The numerical average of a distribution of scores.

means–end analysis heuristic A problem-solving heuristic in which the distance to the goal state is decreased systematically by breaking the problem down into subgoals and achieving these subgoals.

median The score positioned in the middle of a distribution of scores when all of the scores are arranged from lowest to highest.

medulla A brain stem structure involved in many essential body functions, such as heartbeat, breathing, blood pressure, digestion, and swallowing.

memory span The average number of items an individual can remember across a series of memory span trials.

memory span task A memory task in which the participant is given a series of items one at a time and then has to recall the items in the order in which they were presented.

mental set The tendency to use previously successful problem-solving strategies without considering others that are more appropriate for the current problem.

meta-analysis A statistical technique that combines the results of a large number of studies on one experimental question into one analysis to arrive at an overall conclusion.

method of loci A mnemonic in which sequential pieces of information to be remembered are encoded by associating them with sequential locations in a very familiar room or place and then the pieces of information are retrieved by mentally going around the room (place) and retrieving the piece at each location.

misinformation effect The distortion of a memory by exposure to misleading information.

mnemonic A memory aid.

mode The most frequently occurring score in a distribution of scores.

mood disorders Disorders that involve dramatic changes in a person's emotional mood that are excessive and unwarranted.

mood-congruence effect Tendency to retrieve experiences and information that are congruent with a person's current mood.

mood-dependent memory Long-term memory retrieval is best when a person's mood state at time of encoding and retrieval of the information is the same.

motivation The set of internal and external factors that energize our behavior and direct it toward goals.

motor cortex The strip of cortex in each cerebral hemisphere in the frontal lobe directly in front of the central fissure, which allows us to move different parts of our body.

motor neurons Neurons in the PNS that carry movement commands from the CNS out to the rest of the body.

myelin sheath An insulating layer covering an axon that allows for faster neural impulses.

naturalistic observation A descriptive research method in which the behavior of interest is observed in its natural setting, and the researcher does not intervene in the behavior being observed.

nearsightedness A visual problem in which the light waves from distant objects are focused in front of the retina, blurring the images of these objects.

negative correlation An inverse relationship between two variables.

negative punishment Punishment in which an appetitive stimulus is removed.

negative reinforcement Reinforcement in which an aversive stimulus is removed.

nerve deafness Hearing loss created by damage to the hair cells or the auditory nerve fibers in the inner ear.

neurogenesis theory of depression An explanation of depression that proposes that neurogenesis, the growth of new neurons, in the hippocampus stops during depression, and when it resumes, the depression lifts.

neurons Cells that transmit information within the nervous system.

neurotransmitter A naturally occurring chemical in the nervous system that specializes in transmitting information between neurons.

norepinephrine A neurotransmitter involved in levels of arousal and mood, sleep, and eating.

normal distribution A frequency distribution that is shaped like a bell. About 68 percent of the scores fall within 1 standard deviation of the mean, about 95 percent within 2 standard deviations of the mean, and over 99 percent within 3 standard deviations of the mean.

normative social influence Influence stemming from our desire to gain the approval and to avoid the disapproval of others.

obedience Following the commands of a person in authority.

object permanence The knowledge that an object exists independent of perceptual contact with it.

observational learning (modeling) Learning by observing others and imitating their behavior.

obsession A persistent intrusive thought, idea, impulse, or image that causes anxiety.

obsessive-compulsive disorder An anxiety disorder in which the person experiences recurrent obsessions or compulsions that are perceived by the person as excessive or unreasonable, but cause significant distress and disruption in the person's daily life.

occipital lobe The area located in the lower back of each cerebral hemisphere. The primary visual cortex is in this lobe.

Oedipus conflict A phallic stage conflict for a boy in which the boy becomes sexually attracted to his mother and fears the father will find out and castrate him.

operant conditioning Learning to associate behaviors with their consequences. Behaviors that are reinforced (lead to satisfying consequences) will be strengthened, and behaviors that are punished (lead to unsatisfying consequences) will be weakened.

operational definition A description of the operations or procedures that a researcher uses to manipulate or measure a variable.

opponent-process theory A theory of color vision that assumes that there are three opponent-process cell systems (red-green, blue-yellow, and black-white) that process color information after it has been processed by the cones. The colors in each system oppose one another in that if one color is stimulated, the other is inhibited.

oral stage of psychosexual development The first stage in Freud's theory (from birth to 18 months), in which the erogenous zones are the mouth, lips, and tongue, and the child derives pleasure from oral activities such as sucking, biting, and chewing.

overextension The application of a newly learned word to objects that are not included in the meaning of the word.

overjustification effect A decrease in an intrinsically motivated behavior after the behavior is extrinsically reinforced and then the reinforcement is discontinued.

panic disorder An anxiety disorder in which a person experiences recurrent panic attacks.

parasympathetic nervous system The part of the autonomic nervous system that returns the body to its normal resting state after having been highly aroused, as in an emergency.

parietal lobe The area in each cerebral hemisphere in back of the central fissure and above the lateral fissure. The somatosensory cortex is in this lobe.

Parkinson's disease A disease in which the person has movement problems such as muscle tremors, difficulty initiating movements, and rigidity of movement. These movement problems stem from a scarcity of dopamine in the basal ganglia.

partial-reinforcement effect The finding that operant responses that are reinforced on partial schedules are more resistant to extinction than those reinforced on a continuous schedule.

partial schedule of reinforcement In operant conditioning, reinforcing the desired operant response only part of the time.

participant observation A descriptive research method in which the observer becomes part of the group being observed.

peg-word system A mnemonic in which the items in a list to be remembered are associated with the sequential items in a memorized jingle and then the list is retrieved by going through the jingle and retrieving the associated items.

percentile rank The percentage of scores below a specific score in a distribution of scores.

perception The interpretation by the brain of sensory information.

perceptual constancy The perceptual stability of the size, shape, brightness, and color for familiar objects seen at varying distances, different angles, and under different lighting conditions.

perceptual set The interpretation of ambiguous sensory information in terms of how our past experiences have set us to perceive it.

peripheral nervous system (PNS) The part of the nervous system that links the CNS with the body's sensory receptors, muscles, and glands.

permissive parenting A style of parenting in which the parents make few demands and are overly responsive to their children's desires, letting their children do pretty much as they please.

personality A person's internally based characteristic ways of acting and thinking.

personality disorder A disorder characterized by inflexible, long-standing personality traits that lead to behavior that impairs social functioning and deviates from cultural norms.

personality inventory An objective personality test that uses a series of questions or statements for which the test taker must indicate whether they apply to him or her or not.

person-who reasoning Questioning a well-established research finding because one knows a person who violates the finding.

phallic stage of psychosexual development The third stage in Freud's theory (from 3 to 6 years), in which the erogenous zone is located at the genitals, and the child derives pleasure from genital stimulation.

phonemes The smallest distinctive speech sounds in a language.

pituitary gland The most influential gland in the endocrine glandular system. It releases hormones for human growth and hormones that direct other endocrine glands to release their hormones.

place theory A theory of pitch perception which assumes that there is a specific location along the basilar membrane that will maximally respond to a particular frequency, thereby indicating the pitch to the brain. As this location goes down the basilar membrane from the oval window, the pitch goes down from 20,000 Hz to 20 Hz.

placebo An inactive pill or a treatment that has no known effects.

placebo effect Improvement due to the expectation of improving because of receiving treatment.

placebo group A control group of participants who believe they are receiving treatment, but who are only receiving a placebo.

pleasure principle The principle of seeking immediate gratification for instinctual drives without concern for the consequences.

pons A brainstem structure that serves as a bridge between the cerebellum and the rest of the brain and is involved in sleep and dreaming.

population The entire group of people that a researcher is studying.

positive correlation A direct relationship between two variables.

positive punishment Punishment in which an aversive stimulus is presented.

positive reinforcement Reinforcement in which an appetitive stimulus is presented.

positron emission tomography (PET) scan A visual display of the activity levels in various areas in the brain generated by detecting the amount of positron emission created by the metabolization of radioactive glucose in each area.

postconventional level of moral reasoning The last level of reasoning in Kohlberg's theory of moral development in which moral reasoning is based on self-chosen universal ethical principles (with human rights taking precedence over laws) and the avoidance of self-condemnation for violating such principles.

preconscious mind Freud's term for what is stored in your memory that you are not presently aware of but can access.

preconventional level of moral reasoning The first level of reasoning in Kohlberg's theory of moral development in which moral reasoning is based on avoiding punishment and looking out for your own welfare and needs.

preoperational stage The second stage in Piaget's theory of cognitive development, from age 2 to 6, during which the child's thinking becomes more symbolic and language-based, but remains egocentric and lacks the mental operations that allow logical thinking.

primacy effect (1) In memory, the superior recall of the early portion of a list relative to the middle of the list in a one-trial free recall task. (2) In impression formation, information gathered early is weighted more heavily than information gathered later in forming an impression of another person.

primary reinforcer A stimulus that is innately reinforcing.

priming The implicit influence of an earlier presented stimulus on the response to a later stimulus. This influence is independent of conscious memory for the earlier stimulus.

proactive interference The disruptive effect of prior learning on the retrieval of new information.

procedural memory Implicit memory for cognitive and motor tasks that have a physical procedural aspect to them.

projective test A personality test that uses a series of ambiguous stimuli to which the test taker must respond about his or her perceptions of the stimuli.

psychoanalysis A style of psychotherapy originally developed by Sigmund Freud in which the therapist helps the person gain insight into the unconscious sources of his or her problems.

psychology The science of behavior and mental processes.

psychosurgery A biomedical treatment in which specific areas of the brain are destroyed.

psychotherapy The use of psychological interventions to treat mental disorders.

psychotic disorder A disorder characterized by a loss of contact with reality.

punisher A stimulus that decreases the probability of a prior response.

punishment The process by which the probability of a response is decreased by the presentation of a punisher.

random assignment A control measure in which participants are randomly assigned to groups in order to equalize participant characteristics across the various groups in an experiment.

random sampling A sampling technique that obtains a representative sample of a population by ensuring that each individual in a population has an equal opportunity of being in the sample.

range The difference between the highest and lowest scores in a distribution of scores.

rational-emotive therapy A type of cognitive therapy developed by Albert Ellis in which the therapist directly confronts and challenges the person's unrealistic thoughts and beliefs to show that they are irrational.

reaction range The genetically determined limits for an individual's intelligence.

reality principle The principle of finding gratification for instinctual drives within the constraints of reality (norms of society).

recall A measure of long-term memory retrieval that requires the reproduction of the information with essentially no retrieval cues.

recency effect The superior recall of the latter portion of a list relative to the middle of the list in a one-trial free recall task.

recognition A measure of long-term memory retrieval that only requires the identification of the information in the presence of retrieval cues.

reflex A stimulus–response pair in which the stimulus (the unconditioned stimulus) automatically elicits the response (the unconditioned response).

reinforcement The process by which the probability of a response is increased by the presentation of a reinforcer.

reinforcer A stimulus that increases the probability of a prior response.

relearning The savings method of measuring long-term memory retrieval in which the measure is the amount of time saved when learning information for the second time.

reliability The extent to which the scores for a test are consistent.

REM (rapid eye movement) sleep The stage of sleep that is characterized by rapid eye movements and brain wave patterns that resemble those for an awake state and in which most dreaming occurs. REM sleep is sometimes referred to as paradoxical sleep because the bodily muscles are immobilized but much of the brain is highly active.

representativeness heuristic A heuristic for judging the probability of membership in a category by how well an object resembles (is representative of) that category (the more representative, the more probable).

resistance A person's unwillingness to discuss a particular topic during therapy.

reticular formation A network of neurons running up the center of the brain stem that is responsible for our different levels of arousal and consciousness.

retina The light-sensitive layer of the eye that is composed of three layers of cells—ganglion, bipolar, and receptor (rods and cones).

retinal disparity A binocular depth cue referring to the fact that as the disparity (difference) between the two retinal images of an object increases, the distance of the object from us decreases.

retrieval The process of bringing information stored in long-term memory into short-term memory.

retroactive interference The disruptive effect of new learning on the retrieval of old information.

retrograde amnesia The disruption of memory for the past, especially episodic information for events before, especially just before, surgery or trauma to the brain.

reversibility The knowledge that reversing a transformation brings about the conditions that existed before the transformation.

right-skewed distribution An asymmetric frequency distribution in which there are some unusually high scores that distort the mean to be greater than the median.

rods Receptor cells in the retina that are principally responsible for dim light and achromatic vision.

rooting reflex An innate human reflex that leads infants to turn their mouths toward anything that touches their cheeks and search for something to suck on.

sample The subset of a population that actually participate in a research study.

scaffolding According to Vygotsky, a style of teaching in which the teacher adjusts the level of help in relation to the child's level of performance while orienting the child's learning toward the upper level of his or her zone of proximal development.

scatterplot A visual depiction of correlational data in which each data point represents the scores on the two variables for each participant.

Schachter-Singer two-factor theory A theory of emotion proposing that an emotion is determined by cognitive appraisal of the physiological arousal and the entire environmental situation.

schemas Frameworks for our knowledge about people, objects, events, and actions that allow us to organize and interpret information about our world.

schemes Piaget's term for what are now called schemas—frameworks for our knowledge about people, objects, events, and actions that allow us to organize and interpret information about our world.

schizophrenia A psychotic disorder in which at least two of the following symptoms are present most of the time during a 1-month period—hallucinations, delusions, disorganized speech, disorganized or catatonic behavior, or negative symptoms such as loss of emotion.

secondary reinforcer A stimulus that gains its reinforcing property through learning.

secure attachment The type of attachment indicated by the infant exploring freely in the presence of the mother in the Ainsworth strange situation, displaying distress when the mother leaves, and responding enthusiastically when she returns.

selective serotonin and norepinephrine reuptake inhibitors (SSNRIs) Antidepressant drugs that achieve their agonistic effect on serotonin and norepinephrine by selectively blocking their reuptake.

selective serotonin reuptake inhibitors (SSRIs) Antidepressant drugs that achieve their agonistic effect on serotonin by selectively blocking its reuptake.

self-actualization The fullest realization of a person's potential.

self-efficacy A judgment of one's effectiveness in dealing with particular situations.

self-fulfilling prophecy Our behavior leads a person to act in accordance with our expectations for that person.

self-perception theory A theory developed by Daryl Bem that assumes that when we are unsure of our attitudes, we infer them by examining our behavior and the context in which it occurs.

self-reference effect The superior long-term memory for information related to oneself at time of encoding into long-term memory.

self-serving bias The tendency to make attributions so that one can perceive oneself favorably.

self-system The set of cognitive processes by which a person observes, evaluates, and regulates his or her behavior.

semantic memory Explicit memory for factual knowledge.

sensation The initial information gathering and recoding by the sensory structures.

sensorimotor stage The first stage in Piaget's theory of cognitive development, from birth to about age 2, during which infants learn about the world through their sensory and motor interactions with it and develop object permanence.

sensory adaptation Our sensitivity to unchanging and repetitive stimuli disappears over time.

sensory memory (SM) The set of sensory registers, one for each of our senses, that serve as holding places for incoming sensory information until it can be attended to, interpreted, and encoded into short-term memory.

sensory neurons Neurons in the PNS that carry information to the CNS from sensory receptors, muscles, and glands.

serotonin A neurotransmitter involved in levels of arousal and mood, sleep, and eating.

shaping Training a human or animal to make an operant response by reinforcing successive approximations of the desired response.

short-term memory (STM) The memory stage with a small capacity (7 ± 2 chunks) and brief duration (< 30 seconds) that we are consciously aware of and in which we do our problem solving, reasoning, and decision making.

signal detection theory A theory that assumes that the detection of faint sensory stimuli depends not only upon a person's physiological sensitivity to a stimulus but also upon their decision criterion for detection, which is based on non-sensory factors.

social facilitation Facilitation of a dominant response on a task due to social arousal, leading to improvement on simple or well-learned tasks and worse performance on complex or unlearned tasks when other people are present.

social loafing The tendency to exert less effort when working in a group toward a common goal than when individually working toward the goal.

social phobia An anxiety disorder indicated by a marked and persistent fear of one or more social performance situations in which there is exposure to unfamiliar people or scrutiny by others.

social psychology The scientific study of how we influence one another's behavior and thinking.

sociocultural perspective A research perspective whose major explanatory focus is how other people and the cultural context impact on behavior and mental processes.

somatic (skeletal) nervous system The part of the PNS that carries sensory input from receptors to the CNS and relays commands from the CNS to skeletal muscles to control their movement.

somatosensory cortex The strip of cortex in each cerebral hemisphere in the parietal lobe directly in back of the central fissure that allows us to sense pressure, temperature, and pain in different parts of our body as well as the position of our body parts.

source misattribution Attributing a memory to the wrong source, resulting in a false memory.

spacing (distributed study) effect Superior long-term memory for spaced study versus massed study (cramming).

specific phobia An anxiety disorder indicated by a marked and persistent fear of specific objects or situations that is excessive and unreasonable.

Sperling's full-report procedure An experimental procedure in which, following the brief presentation of a matrix of unrelated consonants, the participant has to attempt to recall all of the letters in the matrix.

Sperling's partial-report procedure An experimental procedure in which, following the brief presentation of a matrix of unrelated consonants, the participant is given an auditory cue about which row of the matrix to recall.

spinal cord The conduit between the brain and the PNS for incoming sensory data and outgoing movement commands to the muscles.

spinal reflex A simple automatic action of the spinal cord not requiring involvement of the brain, such as the knee-jerk reflex.

spontaneous recovery (in classical conditioning) A partial recovery in strength of the conditioned response following a break during extinction training.

spontaneous recovery (in operant conditioning) The temporary recovery of the operant response following a break during extinction training.

spontaneous remission Getting better with the passage of time without receiving any therapy.

standard deviation The average extent that the scores vary from the mean for a distribution of scores.

standardization The process that allows test scores to be interpreted by providing test norms.

state-dependent memory Long-term memory retrieval is best when a person's physiological state at time of encoding and retrieval of the information is the same.

Stevens's power law The perceived magnitude of a stimulus is equal to its actual physical intensity raised to some constant power. The constant power is different for each type of sensory judgment.

stimulus discrimination (in classical conditioning) The elicitation of the conditioned response only by the conditioned stimulus or only by a small set of highly similar stimuli that includes the conditioned stimulus.

stimulus discrimination (in operant conditioning) Learning to give the operant response only in the presence of the discriminative stimulus.

stimulus generalization (in classical conditioning) The elicitation of the conditioned response to stimuli that are similar to the conditioned stimulus. The more similar the stimulus is to the conditioned stimulus, the stronger the response.

stimulus generalization (in operant conditioning) Giving the operant response in the presence of stimuli similar to the discriminative stimulus. The more similar the stimulus is to the discriminative stimulus, the higher the operant response rate.

storage The process of maintaining information in a memory stage.

storage decay theory A theory of forgetting that proposes that forgetting is due to the decay of the biological representation of the information and that periodic usage of the information will help to maintain it in storage.

subjective contour A line or shape that is perceived to be present but does not really exist. The brain creates it during perception.

subtractive mixtures Mixtures of wavelengths of light in which some wavelengths are absorbed (subtracted) and so do not get reflected from the mixtures to the retina.

sucking reflex An innate human reflex that leads infants to suck anything that touches their lips.

superego The part of the personality that represents one's conscience and idealized standards of behavior.

survey research A descriptive research method in which the researcher uses questionnaires and interviews to collect information about the behavior, beliefs, and attitudes of particular groups of people.

sympathetic nervous system The part of the autonomic nervous system that is in control when we are highly aroused, as in an emergency, and need to prepare for defensive action.

synaptic gap (synapse) The microscopic gap between neurons across which neurotransmitters travel to carry their messages to other neurons.

systematic desensitization A counterconditioning exposure therapy in which a fear response to an object or situation is replaced with a relaxation response in a series of progressively increasing fear-arousing steps.

tardive dyskinesia A side effect of long-term use of traditional antipsychotic drugs causing the person to have uncontrollable facial tics, grimaces, and other involuntary movements of the lips, jaw, and tongue.

telegraphic speech Using two-word sentences with mainly nouns and verbs.

temperament The set of innate tendencies or dispositions that lead a person to behave in certain ways.

temporal integration procedure An experimental procedure in which two meaningless visual patterns that produce a meaningful pattern if integrated are presented sequentially with the time delay between their presentations varied.

temporal lobe The area in each cerebral hemisphere located beneath the lateral fissure. The primary auditory cortex is in this lobe.

teratogens Environmental agents such as drugs and viruses, diseases, and physical conditions that impair prenatal development and lead to birth defects and sometimes death.

thalamus A part of the brain that serves as a relay station for incoming sensory information.

that's-not-all technique Compliance to a planned second request with additional benefits is gained by presenting this request before a response can be made to a first request.

theory of mind The understanding of the mental and emotional states of both ourselves and others.

thinking The processing of information to solve problems and make judgments and decisions.

third-variable problem An explanation of a correlation between two variables in terms of another (third) variable that could possibly be responsible for the observed relationship between the two variables.

top-down processing The brain's use of knowledge, beliefs, and expectations to interpret sensory information.

trace conditioning A classical conditioning procedure in which the conditioned stimulus precedes the unconditioned stimulus but is removed before the unconditioned stimulus is presented so the two stimuli do not occur together.

traits The relatively stable, internally based characteristics that describe a person.

transcranial magnetic stimulation (TMS) A neurostimulation therapy in which the left frontal lobe is stimulated with magnetic pulses via an electromagnetic coil placed on the patient's scalp. It is only cleared for use in cases of severe depression for which traditional treatment has not helped.

transduction The conversion of physical energy into neural signals that the brain can understand.

transference A person undergoing therapy acts toward the therapist as he or she did or does toward important figures in his or her life, such as parents.

trichromatic theory A theory of color vision that assumes that there are three types of cones, each only activated by wavelength ranges of light corresponding roughly to blue, green, and red. It further assumes that all of the various colors that we can see are mixtures of various levels of activation of the three types of cones. If all three are equally activated, we see white.

unconditional positive regard Unconditional acceptance and approval of a person by others.

unconditioned response (UCR) The response in a reflex that is automatically elicited by the unconditioned stimulus.

unconditioned stimulus (UCS) The stimulus in a reflex that automatically elicits an unconditioned response.

unconscious mind Freud's term for the part of our mind that we cannot become aware of.

underextension The failure to apply a new word more generally to objects that are included within the meaning of the word.

uninvolved parenting A style of parenting in which the parents minimize both the time they spend with their children and their emotional involvement with them, and provide for their children's basic needs, but little else.

validity The extent to which a test measures what it is supposed to measure or predicts what it is supposed to predict.

variable Any factor that can take on more than one value.

variable-interval schedule A partial schedule of reinforcement in which the time that must elapse on each trial before a response will lead to the delivery of a reinforcer varies from trial to trial but averages to a set time across trials.

variable-ratio schedule A partial schedule of reinforcement in which the number of responses it takes to obtain a reinforcer varies on each trial but averages to a set number across trials.

virtual reality therapy A counterconditioning exposure therapy in which the patient is exposed in graduated steps to computer simulations of a feared object or situation.

volley principle Cells taking turns firing will increase the maximum firing rate for a group of cells.

vulnerability–stress model A biopsychosocial explanation of schizophrenia that proposes that genetic, prenatal, and postnatal biological factors render a person vulnerable to schizophrenia, but environmental stress determines whether it develops or not.

wavelength The distance in one cycle of a wave, from one crest to the next.

Weber's law For each type of sensory judgment that we can make, the measured difference threshold is a constant fraction of the standard stimulus value used to measure it. This constant fraction is different for each type of sensory judgment.

well-defined problem A problem with clear specifications of the start state, goal state, and the processes for reaching the goal state.

Wernicke's area An area in the cerebral cortex responsible for comprehension of speech and text. It is in the left temporal lobe of the majority of people, regardless of handedness.

working backward heuristic A problem-solving heuristic in which one attempts to solve a problem by working from the goal state back to the start state.

Yerkes-Dodson law A law describing the relationship between the amount of arousal and the performance quality on a task—increasing arousal up to some optimal level increases performance quality on a task, but increasing arousal past this point is detrimental to performance.

zone of proximal development According to Vygotsky, the difference between what a child can actually do and what the child could do with the help of others.

zygote The fertilized egg that is formed from the union of the sperm and egg cells in human reproduction.

References

Ackerman, D. (2004). *An alchemy of mind: The marvel and mystery of the brain*. New York: Scribner.

Adams, J. L. (1986). *Conceptual blockbusting* (3rd ed.). Reading, MA: Addison-Wesley.

Ainsworth, M. D. S. (1979). Infant-mother attachment. *American Psychologist, 34*, 932–937.

Ainsworth, M. D. S., Blehar, M. C., Waters, E., & Wall, S. (1978). *Patterns of attachment: A psychological study of the Strange Situation*. Hillsdale, NJ: Erlbaum.

Allen, C. T., & Shimp, T. A. (1990). On using classical conditioning methods for researching the impact of ad-evoked feelings. In S. J. Agnes, J. A. Edell, & T. M. Dubitsky (Eds.), *Emotion in advertising: Theoretical and practical explanations* (pp. 19–34). New York: Quorum Books.

Allport, G. W., & Odbert, H. S. (1936). Trait-names: A psycholexical study. *Psychological Monographs, 47* (Whole No. 1).

Allyon, T., & Azrin, N. H. (1968). *The token economy*. New York: Appleton-Century-Crofts.

American Psychiatric Association. (1994). *Diagnostic and statistical manual of mental disorders* (4th ed.). Washington, DC: Author.

American Psychiatric Association. (2000). *Diagnostic and statistical manual of mental disorders* (4th ed., Text Revision). Washington, DC: Author.

Andersen, A. N., Wohlfahrt, J., Christens, P., Olsen, J., & Melbe, M. (2000). Maternal age and fetal loss: Population based linkage study. *British Medical Journal, 320*, 1708–1712.

Anderson, C. A., Berkowitz, L., Donnerstein, E., Huesmann, L. R., Johnson, J. D., Linz, D., et al. (2003). The influence of media violence on youth. *Psychological Science in the Public Interest, 4*(3) [Whole issue].

Anderson, C. A., Lepper, M. R., & Ross, L. (1980). Perseverance of social theories: The role of explanations in the persistence of discredited information. *Journal of Personality and Social Psychology, 39*, 1037–1049.

Andrews, P. W., & Thomson, J. A. (2009). The bright side of being blue: Depression as an adaptation for analyzing complex problems. *Psychological Review, 116*, 620–654.

Andrews, P. W., & Thomson, J. A. (2010, January/February). Depression's evolutionary roots. *Scientific American MIND, 20*, 56–61.

Anthes, E. (2009). *The instant egghead guide to the mind*. New York: St. Martin's Press.

Applebaum, P. S. (2004). One madman keeping loaded guns: Misconceptions of mental illness and their legal consequences. *Psychiatric Services, 55*, 1105–1106.

Asch, S. E. (1955, November). Opinions and social pressure. *Scientific American, 193*, 31–35.

Asher, S. R. (1983). Social competence and peer status: Recent advances and future directions. *Child Development, 54*, 1427–1434.

Atkinson, R. C., & Shiffrin, R. M. (1968). Human memory: A proposed system and its control processes. In K. W. Spence & J. T. Spence (Eds.), *The psychology of learning and motivation: Advances in research and theory* (Vol. 2, pp. 89–195). New York: Academic Press.

Baddeley, A. D. (1992). Working memory. *Science, 255*, 556–569.

Baddeley, A. D. (2001). Is working memory still working? *American Psychologist, 56*, 849–864.

Baddeley, A. D. (2003). Working memory: Looking backward and forward. *Nature Reviews Neuroscience, 4*, 829–839.

Bahrick, H. P. (1984). Semantic memory content in permastore: Fifty years of memory for Spanish learned in school. *Journal of Experimental Psychology: General, 113*, 1–29.

Baillargeon, R. (1987). Object permanence in 3.5- and 4.5-month-old infants. *Developmental Psychology, 23*, 655–664.

Baillargeon, R. (1993). The object-concept revisited: New directions in the investigation of infants' physical knowledge. In C. E. Granrud (Ed.), *Visual perception and cognition in infancy* (pp. 265–315). Hillsdale, NJ: Erlbaum.

Baillargeon, R. (2002). The acquisition of physical knowledge in infancy: A summary in eight lessons. In U. Goswami (Ed.), *Handbook of childhood cognitive development* (pp. 47–83). Malden, MA: Blackwell.

Baldwin, D. A., & Moses, L. J. (2001). Links between social understanding and early word learning: Challenges to current accounts. *Social Development, 10,* 309–329.

Bandura, A. (1965). Influences of models' reinforcement contingencies on the acquisition of imitative responses. *Journal of Personality and Social Psychology, 1,* 589–593.

Bandura, A. (1973). *Social learning theory.* Englewood Cliffs, NJ: Prentice Hall.

Bandura, A. (1986). *Social functions of thought and action: A social-cognitive theory.* Englewood Cliffs, NJ: Prentice Hall.

Bandura, A. (1997). *Self-efficacy: The exercise of control.* New York: W. H. Freeman.

Bandura, A., Ross, D., & Ross, S. A. (1961). Transmission of aggression through imitation of aggressive models. *Journal of Abnormal and Social Psychology, 63,* 575–582.

Bandura, A., Ross, D., & Ross, S. A. (1963a). Imitation of film-mediated aggressive models. *Journal of Abnormal and Social Psychology, 66,* 3–11.

Bandura, A., Ross, D., & Ross, S. A. (1963b). Vicarious reinforcement and imitative learning. *Journal of Abnormal and Social Psychology, 67,* 601–607.

Bangasser, D. A., Waxler, D. E., Santollo, J., & Shors, T. J. (2006). Trace conditioning and the hippocampus: The importance of contiguity. *The Journal of Neuroscience, 26,* 8702–8706.

Bar, M., & Biederman, I. (1998). Subliminal visual priming. *Psychological Science, 9,* 464–469.

Bard, P. (1934). On emotional expression after decortication with some remarks on certain theoretical views. *Psychological Review, 41,* 309–329.

Baron-Cohen, S. (2000). Theory of mind and autism: A fifteen year review. In S. Baron-Cohen, H. Tager-Flusberg, & D. J. Cohen (Eds.), *Understanding other minds: Perspectives from developmental cognitive neuroscience* (pp. 3–20). New York: Oxford University Press.

Bartlett, F. C. (1932). *Remembering: A study in experimental and social psychology.* Cambridge: Cambridge University Press.

Bates, S. C. (2004). Coverage: Findings from a national survey of introductory psychology syllabi. In D. V. Doty (Chair), *What to leave in and out of introductory psychology.* Symposium conducted at the 112th convention of the American Psychological Association, Honolulu, Hawaii.

Baumrind, D. (1964). Some thoughts on ethics of research: After reading Milgram's "Behavioral study of obedience." *American Psychologist, 19,* 421–423.

Baumrind, D. (1971). Current patterns of parental authority. *Developmental Psychology Monograph, 4,* 1–103.

Baumrind, D. (1991). The influence of parenting style on adolescent competence and substance abuse. *Journal of Early Adolescence, 11,* 56–95.

Baumrind, D. (1996). The discipline controversy revisited. *Family Relations, 45,* 405–414.

Beck, A. T. (1976). *Cognitive therapy and the emotional disorders.* New York: International Universities Press.

Beck, J. S., & Beck, A. T. (1995). *Cognitive therapy: Basics and beyond.* New York: Guilford.

Begley, S. (2007). *Train your mind, change your brain: How a new science reveals our extraordinary potential to transform ourselves.* New York: Ballantine Books.

Békésy, G. von (1960). *Experiments in hearing.* New York: McGraw-Hill.

Belmont, L., & Marolla, F. A. (1973). Birth order, family size and intelligence. *Science, 182,* 1096–1101.

Bem, D. J. (1972). Self-perception theory. In L. Berkowitz (Ed.), *Advances in experimental social psychology* (Vol. 6, pp. 1–62). New York: Academic Press.

Ben-Porath, Y. S., & Butcher, J. N. (1989). The comparability of MMPI and MMPI-2 scales and profiles. *Psychological Assessment: A Journal of Consulting and Clinical Psychology, 1,* 345–347.

Berger, K. S. (2006). *The developing person through childhood* (4th ed.). New York: Worth.

Besson, M., Faita, F., Peretz, L., Bonnel, A. M., & Requin, J. (1998). Singing in the brain: Independence of lyrics and tunes. *Psychological Science, 9,* 494–498.

Birdsong, D., & Molis, M. (2001). On the evidence for maturational constraints in second-language acquisition. *Journal of Memory and Language, 44,* 235–249.

Blass, T. (1999). The Milgram paradigm after 35 years: Some things we now know about obedience to authority. *Journal of Applied Social Psychology, 29,* 955–978.

Blass, T. (2004). *The man who shocked the world: The life and legacy of Stanley Milgram.* New York: Basic Books.

Blastland, M., & Dilnot, A. (2009). *The numbers game: The commonsense guide to understanding numbers in the news, in politics, and in life.* New York: Gotham Books.

Boldrini, M., Underwood, M. D., Hen, R., Rosoklija, G. B., Dwork, A. J., Mann, J. J., et al. (2009). Antidepressants increase neural progenitor cells in the human hippocampus. *Neuropsychopharmacology, 34,* 2376–2389.

Bond, C. E., Jr., & Titus, L. J. (1983). Social facilitation: A meta-analysis of 24 studies. *Psychological Bulletin, 94,* 265–292.

Bond, R., & Smith, P. B. (1996). Culture and conformity: A meta-analysis of studies using Asch's (1952b, 1956) line judgment task. *Psychological Bulletin, 119,* 111–137.

Botwinick, J. (1961). Husband and father-in-law: A reversible figure. *American Journal of Psychology, 74,* 312–313.

Bouchard, T. J., Jr., & McGue, M. (1981). Familial studies of intelligence: A review. *Science, 212,* 1055–1059.

Bouchard, T. J., Jr., Lykken, D. T., McGue, M., Segal, N. L., & Tellegen, A. (1990). Sources of human psychological differences: The Minnesota Study of Twins Reared Apart. *Science, 250,* 223–228.

Bouton, M. E. (1994). Context, ambiguity, and classical conditioning. *Current Directions in Psychological Science, 13,* 148–151.

Bowlby, J. (1969). *Attachment and loss: Vol. 1. Attachment.* New York: Basic Books.

Boynton, R. M. (1988). Color vision. *Annual Review of Psychology, 39,* 69–100.

Bregman, E. O. (1934). An attempt to modify the emotional attitudes of infants by the conditioned response technique. *Journal of Genetic Psychology,* 169–198.

Breland, K., & Breland, M. (1961). The misbehavior of organisms. *American Psychologist, 16,* 681–684.

Bronfenbrenner, U. (1993). The ecology of cognitive development: Research models and fugitive findings. In R. H. Wozniak & K. W. Fischer (Eds.), *Development in context* (pp. 3–44). Hillsdale, NJ: Erlbaum.

Brooks, R., & Meltzoff, A. N. (2008). Infant gaze following and pointing predict accelerated vocabulary growth through two years of age: A longitudinal, growth curve modeling study. *Journal of Child Language, 35,* 207–220.

Brown, A. S. (2006). Prenatal infection as a risk factor for schizophrenia. *Schizophrenia Bulletin, 32,* 200–202.

Brown, J. (1958). Some tests of the decay theory of immediate memory. *Quarterly Journal of Experimental Psychology, 10,* 12–21.

Brynie, F. H. (2009). *Brain sense: The science of the senses and how we process the world around us.* New York: AMACOM.

Buchanan, R. W., & Carpenter, W. T. (1997). The neuroanatomies of schizophrenia. *Schizophrenia Bulletin, 23,* 367–372.

Buckley, K. W. (1989). *Mechanical man: John Broadus Watson and the beginning of behaviorism.* New York: Guilford.

Buhs, E., & Ladd, G. (2001). Peer rejection as an antecedent of young children's school adjustment: An examination of mediating processes. *Developmental Psychology, 37,* 550–560.

Burger, J. M. (1986). Increasing compliance by improving the deal: The that's-not-all technique. *Journal of Personality and Social Psychology, 51,* 277–283.

Burger, J. M. (2009). Replicating Milgram: Would people still obey today? *American Psychologist, 64,* 1–11.

Bushman, B. J., & Anderson, C. A. (2001). Media violence and the American public: Scientific facts versus media misinformation. *American Psychologist, 56,* 477–489.

Butcher, J. N., Dahlstrom, W. G., Graham, J. R., Tellegen, A., & Kaemmer, B. (1989). *Manual for the restandardized Minnesota Multiphasic Personality Inventory: MMPI-2.* Minneapolis, MN: University of Minnesota Press.

Calev, A., Gaudino, E. A., Squires, N. K., Zervas, I. M., & Fink, M. (1995). ECT and non-memory cognition: A review. *British Journal of Clinical Psychology, 34,* 505–515.

Campos, J., Anderson, D., Barbu-Roth, M., Hubbard, E., Hertenstein, M., & Witherington, D. (2000). Travel broadens the mind. *Infancy, 1,* 149–219.

Cannon, T. D. (1997). On the nature and mechanisms of obstetric influence in schizophrenia: A review and synthesis of epidemiologic studies. *International Review of Psychiatry, 9,* 387–397.

Cannon, W. B. (1927). The James-Lange theory of emotions: A critical examination and an alternative theory. *American Journal of Psychology, 39,* 106–124.

Cattell, R. B. (1950). *Personality: A systematic, theoretical, and factual study.* New York: McGraw-Hill.

Cattell, R. B. (1965*). The scientific analysis of personality.* Baltimore, MD: Penguin.

Cattell, R. B. (1987). *Intelligence: Its structure, growth and action.* Amsterdam: North-Holland.

Chapman, G. B., & Bornstein, B. H. (1996). The more you ask for, the more you get: Anchoring in personal injury verdicts. *Applied Cognitive Psychology, 10,* 519–540.

Chapman, L. J. (1967). Illusory correlation in observational report. *Journal of Verbal Learning and Verbal Behavior, 6,* 151–155.

Chapman, L. J., & Chapman, J. P. (1967). Genesis of popular but erroneous psychodiagnostic observations. *Journal of Abnormal Psychology, 72,* 193–204.

Chase, W. G., & Simon, H. A. (1973). Perception in chess. *Cognitive Psychology, 4,* 55–81.

Chomsky, N. (1965). *Aspects of the theory of syntax.* Cambridge, MA: MIT Press.

Churchland, P. S., & Ramachandran, V. S. (1996). Filling in: Why Dennett is wrong. In K. Atkins (Ed.), *Perception* (pp. 132–157). Oxford: Oxford University Press.

Cialdini, R. B. (1993). *Influence: Science and practice* (3rd ed.). New York: HarperCollins.

Cialdini, R. B., Cacioppo, J. T., Bassett, R., & Miller, J. A. (1978). Lowball procedure for producing compliance: Commitment then cost. *Journal of Personality and Social Psychology, 36,* 463–476.

Cialdini, R. B., Vincent, J. E., Lewis, S. K., Catalan, J., Wheeler, D., & Danby, B. L. (1975). Reciprocal concession procedure for inducing compliance: The door-in-the-face technique. *Journal of Personality and Social Psychology, 31,* 206–215.

Clark, R. E., & Squire, L. R. (1998). Classical conditioning and brain systems: The role of awareness. *Science, 280,* 77–91.

Cohen, L. B., & Marks, K. S. (2002). How infants process addition and subtraction events. *Developmental Science, 5,* 186–201.

Cohen, N. J., & Eichenbaum, H. (1993). *Memory, amnesia, and the hippocampal system.* Cambridge, MA: MIT Press.

Comer, R. J. (2010). *Abnormal psychology* (7th ed.). New York: Worth.

Corballis, M. C. (2007). The dual-brain myth. In S. Della Sala (Ed.), *Tall tales about the mind and brain: Separating fact from fiction* (pp. 291–314). New York: Oxford University Press.

Cordón, L. A. (2005). *Popular psychology: An encyclopedia.* Westport, CT: Greenwood Press.

Coren, S. (1993). *Sleep thieves: An eye-opening exploration into the science and mysteries of sleep.* New York: Free Press.

Coren, S., Ward, L. M., & Enns, J. T. (2004). *Sensation and perception* (6th ed.). New York: Wiley.

Corina, D. P. (1998). The processing of sign language: Evidence from aphasia. In B. Stemmer & H. A. Whittaker (Eds.), *Handbook of neurolinguistics* (pp. 313–329). San Diego: Academic Press.

Corkin, S. (1968). Acquisition of a motor skill after bilateral medial temporal lobe excision. *Neuropsychologia, 6,* 255–265.

Corkin, S. (1984). Lasting consequences of bilateral and medial temporal lobectomy: Clinical course and experimental findings in H. M. *Seminars in Neurology, 4,* 249–259.

Corkin, S. (2002). What's new with the amnesic patient H. M.? *Nature Reviews Neuroscience, 3,* 153–160.

Costa, P. T., Jr., & McCrae, R. R. (1985). *The NEO Personality Inventory manual.* Odessa, FL: Psychological Assessment Resources.

Costa, P. T., Jr., & McCrae, R. R. (1988). Personality in adulthood: A six-year longitudinal study of self-reports and spouse ratings on the NEO Personality Inventory. *Journal of Personality and Social Psychology, 54,* 853–863.

Costa, P. T., Jr., & McCrae, R. R. (1992). *Revised NEO Personality Inventory (NEO PI) and NEO Five Factor Inventory (NEO FFI) professional manual.* Odessa, FL: Psychological Assessment Resources.

Costa, P. T., Jr., & McCrae, R. R. (2008). The NEO inventories. In R. P. Archer & S. R. Smith (Eds.). *Personality assessment* (pp. 213–246). New York: Routledge.

Craik, F. I. M., & Lockhart, R. S. (1972). Levels of processing: A framework for memory research. *Journal of Verbal Learning and Verbal Behavior, 11,* 671–684.

Craik, F. I. M., & Tulving, E. (1975). Depth of processing and the retention of words in episodic memory. *Journal of Experimental Psychology: General, 104,* 268–294.

Crow, T. J. (1985). The two-syndrome concept: Origins and current status. *Schizophrenia Bulletin, 11,* 471-485.

Damasio, A. R., Grabowski, T. J., Bechara, A., Damasio, H., Ponto, L., & Parvizi, J., et al. (2000). Subcortical and cortical brain activity during the feeling of self-generated emotions. *Nature Neuroscience, 3,* 1049-1056.

Damasio, H., Grabowski, T. J., Frank, R., Galaburda, A. M., & Damasio, A. R. (1994). The return of Phineas Gage: Clues about the brain from the skull of the famous patient. *Science, 264,* 1102-1105.

Dapretto, M., Davies, M. S., Pfeifer, J. H., Scott, A. A., Sigman, M., Bookheimer, S. Y., et al. (2006). Understanding emotions in others: Mirror neuron dysfunction in children with autism spectrum disorders. *Nature Neuroscience, 9,* 28-30.

Darley, J. M., & Latané, B. (1968). Bystander intervention in emergencies: Diffusion of responsibility. *Journal of Personality and Social Psychology, 8,* 377-383.

Darwin, C. J., Turvey, M. T., & Crowder, R. G. (1972). An auditory analogue of the Sperling partial-report procedure. *Cognitive Psychology, 3,* 255-267.

Dasen, P. R. (1994). Culture and cognitive development from a Piagetian perspective. In W. J. Lonner & R. S. Malpass (Eds.), *Psychology and culture* (pp. 145-149). Needham Heights, MA: Allyn & Bacon.

Davey, G. C. L. (1995). Classical conditioning and the acquisition of human fears and phobias: A review and synthesis of the literature. *Advances in Behavior Research and Therapy, 14,* 29-66.

Davis, J. O., & Phelps, J. A. (1995). Twins with schizophrenia: Genes or germs? *Schizophrenia Bulletin, 21,* 13-18.

Davis, K. L., Kahn, R. S., Ko, G., & Davidson, M. (1991). Dopamine in schizophrenia: A review and reconceptualization. *American Journal of Psychiatry, 148,* 1474-1486.

Dawes, R. M. (1994). *House of cards: Psychology and psychotherapy built on myth.* New York: Free Press.

DeCasper, A. J., & Fifer, W. P. (1980). Of human bonding: Newborns prefer their mothers' voices. *Science, 208,* 1174-1176.

DeCasper, A. J., & Spence, M. J. (1986). Prenatal maternal speech influences newborns' perception of speech sounds. *Infant Behavior and Development, 9,* 133-150.

Deci, E. L., Koestner, R., & Ryan, R. M. (1999). A meta-analytic review of experiments examining the effect of extrinsic rewards on intrinsic motivation. *Psychological Bulletin, 125,* 637-668.

DeLeon, A., Patel, N. C., & Crismon, M. L. (2004). Aripiprazole: A comprehensive review of its pharmacology, clinical efficacy, and tolerability. *Clinical Therapeutics, 26,* 649-666.

Delis, D. C., Robertson, L. C., & Efron, R. (1986). Hemispheric specialization of memory for visual hierarchical stimuli. *Neuropsychologica, 24,* 205-214.

DeLisi, L. E. (1997). The genetics of schizophrenia. *Schizophrenia Research, 28,* 163-175.

Dement, W. C. (1999). *The promise of sleep.* New York: Delacorte Press.

DeRubeis, R. J., Hollon, S., Amsterdam, J., Shelton, R., Young, P., Salomon, R., et al. (2005). Cognitive therapy vs medications in the treatment of moderate to severe depression. *Archives of General Psychiatry, 62,* 409-416.

DeValois, R. L., & DeValois, K. K. (1975). Neural coding of color. In E. C. Carterette & M. P. Friedman (Eds.), *Handbook of perception* (Vol. 5, pp. 117-166). New York: Academic Press.

Digman, J. M. (1990). Personality structure: Emergence of the five-factor model. *Annual Review of Psychology, 41,* 417-440.

Dinberg, U., & Thunberg, M. (1998). Rapid facial reactions to emotional facial expressions. *Psychological Science, 11,* 86-89.

Dirix, C. E. H., Nijhuis, J. G., Jongsma, H. W., & Hornstra, G. (2009). Aspects of fetal learning and memory. *Child Development, 80,* 1251-1258.

Domhoff, G. W. (2003). *Finding meaning in dreams: A quantitative approach.* New York: Plenum.

Dowling, J. E. (1998). *Creating mind: How the brain works.* New York: Norton.

Druckman, D., & Swets, J. A. (1988). *Enhancing human performance: Issues, theories, and techniques.* Washington, DC: National Academy Press.

DuJardin, J., Guerrien, A., & LeConte, P. (1990). Sleep, brain activation, and cognition. *Physiology and Behavior, 47,* 1271-1278.

Duncker, K. (1945). On problem solving. *Psychological Monographs, 58* (Whole No. 270).

Dyk, P. H., & Adams, G. R. (1990). Identity and intimacy: An initial investigation of three theoretical models using cross-lag panel correlations. *Journal of Youth and Adolescence, 19,* 91–100.

Ebbinghaus, H. (1964). *Memory: A contribution to experimental psychology* (H. A. Ruger & C. E. Bussenius, Trans.). New York: Dover. (Original work published 1885)

Eddy, D. M. (1982). Probabilistic reasoning in clinical medicine: Problems and opportunities. In D. Kahneman, P. Slovic, & A. Tversky (Eds.), *Judgment under uncertainty: Heuristics and biases* (pp. 249–267). Cambridge: Cambridge University Press.

Egan, L. C., Santos, L. R., & Bloom, P. (2007). The origins of cognitive dissonance: Evidence from children and monkeys. *Psychological Science, 18,* 978–983.

Eich, E. (1995). Searching for mood dependent memory. *Psychological Science, 6,* 67–75.

Eisenberger, R., & Cameron, J. (1996). Detrimental effects of rewards: Reality or myth? *American Psychologist, 51,* 1153–1166.

Ellis, A. (1962*). Reason and emotion in psychotherapy*. New York: Lyle Stuart.

Ellis, A. (1993). Reflections on rational-emotive therapy. *Journal of Counseling and Clinical Psychology, 61,* 199–201.

Ellis, A. (1995). Rational emotive behavior therapy. In R. J. Corsini & D. Wedding (Eds.), *Current psychotherapies* (5th ed., pp. 162–196). Itasca, IL: Peacock.

Elman, J. L., Bates, E. A., Johnson, M., Karmiloff-Smith, A., Paisi, D., & Plunkett, K. (1996). *Rethinking innateness: A connectionist perspective on development.* Cambridge, MA: MIT Press.

Engel, S. A. (1999). Using neuroimaging to measure mental representations: Finding color-opponent neurons in visual cortex. *Current Directions in Psychological Science, 8,* 23–27.

Engle, R. W. (2002). Working memory capacity as executive attention. *Current Directions in Psychological Science, 11,* 19–23.

Erel, O., Oberman, Y., & Yirmiya, N. (2000). Maternal versus nonmaternal care and seven domains of children's development. *Psychological Bulletin, 126,* 727–747.

Eriksen, C. W., & Collins, J. F. (1967). Some temporal characteristics of visual pattern recognition. *Journal of Experimental Psychology, 74,* 476–484.

Erikson, E. H. (1950). *Childhood and society*. New York: Norton.

Erikson, E. H. (1963). *Childhood and society* (2nd ed.). New York: Norton.

Erikson, E. H. (1968). *Identity: Youth and crisis*. New York: Norton.

Erikson, E. H. (1980). *Identity and the life cycle*. New York: Norton.

Eriksson, P. S., Perfilieva, E., Björk-Eriksson, T., Alborn, A., Nordborg, C., Peterson, D. A., et al. (1998). Neurogenesis in the adult human hippocampus. *Nature Medicine, 4,* 1313–1317.

Esser, J. K., & Lindoerfer, J. S. (1989). Groupthink and the space shuttle *Challenger* accident: Toward a quantitative case analysis. *Journal of Behavioral Decision Making, 2,* 167–177.

Etscorn, E., & Stephens, R. (1973). Establishment of conditioned taste aversions with a 24-hour CS-US interval. *Physiological Psychology, 1,* 251–253.

Eysenck, H. J. (1982). *Personality, genetics, and behavior*. New York: Praeger.

Eysenck, H. J. (1990). Biological dimensions of personality. In L. A. Pervin (Ed.), *Handbook of personality: Theory and research* (pp. 244–276). New York: Guilford Press.

Eysenck, H. J. (1997). Personality and experimental psychology: The unification of psychology and the possibility of a paradigm. *Journal of Personality and Social Psychology, 73,* 1224–1237.

Eysenck, H. J., & Eysenck, M. W. (1985). *Personality and individual differences*. New York: Plenum.

Fancher, R. E. (1985). *The intelligence men: Makers of the IQ controversy*. New York: Norton.

Fantz, R. L. (1961, May). The origin of form perception. *Scientific American, 204,* 66–72.

Fantz, R. L. (1963). Pattern vision in newborn infants. *Science, 140,* 296–297.

Festinger, L. (1957). *A theory of cognitive dissonance*. Stanford, CA: Stanford University Press.

Festinger, L., & Carlsmith, J. M. (1959). Cognitive consequences of forced compliance. *Journal of Abnormal and Social Psychology, 38,* 203–210.

Field, T. M., Cohen, D., Garcia, R., & Greenberg, R. (1984). Mother-stranger face discrimination by the newborn. *Infant Behavior and Development, 7,* 19–25.

Fields, R. D. (2004, April). The other half of the brain. *Scientific American, 266,* 55–61.

Fields, R. D. (2009). *The other brain: From dementia to schizophrenia, how new discoveries about the brain are revolutionizing medicine and science.* New York: Simon & Schuster.

Fink, G. R., Halligan, P. W., Marshall, J. C., Frith, C. D., Frackowiak, R. S. J., & Dolan, R. J. (1996). Where in the brain does visual attention select the forest and the trees? *Nature, 382,* 626–628.

Fisher, S., & Greenberg, R. (Eds.). (1997). *From placebo to panacea: Putting psychiatric drugs to the test.* New York: Wiley.

Fleischman, J. (2002). *Phineas Gage: A gruesome but true story about brain science.* Boston: Houghton Mifflin.

Flynn, J. R. (1987). Massive IQ gains in 14 nations: What IQ tests really measure. *Psychological Bulletin, 101,* 171–191.

Flynn, J. R. (1999). Searching for justice: The discovery of IQ gains over time. *American Psychologist, 54,* 5–20.

Flynn, J. R. (2007). *What is intelligence?: Beyond the Flynn effect.* New York: Cambridge University Press.

Folsom, D. P., Fleisher, A. S., & Depp, C. A. (2006). Schizophrenia. In D. V. Jeste & J. H. Friedman (Eds.), *Psychiatry for neurologists* (pp. 59–66). Totowa, NJ: Humana Press.

Fossey, D. (1983). *Gorillas in the mist.* Boston: Houghton Mifflin.

Fowles, D. C. (1992). Schizophrenia: Diathesis-stress revisited. *Annual Review of Psychology, 43,* 303–336.

Freedman, J. L., & Fraser, S. C. (1966). Compliance without pressure: The foot-in-the-door technique. *Journal of Personality and Social Psychology, 4,* 195–202.

Freud, A. (1936). *The ego and the mechanisms of defense* (C. Baines, Trans.). New York: International Universities Press.

Freud, S. (1953a). The interpretation of dreams. In J. Strachey (Ed. & Trans.), *The standard edition of the complete psychological works of Sigmund Freud* (Vols. 4 & 5). London: Hogarth. (Original work published 1900)

Freud, S. (1953b). Three essays on sexuality. In J. Strachey (Ed. & Trans.), *The standard edition of the complete psychological works of Sigmund Freud* (Vol. 7). London: Hogarth. (Original work published 1905)

Freud, S. (1960). Psychopathology of everyday life. In J. Strachey (Ed. & Trans.), *The standard edition of the complete psychological works of Sigmund Freud* (Vol. 6). London: Hogarth. (Original work published 1901)

Freud, S. (1963). Introductory lectures on psycho-analysis. In J. Strachey (Ed. & Trans.), *The standard edition of the complete psychological works of Sigmund Freud* (Vols. 15 & 16). London: Hogarth. (Original work published 1916 & 1917)

Freud, S. (1964). New introductory lectures on psycho-analysis. In J. Strachey (Ed. & Trans.), *The standard edition of the complete psychological works of Sigmund Freud* (Vol. 22). London: Hogarth. (Original work published 1933)

Frith, U. (2003). *Autism: Explaining the enigma* (2nd ed.). New York: Wiley-Blackwell.

Fromkin, V., Krasjen, S., Curtiss, S., Rigler, D., & Rigler, M. (1974). The development of language in Genie: A case of language acquisition beyond the "critical period." *Brain & Language, 1,* 81–107.

Funder, D. C. (2001). Personality. *Annual Review of Psychology, 52,* 197–221.

Furman, W., & Biermam, K. L. (1984). Children's conceptions of friendship: A multi-method study of developmental changes. *Developmental Psychology, 20,* 925–931.

Gabrieli, J. D. E., Corkin, S., Mickel, S. F., & Growdon, J. H. (1993). Intact acquisition and long-term retention of mirror-tracing skill in Alzheimer's disease and in global amnesia. *Behavioral Neuroscience, 107,* 899–910.

Gage, F. H. (2003, September). Brain, repair yourself. *Scientific American, 289,* 46–53.

Galanter, E. (1962). Contemporary psychophysics. In R. Brown, E. Galanter, E. H. Hess, & G. Mandler (Eds.), *New directions in psychology* (Vol. 1, pp. 87–156). New York: Holt, Rinehart, & Winston.

Gamwell, L., & Tomes, N. (1995). *Madness in America: Cultural and medicinal perceptions of mental illness before 1914.* Ithaca, NY: Cornell University Press.

Garb, H. N. (1999). Call for a moratorium on the use of the Rorschach inkblot test in clinical and forensic settings. *Assessment, 6,* 313–315.

Garcia, J. (2003). Psychology is not an enclave. In R. J. Sternberg (Ed.), *Defying the crowd: Stories of those who battled the establishment and won* (pp. 67–77). Washington, DC: American Psychological Association.

Garcia, J., Kimeldorf, D. J., Hunt, E. L., & Davies, B. P. (1956). Food and water consumption of rats during exposure to gamma radiation. *Radiation Research, 4,* 33–41.

Garcia, J., & Koelling, R. A. (1966). Relation of cue to consequence in avoidance learning. *Psychonomic Science, 4,* 123–124.

Gardner, H. (1983). *Frames of mind: The theory of multiple intelligences.* New York: Basic Books.

Gardner, H. (1993). *Multiple intelligences: The theory in practice.* New York: Basic Books.

Gardner, H. (1999). *Intelligence reframed.* New York: Basic Books.

Gardner, H., Kornhaber, M. L., & Wake, W. K. (1996). *Intelligence: Multiple perspectives.* Fort Worth, TX: Harcourt.

Gazzaniga, M. S. (1992). *Nature's mind.* New York: Basic Books.

Gazzaniga, M. S. (2005). Forty-five years of split-brain research and still going strong. *Nature Reviews Neuroscience, 6,* 653–659.

Gazzaniga, M. S. (2008). *Human: The science behind what makes us unique.* New York: HarperCollins.

Gazzaniga, M. S., Ivry, R. B., & Mangun, G. R. (2002). *Cognitive neuroscience: The biology of the mind* (2nd ed.). New York: Norton.

Gegenfurtner, K. R., & Kiper, D. C. (2003). Color vision. *Annual Review of Neuroscience, 26,* 181–206.

Gescheider, G. A. (1976). *Psychophysics: Method and theory.* Hillsdale, NJ: Erlbaum.

Ghim, H. (1990). Evidence for perceptual organization in infants: Perception of subjective contours by young infants. *Infant Behavior and Development, 13,* 221–248.

Gigerenzer, G. (2002). *Calculated risks: How to know when numbers deceive you.* New York: Simon & Schuster.

Gigerenzer, G. (2004). Dread risk, September 11, and fatal traffic accidents. *Psychological Science, 15,* 286–287.

Gigerenzer, G. (2006). Out of the frying pan into the fire: Behavioral reactions to terrorist attacks. *Risk Analysis, 26,* 347–351.

Gigerenzer, G., & Edwards, A. G. K. (2003). Simple tools for understanding risk: From innumeracy to insight. *British Medical Journal, 307,* 741–744.

Gigerenzer, G. Gaissmaier, W., Kurz-Milke, E., Schwartz, L. M., & Woloshin, S. (2007). Helping doctors and patients make sense of health statistics. *Psychological Science in the Public Interest, 8,* 53–96.

Gilbert, S. J. (1981). Another look at the Milgram obedience studies: The role of the gradated series of shocks. *Personality and Social Psychology Bulletin, 7,* 690–695.

Gilhooly, K. J. (1996). *Thinking: Directed, undirected and creative* (3rd ed.). London: Academic Press.

Glanzer, M., & Cunitz, A. R. (1966). Two storage mechanisms in free recall. *Journal of Verbal Learning and Verbal Behavior, 5,* 351–360.

Glass, R. M. (2001). Electroconvulsive therapy: Time to bring it out of the shadows. *Journal of the American Medical Association, 285,* 1346–1348.

Gluck, M. A., Mercado, E., & Myers, C. E. (2008). *Learning and memory: From brain to behavior.* New York: Worth.

Glucksberg, S., & Cowen, G. N., Jr. (1970). Memory for nonattended auditory material. *Cognitive Psychology, 1,* 149–156.

Godden, D. R., & Baddeley, A. D. (1975). Context-dependent memory in two natural environments: On land and underwater. *British Journal of Psychology, 66,* 325–331.

Goldberg, L. R. (1990). An alternative "description of personality": The big-five factor structure. *Journal of Social and Personality Psychology, 59,* 1216–1229.

Goldstein, E. B. (2007). *Sensation and perception* (7th ed.). Belmont, CA: Thomson Wadsworth.

Golinkoff, R. M., & Hirsch-Pasek, K. (2006). Baby wordsmith: From associationist to social sophisticate. *Current Directions in Psychological Science, 15,* 30–33.

Goodall, J. (1986). *The chimpanzees of Gombe: Patterns of behavior.* Boston: Belknap Press of Harvard University Press.

Goodman, J. A., Krahn, L. E., Smith, G. E., Rummans, T. A., & Pileggi, T. S. (1999, October). Patient satisfaction with electroconvulsive therapy. *Mayo Clinic Proceedings, 74,* 967–971.

Gottesman, I. I. (1991). *Schizophrenia genesis.* New York: W. H. Freeman.

Gottfredson, L. S. (1997). Mainstream science on intelligence: An editorial with 52 signatories, history, and bibliography. *Intelligence, 24,* 13–23.

Gottfredson, L. S. (2002a). Where and why *g* matters: Not a mystery. *Human Performance, 15,* 25–46.

Gottfredson, L. S. (2002b). *g:* Highly general and highly practiced. In R. J. Sternberg & E. L. Grigorenko (Eds.), *The general factor of intelligence: How general is it?* (pp. 331–380). Mahwah, NJ: Erlbaum.

Gottfredson, L. S. (2009). Logical fallacies used to dismiss evidence on intelligence testing. In R. Phelps (Ed.). *Correcting fallacies about educational and psychological testing* (pp. 11–65). Washington, DC: American Psychological Association.

Gould, S. J. (1985, June). The median isn't the message. *Discover, 6,* 40–42.

Graf, P., Squire, L. R., & Mandler, G. (1984). The information that amnesic patients do not forget. *Journal of Experimental Psychology: Learning, Memory, and Cognition, 10,* 164–178.

Green, D. M., & Swets, J. A. (1966). *Signal detection theory and psychophysics.* New York: Wiley.

Green, J. T., & Woodruff-Pak, D. S. (2000). Eyeblink classical conditioning: Hippocampal formation is for neutral stimulus associations as cerebellum is for association-response. *Psychological Bulletin, 126,* 138–158.

Greenough, W. T., Black, J. E., & Wallace, C. S. (1987). Experience and brain development. *Child Development, 58,* 539–559.

Greenwald, A. G., Draine, S. C., & Abrams, R. L. (1996). Three cognitive markers of unconscious semantic activation. *Science, 273,* 1699–1702.

Greenwald, A. G., Klinger, M. R., & Schuh, E. S. (1995). Activation by marginally perceptible ("subliminal") stimuli: Dissociation of unconscious from conscious cognition. *Journal of Experimental Psychology: General, 124,* 22–42.

Greenwald, A. G., Spangenberg, E. R., Pratkanis, A. R., & Eskenazi, J. (1991). Double-blind tests of subliminal self-help audiotapes. *Psychological Science, 2,* 119–122.

Gregory, R. L. (1968, November). Visual illusions. *Scientific American, 219,* 66–76.

Griggs, R. A. (2003). Helping students gain insight into mental set. *Teaching of Psychology, 30,* 143–145.

Griggs, R. A., & Cox, J. R. (1982). The elusive thematic materials effect in Wason's selection task. *British Journal of Psychology, 73,* 407–420.

Grossman, R. P., & Till, B. D. (1998). The persistence of classically conditioned brand attitudes. *Journal of Advertising, 27,* 23–31.

Gruneberg, M. M., & Herrmann, D. J. (1997). *Your memory for life.* London: Blanford.

Grunhaus, L., Schreiber, S., Dolberg, O. T., Polak, D., & Dannon, P. N. (2003). A randomized controlled comparison of electroconvulsive therapy and repetitive transcranial magnetic stimulation in severe and resistant nonpsychotic major depression. *Biological Psychiatry, 53,* 324–331.

Hallinan, J. T. (2009). *Why we make mistakes: How we look without seeing, forget things in seconds, and are all pretty sure we are above average.* New York: Broadway Books.

Harkins, S. G., & Jackson, J. M. (1985). The role of evaluation in eliminating social loafing. *Personality and Social Psychology Bulletin, 11,* 457–465.

Harlow, H. F. (1959, June). Love in infant monkeys. *Scientific American, 200,* 68–74.

Harlow, H. F., & Harlow, M. K. (1962, November). Social deprivation in monkeys. *Scientific American, 207,* 136–146.

Harlow, H. F., & Zimmerman, R. R. (1959). Affectional responses in the infant monkey. *Science, 130,* 421–432.

Harris, B. (1979). Whatever happened to Little Albert? *American Psychologist, 34,* 151–160.

Harris, J. R. (1998). *The nurture assumption: Why children turn out the way they do.* New York: Free Press.

Hartigan, J. A., & Wigdor, A. K. (Eds.). (1989). *Fairness in employment testing: Validity generalization, minority issues, and the General Aptitude Test Battery.* Washington, DC: National Academy Press.

Hathaway, S. R., & McKinley, J. C. (1943). *MMPI manual.* New York: Psychological Corporation.

Hefferline, R. F., Keenan, B., & Harford, R. A. (1959). Escape and avoidance conditioning in human subjects without their observation of the response. *Science, 130,* 1338–1339.

Hellige, J. B. (1993). Unity of thought and action: Varieties of interaction between the left and right cerebral hemispheres. *Current Directions in Psychological Science, 2,* 21–25.

Herrnstein, R. J., & Murray, C. (1994). *The bell curve: Intelligence and class in American life.* New York: Free Press.

Hill, W. E. (1915, November) My wife and my mother-in-law. *Puck, 16,* 1.

Hilts, P. F. (1995). *Memory's ghost: The strange tale of Mr. M and the nature of memory.* New York: Simon & Schuster.

Hite, S. (1987). *Women and love: A cultural revolution in progress.* New York: Knopf.

Hobson, J. A. (2003) *Dreaming: An introduction to the science of sleep.* New York: Oxford.

Hobson, J. A., & McCarley, R. W. (1977). The brain as a dream generator: An activation-synthesis hypothesis of the dream process. *American Journal of Psychiatry, 134,* 1335–1348.

Hobson, J. A., Pace-Scott, E. F., & Stickgold, R. (2000). Dreaming and the brain: Toward a cognitive neuroscience of conscious states. *Behavioral and Brain Sciences, 23,* 793–842.

Hoffrage, U., & Gigerenzer, G. (1995). How to improve Bayesian reasoning without instruction: Frequency formats. *Psychological Review, 102,* 684–704.

Hoffrage, U., & Gigerenzer, G. (1998). Using natural frequencies to improve diagnostic inferences. *Academic Medicine, 73,* 538–540.

Hofling, C. K., Brotzman, E., Dalrymple, S., Graves, N., & Pierce, C. M. (1966). An experimental study of nurse-physician relationships. *Journal of Nervous and Mental Disease, 143,* 171–180.

Hogben, J. H., & Di Lollo, V. (1974). Perceptual integration and perceptual segregation of brief visual stimuli. *Vision Research, 14,* 1059–1069.

Holmes, D. S. (1990). The evidence for repression: An examination of sixty years of research. In J. L. Singer (Ed.), *Repression and dissociation: Implications for personality theory, psychopathology, and health* (pp. 85–102). Chicago: University of Chicago Press.

Holsti, L., Grunau, R., & Whitfield, M. (2002). Developmental coordination disorder in extremely low birth weight children at nine years. *Journal of Developmental and Behavioral Pediatrics, 23,* 9–15.

Hood, B. M. (2009). *Supersense: Why we believe in the unbelievable.* New York: HarperCollins.

Horn, J. (1982). The aging of cognitive abilities. In B. B. Wolman (Ed.), *Handbook of developmental psychology* (pp. 847–870). Englewood Cliffs, NJ: Prentice Hall.

Horn, J., & Cattell, R. B. (1966). Refinement and test of the theory of fluid and crystallized general intelligences. *Journal of Educational Psychology, 57,* 253–270.

Horn, J. L., & Cattell, R. B. (1967). Age differences in fluid and crystallized intelligence. *Acta Psychologica, 26,* 107–129.

Horney, K. (1937). *The neurotic personality of our time.* New York: Norton.

Horowitz, A. V., & Wakefield, J. C. (2007). *The loss of sadness: How psychiatry transformed normal sorrow into depressive disorder.* New York: Oxford University Press.

Hubel, D. H., & Wiesel, T. N. (2004). *Brain and visual perception: The story of a 25-year collaboration.* New York: Oxford University Press.

Huff, D. (1954). *How to lie with statistics.* New York: Norton.

Hunt, M. (1993). *The story of psychology.* New York: Doubleday.

Hurvich, L. M., & Jameson, D. (1957). An opponent-process theory of color vision. *Psychological Review, 63,* 384–404.

Huston, A. C., Donnerstein, E., Fairchild, H., Feshbach, N. D., Katz, P. A., & Murray, J. P. (1992). *Big world, small screen: The role of television in American Society.* Lincoln, NE: University of Nebraska Press.

Iacoboni, M. (2005). Neural mechanisms of imitation. *Current Opinion in Neurobiology, 15,* 632–637.

Iacoboni, M. (2009). *Mirroring people: The science of empathy and how we connect with others.* New York: Picador.

Iacoboni, M., & Dapretto, M. (2006). The mirror neuron system and the consequences of its dysfunction. *Nature Reviews Neuroscience, 7,* 942–951.

Inhelder, B., & Piaget, J. (1958). *The growth of logical thinking from childhood to adolescence* (A. Parsons & S. Milgram, Trans.). New York: Basic Books.

Izard, C. E. (1990). Facial expressions and the regulation of emotions. *Journal of Personality and Social Psychology, 58,* 487–498.

Jackson, S. L. (2009). *Research methods and statistics: A critical thinking approach* (3rd ed.). Belmont, CA: Wadsworth.

Jacobs, B. L. (2004). Depression: The brain finally gets into the act. *Current Directions in Psychological Science, 13,* 103–106.

Jacobs, B. L., van Praag, H., & Gage, F. H. (2000b, July/August). Depression and the birth and death of brain cells. *American Scientist, 88,* 340–345.

Jacobsen, T., & Hoffman, V. (1997). Children's attachment representations: Longitudinal relations to school behavior and academic competency in middle childhood and adolescence. *Developmental Psychology, 33,* 703–710.

Jang, K. L., Livesley, W. J., & Vernon, P. A. (1996). Heritability of the Big Five personality dimensions and their facets: A twin study. *Journal of Personality, 64,* 577–591.

Janis, I. L. (1972). *Victims of groupthink.* Boston: Houghton Mifflin.

Janis, I. L. (1983). *Groupthink: Psychological studies of policy decisions and fiascoes* (2nd ed.). Boston: Houghton Mifflin.

Jiang, X., & Cillessen, A. (2005). Stability of continuous measures of sociometric status: A meta-analysis. *Developmental Review, 25,* 1–25.

John, O. P. (1990). The "Big Five" factor taxonomy: Dimensions of personality in the natural language and in questionnaires. In L. A. Pervin (Ed.), *Handbook of personality: Theory and research* (pp. 66–100). New York: Guilford.

Johnson, J., & Newport, E. (1989). Critical period effects in second language learning: The influence of maturational state on the acquisition of English as a second language. *Cognitive Psychology, 21,* 60–99.

Jones, M. C. (1924). A laboratory study of fear: The case of Peter. *Pedagogical Seminary, 31,* 308–315.

Jones, R. A. (1977). *Self-fulfilling prophecies.* Hillsdale, NJ: Erlbaum.

Julien, R. M. (2008). *A primer of drug action* (11th ed.). New York: W. H. Freeman.

Kail, R. (1991). Developmental change in speed of processing during childhood and adolescence. *Psychological Bulletin, 109,* 490–501.

Kalat, J. W. (2007). *Biological psychology* (9th ed.). Belmont, CA: Wadsworth.

Kanizsa, G. (1976, April). Subjective contours. *Scientific American, 234,* 48–52.

Karau, S. J., & Williams, K. D. (1993). Social loafing: A meta-analytic review and theoretical integration. *Journal of Personality and Social Psychology, 65,* 681–706.

Kaufman, A. S. (2000). Tests of intelligence. In R. J. Sternberg (Ed.), *Handbook of intelligence* (pp. 445–476). New York: Cambridge University Press.

Kaufman, A. S. (2009). *IQ testing 101.* New York: Springer.

Kazdin, A. E. (2001). *Behavior modification in applied settings* (6th ed.). Belmont, CA: Wadsworth.

Kellman, P. J., & Arterberry, M. E. (1998). *The cradle of knowledge: Development of perception in infancy.* Cambridge, MA: MIT Press.

Kellman, P. J., & Banks, M. S. (1998). Infant visual perception. In W. Damon (Series Ed.) & R. Siegler & D. Kuhn (Vol. Eds.), *Handbook of child psychology: Vol. 2. Cognition, perception, and language* (5th ed., pp. 103–146). New York: Wiley.

Kempermann, G., & Gage, F. H. (1999, May). New nerve cells for the adult brain. *Scientific American, 280,* 48–53.

Kessler, R. C., Berglund, P., Demler, O., Jin, R., Koretz, D., Merikangas, K. R., et al. (2003). The epidemiology of major depressive disorder: Results from the National Comorbidity Survey Replication (NCS-R). *JAMA: Journal of the American Medical Association, 289,* 3095–3105.

Kessler, R. C., McGonagle, K. A., Zhao, S., Nelson, C. B., Hughes, M., Eshleman, S., et al. (1994). Lifetime and 12-month prevalence of DSM-III-R psychiatric disorders in the United States. *Archives of General Psychology, 51,* 8–19.

Kirkpatrick, E. A. (1894). An experimental study of memory. *Psychological Review, 1,* 602–609.

Kirsch, I. (2010). *The emperor's new drugs: Exploding the antidepressant myth.* New York: Basic Books.

Klein, S. B., & Kihlstrom, J. F. (1998). On bridging the gap between social-personality psychology and neuropsychology. *Personality and Social Psychology Review, 2,* 228–242.

Klüver, H., & Bucy, P. C. (1939). Preliminary analysis of functions of the temporal lobes in monkeys. *Archives of Neurology and Psychiatry, 42,* 979–1000.

Knight, D. C., Nguyen, H. T., & Bandettini, P. A. (2003). Expression of conditional fear with and without awareness. *Proceedings of the National Academy of Sciences, 100,* 15280–15283.

Knoblich, G., & Oellinger, M. (2006, October/November). Aha! The Eureka moment. *Scientific American MIND, 17,* 38–43.

Kohlberg, L. (1976). Moral stages and moralization: The cognitive-developmental approach. In T. Lickona (Ed.), *Moral development and behavior: Theory, research, and social issues* (pp. 31–53). New York: Holt, Rinehart, & Winston.

Kohlberg, L. (1984). *Essays on moral development, Vol. 2. The psychology of moral development: The nature and validity of moral stages.* San Francisco: Harper & Row.

Kolb, B., & Whishaw, I. Q. (2001). *An introduction to brain and behavior.* New York: Worth.

Koop, J. (2009). *The root of thought.* Upper Saddle River, NJ: Pearson Education.

Krijn, M., Emmelkamp, P. M. G., Olafsson, R. P., & Biemond, R. (2004). Virtual reality therapy of anxiety disorders: A review. *Clinical Psychology Review, 24,* 259–281.

Krupa, D. J., Thompson, J. K., & Thompson, R. F. (1993). Localization of a memory trace in the mammalian brain. *Science, 260,* 989–991.

Kuhl, P. K. (2004). Early language acquisition: Cracking the speech code. *Nature Reviews Neuroscience, 5,* 831–843.

Kuhl, P. K., Tsao, F.-M., & Liu, H.-M. (2003). Foreign-language experience in infancy: Effects of short-term exposure and social interaction on phonetic learning. *Proceedings of the National Academy of Sciences, 100,* 9096–9101.

Lachman, M. E., & Weaver, S. L. (1998). The sense of control as a moderator of social class differences in health and well-being. *Journal of Personality and Social Psychology, 74,* 763–773.

Lambert, K., & Kinsley, C. H. (2005). *Clinical neuroscience: The neurobiological foundations of mental health.* New York: Worth.

Lang, P. J. (1994). The varieties of emotional experience: A meditation on the James-Lange theory. *Psychological Review, 101,* 211–221.

Lange, C. G., & James, W. (1922). *The emotions* (I. A. Haupt, Trans.). Baltimore: Williams & Wilkins.

Langer, E. J. (1989). *Mindfulness.* Reading, MA: Addison-Wesley.

Langer, E. J. (1997). *The power of mindful learning.* Reading, MA: Addison-Wesley.

Larsen, R. J., & Buss, D. M. (2000). *Personality psychology: Domains of knowledge about human nature.* New York: McGraw-Hill.

Latané, B., & Darley, J. M. (1968). Group inhibition of bystander intervention. *Journal of Personality and Social Psychology, 10,* 215–221.

Latané, B., & Darley, J. M. (1970). *The unresponsive bystander: Why doesn't he help?* New York: Appleton-Century-Crofts.

Latané, B., & Nida, S. (1981). Ten years of research on group size and helping. *Psychological Bulletin, 89,* 308–324.

Latané, B., & Rodin, J. (1969). A lady in distress: Inhibiting effects of friends and strangers on bystander intervention. *Journal of Experimental Social Psychology, 5,* 189–202.

Latané, B., Williams, K. D., & Harkins, S. G. (1979). Many hands make light work: The causes and consequences of social loafing. *Journal of Personality and Social Psychology, 37,* 822–832.

LeDoux, J. E. (1996). *The emotional brain: The mysterious underpinnings of emotional life.* New York: Simon & Schuster.

LeDoux, J.E. (2000). Emotional circuits in the brain. *Annual Review of Neuroscience, 23,* 155–184.

Lehrer, J. (2009). *How we decide.* New York: Houghton Mifflin Harcourt.

Lepper, M. R., Greene, D., & Nisbett, R. E. (1973). Undermining children's intrinsic interest with extrinsic rewards. *Journal of Personality and Social Psychology, 28,* 129–137.

Lepper, M. R., & Henderlong, J. (2000). Turning "play" into "work" and "work" into "play": 25 years of research on intrinsic versus extrinsic motivation. In C. Sansone & J. M. Havackiewicz (Eds.), *Intrinsic and extrinsic motivation: The search for optimal motivation and performance* (pp. 257–307). San Diego: Academic Press.

Lerner, M. J. (1980). *The belief in a just world: A fundamental delusion.* New York: Plenum.

Levenson, R. W. (1992). Autonomic nervous system differences among emotions. *Psychological Science, 3,* 23–27.

Levine, R. (2003). *The power of persuasion: How we're bought and sold.* New York: Wiley.

Li, C. (1975). *Path analysis: A primer.* Pacific Grove, CA: Boxwood Press.

Lichtenstein, S., Slovic, P., Fischhoff, B., Layman, M., & Combs, B. (1978). Judged frequency of lethal events. *Journal of Experimental Psychology: Human Learning and Memory, 4,* 551–578.

Lilienfeld, S. O., Lynn, S. J., Ruscio, J., Beyerstein, B. L. (2010). *50 great myths of popular psychology: Shattering widespread misconceptions about human behavior.* Malden, MA: Wiley-Blackwell.

Lilienfeld, S. O., Wood, J. M., & Garb, H. N. (2000). The scientific status of projective techniques. *Psychological Science in the Public Interest, 1,* 27–66.

Linn, R. L. (1982). Admissions testing on trial. *American Psychologist, 37,* 279–291.

Loehlin, J. C. (1992). *Genes and environment in personality development.* Newbury Park, CA: Sage.

Loehlin, J. C., McCrae, R. R., Costa, P. T., Jr., & John, O. P. (1998). Heritabilities of common and measure-specific components of the Big Five personality factors. *Journal of Research in Personality, 32,* 431–453.

Loftus, E. F., Coan, J., & Pickrell, J. E. (1996). Manufacturing false memories using bits of reality. In L. Reder (Ed.), *Implicit memory and metacognition* (pp. 195–220). Mahwah, NJ: Erlbaum.

Loftus, E. F., & Ketcham, K. (1991). *Witness for the defense.* New York: St. Martin's.

Loftus, E. F., & Ketcham, K. (1994). *The myth of repressed memory: False memories and accusations of sexual abuse.* New York: St. Martin's.

Loftus, E. F., & Palmer, J. C. (1974). Reconstruction of automobile destruction: An example of the interaction between language and memory. *Journal of Verbal Learning and Verbal Behavior, 13,* 585–589.

Lourenco, O., & Machado, A. (1996). In defense of Piaget's theory: A reply to 10 common criticisms. *Psychological Review, 103,* 143–164.

Lynch, G., & Granger, R. (2008). *Big brain: The origins and future of human intelligence.* New York: Palgrave Macmillan.

MacFarlane, A. (1975). Olfaction in the development of social preferences in the human neonate. *Parent-infant interaction* (CIBA Foundation Symposium, No. 33). Amsterdam: Elsevier.

Macmillan, M. (2000). *An odd kind of fame: Stories of Phineas Gage.* Cambridge, MA: MIT Press.

MacNeilage, P. F., Rogers, L. J., & Vallortigara, G. (2009, July). Origins of the left & right brain. *Scientific American, 30,* 60–67.

Mahler, D. A., Cunningham, L. N., Skrinar, G. S., Kraemer, W. J., & Colice, G. L. (1989). Beta-endorphin activity and hypercapnic ventilatory responsiveness after marathon running. *Journal of Applied Physiology, 66,* 2431–2436.

Main, M., & Solomon, J. (1990). Procedures for identifying infants as disorganized/disoriented during the Ainsworth Strange Situation. In M. T. Greenberg, D. Cicchetti, & E. M. Cummings (Eds.), *Attachment in the preschool years* (pp. 121–160). Chicago: University of Chicago Press.

Manning, R., Levine, M., & Collins, A. (2007). The Kitty Genovese murder and the social psychology of helping: The parable of 38 witnesses. *American Psychologist, 62,* 555–562.

Marcel, A. (1983). Conscious and unconscious perception: Experiments on visual masking and word recognition. *Cognitive Psychology, 15,* 197–237.

Maslow, A. H. (1968). *Toward a psychology of being* (2nd ed.). New York: Harper & Row.

Maslow, A. H. (1970). *Motivation and personality* (2nd ed.). New York: Harper & Row.

Matlin, M. W., & Foley, H. J. (1997). *Sensation and perception* (4th ed.). Needham Heights, MA: Allyn and Bacon.

Mazur, J. E. (1998). *Learning and behavior* (4th ed.). Upper Saddle River, NJ: Prentice-Hall.

McCrae, R. R., & Costa, P. T., Jr. (1997). Personality trait structure as a human universal. *American Psychologist, 52,* 509–516.

McCrae, R. R., & Costa, P. T., Jr. (1999). A five-factor theory of personality. In L. A. Perrin & O. P. John (Eds.), *Handbook of personality: Theory and research* (pp. 139–153). New York: Guilford.

McCrae, R. R., & Costa, P. T., Jr. (2001). Trait psychology and culture. *Journal of Personality, 69,* 819–846.

McCrae, R. R., & Costa, P. T., Jr. (2003). *Personality in adulthood: A five-factor theory perspective* (2nd ed.). New York: Guilford.

McCrae, R. R., Costa, P. T., Jr., & Martin, T. A. (2005). The NEO-PI-3: A more readable revised NEO personality inventory. *Journal of Personality Assessment, 84,* 261–270.

McGue, M., Bouchard, T. J., Jr., Iacono, W. G., & Lykken, D. T. (1993). Behavioral genetics of cognitive ability: A life-span perspective. In R. Plomin

& G. E. McClearn (Eds.), *Nature, nurture, and psychology* (pp. 59–76). Washington, DC: American Psychological Association.

McKinnon, J. W., & Renner, J. W. (1971). Are colleges concerned with intellectual development? *American Journal of Psychology, 39,* 1047–1052.

McNally, R. J. (1987). Preparedness and phobias: A review. *Psychological Bulletin, 101,* 283–303.

McNally, R. J. (2003). *Remembering trauma.* Cambridge, MA: Harvard University Press.

Messer, W. S., & Griggs, R. A. (1989). Student belief and involvement in the paranormal and performance in introductory psychology. *Teaching of Psychology, 16,* 187–191.

Mezulis, A. H., Abramson, L. Y., Hyde, J. S., & Hankin, B. L. (2004). Is there a universal positivity bias in attributions? A meta-analytic review of individual, developmental, and cultural differences in self-serving attributional bias. *Psychological Bulletin, 130,* 711–747.

Milgram, S. (1963). Behavioral study of obedience. *Journal of Abnormal and Social Psychology, 67,* 371–378.

Milgram, S. (1964). Issues in the study of obedience: A reply to Baumrind. *American Psychologist, 19,* 848–852.

Milgram, S. (1965). Some conditions of obedience and disobedience. *Human Relations, 18,* 57–76.

Milgram, S. (1974). *Obedience to authority.* New York: Harper & Row.

Miller, B., & Gentile, B. F. (1998). Introductory course content and goals. *Teaching of Psychology, 25,* 89–96.

Miller, G. (2005). How are memories stored and retrieved? *Science, 309,* 92.

Miller, G. A. (1956). The magical number seven, plus or minus two: Some limits on our capacity for processing information. *Psychological Review, 63,* 81–97.

Miller, P. H. (2011). *Theories of developmental psychology* (5th ed.). New York: Worth.

Milton, J., & Wiseman, R. (1999). Does psi exist? Lack of replication of an anomalous process of information transfer. *Psychological Bulletin, 125,* 387–391.

Mlodinow, L. (2008). *The drunkard's walk: How randomness rules our lives.* New York: Pantheon Books.

Montcrief, J. (1997). Lithium: Evidence reconsidered. *British Journal of Psychiatry, 171,* 113–119.

Moore, T. E. (1988). The case against subliminal manipulation. *Psychology and Marketing, 5,* 297–316.

Moore, T. E. (1992, November/December). Subliminal perception: Facts and fallacies. *Skeptical Inquirer, 16,* 273–281.

Morgan, C. D., & Murray, H. A. (1935). A method for investigating fantasies: The Thematic Apperception Test. *Archives of Neurology and Psychiatry, 34,* 289–306.

Morris, J. S., Öhman, A., & Dolan, R. J. (1998). Conscious and unconscious emotional learning in the human amygdala. *Nature, 393,* 467–470.

Moruzzi, G., & Magoun, H. W. (1949). Brain stem reticular formation and activation of the EEG. *Electroencephalography and Clinical Neurophysiology, 1,* 455–473.

Moshman, D., & Franks, B. A. (1986). Development of the concept of inferential validity. *Child Development, 57,* 153–165.

Murray, J. P. (2008). Media violence: The effects are both real and strong. *American Behavioral Scientist, 51,* 1212–1230.

Myers, D. G. (2001, December). Do we fear the right things? *American Psychological Society Observer, 14,* 3.

Myers, D. G. (2002). *Social psychology* (7th ed.). New York: McGraw-Hill.

Myers, I. B., & McCaulley, M. H. (1985). *Manual: A guide to the development and use of the Myers-Briggs Type Indicator.* Palo Alto, CA: Consulting Psychologists Press.

Napolitan, D. A., & Goethals, G. R. (1979). The attribution of friendliness. *Journal of Experimental Social Psychology, 15,* 105–113.

Nathan, P. E., & Lagenbucher, J. W. (1999). Psychopathology: Description and classification. *Annual Review of Psychology, 50,* 79–107.

Navon, D. (1977). Forest before trees: The precedence of global features in visual perception. *Cognitive Psychology, 9,* 353–383.

Neimark, J. (1996, January). The diva of disclosure, memory researcher Elizabeth Loftus. *Psychology Today, 29,* 48–80.

Neisser, U. (Ed.). (1998). *The rising curve: Long-term gains in IQ and related measures.* Washington, DC: American Psychological Association.

Neisser, U., Boodoo, G., Bouchard, T. J., Jr., Boykin, A. W., Brody, N., Ceci, S. J., et al. (1996).

Intelligence: Knowns and unknowns. *American Psychologist, 51,* 77–101.

Newport, E. (1991). Contrasting concepts of the critical period for language. In S. Carey & R. Gelman (Eds.), *The epigenesis of mind: Essays on biology and cognition* (pp. 111–132). Hillsdale, NJ: Erlbaum.

NICHD Early Child Care Research Network. (1997). The effects of infant child care on infant-mother attachment security: Results of the NICHD Study of Early Child Care. *Child Development, 68,* 860–879.

NICHD Early Child Care Research Network (2001). Child-care and family predictors of preschool attachment and stability from infancy. *Developmental Psychology, 37,* 347–862.

Nickerson, R. S. (1998). Confirmation bias: A ubiquitous phenomenon in many guises. *Review of General Psychology, 2,* 175–220.

Nickerson, R. S., & Adams, M. J. (1979). Long-term memory for a common object. *Cognitive Psychology, 11,* 287–307.

Niemi, M. (2009, February/March). Cure in the mind. *Scientific American MIND, 20,* 42–49.

Nisbett, R. E., & Ross, L. (1980). *Human inference: Strategies and shortcomings of social judgment.* Englewood Cliffs, NJ: Prentice-Hall.

Noice, T., & Noice, H. (1997). *The nature of expertise in professional acting: A cognitive view.* Mahwah, NJ: Erlbaum.

Oatley, K., & Duncan, E. (1994). The experience of emotions in everyday life. *Cognition and Emotion, 8,* 369–381.

Öhman, A., & Mineka, S. (2001). Fear, phobias, and preparedness: Toward an evolved module of fear and fear learning. *Psychology Review, 108,* 483–522.

O'Kane, G., Kensinger, E. A., & Corkin, S. (2004). Evidence for semantic learning in profound amnesia: An investigation with patient H. M. *Hippocampus, 14,* 417–425.

Olson, M. A., & Fazio, R. H. (2001). Implicit attitude formation through classical conditioning. *Psychological Science, 12,* 413–417.

Olsson, A., & Phelps, E. A. (2004). Learned fear of "unseen" faces after Pavlovian, observational, and instructed fear. *Psychological Science, 15,* 822–828.

Ornstein, R. (1991). *The evolution of consciousness: Of Darwin, Freud, and cranial fire—the origins of the way we think.* Englewood Cliffs, NJ: Prentice-Hall.

Osherson, D. N., & Markman, E. M. (1975). Language and the ability to evaluate contradictions and tautologies. *Cognition, 2,* 213–226.

Packer, D. J. (2008). Identifying systematic disobedience in Milgram's obedience experiments: A meta-analytic review. *Perspectives on Psychological Science, 3,* 301–304.

Pascual-Leone, J. (1989). Constructive problems for constructive theories: The current relevance of Piaget's work and a critique of information-processing simulation psychology. In R. Kluwe & H. Spada (Eds.), *Developmental models of thinking* (pp. 263–296). New York: Academic Press.

Paulos, J. A. (2003). *A mathematician plays the stock market.* New York: Basic Books.

Paulos, J. A. (2006, August 6). Who's counting: It's mean to ignore the median. Retrieved from http://www.abcnews.com/Technology/WhosCounting.

Paulus, J. (2007, April/May). Lithium's healing power. *Scientific American MIND, 18,* 70–75.

Pavlov, I. P. (1960). *Conditioned reflexes: An investigation of the physiological activity of the cerebral cortex* (G.V. Anrep, Trans.). New York: Dover. (Original work published 1927)

Payne, D. G., & Wenger, M. J. (1996). Practice effects in memory: Data, theory, and unanswered questions. In D. Herrmann, C. McEvoy, C. Hertzog, P. Hertel, & M. K. Johnson (Eds.), *Basic and applied memory research: Practical applications* (Vol. 2, pp. 123–138). Mahwah, NJ: Erlbaum.

Penfield, W., & Rasmussen, T. (1968). *The cerebral cortex of man: A clinical study of localization of function.* New York: Hafner.

Pert, C. B. (1999). *Molecules of emotion.* New York: Simon & Schuster.

Pert, C. B., & Snyder, S. H. (1973). Opiate receptors: Demonstration in the nervous tissue. *Science, 179,* 1011–1014.

Pessiglione, M., Petrovic, P., Daunizeau, J., Palminteri, S., Dolan, R. J., & Frith, C. D. (2008). Subliminal instrumental conditioning demonstrated in the human brain. *Neuron, 59,* 561–567.

Peterson, C., Maier, S. F., & Seligman, M. E. P. (1993). *Learned helplessness: A theory for the age of personal control.* New York: Oxford.

Peterson, C., & Seligman, M. E. P. (1984). Causal explanations as a risk factor for depression: Theory and evidence. *Psychological Review, 91,* 347–374.

Peterson, L. R., & Peterson, M. J. (1959). Short-term retention of individual verbal items. *Journal of Experimental Psychology, 58,* 193–198.

Pettinati, H. M., Tamburello, B. A., Ruetsch, C. R., & Kaplan, F. N. (1994). Patient attitudes toward electroconvulsive therapy. *Psychopharmacology Bulletin, 30,* 471–475.

Phipps, M., Blume, J., & DeMonner, S. (2002). Young maternal age associated with increased risk of postneonatal death. *Obstetrics and Gynecology, 100,* 481–486.

Piaget, J. (1929). *The child's conception of the world.* New York: Harcourt, Brace. (Original work published 1926)

Piaget, J. (1932). *The moral judgment of the child.* New York: Harcourt, Brace.

Piaget, J. (1952). *The origins of intelligence in children.* New York: International Universities Press. (Original work published 1936)

Piaget, J. (1972). Intellectual evolution from adolescence to adulthood. *Human Development, 15,* 1–12.

Piaget, J. (1983). Piaget's theory. In P. H. Mussen (Series Ed.) and W. Kessen (Vol. Ed.), *Handbook of child psychology: Vol. 1. History, theory, and methods* (4th ed., pp. 103–126). New York: Wiley.

Pinker, S. (1994). *The language instinct: How the mind creates language.* New York: William Morrow.

Pliner, P., Hart, H., Kohl, J., & Saari, D. (1974). Compliance without pressure: Some further data on the foot-in-the-door technique. *Journal of Experimental Social Psychology, 10,* 17–22.

Plomin, R., DeFries, J. C., McClearn, G. E., & Rutter, M. (1997). *Behavioral genetics.* New York: W. H. Freeman.

Plous, S. (1993). *The psychology of judgment and decision making.* New York: McGraw-Hill.

Powell, R. A., Symbaluk, D. G., & MacDonald, S. E. (2002). *Introduction to learning & behavior.* Belmont, CA: Wadsworth.

Pratkanis, A. R. (1992, Spring). The cargo-cult science of subliminal persuasion. *Skeptical Inquirer, 16,* 260–272.

Pratkanis, A. R., & Greenwald, A. G. (1988). Recent perspectives on unconscious processing: Still no marketing applications. *Psychology and Marketing, 5,* 337–353.

Raphael, B. (1976). *The thinking computer.* San Francisco: W. H. Freeman.

Rapoport, J. L. (1989, March). The biology of obsessions and compulsions. *Scientific American,* 83–89.

Rapoport, J. L. (1991). Recent advances in obsessive-compulsive disorder. *Neuropsychopharmacology, 5,* 1–10.

Raskin, N. J., & Rogers, C. R. (1995). Person-centered therapy. In R. J. Corsini & D. Wedding (Eds.), *Current psychotherapies* (5th ed., pp. 144–149). Itasca, IL: Peacock.

Ratey, J. J. (2001). *A user's guide to the brain: Perception, attention, and the four theaters of the brain.* New York: Pantheon.

Reber, P. (2010, May/June). Ask the Brains. *Scientific American MIND, 21,* 70.

Redelmeier, D. A., & Tversky, A. (1996). On the belief that arthritis pain is related to the weather. *Proceedings of the National Academy of Sciences, 93,* 2895–2896.

Rescorla, R. A. (1988). Pavlovian conditioning: It's not what you think it is. *American Psychologist, 43,* 151–160.

Rescorla, R. A. (1996). Preservation of Pavlovian associations through extinction. *Quarterly Journal of Experimental Psychology, 49B,* 245–258.

Restle, F. (1970). Moon illusion explained on the basis of relative size. *Science, 167,* 1092–1096.

Ridley-Johnson, R., Cooper, H., & Chance, J. (1983). The relation of children's television viewing to school achievement and IQ. *Journal of Educational Research, 76,* 294–297.

Ritov, I. (1996). Anchoring in simulated competitive market negotiation. *Organizational Behavior and Human Decision Processes, 67,* 16–25.

Rivas-Vasquez, R. A. (2003). Aripiprazole: A novel antipsychotic with dopamine stabilizing properties. *Professional Psychology: Research and Practice, 34,* 108–111.

Rizzolatti, G., & Arbib, M. A. (1998). Language within our grasp. *Trends in Neuroscience, 21,* 188–194.

Rizzolatti, G., & Craighero, L. (2004). The mirror-neuron system. *Annual Review of Neuroscience, 27,* 169–192.

Rogers, C. R. (1951). *Client-centered therapy: Its current practices, implications, and theory.* Boston: Houghton Mifflin.

Rogers, C. R. (1961). *On becoming a person: A therapist's view of psychotherapy.* Boston: Houghton Mifflin.

Rogers, T. B., Kuiper, N. A., & Kirker, W. S. (1977). Self-reference and the encoding of personal information. *Journal of Personality and Social Psychology, 35,* 677–688.

Rohrer, J. H., Baron, S. H., Hoffman, E. L., & Swander, D. V. (1954). The stability of autokinetic judgments. *Journal of Abnormal and Social Psychology, 49,* 595–597.

Rosch, E. H. (1973). Natural categories. *Cognitive Psychology, 4,* 328–350.

Rosenhan, D. L. (1973). On being sane in insane places. *Science, 179,* 250–258.

Rosenthal, A. M. (1964). *Thirty-eight witnesses.* New York: McGraw-Hill.

Rosenthal, R. (1966). *Experimenter effects in behavioral research.* New York: Appleton-Century-Crofts.

Rosenthal, R. (1994). Interpersonal expectancy effects: A 30-year perspective. *Current Directions in Psychological Science, 3,* 176–179.

Rosenthal, R., & Jacobson, L. (1968). *Pygmalion in the classroom: Teacher expectation and pupils' intellectual development.* New York: Holt, Rinehart & Winston.

Ross, L. (1977). The intuitive psychologist and his shortcomings: Distortions in the attribution process. In L. Berkowitz (Ed.), *Advances in experimental social psychology* (Vol. 10, pp. 173–220). New York: Academic Press.

Rotter, J. B. (1966). Generalized expectancies for internal versus external control of reinforcement. *Psychological Monographs, 80* (1, Whole No. 609).

Rotter, J. B. (1990). Internal versus external control of reinforcement: A case history of a variable. *American Psychologist, 45,* 489–493.

Rundus, D., & Atkinson, R. C. (1970). Rehearsal processes in free recall: A procedure for direct observation. *Journal of Verbal Learning and Verbal Behavior, 9,* 99–105.

Sabbagh, L. (2006, August/September). The teen brain, hard at work. No, Really. *Scientific American MIND, 17,* 20–25.

Sackett, P. R., Bornerman, M. J., & Connelly, B. J. (2008). High-stakes testing in higher education and employment: Appraising the evidence for validity and fairness. *American Psychologist, 63,* 215–227.

Sackett, P. R., Schmitt, N., Ellingson, J. E., & Kabin, M. B. (2001). High-stakes testing in employment, credentialing, and higher education: Prospects in a post-affirmative action world. *American Psychologist, 56,* 302–318.

Saufley, W. H., Otaka, S. R., & Bavaresco, J. L. (1985). Context effects: Classroom tests and context independence. *Memory and Cognition, 13,* 522–528.

Schachter, S., & Singer, J. E. (1962). Cognitive, social, and physiological determinants of emotional state. *Psychological Review, 69,* 379–399.

Schacter, D. L. (2000). *The seven sins of memory: How the mind forgets and remembers.* New York: Houghton Mifflin.

Schafe, G. E., Sollars, S. I., & Bernstein, I. L. (1995). The CS-UCS interval and taste aversion learning: A brief look. *Behavioral Neuroscience, 109,* 799–802.

Schaie, K. W. (1994). The life course of adult intellectual development. *American Psychologist, 49,* 304–313.

Schaie, K. W. (1995). *Intellectual development in adulthood: The Seattle Longitudinal Study.* New York: Cambridge University Press.

Schank, R. C., & Abelson, R. P. (1977). *Scripts, plans, goals, and understanding: An inquiry into human knowledge structures.* Hillsdale, NJ: Erlbaum.

Schmidt, D. P., Allik, J., McCrae, R. R., & Benet-Martinez, V. (2007). The geographic distribution of big five personality traits: Patterns and profiles of human self-description across 56 nations. *Journal of Cross-Cultural Psychology, 38,* 173–212.

Schmidt, F. L., & Hunter, J. E. (1998). The validity and utility of selection methods in personnel psychology: Practical and theoretical implications of 85 years of research findings. *Psychological Bulletin, 124,* 262–274.

Schneider, B. H., Atkinson, L., & Tardif, C. (2001). Child-parent attachment and children's peer relations: A quantitative review. *Developmental Psychology, 37,* 86–100.

Schneider, W. (1993). Domain-specific knowledge and memory performance in children. *Educational Psychology Review, 5,* 257–273.

Schultz, D. (2001). *Theories of personality* (7th ed.). Pacific Grove, CA: Brooks/Cole.

Schwartz, N. (1999). Self-reports: How the questions shape the answers. *American Psychologist, 54,* 93–105.

Scott, B. W., Wojtowicz, J. M., & Burnham, W. M. (2000). Neurogenesis in the dentate gyrus of the rat following electroconvulsive shock seizures. *Experimental Neurology, 165,* 231–236.

Scoville, W. B., & Milner, B. (1957). Loss of recent memory after bilateral hippocampal lesions. *Journal of Neurology, Neurosurgery and Psychiatry, 20,* 11–21.

Segall, M. H., Campbell, D. T., & Herskovits, M. J. (1963). Cultural differences in the perception of geometric illusions. *Science, 193,* 769–771.

Segall, M. H., Campbell, D. T., & Herskovits, M. J. (1966). *The influence of culture on visual perception.* Indianapolis, IN: Bobbs-Merrill.

Segall, M. H., Dasen, P. R., Berry, J. W., & Poortinga, Y. H. (1990). *Human behavior in a global perspective: An introduction to cross-cultural psychology.* New York: Pergamon.

Seligman, M. E. P. (1971). Phobias and preparedness. *Behavior Therapy, 2,* 307–320.

Seligman, M. E. P. (1975). *Helplessness: On depression, development, and death.* San Francisco: W. H. Freeman.

Seligman, M. E. P. (1994). *What you can change and what you can't: The ultimate guide to self-improvement.* New York: Knopf.

Seligman, M. E. P., Walker, E. F., & Rosenhan, D. L. (2001). *Abnormal psychology* (4th ed.). New York: Norton.

Senghas, A., & Coppola, M. (2001). Children creating language: How Nicaraguan sign language acquired a spatial grammar. *Psychological Science, 12,* 323–328.

Shadish, W. R., Matt, G. E., Navarro, A. M., & Phillips, G. (2000). The effects of psychological therapies under clinically representative conditions: A meta-analysis. *Psychological Bulletin, 126,* 512–529.

Shepard, R. N. (1990). *Mind sights: Original visual illusions, ambiguities, and other anomalies.* New York: W. H. Freeman.

Sherif, M. (1937). An experimental approach to the study of attitudes. *Sociometry, 1,* 90–98.

Sherif, M., & Sherif, C. W. (1969). *Social psychology.* New York: Harper and Row.

Simpkins, S., Parke, R., Flyr, M., & Wild, M. (2006). Similarities in children's and early adolescents' perceptions of friendship qualities across development, gender, and friendship qualities. *Journal of Early Adolescence, 26,* 491–508.

Skinner, B. F. (1938). *The behavior of organisms: An experimental analysis.* New York: Appleton-Century-Crofts.

Skinner, B. F. (1956). A case history in the scientific method. *American Psychologist, 45,* 1206–1210.

Slovic, P., & Fischhoff, B. (1977). On the psychology of experimental surprises. *Journal of Experimental Psychology: Human Perception and Performance, 3,* 544–551.

Smith, M. B. (1978). Psychology and values. *Journal of Social Issues, 34,* 181–199.

Smith, C. N., & Squire, L. R. (2009). Medial temporal lobe activity during retrieval of semantic memory is related to the age of the memory. *The Journal of Neuroscience, 29,* 930–938.

Smith, M. L., Glass, G. V., & Miller, T. I. (1980). *The benefits of psychotherapy.* Baltimore, MD: Johns Hopkins University Press.

Smith, S. M., Glenberg, A., & Bjork, R. A. (1978). Environmental context and human memory. *Memory and Cognition, 6,* 342–353.

Snarey, J. R. (1985). Cross-cultural universality of social-moral development: A critical review of Kohlbergian research. *Psychological Bulletin, 97,* 202–232.

Soussignan, R. (2002). Duchenne smile, emotional experience, and autonomic reactivity: A test of the facial-feedback hypothesis. *Emotion, 2,* 52–74.

Spearman, C. (1927). *The abilities of man.* New York: Macmillan.

Sperling, G. (1960). The information available in brief visual presentations. *Psychological Monographs, 74* (Whole No. 498).

Springer, S. P., & Deutsch, G. (1998). *Left brain, right brain* (5th ed.). New York: W. H. Freeman.

Squire, L. R. (2004). Memory systems of the brain: A brief history and current perspective. *Neurobiology of Learning and Memory, 82,* 171–177.

Squire, L. R. (2009). The legacy of patient H. M. for neuroscience. *Neuron, 61,* 6–9.

Squire, L. R., & Cohen, N. J. (1984). Human memory and amnesia. In G. Lynch, J. L. McGaugh, & N. M. Weinberger (Eds.), *Neurobiology of learning and memory* (pp. 3–64). New York: Guilford Press.

Staddon, J. E. R., & Ettinger, R. H. (1989). *Learning: An introduction to the principles of adaptive behavior.* San Diego: Harcourt.

Stanovich, K. E. (2004). *How to think straight about psychology* (7th ed.). Needham Heights, MA: Allyn and Bacon.

Stanovich, K. E. (2009a, November/December). Rational and irrational thought: The thinking that IQ tests miss. *Scientific American MIND, 20,* 34–39.

Stanovich, K. E. (2009b). *What intelligence tests miss: The psychology of rational thought.* New Haven, CT: Yale University Press.

Stern, W. (1914). *The psychological methods of testing intelligence* (G. M. Whipple, Trans.). Baltimore: Warrick and York.

Sternberg, R. J. (1985). *Beyond IQ: A triarchic theory of intelligence.* New York: Cambridge University Press.

Sternberg, R. J. (1988). *The triarchic mind: A new theory of human intelligence.* New York: Viking.

Sternberg, R. J. (1999). The theory of successful intelligence. *Review of General Psychology, 3,* 292–316.

Sternberg, R. J., & Davidson, J. E. (1982, June). The mind of the puzzler. *Psychology Today, 16,* 37–44.

Stevens, S. S. (1962). The surprising simplicity of sensory metrics. *American Psychologist, 17,* 29–39.

Stevens, S. S. (1975). *Psychophysics: Introduction to its perceptual, neural, and social prospects.* New York: Wiley.

Stevenson, H. W., Chen, C., & Lee, S. (1993). Mathematics achievement of Chinese, Japanese, and American schoolchildren: Ten years later. *Science, 259,* 53–58.

Stevenson, H. W., & Stigler, J. W. (1992). *The learning gap.* New York: Summit.

Stewart, N. (2009). The cost of anchoring. *Psychological Science, 20,* 39–41.

Stewart, V. M. (1973). Tests of the "carpentered world" hypothesis by race and environment in America and Zambia. *International Journal of Psychology, 8,* 83–94.

Stewart-Williams, S. (2004). The placebo puzzle: Putting together the pieces. *Health Psychology, 23,* 198–206.

Stickgold, R., & Ellenbogen, J. M. (2009, August/September). Quiet! Sleeping brain at work. *Scientific American MIND, 19,* 22–29.

Stickgold, R., Hobson, J. A., Fosse, R., & Fosse, M. (2001). Sleep, learning, and dreams: Off-line memory reprocessing. *Science, 294,* 1052–1057.

Swets, J. A. (1964). *Signal detection and recognition by human observers.* New York: Wiley.

Symons, C. S., & Johnson, B. T. (1997). The self-reference effect in memory: A meta-analysis. *Psychological Bulletin, 121,* 371–394.

Takei, N., Van Os, J., & Murray, R. M. (1995). Maternal exposure to influenza and risk of schizophrenia: A 22 year study from the Netherlands. *Journal of Psychiatric Research, 29,* 435–445.

Talmi, D., Grady, C. L., Goshen-Gottstein, Y., & Moscovitch, M. (2005). Neuroimaging the serial position curve: A test of single-store versus dual-store models. *Psychological Science, 16,* 716–723.

Tang, S., & Hall, V. C. (1995). The overjustification effect: A meta-analysis. *Applied Cognitive Psychology, 9,* 365–404.

Tavris, C., & Aronson, E. (2007). *Mistakes were made (but not by me): Why we justify foolish beliefs, bad decisions, and hurtful acts.* New York: Harcourt.

Teghtsoonian, R. (1971). On the exponents in Stevens's law and the constant in Ekman's law. *Psychological Review, 78,* 71–80.

Teigen, K. H. (1986). Old truths or fresh insights? A study of students' evaluation of proverbs. *British Journal of Social Psychology, 25,* 43–50.

Teplin, L. A. (1985). The criminality of the mentally ill: A deadly misconception. *American Journal of Psychiatry, 142,* 593–598.

Terman, L. M. (1916). *The measurement of intelligence.* Boston: Houghton Mifflin.

Thaler, R., & Sunstein, C. (2008). *Nudge: Improving decisions about health, wealth, and happiness.* New Haven, CT: Yale University Press.

Thelen, E. (1995). Motor development: A new synthesis. *American Psychologist, 50,* 79–95.

Thompson, R. F. (2000). *The brain: A neuroscience primer* (3rd ed.). New York: Worth.

Thorndike, E. L. (1898). Animal intelligence: An experimental study of the associative processes in animals. *Psychological Review Monograph Supplement, 2,* (No. 8).

Thorndike, E. L. (1911). *Animal intelligence: Experimental studies.* New York: Macmillan.

Thurstone, L. L. (1938). *Primary mental abilities.* Chicago: University of Chicago Press.

Tolman, E. C., & Honzik, C. H. (1930a). Degrees of hunger, reward and non-reward, and maze learning in rats. *University of California Publications in Psychology, 4,* 241–256.

Tolman, E. C., & Honzik, C. H. (1930b). "Insight" in rats. *University of California Publications in Psychology, 4,* 215–232.

Tolman, E. C., & Honzik, C. H. (1930c). Introduction and removal of reward, and maze performance in rats. *University of California Publications in Psychology, 4,* 257–275.

Tomasello, M. (2003). *Constructing a language: A usage-based theory of language acquisition.* Cambridge, MA: Harvard University Press.

Tomasello, M., Strosberg, R., & Akhtar, N. (1996). Eighteen-month-old children learn words in non-ostensive contexts. *Journal of Child Language, 23,* 157–176.

Torrey, E. F., Miller, J., Rawlings, R., & Yolken, R. H. (1997). Seasonality of births in schizophrenia and bipolar disorder: A review of the literature. *Schizophrenia Research, 28,* 1–38.

Trappey, C. (1996). A meta-analysis of consumer choice and subliminal advertising. *Psychology and Marketing, 13,* 517–530.

Tsuang, M. T., & Faraone, S. V. (1990). *The genetics of mood disorders.* Baltimore, MD: Johns Hopkins University Press.

Tuddenham, R. D. (1948). Soldier intelligence in World Wars I and II. *American Psychologist, 3,* 54–56.

Tulving, E. (1972). Episodic and semantic memory. In E. Tulving & W. Donaldson (Eds.), *Organization of memory* (pp. 381–403). New York: Academic Press.

Tulving, E. (1974, January/February). Cue-dependent forgetting. *American Scientist, 62,* 74–82.

Tulving, E. (1983). *Elements of episodic memory.* New York: Oxford University Press.

Tulving, E., Schacter, D. L., & Stark, H. (1982). Priming effects in word-fragment completion are independent of recognition memory. *Journal of Experimental Psychology: Learning, Memory, and Cognition, 8,* 336–342.

Tversky, A., & Kahneman, D. (1971). Belief in the law of small numbers. *Psychological Bulletin, 76,* 105–110.

Tversky, A., & Kahneman, D. (1973). Availability: A heuristic for judging frequency and probability. *Cognitive Psychology, 5,* 207–232.

Tversky, A., & Kahneman, D. (1974). Judgment under uncertainty: Heuristics and biases. *Science, 185,* 1124–1131.

Tversky, A., & Kahneman, D. (1983). Extensional versus intuitive reasoning: The conjunction fallacy in probability judgment. *Psychological Review, 90,* 293–315.

Twitmyer, E. B. (1974). A study of the knee jerk. *Journal of Experimental Psychology, 103,* 1047–1066.

Valenstein, E. S. (1986). *Great and desperate cures: The rise and decline of psychosurgery and other radical treatments.* New York: Basic Books.

Valenstein, E. S. (1988). *Blaming the brain: The truth about drugs and mental health.* New York: Free Press.

Valenstein, E. S. (2005). *The war of the soups and sparks: The discovery of neurotransmitters and the dispute over how nerves communicate.* New York: Columbia University Press.

Valenza, E., Simion, F., Cassia, V. M., & Umilta, C. (1996). Face preferences at birth. *Journal of Experimental Psychology: Human Perception & Performance, 22,* 892–903.

van Praag, H., Schinder, A. F., Christie, B. R., Toni, N., Palmer, T. D., & Gage, F. H. (2002). Functional neurogenesis in the adult hippocampus. *Nature, 415,* 1030–1034.

Vasta, R., Miller, S. A., & Ellis, S. (2004). *Child psychology* (4th ed.). New York: Wiley.

Vertosick, F. T., Jr. (1997, October). Lobotomy's back. *Discover, 18,* 66–68, 70–72.

Vygotsky, L. S. (1978). *Mind in society: The development of higher psychological processes.* Cambridge, MA: Harvard University Press. (Original work published 1930, 1933, & 1935)

Vygotsky, L. S. (1986). *Thought and language.* Cambridge, MA: MIT Press. (Original work published 1934)

Vyse, S. A. (1997). *Believing in magic: The psychology of superstition.* New York: Oxford University Press.

Waber, R. L., Shiv, B., Carmon, Z., & Ariely, D. (2008). Commercial features of placebo and therapeutic efficacy. *Journal of the American Medical Association, 299,* 1016–1017.

Wald, G. (1964). The receptors of human color vision. *Science, 145,* 1007–1017.

Waldman, M., Nicholson, S., Adilov, N., & Williams, J. (2008). Autism prevalence and precipitation rates in California, Oregon, and Washington counties. *Archives of Pediatric and Adolescent Medicine, 162,* 1026–1034.

Wason, P. C. (1960). On the failure to eliminate hypotheses in a conceptual task. *The Quarterly Journal of Experimental Psychology, 12,* 129–140.

Wason, P. C. (1966). Reasoning. In B. M. Foss (Ed.), *New horizons in psychology* (pp. 135–151). Harmondsworth, England: Penguin.

Wason, P. C. (1968). Reasoning about a rule. *The Quarterly Journal of Experimental Psychology, 20,* 273–281.

Watkins, C. E., Campbell, V. L., Nieberding, R., & Hallmark, R. (1995). Contemporary practice of psychological assessment by clinical psychologists. *Professional Psychology: Research and Practice, 26,* 54–60.

Watson, J. B. (1913). Psychology as the behaviorist views it. *Psychological Review, 20,* 158–177.

Watson, J. B. (1919). *Psychology from the standpoint of the behaviorist.* Philadelphia: Lippincott.

Watson, J. B., & Rayner, R. (1920). Conditioned emotional reactions. *Journal of Experimental Psychology, 3,* 1–14.

Weiner, I. B., & Greene, R. L. (2008). *Handbook of personality assessment.* New York: Wiley.

Weisberg, R., & Alba, J. W. (1981). An examination of the alleged role of "fixation" in the solution of several "insight" problems. *Journal of Experimental Psychology: General, 110,* 169–192.

Weissman, M. M., Bland, R. C., Canino, G. J., Faravelli, C., Greenwald, S., Hwu, H. G., et al. (1996). Cross-national epidemiology of major depression and bipolar disorder. *Journal of the American Medical Association, 276,* 293–299.

Weisstein, E. W. (2009). Young girl-old woman illusion. From *MathWorld*—A Wolfram Web Resource. Retrieved from http://www.mathworld.wolfram.com/YoungGirl-OldWomanIllusion.html.

Wellman, H. M., Cross, D., & Watson, J. (2001). Meta-analysis of theory-of-mind development: The truth about false belief. *Child Development, 72,* 655–684.

Westly, E. (2010, May/June). Different shades of blue. *Scientific American MIND, 21,* 30–37.

Westen, D. (1998). The scientific legacy of Sigmund Freud: Toward a psychodynamically informed psychological science. *Psychological Bulletin, 124,* 333–371.

Whitehurst, G. J., & Valdez-Menchaca, M. C. (1988). What is the role of reinforcement in early language acquisition? *Child Development, 59,* 430–440.

Wickelgren, W. A. (1974). *How to solve problems: Elements of a theory of problems and problem solving.* San Francisco: W. H. Freeman.

Widiger, T. A. (2005). Classification and diagnosis: Historical development and contemporary issues. In J. Maddux & B. Winstead (Eds.), *Psychopathology: Foundations for a contemporary understanding* (pp. 63–83). Mahwah, NJ: Erlbaum.

Wigdor, A. K., & Garner, W. R. (Eds.). (1982). *Ability testing: Uses, consequences, and controversies.* Washington, DC: National Academy Press.

Wiggins, J. S. (Ed.). (1996). *The five-factor model of personality: Theoretical perspectives.* New York: Guilford.

Williams, J. H., Whiten, A., Suddendorf, T., & Perrett, D. I. (2001). Imitation, mirror neurons and autism. *Neuroscience and Biobehavioral Review, 25,* 287–295.

Williams, K. D., Harkins, S. G., & Latané, B. (1981). Identifiability as a deterrent to social loafing: Two cheering experiments. *Journal of Personality and Social Psychology, 40,* 303–311.

Wilcoxon, H. C., Dragoin, W. B., & Kral, P. A. (1971). Illness-induced aversions in rats and quail: Relative salience of visual and gustatory cues. *Science, 171,* 826–828.

Woloshin, S., Schwartz, L. M., & Welch, H. G. (2008). *Know your chances: Understanding health statistics.* Berkeley, CA: University of California Press.

Wolpe, J. (1958). *Psychotherapy by reciprocal inhibition.* Stanford, CA: Stanford University Press.

Woodruff-Pak, D. S. (1993). Eyeblink classical conditioning in H. M.: Delay and trace paradigms. *Behavioral Neuroscience, 107,* 911–925.

Wright, P., Takei, N., Rifkin, L., & Murray, R. M. (1995). Maternal influenza, obstetric complications, and schizophrenia. *American Journal of Psychiatry, 152,* 1714–1720.

Wynn, K. (1992). Addition and subtraction by human infants. *Nature, 358,* 749–750.

Yates, F. A. (1966). *The art of memory.* Chicago: University of Chicago Press.

Yerkes, R. M., & Dodson, J. D. (1908). The relation of strength of stimulus to rapidity of habit-formation. *Journal of Comparative and Neurological Psychology, 18,* 459–482.

Zajonc, R. B. (1965). Social facilitation. *Science, 149,* 269–274.

Zimbardo, P. G. (1970). The human choice: Individuation, reason, and order versus deindividuation, impulse, and chaos. In W. J. Arnold & D. Levine (Eds.), *Nebraska Symposium on Motivation, 1969* (pp. 237–307). Lincoln, NE: University of Nebraska Press.

Zimbardo, P. (2007). *The Lucifer effect: Understanding how good people turn evil.* New York: Random House.

Zuckerman, M. (1979). *Sensation seeking: Beyond the optimal level of arousal.* Hillsdale, NJ: Erlbaum.

Zwislocki, J. J. (1981, March/April). Sound analysis in the ear: A history of discoveries. *American Scientist, 69,* 184–192.

Name Index

Subject Index